D1103936

WTO AT THE MARGINS

At a pivotal point in the history of the World Trade Organisation, when development issues are at the heart of negotiations, how the larger and more powerful WTO Members address the legitimate concerns of its poorest and most vulnerable members will shape the perception of the institution throughout much of the century. This book aims not only to document almost ten years of experience of small, vulnerable states with the WTO, but also to explain why these experiences have occurred.

The book takes an evidential theory approach to explaining the inherent features characteristic to the trade and economic development of small island states. It then proceeds to highlight the particular issues of concern to these states in relation to multilateral trade negotiations at the WTO. A section is devoted to discussing the experience of the African Caribbean and Pacific (ACP) countries with the WTO dispute settlement mechanism, in the context of the impact and implications of EU reform in the sugar, banana and tuna industries. The book ends with a discussion of key negotiating issues for the island states and institutional arrangements which will facilitate reform.

ROMAN GRYNBERG is Advisor and Head of International Trade and Regional Co-operation for the Economic Affairs Division of the Commonwealth Secretariat.

WTO AT THE MARGINS

Small States and the Multilateral Trading System

Edited by

ROMAN GRYNBERG

CAMBRIDGE UNIVERSITY PRESS
Cambridge, New York, Melbourne, Madrid, Cape Town, Singapore, São Paulo

Cambridge University Press
The Edinburgh Building, Cambridge CB2 2RU, UK

Published in the United States of America by Cambridge University Press, New York

www.cambridge.org
Information on this title: www.cambridge.org/9780521861434

First published 2006

Printed in the United Kingdom at the University Press, Cambridge

A catalogue record for this publication is available from the British Library

ISBN-13 978-0-521-86143-4 hardback
ISBN-10 0-521-86143-8 hardback

CONTENTS

LIST OF FIGURES AND APPENDICES

LIST OF TABLES

LIST OF CONTRIBUTORS

Elizabeth Bennett is a researcher with IDDRA (UK) Ltd.

Richard L. Bernal is the Director General, Caribbean Regional Negotiating Machinery and Hon. Professor, Sir Arthur Lewis Institute of Social and Economic Studies, University of the West Indies, Jamaica.

Michael Davenport is a consultant on international trade based in London.

Carol C. George is currently with the law firm of Baker and McKenzie, London.

Roman Grynberg is the Deputy Director, International Trade and Regional Co-operation Section, Economic Affairs Division, Commonwealth Secretariat.

Virginia Horscroft is a consultant to the Commonwealth Secretariat and a former ODI Fellow, and is based at Queen Elizabeth House and New College, Oxford.

David Joiner is currently Assistant Professor of Computational Finance at the New Jersey Center for Science and Technology Education at Kean University in Union, NJ.

Roy Mickey Joy is the Director of Trade in Port Villa, Vanuatu.

Edwin Laurent is the former Ambassador of Dominica, St Kitts and Nevis, St Vincent and the Grenadines to the European Commission and is now a consultant on international trade, based in Brussels.

Pedro M. G. Martins is currently with the School of Social Sciences, University of Sussex.

Chris Milner is currently a Professor of International Economics in the School of Economics, and Fellow of the Centre for Research on Economic Development and International Trade (CREDIT), University of Nottingham.

Wyn Morgan is currently a Professor in the School of Economics, University of Nottingham.

Stephen J. Orava was formerly with the law firm of Baker and McKenzie, London.

Claudius Preville is presently the Technical Advisor on Trade Policy to the OECS Secretariat for the Caribbean Regional Negotiating Machinery (CRNM).

Mohammad A. Razzaque is currently a Lecturer for the Department of Economics, University of Dhaka.

Stephen Redding is with the Department of Economics, London School of Economics.

Jan Yves Remy was formerly a Research Assistant with the Economic Affairs Division, Commonwealth Secretariat and is currently a Services Analyst with the Caribbean Regional Negotiating Machinery (CRNM).

Helene Rey-Valette is with the University of Montpellier, France.

David Robertson is currently a solicitor and a consultant on international trade based in London.

Sacha Silva is a consultant on international trade, currently working for the Commonwealth Secretariat.

Marcia Thomas is currently the Director of the Foreign Trade Department, Ministry of Foreign Affairs and Foreign Trade, Jamaica.

Anthony J. Venables is with the Department of Economics, London School of Economics.

Zhen Kun Wang is an international trade consultant based in London.

Michael Weatherhead is presently an ODI Fellow, working in Guyana.

Ganeshan Wignaraja is currently with the Asian Development Bank, Manila, Philippines.

L. Alan Winters was formerly a Professor for the School of Social Sciences, University of Sussex and is currently the Director of Research for the World Bank.

Evious Zgovu is with the School of Economics, University of Nottingham and is a consultant with the Commonwealth Secretariat.

Introduction

ROMAN GRYNBERG

This book aims not only to document almost ten years' experience of small vulnerable states with the WTO but also to explain why the experiences have occurred. Since the formation of the WTO in 1995, small states have become increasingly vocal in their criticism of what they see as onerous rules from which they feel that they have not benefited. Now at this pivotal point in the history of the WTO when development issues are at the heart of negotiations, how the larger and more powerful WTO members address the legitimate trade concerns of its poorest and most vulnerable members will shape the perception of the institution throughout much of the century. If the Doha Development Agenda fails to address these concerns in a constructive manner that recognises the particular vulnerabilities of various groups, it will leave the WTO further weakened and undermined from the perspective of a group of countries that are emerging as the majority of its members.

Small vulnerable states and, in particular, small island states have endowed or inherent handicaps that have shaped their trade and economic development as well as the policy of the international community since the colonial era. The combination of smallness, isolation and dispersion of small pockets of population has shaped the range and type of products and services that these countries have been able to export. What the export activities of small vulnerable states have in common is that a surplus or quasi-rent has been needed to cover the inherent cost disadvantage faced by the private investor who has chosen to locate in small vulnerable states. This quasi-rent has been provided through legal instruments such as trade preferences which provided subventions to those investors in export-oriented activities. Other legal instruments such as tax concessions, and even the very sovereignty of these states, have provided the possibility for creating surpluses or quasi-rents that were needed for the survival of internationally competitive export-oriented production.

It has not just been legal institutions that create this surplus, the market has also provided quasi-rents through niche exports or through booming sectors which have provided fuel for the development of what would otherwise be an uncompetitive private sector. It is the dismantling of the special trade and economic arrangements at the WTO that has served to so undermine the position of small states and resulted in their perception of the WTO as an institution that has, by and large, not served their economic interests.

What remains a common thread throughout much of the previous academic and policy research on small vulnerable states is that these countries do not generally have a special economic and trade problem. These studies have observed that small vulnerable states have high incomes, have achieved relatively high economic growth and, despite their recognised vulnerabilities, are generally not in need of assistance and policy advice that is in any way different from that of other developing states. This position certainly reached its pinnacle in the work of Easterly and Kray (see chapter 2) whose paper 'Small States, Small Problems' encapsulated the dominant position throughout the 1990s on small states. While there has been a shift in thinking on the subject recently, there has been precious little understanding or sympathy for the predicament of these states. The global consensus that emerged was that small vulnerable states are low- to middle-income countries and, in comparison to the economic constraints facing the least developed, the problems of small vulnerable states remain less challenging. Yet, despite the consensus of economic thinking, the problem of adjusting from trade preference dependence to a liberalised global trading environment has proved daunting.

Small vulnerable states have high-cost structures that stem not from poor policy but from inherited cost disadvantages. There can be no guarantee that, given the magnitude of these disadvantages, there exists any above-zero wage or factor price that will induce investors, whether local or foreign, to invest in these countries once the benefits of trade preferences and other sources of quasi-rent are removed. Only if these countries are able to develop niche market activities will they be able to survive in a far more liberalised world that will almost certainly follow the completion of the Doha Round.

The empirical studies of the impact of smallness, isolation and distance (chapters 3 and 5) for the first time provide quantitative evidence of the magnitude of the disadvantages faced by these states. The chapter by Winters and Martins also provides important policy advice on how the international community may wish to address some of the concerns facing the most disadvantaged. This includes the provision of possible temporary labour market access for nationals. Redding and Venables suggest the need for more infrastructure in their analysis of isolation and distance.

The trade performance of small vulnerable states over the last three decades is considered in chapter 6 where the results of analysis of trade data for the last thirty to fifty years shows a continual pattern of marginalisation in trade in both goods and services. While a declining share of world trade does not necessarily imply declining welfare for a state, it does measure, in one summary statistic, several aspects of the performance of the state and of the global trading system as a whole. First, the share of world trade reflects the productive efficiency of a country, i.e. countries that maintain growth levels of international trade above the global average by definition do not become marginalised. Second, secular declines in the share of world trade reflect the distributional equity of the trading system. If a large group of low-income countries, for example, are experiencing a secular decline in their share of world trade while high-income ones are experiencing an increase, the distribution of welfare benefits of the trading system will follow. Third, marginalisation, i.e. a decline in share of world trade, also reflects the political significance of a state. It was furthermore observed that investment share and aid levels are also in decline. The marginalisation of small states in the trade in goods has been pronounced irrespective of the time period considered.

The chapter by Winters and Martins reflects the high level of concern regarding the trade competitiveness of small vulnerable states. The chapter by Wignaraja and Joiner (chapter 4), which has developed a Small States Manufactured Export Competitiveness Index to measure the competitiveness of small states in the industrial sector, exhibits interesting results. It shows that despite serious cost disadvantages, some small states such as the Fiji Islands, Mauritius, Trinidad and Tobago have successfully developed from a state of vulnerability to a situation where they have a viable, internationally competitive industrial sector. While their experience is testimony that the predicament of some small vulnerable economies is not without hope for achieving competitiveness, concerns over the vulnerable situation of other small states, which have performed poorly on the export competitiveness index, remain.

The characteristics of small economies, centred on their size, vulnerability and governance capacity, combine to yield significant cost disadvantages that are large enough to undermine these states' capacities to participate in trade on a remunerative basis, even in their areas of comparative advantage. Diminishing trade possibilities serve primarily to compound the deleterious effects of small size on their economic welfare. The chapter by Horscroft (chapter 7) highlights the need to adjust multilateral trade rules to accommodate the concerns of small economies. The special characteristics of small economies also undermine the bargaining power of small states significantly, and therefore affect the likelihood of their achieving beneficial outcomes from the interstate negotiating process that determines global trade rules.

In chapters 8 and 9 the small vulnerable economy issue at the WTO is addressed in quite different ways. The fraught question of definition of small vulnerable states is addressed, with possibilities considered for an appropriate quantitative definition. Significantly the chapter by Davenport (chapter 10) shows how minor the consequences would be for the multilateral trading system of providing improved market access for small states. The chapter also shows that, on the basis of cluster analysis, there is much in common between small states and the least developed states, which are the only group of WTO members that are provided with substantial market access improvements.

It is the tangible experience of small vulnerable states with the most important and powerful of the WTO institutions, its dispute settlement mechanism, which has, more than anything else shaped perceptions of the organisation as being antithetical to the interests of its smallest members. The banana dispute, and its impact on the Caribbean, is considered in three chapters that should be read together to grasp the full breadth of the dispute. This is a dispute that has completely undermined the trade provisions of the Lomé Convention and necessitated the wholesale reform of trade relations between Europe and the African, Caribbean and Pacific (ACP) nations under the Cotonou Agreement which envisages negotiations with Free Trade Areas (FTAs) and/or Economic Partnership Agreements (EPAs). The EPAs will oblige these small states to provide free market access to EU goods in return for maintaining the existing market access. Throughout the ACP group this will necessitate a complete reform of taxation and trading systems that will occupy economic policy matters in these countries in the first decades of the century.

However, it is not just the well-documented banana dispute that has served to erode confidence in the WTO as a system of law, readily able to adapt to the economic realities of its weakest members. Recently the EU's sugar regime has been challenged by Brazil, Australia and Thailand. Many of the same ACP states that were dependent upon the preference arrangements available for their exports of bananas to the EU are similarly – and in some cases (Mauritius, Fiji and Guyana) more – dependent upon the sugar protocol. While there has, at the time of writing, been no decision by a WTO panel, an adverse outcome could seriously undermine the economies of the sugar-producing ACP states. Chapters 14 and 15 consider the legal and economic implications of the dispute.

If small states felt that two key export sectors were threatened by the dispute settlement mechanism, the need for a WTO waiver that resulted from the banana dispute exposed their economies to further risks. When the ACP and the EU sought an extension of the existing GATT waiver for the preferences temporarily available under the terms of the Cotonou Agreement at the Doha Ministerial Conference in 2001, the Philippines and Thailand, two developing countries with considerable export interests in canned tuna, held up the consensus on the waiver until the EU agreed to mediation over the access provided to Thai and Philippine canned tuna. Under the EU's Generalised System of Preferences (GSP), Thai and Philippine tuna is exported to the EU with the full most-favoured nation (MFN) tariff (24 per cent) while ACP tuna enters duty free. Chapter 16 provides an analysis of the impact on ACP states of the tariff quota that was eventually provided by the EU, ostensibly to Thailand and the Philippines. This initial tariff quota clearly presages a further reduction in the margins of trade preference available to ACP states which will undermine an export sector of vital interest to Indian Ocean and Pacific Island states.

The experience of the small states in general and the ACP in particular with the WTO's dispute settlement mechanism (DSM) has not been entirely negative. The DSM has provided for small WTO members a mechanism whereby they can, at least in theory, challenge much larger states and where, as aggrieved parties, they can seek redress which would certainly not be possible outside the WTO's legal system. Indeed, the success of Costa Rica in using the DSM has been proof that small states are capable of using it in their favour. Recently the small island state of Antigua and Barbuda has taken the US to the DSM over market access for internet gambling. It was widely reported that Antigua had won the dispute with the US, but at the time of writing the parties have agreed to suspend the dispute pending further consultation. If the US does not agree to bring its trade regime on internet gambling into conformity with its WTO obligations, the option available to Antigua is to impose trade sanctions on the US. The absurdity of such an outcome only serves to underline the clear limitation of the current DSM as it pertains to small states.

While the DSM has afforded opportunities for small states, it has simultaneously set off a chain reaction, beginning with the various banana disputes, that has served to undermine the economic base of many small states. Indeed, the ongoing negotiations between the six ACP regions and the EU for the completion of Economic Partnership Agreements which are ostensibly free trade areas stems from the banana dispute and the need to maintain a WTO-compatible trade regime. This will necessitate a painful adjustment of trade and taxation regimes of most ACP states and, because of the multiplicity of trade agreements with their explicit and implicit MFN obligations with other developed countries and regions, the ACP states will need to negotiate similar arrangements with other trading partners as well. Thus the banana dispute and what followed directly from it can be characterised as the dispute which completely changed North–South trade relations. What is peculiar is that the banana dispute, like the subsequent sugar dispute, included the small states only as third parties. They were not the 'object' of the disputes but rather suffered collateral damage in disputes between larger WTO members. This has added to the pervasive sense of powerlessness of the small states.

The book also considers new and emerging WTO issues of significance to small states. Three issues in particular are considered where the development of new rules or the implementation of existing rules creates serious challenges for small states. The first is the negotiation of potential new disciplines in the area of fisheries subsidies (chapter 17) which could have very damaging effects upon the economies of some of the smallest and poorest island states in the Pacific. Again, the impact is by way of 'collateral damage' where these countries, which are not even WTO members, may have their economic foundation undermined by virtue of disciplines negotiated in Geneva.

The second issue is the export of financial services which has emerged over the last twenty years as a growing and viable offshore financial sector (chapter 18). The development of regulations essentially by OECD countries, which have not consulted or taken into account the interests of small vulnerable states, has served to weaken their position and undermine the commercial advantage of the offshore financial sector in small vulnerable states. The need for WTO disciplines on the formation and imposition of essentially plurilateral standards by institutions dominated by developed countries was raised by small vulnerable states at the WTO. The development of the Harmful Tax Initiative, the work of the Financial Action Taskforce and the Basel Committee are considered in relation to the development of the financial services sector in small vulnerable states.

The third issue is the impact that the Agreement on Subsidies and Countervailing Measures could have on those developing countries, small or otherwise, that maintain export processing zones (EPZs) (chapter 19). Clearly, for those that are not LDCs or low-income countries, there remains the considerable risk that their EPZ regimes are not compatible with their WTO obligations. The phasing out of export subsidies constitutes a further diminution of the rents available to exporters operating in small states.

The final chapter addresses two specific institutional issues and the actual experience of small states – the first is accession to the WTO and the second the advice being offered to small states during the WTO's Trade Policy Review. For almost ten years, small developing states which, during the years of the GATT, were either not members of the organisation or played no noticeable role, have simultaneously complained about their inability to implement what they perceive as burdensome and onerous obligations of the Uruguay Round while lining up in large numbers to join the WTO. This apparent contradiction is explored in part in the experience of Vanuatu – a small LDC in the South Pacific which has had a particularly traumatic experience with its accession to the WTO. For many observers, there seems little direct trade benefit to countries like Vanuatu from accession as they would not be able to negotiate improved market access for their limited range of exports. However, there are numerous reasons why small developing countries choose to undergo the difficult and intrusive process of accession that are specific to the geopolitics of their region. However, in the case of Vanuatu, accession, unlike in many post-Soviet transition economies, was motivated neither by trade nor by political considerations. Accession to the WTO means an ability to participate in what has in effect become a global parliament where the world's commercial laws are negotiated. Membership of GATT, where negotiations were simply about border measures, by micro-states like Vanuatu certainly made no commercial sense. However, now that the WTO has become increasingly involved in negotiating what eventually become national commercial laws, membership becomes an imperative to all those who wish to have any impact on their own domestic laws.

To say the least, the experience of small vulnerable states with the rules-based multilateral system has not been an entirely happy one. The Doha Development Agenda, as the Doha Round is called, is an opportunity to address the legitimate concerns of such states. These states are, however, so politically weak that they are easily overlooked and, if developed countries are able to come to mutually acceptable terms with the large developing countries, i.e. India, Brazil, China, South Africa, etc., it is entirely plausible that bilateral pressures from the large developing countries can be used to induce small states to agree to another agreement that they perceive is not in their economic interest. Such an outcome would serve not only to marginalise and alienate a large number of the WTO's weakest members, it would also further erode confidence in the multilateral trading system and leave it in disrepute.

PART I

Theory and evidence

1

A theory of trade and development of small vulnerable states

ROMAN GRYNBERG

1.1 Introduction: the theory of comparative advantage *ad extremum*

The purpose of this chapter is to attempt to draw together the common thread of the historical experience of trade and development of the small island states of the central and western Pacific within the context of economic theory. The theory of comparative advantage has, since Ricardo, been enunciated as a positive statement that nations will trade in those areas where they have a comparative advantage even if they have an absolute disadvantage in all areas. If a theory is to be general in nature, it must apply to all cases. There is perhaps nowhere better to challenge any theory than considering its applicability *ad extremum.* Indeed the smallest, most disadvantaged and remote of the micro-states of the central and western Pacific, e.g. Tuvalu, Kiribati and Niue,[1] constitute a fascinating test of Ricardian trade theory for they provide examples of states which do not consistently trade in either goods or services, and maintain existing consumption levels from migration, remittances and aid. In such extreme cases, it is difficult to see how Ricardian theory of comparative advantage applies as an explanation of observed behaviour. Those who are wedded to Ricardian theory of trade as a 'tautology of impregnable circularity' would explain the observations from the remote islands of the South Pacific as merely a case of high transaction cost stemming from transport and the absence of economies of scale.

These are the views of the author and not necessarily those of the Commonwealth Secretariat or any of its member governments.

[1] Kiribati consistently exports seaweed and Niue and Tuvalu have only minor and ad hoc exports of products such as taro or copra but in all cases production for export or for subsistence consumption constitutes only a very minor proportion of the observed subsistence of the population. Consumption is determined largely by aid levels. At least two other countries of the central Pacific, Nauru and the Marshall Islands, have virtually no production and subsist largely from remittances and aid.

At least two of these three countries (Kiribati and Tuvalu) have in the past had a comparative advantage in the production of copra, for example, but now do not trade as prices are too low to compensate for the disadvantages of scale, isolation and dispersed pockets of production. What little production occurs is for the non-monetised physical subsistence of those remaining inhabitants. What are equally interesting are the cases of a number of larger central Pacific countries which currently export but are at the very margins of commercially viable production and are facing future prospects not dissimilar to those micro-states that are now in effect subsistence economies supplemented by transfers. What this chapter attempts to do is to explain trade patterns not within the Ricardian tradition but within the tradition of economic theory of rents and quasi-rents.

It is argued that the development experience of the small states of the central and western Pacific over the last half century follows from their inherent structural characteristics of smallness, isolation and physical dispersion and poor human resource development which render otherwise competitive industries structurally uncompetitive. The high-cost structure has necessitated market-generated quasi-rents or *de jure* rents on an ongoing basis in all sectors of economic activity as a precondition for private sector investment. Rents are defined by the normal neoclassical version, i.e. payments to any factor of production above its opportunity cost. Quasi-rents are temporary or monopoly rents. Without these rents, the high operating costs would not be covered but, more significantly, capital and entrepreneurship could not be induced to enter the market. Thus what would normally be deemed to be rent in other larger and less disadvantaged economies is, in the context of such remote and high-cost countries, an offset payment to compensate for the inherent disadvantage of location.

Two distinct sources of rents have in the past fuelled what development has occurred in the island states of the central and western Pacific. These include *de jure* sources of rent stemming from trade preferences, tax concessions and sovereignty (significant for the smallest of micro-states) and market-based quasi-rent sources stemming from booming sectors. From a development perspective, the system of trade preferences has been far more significant for the longer-term development of the region than market-based sources of rent because it has allowed the development of stable economic linkages that stem from a substantial and long-term economic activity. While market-based sources have been important and will become more important as economic globalisation advances, they are unlikely to give rise to sustained development because of their failure to create linkages with other sectors. These niche market activities, while not creating traditional economic linkages, do create marketing links which in turn shape the nature of development which, by their nature, will be predicated upon the relationship with the outside world. Both booming sectors and niche markets are more likely to generate 'Dutch disease' effects in small economies which tend to undermine their long-term economic development.

1.2 Characteristics of efficient national economies in a global market

Societies, like individuals, that prove most able to take advantage of the market opportunities created by a more liberalised and globalised market environment are those that are adept at moving resources and changing economic activities with changing market opportunities. Economists normally associate several features or characteristics with societies that are best able to adjust to the global market. The first of these is a pool of freely traded and specialised land, labour and capital that are mobile, with low transaction costs when involved in inter-sectoral mobility. Second, for a market to function efficiently an efficient information system that disseminates relevant market information rapidly and at low cost is essential. The third feature is a physical infrastructure that permits efficient movement of goods, services, resources and natural persons. A final feature is a social and political infrastructure conducive to predictable legal outcomes.

In all economies, two broad types of factors are responsible for the absence of these characteristics. The first are those factors induced by domestic policy and the second, exogenous or inherent factors that are beyond the immediate policy purview of national governments or multilateral agencies. Market-oriented structural adjustment programmes are necessary to deal with the policy-induced sources of inefficiency and market failure. However, multilateral financial institutions are increasingly blurring the distinction between exogenous and endogenous policy variables. Other, possibly multilateral, forms of policy intervention by the global community are necessary if small vulnerable states are to cope with those of their inherent cost disadvantages that cause economic marginalisation.

Through a combination of historical circumstance and the evolution of commercial advantage, exports from these small isolated countries have tended to remain largely confined to a limited number of agricultural, forestry and marine products. Small states face fundamental barriers to adjustment that stem from the high cost of sectoral shift from what are often agricultural monocultures to economic structures attuned to a more liberal economic environment. What makes small states and enterprises in those states so fundamentally different from those in larger states of a similar development status is the very limited pool of specialised and competitive domestic human resources available to firms. The absence of such a pool in turn raises the costs of investments that are necessary for sectoral and structural change. Moreover, the high degree of economic specialisation resulting from limited export and domestic market production has meant that adjustment away from these sectors is all the more difficult.

A well-known and understood list of inherent characteristics is at play in many small and highly vulnerable economies. These characteristics or factors when operating together render markets in small economies less capable of adaptation to global market change than those larger developing countries of a similar development status. This list of inhibiting factors includes the absence of economies of scale in production for both domestic and export markets and the physical dispersion of small pockets of resources, products and persons (especially in island states). These two factors are frequently combined with physical isolation from resource and export markets. However, the limitations on the capacity of island states to adjust which stem from inherent physical characteristics are compounded by several factors which stem from the level of development and economic integration and are hence amenable to resolution with the passage of time. The most significant is a lack of trade integration which means that these small isolated economies are frequently unable to acquire domestically scarce resources at the internationally competitive market price. This is particularly so for human resources when the acquisition of domestically scarce skilled labour, management and entrepreneurship requires a significant premium over the world market price. This, when combined with the poor development of human resources, especially of skilled labour and entrepreneurial skills, often creates overarching barriers to the development of industry. These island states frequently are further hampered by poor physical and communications infrastructure and a high degree of vulnerability of that infrastructure to the economic impact of natural disasters.

This list of characteristics which impede market integration is frequently produced, but less common is an understanding of the dynamic interaction between these characteristics in creating cost disadvantages for firms operating in this environment. The interaction between these disadvantages is not necessarily linear, and often produces exponential increases in the costs of production facing firms operating in small isolated states. A simple example may suffice to demonstrate the nature of the interaction. In the early 1990s, the Government of Fiji was considering diversification into the export of cut flowers. The cost of airfreight of cut flowers from Hawaii (one of the principal Pacific suppliers) to Tokyo was approximately USD 1/kg. To export a similar quantity of cut flowers from Fiji to Tokyo was USD 4/kg. In other words, while the distance between Fiji and Tokyo is double that between Hawaii and Tokyo, the airfreight was quadruple. However, as is well understood in transport issues, economies of scale are often far more important than distance in determining freight rates. Export from Hawaii to Tokyo is frequently done in large specialised air freighters because the economies of scale exist to permit this type of development. In Fiji the export of cut flowers (and chilled fish) could only be done in the cargo hold of passenger flights. Thus the absence of economies of scale combine with isolation and distance from markets to render sub-economic the development of an export-oriented cut flower industry. This problem can be overcome, as was the case with some Asian exporters which developed a cut flower export industry by subsidising airfreight in the initial stages until volumes were adequate to assure the development of specialised air services. However, under WTO rules, direct export subsidies are prohibited for all members except LDCs or countries with a GNP/capita of USD 1,000 or less. Fiji, by virtue of its GNP/capita, is prohibited from providing such export subsidies.

Smallness per se is not necessarily an overarching barrier to a country's ability to shift resources and products between users and markets, which is the essence of the adjustment required in order to prepare for a liberalised market. It could readily be argued that more developed small states are in fact better able to shift resources because of the physical proximity of social and physical infrastructure. It is commonly argued that smallness is not a problem because if resources are required for change but are not available domestically they can be acquired through international trade from related or associated countries. However, their acquisition from global markets is often in small volumes, which in turn means that firms frequently pay a premium on top of the world price. This high cost of imported inputs is a particular problem where firms need to acquire skilled labour and managerial talent, and this in turn results in relatively high unit costs of production in small and isolated locations.

Enterprises originating within those small states also suffer from a further dynamic disadvantage in that they are unable to undertake what has long been considered a normal corporate development path in larger economies, i.e. from supplying the local market, usually with some measure of government protection, to supplying the export sector. This is not possible for firms in these very small states, as the domestic market in which they operate is too small to provide a useful commercial education for the entrepreneur. Hence, these firms are often unable to acquire the necessary experience and market skills before entering much more competitive international markets. Thus the natural learning curve that has been the basis for corporate development in larger economies is not available to firms located in small states. The denial of access to this dynamic process in small states constitutes one very important reason for the lack of entrepreneurial talent outside the agricultural and staple goods sector.

To suggest that the development of new export staples requires the existence of rents is in effect axiomatic as it would describe the early phase of the product life cycle of every new staple, whether it be wheat from Australia or cod fish from Canada. What is different is that in the small states of the central and western Pacific the resource base is generally inadequate and the cost structure too high for these exports to survive even in the longer term without rents. While rents are needed in the initial phase of any new staple development, they remain necessary throughout the entire life cycle of products produced in the island states. The high operating costs therefore create a short product life cycle in comparison to larger economies. In turn the linkages that the short staple life cycle creates means there is limited potential for the development of other sectors of the economy. More importantly, the sharp booms associated with these rents tend to be far more destructive of other non-booming sectors because of Dutch disease effects than in other larger economies.

1.3 The nature and consequence of rent-based development

The traditional economic response to the inherent barriers of smallness, isolation and less developed factor markets, and indeed any other undesirable qualities, has been to argue that domestic factor prices in such economies must be adjusted downwards to reflect these cost disadvantages. Adjusting factor prices sufficiently to compensate for these disadvantages, it is argued, would induce firms operating in competitive industries to locate in small and highly disadvantaged states.

This raises an important but nonetheless highly heretical empirical question. In small, highly vulnerable economies, does there in fact exist sufficient domestic value added (over and above the subsistence reservation wage in the case of labour, the zero-risk rate of return on capital and a zero rent for land and resources) to compensate potential investors for the cumulative cost disadvantages faced by the private sector in such economies? In other words, normal structural adjustment programmes alone may not alleviate the commonly noted absence of bankable private sector investment projects in small vulnerable economies. Such programmes act to lower factor prices to market-determined levels as there may be insufficient domestic value added to compensate for the plethora of inherent disadvantages associated with these economies.

The proponents of the doctrinaire free-market approach to development, when confronted with the possibility that normal competitive industries cannot develop because factor prices cannot adjust sufficiently normally, offer a second line of defence. They argue that if normal competitive industries cannot be readily established in these small, highly vulnerable economies, then this still does not justify any market-distorting intervention by the international community. It is argued that small, highly vulnerable countries may be able to develop their productive capacity in niche market sectors. Such a possibility is again predicated upon the existence of quasi-rents, which permit production at costs that are above normal competitive levels. However, while in other economies these quasi-rents constitute a basis for super-normal profits, in small states they are often a precondition for productive commercial activity as rents are necessary to cover inherently high operating costs.

The history of the post-independence period in the Pacific islands – a region where many of the other disadvantages frequently associated with smallness are found – produces abundant evidence that the emergence and continued existence of virtually every commodity export sector has been associated with the different forms of rents described above.

1.3.1 *Market-based sources of quasi-rent*

Shifts in global commodity markets have had profound effects upon the development of the Pacific island states from the time of the earliest contact that the region had with European explorers. Perhaps the first wave of commodity trade in the region stems from the mid-nineteenth century when sandalwood traders came to the central Pacific in search of sources of supply of the scarce and fragrant timber that were no longer available from the traditional sources of supply in South-East Asia. This pattern of resource development that was experienced during the nineteenth-century sandalwood trade was replicated later in the century with trade in copra, trochus, beche de mere and other tropical marine products. The island states of the central and western Pacific only became sources of supply when the more proximate sources were exhausted as a result of the rapacious exploitation of resources for Asian and European markets. Indeed, it is arguable that this pattern of resource development has not fundamentally changed over 150 years. Without quasi-rents resource developers do not normally enter these markets and the booms induced by termination of supply from other regions generate the quasi-rents needed to induce entry in a difficult and remote region.

In the recent history of the region two different varieties of market-induced quasi-rents have affected the development of the Pacific.

1.3.1.1 Booming sectors

The development of both the Papua New Guinea (PNG) oil and gold deposits and the PNG and Solomon Islands forestry sectors followed immediately after price peaks which induced the exploration and development of very-high-cost green field developments. Both the Solomon Islands and PNG are very-high-cost locations for exploration for oil and gold and the development of logging. In the case of the development of gold mines and oil and natural gas deposits in PNG, the main spur to exploration was the boom in oil and gold prices in 1979–80. The rapid expansion of logging in the Solomon Islands, and also in PNG, is directly a result of the contraction of supply from Sabah and Sarawak and a consequent price peak in the South Sea log market in the early 1990s.

While these quasi-rents have been necessary in small vulnerable states in order to establish new industries, they have all, in quite different ways, created serious impediments to development. Booming sectors have been widely recognised as having negative impacts, through Dutch disease effects upon the non-traded goods sectors of the economy. This has certainly been true in the case of both the Solomon Islands and PNG. While in theory it remains possible to manage resource booms effectively through various macroeconomic instruments such as sterilisation, small countries are particularly vulnerable to such phenomena. Thus there is a far greater tendency for these economies to suffer the economic consequences of Dutch disease and their market-driven successes to result in an economic implosion. Even in sectors where small states have been successful, their small size renders them more prone to Dutch disease effects, which often result in the destruction of non-booming traded goods sectors of the economy and even occasion deleterious effects upon the booming sectors themselves. For example, Tonga's squash boom drew labour away from the manufacturing sector, which resulted in a downturn in export-oriented manufacturing activities as well as the state sector.

Very small developing countries are also less adept at making the type of difficult political and economic decisions needed to manage such booms effectively. In small societies where economic and political actors know each other personally, and few have the economic literacy to understand why revenues from booms should not be spent immediately, it is difficult to convince a parliament not to spend these much-needed resources at once. It is precisely because of their smallness that these island states are more prone to Dutch disease from even small booms that would hardly be felt in other, larger economies.

These booming sectors in high-cost small states also provide a relatively short time period for the development of economic linkages and, as a result, a diminished potential to develop normal economic linkages. Because of their high costs, these sectors (usually natural resources) tend to be developed only when the market has reached a point where the price is sufficiently high to cover operating costs in these small and remote locations. Thus the development of oil and gold reserves as well as forest and marine resources has only occurred when supplies from locations nearer to markets no longer exist. Being high-cost locations, they also tend to be amongst the last countries to enter the sector and the first to exit when the price declines.

The nature of these booming natural resource sectors has also tended to influence the type of entrepreneur attracted to the region. In general, high-risk high-return resource developers are drawn to the region and these tend not to be entrepreneurs interested in other related economic activities which generate lower profits than the booming sector. Within other larger and more advanced economies where there is abundant domestic entrepreneurial talent this would not be a problem as low-risk domestic entrepreneurs would enter to provide those linkages. In the islands, where entrepreneurial talent is at a great premium, this has been particularly problematic. Significantly, those indigenous entrepreneurs that do exist have tended to gain their experience from these booming resource sectors and as a result have a higher risk profile than would normally be expected.

1.3.1.2 Niche market activities

Niche market activities, also generating quasi-rents, are different in that they stem from a temporary market failure caused by the inability of entrepreneurs to combine specialised inputs that are able to produce a particular product or service. These markets are by their nature short-lived and the quasi-rents generated have been transitory, surviving only until such time as entrepreneurs are able to combine inputs and enter a quasi-rent-generating niche market. The history of the island states of the western Pacific is littered with numerous such cases. Perhaps the best example of a quasi-rent-gathering 'niche market economy' is to be found in Tonga which currently exports squash to Japan during a two-month window in November/December when premium prices are paid because few other suppliers have the climatic conditions to supply the Japanese market at this time. Squash is now Tonga's main export. Indeed, Tonga more than any other economy in the region has moved from the market gardening of one product to another in a most entrepreneurial manner, shifting production whenever the demand for a particular product declines. It has shifted throughout its history from exporting bananas, to taro, watermelons, vanilla and squash.

One of the most significant recent examples of successful niche marketing in the region has been the successful export of *sashimi* grade tuna to Japan from Fiji and to a lesser degree from the Marshall Islands and the Solomon Islands. This trade, using local fishermen and capacity, has been based on the high prices that are paid for premium fresh tuna in Japan, the USA and Korea. Without these premiums, the Fiji producers would face the same problems that have been faced in the highly competitive canned tuna market where Pacific island producers have not been as successful as those, such as Thailand and the Philippines, which export to markets such as the EU without the benefit of trade preferences.

The rapid emergence of the traditional Pacific beverage *kava* as a natural sedative in high demand in Northern Europe has also been associated with very high export prices. In Fiji, Vanuatu and Samoa the export of this root crop has provided a massive stimulus to agriculture because of the high quasi-rents associated with this current market niche. However, this niche will no doubt disappear as other countries propagate the traditional Pacific beverage for export. This has already commenced in both Central America and Australia, though given the time taken to grow kava this may take several years. In the interim the price boom has created a substantial incentive for farmers to shift from traditional exports to the export of high-rent-earning kava with little consideration that future prices may not match current observed market prices. Significantly, a recent ban placed on the consumption of kava in several Northern European countries, based on highly contentious scientific analysis, has had devastating effects on several Pacific island states and has underlined their vulnerability to change in such small niche markets.

Niche market activity can constitute a foundation for trade policy in small states. However, the information flows and international marketing links that are necessary are often not available in small vulnerable states, particularly in isolated small island countries. As a result, some highly vulnerable small states, which may be more able to make the change from a trade-preference-dependent economy to a niche-market-based economy, are not obvious candidates for the use of niche markets as a foundation for trade policy. They are frequently disqualified by the lack of a suitable information infrastructure and sophisticated and well-established marketing links. Significantly, it is the existence of labour migration that has been so important in the development of the Tongan squash industry and the creation of the marketing links and information flows that have facilitated the peculiar nature of the Tongan economy as a highly flexible market gardening economy. In economies where that flow of labour and information does not exist, as is the case in so many of the Melanesian economies of the Western Pacific, the development of niche marketing activities seems highly unlikely.

Niche market activities are by their nature highly variable and require rapid adaptation to changing market conditions. The existence of quasi-rents, which by definition characterise niche markets, attracts the entry of competitors. Thus what in one year or season may be a highly profitable niche market may very soon become a crowded low-profit activity associated with high private and social exit costs. This in turn means that a society which has such a basis for its economic development on niche markets will have a radically different development path from those which follow more traditional staples export paths, with often far more volatile macroeconomic environments as entrepreneurs shift from one sector to another, causing short-term dislocation.

In the past and in other societies, a staple export sector could reasonably be expected to generate both backward and forward linkages depending upon the size of the economy, the length of the life cycle and the relative significance of the staple good sector in the economy. These linkages, along with the growth of the staple export sector itself, were frequently responsible for the transformation, if not economic development, of many staples-dependent societies. In the case of niche market products, these life cycles are frequently short and hence traditional economic linkages, the foundation of economic development in so many staples-dependent economies, are not possible. However, niche markets develop and result from non-traditional economic linkages. As niche marketing is by its nature 'marketing intensive', those societies where entrepreneurs develop global linkages will tend to pave the way for new niche products.

1.3.2 De jure sources of rent

The three main sources of rent that have been the most solid foundations for the economies of the region have been trade preferences, preferential taxation regimes and, in the case of the very smallest micro-states, sovereignty. Virtually all the manifestations of these *de jure* rents in the island states have fallen into disrepute within an international community which sees the market as the only valid measure of value and justification for rents. As a result, policy measures are being put in place that will eventually erode the commercial value or application of all these sources of quasi-rent.

1.3.2.1 Trade preferences

Trade preference arrangements have been extremely important in the early development of tropical agricultural exports but have been less significant as liberalisation has eroded the margin of preference in export markets. This has been particularly so in the case of Melanesian tropical tree crop exports such as palm oil, cocoa and coffee. Without what were even in the early post-independence period small margins of trade preference in the European market for tropical tree crop products, the exporters from Melanesia would not have been able to compete with more proximate and competitive suppliers in Asia and Latin America. These small margins of trade preference which are now no larger than 3–5% of the c.i.f. value were often enough to compensate for the isolation of these suppliers, especially when they concerned relatively low value to weight items such as tropical tree crop products.

The main contemporary impact of trade preferences has been in the diversification into garment exports to New Zealand and then Australia from Fiji under the terms of Sparteca in the wake of the 1987 coups. Canned tuna exports from three Melanesian countries (PNG, the Solomon Islands and Fiji) occur under the 24% trade preference margin of the Lomé Convention and its successor the Cotonou Agreement. This has been one of the most conspicuous successes of export diversification of the Lomé Convention. Electrical harnesses for automobiles are exported from Samoa to Australia under Sparteca. Employment has recently been as high as 2,000 workers in Samoa's largest private sector employer.

Trade preferences in the Pacific have played a vital role in providing a stable, predictable and long-term source of quasi-rents that have successfully induced investment in agriculture and manufacturing in these small, vulnerable states. However, even large margins of trade preference had little effect in the case of the most vulnerable and disadvantaged economies, e.g. Tuvalu, Kiribati and Tonga, although larger countries such as Fiji, Samoa, the Solomon Islands and PNG have taken advantage of trade preferences. It is, nevertheless, clear that while trade preferences are extremely important to small states, they cannot long remain a basis for the development of these states. What they can do is provide substantial economic rents which can induce export-oriented investment and commence the necessary process of learning that will enable societies to move to less-rent-dependent activity. The critics of trade preference are correct in arguing that it can neither act as a long-term stimulus nor as a substitute for competitiveness. The economic benefits of trade preference were gained early in the life cycle of those products where high margins or trade preference existed.

What has been noted, as is so frequently the case with all forms of protection and subvention, is that governments in the island states of the western Pacific have behaved as though these trade preferences are permanent and have failed to undertake the difficult measures necessary to shift to less-preference-dependent growth. While this observation is factually correct, one can legitimately ask whether any such measures would have been successful at so early a stage in their development given the cost disadvantages suffered by these countries.

It has been noted by the critics of trade-preference regimes that the greatest beneficiaries of these trade preferences have not even maintained their market share in their traditional export markets in comparison to those which receive no or much less preference.[2] While there is no disputing the decline in market share, the critics of trade preference fail to recognise the possibility that in such economies, in the absence of trade preference, no monetised activity would have occurred. Here the proponents of the emerging trade regime depend upon a thoroughly dubious optimism devoid of any understanding of commercial reality. They argue that even the most disadvantaged societies can become competitive and thus trade preference cannot have a long-term place in development strategy. This is an empirical assertion that remains unproven.

Irrespective of the value of trade preferences in the past, they are undeniably eroding over time as a result of WTO and unilateral liberalisation. It is thus imperative that the international community devise appropriate interventions that will replicate the results of trade preference while avoiding some of the more market-distorting consequences. The difficulty rests less with technical problems of engineering such a facility, than in the political will to recognise and resolve the problem of marginalisation in a globalised economy.

1.3.2.2 Tax concessions

The provision by fiat of tax concessions and other subsidies to exporters that establish or maintain export-oriented production has also fallen into disrepute. Given the ad hoc and frequently opaque application of this instrument in the western Pacific, it is unsurprising that the international community, increasingly driven by corporate governance issues, has pursued a policy of assisting these states to dismantle these regimes. These tax policies have nonetheless been instrumental in assuring export-oriented investment.

Perhaps the single largest expansion of export-oriented investment in the western Pacific occurred in Fiji with the growth and development of the garment export industry in the wake of the 1987 coups. It was the liberalisation of garment imports from island countries into New Zealand and

[2] It is ironic that it is the OECD that has been amongst the strongest critics of trade-preference regimes for developing countries at a time when its members have concluded more preferential trading agreements than at any other time.

then Australia in 1988 that created the push factor for domestic producers to locate in the islands. The liberalisation created a massive margin of trade preference which was then eroded by the rapid MFN liberalisation of the sector. However, it was the tax-free factory system implemented in Fiji after the coups, along with massive devaluation of the currency, that pulled those producers towards what was then a highly politically unstable environment.

Tax concessions were one of the key factors that pulled New Zealand and Australian manufacturers to Fiji rather than one of the twelve other island states that benefited from duty-free access to the Australian and New Zealand garment market. Tax concessions have also been important in far less benign cases such as that of the gold mining industry in Fiji which has operated under secret tax agreements with the state since 1980. These agreements have effectively rendered these gold mines tax free. It is this opaque use of tax concessions that has pushed the international community to pressure developing countries in the western Pacific to eliminate tax concessions and move to a low rate for both domestic and export-oriented production. By and large this policy advice has been strongly resisted by these states.

It has not just been Fiji that made use of ad hoc tax concessions to induce foreign investment. Samoa and the Solomon Islands have made extensive use of tax concessions in promoting export-oriented production both in manufacturing and in agriculture and marine-product exports. In the Northern Pacific as well, tax concessions for investors are seen as a vital ingredient in compensating investors who chose to locate in such disadvantaged areas.

1.3.2.3 Sovereignty: from de jure to nefarious rents

Much of the economic activity in the very smallest micro-states of the central and western Pacific does not stem from trade preferences or tax concessions or from booming sectors or even niche markets. Indeed, in many of these countries there is almost no staples production at all. The sole source of export earnings stems from the provision of services which are deliverable solely by virtue of the sovereignty of these states. Indeed, the sale of stamps, domain names for the internet (e.g. tv for Tuvalu and Nu for Niue) and flags of convenience for shipping, e.g. in the Marshall Islands, are examples of relatively benign rent-generating service activities in the region.

However, the sovereignty-related services provided by small states in the Pacific have not all necessarily been benign nor even legal. Indeed, some of these activities – such as the sale of passports – have been of the most questionable domestic legality even though they have, in the past, been systematically organised at relatively high levels of government. Some seven of the fourteen Pacific Island Forum countries also run finance centres with varying degrees of success. The two most notable successes have been those of the Cook Islands and Vanuatu. While many of the activities of companies operating in these finance centres are no doubt perfectly legal, some involve money laundering activities. As the OECD moves to impose greater controls on tax constituencies that provide 'harmful tax competition', i.e. tax havens, the revenue that small states derive from these rents will decline.

Increasingly the fertile high islands of Melanesia, such as PNG and Fiji, have become source countries for illegal drugs such as cannabis which is exported to Australia and New Zealand. However, more significantly these countries as well as other Pacific island countries have become entrepôts for other more dangerous drugs that are being smuggled into Australia and New Zealand from Asia and South America. It is clear that as the legal economic opportunities to obtain the rents necessary to maintain economic activity evaporate in the face of globalisation, those in small states will turn increasingly and more actively to nefarious activities at the margins of the global production process. This is likely to lead to the increasing criminalisation of these states.

1.3.3 The conundrum of copra and tourism

What has been proposed above is a general theory of trade and development and therefore if it is to have empirical validity then all industries must be covered. There are two particular cases where it can be argued that the theory does not appear to apply. Indeed both copra exports and tourism, the region's oldest and newest export sectors, appear to be counter-examples to the general rent theory of trade and development. However, these counter-examples may be more apparent than real.

Even a cursory reading of the history of the copra trade in the South Seas will show that it started, like all staples, during the boom in the late nineteenth century and developed more significantly again with the boom in the post-First World War era. Since the 1920s copra production has been in decline in the Pacific. Production is now based purely on competitive prices with almost no subventions and no trade preferences. However, production now occurs only in those locations where the soil has few alternative uses and labour remains cheap because there is no alternative monetised activity. Indeed, in many remote islands where copra production continues, the cost of production is actually quite low and the payment to resource owners for copra is pure rent as their land and labour have no alternative uses. In some central and western Pacific countries even copra production has ceased. With the exception of some plantations which continue to operate in Melanesia, where alternatives exist to copra production in the South Pacific it has by and large ceased.

Tourism can also be seen as a counter-example to the theory that normal competitive industries cannot survive without rents in the central and western Pacific. In most countries of the region it remains a niche activity geared towards wreck divers, war veterans and culture and adventure tourists. These are all clearly niche markets. Only in the case of Fiji is there anything that can be considered a mass tourism destination. This is both a counter-example and simultaneously further evidence of the theory's validity. Tourism in Fiji is generally highly competitive and it competes on the international market without major subvention (except for tax concessions), either market-based or de jure. Yet it competes only on the Australia and New Zealand market as a mass destination and this is because this is the one sector where Fiji is no longer remote. Indeed, as a destination for Australian and New Zealand tourists Fiji remains more proximate than its principal Asian competitors in Bali and Thailand. For other source markets such as the USA and Japan, Fiji remains a tiny niche. Thus it is the violation of the condition of distance and isolation that renders Fiji able to develop a mass and competitive market for tourism services.

1.4 Conclusion

The dependence of these small and remote vulnerable states on rent and quasi-rent as a basis for monetised export-oriented production raises several profound and disturbing economic and policy questions, the resolutions of which are beyond the scope of this chapter. If the rent theory is correct then the question arises of how these countries will respond to the consistent erosion of those rents that results from liberalisation and the demise of sovereignty and tax concessions. The response of the international community has been to argue that trade liberalisation necessitates structural adjustment, and yet there has been no analysis of whether there exists sufficient domestic value added in these small vulnerable states that can be adjusted downwards to compensate for the inherent disadvantages of smallness, isolation and physical dispersion. Moreover, the international community has not addressed the more difficult policy issue that possibly prices cannot be adjusted to attract investment and that, as a result, some of these small vulnerable countries may not be structurally viable in a globalised and liberalised economy. If this is the case and structural adjustment cannot work to attract investment, at what point will the international community shift its policy, or will we continue to see, as has been the case in the last few years, demands for ever greater and more politically intrusive structural adjustments when private sector investment fails to materialise?

It is often only at the world's very edges that one can see the impact of historical changes with some clarity. For the central and western Pacific states the impact of liberalisation and globalisation on their current trading regime could not be of greater significance. While we have pointed to several countries which are so small as to render sub-economic all commercial production of goods and services, the impact of globalisation may well create even more such countries. In these societies remittances, aid and migration become the only basis for consumption above physical subsistence. At the very least, for those who optimistically argue that these countries can develop on an unstable base of niche market activities there is a need to rethink the nature of assistance that is provided to these societies to assure that it reflects this reality.

2

Small countries: a survey of the literature

MICHAEL WEATHERHEAD

2.1 Introduction

The study of the economic consequences of being a small state has received a large amount of attention from policy-makers, academics and researchers over the years. This is due in the main to the many arguments put forward attesting to the economic disadvantages countries suffer as a result of their size. These range from low returns to scale in the private economy to export dependence, increased vulnerability and volatility as well as the costs of isolation.

The objective of this chapter is to review these different strands of the literature taking each of the major areas of interest in turn. After an examination of the different concepts of country size presented in the literature, the author will review the range of constraints to growth for small countries that stem from the limited size of small country domestic markets. These include limits to the ability to develop a manufacturing sector (Pryor, 1972; Banerji, 1977) to financial constraints (Fry, 1982; Khatkhate and Short, 1980) and export dependence (Kuznets, 1960). The literature dealing with the constraints is advanced in both a theoretical way, reminiscent of the earlier literature, and also a more empirically based manner, one that marries both the theoretical and the empirical.

The chapter goes on to look at the literature concerned with the issue of volatility, which arises out of the greater openness characteristic of small country economies, and its possible effects on growth. The issue of isolation and the costs it presents to small countries in terms of higher input costs (Redding and Venables, 2001) is also an area of the literature on small economies which has had much attention paid to it. The costs of isolation in conjunction with those resulting from higher volatility combine to provide two elements in another field of study related to small economies, that of vulnerability. Recent development of a number of vulnerability indices has shown a new way of looking at the state of a country's economy (Atkins et al., 2001; Briguglio, 1995).

Having reviewed the arguments put forward for the economic disadvantages perceived to be inherent in small economies, the chapter will examine the empirically based literature that focuses on measuring the relationship between size and growth. Many of the empirical studies use regression-based analysis in examining the growth of small nations (Milner and Westaway, 1993; Easterly and Kraay, 2001; Khalaf, 1979). These studies appear to contradict the theories (outlined above) of how small countries are economically at a disadvantage as a result of their size. Reasons for the apparent discrepancy between the theory and evidence are also reviewed in this section (Easterly and Kraay, 2001; Romer, 1986; Blake, 2001).

In the final section of the chapter, the proposals various authors have made with regard to the strategies small countries might adopt for self-development are reviewed. Issues of economic management rather than economic characteristics are the primary focus – is it the policies rather than the size of countries that have led to some doing better than others?

2.1.1 Concepts of size

A good place to start a review of the literature on country size and economic performance is to examine the concept of size. Country size can be measured in a multitude of ways, although the different measurements can generally be classified into one of two categories – geographic or economic. This variety of measurements does of course make comparisons between papers difficult. For instance, even within the same measure, cut-off points are often made on a quite arbitrary basis.

2.1.1.1 Geographic

Country size as measured in terms of either population or actual physical land mass is a common form of measurement amongst many of the papers reviewed here. Kuznets (1960) decides on population size as his measure of smallness: 'By a small nation I mean an independent sovereign state, with a population of ten million or less.'[1] He openly admits though, that this cut-off point is simply a rough decision. Other authors such as Srinivasan (1986) determine countries with fewer than 1.5 million people as very

[1] Kuznets (1960), p. 14.

small, and those with populations between 1.5 million and 5 million as small. Cherney and Syrquin (1975) classify countries with fewer than 5 million people as small whereas Easterly and Kraay (2001) define smallness for their measurement purposes as below 1 million; Armstrong and Read (1998) use 3 million as their cut-off value.

The most widely held view of recent times is to consider those countries that have populations of less than 1.5 million (with the exception of Botswana, Jamaica, Mauritius and Papua New Guinea) as small states. Even when the same cut-off is used, as in the works by Easterly and Kraay (2001) and Atkins et al. (2001), the sample of small countries used can vary quite substantially. For instance, Easterly and Kraay (2001) include high-income countries (with small populations) such as Qatar, Luxembourg and Iceland in their calculations, countries not found in the work of Atkins et al. (2001).

It is not of course automatically the case that population size and land area will be correlated measures. For the main reason that population size – due to its reference to labour – is possibly more closely connected with potential economic concepts of country size, it is this measure that has prevailed over land area as the most widely used measure in terms of a country's natural characteristics. Land area is not necessarily a redundant measure, but the fact that a number of LDCs have small populations but an extremely large land area makes it less attractive in terms of the exercise being conducted here.

2.1.1.2 Economic

Despite its obvious limitations for measuring the development of a nation state, GDP is the economic measure of size most often used in the literature when examining the question, does country size play any part in determining the level of development or economic performance of a country? It is however often used as a secondary measure to population size for these purposes. With respect to LDCs, the arguments against the exclusive use of GDP are those that led to the creation of the United Nations Index of human development.

An alternative to GDP is a country's real gross national product (GNP), as preferred by Khalaf (1979), which can often produce quite a different value to GDP if, for instance, many of a country's nationals are expatriates who remit money to relatives back home. Gross domestic expenditure (GDE) is another alternative. As Srinivasan (1986) makes clear, 'a poor country with lower per capita income could still have a large GNP (because of its population size). But it would still be only a small potential market, because the bulk of its population is too poor to be potential demanders of anything but basic commodities.'[2]

Davenport (2001) examines smallness in terms of trade flows, proposing a definition of smallness as being below a certain percentage share of world trade, whether by aggregate trade flows or on a sectoral basis. Similarly another economic concept of size put forward by the international trade literature is the market power a country displays. As described by Srinivasan (1986), it is 'the ability of an economy to affect its terms of trade by changing its volume of exports and imports'.[3] This is an interesting definition of smallness. All open macroeconomics models are based on this particular assumption although empirical economists provide minimal support in favour of this, e.g. estimates by Senhandji and Montenegro (1998) show price elasticity of export demand for all countries, whether large or small, to be very small and in most cases less than one (absolutely). This would suggest considerable market power of even apparently small countries. Without going into this debate some qualifications can be made about the terms of trade (TOT) definition of smallness. TOT can be commodity specific and even a small country might affect the international price of a particular commodity. However, if the commodity in question happens to occupy the lion's share in a small state's export bundle, the overall TOT might be influenced by the country's own supplies.

With this last definition and the previous comment made about the ability of a population actually to purchase items produced dictating the size of the market, we come to one of the main areas of discussion around the topic of smallness, namely, the size of the domestic market.

2.2 Constraints to growth and development

Many of the perceived economic disadvantages attributed in the literature to a country's size are interlinked. The starting point for the majority of these problems is the limited size of the small country domestic market. Much of the literature covered in this section features the multiple effects this feature of small countries has on their growth and development prospects. The following flow diagram (figure 2.1) helps identify the different linkages between the various areas of study as described in the papers reviewed, and

[2] Srinivasan (1986), p. 205. [3] Ibid., p. 205.

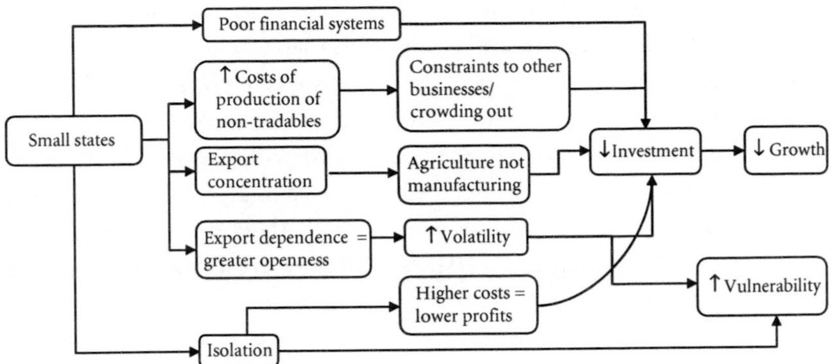

Figure 2.1 Flow diagram of causes of small country disadvantages

how they lead to the authors' conclusions that smallness constrains growth and development. It provides a route map for the literature foci that follow.

2.2.1 *Export dependence*

Many of the arguments put forward for the inherent disadvantage of being a small nation in the traditional literature are based around the idea of limited domestic market size. The main impediment of having either a small domestic population or limited natural resources is that it is not economically efficient to cater for the home market and that is why many small states are so export focused. At first glance, one might question why this might be considered a problem, but as Kuznets (1960) points out, 'While foreign trade permits concentration of a small country's activity in the economically advantageous sectors, not all goods needed for domestic use can be imported; nor can a country's economic growth be securely built upon exports to a few countries of destination.' The old adage of not having all your eggs in one basket applies very much to small economies. The Joint Task Force report (2000) highlights this dependence amongst small countries, with trade to GDP ratios above 110 per cent for small countries; this compares with 38 per cent in all low income countries.

2.2.2 *Export concentration*

Stemming from the export dependence that characterises the shape of small country economies is the fact that small countries often find themselves focused on just a small number of export products destined for a small number of recipient countries. The limited available labour force means production of a broad range of export products is less likely in small countries. Often the exports of small nations are agriculture-based. A possible reason for this, outlined in a survey[4] in Kuznets (1960), is that, certainly in the first half of the twentieth century, there was a very strong political link between exporting small countries and the large countries their exports were destined for. This is not a great surprise. Many small states were former colonies of the European powers in previous centuries and their economies at that time were often geared towards producing items for the colonial power's home market. Sugar is a good example of this. Many small states in the Caribbean, Africa and Pacific regions had their economies organised by the United Kingdom for the sole export of sugar to the British market. Movements away from exports of raw sugar into, for example, refining of raw sugar (where the greatest value addition is to be achieved) was discouraged in these countries via the imposition of high tariffs. In the second half of the twentieth century, after independence was gained, many preferential trade agreements were established between the large European countries and their former colonies, contributing towards the continuation of dependence on small numbers of agricultural exports with a small number of destinations for those exports. With commodity prices having fallen relative to manufactures and services in the past and likely to continue to do so (Hewitt and Page, 2002), there is a real threat that focusing on these products will inhibit growth and development.

Concentrating on a sector other than agriculture does not necessarily improve a small country's prospects however. For instance, the economies of the Caribbean have been very badly affected by the events of 11 September. This is because of their export concentration in tourism, which accounts for 76 per cent of total exports in St Lucia, 61 per cent in Antigua and Barbuda and 55 per cent in Barbados, for example (Joint Task Force, 2000). The reduced number of Americans flying has had serious implications for their economies' overall growth.

2.2.3 *Size and manufacturing*

Because of the research done on basic commodity prices,[5] it is now widely accepted that the economic development of a country cannot rely on

[4] Kuznets (1960), p. 22. [5] See bibliography of Hewitt and Page (2002).

agricultural expansion alone. Industrialisation and manufacturing is seen by many as the next rung on the ladder of development for low-income countries. A range of potential reasons why countries have shown different levels of development of their manufacturing bases (in terms of plant size) has been offered by a number of studies. Both theory and evidence point to a number of factors that are complicit in this finding. These constraints on manufacturing development include the size of the market (Pryor, 1972), poor financial systems (Fry, 1982), tariff barriers in export markets and the cost of transportation of inputs (Redding and Venables, 2001).

Under the simple assumptions of homothetic production functions and invariant factor price ratios across countries, the result that average plant size in a country is limited due to the size of its market and capability of its financial sector is an obvious one. Banerji (1977) postulates, however, that production functions of manufacturing may be non-homothetic – meaning there may be more than one expansion path in a given industry which could mean different returns to scale; combined with the assumption that relative factor costs may well vary between countries (particularly developed and less developed), then manufacturers in different countries could be on different paths. Assuming, as is reasonable, that the relative factor price of capital to labour is lower in developed countries, then these manufacturers will pursue a more capital-intensive path, whilst LDCs adopt a more labour-intensive route. With the common belief that the capital intensive expansion path is associated with higher returns to scale, then this will lead to a greater average plant size amongst capital-intensive countries and greater levels of profit for those in capital-intensive manufacturing.

The relative factor prices of small countries are therefore critical in dictating which expansion path they are likely to follow, and thus the levels of returns achievable. The relative factor prices of capital and labour of small countries will depend on factors including the level of development, which will to a degree dictate the relative factor prices of a small LDC, and its resource base or capacity to obtain competitively priced capital. Except for the exceptional success stories amongst small countries, namely Hong Kong, Singapore and small European states, it is reasonable to assume that labour is cheaper relative to capital in small countries, which would lead to a more labour-intensive form of manufacturing and therefore a lower return and restricted growth opportunities.

Banerji's findings show his hypothesis to hold. This then bodes ill not only for domestic production of non-tradables in small countries – such as infrastructure which requires large-scale capital-intensive operations in order to reap the benefits of scale economies, but also for export production, implying that development of the export sector may well be limited for small countries in manufacturing, therefore reducing a small country's ability to develop in higher 'value added' directions.

The author's findings (as he himself admits) are limited by the data available and the proxies used. Indicative rather than definitive is the description he likes to give his results. An interesting point to note in the discussion on relative capital intensity of manufacturing, in one of the findings of Banerji, is that in textiles (a form of light manufacture many commentators believe is the first rung of the manufacturing ladder for agrarian-based LDC economies) average plant size is the same in both the developed and the less-developed world. This form of manufacturing (which is less capital/more labour intensive than others) therefore shows that it lends itself equally to production in the developed and the less-developed world.

2.2.4 *Domestic production of non-tradables*

As touched on above, a disadvantage facing small economies alluded to in Kuznets (1960), Srinivasan (1986) and Armstrong (1993) is the possibility of higher per unit costs of various services that for economic and social reasons cannot be imported. Whereas Kuznets (1960) suspected that smallness did not prove a particular obstacle in the provision of a number of different non-tradables such as health care and education (which he believed were small scale in nature the world over), he did concede that in areas such as infrastructure smallness might be an issue.

The capital-intensive nature of infrastructure manufacturing – materials, machinery etc. – demonstrates why it is less developed as an industry in smaller countries and thus more expensive to undertake. The higher per unit cost of infrastructure partly explains the proportionately larger size of small country governments, which can lead to crowding out of the private sector in terms of investment (Gutierrez, 1996). The resultant lack of infrastructure is most serious for a small country in terms of costs for other business. An example of one industry in which a number of small ACP countries are involved and where good overland transport linkages as well as port facilities are vital is the sugar industry. Poor infrastructure can lead to higher costs and less growth in the sector. Good infrastructure in Australia for instance and the recent privatisation and improvement of transport and port facilities in Brazil help these countries to be amongst the most efficient sugar exporters in the world (ABARE 1999).

Continuing the theme of small countries' lack of ability to exploit economies of scale in certain non-tradables, Armstrong (1993) identify retail as another sector that fails to exploit economies of scale in situations of limited domestic market size. He finds that the Isle of Man has more single outlet firms and few larger superstores relative to the UK. Energy distribution and electricity generation are also areas where small-scale production has led to higher costs. Whether this is more a feature of island economies or simply small economies may be dependent on the region in which the small country is located and on the available supplies.

2.2.5 *Size and matters of finance*

The predicted effect on growth of the above-mentioned chain of problems is compounded when one considers the effects size has on the financial sector of small countries. Often dominated by foreign commercial banks, their financial sectors are invariably uncompetitive (Fry, 1982). This has serious implications for the ability of individuals and organisations to get funding for investment purposes. The fact that many countries export primary commodities with falling prices reduces the returns to these sectors and further contributes to the problems of low investment. Small countries, particularly those prone to natural shocks, can also often be seen as highly risky by foreign investors. Crowding in can be a positive externality of official aid (Collier and Dollar, 1999), but other reasons such as costs of information collection, detailing capacity to repay a loan as well as the cost of enforcing contracts have a negative effect on willingness to invest.

The particular economic characteristics of small countries also tend to circumscribe the monetary policy options available to a central bank. Economic delineation of country size for financial purposes can be measured as the size of domestic production destined for domestic consumption versus the amount produced for export. As Khatkhate and Short (1980) explain, the greater the amount produced for export, the smaller the control a central bank has over its economic targets. This control is often further decreased in small countries because many of the services being supplied domestically are designed to cater for the tourism trade.

The authors go on to hypothesise that if one is an export price taker, as small countries invariably are, then one cannot control the value of one's exports. Similarly, control over import inflation is also beyond the power of the central bank. All these factors can lead to a greater vulnerability in financial terms for small countries and greater vulnerability is often reflected in greater volatility, which has the potential to constrain growth. Gylfason (1999) also finds that, up to a point, higher inflation (during the period under review in his article) tended to be associated with lower exports as a proportion of GDP and also with slow growth of countries.

Capital mobility and fixed exchange rates render the actions of a small open economy central bank particularly ineffective. An example (along the lines of the Mundell-Fleming model for small open economies) of this ineffectiveness is the case of the central bank increasing money supply and simultaneously reducing interest rates – an expansive monetary policy often used as a stimulus to the economy. In the small country case, these actions will lead to an increase in aggregate demand for imports and non-traded commodities. The lower interest rates will lead to a capital outflow. With remittances often contributing significantly to the GNP of small countries, lower interest rates will encourage more rapid outward remittances or slower inward remittances. All of these factors will reduce the small countries' foreign reserves, which reduces commercial bank reserves, forcing the authorities to undertake to decrease the money supply and raise interest rates to protect exchange reserves.

In terms of fiscal policy, small countries tend to rely more heavily on trade taxes than on income taxes – the primary revenue source of large country governments (Codrington, 1989). With the international movement towards free trade, reductions in import duties and export taxes will have serious consequences for levels of revenue and a country's ability to fund production of its non-tradables.

All of this is not to say that small countries' central banks have no options. Suggestions made in Khatkhate and Short (1980) with regard to different policy initiatives designed to compensate for these monetary disadvantages are examined in the concluding section of this chapter.

2.2.6 Volatility

As just mentioned, the limited control of small economies' central banks can leave them exposed to financial volatility. In the preceding discussion, we saw how small countries, due to their limited market size, become more export orientated and more open.

Greater openness (as measured by trade/GDP) brings a greater reliance on events outside one's control and subsequently greater exposure to variations in the global economy. An exogenous shock to a large country on the other side of the world importing goods from a small country may well result in the small country feeling the effects of the shock just as much as, if not more strongly than, the large country. Although dwarfed in volumetric terms, it is because the proportionate size of small countries' exports to GDP is often far higher than that of larger more developed countries that the effect might be greater for the small, rather than the large country. Growth, up to a point, can be sustained in large countries due to their large domestic market, which reduces reliance on exports. Even though countries such as the USA and Japan are amongst the largest exporters in the world, their proportion of exports to GDP is amongst the smallest.

The possibility of greater volatility, as figure 2.1 shows, can have two effects. It might lead to lower investment and in turn lower growth. It could also lead to greater vulnerability.

The link between volatility and smallness (assuming small equates to open) is tested in Easterly and Kraay (2001). Their regressing of TOT volatility[6] on a number of dummy variables, including one for small countries, shows the small country dummy to be significant. They account for this result by saying that it is due to the unavoidably highly open nature of small economies. Evidence from the authors' regression results that concentration of export products by small countries could account for the volatility is deemed inconclusive.

Having already established that smaller countries suffer higher growth rate volatility, the authors attempt to analyse to what extent TOT volatility contributes to the higher volatility of small countries' overall growth rates. TOT volatility is included as an explanatory variable in their growth regression featured in the second section. The significance of the 'standard deviation of growth' variable in explaining average annual real per capita GDP growth – despite controlling for TOT volatility (and hence small countries' greater openness) – signifies that other factors are also responsible for the higher volatility of the growth experienced by smaller countries. One possible factor, which will be examined later, is proneness to natural disasters.

[6] They define terms-of-trade volatility as the standard deviation of the growth in the local currency price of exports multiplied by the share of exports in GDP minus the (similarly calculated) price growth of imports multiplied by import share of GDP.

2.2.6.1 Volatility and growth

The fact that small countries suffer higher volatility of growth is an important relationship to have established. It links to research which, until the 1980s, had treated growth theory and business-cycle theory as dichotomous. Little attention had been paid to the possibility that business-cycle volatility may have an effect on growth. Romer (1986) proposes that it is difficult to judge the success of growth theories, due to these theories assuming away any variation in output from the business cycle. As highlighted in the previous section, analysis of long-run trends in growth patterns showed an increase in productivity growth rate, not a decrease (decreasing returns being a fundamental assumption of standard growth theories).

Ramey and Ramey (1995) attempt to clarify the relationship between the two theories, through use of regression techniques. Their analysis of a ninety-two-country sample covering the 1960s–1980s amounts to a simple regression of the mean growth of the countries on the standard deviation of growth. Their overall results (fig. 2.2) show a negative relationship, i.e. that a higher volatility of growth results in lower growth rates.

Testing the robustness of this result is vital as the conclusion appears to throw up a paradox: that small countries with higher volatility rates have lower mean growth rates, which, as we shall see, is in direct conflict with the results of many empirical studies. Robustness of the model is built up through the introduction of a vector of control variables designed to account for other characteristics of the countries whose contribution to the result may be masked in their absence from the regression.

Variables we have seen before (included in growth regressions in previous sections), such as initial GDP (to account for convergence), the level of investment as a share of GDP and the level of human capital[7] at the beginning of the sample period, are identified by Levine and Renelt (1992) as being robust across specifications.[8] Their inclusion strengthens the result found by Ramey and Ramey, producing a ratio of a 0.5 per cent change in mean growth from a 1 per cent change in the standard deviation. Despite this, both investment share and initial GDP are larger in terms of economic magnitude – both exhibiting positive relationships with growth.

[7] As is usual in these regressions, the proxy used for initial level of human capital is a measure of the numbers in school at a certain date.

[8] Reference to this type of sensitivity analysis for variable selection in growth regressions where so many variables could seem to be an influence.

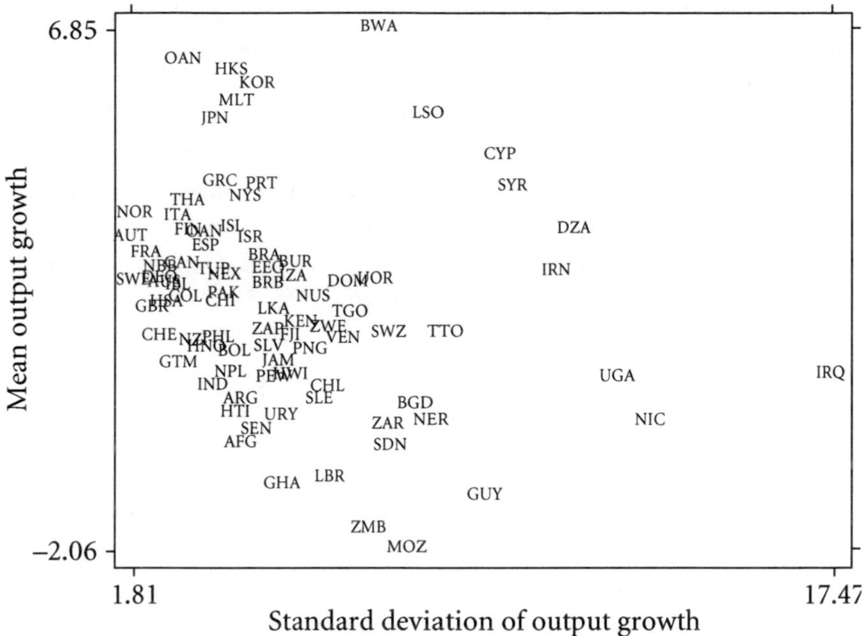

Source: Ramey and Ramey (1995)

Figure 2.2 Simple correlation of growth and volatility

2.2.6.2 Investment: is it the key?

Many authors believe it is investment that links high volatility and low growth. The theoretical background for such an assertion is that of the 'irreversibilities' in investment. That is to say, increased volatility leads to lower investment and therefore lower growth rates. 'When projects are irreversible, agents must make investment timing decisions that trade off the extra returns from early commitment against the benefits of increased information gained by waiting. In an environment in which the underlying stochastic structure is itself subject to random change, events whose long-run implication are uncertain can create an investment cycle by temporarily increasing the returns to waiting for information.'[9] In other words, it is safer to wait, in an uncertain world. Ramey and Ramey (1991) demonstrate that if firms have to commit to their investment ahead of time then volatility can lead to lower growth due to firms operating at sub-optimal levels ex post.

[9] Bernanke (1983), p. 81.

Arguments of a positive relationship between volatility and growth also have investment acting as a bridge, this time as a result of higher precautionary savings (resulting from higher volatility) leading to higher investment and thus higher growth – the theory resting on the assumption that the increased investment will be fully reflected in higher output.

In testing the empirical strength of the argument that investment acts as the link, Ramey and Ramey (1995) include different measures of investment in their original equation for testing the relationship between volatility and mean growth. The different measurements of investment alter the results in an insignificant way, thus leading to the conclusion that investment is not the means by which increased volatility is transmitted into lower growth.

With investment ruled out (empirically) as a candidate for the throughflow of higher volatility to lower growth, innovation variance[10] – a measure more closely connected to the idea of uncertainty – is examined. Empirically it is found that countries with higher innovation variances have lower mean conditional growth rates.

The paradox (mentioned above) presented by the results of Ramey and Ramey (1995) and various studies (in section 2.3) arises from separate regression findings. First, higher volatility has a negative effect on growth; secondly, small countries experience higher volatility; and thirdly small states do not have lower growth rates. In this instance it is not axiomatic that because A results in B and B results in C, A will result in C. The general theme and conclusions from different papers reviewed on the subject of volatility does however point to a consensual view of small countries suffering from greater volatility as a result of their size. The resultant uncertainty that would cause could then act as an impediment to the development process.

2.2.7 Isolation and geographic surroundings

From figure 2.1 we can see the possible effects isolation can have on a country's growth performance either in terms of higher costs resulting in lower profits, thus lower investment and lower growth, or in terms of vulnerability. The topic of isolation is one that features in many of the areas of

[10] For a detailed breakdown of the definition of 'innovation variance' as used by Ramey and Ramey (1995), see ibid., pp. 1143–4.

research related to country size. It is often examination of small island economies that precipitates discussion on the issue. Many studies though examine isolation in the context of its potential influence on GDP through the flow of ideas, goods and factors of production, regardless of island status,[11] a country can be landlocked or an island, but if it is far away from the markets it interacts with economically, then the same problems are faced.

One of the oft-mentioned problems is higher transportation costs. These higher costs can be as a result of smaller cargoes to small countries being off main transportation routes or a lack of resources to develop facilities to accommodate large ships. The median value of the ratio of insurance and freight costs to import values in the Joint Task Force report (2000) is higher for small island and landlocked states than for all developing countries. If of course a country is landlocked, then by definition, it is surrounded by a regional market. For island economies too (though sometimes to a lesser extent), regional markets are a feature of their location. The strength of regional markets and how this may impact on the growth/development of a small country has also been examined in a number of studies.

2.2.7.1 Isolation

A recent paper by Redding and Venables (2001) examines the importance of isolation in determining differences in levels of per capita income across countries. The authors use a structural model using per capita income, bilateral trade and relative manufacturing prices in order to find the effects of geography on variation of per capita income across a range of countries, measuring bilateral trade flows via a gravity model in order to obtain a meaningful estimation of market and supplier access for countries.

The overall results of the study confirm what a number of other studies have found in relation to geography and national income, that geographic factors affecting market and supplier access have an important bearing on variations in per capita income, in this instance accounting for 70 per cent of the cross-country variation in per capita income. The authors' finding that the relative price of manufacturing goods is negatively related to a country's supplier access demonstrates the through-flow of the effects of isolation to lower income levels as shown in figure 2.1.

[11] For a list of studies analysing the effects of market access on factor incomes, see Redding and Venables (2001), p. 4.

Inclusion of variables to control for technology and the price of factors of production allows the authors to demonstrate the robustness of their results. Prediction by the model of the effect of a number of these variables, such as landlocked or island status, shows the former to contribute negatively to trade, the latter positively. Redding and Venables (2001) also find that manufacturing costs are negatively associated with a country's supplier access. Whether this is a problem that would affect all small countries, not just remote ones, is an issue not just of transport costs, but also business practices – reduced prices for bulk purchases, etc.

The finding that the bilateral trade flows predicted by the model show a positive relationship with the trade policy-based measure of openness as developed by Sachs and Warner (1995) is highlighted here due to the criticisms that that measure of openness has faced.[12] As a result, conclusions drawn from the findings of the Redding and Venables paper that increased openness leads to a 60–70 per cent increase in per capita GDP should bear this criticism of openness in mind.

As figure 2.3 demonstrates, countries with greater access to foreign markets in terms of geographic proximity have higher levels of per capita GDP. Thus, despite the continuing integration of world goods and financial markets, which standard neo-classical growth theory predicts would lead to increased levels of Foreign Direct Investment (FDI) through the increased mobility of firms and convergence of country income levels, large differences remain between the income levels of countries.

The findings of the paper do not preclude the future shift in location of large centres of manufacturing which could alter the results.

2.2.7.2 Geographic surroundings

As mentioned earlier in this section, it is not just geographic isolation in terms of distance from major economic markets that can be a factor in determining per capita GDP, but also the region a country is situated in.

Armstrong (1998) looks at the differences in economic performance (in terms of various income measures) between small countries in different regions. He utilises a standard neo-classical growth model with a number of variables – binary, ordinal and quantitative – for assessing various features of the small economies examined in the cross-country analysis. An ordinal variable is used as a proxy for region.

[12] Footnote 13 of Subramanian and Roy (2001).

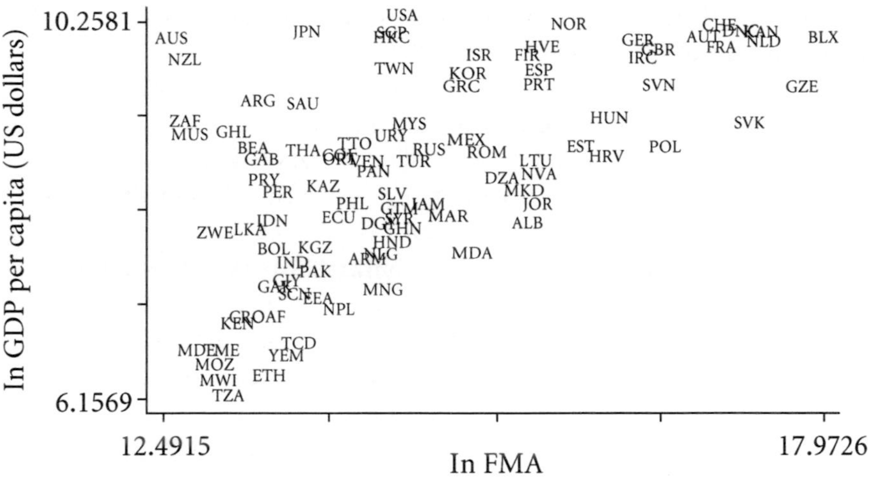

Source: Redding and Venables (2001)
Figure 2.3 GDP per capita and foreign market access

Values between one and eight are used for coding, the highest being for North America, the lowest for Southern Asia. He finds this variable to be significant, with a strong positive effect on performance, i.e. that the region in which a small country is based does have an effect on its level of per capita income. It must be remembered, however, that the use of any dummy variable is more a sign that the author is missing something in the regression than anything else. It says that something about the location is important, but not what that something is. It could therefore be simply reinforcing the isolation hypothesis as defined as distance from major centres of economic activity. Looking behind what might explain the better performance of small countries in certain regions of the world is what is needed for assessing how regional positioning is important – an area of the literature reviewed in section 2.4.

2.2.8 Vulnerability

The disadvantages of smallness described so far, namely the higher volatility of growth rates resulting from the need to be more economically open as well as the higher costs associated with isolation, are both factors which feature in the alternative measure of the state of the economy of a country, that of the level of vulnerability.

The idea for the construction of a vulnerability index which encompasses characteristics of economies that measures such as GDP per capita often conceal has been around for a number of years. The static nature of the GDP/capita measure that disguises so many of the dynamic features (important for describing the true nature of an economy) has led to the construction of a broader measure. It was only really in the 1990s, though, that serious attempts were made to construct vulnerability indices. The idea for them runs along similar lines to the UN human development index: a tool which provides policy-makers with a broader, more detailed picture of the true state of a nation or its people.

Attempts have been made recently to construct indices both for small states (Atkins et al., 2001) defined by population size, and also specifically for small island developing states (Briguglio, 1995). The level of scientific approach applied in the construction process of the indices varies. The vulnerability index constructed with small island developing countries in mind, for example, uses theoretical assumptions for deciding which variables to choose to form the composite index before comparing those variables with each of the ranking of GDP/capita. The paper by Atkins et al. (2001) takes output volatility as their starting point, believing this to be the clearest indicator of a country's vulnerability, and then tests empirically[13] a number of possible factors that may contribute to vulnerability – openness of the economy, mentioned previously, being one of the prominent ones. The most significant of these variables is then used in the construction of the composite vulnerability index. Alternatives to this approach are outlined in Guillaumont (1999), who proposes a measure of the instability of agricultural production, and Pantin (1997), who suggests examination of the impact of natural disasters on some macroeconomic indicators. Both approaches suffer from the problem of isolating the effect of the natural disaster, as the suggested indicators can be affected by other factors as well.

2.2.8.1 Measuring vulnerability index components

A strong reason for the non-inclusion of a number of factors that may result in the greater vulnerability of a country is the difficulty of

[13] The authors use weighted least squares in their regression analysis of output volatility due to the different distributional properties small and large countries exhibit.

measurement. Accurate data and reasonable proxies simply do not exist and cannot be represented in empirical analysis. Briguglio (1995), for instance, acknowledges the importance of environmental factors, such as fragility of coastal areas, but the serious difficulty in obtaining environmental data precludes their use in the index.

One of the three measurable factors found to be significant in regression analysis of determinants of output volatility is *openness* – exposure to foreign economic conditions. This measure – found by Atkins et al. to be a significant determinant of output volatility – is used by both sets of authors in their index construction. The ratio of exports and imports to GDP is the accepted proxy here.

Another of the factors present in both indices and found to be a significant factor in explaining output volatility is *proneness to natural disasters.* This is one of the hardest factors to measure. The proxy used to represent this factor utilises historical data in its assessment of the danger of disasters. A 1990 UNDRO report, utilised by Briguglio in his index, makes its estimations from historical data, similar to the calculations made by Atkins et al. (2001) who measure the proportion of the population affected by such events estimated over a relatively long period of time. Guillaumont (1999) stresses however that proneness to natural disasters is more than just about the probability of a country suffering a disaster. It is about the size and likelihood of the shock, the exposure to the shock and the ability of the country to react to the shock. Factors independent of the will of policy-makers should be the yardstick for measurement.

The third significant measurable variable used in the composite vulnerability indices is that of *remoteness* as measured by international transportation costs. As already mentioned, certain aspects of this factor could be seen more as an impediment to growth rather than a cause of volatility. Its significance, however, as a source of output volatility and hence vulnerability has made it a feature of both the small island vulnerability index and the general small country index.

Weighting of the three variables in the composition of the index is a subjective decision. Briguglio (1995) looks at both an equal weighting scenario and a 50–40–10 per cent split (openness, transport, disasters respectively). Atkins et al. (2001) use the value of the coefficient of each variable in their output volatility regression to represent each factor's importance.[14]

[14] For empirical details see Atkins et al. (2001), pp. 79–80.

2.2.8.2 Indices results

Small countries are heavily represented in the top positions in both vulnerability indices, filling all but two of the top thirty places in a sample size of 111 developing countries in Atkins et al. (2001). Large countries fill the lowest thirty scores (table 2.1).

When making comparisons with levels of GDP per capita, little correlation is found between countries' income levels and their vulnerability scores. This matches the previous income level study findings (Easterly and Kraay, 2001) which show small countries (those found to have generally higher vulnerability scores) not to have particularly worse levels of income per capita levels than other countries. Possible reasons put forward for this include the preferential arrangements many small developing countries benefit from with former colonial European countries (Briguglio) as well as the greater exploitation of their comparative advantage over larger countries (Srinivasan, 1986). Interestingly though, and of importance for policy-makers, is that a number of countries who are close to graduating from LDC status (and thus losing certain concessionary privileges) have very high vulnerability scores. Incorporation of a country's vulnerability score in the decision-making process with regard to eligibility for concessions by international organisations could therefore have an important bearing on a country's status.

Testing for correlation between growth rates and vulnerability, despite not being undertaken by the authors reviewed here, may well not have produced a particularly strong relationship as correlation between Atkins et al.'s vulnerability index and the output volatility index (table 2.1) shows mixed results. Hence the link between output volatility and lower growth made in the previous section by Ramey and Ramey (1995) may not carry over to vulnerability. Possible reasons for differences in output and vulnerability indices could be that, due to the nature of a composite index, some of the vulnerability components cancel each other out, thus disguising the link with volatility – though exactly why this might happen with three variables all strongly positively correlated with output volatility would need to be examined on a case-by-case basis.[15]

[15] Which Atkins et al. (2001) do for a number of the countries in their sample.

Table 2.1 *Composite vulnerability index and other indices ordered according to vulnerability score*

Country	Population ('000s)	Real per capita GDP ($)	Rank	Output volatility index	Rank	Composite vulnerability index	Rank
Top ten countries							
Vanuatu	161	2,500	53	3.61	90	13.295	1
Antigua & Barbuda	65	5,369	86	13.38	3	11.246	2
Tonga	93	3,740	73	13.18	4	10.439	3
Bahamas	268	16,180	110	7.37	25	10.433	4
Botswana	1,401	5,220	85	10.21	12	10.158	5
Swaziland	809	2,940	58	11.17	10	9.633	6
Gambia	1,042	1,190	27	7.67	22	9.331	7
Fiji	758	5,530	89	6.84	32	8.888	8
Maldives	236	2,200	47	2.97	97	8.654	9
Singapore	2,821	19,350	111	3.35	94	8.651	10
Bottom five countries							
India	901,459	1,240	28	2.12	109	3.782	107
China	1,196,360	2,330	51	4.84	66	3.744	108
Argentina	33,780	8,350	98	6.19	40	3.539	109
Brazil	156,486	5,500	88	4.25	78	3.433	110
Mexico	90,027	7,010	97	5.05	64	3.194	111

Source: Atkins et al. (2001)

2.3 Measuring the relationship between size and growth

2.3.1 Theoretical work

The issues raised in section 2.2 are legitimate concerns for small countries but tend to be dynamic features of small economies and thus not always captured in static examinations of the possible effects of size on growth. As Bhaduri and Sengupta (1982) make clear, you can have both a dynamic framework for measuring size, addressing issues of scale effects, and a static framework, which tends to analyse relative factor endowments. They argue that to make an economically integrated approach, one must look at the rate of growth of labour productivity in relation to the two concepts of comparative advantage and increasing returns. One needs to examine *sustainable* growth in labour productivity in a small country.

The authors do this using a Harrod–Domar formulation, but with the introduction of employment for identification of critical minimum size. Assumptions they make in their modelling are that productivity of labour and other material inputs are positively related to the size of investment. They also assume that ratio of investment to national income is constant through time. With these assumptions, they can then define their dynamic growth path. Their analysis interestingly shows that a larger volume of labour invariably has a positive impact on the rate of growth in labour productivity. This, they note, conforms to the empirically observed 'Kaldor–Verdoorn' law.

In identifying a critical size for sustainable labour productivity growth, the authors create a function separating all the different combinations of investment and employment possible. They demonstrate that the economic size of a country may be a critical constraint on a country's international trading position. With dynamic increasing returns governing increases in labour productivity and dynamic comparative advantage governed by increases in labour productivity, any constraint to dynamic increasing returns, such as limited population or income size or low investment level, could move a country off a sustainable labour productivity growth path. These of course are all potential characteristics of small economies.

2.3.2 *Empirical work*

The work done by Bhaduri and Sengupta (1982) is an important contribution in bridging the gap between the theoretical posturing of much of the traditional literature and the much more empirically 'hard nosed' approach of much of the size and growth literature of the 1990s.

Large-scale cross-country growth regression analysis is a phenomenon that itself grew substantially during the 1990s. Much of the work was not explicit in its investigation of the relationship between size and growth but, due to the focus on how growth rates differ between nations, differentiated by their level of GDP, this work is in tune with the topic of size and growth. An important point to bear in mind with regard to these regression studies is that interpretation of the factors behind the growth figures needs to be done carefully as, when use is made of interactive terms (slope dummies), the results can be ambiguous – i.e. does one of the variables in the interactive term affect the other or vice versa? Due to the large number of variables potentially involved in growth regressions, there is a strong case for sensitivity analysis[16] in papers using such regressions.

A number of studies have used the large cross-country growth regression analysis approach in looking at the question of whether size affects the growth potential of small countries. Studies by Easterly and Kraay (2001), Armstrong and Read (1998), Milner and Westaway (1993) and Khalaf (1979) all take an empirical approach to analysing the subject of size and growth. In all these studies population is used as the yardstick for the size of a country, although for instance Milner and Westaway (2001) expand their regressions to incorporate other measures of size such as area and GDP as well. The importance of population size in explaining growth in these studies is measured via use of either a dummy variable, representing a cut-off for small country size, or a continuous variable representing population.

2.3.3 Growth and size regressions findings

All the four studies mentioned above find there to be no significant relationship between country size and growth.[17] Each paper utilises a different form of econometric analysis as each has a different focus. Milner and Westaway (1993) utilise a correlation matrix to examine the relationship between size (represented by a number of different proxies including population, GDP and area) and GDP growth but find no strong correlation between them. Easterly and Kraay (2001) demonstrate the insignificance of the relationship through two methods: by way of a scatter graph of countries with per capita growth on one axis and population on the other, they surmise that small states have the same range of growth experiences as other countries. They reinforce this conclusion through use of a regression with average annual real per capita GDP growth as the dependent variable (for 147 countries between 1960 and 1995) and a small state dummy variable. Khalaf (1979) tests the effects of size (both in terms of population and GNP) on GNP growth and levels of economic development[18] through the use of multiple correlation analysis (from a sample of 145 countries). He too finds no significant relationship. Armstrong and Read (1998) employ a neo-classical

[16] See Sala-I-Martin (1997).

[17] Population size is either used as a continuous variable or a cut-off point chosen and used as a dummy variable representing smallness.

[18] As measured by average per capita GNP.

conditional convergence growth model, finding the population variable to be insignificant. The insignificance of the results is represented in the rows containing population and the small state dummy in table 2.2.

The findings (of all these studies) that small nations do not exhibit disproportionately lower rates of growth than other countries are reinforced by Srinivasan (1986) who simply takes data for 158 countries between 1970 and 1980 and brackets them according to size and growth rate of real GNP per capita.

One caveat that needs to be mentioned here is that regressions that include GNP as the dependent variable (such as Khalaf, 1979 and Armstrong and Read, 1998) therefore include remittances in their dependent variable. Remittances are for many LDCs very important sources of income, but are of course not necessarily a source of growth that some consider a reflection of the true economic health of the inhabitants of the country to which the remittances are being sent.

2.3.4 Behind the growth results: sources of growth

There does therefore appear to be agreement empirically that small states do not suffer a disadvantage in terms of growth purely on account of their size. As Milner and Westaway (1993) point out however, 'it is not evident from this type of comparison whether the nature or the "sources" of economic growth are affected by country size or remoteness characteristics'.[20] Thus although the studies found there to be no apparent link between size and growth, that result does not tell us how size may affect the fundamentals of growth for countries. All the studies look beyond the simple regression results of growth and size and at the possible sources of growth in small countries.

2.3.4.1 Openness

Openness is one factor that a number of studies measure with respect to the growth of countries. Both Easterly and Kraay (2001) and Khalaf (1979) examine whether it is a potential source of growth through adoption of it as an independent variable in their analyses. The authors produce, however, different findings. Whereas Easterly and Kraay (2001) find openness to be a significant positive factor for growth, Khalaf (1979) finds it to be

[20] Milner and Westaway (1993), p. 203.

Table 2.2 *The impact of size on growth in four growth regressions*

Author(s)	Easterly and Kraay	Armstrong and Read	Milner and Westaway	Khalaf
	Average annual real per capita GDP growth	Per capita GNP growth	GDP growth	GNP growth
Dependent variables				
Sample size	157	133	48	30
Period covered	1960–1985	1980–1993	1975–1985	1951–1957
Independent variables				
Population		0.00001[0.0000008]	0.153*	0.0231[0.027]
Small state dummy	0.002[0.005]			
Initial GDP per capita	−*0.017[0.004]*	*0.0167[0.003]*		
% GDP in agriculture		−*0.0014[0.0001]*	−0.0096[0.139]	
% GDP not in agriculture		−0.0001[0.002]	*0.228[0.138]*	
Level of openness	*0.012[0.003]*			−0.0072[0.022]
Level of education	*0.0003[0.0001]*			
Volatility of GDP growth	−*0.179[0.082]*			
Commodity export concentration				0.0831[0.036]
Geographic export concentration				−0.013[.035]

* correlation value taken from correlation matrix.

Notes:

The dependent variable and a selection of independent variables[19] used in the regressions by the above-mentioned authors are listed in table 2.2. Coefficient values for each variable are shown along with the standard deviation in parenthesis. Significant results (i.e. those showing that the variable does influence the growth rate) at the 90 per cent confidence level are shown in italics. Both Easterly and Kraay and Khalaf measure level of openness as percentage of exports and imports in GDP. Education is measured as average secondary school enrolment rate, volatility of GDP growth as its standard deviation.

[19] Regional dummy variables are used by Armstrong and Read (1993) and Easterly and Kraay (2001) but the latter do not list their results relating to these variables.

insignificant. He also finds there to be no clear relationship between it and the level of economic development of a country. Khalaf's result also contradicts the findings of Redding and Venables (2001) on the effects of openness though it does suggest, as they do, that globalisation in its many forms (mobility of firms, increased openness to trade) is not necessarily the driving force for growth and development in all countries that it is sometimes credited with.

The apparent positive effect of openness on growth found by Easterly and Kraay (2001) is counterbalanced by the negative effect of volatility on growth openness produces. It is the insignificant net effect from the different factors balancing each other out that the authors conclude explains the insignificance of their size and growth findings. By showing that openness can compensate in growth terms for the negative effects of volatility, Easterly and Kraay (2001) present a possible explanation as to why a study purely focused on the link between volatility and growth, such as that by Ramey and Ramey (1995), may show a negative relationship between growth and volatility. The paradox that the findings of Ramey and Ramey (1995) threw up with respect to those of Easterly and Kraay (2001) may be as a result of their study's singular focus on just one relationship. It may also be simply due to the different sample of countries chosen for the different studies undertaken.

Concerns raised in section 2.2 about the potential effect openness and export concentration could have as sources of instability and thus a constraint on growth on small countries is tested by Khalaf (1979) through use of a multiple correlation analysis. As with the findings of Easterly and Kraay (2001) (with respect to the importance of export concentration in causing higher volatility), none of Khalaf's hypotheses tested appear to have a significant bearing on the relationship between growth and size and the level of economic development and size. The relationship is unclear, as both positive and negative effects are found for the different factors with respect to growth and development – though none being significant.

2.3.4.2 Fundamentals

Milner and Westaway (1993), when looking behind their initial size and growth results at possible sources of growth, test four hypotheses addressing the fundamentals of any economy to see whether country size is an influence on the medium-term growth process. They examine *capital shallowing* (differing marginal products of capital due to the perceived extra riskiness of smaller economies), *restricted ability to change structurally*, *barriers to international catch-up* and *limited domestic technological diffusion*. To test these hypotheses they employ a model of disequilibrium growth – allowing for structural change, differential technological progress and technological diffusion (representations of each of the hypotheses being tested).

In order to model the influences outlined above, they employ a methodology[21] that allows the identification of the significance of country size when each variable's importance to the growth rate is calculated. Comparison of the statistical robustness of slope and intercept dummies allows the authors to examine whether country size has a greater impact on 'explained' or 'exogenous' growth sources.

Their findings show only the first hypothesis – that of capital shallowing – to be significantly linked to size. This result could be indicative of the increased difficulties experienced by small firms in obtaining investment outlined in section 2.2. This finding, however, is predicted to be offset by the benefits of greater openness, a measure that also features as a positively significant independent variable in the regressions of Easterly and Kraay (2001).

2.3.4.3 Sectors

Armstrong and Read (1998) look behind their initial finding of no significant relationship between size and growth by looking for sectoral explanations for the wide variety in growth and income performance exhibited by small countries. Use of a number of binary and ordinal variables representing agriculture, tourism and the state of the financial service sector shows that the different sectors promoted by different small countries play a large part in explaining the differences in performance between these countries. Tourism and a developed financial sector are areas identified by Armstrong and Read (1998) as having strong positive effects on growth. Thus diversification by small countries into these sectors would appear wise, a suggestion also made by Bhaduri and Sengupta (1982) as a possible route for growth and development of small states. Agriculture is shown to have a negative influence on performance. This negative result is shared with Milner and Westaway (1995), though without significance. The negative effect of agriculture is an important finding, if concentration on agricultural export markets is being advised by international bodies, or, as is often the case,

[21] The technique used is a dummy variable/spline function methodology. Basically they use intercept and slope dummies to identify country size in the hypotheses they make.

agriculture is a major part of the economy of many small states, for smallness, as seen in section 2.2, can provide impediments to the movement out of this sector into, for example, manufacturing. This problem may have implications for the possible convergence of LDC economies.

2.3.4.4 Convergence

Convergence is a phenomenon predicted by classical growth theory – that poorer countries will catch up richer countries through their higher growth rates. It often features in growth regressions – the effect identified by including a variable denoting the level of income of each country at the beginning of the sample period. It is measured in both the growth regressions of Easterly and Kraay (2001) and Armstrong and Read (1998), though with different results. As mentioned below, Easterly and Kraay find it to have a negative effect on growth (though this result they attribute to their findings of higher average income levels amongst small countries). Armstrong and Read find it to be significant and positive with respect to growth. Romer (1986) however questions the assumption of diminishing returns to per capita output made by the neo-classical growth models used by the above authors. He states that if knowledge were considered an input in production with increasing marginal productivity, then we would not necessarily witness the convergence of LDCs with richer countries. For the thirteen LDC nations classified by UNCTAD as small, this would have serious implications for their growth and development prospects.

2.3.5 Income level and size regression findings

As mentioned above, some of the studies that examine the relationship between size and growth also look at the relationship between size and level of economic development (most often measured as per capita income). The finding that there exists no particular disadvantage from size for small countries in terms of growth also seems to extend to the area of income per capita (Khalaf, 1979). Easterly and Kraay (2001) in fact find per capita income levels for small states to be on average 40 per cent higher. This result would explain the negative coefficient for convergence in their growth regression. Such a result would at first appear to be at odds with the data produced by Srinivasan (1986) who points out that, of the thirty-six countries classified as LDCs by the UN, twenty-one (a clear majority) have populations of less than 5 million. The different cut-off values for smallness could of course account for the difference here (Easterly and Kraay defining small as a population less than 1.5m).

2.3.6 *Behind the income results: preferential arrangements*

Easterly and Kraay (2001) examine the hypothesis made by Bhaduri and Sengupta (1982) that small countries could struggle in terms of productivity due to their size. The authors use a Solow growth model to examine this question. Their findings show two-thirds of the income advantage enjoyed by small countries (mentioned above) is as a result of a productivity advantage, directly challenging Bhanduri and Sengupta's theoretical analysis. Their results show there to be higher investment rates and not significantly lower population growth rates – the two potential bottlenecks for labour productivity identified by Bhanduri and Sengupta's analysis. They do however acknowledge that the results showing that investment may account for a third of the income advantage of small countries should be taken 'with more than a grain of salt'.[22]

A number of arguments outlined by Blake (2001) as to why there is no perceived disadvantage of small countries in terms of income levels as well as growth performance include the access small countries have to concessional or grant financing for capital and infrastructural development. The preferential access to export markets enjoyed by many small nations (either as a result of political ties or from LDC status) and the stability of export earnings that various agreements such as the Lomé Convention of the EU provides to ACP members as well as the importance of natural resources of small countries at different times in the expansion of global production and trade, e.g. petroleum-based energy and bauxite, also contribute.

All the results of the studies reviewed here are dependent on accurate country data. Representation of a broad spectrum of countries is often hindered by lack of data, especially from LDCs. This point needs to be remembered in the conclusions drawn from the results of empirical work. It may be the case that a number of small countries never make it into samples due to the impoverished nature of their data. As mentioned in the first part of this chapter, different samples of small countries may account for some of the differences in the results found in the literature.

[22] Easterly and Kraay (2001), p. 101

2.4 Conclusions and policy implications

In section 2.2 of this chapter, the literature reviewed pointed to the size of small nations as causing sub-optimality in terms of economic production and also economic policy-making for a number of reasons. Econometric findings reviewed in section 2.3 dispute to a large degree these presumptions. As noted in the same section though, there may be various special arrangements, which disguise the disadvantages of small states in the regressions run; this is combined with the static nature of cross-country regressions. Obtaining accurate data for a sufficiently wide sample of countries is also seen to be problematic. If one does therefore believe that in a world moving towards freer trade and a reduction in the number of special arrangements between countries, small country disadvantages will provide a real impediment to development and growth, then the question arises of whether there are particular policies a small country might be able to pursue in order to offset some of these disadvantages.

2.4.1 Sectoral focus

The question of why it is that some small countries have done better than others was touched on in section 2.3 with a number of studies examining sectoral specialisation as a possible cause. Armstrong (1995, 1998) find (through use of a number of sector variables) tourism and the banking sector to be sectors positively related to growth. Agriculture is found to impact on growth in a negative fashion. A good natural resource base is also seen to influence growth strongly. With these results, the message would appear to be that movement into banking and tourism as well as exploitation of natural resources is a possible solution for under-performing small countries. Whether development of these sectors is viable for certain small countries can only be answered on a case-by-case basis. Becoming more competitive by either re-specialising in activities that are 'globally' competitive or specialising in goods or services particular to the country and looking for a niche in the international market is how Encontre (1999) sees small countries' path to growth and development.

The encouragement of small countries to move into the service sector is one made by Bhaduri and Sengupta (1982). The arguments they put forward (in section 2.3), combined with those put forward by Banerji

(1977) (in section 2.2) concerning the limitations of small countries' development of their manufacturing sector, do suggest the service sector path to growth might be their best option.

In the case of natural resource exploitation, little detail is given in Armstrong (1995) as to the type of natural resource measured and thus it is not possible to draw conclusions as to the potential of any one particular type. Certainly, trying to move away from agricultural dependence would seem wise, Bhaduri and Sengupta (1982) also noting the low returns to scale from agriculture. How easy that is, of course, depends on the ability of a country to set up new industries. As listed in section 2.2, small countries may face a number of different obstacles in achieving this aim. Obstacles range from a lack of financial resources to a failure to capture economies of scale to lower returns for manufacturing and loss of skilled labour through migration, this last point highlighted for Pacific Island economies by Cashin and Loayza (1995). The locating of niche markets and the strong environmental impact production of globally competitive goods can have are constraints listed by Encontre (1999) to the approaches he suggests. All of these factors can reduce the chances of a successful diversification strategy.

2.4.2 Openness

Openness (as measured by imports and exports as a percentage of GDP) is undoubtedly a feature of small country economies. With a number of studies (e.g. Sachs and Warner, 1995; Easterly and Kraay, 2001) finding a strong correlation between growth and openness, advocating a more open trade policy approach has gained momentum in recent years. Advocating trade policies, such as a move towards lowering trade barriers, does not always marry with the reality of the situation however. Question marks exist over how classification of countries as open or closed is made in certain studies. Sachs and Warner's use of numerous trade policy indicators, for instance, classified Mauritius as open, whereas 'an alternative scheme of classification that has been devised in the Fund ranked Mauritius as one of the most protected economies in the early 1990s'.[23] Hence closer inspection of this small country success story is required.

[23] Subramanian and Roy (2001), p. 15.

2.4.3 *EPZs and a heterodox trade strategy: the example of Mauritius*

Subramanian and Roy's review (2001) of the different explanations for the success of Mauritian economic development over the last two decades is enlightening in its observations regarding the trade strategies adopted to overcome any handicaps of being a small country. The theory of a heterodox opening trade strategy advocated in Subramanian and Roy (2001) by Rodrik sees the effective segmentation of export and import competing sectors as vital to its growth. By isolating the export sector from other sectors of the economy it allowed the pursuit of a restrictive trade policy with regard to imports (from which incidence analysis would normally predict a reduction in exports) without the attraction of resources away from the export sector.

This theme is continued in Romer's attributing of Mauritius's success to the creation of Export Processing Zones (EPZs). These zones had different tax incentives, labour market rules and duty-free access to imported inputs, enabling fast development of industries to optimal production sizes.

Of course the attracting away of factors of production from exports to import substitutes is not a feature unique to small countries, but, due to the limited factors of production available to them, any switch of resources resulting in sub-optimal output levels amongst the export industries would not be so easily restored.

The appearance therefore of a policy mix that can help small countries overcome a size disadvantage they might experience has to be tempered by the realisation that a vital source of the development of Mauritius has been the preferential access it enjoys to EU markets for its primary agricultural export, sugar.

2.4.4 *Integration*

Integration in terms of both regional multilateral agreements and financial integration is considered here for small countries. Gutierrez (1996) sees financial integration as the primary form of integration to bestow the greatest benefits for small countries. She also notes that activities related to the concentration of exports, such as infrastructure, transportation, marketing, education, health, insurance and research and development (R&D), require a minimum scale which a country will not be able to get through openness to trade and investment, thus making economic integration an attractive option.

A number of the benefits of financial integration afforded to members of a monetary union illustrated in Khatkhate and Short (1980) include greater stability and thus higher levels of domestic investment (an important benefit due to the increased volatility experienced by small countries), the reduced amount of foreign reserves each country would have to hold and the possibility for risk-pooling. The authors note, however, that a full cost–benefit analysis would need to be undertaken prior to the formation of any monetary union and that the benefits may well not be evenly distributed between the possible members.

With respect to regional multilateral integration agreements, one of the most prominent featuring small countries is that between the EU and the African, Caribbean and Pacific (ACP) countries. Such agreements have brought benefits to small countries such as preferential access to developed country markets (Lomé Convention) though do not generally encourage economic diversification, which could be seen as storing up trouble for the future in the face of WTO challenges to these preferential agreements. Other types of arrangements that exist involve 'south–south' groupings of countries. Schiff (2001) examines the advantages and disadvantages for small country involvement in these arrangements. The spectre of trade diversion leading to welfare reduction from the creation of such customs unions is widely believed to affect smaller countries more than larger members of such groupings. Intra-regional transfer mechanisms can help offset any such welfare reductions. Cooperation on public goods such as infrastructure and energy however has the potential to benefit smaller members greatly. The primary benefit to small countries of such arrangements, however, is the increase in bargaining power in the international arena. The example of CARICOM (the Caribbean Community and Common Market) demonstrates the increased effectiveness and benefits of reductions in fixed costs and the strengthening of relatively weak individual bargaining positions such south–south groupings can bring to small countries.

Thus we see a range of policy options open to small countries looking to improve their economic performance. Whether a combination of them is required or just single measures will suffice is an issue for the individual country. These policies build on those mentioned over forty years before by Kuznets (1960) about the challenge of using the stronger sense of community, closer coherence of the population and the greater elasticity of social institutions in small countries to overcome the disadvantage of smallness.

Appendix 2.1 Annotated bibliography

Armstrong and Read (1995)

Objective	Examination of economic performance of EU's micro-states and autonomous regions
Methodology	Combine six binary/ordinal variables in linear discriminant function for partial analysis of reasons behind performance
Results	Micro-states display large variance in GDP/capita. Often did better than their neighbours. Tourism, financial sector and natural resources important
Conclusions/policy implications	Isolation does not seem to be an issue. Because of sectoral results, tourism and financial sector development are good for performance

Armstrong, De Kervenoael and Read (1998)

Objective	Quantitatively check how small country economic performance compares with larger countries'. Examine whether different economic structures are the reason
Methodology	Use neo-classical conditional convergence growth model. Sectoral investigation through inclusion of variables representing different structural aspects
Results	Population size has no bearing on performance. Region, tourism, financial sector and resources important. Agriculture has a negative impact and manufacturing effect is weak
Conclusions/policy implications	Regional placement accounts for much of the variation among micro-states. Certain sectors are better to specialise in

Armstrong and Johnes (1993)

Objective	Examine whether transport costs account for price differential in retail and energy supplies between the Isle of Man and the UK
Methodology	Examination of costs that contribute towards final product price
Results	Only a small amount of price differential attributable to transport costs
Conclusions/policy implications	Other factors cause differential: higher stockholding costs, failure to exploit economies of scale and a lack of competition

Atkins, Mazi and Easter (2001)

Objective	Present a composite index to identify vulnerable small states
Methodology	Regression of output volatility on variables thought to cause vulnerability. Three most significant – openness, remoteness and proneness to natural disasters – then used to construct vulnerability index
Results	All but two of top thirty in vulnerability rankings are small countries. Bottom thirty are all large countries. Lack of correlation between output volatility rankings and vulnerability rankings
Conclusions/policy implications	Shows importance of treating small countries differently. Important measure for small countries about to graduate from LDC status

Banerji (1978)

Objective	Demonstrate non-homothetic production function in manufacturing means plant size as a result of both economic development and physical capital intensity
Methodology	Log normal distribution fitted to observed size distributions of plants. Average size of plants in an

	industry then derived from estimated parameters of the fitted distribution. Incorporates elements of both systematic and random effects
Results	Middle- and low-income countries' average plant size tends to be smaller than high-income countries'
Conclusions/policy implications	Many factors affect plant size. With capital-intensity correlated to size of plants then non-homothetic hypothesis may also contribute to size

Bhaduri, Mukhedi and Sengupta (1982)

Objective	Theoretical analysis of whether smallness causes problems for long-term growth prospects of small countries
Methodology	Use of a Harrod–Domar formulation, but with introduction of employment for identification of a minimum critical size
Results	Analysis shows the critical role of economic size – either in terms of minimum employment level or investment level – in maintaining labour productivity growth
Conclusions/policy implication	To maintain its international competitive position, a small country has to maintain a minimum growth in labour productivity which, due to its economic size, it may not be able to do. Should focus on services

Briguglio (1995)

Objective	Construction of a composite vulnerability index
Methodology	Combining of three variables – openness, remoteness and proneness to natural disasters – in different ratios to form vulnerability ranking
Results	Small Island Developing States (SIDS) score highly on ranking. Poor correlation between vulnerability scores and per capita GDP rankings
Conclusions/policy implications	SIDS should concentrate on niche export markets, flexible specialisation and economic deregulation

Cashin and Loayza (1995)

Objective	Examine growth experience of nine Pacific islands. Examine whether convergence has taken place
Methodology	Use Cobb–Douglas Production Function to capture convergence measure. Use time-series estimation of convergence. Use Chamberlin Matrix to correct for problems in Ordinary Least Squares (OLS) regression, for determining speed of approach to steady-state level of income
Results	Inclusion of Australia and New Zealand results in divergence. Excluding them and using Matrix leads to convergence in GDP measure. Migration a factor in the effect of convergence
Conclusions/policy implications	Model predicts convergence of neo-classical growth model. Private and official net transfers help prevent dispersion of GNP

Codrington (1989)

Objective	Examine issues of size and taxation in poor countries
Methodology	Examination of different sources of taxes and methods of collection in different sized countries
Results	Small countries tend to get more of their tax from trade taxes, large countries get their revenue from a broader range of taxes which focus more on income. Tax levels per capita higher in smaller countries
Conclusions/policy implications	Higher per capita taxes needed in smaller countries due to market failures. Country size is an important determinant of taxation in LDCs

Easterly and Kraay (2001)

Objective	Test empirically whether small states are different to large states in terms of income, growth and volatility
Methodology	Large cross-country growth regression employing dummy variables to capture smallness and other factors

Results	Show same variance of growth and income rates as large countries. Show greater volatility of growth rates for small countries
Conclusions/policy implications	Because of similarities in performance figures, does not believe small countries should have preferential treatment

Gutierrez (1996)

Objective	Analysis of specific problems and ways to facilitate integration of smaller countries into the free trade area of the Americas
Methodology	Examination of particular features of small country economies and what potential benefits size may constrain
Results	Large governments squeeze out private sector. Trade dependence and concentration a feature of small economies. Heavy dependence on international trade tax for government revenue
Conclusions/policy implications	In small economies integration has a greater influence on macro-economic management than in large countries. Adjustment costs should be a concern for small countries. Integration may or may not narrow inequalities in terms of income and human development

Khalaf (1979)

Objective	To assess the relationship between country size and rates of economic growth and levels of economic development, and the possible effects of trade concentration and dependence on trade on this relationship
Methodology	Use of multiple correlation analysis to test propositions
Results	Find size and dependence on trade not linked to level of development. Only significant result is export concentration negatively related to development levels. Lot of other non-significant results

Conclusions/policy implications	Size not an issue with regard to growth. No clear relationship between growth and trade dependence. Also, concentration not important

Khatkhate and Short (1980)

Objective	Examination of what small countries can do to overcome the constraints on monetary policy imposed on them by their size
Methodology	Examination of monetary unions and systems of currency issue
Results	Benefits could be unfairly distributed amongst members of a monetary union. Adopting a currency can bring about a stable relationship between output and money which facilitates the inflow of capital for domestic investment and growth. Removes flexibility of currency issue
Conclusions/policy implications	Any decision on a currency union should be taken after a full-scale cost–benefit analysis. Think use of a currency board may be a better option for mini states as a system of currency issue

Kuznets (1960)

Objective	Examine possible relationship between small countries and growth
Methodology	Examination of features of small economies
Results	Small states at a disadvantage because of limited area and variety of resources, limited population and greater security issues
Conclusions/policy implications	Can compensate for disadvantages by the quality of their people and social institutions

Kwan and Beladi (1993)

Objective	Investigation of optimal trade policies for small economies with unemployment

Methodology	Employ a general unemployment model to investigate optimal trade policies for a small open economy with unemployed resources
Results	With factor price rigidity, random foreign prices result in random unemployment of resources. A full-employment tariff would be higher than an optimal tariff
Conclusions/policy implications	Looking at the third best alternatives, if in certain circumstances, the optimal composite tariff dominates the optimal target price, which in turn dominates the optimal quota

Milner and Westaway (1993)

Objective	Examine the relationship between country size and growth. Test a number of hypotheses that can be put forward about the influence of country size on medium-term growth
Methodology	Use of zero-order correlation matrix to test for size–growth correlation. Employ a model of disequilibrium growth – allowing for structural change, differential technological progress and technological diffusion to test hypotheses
Results	No correlation between size and growth. Only the capital shallowing (different marginal products of capital in different sized countries) hypothesis is significant
Conclusions/policy implications	No obvious link between medium-term growth performance and a range of attributes of country size and performance

Ramey and Ramey (1995)

Objective	To see whether the standard dichotomy of growth from the volatility of economic fluctuations is evident from a ninety-two-country study
Methodology	Regression of mean growth on the standard deviation of growth. Incorporation of a vector of control

	variables that control for other characteristics. Examine growth and variance of innovations by use of a forecasting equation for growth
Results	Discover that investment share of GDP plays little role in the link between volatility and growth. Negative effect mainly from innovation variance which reflects uncertainty
Conclusions/policy implications	Standard dichotomy between growth and volatility of economic fluctuations is not supported by the data. Results confirm theoretical ideas that costs of volatility directly linked to uncertainty induced planning errors by firms

Romer (1986)

Objective	Examination of a fully specified model of long-run growth in which knowledge is assumed to be an input in production that has increasing marginal productivity
Methodology	Calculation of a social optimum, which is equivalent to solving a maximisation problem
Results	In contrast to model of diminishing returns, growth rates can be increasing over time, and thus large countries may always grow faster than small countries
Conclusions/policy implications	Can look at an equilibrium situation of increasing marginal productivity of knowledge and decreasing marginal productivity of physical capital. Large countries may always grow faster than small countries

Srinivasan (1986)

Objective	Consider the problems that small economies are most often alleged to face – failure to achieve economies of scale, vulnerability, remoteness and macro-economic policy dependence
Methodology	Examination of arguments put forward
Results	Not hindered on the whole from a lack of economies of scale. Remoteness not a small country issue; no difference in incomes of small and large countries;

	exploitation of comparative advantage can offset higher international exposure due to openness
Conclusions/policy implications	Either good policies are needed, or the alleged problems are not peculiar to small countries

Venables and Redding (2001)

Objective	Examination via a structural model using per capita income, bilateral trade and relative manufacturing prices, of whether geography plays a part in explaining variation of per capita income across a cross-section of countries
Methodology	Development of a trade model incorporating trade equation to measure bilateral trade, wage equation to estimate relationship between actual and model predicted wages due to market access and a price index to see how prices of manufactures should vary with supplier access. Use of instrumental variable to back up hypothesis
Results	Geographic factors affecting market and supplier access have an important bearing on variations in per capita income
Conclusions/policy implications	Isolation is a problem for growth rates of countries which are situated far away from centres of economic activity

Bibliography

ABARE (1999), *Sugar: International Policies Affecting Market Expansion*, Australian Bureau of Agricultural Research Establishment research paper 99.14. Canberra: Australian government publishing service

Alesina, A. and Spolaore, E. (1997), 'On the Number and Size of Nations', *Quarterly Journal of Economics*, November

Armstrong, H., De Kervenoael, R., Li, X. and Read, R. (1998), 'A Comparison of the Economic Performance of Different Micro-States, and Between Micro-States and Larger Countries', *World Development*, vol. 26, no. 4, pp. 639–56

Armstrong, H. and Johnes, G. (1993), 'The Role of Transport Costs as a Determinant of Price Level Differentials Between the Isle of Man and the United Kingdom, 1989', *World Development*, vol. 21, no. 2, pp. 311–18

Armstrong, H. and Read, R. (1995), 'Western European Micro-States and EU Autonomous Regions: The Advantages of Size and Sovereignty', *World Development*, vol. 23, no. 7, pp. 1229–45

Atkins, J. P., Mazi, S. and Easter, C. D. (2001), 'Small States: A Composite Vulnerability Index', in Peretz, Faruqi and Kisanga (eds.), *Small States in the Global Economy*. London: Commonwealth Secretariat.

Augier, G. C. (1980), 'Sizes of Firms, Exporting Behaviour and the Structure of French Industry', *Journal of Industrial Economics*, vol. 29, pp. 203–18

Banerji, R. (1978), 'Average Size of Plants in Manufacturing and Capital Intensity', *Journal of Development Economics*, vol. 5, pp. 155–61

Barro, R. and Sala-I-Martin, X. (1995), *Economic Growth*. New York: McGraw-Hill

Baumol, W. J. (1985), 'Productivity Growth, Convergence and Welfare: What the Lond Run Data Show', Research Report no. 85–27. New York: New York University, C. V. Starr Centre

Bernanke, B. (1983), 'Irreversibility, Uncertainty, and Cyclical Investment', *Quarterly Journal of Economics*, vol. 98(1), pp. 81–106

Bhaduri, A., Mukhedi, A. and Sengupta, R. (1982), 'Problems of Long-term Growth in Small Economies: A Theoretical Analysis', in B. Jalan (ed.), *Problems and Policies in Small Economies*. Beekenham: Croom Helm for the Commonwealth Secretariat

Blake, B. (2001), 'Comments on "Small States: A Composite Vulnerability Index" and "Small States, Small Problems?"' in Peretz, Faruqi and Kisanga (eds.), *Small States in the Global Economy*. London: Commonwealth Secretariat

Briguglio, L. (1995), 'Small Island Developing States and Their Economic Vulnerabilities', *World Development*, vol. 23, no. 9, pp. 1615–32

Cashin, P. and Loayza, N. (1995), 'Paradise Lost? Growth, Convergence, and Migration in the South Pacific', *IMF Staff Papers*, vol. 42, no. 3, September

Cherney, H. B. and Taylor, L. (1968), 'Development Patterns: Among Countries and Over Time', *Review of Economics and Statistics*, November

Codrington, H. (1989), 'Country Size and Taxation in Developing Countries', *Journal of Development Studies*, vol. 25, no. 4, July

Collier, P. and Dollar, D. (1998), 'Aid Allocation and Poverty Reduction', Policy Research Working Paper, no. 2041, World Bank

Commonwealth Secretariat and World Bank (2000), *Small States: Meeting Challenges in the Global Economy*, Report of the Commonwealth Secretariat–World Bank Joint Task Force on Small States. London: Commonwealth Secretariat; Washington D.C.: World Bank

Davenport, M. (2001), 'A Study of Alternative Special and Differential Arrangements for Small Economies', Interim Report, Commonwealth Secretariat

Easterly, W. and Kraay, A. (2001), 'Small States, Small Problems? Income, Growth and Volatility in Small States', in Peretz, Faruqi and Kisanga (eds.), *Small States in the Global Economy*. London: Commonwealth Secretariat

Easterly, W. and Levine, R. (1997), 'Africa's Growth Tragedy: Policies and Ethnic Divisions', *Quarterly Journal of Economics*, November

Fry, M. (1982), 'Financial Sectors in Some Small Island Developing Economies', in B. Jalan (ed.), *Problems and Policies in Small Economies*. Beekenham: Croom Helm for the Commonwealth Secretariat

Grynberg, R. (2001), 'Trade Policy Implications for Small Vulnerable States of the Global Trade Regime Shift' in Peretz, Faruqi and Kisanga (eds.), *Small States in the Global Economy*. London: Commonwealth Secretariat

Guillaumont, P. (1999), 'On the Economic Vulnerability of Low Income Countries', mimeo, CERDI-CNRS. Universite d'Auvergne, France

Gutierrez, M. (1996), 'Is Small Beautiful for Economic Integration?', *Journal of World Trade*, vol. 30.

Gylfason, T. (1999), 'Exports, Inflation and Growth', *World Development*, vol. 27, no. 6, pp. 1031–57

Hewitt, A. and Page, S. (2001), *World Commodity Prices: Still a Problem for Developing Countries?* Special Report, Overseas Development Institute, London

Keesing, D. B. and Sherk, D. R. (1971), 'Population Density in Patterns of Trade and Development', *American Economic Review*, December

Khalaf, N. (1979), 'Country Size and Economic Growth and Development', *Journal of Development Studies*, no. 16

Khatkhate, D. and Short, B. (1980), 'Monetary and Central Banking Problems of Mini States', *World Development*, vol. 8, pp. 1017–25

Kuznets, S. (1960), 'Economic Growth of Small Nations', in E. A. G. Robinson (ed.), *The Economic Consequences of the Size of Nations: Proceedings of a Conference held by the International Economic Association*. London: Macmillan

Kwan, E. and Beladi, H. (1993), 'Optimal Trade Policies for a Small Open Economy', *Economica*

Leamer, E. (1997), 'Access to Western Markets and Eastern Effort', in S. Zecchini (ed.), *Lessons from the Economic Transition, Central and Eastern Europe in the 1990s*. Dordrecht: Kluwer Academic Publishers, pp. 503–26

Levine, R. and Renelt, D. (1992), 'A Sensitivity Analysis of Cross-Country Growth Regressions', *American Economic Review*, vol. 82, no. 4, September, pp. 942–63

Limao, N. and Venables, A. J. (2001), 'Infrastructure, Geographical Disadvantage, Transport Costs and Trade', *World Bank Economic Review*

Milner, C. and Westaway, T. (1993), 'Country Size and the Medium-Term Growth Process: Some Cross-Country Evidence', *World Development*, vol. 21, no. 2, pp. 203–11

Pantin, D. A. (1997), 'Alternative Ecological Vulnerability Indices for Developing

Countries with Special Reference to SIDS', report for the United Nations Department of Economic and Social Affairs. Trinidad: University of West Indies

Pryor, F. L. (1972), 'The Size of Production Establishments in Manufacturing', *Economic Journal*, vol. 82, pp. 547–66

Ramey, G. and Ramey, V. (1991), 'Technology Commitment and the Cost of Economic Fluctuations', *National Bureau of Economic Research*, Cambridge, MA, Working Paper No. 3755

Ramey, G. and Ramey, V. (1995), 'Cross-Country Evidence on the Link Between Volatility and Growth', *American Economic Review*, vol. 85, no. 5, December

Redding, S. and Venables, A. (2001), 'Economic Geography and International Inequality', *CEPR*, London

Robinson, E. A. G. (ed.) (1960), *The Economic Consequences of the Size of Nations: Proceedings of a Conference held by the International Economic Association.* London: Macmillan

Rodrik, D. (1998), 'Who Needs Capital Account Convertibility?', in Peter Kenen (ed.), *Should the IMF Pursue Capital-Account Convertibility?* Princeton Essays in International Finance, no. 207

Romer, P. (1986), 'Increasing Returns and Long-Run Growth', *Journal of Political Economy*, vol. 94, no. 5

Sachs, J. and Warner, A. (1995), 'Economic Reform and the Process of Global Integration', *Brookings Paper on Economic Activity*, pp. 1–95. Washington: Brookings Institution

Sala-I-Martin, X. (1997), 'I Just Ran Two Million Regressions', *American Economic Review, Papers and Proceedings*, vol. 87, no. 2

Schiff, M. (2001), 'Regional Integration and Development in Small States', World Bank Policy Research Working Paper

Senhandji, A. and Montenegro, C. (1998), 'Time Series Analysis of Export Demand Equations: A Cross-Country Analysis', IMF Working Paper WP/98/149

Srinivasan, T. N. (1986), 'The Costs and Benefits of being a Small, Remote, Island, Landlocked or Ministate Economy', *World Bank Research Observer*, vol. 1, no. 2, pp. 205–18

Subramanian, A. and Roy, D. (2001), 'Who Can Explain the Mauritian Miracle: Meade, Romer, Sachs or Rodrik?', IMF Working Paper

Svennilson, L. (1960), 'The Concept of the Nation and Its Relevance to Economic Analysis', in E. A. G. Robinson (ed.), *The Economic Consequences of the Size of Nations: Proceedings of a Conference held by the International Economic Association.* London: Macmillan

Tarshis, L. (1960), 'The Size of the Economy and its Relation to Stability and Steady Progress', in E. A. G. Robinson (ed.), *The Economic Consequences of the Size of Nations: Proceedings of a Conference held by the International Economic Association.* London: Macmillan

3

When comparative advantage doesn't matter: business costs in small economies

L. ALAN WINTERS AND PEDRO M. G. MARTINS

3.1 Background

For a small economy in isolation, the most obvious economic constraint is scale. With a small market, small scale would follow, and with it, almost inevitably, inefficiency in the rate at which inputs can be transformed into outputs. In seeking to identify the disadvantages of smallness empirically one would need to consider minimum efficient scales and look at differences in production functions and overall efficiency across different sized countries.

The problem addressed in this chapter is rather different. We consider a trading economy in which in principle the scale problem can be obviated by trading with the rest of the world. Imports can be purchased from the world's most efficient producer (or, at least, at prices dictated by that producer), while exporting to a huge world market allows an economy to reap full economies of scale in export sectors. The potential problem now is that trade with the rest of the world is more costly for small and remote countries.[1] Because of a mixture of small consignment size, poor infrastructure, a lack of competition and weak regulatory arrangements, small countries' costs of trade may be inflated, and so the physical cost of goods and services in small economies will always exceed world minima. (By physical cost we mean the inputs required to deliver a unit of consumption measured in physical terms.) Either consumers need to fund the costs of importing in addition to the minimum price of the good in world markets, or the trading cost of importing will be so great that local production is preferable, in which case local scale re-emerges as the constraint. Moreover, delivering a unit of exports is also more costly for a small country. The small country has to find

[1] Separating the effects of smallness and remoteness is a serious issue, to which we return below. For now we will be a little vague about which matters.

not only the resources necessary for production (even if it is the most efficient producer), but also those to deliver it to market – i.e. the cost of trading.

In identifying the potential commercial disadvantages of smallness in the global economy one is thus interested in (a) the excess costs of international transactions for small and remote countries and (b) the excess costs of non-traded inputs into efficient industries. This is the agenda of the present study.

Such excess costs imply, first, that *ceteris paribus* incomes will be lower in small economies and, second, that the sets of goods that are traded internationally may be smaller for smaller economies. Nothing in these circumstances suggests that countries will over-trade (and hence benefit from curtailing trade with the rest of the world) or that they will trade in the wrong goods (and hence benefit from policies designed to alter the bundle of traded goods). That is, provided that a country continues to trade internationally, the law of comparative advantage will determine its welfare-maximising trade. But the provision is important: comparative advantage does not matter if either you do not trade internationally or you cannot survive (literally) when you do.

We do not challenge the proposition that, by definition, there must be some good in which a country is, relatively speaking, least inefficient, but we consider the possible routes through which 'least inefficient' does not translate into effective exporting, and clothe them, for the first time, we believe, in real data. We hypothesise that very small economies might lack sufficient absolute comparative advantage for trade – i.e. have no good or service which they can export competitively – because either their transactions costs or their real production costs are too high to permit any trade on a commercial basis. Taking world prices as given and subtracting the minimum costs of trading and/or of intermediate inputs leaves nothing over for value added, or, perhaps, too little for subsistence. Free trade would lead to no trade.

3.2 The approach

Our approach to testing whether small economies can sustain acceptable incomes is conceptually unsophisticated. We collect data on a wide range of the costs of doing business across a range of differently sized economies and seek regularities in the relationship between cost and size. We also collect data on certain policy variables to test whether small countries' problems stem from obvious shortcomings in policy.

Since countries' size varies only slowly, we rely on cross-country variance to identify the size effect. We define size in terms of population – the traditional measure – although for some costs we also include GDP per capita among our explanatory variables so that there may be aggregate income effects too.[2] Where we need size categories we use the following definitions:

1 Below 400,000 inhabitants
2 Between 400,000 and 2 million inhabitants
3 Between 2 and 10 million inhabitants
4 Between 10 and 50 million inhabitants
5 More than 50 million inhabitants

The boundary between our second and third categories (2 million) accords well with the semi-official definition of smallness used by the Commonwealth Secretariat and agreed by the Commonwealth Advisory Group in 1997. The latter proposes 1.5 million as the threshold, but includes within the group Jamaica (which has a population of 2,633,000 in our data), Lesotho (2,035,000), Namibia (1,757,000) and Papua New Guinea (5,130,000).

Our sample of ninety-two countries is defined in table 3.1, along with information about their survey organisation (see below), their population, GDP and GDP per capita in 2000.

Size is not the only feature of an economy that potentially affects its performance and business costs. There are strong reasons for believing that location also matters in terms of both who are your neighbours (e.g. Vamvakidis, 1998) and how isolated you are from the main centres of economic activity (Redding and Venables, 2002a).[3]

We try to separate locational factors from size factors in a variety of ways below. For transportation and communications costs, where the data refer to links with specific main centres (e.g. London or Tokyo), we include distance to those centres. Moreover, for sea transportation we include land distances to the port of entry/exit and seek qualitative differences for cases where this exceeds a threshold or where it involves crossing an international border. Isolation effects are explored by the use of an island dummy in some relationships.[4]

[2] Population is also better measured and more likely to be exogenous than GDP.

[3] See Redding and Venables (2002b) for an overview.

[4] See Winters and Martins (2004a) (hereafter 'WM1') for a discussion of the definition of an island.

Table 3.1 *Summary statistics of the sample of countries*

Country	City	Sampling organisation	Population million	GDP $ million	GDPpc $
Anguilla	The Valley	C	0.01	108	8,869
Antigua & Barbuda	St John's	C	0.07	689	10,125
Argentina	Buenos Aires		37.03	284,960	7,695
Australia	Sydney		19.18	390,110	20,337
Austria	Vienna		8.11	189,030	23,308
Bangladesh	Dhaka		131.05	47,106	359
Barbados	Bridgetown	C	0.27	2,600	9,736
Belgium	Brussels		10.25	226,650	22,108
Belize	Belize City	C	0.24	821	3,419
Botswana	Gaborone	I	1.60	5,285	3,299
Brazil	São Paolo		170.41	595,460	3,494
Cameroon	Douala		14.88	8,879	597
Canada	Toronto		30.75	687,880	22,370
Chile	Santiago		15.21	70,545	4,638
China	Shanghai		1,262.50	1,079,900	855
Colombia	Bogotá		42.30	81,283	1,922
Cook Islands	Rarotonga	P	0.02	85	5,264
Côte d'Ivoire	Abidjan		16.01	9,370	585
Czech Republic	Prague		10.27	50,777	4,943
Denmark	Copenhagen		5.34	162,340	30,424
Dominica	Roseau	C	0.07	270	3,700
Ecuador	Quito		12.65	13,607	1,076
Fiji	Suva	P	0.81	1,495	1,842
Finland	Helsinki		5.18	121,470	23,463
France	Paris		58.89	1,294,200	21,976
Gabon	Libreville		1.23	4,932	4,010
Germany	Berlin		82.15	1,873,000	22,800
Greece	Athens		10.56	112,650	10,668
Grenada	Saint Georges	C	0.10	410	4,187
Guyana	Georgetown	C	0.76	712	936
Hong Kong	Hong Kong		6.80	162,640	23,928
Hungary	Budapest		10.02	45,633	4,553
India	Mumbai		1,015.90	456,990	450
Indonesia	Jakarta		210.42	153,260	728
Ireland	Dublin		3.79	93,865	24,740
Italy	Rome		57.69	1,074,000	18,617
Jamaica	Kingston	C	2.63	7,403	2,812
Japan	Tokyo		126.87	4,841,600	38,162
Kenya	Nairobi	I/E	30.09	10,357	344

Table 3.1 (*cont.*)

Country	City	Sampling organisation	Population million	GDP $ million	GDPpc $
Kiribati	Tarawa	P	0.09	43	475
Lesotho	Maseru	I	2.04	899	442
Malawi	Blantyre	I	10.31	1,697	165
Malaysia	Kuala Lumpur		23.27	89,659	3,853
Marshall Islands	Majuro	P	0.05	96	1,844
Mauritius	Port Louis	I	1.19	4,381	3,694
Mexico	Mexico City		97.97	574,510	5,864
Micronesia	Kolonia	P	0.12	228	1,932
Mozambique	Maputo	I	17.69	3,754	212
Namibia	Windhoek	I	1.76	3,479	1,980
Nauru	Yaren	P	0.01	50	4,348
Netherlands	Amsterdam		15.92	364,770	22,914
New Zealand	Auckland		3.83	49,903	13,027
Nigeria	Lagos		126.91	41,085	324
Niue	Alofi	P	0.00	7	3,763
Norway	Oslo		4.49	161,770	36,021
Pakistan	Karachi		138.08	61,638	446
Palau	Koror, Palau	P	0.02	144	7,600
Papua New Guinea	Port Moresby	P	5.13	3,818	744
Peru	Lima		25.66	53,466	2,084
Philippines	Manila		75.58	74,733	989
Poland	Warsaw		38.65	157,740	4,081
Portugal	Lisbon		10.01	105,050	10,497
Samoa	Apia	P	0.17	236	1,387
Senegal	Dakar		9.53	4,371	459
Seychelles	Victoria	I	0.08	614	7,554
Singapore	Singapore		4.02	92,252	22,960
Solomon Islands	Honiara	P	0.45	275	614
South Africa	Durban	I	42.80	125,890	2,941
South Korea	Seoul		47.28	457,220	9,672
Spain	Madrid		39.47	558,560	14,153
Sri Lanka	Colombo		19.36	16,305	842
St Kitts and Nevis	Basseterre	C	0.04	314	7,660
St Vincent & the Grenadines	Kingstown	C	0.12	333	2,895
Suriname	Paramaribo	C	0.42	846	2,029
Swaziland	Mbabane	I	1.05	1,478	1,415

Table 3.1 (*cont.*)

Country	City	Sampling organisation	Population million	GDP $ million	GDPpc $
Sweden	Stockholm		8.87	227,320	25,631
Taiwan	Taipei		22.40	309,000	13,795
Tanzania	Dar Es Salaam	I	33.70	9,028	268
Thailand	Bangkok		60.73	122,170	2,012
Tonga	Nuku'alofa, Tongatapu	P	0.10	153	1,529
Trinidad & Tobago	Port of Spain	C	1.30	7,312	5,620
Turkey	Istanbul		65.29	199,940	3,062
Tuvalu	Fusi, Funafuti	P	0.01	14	1,167
Uganda	Kampala	I	22.21	6,170	278
United Kingdom	London		59.74	1,414,600	23,680
United States	New York		281.55	9,837,400	34,940
Uruguay	Montevideo		3.34	19,715	5,908
Vanuatu	Port-Vila	P	0.20	212	1,074
Venezuela	Caracas		24.17	120,480	4,985
Vietnam	Ho Chi Minh City		78.52	31,344	399
Zambia	Lusaka	I	10.09	2,911	289
Zimbabwe	Harare	I/E	12.63	7,392	585
mean			52.83	320,534	7,831
std dev			170.85	1,162,932	9,613
median			10.06	25,530	3,697
number	92				

Note:
Under Sampling Organisation, 'I' denotes Imani Capricorn, 'C' Caricom, 'P' Pacific Islands Forum, 'I/E' Imani and EIU, and blank denotes Economist Intelligence Unit.
Source: EIU, Business Cost Survey, World Development Indicators

Since completing the analysis data for St Lucia have been located. Its row of this table would read:

Country	City	Sampling organisation	Population million	GDP $ million	GDPpc $
St Lucia	Castries	C	0.16	866	5,413

Table 3.2 *Sample countries cross-classified by size, region and insularity*

	Population categories				
	1	2	3	4	5
Region					
Pacific	11	2	1	–	–
Carribbean	8	3	1	–	–
Sub-Saharan Africa	1	5	2	10	1
Latin America	–	–	1	6	1
South Asia	–	–	–	1	3
Rest Asia	–	–	2	2	5
OECD	–	–	7	11	8
Geographical status					
Continental	1	6	13	30	18
Island	19	4	1	–	–

Unfortunately, however, size, region and insularity are highly collinear. The Pacific and Caribbean regions are almost wholly comprised of small countries and together comprise nearly the whole of our sample of small countries – see table 3.2. These two regions similarly provide nearly all our island economies and contain very few continental countries, and smallness and insularity also go very closely together. The correlations between these features are given in table 3.3. Indeed, arguably, the correlation between size and insularity is no accident, for there is a clear historical tendency for small administrations on the same land mass to coalesce – e.g. the USA, Germany, the United Kingdom. Even remoteness could enter the same nexus, since islands close to larger countries will often become part of them.

These collinearities essentially reflect a lack of information. Because the variables move together we cannot ascertain with certainty which of them provides the explanation for the phenomena we observe, e.g. the level of freight costs. Future researchers might try to solve the problem by enlarging the sample (e.g. to collect data for more islands and small economies outside the Pacific or Caribbean, to consider more continental small countries such as Andorra, and to study islands within countries to ascertain the costs of physical separation). For the present, however, the only palliatives are theory and parsimony – exploiting theory to try to separate the different effects and recognising the fundamental problem by not seeking too fine a degree of explanation. The policy problem is, after all, also

Table 3.3 *Correlations between size, region and insularity*

	Correlation with	
	log (population)	log (GDP)
Pacific Region	−0.60	−0.63
Caribbean	−0.43	−0.36
Island	−0.81	−0.75

collinear; we are mostly concerned about economies that are both small and remote.

3.3 The business cost data

Our business cost data come from four sources. The main one is the Economist Intelligence Unit, which administers a six-monthly survey in fifty-four major capitals and business centres. We use their survey results from mid-2002 and supplement them with surveys commissioned by the Commonwealth Secretariat from regional organisations in various (mostly small) economies: Imani Capricorn in Africa, the Caribbean Community Secretariat/Caricom Secretariat in the Caribbean and the Pacific Islands Forum in the Pacific. These surveys were also completed in mid-2002. The survey instrument is given in WM1.

The data on costs come in two forms. Some are measured as continuous variables – e.g. the nominal wage for a kitchen porter or the cost of a unit of electricity – while others are categorical – 'does the power fail once a week, once a month, once a quarter, or never?'. The former costs are analysed by simple regressions of the cost variable on the country's size and other variables which we believe might affect it (and which are reasonably readily available). For the categorical variables, where the cost categories imply a natural ordering, as with the power failure example above, we estimate an ordered logit equation which asks whether a country's chance of falling into any particular cost category depends on its size. If so, we see that size is either an advantage, reducing the chances of falling into a costly category, or a disadvantage, increasing those chances. We cannot easily convert the categories for these cost variables into dollars and cents in the way that we can the continuous variables, but these results help to inform us about the qualitative advantages or disadvantages of size.

All survey data are subject to error and ours are no exception. Considerable effort was required to interpret and clean them and, in order to increase the value of the data, we have corrected the most obvious of the errors – for example, re-scaling prices that have been reported in cents rather than dollars. Nonetheless, a number of difficulties remain, which we note very briefly as we come to them below. Full details of the problems and adjustments made are available in WM1. Although our intention was to make the data available to other researchers the requisite permissions have not yet been received.

Even after the first round of cleansing, the data still contain a number of obvious surprises and outliers. Where possible we have verified these from secondary sources, but where we could not we have not overridden the reported values. We have, however, omitted them from our empirical analysis below. In addition, during the analysis further outliers were sometimes identified in the form of absolutely large residuals from our estimated relationships. Since our aim is to test the relationship between the various business costs and size, we have in general eliminated these from the regressions in order to preserve the normality of the residuals and hence the legitimacy of the statistical inference. In all cases, however, we report the direction in which the observation is outlying and check that the nature of the estimated relationship is not greatly changed by the elimination. If it is, we – and our readers – should exercise great caution in drawing conclusions.

The main source for GDP, GDP PPP (Power Purchasing Parity) and population was the World Development Indicators 2002, although other sources were also used to complement this information where necessary (Global Business Cost Survey and Asian Development Bank). For information on air and sea distances, please see WM1.

The continuous data from the survey that we explore below are given in table 3.4.[5]

All values are reported in or converted to current US dollars and all refer to mid-2002. The data on passenger travel costs were obtained from the Commonwealth Secretariat's travel agents. They represent the cost of an economy return ticket from each capital to the respective destination.

The usable categorical data from the survey are given in table 3.5.

[5] Certain collected data proved unusable – see WM1 for details.

Table 3.4 *The continuous variables from the survey*

Airfreight	Airfreight costs of transporting 100 kilograms of general cargo 'to' and 'from' London, Tokyo and New York
Sea freight	Shipping costs of transporting a standard 20ft Full Container Load (FCL) of general cargo 'to' and 'from' Rotterdam, Yokohama and New York
Wages	Average hourly wage for unskilled jobs and annual salary for the rest
Telephone	– Rate per minute of local calls during peak hour – Rate per minute of international calls during peak hour – Installation fee for a standard commercial line – Line rental fee for a standard commercial line
Electricity	– Costs of electricity for a standard commercial line (KWh) – Connection fee for a standard commercial line
Water	– Costs of water for standard commercial rate (per 1,000 litres) – Standard commercial connection fees
Fuel	– Retail price of diesel per litre – Retail price of petrol per litre
Land	– Average annual cost of per square metre of industrial (factory) space (average industrial estate) – Average annual rent of per square metre of office space in the prime location
Bank	– Prime commercial bank lending interest rate – Prime commercial bank deposit interest rate
Corporate tax	– Corporate tax rate for residents – Corporate tax rate for non-residents
Import duties	– Unweighted average (nominal) tariff rate – Import weighted (nominal) tariff rate – Receipts from import duties and taxes (including customs duties, VAT, sales taxes, supplementary duties, etc.) as percentage of total government tax revenues as available for the latest year
Personal air travel	Cost of economy return from London, Tokyo or New York (separate source)

Table 3.5 *The categorical variables from the survey*

Are unskilled/semi-skilled/ skilled workers domestically available or do they have to be hired from abroad?	**(1)** Domestically available and there is no need to import them from abroad **(2)** There are enough workers domestically available *to* satisfy most of the demand; however, occasionally workers need to be imported from abroad **(3)** Workers are available domestically, but many need to be imported from abroad to satisfy demand **(4)** Some workers are domestically available, but most need to be imported from abroad **(5)** Few workers are available domestically. The vast majority of workers are imported from abroad
How long does it take to get a new connection?	**(1)** <72 hours, **(2)** <1 week, **(3)** 1 week – 1 month, **(4)** >1 month, **(5)** Not available (i.e. indefinite delays)
How frequently does one experience disruptions?	**(1)** No disruption, **(2)** Very rare, **(3)** Rare, **(4)** Quite frequently, **(5)** Most frequently
How long does it take, in general, to have a broken line repaired? (Telephone only)	**(1)** 48 hours, **(2)** 5 working days, **(3)** 2 weeks, **(4)** >2 weeks
Are tax incentives available for exporters and other businesses?	YES/NO
Export duty rate (duties from exports as percentage of total government tax revenues)	Converted into YES/NO since there were too few values (different from 0) to run a regression
Is there a special exchange rate for exports?	YES/NO

3.4 The regressions results

This section gives a brief account of our attempts to locate country-size effects in our data. Full details are given in WM1 and Winters and Martins (2004b) (here after 'WM2'). Our general strategy was to fit log-linear models between the business variables cost and population as a measure of size, including, as necessary, other obvious regressors such as distance in the transportation cost equations. Where appropriate we made allowances for insularity and for likely differences between high- and low-income countries.

All equations were subject to a number of standard econometric diagnostic tests, including for normality, functional form and heteroscedasticity, and also tests for the robustness of the reported equations. In the few cases where we could not eliminate the problems, the reservations are noted and discussed in WM1 and WM2. Here we merely report our best estimates of the relationships between cost and size.

Our basic estimating equation for the continuous variables was:

$$\text{Ln (costs)} = \alpha_0 + \alpha_1 \text{ Ln (Popn)} + \alpha_2 \text{ [Ln(Popn)]}^2 + \text{other variables}$$

Where costs were zero, observations had to be dropped, but we took a great deal of care to identify cases where this might have changed the results. Similarly, where missing observations (zeros) may have been influential, we flag that fact when discussing the results below.

For the policy variables – various tax, subsidy and interest rates – we use a linear-log specification since the policy variables are expressed as percentages, which are, broadly speaking, scale free. These equations also include GDP per head, Ln(GDPpc).

For the categorical information on the frequency of disruptions or length of waits for connection or repair we estimate size effects from Ordered Logits, since the data can be ordered (i.e. it is better to have fewer disruptions than more). We thus calculate the probability of a country falling into a particular class of disruption according to its individual characteristics (e.g. income and size) as:

$$\text{Prob(country i is in class} = \text{j)} = \frac{\exp(\mu_j + \beta' x_i)}{\Sigma \exp(\mu_\lambda + \beta' x_i)}$$

$$\text{where } \beta' x_i = \alpha_1 {}^* \text{Ln(GDPpc)}_i + \alpha_2 {}^* \text{Ln(Pop)}_i$$

The main results are summarised in table 3.6. This reports, in column order: the regression coefficients on population and population squared, the joint test of their statistical significance, the co-efficients on distance, GDP pc, an inland transportation dummy, an OECD dummy, R^2 and the number of observations. Finally come the cost disadvantages implied by the equations for three example countries: those in italics are based on statistically insignificant estimates of size effects, while where we think there is *no* evidence of size effects we write 0. These are the columns that will underpin the competitiveness exercise in the subsequent parts of the chapter.

The cost disadvantage ratios summarise the costs of smallness by presenting for three representative countries the percentage excess costs of an input relative to that of the median country. The exemplar countries are located fourth, eighteenth and thirty-sixth in our ranking by size, expressing their percentage disadvantage relative to the median country, ranked forty-sixth. To make the examples concrete, they correspond to the populations of:

micro-economies	Anguilla	12.13 thousand
very small	Vanuatu	197 thousand
small	Singapore	4,018 thousand
median	Hungary	10,022 thousand

The estimates for **airfreight costs** suggest that there are significant size effects for outward transportation (as shown by the joint significance F-tests in column 3 of table 3.6). The negative sign on population and positive sign on the squared term implies a u-shaped relationship between population and costs – as illustrated in figure 3.1. The turning points vary between 1.5 million inhabitants and 3.5 million inhabitants (for the outward regressions), which leaves at least thirty small economies on the downward part of the curve.

A surprise is the apparent absence of significant size effects in the inbound freight rates (from London etc.). Inbound rates are generally significantly higher than outbound ones, and we speculate that the difference arises because of different practices in consolidating consignments. Outbound, export agents seek to consolidate and so are able to do something to overcome the disadvantages of small size. This is feasible for them because exports are not highly diversified and stem from a small number of economic entities. Inbound, on the other hand, the co-ordination problems are greater, with greater diversity of goods, entities and origins and also great distance between national agents at home and the place where consolidation must be done (i.e. in the partner country).

Turning to **sea freight costs**, there are strong size effects for all regressions: the coefficients on population are always significantly negative and the joint significance of the population variables very high. In this case the 'U' is much steeper and the turning points much higher: in two cases they are far beyond any existing country's size. That is, sea freight shows much

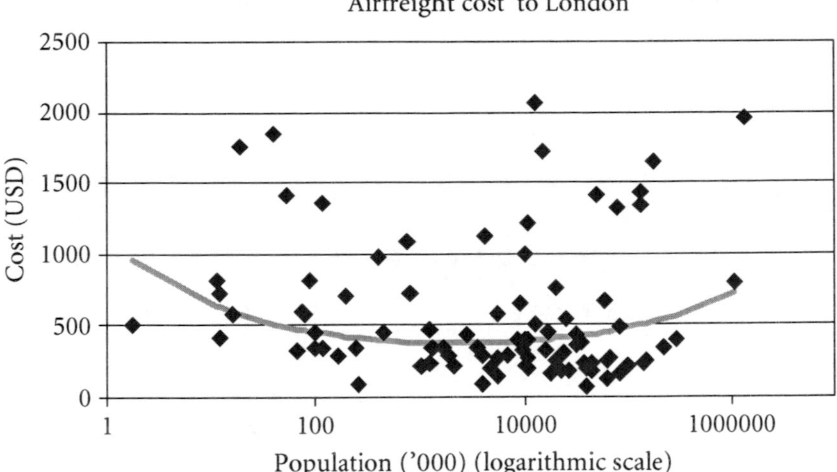

Figure 3.1 Airfreight costs 'to London' vs. population

higher minimum efficient scale than airfreight – see figure 3.2. (We decided to keep the two insignificant squared terms to maintain the same functional form for all sea freight regressions.)

Distance here includes both sea and land distances and is almost always significant (the exception is 'from NY'). It is supplemented by the dummy variable L500, which takes a value of 1 when the trade is subject to internal transportation between capital and port of at least 500 km. This takes a positive sign (except 'to NY' where it is not significant) and is significant in three cases. We also tested for the effects of land-lockedness by including for crossing an international border: surprisingly it was not significant. The OECD dummy always assumes a negative sign and is significant in five of the six cases. It reflects, we hypothesise, different infrastructures and institutions in these countries.

The samples for the **nominal wage** regressions exclude the OECD and the three high-income Asian countries. This decision followed a careful examination of data plots that displayed very great differences between the rich and poor sub-samples. Among developing countries the relationship between size and wages is log linear (since none of the squared terms for population was statistically significant). GDPpc is always positive and significant at 1 per cent. Coincidently, the regressions for bank clerks and bank managers had significantly worse fit than the rest of the estimates, a fact which we attribute to the multinationality of the banking sector. Inter-country

Table 3.6 *Summary of the size regressions for continuous variables*

	Regression	Ln (Pop)	[Ln (Pop)]^2	F-test (Pop)	Ln (Distance)	Ln (GDPpc)	L500	OECD	R-Sq.	Obs.	Cost disadvantages Micro	V. Small	Small
Airfreight	To London	−0.281**	0.018**	2.565*	0.248***	–	–	–	0.19	91	60.3	8.2	−3.1
	From London	−0.189	0.010	0.770	0.369***	–	–	–	0.23	83	*62.1*	*18.9*	*1.3*
	To Tokyo	−0.326***	0.020***	4.007**	0.336***	–	–	–	0.14	84	85.3	15.2	−2.2
	From Tokyo	−0.057	0.004	0.469	0.372***	–	–	–	0.09	80	*7.1*	*−0.4*	*−1.2*
	To NY	−0.278***	0.019***	5.179***	0.499***	–	–	–	0.36	84	45.2	1.0	−4.9
	From NY	−0.211	0.014	0.886	0.533***	–	–	–	0.17	82	*37.2*	*3.2*	*−3.1*
Sea freight	To Rotterdam	−0.290***	0.011*	16.601***	0.218***	–	0.419**	−0.355**	0.61	70	195.3	67.0	9.3
	From Rotterdam	−0.307**	0.009	29.268***	0.135*	–	0.727***	−0.416**	0.70	62	287.4	100.1	14.6
	To Yokohama	−0.406***	0.017**	29.450***	0.548***	–	0.310**	−0.291**	0.60	78	301.5	87.2	10.4
	From Yokohama	−0.316**	0.011	24.973***	0.678***	–	0.126	−0.357***	0.64	75	251.6	85.0	11.9
	To NY	−0.311**	0.015**	5.819***	0.202**	–	−0.131	−0.177	0.29	75	148.3	44.4	4.5
	From NY	−0.302**	0.015**	11.303***	0.048	–	0.111	−0.378*	0.22	75	133.7	39.4	3.7
Wages	CW	−0.075***	–	–	–	0.525***	–	–	0.67	*63*	65.5	34.3	7.1
	CO	−0.054***	–	–	–	0.489***	–	–	0.67	*63*	43.7	23.6	5.1
	KP	−0.080***	–	–	–	0.452***	–	–	0.76	*63*	71.1	36.9	7.6
	BCL	−0.050*	–	–	–	0.257***	–	–	0.39	*58*	39.9	21.7	4.7
	BCF	−0.040	–	–	–	0.229***	–	–	0.29	*59*	*30.8*	*17.0*	*3.7*
	GM	−0.060**	–	–	–	0.461***	–	–	0.63	*63*	49.6	26.6	5.6
	PC	−0.012	–	–	–	0.543***	–	–	0.60	*63*	*8.4*	*4.8*	*1.1*

	QT	−0.047**	–	–	–	0.532***	–	–	0.73	*63*	37.1	20.3	4.4
	BML	−0.064**	–	–	–	0.298***	–	–	0.35	*58*	53.7	28.6	6.0
	BMF	−0.046	–	–	–	0.291***	–	–	0.26	*58*	*36.2*	*19.8*	*4.3*
	GRN	−0.071***	–	–	–	0.515***	–	–	0.73	*61*	61.1	32.2	6.7
Telephone	London	−0.101***	–	–	0.418***	−0.227***	–	–	0.61	89	97.1	48.7	9.7
	Tokyo	−0.117***	–	–	0.001	−0.196***	–	–	0.36	89	119.4	58.4	11.3
	NY	−0.152***	–	–	0.169	−0.393***	–	–	0.61	90	177.6	81.7	14.9
	Local	−0.073*	–	–	–	−0.074	–	–	0.05	81	0.0	0.0	0.0
	Inst. fee	0.058*	–	–	–	0.106	–	–	0.06	90	−32.3	−20.4	−5.2
	Line rent	−0.026	–	–	–	0.364***	–	–	0.42	88	*19.1*	*10.8*	*2.4*
Electricity	Usage	−0.098***	–	–	–	−0.021	–	–	0.19	84	93.1	47.0	9.4
	Connect	0.103	–	–	–	−0.223	–	–	0.07	67	*0.0*	*0.0*	*0.0*
Water	Usage	−0.184***	–	–	–	0.024	–	–	0.14	82	0.0	0.0	0.0
	Connect	0.219***	–	–	–	0.409***	–	–	0.35	63	−77.0	−57.7	−18.1
Fuel	Diesel	−0.084***	–	–	–	−0.110**	–	–	0.32	*62*	75.8	39.1	8.0
	Petrol	−0.041**	–	–	–	−0.025	–	–	0.11	*61*	31.7	17.5	3.8
Passenger travel	London	−0.116***	–	–	0.641***	−0.160***	–	–	0.93	86	118.0	57.7	11.2
	Tokyo	−0.106***	–	–	0.455***	−0.285***	–	–	0.58	88	103.8	51.7	10.2
	NY	−0.121***	–	–	0.871***	−0.213***	–	–	0.76	87	125.4	60.9	11.7
Land	Office	−0.399	0.035**	16.349***	–	0.729***	–	–	0.51	86	−7.0	−34.4	−17.8
	Factory	0.040	–	–	–	0.256***	–	–	0.29	73	0.0	0.0	0.0
Bank	Lending	1.561**	−0.107**	5.812*	–	−2.630***	–	–	0.50	82	−2.1	0.0	0.3
	Deposit	0.322***	–	–	–	−1.078***	–	–	0.29	83	−2.2	−1.3	−0.3

Table 3.6 (*cont.*)

	Regression	Ln (Pop)	$[\text{Ln (Pop)}]^2$	F-test (Pop)	Ln (Distance)	Ln (GDPpc)	L500	OECD	R-Sq.	Obs.	Cost disadvantages Micro	V. Small	Small
Corp. tax	Residents	0.373	–	–	–	−0.091	–	–	0.03	84	*−2.5*	*−1.5*	*−0.3*
	Non-residents	0.113	–	–	–	−0.767*	–	–	0.04	84	*0.8*	*0.4*	*0.1*
Import duties	Weighted	−0.193	–	–	–	−3.492***	–	–	0.47	51	*1.3*	*0.8*	*0.2*
	Unweighted	−0.057	–	–	–	−3.623***	–	–	0.58	47	*0.4*	*0.2*	*0.1*
	% Revenue	−6.051***	–	–	–	−7.028***	–	–	0.55	65	40.6	23.8	5.5

Obs. – Refers to the number of observations used in the final regressions

Cost disadvantages – These are based on the ratio between the costs of each of the three exemplar countries (chosen to represent different population categories) and the median country. For the cost regressions these represent percentage deviations from a fictional median country with around 10 million inhabitants. For the policy variables, these disadvantages are actually expressed in percentage points. The cases where the evidence of a population effect is insignificant but different from zero are in italics. The zeros are cases where there is no convincing case for cost disadvantages (based on the significance of the population effects and sensitivity tests undertaken to assess the impact of the exclusions of the '0' observations).

* Significance at 10%; ** Significance at 5%; *** Significance at 1%

Wages

CW – Construction worker	BCL – Bank clerk/Teller in local bank	PC – Payroll clerk	BMF – Bank manager in foreign bank
CO – Checkout operator	BCF – Bank clerk/Teller in foreign bank	QT – Qualified teacher	GRN – General registered nurse
KP – Kitchen porter	GM – Garage mechanic	BML – Bank manager in local bank	

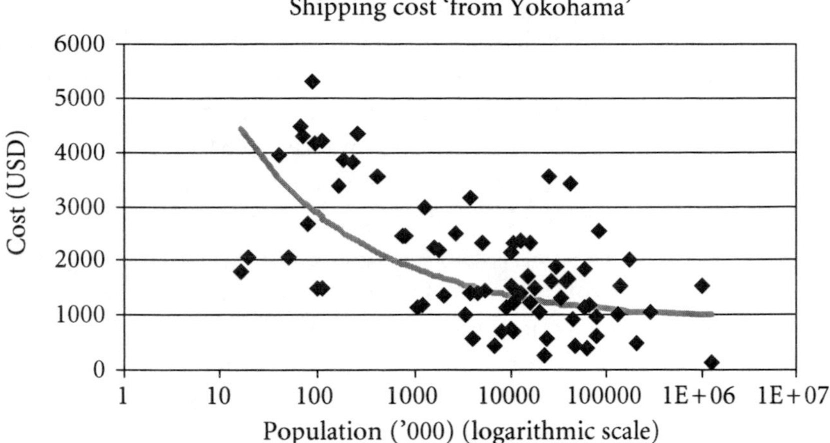

Figure 3.2 Shipping costs 'from Yokohama' vs. population

comparisons are much easier within a company than between companies and so the relationship of the wage with national variables is more readily 'contaminated' by spillovers between countries. Population is significant in eight of the eleven wage regressions (seven at 5 per cent) and the respective coefficients range from −0.047 to −0.080. Nevertheless, all eleven regressions suggest a negative relationship between size and wages. The fact that two out of the three non-significant regressions refer to foreign banks (bank clerk and bank manager) again, we believe, reflects multinationality.

Nominal wages may be higher in small countries because the cost of living is higher for precisely the sort of reasons we are discussing in this chapter. To explore this we also included the PPP adjustment factor in the equation to capture 'real' price differences. This is strongly correlated with size and absorbed some of the size effects. However, all the population effects remained negative and three remained significantly different from zero. Once we allow for the negative relationship between population and PPP factor, the net effect of population on wages is almost identical whether we break out the price effects or not.

For **utilities** we ran regressions for both fixed and variable costs. The main problem faced with the utilities was the high number of zeros reported. Since our log-linear regressions are highly sensitive to this issue we were very careful with the interpretation of the results, and apply sensitivity tests to assess the importance of dropping these observations – see WM1 and WM2.

For international telephone costs, population is always significantly negative at 1 per cent but distance is not important except 'to London'. As for virtually all utilities' marginal costs, the coefficients on GDPpc are robustly negative, indicating that people in richer countries pay less than those in poorer countries. The estimates for local telephone costs are much weaker and we feel that we cannot identify convincing size effects for this variable. Turning to the fixed costs of telephones, installation fees proved to have a weak but positive relationship with size (at 10 per cent), although not with GDPpc. Finally, for line rental fees, we found that GDPpc has a strong impact, but that population is not a significant determinant (although the estimate suggests a negative relationship between size and line rental costs).

The results for electricity marginal costs indicate a significantly negative population coefficient. We cannot prove the existence of a relationship between size and electricity connection costs however, although the coefficient suggests a positive relationship. There were nine zeros (for countries ranging from Nauru and Senegal to Sweden and Australia), and different ways of treating them gave different results, so a good deal of caution is required here.

Turning to water, we find a negative relationship between size and usage costs, while GDPpc was not significant. However, again the zeros look influential so we do not include these results in the cost disadvantage exercise. For water connection fees, we found a positive size effect on the regression, and that GDPpc was significant at 1 per cent. The eleven zeros would probably attenuate this result since most of these are for large countries. Nevertheless, to be conservative we do carry these estimates forward.

In the **fuel** regressions, we again had to exclude the OECD and three high-income Asian countries based on various data plots – a procedure we justify by appealing to different environmental and safety standards. The results illustrate a negative significant relationship between size and the cost of fuel.

The exercise on **passenger travel** used data provided by the Commonwealth Secretariat's travel agents. The results are pretty much consistent across the three different destinations. The coefficient on population varies from -0.106 to -0.121, while those on GDPpc were negative and those on distance positive as experience would predict.

The last of the log-log regressions was on **land rents**. Here we had severe problems with missing observations and outliers. We managed to estimate a relationship for the costs of office space, but the same was not possible for factory space. For office space, the population variables are jointly significant, but since the coefficient on population is small (and insignificant) the turning point occurs very early. Hence the predominant relationship between size and office costs is positive. For factory rentals, we were unable to find a significant relationship with size, especially given the numerous outliers in the sample. The estimates, however, suggest again a positive relationship. At first sight these results might look as if they show advantages to being small. However, the Ricardian theory of rents suggests that land rents reflect the surplus between earnings and costs, and hence that low rents merely serve to confirm the disadvantages of small size seen above.

For the **categorical variables** we estimate ordered logits to explore the relationships between size (population) and the different categories of disruption or waiting time. Table 3.7 reports the results. For each issue it reports the coefficients on population and GDPpc, the population thresholds between categories 1 and 2 and between categories 2 and 3 assuming a GDPpc of $10,000, a measure of fit and the number of observations used.

We start with the availability of workers. We ran regressions relating the availability of each of three types of workers (unskilled, semi-skilled and skilled) to size (logged population) and (logged) GDPpc. Although, as we would expect, we do not have strong evidence for unskilled workers, for semi-skilled and skilled workers there are clear reported shortages in small countries. The minus sign attached to the population coefficient represents the greater dependence of small economies on the import of semi-skilled and skilled labour (lower categories mean less need to import workers from abroad). It is comforting to note the GDPpc effects suggest that richer countries lack unskilled workers, and semi-skilled workers to a lesser extent (evidenced by a positive sign in GDPpc), but, relatively speaking, have an abundance of skilled workers. The thresholds between categories 1 and 2 are 1.8 and 15.8 million respectively for semi-skilled and skilled workers. This suggests that a large range of countries are small enough to have shortages of skills, especially since the thresholds are evaluated at a gap of $10,000pc and the skills shortages will be greater at lower incomes.

For telephones, we found that while there were no significant size effects for connection and repair times, there was evidence that disruptions tend to occur more frequently in small countries. This conclusion is repeated precisely for water and electricity. For quite understandable reasons,

Table 3.7 *Estimates for the ordered logit equations on categorical variables*

Regression		Ln(Pop)	Ln(GDPpc)	Cat = 1/2 pop ('000)	Cat = 2/3 pop ('000)	McFadden Pseudo R-Sq.	Obs.
Workers' availability	Unskilled	−0.169*	1.003***	340.8078	0.7730	0.150	92
	Semi-skilled	−0.361***	0.367**	1892.8546	3.7076	0.142	92
	Skilled	−0.392***	−0.331**	15803.2397	55.1362	0.134	92
Telephone	Connection	−0.064	−0.620***	–	–	0.079	92
	Disruption	−0.176**	−0.827***	9169.5955	0.0003	0.152	92
	Repair	−0.098	−0.445**	–	–	0.051	92
Electricity	Connection	−0.021	−0.479***	–	–	0.048	91
	Disruption	−0.242***	−1.129***	56832.1320	1.4408	0.211	92
Water	Connection	0.055	−0.417***	–	–	0.040	90
	Disruption	−0.271***	−1.042***	3205.8005	0.3942	0.194	91

Cat = 1 and Cat = 2 are based on a GDPpc = \$10,000

*Significance at 10%

**Significance at 5%

***Significance at 1%

small countries are more vulnerable to utilities disruptions than are larger countries.[6]

The second substantive question to address is whether **policy** is 'worse' in small countries. We used linear-log regressions for the policy variables, since these were variables represented by percentages. There were severe problems with outliers in almost all the regressions, but some tentative conclusions can be drawn. There appear to be significant relationships between size and bank lending and bank deposit rates. Thus, small countries appear to have lower deposit rates than the median country, but for lending rates we can say that only for very small countries.[7] The effect of GDPpc is significantly negative in both equations, meaning that high per capita income countries have lower interest rates.

With reference to corporate tax, we could not establish a convincing relationship between either size or GDPpc and the tax rate. Thus, although we are clearly not capturing much of the explanation of tax rates (see the very low R-squares), the results certainly do not suggest that small countries tax more.

The final block on table 3.6 concerns import duties. Although we find strongly significant coefficients for GDPpc, we were unable to establish a convincing relationship between size and import duty rates. On the other hand, receipts from import duties as a percentage of tax revenue did prove to be robustly and significantly higher in small countries. GDPpc was also negative and significant at 1 per cent, confirming that in richer countries import duties provide a smaller share of total tax revenue. The relationship with size seems intuitively plausible, for in small economies very large shares of consumption are imported (increasing the numerator and reducing the denominator of the fraction to be explained). Indeed, in the limit, if imported inputs into industry are exempted, as they frequently are, import duties become very similar to consumption taxes and thus probably rather efficient sources of revenue.

Finally, we have dichotomous data on three policy variables – the existence of special interest rates or tax incentives for exporters, and the existence of export duties. Testing (through binary logits) for differences in the sizes of the economies that display these features and those that do not,

[6] In WM1 we also present cross tabulations of disruption and waiting times by size class. They confirm these results.

[7] Because the relationships are linear-log the disadvantage ratios are expressed in percentage points not percentage terms.

the only significant difference is that small economies are less likely to give tax incentives for exports.

We did also collect information on general indirect tax rates and budget deficits, but, unfortunately, neither were usable – the former because the quoted ranges were too large (e.g. 0–350 per cent for Brazil) and the latter because the survey did not specify whether to include a minus sign on the deficit, which may have induced some correspondents into mistake.

3.5 The disadvantages of smallness: cost inflation factors and income penalties

Tables 3.6 and 3.7 leave a strong impression of the excess transactions and input costs arising from small size, especially for micro and very small economies. However, we still need to confirm that these excess costs add up to a material competitive disadvantage on world markets. To do this we estimate the cost structures of three export industries typical of developing countries – electronic assembly, clothing manufacture and hotels and tourism – and use them to weight together the cost disadvantages above to create a single cost inflation factor for each product.

The cost structures are based on the input–output tables from the Global Trade Analysis Project (GTAP) consortium. For each industry we collapsed the input structure into three primary factors – skilled and unskilled labour and capital – and about a dozen intermediates. We then arrayed the (value) input shares across the sixty-five countries for which data were provided (there is considerable variance) and tried to infer the likely shares for the median-sized developing country. The valuation is at producer prices – i.e. essentially the same basis as our collected cost data – and so the shares provide the weights required for creating base-weighted indices of the cost disadvantages relative to the median in the exemplar economies.

To create the indices we need to distil the results in the last three columns of table 3.6 into a single figure for each identified input. In general we use the averages in that table and further weight them together using crude a priori weights. Whenever a cost disadvantage is not statistically significant in the table, we assume the value to be zero here. We took averages of outbound and inbound transport costs separately for exports and imports respectively (weighting airfreight one-third and sea freight two-thirds). For skilled labour we used the cost disadvantage for skilled labour above, and for 'unskilled labour' the weighted average of our original results for unskilled and semi-skilled (one-third for semi-skilled and two-thirds for unskilled). This fits reasonably well with the GTAP definitions of skills. Finally, for the cost of utilities we consider the averages only for the marginal cost component, ignoring the connection fee (which means we overstate the costs of smallness) and the costs of disruption (which means we understate them).

Second, we need to determine what proportion of the cost of each input is exposed to the disadvantage factors. We distinguish five different treatments:

(1) Internationally traded intermediates are assumed to be available at the price of the median country plus the excess transport costs identified above assuming that 8 per cent of the gross value of these goods is accounted for by transport. We apply the same transport cost disadvantage factors to the full value of small economies' exports of electronics and clothing.

(2) Inputs of labour bear their own cost disadvantage factors and we assume that the same factors apply to inputs of essentially non-tradable services. For the tradable component of services categories we assume that foreign competition imposes some discipline (or displacement), and hence we halve the labour disadvantage factors when applying them to each service in aggregate. We make no further allowances for the labour availability disadvantages identified above.

(3) For capital our measured cost disadvantage factors – bank lending rates – are not very appropriate. We assume conservatively that capital costs are 15 per cent, 10 per cent and 5 per cent above median values for our three exemplar small economies respectively. These excesses essentially reflect investors' ignorance of small economies and the greater variability that the latter, almost inevitably, face. They are not large: if the cost of capital is 10 per cent in the median country we make it 11.5 per cent, 11 per cent and 10.5 per cent for the three exemplar countries.

(4) For utilities we use the cost disadvantage factors from the table directly, ignoring both the connection fees and the excess disruptions that small economies face.

(5) Finally, for exports of tourism we assume that visitors have to pay the excess personal travel costs identified in the table and that these account for 25 per cent of the costs of a visit. Hence for recreation we

have an exposure factor of 25 per cent and a cost disadvantage factor of 116 per cent for the smallest economies.[8]

Table 3.8 summarises the cost disadvantage information that we use in our subsequent calculations on electronics. It reports our estimates of (a) the cost shares of each input, (b) the assumed exposure to the disadvantage factors, and (c) the summary disadvantage factors for each input for each of our three exemplar small countries.

To put the cost disadvantage factors into context we also calculate the income penalties that they entail. Assuming that exports must be delivered at the same price as the median country would charge, the excess costs eat into small countries' returns to economic activity. By how much depends on which inputs face excess costs and which returns can be squeezed to restore competitiveness.

We define five concepts of the income penalty, progressively enlarging the set of inputs with unavoidable cost disadvantages and correspondingly shrinking the set which can be squeezed to accommodate the excess costs if exports are to be competitive:

Concept	Inputs bearing the costs of inefficiency	Inputs assumed to have unavoidable cost disadvantages
1	all domestic supplies – primary factors, services and non-tradedintermediates	internationally traded intermediate inputs
2	primary factors and services	traded intermediate inputs and utilities
3	primary factors	all intermediate inputs including services
4	capital	all intermediate inputs and labour
5	labour	all intermediate inputs and capital

If all domestically supplied factors, utilities and services (i.e. everything except those goods that are directly traded internationally) can be squeezed to absorb the excess transactions costs of smallness, the relatively small cost disadvantages on intermediate inputs are spread over relatively large flows

[8] In retrospect, we accept that these factors may be a bit large, given that many tourists travel on package holidays, which helps agents avoid the costs of small consignments.

Table 3.8 *Cost structures for electronics and cost disadvantage ratios*

	Central estimate	Share subject to	Cost disadvantage factors (%)			
	%	inflation	Micro	V. Small	Small	Comment
Unskilled labour	12.5	1	47.5	25.1	5.3	(Unskilled & Semi-skilled)
Skilled labour	4	1	38.0	20.3	4.3	(Skilled)
Capital	14	1	15.0	10.0	5.0	
ElectronicEq	22	0.08	149.5	49.9	6.7	(Av. import – Transport)
Machinery	15.5	0.08	149.5	49.9	6.7	(Av. import – Transport)
MetMinerals	6.5	0.08	149.5	49.9	6.7	(Av. import – Transport)
Chemical	4	0.08	149.5	49.9	6.7	(Av. import – Transport)
Energy	1	1	73.4	37.7	7.7	(Electricity and fuel)
Trade	7.5	1	22.2	11.7	2.5	(labour*0.5)
Transport	2.5	1	157.0	48.4	5.5	(Airfreight and sea freight)
Communication	0.5	1	98.5	47.2	9.0	(Telephone)
FinBusServ	5	0.5	22.2	11.7	2.5	(labour*0.5)
Other goods	2.5	0.08	149.5	49.9	6.7	(Av. import – Transport)
Other services	2.5	0.5	22.2	11.7	2.5	(labour*0.5)
Export transport factor	2.5	0.08	164.6	46.8	4.2	(Av. export – Transport)

of income (revenue), and so the proportionate penalty is relatively small. Concept 2 accepts that utilities' costs in small countries are not reducible. Hence it implies larger cost disadvantages loaded onto a smaller base than does concept 1. Concept 3 follows the effective protection literature and takes all intermediates' prices as fixed (by trade or the limits of small-scale technology) and takes value added (primary factors of production) as the residual claimants. In concept 4 an individual investor considers the 'excess costs' of workers as given, and that she herself is the residual claimant on income. Concept 5 asks essentially a public policy question. If small economies cannot force down the prices of intermediate inputs and if they have to pay a premium to borrow on international capital markets, how much income can they generate for the local population qua workers?

Table 3.9 presents the core results of our study in the first row: the cost inflation factors. Subject to inevitably wide margins of error, micro-economies face very large competitive challenges indeed. Our central estimates suggest that micro-economies have a cost inflation factor for manufacturing of 36 per cent, and that for tourism the factor is 58 per cent! The last is driven substantially by our high cost-disadvantage estimates for personal travel (and the high share of such travel in overall packages), but even without that problem, tourism in micro-economies would be some 29 per cent more expensive than in an equivalent median-sized economy. For very small economies the cost inflation factors are still a significant 14 per cent and 29 per cent for manufacturing and tourism respectively, although for small economies they are a mere 3–6 per cent, well within the range of estimation error and small enough to be overcome by good management.

The 'income penalties' in the remaining rows report the extent to which particular elements of the cost structure would have to accept *below* median prices or returns if the target economies were to supply exports at median-country prices. Consider electronics in a micro-economy. If every element of cost were 'squeezable', except for internationally traded intermediates and export freight costs, they would all have to accept 39 per cent lower returns than in the median country. If we next assume that utilities' prices cannot be squeezed either, the remaining elements (factors and service suppliers) would need to take a 43 per cent cut.[9]

[9] As we move down the column the figures increase because we are both adding further cost disadvantages to the numerator of equation (2) and removing flows from the denominator, so that the penalties have to be borne on a smaller and smaller base.

Table 3.9 *Central case cost inflation factors and income penalties*

	Electronic assembly			Clothing			Hotels and tourism		
	micro	V. small	small	micro	V. small	small	micro	V. small	small
cost inflation factor	36.4	14.3	2.7	36.3	14.3	2.7	57.5	28.5	6.2
income penalty – % of median country's income flow									
all domestic supplies	−38.8	−11.6	−1.2	−40.1	−12.0	−1.3	−36.2	−17.4	−3.3
factors and services	−42.6	−13.3	−1.5	−44.7	−14.0	−1.6	−46.3	−22.3	−4.3
value added	−88.0	−29.2	−3.8	−86.0	−28.6	−3.7	−71.9	−34.0	−6.5
capital	−245.1	−91.8	−14.1	−263.9	−99.9	−15.6	−202.1	−98.4	−19.2
labour	−175.5	−62.5	−11.2	−161.0	−57.3	−10.2	−116.5	−56.6	−12.4

The big step occurs if we take services as unavoidably more expensive in small countries. Now the primary factors of production in electronics would earn 88 per cent less than in the median country – that is only 12 per cent of what median factors owners earn. Specialising the burden further to fall only on labour or capital, the other receiving its excess returns indicated by our cost-disadvantage estimates, generates income penalties exceeding 100 per cent. That is, if all inputs except capital received the predicted excess prices (returns), capital owners would make losses larger than the profits the median-country capitalists received. If all inputs except labour received the excess prices/costs, there would be nothing to pay the labour with and prices would still exceed median-country levels! While, with our fixed weight indices and no allowance for niche marketing, we may have exaggerated the losses, it is difficult to believe that we have the basic story wrong.

Of course, at present small economies manifestly do not suffer these huge income penalties. One reason is presumably that they do not undertake these activities, but rather produce and export other goods or services. There is some truth in this – e.g. the small island economies specialising in fishing – but these alternatives also face excess costs of similar magnitudes and so this cannot be the answer. Another reason is that the economies produce virtually no exports, but rather depend on remittances, aid or asset returns to fund essential imports.[10] The third possibility is that preferences on their exports or product differentiation into niche markets allow them to earn prices above those of the median country, or that they have benefactors who will accept below market rates of return on their capital, or labour in return for various non-pecuniary benefits of living in a small economy. Finally, regulation may be more flexible and more cheaply achieved in small economies than in large ones, leaving more surplus for real incomes. This continuing advantage is independent of the trading regime they face and so is not vulnerable to removal. Equally, however, it cannot extend to compensate for any loss of trading advantages.

In WM1 we conduct extensive sensitivity tests on these results and find them robust with respect to changes in weights, and clearly they are proportional to the cost overall level of disadvantage. The most sensitive issue is the transportation cost factor because it is applied to the full value of the export and, for tourism, to 25 per cent of the value of a package. This is

[10] It is well known, for example, that aid per head is much higher for small economies than for large ones.

clearly an area towards which both future research and policy consideration should be directed.

3.6 Policy conclusion

The message of this chapter is robust and stark. While circumstances vary by economy and class of economy it is clear that, on average, micro- and very small economies face huge competitive challenges. These economies will not be suitable locations for industry or even tourism unless they have very specific advantages that allow them to charge substantially higher prices than the median country. For hotels and tourism the attractions of small tropical islands are plausible and we do, indeed, see viable tourist industries on them. Our results merely indicate that they will need to manage costs carefully and will never achieve mass market penetration.

For manufacturing, on the other hand, the barriers look very high indeed, and if we wish such industries to develop, the leverage of any corrective policies will need to be correspondingly high. One common response is that since the costs of trading are so high, small countries need the right to protect their industries. This is completely misguided. The problem is not that imports can get in too easily but the very opposite. Adding barriers to trade will exacerbate not relieve the problems of smallness. Even where local industries could be successfully established behind tariff walls there is nothing in the foregoing analysis to suggest that such an approach would be economically beneficial. Theory still suggests that following comparative advantage maximises real income: only not sufficiently to provide an adequate income.

A related response has been to suggest subsidising business investment in order to overcome the cost disadvantages of smallness. There are many arguments in the policy-making literature for subsidising business in an economy. We do not accept many of them, but, even if we did, smallness adds nothing to them. If you would not subsidise business in a large economy, neither should you do so in an equivalent small one, for precisely the reasons outlined in the previous paragraph. Smallness does not introduce marginal distortions that need to be countervailed, but an overall feasibility constraint. If income is insufficient when you maximise it, it will certainly be insufficient if you do not; and in the absence of the market failures usually adduced to justify subsidising manufacturing, subsidies will reduce income.

The conclusion must be that if unviable economies are to be made viable, an additional source of income must be found and, presuming the absence of free technological or organisational lunches, that means from abroad.[11] One source internal to the set of small economies themselves is to economise on the costs of economic management or even of statehood. Andriamananjara and Schiff (2001) and Schiff and Winters (2003) argue strongly that by combining various functions of government small states can both economise on costs and, possibly, exert a greater influence on their environments. Whether such efficiencies are sufficient to overcome the disadvantages we have noted here, we rather doubt, but there is undoubtedly a case for seeking such efficiency gains in any case. We also note that in the cases where smallness appears not to matter – e.g. Luxembourg, Liechtenstein, Andorra – the secret appears to be to integrate extremely closely with the neighbouring large countries.

In the end, however, we suspect that the sources of income necessary to keep very small economies going must be external – that ultimately the international community will have to provide the compensating flows. Merely subsidising capital costs will not generally be sufficient – there are too many other continuing disadvantages. Thus, while international capital transfers – either bilateral or via international financial institutions and development banks – will clearly help to reduce costs by improving infrastructure and perhaps utilities, most of the disadvantages we see above are on the current account – e.g. shipping costs, thin markets for skills etc. The most favourable case for infrastructural salvation is probably communications links. If these are excellent and cheap, services relying on electronic interchange may become competitive. But even so, the costs of importing goods will still be high and even in 'electronic services' personal contacts are important so small remote economies will be disadvantaged by their high travel costs and long travel times. Thus, we believe that one probably needs continuing current transfer to confer lasting viability.

One superficially promising route is via some sort of preferences for small countries' exports, allowing them to sell at tariff-inclusive prices in industrial country markets rather than at world prices. This source of rent has historically been very important – as, for example, with banana or tuna exports to the EU or clothing exports from the Caribbean to the USA.

[11] Our brief discussion of policy certainly did not suggest that the disadvantages of smallness stemmed from policy inadequacy.

The problems are, first, that other developing countries have become more hostile to these preferences, as with Latin American challenges to banana preferences and East Asian challenges to those on tuna, and that the more legalistic regime of the WTO makes them far harder to defend than they were under the GATT. Second, as donors discover new favourites the preferences of the old are eroded: consider Pakistan's recent advantages under the textile quotas and the way in which NAFTA and now African Growth Opportunity Act (AGOA) reduced the advantages of the Caribbean countries in the USA. Third, industrial countries are gradually liberalising their trade regimes anyway, so that the benefits of preferences are gradually declining. In all these cases, as rents are reduced, very small economies face large income penalties. A salutary thought is that if very small economies are dependent on rents, the erosion of legal rents could presage a search for less social sources. Very small countries are inherently difficult to police if their governments are not sympathetic to global objectives.

An alternative route could be for industrial countries to subsidise small country trade explicitly – either their exports or their imports or both. This would require conscious policy-shifts in the major capitals and also derogations from WTO agreements. A similar route would be straight income transfers. In either case the issue for the recipients would be the security of such transfers. As we noted above, we believe that they would need to be permanent and so could not be dressed up merely as transitional financing to encourage structural adjustment.

Explicit subsidies to micro- and very small economies raise their own very particular political challenges. Specifically, many of the cost disadvantages we have identified must also apply to insular or isolated parts of larger countries. These disadvantaged regions are often subsidised via regional policies. But if small economies were permitted to have export subsidies, one would need to argue why this privilege should not be extended to parts of larger economies, for if it were it would probably fatally undermine subsidies discipline in the WTO. The reason is not hard to formulate, but it may be uncomfortable: within a country, people can move out of uneconomic locations. Ultimately if the current preferences that small countries receive are eroded and we do not somehow support their incomes in other ways, many of their inhabitants will seek to work abroad. We have argued elsewhere that liberalising the temporary movement of labour within the world economy – mode 4 of the GATS – promises huge economic gains (Winters et al., 2003). This could be a key factor for very small economies, essentially allowing residents to earn abroad but live and consume at home. Temporary workers from small countries would still be at a disadvantage relative to those from larger ones: they would face higher transport costs, less effective networks for finding jobs and easing migratory strains, and higher consumption costs at home. However, particularly if they had preferential access – e.g. guaranteed quotas – the benefits would be large enough to cover the disadvantages. But again the sustainability of preferences would fall under question.

The alternative to temporary mobility would be permanent migration. In the current political climate this appears to combine the nightmares of both sides: of immigration in most developed countries and of depopulation, and maybe eventual cultural extinction, in the very small economies.[12] Such nightmares should fuel our search for alternative solutions.

The title of Easterly and Kraay's (2000) important paper 'Small States, Small Problems' upset many commentators on the problems of small size: the problems, they said, are very large if you face them. But the title contains a silver lining: 'small problems, small solutions'. Particularly if we limit transfers to the micro- and very small economies they will need to be only very small in aggregate – small amounts of money, small flows of people etc. If there is a political will to offer them – not only in the developed donor countries but also among developing countries, especially those which are only just too big to receive them – they would be perfectly manageable. Around 3.1 million people (0.05 per cent of the world's population) live in countries of below 200,000 population, 6.3 million in those below 400,000 and 16.4 million in those below 1 million population. These are not insurmountable by any yardstick.

References

Andriamananjara, S. and Schiff, M. (2001) 'Regional Cooperation Among Microstates', *Review of International Economics*, vol. 9, no. 1, pp. 42–51

Easterly, W. and Kraay, A. (2000) 'Small States, Small Problems? Income, Growth, and Volatility in Small States', in *World Development*, vol. 28, no. 11, pp. 2013–27, November, Elsevier Science Ltd

[12] This nightmare also shows why subsidising human capital formation is at best a very partial answer for very small economies: the highly skilled will leave, returning the small economy to square one.

Redding, S. and Venables, A. (2002a) *The Economics of Isolation and Distance*, mimeo, Commonwealth Secretariat

Redding, S. and Venables, A. (2002b) *Economic Geography and International Inequality*, CEPR Discussion Paper No. 2568

Schiff, M. and Winters, L. A. (2003) *Regional Integration and Development*, Oxford University Press for World Bank

Vamvakidis, A. (1998) 'Regional Trade Agreements or Broad Liberalization: Which Path Leads to Faster Growth?', IMF Staff Paper, vol. 46, no. 3 (September/December 1999)

Winters, L. A. and Martins, P. M. G. (2004a) 'Beautiful but Costly: Business Costs in Small Economies', mimeo, Department of Economics, University of Sussex, to be published by Commonwealth Secretariat [WM1]

Winters, L. A. and Martins, P. M. G. (2004b) 'When Comparative Advantage is Not Enough: Business Costs in Small Developing Economies', mimeo, Department of Economics, University of Sussex [WM2]

Winters, L. A., Walmsley, T., Wang, Z. and Grynberg, R. (2003) 'Negotiating the Temporary Movement of Natural Persons: An Agenda for the Development Round', *The World Economy*, vol. 26(8), pp. 1137–62

4

Can small states compete in manufacturing?

GANESHAN WIGNARAJA AND DAVID JOINER

4.1 Introduction

There is little doubt that globalisation has a profound impact on the economic prosperity of the world's smallest economies. Much of the recent policy and academic literature has tried to show that small states do face specific problems and that their small size can constrain economic development in a global world economy. Several studies highlight the existence of an inverse relationship between country size and susceptibility to economic, political and environmental risks and threats (Commonwealth Consultative Group, 1985; Commonwealth Secretariat, 1997; Streeten, 1993; Briguglio, 1995; Atkins et al., 2001; Grynberg, 2001; Winters and Martins, 2003). This literature concludes that small states are more vulnerable than larger economies because of higher exposure to external shocks from higher trade openness and single primary commodity dependence; have less access to international financial markets and aid due to limited creditworthiness; face higher transport costs due to remoteness; and are more exposed to environmental risks due to their geographical location.

These arguments have fuelled calls by small states' representatives in international fora for increased foreign aid and trade preferences to facilitate economic adjustment to globalisation. However, the success of such efforts to date, and the prospect for future success, is at best limited, and even if it were to improve significantly the underlying trends of globalisation are unlikely to change. Realistically, small states will increasingly have to compete on world markets for exports and foreign investment, and will receive less in aid and special treatment. Relatively little academic and policy attention, however, has been devoted to the competitiveness in small states (particularly in the manufacturing sector) and the factors explaining success.[1]

[1] Recent studies on competitiveness in small states include: Wignaraja, 1997; Wint, 2003; Holden et al., 2004; and Briguglio and Cordina, 2004.

This chapter deals with the pressing policy question of whether small states can compete in manufacturing in a global world. It measures the industrial competitiveness record of small states using a composite index and benchmarks them against each other. Benchmarking exercises of this type allow small states to assess their country's performance in relation to: (i) countries at a similar level of development, or of similar characteristics, which they would like to outperform; and (ii) countries at a higher level of development, whose performance they wish to emulate, and whose policy strategies they could learn from in order to achieve it.

Section 4.2 explores popular efforts to benchmark competitiveness and highlights the lack of coverage of small economies in these exercises. Section 4.3 constructs a small states manufactured export competitiveness index (SSMECI) and presents the results. This is a simple composite index made up of three variables (manufactured exports per capita, growth rate of manufactured exports, and share of manufacturing in gross domestic product (GDP)). Section 4.4 undertakes a T-test to shed light on the performance of small states, while section 4.5 concludes.

There are many ways (e.g. GDP, population and surface area) to define a small state and each has merits depending on the purpose at hand. Following the Commonwealth Secretariat (1997), this study defines a small state as an economy with 1.5 million people or fewer. Accordingly, forty economies are considered small states in this study.[2]

4.2 Current benchmarking initiatives and their appropriateness for small states

The concept of competitiveness is somewhat elusive, particularly at the national level, and has been intensely debated to clarify its meaning and economic relevance. It has often been equated with macroeconomic issues (e.g. changes in exchange rates or wages) or microeconomic issues (e.g. entrepreneurship, economic incentives and bureaucratic regulations on business, and firm-level technological capabilities and institutional support) (see Faggerberg, 1988; Porter, 1990; Corden, 1994; Krugman, 1994; Dahlman and Aubert, 2001; Lall, 2001a; and ADB, 2003). An examination of the

[2] Included in this group are five somewhat larger states (Botswana, Jamaica, Lesotho, Namibia and Papua New Guinea), which share many of the physical and economic characteristics of small states in their respective regions. The table in the appendix contains a basic profile of the forty small states.

theoretical debate on competitiveness is beyond the scope of this chapter. Suffice it to say that both macroeconomic and microeconomic approaches to competitiveness offer valuable insights, depending on the purpose at hand. There is increasing recognition that building technological capabilities at the firm level is associated with competitiveness performance in a world of rapid globalisation and technological progress. Furthermore, appropriate economic incentives and supportive institutions can help firms to overcome market and systems failures in technological learning. This chapter's focus is on the empirical literature on competitiveness, particularly on recent exercises to benchmark competitiveness performance across countries using different composite indices.[3] These include the following:

(i) World Economic Forum's *Global Competitiveness Report* (WEF, 2003);
(ii) International Institute for Management Development's *World Competitiveness Yearbook* (IMD, 2003);
(iii) United Nations Industrial Development Organisation's *World Industrial Development Report 2002/2003* (UNIDO, 2002); and
(iv) Wignaraja and Taylor (2003).

Table 4.1 summarises the key features of these four initiatives.

The work of the WEF and the IMD, both based in Switzerland, has largely dominated the global competitiveness benchmarking industry. Annual rankings of competitiveness in developed and developing countries have been produced for twenty-four years by the WEF's *Global Competitiveness Report* and for thirteen years by the IMD's *World Competitiveness Yearbook*. Both indices focus on the micro-level business perspective, and examine the extent to which nations provide an environment in which enterprises can compete. In line with this, rather than focusing on trying to calculate a measure of *actual* competitive performance, both adopt an approach of looking at a wide range of factors that could *affect* national competitiveness. To this end they use a large basket of variables (160 for WEF and 321 for IMD in 2003), which include both 'hard' published statistics and 'soft' data from surveys of businessmen. The sample size of these surveys is rapidly increasing, with 7,741 responses to the WEF 'Executive Opinion Survey' in 2003, as opposed to 4,600 in 2001.

[3] Composite indices of the type used in this chapter are only one possible way to capture competitiveness. Other popular methods include labour productivity, unit labour cost, real effective exchange rates, and revealed comparative advantage. See ADB (2003) for a discussion of the different methods.

Table 4.1 *Features of recent competitiveness indices*

	World Economic Forum (2003)	Institute for Management Development (2003)	UNIDO (2003)	Wignaraja and Taylor (2003)
Name of index	Growth competitiveness index	World competitiveness scoreboard	Competitive industrial performance index	Manufactured export competitiveness index
Concept	Business school approach to measuring national level competitiveness, using both performance and explanatory variables	Business school approach to measuring national level competitiveness, using both performance and explanatory variables	Focus on industrial performance and national ability to produce manufactures competitively	Focus on industrial performance and national ability to produce manufactures competitively
Number of variables	160	321	4	3
Weighting system	Two-tier approach based on a concept of 'core' or 'non-core' innovator countries; different aggregations and weightings apply to each group in the final index	20 categories each weighted at 5 per cent	4 variables, equally weighted	3 variables weighted at 30, 30 and 40 per cent (with technology intensity of exports weighted more)
Data source type	Published data and entrepreneur surveys (7,741 responses)	Published data and entrepreneur surveys (over 4,000 responses)	Published data	Published data

Table 4.1 (*cont.*)

	World Economic Forum (2003)	Institute for Management Development (2003)	UNIDO (2003)	Wignaraja and Taylor (2003)
Country coverage (including small states)	Covers 102 countries (8 small states)	Covers 59 countries (0 small states)	Covers 87 countries (3 small states)	Covers 80 countries (11 small states)
First published/ frequency	Yearly since 1979	Yearly since 1990	2002 and henceforth periodically	2003

Both indices are widely used, gaining widespread media attention. They have also generated a wealth of empirical data. What light then can they shed on the competitiveness of small states? Unfortunately the answer is very little. Despite increasing its coverage from 80 to 102 countries, the WEF index only has eight countries that are among the forty small states in this study. The situation with the IMD index is even worse, with no small states among the fifty-nine countries included. The precise reasons for this lack of coverage are unknown, and without discussion with the institutions involved, any attempts to determine such reasons remain simple guesses. However, one of the most significant factors is likely to be that the very complexity of both the indices means that the data requirements simply cannot be met in small states. With small populations and often underdeveloped institutions, there is simply no capacity or demand to collect the data required.

The specific issues of small states may also mean that the general theory of competitiveness espoused by both the WEF and IMD is perhaps inappropriate for the measurement of competitiveness in the small states context. In small, developing economies, focus on the basic economic fundamentals (e.g. macroeconomic stability, outward-oriented trade policies, high levels of human capital and efficient infrastructure) is perhaps more appropriate than worrying about the 200 subcomplexities found in sophisticated multisectoral economies of the developed world.

Quite apart from the lack of attention given to small states, the WEF and IMD competitiveness indices have attracted criticism on technical grounds. Lall (2001b) provides a comprehensive analysis of the WEF index of 2000 and finds flaws in its definition of competitiveness, model specification, choice of variables, identification of casual relations, and use of data. Lall goes on to offer some insights into the construction of competitiveness indices, and while not writing with small states in mind, his comments are perhaps particularly relevant in the context of small states:

> To be analytically acceptable, however, all such efforts should be more limited in coverage, focusing on particular sectors rather than economies as a whole and using a smaller number of critical variables rather than putting in everything the economics, management, strategy and other disciplines suggest. They should also be more modest in claiming to quantify competitiveness: the phenomenon is too multifaceted and complex to permit easy measurement (Lall, 2001b, 1520).

The Asian Development Bank (ADB, 2003) points out similar flaws in the WEF competitiveness index. For instance, ADB notes that the weights used to construct the WEF index are arbitrary and the index displays an overly negative view of the role of government. Furthermore, it relies extensively on qualitative data obtained through questionnaires that are only tenuously related to the notion of competitiveness.

Wignaraja and Taylor (2003) also offer a critique of the theory and methodology used by the WEF and IMD, including a detailed exploration of the IMD index of 2001. In summary they find that the IMD rankings have:

(i) *Ambiguous theoretical basis.* The theoretical linkages between the input determinants and national competitiveness are weak. The 'fundamentals' of the IMD 2001 index (IMD 2001, 43–9), which details the 'four fundamental forces of competitiveness', are more of a schema than a theory.
(ii) *Problems of index construction.* The justification for the weightings given to each of the indicators is sometimes weak and often nontransparent. There also seems to be a lack of distinction between variables that indicate competitiveness and those that determine it, with both types used. These lead to problems in interpreting the results and applying lessons to other countries.
(iii) *Ad hoc data and proliferation of components.* The use of survey data can be problematic in that the perceptions of businessmen in one country cannot be directly compared with the views of businessmen in another country without some kind of moderation. The justification of the recent proliferation of indicators is also weak, with no explanation as to what is being gained by their addition.

Building on this critique, and the argument that such indices need to be less ambitious and analytically simpler, recent work by UNIDO (2003) and Wignaraja and Taylor (2003) has emphasised the industrial competitiveness performance of developing countries.[4] This is a departure from the somewhat broader (and more vague) concept of national competitiveness implicit in the WEF and IMD work. The two newer indices were developed from a general developing country perspective, rather than being small-

[4] The UNCTAD/WTO International Trade Centre (ITC) also produces a Trade Performance Index, which benchmarks across developing countries at an industry/product level (see ITC, 2000). It is not discussed here due to the current chapter's focus on national level competitiveness, rather than individual industries/products. However, for policymakers interested in such detail it can be a valuable tool.

states specific, but come closer to the methodology appropriate for the focus of this study and in the context of data-sparse small states.

The UNIDO Competitive Industrial Performance Index focuses on national ability to produce manufactures competitively, and is constructed from four basic indicators of industrial performance (see UNIDO, 2003):

(i) manufacturing value added (MVA) per capita
(ii) manufactured exports per capita
(iii) share of medium- and high-tech activities in MVA
(iv) share of medium- and high-tech products in manufactured exports.

The UNIDO index provides valuable insights into the industrial record of the developing world. Unfortunately, out of eighty-seven countries listed in the index, only three are small states as defined in this study. Again, the reasons are unclear, but perhaps even such a simplified index still poses data availability problems.

Wignaraja and Taylor (2003) found a similar analytical underpinning to the UNIDO work and construct a Manufactured Export Competitiveness Index (MECI) of eighty developing countries using three variables:

(i) manufacturing exports per capita (1999)
(ii) average manufactured export growth per annum (1980–99)
(iii) technology-intensive exports as a percentage of total merchandise exports (1998).[5]

Of the eighty countries in the MECI, eleven are small states. The results for these economies are shown in table 4.2. The top and bottom three results in the overall MECI are also shown in order to give context to the data and index values for small states.

The eleven small states are fairly evenly spread through the middle section of the index, but even the highest performers have MECI values substantially below East Asian tiger economies (such as Malaysia, Singapore and Taipei, China) at the top of the rankings, putting perspective on the performance of small states. One of the reasons for this is perhaps the universally low level of high-technology exports in the small states (whether due to lack of such productive capacity or lack of data). While the share of high-technology exports was an appropriate variable

[5] Technology-intensive exports include electronics, petrochemicals and chemicals, iron and steel, engineering, plastics and industrial ceramics.

Table 4.2 *Summary of results from MECI*

			Manufactured exports per capita, 1999		Average manufactured export growth, 1980–99		Technology-intensive exports, 1998 (percentage of total merchandise exports)	
Overall rank	Economy	MECI value	Rank	Value (current US$)	Rank	Value (%)	Rank	Value (%)
1	Singapore	0.93	1	25,039	13	13.4	1	70
2	Malaysia	0.82	5	2,988	3	19.2	4	55
3	Taipei, China	0.79	3	5,477	31	9.4	3	58
15	Trinidad and Tobago	0.52	16	645	37	7.7	14	23
24	Mauritius	0.45	12	984	15	12.8	43	3
26	Cyprus	0.45	15	684	62	3.1	23	17
30	Bahrain	0.42	13	953	19	11.6	65	0
38	Dominica	0.38	21	393	34	9.2	65	0
45	Jamaica	0.35	22	377	64	2.8	43	3
50	St Kitts and Nevis	0.33	26	300	57	3.8	65	0
55	Grenada	0.31	52	45	42	7.2	65	0
58	Belize	0.29	41	86	69	0.4	49	2
61	Guyana	0.27	53	37	67	0.9	43	3
67	Tonga	0.24	72	6	50	5.9	65	0
78	Congo, DR	0.15	76	1	74	−2.1	58	1
79	Nigeria	0.13	80	1	71	−1.2	58	1
80	Yemen, Rep. of	0.00	78	1	80	−18.0	65	0

Source: Wignaraja and Taylor (2003)

for the study of eighty developing countries, its applicability for work that focuses on small states exclusively is called into question, as it is either not available or not distinctive enough among a small-states sample.

Significant differences in the performance of individual small states are visible. Cyprus, Mauritius and Trinidad and Tobago stand out among the sample of eleven small states in the MECI rankings. In contrast, smaller Caribbean economies (Belize, Grenada, Guyana and St Kitts and Nevis) and Tonga in the Pacific have performed poorly compared to the three leading small states.

4.3 A small-states specific competitiveness index

Bearing in mind the limited coverage of small states in the mainstream competitiveness literature and the specific issues surrounding measurement of their performance, efforts to benchmark the export performance of small states requires a new small-states specific index. As many of the existing methodologies are inappropriate for small states, the design of such an index and the interpretation of its results need to be handled with care. Building on the empirical work of Wignaraja and Taylor (2003), a simple, transparent SSMECI was developed. The key features of this index are highlighted in box 4.1, while the rest of the section presents the results by country and various aggregate categories.

Box 4.1 The small states manufactured export competitiveness index (SSMECI)

The small states manufactured export competitiveness index (SSMECI) emphasises the ability to produce manufactures competitively in the world's smallest economies. It has been designed in light of the problems with data availability in some small states and the need to build in realistic data requirements in order to make the country coverage of the index as wide as possible. The SSMECI is composed of just three variables, each of which captures a different aspect of industrial competitiveness and which combine to create a simple but effective snapshot of the economy's overall international competitiveness in this area. The three factors captured are:

(i) current performance in world export markets scaled by size
(ii) dynamism of this performance over time, i.e. growth rates

(iii) size of the manufacturing base in the structure of the wider economy.

The first factor captures an economy's actual record of competing in international markets rather than simply alluding to an ability to be competitive. The second captures how dynamic this performance is, and whether the economy's performance is on an upward or downward trend. The third looks at more structural issues, recognising that in a small state where economies of scale are such an issue, a larger manufacturing base is likely to reflect an advantage in achieving competitiveness. To reflect these three concepts and in light of the data issues, three specific variables were selected for the small states index, namely:

(i) manufactured export value per capita in 2001 (US$)
(ii) average manufactured export growth per annum 1990–2001
(iii) manufacturing value added as a percentage of GDP in 1999.

Using these variables, the SSMECI was constructed for forty small states in the sample set. This sample size is sufficient to permit basic statistical analysis of determinants. Calculations were performed to give each country a value between 0 and 1 for each of the three variables, and these were then weighted to produce a final index figure for each country, which could then be ranked. Higher values in the SSMECI indicate greater levels of competitiveness: thus, for example, Malta, with a SSMECI of 0.72 is perceived to be more competitive than Djibouti with a SSMECI of 0.22 in Table 4.4.

In interpreting the findings, readers should be aware of the sensitivity of results in small states. When the overall production base is so small, the establishment or closure of a single factory can substantially affect the overall figures for that year. The quality/reliability of the data obtained can also often be poor, due to underdeveloped/ understaffed statistics institutions in small states. To a degree, such factors may have influenced the overall rankings and led to marginally higher or lower placement than would be expected. This needs to be taken into account when interpreting the results, though it is unlikely to change the basic patterns observed.

Full details of data sources, definitions and the specific methodology used to construct the SSMECI are given in the appendix.

4.3.1 Country-level findings

Country-level rankings of competitiveness generate considerable interest in academic and policy circles. Of particular interest are the top performers. Before considering the composite SSMECI rankings, it is useful to start with a brief look at the component variables. Table 4.3 shows the top ten performers for each of the three component variables in the SSMECI. It is noticeable that there is considerable difference in the ranking of the three variables, and that top performers in one component are not necessarily the top in others. However, some countries rank consistently high, for example Estonia, which ranks third, third and fourth respectively. The Seychelles also figures in all three lists, albeit at the bottom end. Some countries that figure highly in two of the components, such as Mauritius in per capita manufactured exports and manufacturing value added (MVA) as a percentage of GDP, do not figure well in the third (average manufactured export growth) and this ultimately leads to a lower overall ranking in the SSMECI. At the same time, a particularly high ranking on a single variable can push up a country on the overall SSMECI rankings. Swaziland, which is at the top in terms of share of manufacturing in GDP, is a case in point.[6]

Table 4.4 shows the full SSMECI ranking for the forty small states, with the component indices, the ranking in each individual variable, and the underlying data values.

As might have been expected, results show that two European countries, Malta and Estonia, occupy the first two places in the ranking, perhaps reflecting both the greater access to market and the positive effect of sustained competitive pressure from their large European neighbours.[7] The rest of the top ten is made up of some of the traditional small state powerhouses of the various regions, such as Mauritius from the Indian Ocean, Trinidad and Tobago from the Caribbean, and Fiji Islands from the Pacific.

[6] Swaziland's large share of manufacturing in GDP seems to be due to the following: (i) twenty-six garment factories established by Taipei, China investors to take advantage of the Africa Growth and Opportunities Act, which provides ready access to the American market; (ii) one of Coca Cola's five worldwide plants that produces coke concentrate; (iii) various sugar pulp factories; and (iv) other light industries established by South African investors to take advantage of the South African Customs Union market.

[7] Calculations were also done to include Costa Rica, Singapore and Taipei, China, in order to check the robustness of the theory, and to set context to the SSMECI figures. Not surprisingly, these three economies came out at the top of the index.

Table 4.3 *Country rankings for the three separate variables*

Manufactured exports per capita 2001			Average manufactured export growth, 1990–2001			Manufacturing value added as percentage of GDP, 1999		
Rank	Country	Value (current US$)	Rank	Country	Value (%)	Rank	Country	MVA
1	Malta	4,469	1	Brunei	19.50	1	Swaziland	31.69
2	Botswana	2,891	2	Maldives	17.07	2	Mauritius	24.56
3	Estonia	2,203	3	Estonia	16.86	3	Namibia	15.45
4	Trinidad and Tobago	1,666	4	Lesotho	15.70	4	Estonia	15.43
5	Qatar	1,331	5	Trinidad and Tobago	13.25	5	Lesotho	15.13
6	Bahrain	1,080	6	Bahamas	12.89	6	Belize	14.81
7	Mauritius	940	7	Fiji Islands	12.75	7	Fiji Islands	14.11
8	Brunei	773	8	Grenada	12.48	8	Jamaica	13.93
9	Cyprus	605	9	Seychelles	11.19	9	Seychelles	13.73
10	Seychelles	576	10	Suriname	10.36	10	Malta	12.03

Sources: Data primarily from ITC, using COMTRADE Database, *World Development Indicators* (2001, 2002, 2003) and other regional and national sources. See appendix for full details of data sources and methodology.

Of noteworthy interest is the performance of the 'BLNS' countries that make up the Southern African Customs Union with South Africa. In the rankings all four score highly: Swaziland is third, Lesotho eighth, Botswana ninth and Namibia eleventh. This high performance may again be due in part to proximity to large markets, and the trade and investment stimulus that an agreement such as the Southern African Customs Union produces for its 'satellites'.

Some countries do not perform as well as might be expected. For example, Cyprus, ranked twenty-three, did not perform as well as the other European countries in the sample. While it scored fairly highly in terms of per capita exports and MVA, manufactured exports have actually fallen over the last ten years, possibly reflecting a fall in comparative competitiveness, and this negative average growth brings down the overall SSMECI ranking score.

4.3.2 Findings by region, income group and country size

In an attempt to establish patterns of performance and provide analytical insights, the forty small states have been grouped into various categories as follows:

(i) geographical region to facilitate comparisons across regions
(ii) income per head to permit analysis of different income groups
(iii) population to enable analysis by country size.

In each case, the group values for each of the three variables have been calculated using weighted averages, which have then been indexed, using the same methodology as before. Simple averages are also shown for each grouping, calculated using average index values for each country in the group. Table 4.5 aggregates the results according to geography, allowing the regional breakdown of the results to be analysed.

The high performance of the European region is probably to be expected, as discussed above. In comparison, the relatively high performance of the African region is more surprising, and closer inspection shows that there are in fact two tiers of performance within the region. At the top level, the four BLNS countries, Mauritius and the Seychelles are all in the top eleven of the SSMECI rankings. At the other end, a number of African countries, particularly in Western Africa, are among the bottom ten positions. Overall, the contributions of the top-tier performers are enough to obtain a high average in comparison to the other regions. Also of

Table 4.4 *Overall SSMECI ranking*

			Manufactured exports per capita, 2001[a]		Average manufactured export growth, 1990–2001[b]		Manufacturing value added as percentage of GDP, 1999[c]	
Overall rank	Country	SSMECI value	Rank	Value (current US$)	Rank	Value (%)	Rank	MVA
1	Malta	0.72	1	4,469	16	5.36	10	12.03
2	Estonia	0.71	3	2,203	3	16.86	4	15.43
3	Swaziland	0.69	17	299	12	7.10	1	31.69
4	Mauritius	0.65	7	940	22	3.14	2	24.56
5	Trinidad and Tobago	0.59	4	1,666	5	13.25	22	7.99
6	Brunei	0.58	8	773	1	19.50	19	8.42
7	Seychelles	0.57	10	576	9	11.19	9	13.73
8	Lesotho	0.56	24	113	4	15.70	5	15.13
9	Botswana	0.55	2	2,891	25	2.25	34	4.97
10	Fiji Islands	0.55	18	266	7	12.75	7	14.11
11	Namibia	0.51	14	398	26	2.15	3	15.45
12	Bahrain	0.51	6	1,080	21	3.25	15	9.88
13	Qatar	0.49	5	1,331	28	1.73	23	7.30
14	Guyana	0.49	19	207	11	10.02	14	10.15
15	Grenada	0.49	16	319	8	12.48	24	7.26
16	Maldives	0.49	23	116	2	17.07	26	6.46
17	St Kitts and Nevis	0.48	11	514	20	3.82	13	10.33
18	Jamaica	0.48	26	105	18	4.51	8	13.93
19	Bahamas	0.47	12	508	6	12.89	38	3.20

20	Barbados	0.46	13	468	23	2.82	16	9.32
21	Belize	0.46	22	122	30	0.00	6	14.81
22	Bhutan	0.46	28	59	14	6.86	11	11.56
23	Cyprus	0.46	9	605	31	−1.68	12	10.54
24	Dominica	0.45	15	357	19	3.94	17	8.48
25	Suriname	0.43	30	21	10	10.36	21	8.12
26	St Vincent/Grenadines	0.41	25	111	17	5.16	25	6.54
27	Gabon	0.39	29	48	13	6.89	32	5.16
28	Solomon Islands	0.39	21	148	27	1.89	33	5.12
29	Samoa	0.37	34	9	15	5.53	28	6.02
30	Vanuatu	0.34	33	9	29	0.53	27	6.35
31	Papua New Guinea	0.32	32	10	33	−5.37	20	8.28
32	Tonga	0.31	35	4	24	2.33	36	3.89
33	St Lucia	0.31	27	83	34	−9.79	29	5.96
34	Cape Verde	0.30	31	21	36	−10.96	18	8.45
35	Antigua and Barbuda	0.27	20	197	37	−13.97	39	2.25
36	São Tomé and Principe	0.24	39	0	32	−3.65	35	4.52
37	Djibouti	0.22	37	2	35	−10.90	37	3.60
38	The Gambia	0.20	36	2	38	−16.74	30	5.60
39	Comoros	0.13	38	1	39	−26.09	31	5.43
40	Kiribati	0.00	40	0	40	−29.07	40	0.99

[a] In some cases where data from 2001 was not available, 2000 or 1999 data was used. See appendix for full details.

[b] Where data was not available for 1990 or 2001, data for the nearest available year was used. Growth rates were calculated using a compound method, adjusting for length of time period as appropriate. See appendix for full details.

[c] Where 1999 data was not available, 1998 or 2000 data was used. See appendix for full details.

Sources: Data primarily from ITC, using COMTRADE Database, *World Development Indicators* (2001, 2002, 2003) and other regional and national sources. See appendix for full details of data sources and methodology.

Table 4.5 *SSMECI performance by region*

					Manufactured exports per capita, 2001		Average manufactured export growth, 1990–2001		Manufacturing value added as percentage of GDP, 1999	
Rank	Regional grouping[a]	No.	Weighted average SSMECI[b]	Simple average SSMECI	Rank	Value (current US$)	Rank	Value (%)	Rank	MVA
1	Europe	3	0.79	0.63	1	2,076	3	8.70	2	12.24
2	Africa	12	0.49	0.42	3	602	5	2.74	1	12.86
3	Asia	3	0.45	0.51	5	351	1	16.95	5	8.46
4	Caribbean/Latin America	13	0.37	0.45	4	481	2	9.84	4	9.04
5	Middle East	2	0.28	0.50	2	1,200	6	2.41	6	8.21
6	Pacific	7	0.14	0.33	6	51	4	5.01	3	9.53

[a] Regional groupings according to *World Development Indicators 2002* (World Bank, 2002).

[b] Group values calculated from weighted components of subindices for members of each region. Where original data for manufactured exports for 1990 and 2001 were not available, data for these years have been extrapolated using average growth rates for that country. SSMECI values were calculated using sample maximum and minimum levels.

Sources: Author's calculations, COMTRADE Database, *World Development Indicators* (2001, 2002, 2003) and other regional and national sources. See also the appendix for full details of data sources and methodology.

note is the particularly poor performance of the Pacific region, which was not strong in any of the three variables, and significantly lower in the SSMECI rankings.[8] Apart from the Fiji Islands at position ten in the overall SSMECI, the other countries of the Pacific were all in the bottom fifteen.

Table 4.6 shows the performance by income grouping, which reveals some very interesting results. Rather than running from high income down to low income in a linear fashion, the performance of the four groups is more erratic. High-income countries perform only third best out of the four, with the lowest average growth rates in manufacturing exports, and the lowest MVA as a percentage of GDP. They do have the second highest manufactured exports per capita though, which prevents them from being below the low-income countries. This pattern of results could reflect 'mature' economies that have developed a manufacturing export base, as shown in the high per capita figures, but have then diversified their economies into other sectors such as services, particularly financial services and high-end tourism. In such a case, the per capita exports in manufacturing would still be relatively high, but growth in manufacturing exports would slow, and value added in manufacturing as a share of total GDP would fall.

Table 4.7 shows the SSMECI performance grouped by population size. This distinction is particularly important to capture the record of tiny, micro-states compared to larger small states. In the absence of a universally accepted definition of subcategories by size, the sample was divided into countries with populations under 250,000 (micro-states); between 250,000 and 1 million; and over 1 million. The striking finding is that the micro-states record a particularly weak competitiveness performance. This suggests that even within the world's smallest economies, country size matters for industrial competitiveness. Perhaps unsurprisingly, the performance of the larger states was better than the smaller two categories, though the magnitude of this is perhaps unexpected. Many factors probably explain the gap in industrial competitiveness performance between larger states and

[8] There are about twelve small states in the Pacific by our definition but five could not be included in the final SSMECI due to data constraints. As a result, the sample for the Pacific is not complete and may be biased. However, lack of data is often correlated to poor performance, and it is unlikely that inclusion of these countries, if data were available, would significantly improve overall regional performance. See Holden et al. (2004) for an analysis of constraints facing the private sector in the Pacific. These include a weak macroeconomic environment, poor governance, frequent political instability, excessive state involvement combined with weak regulation, underdeveloped financial markets and a poor investment policy environment for business.

Table 4.6 *SSMECI performance by income grouping*

					Manufactured exports per capita, 2001		Average manufactured export growth, 1990–2001		Manufacturing value added as percentage of GDP, 1999	
Rank	Regional grouping[a]	No.	Weighted average SSMECI[b]	Simple average SSMECI	Rank	Value (current US$)	Rank	Value (%)	Rank	MVA
1	Upper middle income	11	0.84	0.52	1	1,520	1	6.23	2	11.06
2	Lower middle income	14	0.55	0.40	3	193	2	4.93	1	13.98
3	High income	8	0.36	0.50	2	1,308	4	3.80	4	8.49
4	Low income	7	0.13	0.33	4	38	3	4.62	3	9.09

[a] Income groupings according to *World Development Indicators 2003* (World Bank, 2003).

[b] Group values calculated from weighted components of subindices for members of each income group. Where original data for manufactured exports for 1990 and 2001 were not available, data for these years have been extrapolated using average growth rates for that country. SSMECI values were calculated using sample maximum and minimum levels.

Sources: Author's calculations, COMTRADE Database, *World Development Indicators* (2001, 2002, 2003) and other regional and national sources. See also the appendix for full details of data sources and methodology.

Table 4.7 *SSMECI performance by population size grouping*

					Manufactured exports per capita, 2001		Average manufactured export growth, 1990–2001		Manufacturing value added as percentage of GDP, 1999	
Rank	Regional grouping[a]	No.	Weighted average SSMECI[b]	Simple average SSMECI	Rank	Value (current US$)	Rank	Value (%)	Rank	MVA
1	More than 1m	11	1.00[c]	0.52	1	615	1	5.96	1	12.42
2	250,000 to 1m	16	0.63[c]	0.45	2	592	2	4.34	2	8.72
3	Less than 250,000	13	0.00[c]	0.36	3	123	3	0.48	3	8.27

[a] Population groups as per authors' definition.

[b] Group values calculated from weighted components of subindices for members of each population group. Where original data for manufactured exports for 1990 and 2001 were not available, data for these years have been extrapolated using average growth rates for that country. SSMECI values were calculated using sample maximum and minimum levels.

[c] The extreme range of the weighted average SSMECI index values obtained (1.00 and 0.00) reflects the strength of the correlation. The group with population of over 1 million was ranked first in all three variables, thus achieving an index value of 1.00 for all three variables. When weighted, this gives an overall SSMECI of 1.00. For the group with a population under 250,000 the reverse is true, with last place rankings in each variable giving 0.00 index values, and an overall SSMECI of 0.00.

Sources: Author's calculations, COMTRADE Database, *World Development Indicators* (2001, 2002, 2003) and other regional and national sources. See also the appendix for full details of data sources and methodology.

micro-states. These include the facts that the larger small states have somewhat bigger markets than smaller ones; have access to a larger pool of technical and managerial skills; are more attractive to inflows of foreign direct investment (FDI); are better able to finance costly infrastructure projects (e.g. setting up a national airline); and, possibly, are less susceptible to natural disasters.

4.3.3 Comparison of results with other indices

As stated earlier, one of the reasons for developing the SSMECI is the lack of coverage that existing work gives to small states. The IMD index contains none of the small states in the SSMECI, so comparison of results is not possible. The WEF index however, has eight common countries, and the MECI of Wignaraja and Taylor (2003) has eleven similarities. A comparison of the resulting rankings is given in table 4.8.

Only three countries appear in all three indices, and so comparison across all at the same time is difficult. However, if the SSMECI is compared individually against each of the others, the results, while not identical, show some correlation. Against the WEF, the results are broadly similar, and while Botswana and The Gambia fare slightly better in the WEF rankings than in the SSMECI, the rankings are otherwise fairly similar. The correlation with the MECI is somewhat surprisingly less strong, with a number of countries having significantly different rankings. However, if these outliers – including Cyprus, Dominica, and Guyana – are excluded, the overall pattern of correlation is again visible.

4.4 Explaining industrial competitiveness performance

Ranking intercountry patterns of competitiveness performance is only the first step in analysing competitiveness. A second and more interesting step is investigating what factors led to high, or low, performance. In other words, what are the determinants of manufacturing export competitiveness and what lessons can be learned for future policy development?

4.4.1 T-test and variables

The analysis of the determinants of competitiveness in small states has been conducted using a simple statistical test, a two sample t-test of the variable

Table 4.8 *Comparison of results from SSMECI, MECI, and WEF growth competitiveness index*

Country	SSMECI ranking	MECI (Wignaraja and Taylor, 2003)	WEF growth competitiveness ranking, 2003
Malta	1	...	19
Estonia	2	...	22
Mauritius	4	24	46
Trinidad and Tobago	5	15	49
Botswana	9	...	36
Namibia	11	...	52
Bahrain	12	30	...
Guyana	14	61	...
Grenada	15	55	...
St Kitts and Nevis	17	50	...
Jamaica	18	45	67
Belize	21	58	...
Cyprus	23	26	...
Dominica	24	38	...
Tonga	32	67	...
The Gambia	38	...	55

Notes:
. . . means not available
Sources: WEF (2003), authors' calculations

means.[9] It analyses whether the two sample means are equal, and thus whether the two groups are distinct in statistical terms. By using the top twenty and the bottom twenty performers in the SSMECI as our two samples, we can determine whether the mean for a particular determinant is different in the two groups. If, for example, the mean value for a particular determinant (e.g. foreign investment) is higher in the top twenty sample to a level that is statistically significant, this would imply that high levels of foreign investment are associated with high SSMECI performance, which further implies that it has an impact on competitiveness.[10]

[9] Recent attempts at statistical analysis of the factors affecting competitiveness in developing countries include Ul Haque (1995), James and Romijn (1997), Wignaraja and Taylor (2003) and Wint (2003).

[10] An important qualification about the testing procedure should be noted. The simple t-test shows significantly different means between two samples for individual variables. However, it

Tests of this nature were conducted on twenty-five separate variables, to see which factors were statistically significant. The variables utilised are divided into eight subcategories:

(i) *Macro-environment.* A stable and predictable macroeconomic environment, characterised by low inflation and interest rates, sustained GDP growth, and high levels of saving and investment, is widely accepted as a fundamental condition for business activity. Five variables are used in this category covering a wide range of macroeconomic variables.
(ii) *Country size.* Recent literature has shown that country size is inversely correlated with susceptibility to economic, political and environmental risks. Traditional economic theory would also suggest that larger country size may allow greater economies of scale and scope. Population is used as the proxy for country size as this has been shown to have the same result as more complex indices based on variables such as total GNP, population and total arable land.
(iii) *Trade and investment regime.* An open trade and investment regime exposes the business sector to overseas competition, encourages economies of scale through increased market access and facilitates technological transfer. Three proxies of openness are used as well as inward FDI stock.
(iv) *Vulnerability.* 'Vulnerability', whether in the form of susceptibility to natural disasters or over-reliance on one commodity, may hamper the competitiveness of economies. Six variables are used to test this hypothesis, including both singular and composite measures of vulnerability.
(v) *Structure.* The overall structure of economic activity may impact competitiveness, with a move away from low value-adding agriculture into manufacturing and services, freeing labour and benefiting the overall competitiveness of the economy. However, conversely at the opposite extreme, a lack of agricultural and mineral activity may prevent exploitation of potential for value-added industries based on natural resources. Two basic measures of economic structure are used.

does not indicate causality, and is thus less powerful than full econometric analysis. That said, it does provide insights into those underlying factors correlated with competitive success in comparisons of strong and weak national performance.

(vi) *Infrastructure.* Efficient and cost-competitive physical infrastructure allows businesses to compete in the global market without constraint, and for small states modern ICT infrastructure particularly allows the possibility to escape the 'tyranny of distance' and stay abreast of the latest technological innovation and production techniques. Three variables of modern ICT infrastructure are used.

(vii) *Human capital.* A strong base of productive human capital is recognised as the basis for industrial innovation and competitiveness. Education and training provide productive numerate workers with the skills to compete successfully. Four variables are used, covering enrolment rates at different stages of education and adult literacy.

(viii) *'Development'.* While not strictly a 'determinant' of competitiveness, a country's level of development would be expected to be correlated with its level of competitiveness, even if the direction of causality is complicated. As such, three variables are used to proxy for overall 'development'.

4.4.2 The t-test results

Table 4.9 shows the results of the t-tests on the means of the variables for high-performing sample countries (top twenty) and the low performers (bottom twenty). Data availability determined the sample size for a given t-test. In some cases the sample size would ideally have been higher, but all have enough for statistical relevance and are not low by cross-national statistical analysis standards.

The main findings are as follows:

(i) *Macro-environment.* The higher-performing sample countries had significantly higher average savings ratios and lower interest rates (both at the 5 per cent confidence level). This may suggest that cost and availability of capital is a driver of SSMECI performance. The means of GDP growth of the two samples are statistically different at the 5 per cent level (5.6 compared to 3.5 per cent between 1990 and 1999). While the high-performing sample countries do have a lower mean inflation rate, the difference is not statistically significant at the 10 per cent level, nor was the gross capital formation ratio.

Table 4.9 *T-tests to examine significance of determinants*

Determinants	High performers (top 20)		Low performers (bottom 20)		T-stat	Significant at 5% (* also at 1% level)
	Mean	Observations	Mean	Observations		
Macro fundamentals						
Inflation, average 1996–2000 (%)[b]	4.4	20	12.0	20	−1.10	
GDP growth, average 1990–9 (%)[b]	5.6	17	3.5	19	1.75	☑
Interest rate, 1999 (%)[b,c]	13.1	17	16.8	15	−1.75	☑
Gross domestic saving as % GDP (1999)[b]	20.8	16	12.8	16	2.14	☑
Gross capital formation as % GDP (1999)[a]	26.4	16	25.9	16	0.15	
Country size						
Population (2001)[a]	886,869	20	666,785	20	0.73	
Population (excluding PNG)[a]	886,869	20	425,429	19	2.49	☑*
Trade and investment regime						
FDI inward stock as % GDP (2000)[d]	75.4	18	42.8	18	1.86	☑
Imports as % GDP (1999)[b]	62.5	20	66.1	20	−0.31	
Exports as % GDP (1999)[b]	51.4	19	30.9	20	2.10	☑
Imports/exports as % GDP (1999)[b]	111.3	20	97.0	20	0.92	
Vulnerability						
Vulnerability to natural disasters[e]	127	17	170	20	−0.72	
Composite vulnerability index[e]	7.55	17	7.41	20	0.21	
Export dependence[e]	64.66	17	43.49	20	2.66	☑*
UNCTAD diversification index (2000)[f]	0.77	15	0.69	13	1.97	☑
UNCTAD concentration index (2000)[f]	0.46	16	0.51	14	−0.76	
No. of commodities exported (2000)[f]	81.9	16	25.3	14	3.62	☑*
Structure						
Agriculture value added, 1999 (% GDP)[b]	7.9	18	18.4	19	−3.28	☑*
Services value added, 1999 (% GDP)[b]	59.4	18	58.9	18	0.09	

Infrastructure						
Telephones/mobiles per 1,000 population (2000)[a]	379	20	220	17	1.90	☑
Internet users (2001)[a]	46,000	20	33,974	19	0.50	
Personal computers per 1,000 population (2001)[a]	87.2	17	79.4	16	0.33	
Human capital						
Adult literacy as % population, 1999[a]	88.6	18	71.5	13	3.07	☑*
Secondary enrolment, 2000[a]	66.2	13	57.8	11	0.90	
Tertiary enrolment, 2000[a]	14.9	13	11.5	10	0.62	
Development						
GDP per capita, 2001 (Current US$)[a]	6,833	20	2,531	20	2.62	☑*
GDP per capita, 2001 (PPP US$)[g]	10,203	20	5,145	18	3.07	☑*
HDI value, 2003[g]	0.76	20	0.67	18	2.34	☑

Sources:

[a] *World Development Indicators* (World Bank, 2003)

[b] *Small States, Economic Review and Basic Statistics* (Commonwealth Secretariat, 2002)

[c] IMF, various country reports

[d] UNCTAD, *World Investment Report 2002*

[e] Atkins, Mazzi and Easter (2001)

[f] *Handbook of Statistics* (UNCTAD, 2002)

[g] *Human Development Report* (UNDP, 2003)

(ii) *Country size.* Using the full data set, the difference in the means of population size for the two samples was not statistically significant. However, if Papua New Guinea is not included in the sample (at 5.25 million, it is something of an outlier in the group), then the means are highly significant at the 1 per cent confidence level. This backs up the theory that size, even within the small states grouping, is a significant factor in SSMECI performance.

(iii) *Trade and investment regime.* The high-performing sample countries have significantly greater means for FDI stock (at the 5 per cent confidence level), which would confirm the suggestion that FDI is a driver of competitiveness, through generation of export production and technological transfer. Unsurprisingly, openness as measured by the exports/GDP ratio was significant. However, imports/GDP and the combination of exports and imports to GDP were not significant. This is surprising but perhaps reflects that all small states are by nature fairly reliant on imports, perhaps even more so if lacking competitiveness.

(iv) *Vulnerability.* Some measures of vulnerability showed high levels of significance, particularly those relating to the structure and diversity of production. Dependence on exports and the number of commodities exported were both significant at the 1 per cent level, while the UNCTAD diversification measure was significant at the 5 per cent level. Perhaps surprisingly, the recent attempts to produce vulnerability indices were not significant, with neither the Natural Disasters vulnerability index, nor the composite vulnerability index producing statistically significantly different means across the samples.

(v) *Structure.* The structural variable showed that high-performing SSMECI countries had a significantly lower mean for the share of agricultural value added in GDP than the lower-performing group (at the 1 per cent confidence level). Given the nature of the index, this is perhaps not surprising and represents the traditional shift from agricultural production to manufacturing and industry. The share of services value added in GDP was not significant at the 10 per cent level.

(vi) *Infrastructure.* In the area of modern infrastructure the difference in means for telephone connections (fixed lines and mobile) was significant at the 5 per cent level, suggesting that communication and information flow is a factor in competitiveness. The number of Internet connections and PCs was not significant however, and this may be because it is too early for such new technology to be feeding through to the indicators found in the SSMECI.

(vii) *Human capital.* The importance of human capital in determining competitiveness may be suggested by the high significance (at the 1 per cent confidence level) in the difference in means between samples for levels of adult literacy. For both secondary and tertiary level education enrolment rates, the higher-performing SSMECI countries had greater means than the lower. However, this was not statistically significant at the 10 per cent level. This lack of significance may have been affected by poor data availability in these data sets.

(viii) *Development.* As expected, the relationship between overall development and performance in the SSMECI was strong. Both measures of GDP per capita had significantly higher means in the top-performing SSMECI countries (at the 1 per cent confidence level), while for the Human Development Index (HDI) the means were significantly different at the 5 per cent confidence level.

4.5 Conclusions

International exercises to benchmark competitiveness have made little attempt to include small states, let alone focus on them particularly. This chapter presents a first attempt at such an index, and develops a simple small state manufactured export competitiveness index (SSMECI). As ever with work of this kind, some results are expected and fit with *a priori* expectations. However, other results take more analysis and explanation. The very size of the countries in question leads to increased data volatility, and this may affect the results, perhaps causing a few anomalies and raised eyebrows. This can never be avoided, but while one or two may have performed above or below expectations, the general pattern of results is sound, and provides insight.

Not surprisingly, the European small states (e.g. Malta and Estonia) perform well, as do other traditional regional small state 'powerhouses', such as Fiji Islands, Mauritius and Trinidad and Tobago. The high performance of Botswana, Lesotho, Namibia and Swaziland in the Southern African Customs Union is of note, and points to the benefits of integrated trade and investment relationships with larger neighbours. This shows *that some small states have successfully transited from a state of vulnerability to developing a viable, internationally competitive industrial sector.* These economies have reaped positive aspects of globalisation such as access to new markets, capital, industrial skills and technologies and have been able to cope with increased international competition. In spite of possible vulnerabilities and cost disadvantages associated with country size, globalisation has not been a zero-sum game for all small states. Success does co-exist, however, with a long tail of underperformance. Indeed, many small states in the Pacific, Caribbean and Western Africa lag behind the industrial leaders. Tiny micro-states record a particularly poor performance and industrialisation may not be a viable option for them. Factors like the lack of domestic markets, technical manpower, foreign direct investment and limited industrial experience may help to explain the lacklustre performance of micro-states. Thus, in the final analysis, small country size may hinder the creation of industrial competitiveness but does not rule it out altogether for small states.

Unfortunately, greater use of econometric techniques was hampered by the lack of data on key variables, and so the ability to analyse the determinants of competitiveness was constrained. However, simple t-test analysis indicates that the determinants of competitiveness include several policy environment and supply side factors. High-performing small states had better macroeconomic conditions, higher levels of FDI, more trade openness, better levels of education and modern infrastructure. This suggests that the adoption of a coherent, market-oriented competitiveness strategy in small states is vital to success on international markets.[11]

Ultimately, even with better data availability that would have enabled more complex econometric analysis to be undertaken, exercises of this type can only begin to shed light on competitive performance and its drivers. The complex nature of factors involved in export competitiveness, and the particular circumstances and constraints of different countries, mean that the lessons a particular policymaker can draw are normally only at the macro-level. To truly understand the drivers of competitiveness, there is a need for greater exploration of specific policy environment,

[11] See Wignaraja (1997 and 2003) and Wignaraja et al. (2004) for more details of these and other elements of a coherent competitiveness strategy.

and institutional and firm-level competitiveness factors, which requires detailed case studies of individual small states.[12]

Appendix 4.1 Construction of the SSMECI

This appendix covers the technical details of the methodology used to construct the small states manufacturing export competitiveness index (SSMECI), along with notes on data sources and definitions.

Data definitions and sources

Definition of 'manufacturing'

The commonly used international definition of manufacturing is used throughout, using the Standard International Trade Classification (SITC) codes. The manufacturing sector is represented by the addition of the values for SITC code levels 5, 6, 7 and 8, minus the value of code level 68.

The use of such a definition has both benefits and costs, but in light of the data constraints of small states, was the only realistic option. In order to put together data for as many countries as possible, a variety of sources had to be used (see below). The use of an international definition made this task both more accurate in terms of common definitions across multiple sources, and more realistic as far as availability is concerned.

Ideally, it would have been useful to define manufacturing to include more of the food processing industry, as this is often a large component of small states' export production. However, without access to disaggregated data for each country this was not possible, and in the interest of larger samples, a more standardised definition was more appropriate.

Definition of small states and countries used

The standard Commonwealth definition of small states has been used throughout this chapter, and is again used here. From this thirty-two small states are identified that are Commonwealth members. This includes four countries with small-state characteristics despite their larger populations (Lesotho, Namibia, Papua New Guinea and Swaziland).

[12] For recent examples of detailed competitiveness studies on small states such as Jamaica, Malta and Mauritius, see World Bank (1994), Harris (1997), Lall and Wignaraja (1998) and Malta Ministry of Economic Services (1999). On Singapore, see Singapore Ministry of Trade and Industry (1998).

To increase the sample size slightly further, the IMF definition of small states was also used; this identifies forty-three small states, and, when combined with the Commonwealth list, produces a sample of forty-seven countries. Data constraints meant, however, that a final sample of forty was available for this study.

Data sources

As mentioned above, given the difficulties of obtaining data in many small states, a number of sources were used. For the first two variables, the main source was the International Trade Centre, with data extracted from the COMTRADE database. This was supplemented using data from UNCTAD's *Handbook of Statistics*, ITC's *PC-TAS* and the World Bank *World Development Indicators.* National sources were also used where there were gaps in the data, or to verify data. In certain circumstances, gaps in data have been estimated using standard imputation techniques from other data from that country.

Construction of the SSMECI

The SSMECI is a composite index constructed using a methodology similar to that used for the UNDP Human Development Index (HDI).

Indexing the variables

For each of the three variables an index value was calculated using the following general formula:

$$\text{Index} = \frac{\text{Actual Value} - \text{Minimum Value}}{\text{Maximum Value} - \text{Minimum Value}}$$

A key consideration in such a calculation was determining the minimum and maximum values that were appropriate. In the absence of a theoretical rationale suggesting definite alternatives, the maximum and minimum values in the relevant sample set were used. For example: value added from manufacturing (MVA) as a percentage of GDP of the Fiji Islands was 14.11 per cent in 1999, the sample maximum is 31.69 in Swaziland, and the sample minimum 1 per cent in Kiribati. The index for Fiji is therefore:

$$\text{MVA Index} = \frac{14.11 - 1}{31.69 - 1} = 0.43$$

Appendix table 4.1 *Basic profile of small states, most recent estimates*

Country	Population (2001)	GDP per capita (current US$ 2001)	GDP per capita (PPP US$ 2001)	HDI rank (2003)[a]	HDI value (2003)
Antigua and Barbuda	68,490	9,961	10,170	56	0.798
Bahamas	309,840	15,550	16,270	49	0.812
Bahrain	651,000	12,189	16,060	37	0.839
Barbados	268,190	10,281	15,560	27	0.888
Belize	247,110	3,258	5,690	67	0.776
Bhutan	828,040	637	1,833	136	0.511
Botswana	1,695,000	3,066	7,820	125	0.614
Brunei	344,000	14,088	19,210	31	0.872
Cape Verde	446,400	1,264	5,570	103	0.727
Comoros	571,890	386	1,870	134	0.528
Cyprus	760,650	12,004	21,190	25	0.891
Djibouti	644,330	894	2,370	153	0.462
Dominica	71,870	3,607	5,520	68	0.776
Estonia	1,364,000	4,051	10,170	41	0.833
Fiji Islands	817,000	2,062	4,850	81	0.754
Gabon	1,260,790	3,437	5,990	118	0.653
Gambia, The	1,340,770	291	2,050	151	0.463
Grenada	100,410	3,965	6,740	93	0.738
Guyana	766,260	912	4,690	92	0.740
Jamaica	2,590,000	3,005	3,720	78	0.757
Kiribati	92,810	430	–	–	–

Appendix table 4.1 (*cont.*)

Country	Population (2001)	GDP per capita (current US$ 2001)	GDP per capita (PPP US$ 2001)	HDI rank (2003)[a]	HDI value (2003)
Lesotho	2,061,730	386	2,420	137	0.510
Maldives	280,320	2,229	4,798	86	0.751
Malta	395,000	9,150	13,160	33	0.856
Mauritius	1,200,000	3,771	9,860	62	0.779
Namibia	1,792,060	1,730	7,120	124	0.627
Papua New Guinea	5,252,530	552	2,570	132	0.548
Qatar	597,550	27,536	19,844	44	0.826
Samoa	174,000	1,404	6,180	70	0.775
São Tomé and Príncipe	151,100	311	1,317	122	0.639
Seychelles	82,420	6,912	17,030	36	0.840
Solomon Islands	430,760	683	1,910	123	0.632
St Kitts and Nevis	45,050	7,609	11,300	51	0.808
St Lucia	156,700	4,222	5,260	71	0.775
St Vincent/Grenadines	115,880	3,007	5,330	80	0.755
Suriname	419,660	1,803	4,599	77	0.762
Swaziland	1,067,940	1,175	4,330	133	0.547
Tonga	100,720	1,371		–	–
Trinidad and Tobago	1,309,610	6,983	9,100	54	0.802
Vanuatu	201,190	1,096	3,190	128	0.568

[a] Rank out of 175 countries in HDI Sample.

Source: UNDP Human Development Report 2003, World Development Indicators 2003

This method was used for the MVA variable and the growth of manufactured exports variable. However, for the manufactured exports per capita variable, the extreme high values of some countries in the sample meant that all, except for three countries, had an index value of below 0.4. This has the effect of introducing a large bias in the overall index in favour of the top three countries. In order to discount these extreme variables, logarithms were used in the calculations. However, this overcompensated for the bias, and even low performers were attaining index values of above 0.8. In order to even out the effect, an average of the two was used, i.e. the average of the two values produced from using logarithms and from not using them.

Rank correlation calculations were used to measure the effect of the use/non-use of logarithms on the SSMECI order. The rank correlation between the SSMECI based on a logarithmic approach and the 'average' method above is 0.985, while the rank correlation between the SSMECI based on a non-logarithmic approach and the 'average' method above is 0.993. Thus, while the average method refines the index, its overall impact is relatively limited.

Weighting the indices

The three variables were weighted 40:30:30 per cent, with manufacturing exports per capita gaining the largest 40 per cent weight. This approach has been adopted, rather than perhaps the more obvious choice of equal thirds, given the particular interest in current performance and the need to account for the varying sizes of the countries involved.

As above, the ranking is robust compared to the use of an equal weighting, with a rank correlation of 0.993 between the results of the two methods.

References

Asian Development Bank (ADB), 2003, 'Special Chapter: Competitiveness in Developing Asia'. In *Asian Development Outlook 2003*. Oxford: Oxford University Press for the Asian Development Bank

Atkins, J. P., S. Mazzi and C. D. Easter, 2001, 'Small States: A Composite Vulnerability Index'. In D. Peretz, R. Faruqi and E. Kissanga, eds., *Small States in the Global Economy*. London: Commonwealth Secretariat

Briguglio, L., 1995, 'Small Island Developing States and their Economic Vulnerabilities', *World Development*, 23:9, pp. 1615–32

Briguglio, L. and G. Cordina, eds., 2004, *Competitiveness Strategies for Small States.* Formatek Ltd, Malta

Commonwealth Consultative Group, 1985, *Vulnerability: Small States in the Global Society.* London: Commonwealth Secretariat

Commonwealth Secretariat, 1997, *A Future for Small States: Overcoming Vulnerability.* Report of a Commonwealth Advisory Group. London: Commonwealth Secretariat

Commonwealth Secretariat, 2002, *Small States, Economic Review and Basic Statistics.* London: Commonwealth Secretariat

Corden, M., 1994, *Economic Policy, Exchange Rates and the International System.* Oxford: Oxford University Press

Dahlman, C. J. and J. E. Aubert, 2001,*China and the Knowledge Economy: Seizing the 21st Century.* Washington DC: World Bank Institute

Faggerberg, J., 1988, 'International Competitiveness'. *Economic Journal* 98 (June): 355–74

Gounder, R. and V. Xayavong, 2001, 'Globalisation and the Island Economies of the South Pacific'. United Nations University World Institute for Development Economic Research (UNUWIDER), Discussion Paper No. 2001/41, Helsinki

Grynberg, R., 2001, 'Trade Policy Implications for Small Vulnerable States of the Global Trade Regime Shift', in D. Peretz, R. Faruqi and E. Kissanga, eds., *Small States in the Global Economy.* London: Commonwealth Secretariat, pp. 267–328

Harris, D. J., 1997, 'Jamaica's Export Economy: Towards a Strategy of Export-Led Growth'. Critical Issues in Caribbean Development Series No. 5, Ian Randle Publishers, Kingston

Holden, P., M. Bale and S. Holden, 2004, 'Swimming Against the Tide? An Assessment of the Private Sector in the Pacific'. Pacific Studies Series, Asian Development Bank, Manila, Philippines

IMD, various years, *The World Competitiveness Yearbook.* International Institute for Management Development, Lausanne

ITC, 2000, 'The Trade Performance Index: Background Paper'. Market Analysis Section, UNCTAD/WTO International Trade Centre, Geneva

James, J. and H. Romijn, 1997, 'Determinants of Technological Capability: A Cross-Country Analysis'. *Oxford Development Studies* 25(2): 189–207

Jessen, A., and E. Rodriguez, 1999, 'The Caribbean Community: Facing the Challenges of Regional and Global Integration'. INTAL–ITD Occasional Paper 2 (Institute for the Integration of Latin America and the Caribbean, INTAL, and Inter-American Development Bank, IDB). Available: http://www.iadb.org/int/pub

Krugman, P., 1994, 'Competitiveness: A Dangerous Obsession'. *Foreign Affairs* 73(2): 28–44

Lall, S., 2001a, *Competitiveness, Technology and Skills.* Aldershot, UK: Edward Elgar

Lall, S., 2001b, 'Competitiveness Indices and Developing Countries: An Economic Evaluation of the Global Competitiveness Report'. *World Development* 29(9): 1501–25

Lall, S. and G. Wignaraja, 1998, 'Mauritius: Dynamising Export Competitiveness'. Commonwealth Economic Paper No. 33. London: Commonwealth Secretariat

Malta Ministry of Economic Services, 1999, *Prosperity in Change: Challenges and Opportunities for Industry.* Ministry of Economic Services, Malta

Peretz, D., R. Faruqi and E. Kissanga, eds., 2001, *Small States in the Global Economy.* London: Commonwealth Secretariat

Porter, M. E., 1990, *The Competitive Advantage of Nations.* London: Macmillan Press

Singapore Ministry of Trade and Industry, 1998, *Committee on Singapore's Competitiveness.* Ministry of Trade and Industry, Singapore

Streeten, P., 1993, 'The Special Problems of Small Countries', *World Development,* 21(2): 197–202

Ul Haque, I., 1995, 'Introduction'. In I. Ul Haque, ed., *Trade, Technology and International Competitiveness.* Economic Development Institute, World Bank, Washington DC

UNCTAD, 2002, *World Investment Report,* United Nations Conference on Trade and Development, Geneva

UNCTAD, various years, *Handbook of International Trade Statistics.* United Nations Conference on Trade and Development, Geneva

UNDP, 2003, *Human Development Report.* New York: Oxford University Press

UNIDO, 2003, *World Industrial Development Report 2002/2003: Competing Through Innovation.* United Nations Industrial Development Organization, Vienna

WEF, 2003, *Global Competitiveness Report 2003.* Oxford University Press for the World Economic Forum: New York. Available: http://www.weforum.org

Wignaraja, G., 1997, 'Manufacturing Competitiveness With Special Reference to Small State'. In *Small States: Economic Review and Basic Statistics,* vol. 3. London: Commonwealth Secretariat

Wignaraja, G., 2003, 'Competitiveness Analysis and Strategy'. In G. Wignaraja, *Competitiveness Strategy in Developing Countries.* London: Routledge

Wignaraja, G., 2004, 'Building Business Competitiveness'. Session paper prepared for UNCTAD XI. Sao Paolo, Brazil. Available: http://www.intracen.org/UNCTADXI/welcome.htm

Wignaraja, G., and A. Taylor, 2003, 'Benchmarking Competitiveness: A First Look at the MECI'. In G. Wignaraja, *Competitiveness Strategy in Developing Countries.* London: Routledge

Wignaraja, G., M. Lezama and D. Joiner, 2004, *Small States in Transition: From Vulnerability to Competitiveness.* London: Commonwealth Secretariat

Wint, A. G., 2003, *Competitiveness in Small Developing Economies: Insights from the Caribbean.* Kingston: University of West Indies Press

Winters, L. A. and Martins, P. M. G., 2003, *Beautiful But Costly: An Analysis of Operating Cost of Doing Business in Small Economies.* London: Commonwealth Secretariat and Geneva: UNCTAD, mimeo

World Bank, 1994, 'Mauritius: Technology Strategy for Competitiveness'. Report No. 12518-MAS, World Bank, Washington DC

World Bank, various years, *World Development Indicators.* New York: Oxford University Press

WTO, 2002, *World Trade Statistics.* World Trade Organization, Geneva

5

The economics of isolation and distance

STEPHEN REDDING AND ANTHONY J. VENABLES

A recent programme of research at the Centre for Economic Performance at the London School of Economics addresses the role of geography in determining trade flows, the location of economic activity, and the extent of income differentials between countries.[1] Although not directed especially at the problems faced by small or isolated economies, the central issues researched are the interactions between scale and proximity. There are benefits from being large and from being close to centres of economic activity, and the research seeks to understand these benefits, assess their magnitude, and evaluate the rate at which they fall off with distance from the centre. The purpose of this chapter is to draw out some of the implications of this research for small and isolated economies that are deprived of these benefits.

The point of departure is to pose the question, why do isolation and distance matter for economic performance? There are several main considerations. The first is simply that having good access to markets is valuable for firms. The access can derive from two sources: one is proximity to other countries that can bring good access to export markets, and the other is domestic scale, i.e. the extent to which the home market can provide an alternative to exports. Countries that are both remote and small forgo both these sources of market access. The second consideration is access to suppliers of intermediate and capital goods. Again, the supply of these goods can be from imports or domestic supply, and remoteness and smallness will have the effect of impeding the supply and raising the prices of these goods.

This chapter is based on a talk prepared for a WTO meeting on Small Economies, Geneva, 21 February 2002.

[1] The main analytical work is summarised in Fujita, Krugman and Venables (1999); see also Limao and Venables (2002). Empirical work is summarised in Overman, Redding and Venables (2001), and see also Redding and Venables (2001). This chapter is based partly on Venables (2002). The Centre for Economic Performance is funded by the UK Economic and Social Research Council.

A further penalty may arise if the flow of ideas and technologies is curtailed with distance. Although the determinants of these flows are not well understood, there is a good deal of evidence that proximity to centres of technology matters in both the development and application of R&D. We present some of this evidence below.

These forces can give rise to spatial clustering of economic activity, showing up both at the level of a single industry (e.g. electronics in Silicon Valley or financial services in London) and at a more aggregate level (the formation of cities and industrial districts). There is evidence – derived from studies of subnational data in both the US and the EU – that productivity levels are higher where economic activity is dense, with causality running from density to productivity.[2] This effect can be a source of benefit for small and densely populated city states – a Singapore or Hong Kong effect. However, many more countries lack the scale to develop their own clusters of activity, and suffer the cost of remoteness from existing centres.

Although this is not an exhaustive list of the costs of smallness the remainder of the chapter will focus on drawing out some of the facts that have been established concerning these forces.[3] We look first at the direct effects of distance on economic interactions, particularly the costs of making trades across space. We then turn to their implications for per capita income levels. Finally, we present a few ideas on the possible effects of new technologies on these relationships.

5.1 The direct costs of distance

5.1.1 Distance and economic interactions

However much we hear about globalisation, a startling feature of economic life is how local most economic interactions are, and how sharply they decline with distance. Trade economists have explored this relationship with 'gravity models' in which bilateral trade flows between countries are explained by economic mass (e.g. GDP) of the exporter and importer countries, and 'between-country' variables such as distance, and perhaps also by whether they share a common border, language or membership of a regional

[2] Ciccone and Hall (1996) for the US, Ciccone (2002) for the EU.

[3] Other factors that are important are economies of scale in public sector activities and the commodity concentration of small countries' exports, with the associated high levels of variability of export earnings.

Table 5.1 *Economic interactions and distance*
(Flows relative to their magnitude at 1000km)

	Trade (0 = −1.25)	Equity flows (0 = −0.85)	FDI (0 = −0.42)	Technology
1,000km	1	1	1	1
2,000km	0.42	0.55	0.75	0.65
4,000km	0.18	0.31	0.56	0.28
8,000km	0.07	0.17	0.42	0.05

Sources: see text

integration agreement. Extensive data permit the gravity trade model to be estimated on the bilateral trade flows of 100 or more countries, and studies find that the elasticity of trade flows with respect to distance is around −0.9 to −1.5. This implies that volumes of trade decline relative to their magnitude at 1,000km: with a representative value of this elasticity −1.25, doubling distance more than halves trade flows; by 4,000km volumes are down by 82 per cent and by 8,000km down by 93 per cent.

Similar methodologies have been used to study other sorts of economic interactions and are also reported in table 5.1. Portes and Rey (1999) study cross-border equity transactions (using data for fourteen countries accounting for around 87 per cent of global equity market capitalisation, 1989–96). Their main measure of countries, mass is stock market capitalisation, and their baseline specification gives an elasticity of transactions with respect to distance of −0.85. This indicates again how controlling for the characteristics of the distance matters. Other authors have studied foreign direct investment flows. Data limitations mean that the set of countries is quite small, and the estimated gravity coefficient is smaller, although still highly significant; for example, Di Mauro (2000) finds an elasticity of FDI flows with respect to distance of −0.42. The effect of distance on technology flows has been studied by Keller (2001) who looks at the dependence of total factor productivity (TFP) on R&D stocks (i.e. cumulated R&D expenditures) for twelve industries in the G7 countries, 1971–95. The R&D stocks include both the own country stock and foreign country stocks weighted by distance.[4] Both own and foreign country stocks are significant determinants of each country's TFP and so too is the distance effect, with

[4] Distance weighting according to exp ($-\text{distance}_{ij}$).

R&D stocks in distant economies having much weaker effects on TFP than do R&D stocks in closer economies. The final column in table 5.1 illustrates his results by computing the spillover effects of R&D in more distant economies relative to an economy 1,000km away; the attenuation due to distance is once again dramatic.[5]

In addition, we know that borders have a major effect in reducing economic interactions. Evidence from Canadian–US trade suggests that even that most innocuous of borders has a huge impact. On average, the exports of Canadian provinces to other Canadian provinces are some twenty times larger than their exports to equivalently situated US states (Helliwell, 1997), and evidence from urban price movements suggests that the border imposes barriers to arbitrage comparable to 1,700 miles of physical space (Engel and Rogers, 1996). Overall then, these facts tell us that geography still matters greatly for economic interaction.

5.1.2 *The magnitude of shipping costs*

Underlying the rate of decline of these interactions are a variety of costs. The easiest to measure and observe are freight charges, although other costs of time in transit and information costs are quite possibly more important.

Shipping costs on short or heavily used routes are typically quite low. For the US, freight expenditure incurred on imports was only 3.8 per cent of the value of imports; equivalent numbers for Brazil and Paraguay are 7.3 per cent and 13.3 per cent (Hummels 1999a, from customs data). However, these values incorporate the fact that most trade is with countries that are close, and in goods that have relatively low transport costs. Looking at transport costs unweighted by trade volumes gives much higher numbers. Thus, if we take all possible bilateral trade flows for which data is available (some 20,000 combinations of importer and exporter countries) the median cif/fob ratio is 1.28, implying transport and insurance costs amounting to 28 per cent of the value of goods shipped. Looking across

[5] To try and identify the channels through which technical knowledge is transmitted Keller investigates not just distance between countries, but also the volume of trade between them, their bilateral FDI holdings and their language skills (the share of the population in country *I* that speaks language *J*). Adding these variables renders simple geographical distance insignificant; around two-thirds of the difference in bilateral technology diffusion is accounted for by trade patterns, and one-sixth each through FDI and language. However, all these variables are themselves declining with distance.

commodities, an unweighted average of freight rates is typically two to three times higher than the trade weighted average rate.

5.1.3 Determinations of shipping costs

Estimates of the determinants of transport costs are given in Hummels (1999b) and Limao and Venables (2001). These studies typically have elasticities of transport costs with respect to distance of between 0.2 and 0.3, meaning that a doubling of the distance over which goods are shipped increases freight costs by around 20 per cent. Sharing a common border substantially reduces transport costs and overland distance is around seven times more expensive than sea distance.

In addition to the effects of distance and mode of transport, shipping costs are highly route specific, reflecting densities of traffic flow and monopoly power. For example, the cost of shipping a standard container from Baltimore to Durban is $2,500; shipping the 1,600km further to Lusaka costs an additional $2,500, while the 347km from Durban to Maseru (Lesotho) costs an additional $7,500 (quotes from the shipping company used by the World Bank, cited in Limao and Venables, 2001). Fink, Mattoo and Neagu (2000) study the impact of anti-competitive practices in the shipping industry, and estimate that these raise prices by more than 25 per cent: the break-up of private carrier agreements would, they estimate, save transport costs of $2 billion pa on imports to the US alone.

5.1.4 Landlocked countries

Landlocked countries face severe cost penalties. Research by Limao and Venables (2001) indicates that a representative landlocked country has transport costs approximately 75 per cent greater than those of a representative coastal economy. Infrastructure quality (as measured by a composite index of transport and communications networks) is also important. While this matters for all countries, it is particularly important for landlocked countries. Dependence on both their own and their transit countries' infrastructure (at the seventy-fifth percentile of the distribution) makes landlocked countries' transport costs a full 75 per cent higher than those of a representative coastal economy.

These higher transport costs have a large impact on trade flows. The median landlocked economy (controlling for other factors) has trade flows

60 per cent lower than the median coastal economy. If, in addition, there is poor own infrastructure and transit country infrastructure, then trade is 75 per cent lower than for the median coastal economy.

5.1.5 The costs of time in transit

Direct shipping costs are only part of the costs of distance. Also important are costs of search, i.e. finding and identifying trading partners and coordinating trades. Time in transit is important, and perhaps increasingly important as firms seek to apply 'just-in-time' management methods. Recent work by Hummels (2000) provides interesting evidence on the magnitude of time costs. He analyses data on some 25 million observations of shipments into the US, some by air and some by sea (imports classified at the ten-digit commodity level, by exporter country, and by district of entry to US for twenty-five years). Given data on the costs of each mode and the shipping times from different countries, he is able to estimate the implicit value of time saved by using air transport. The numbers are quite large. The cost of an extra day's travel is (from estimates on imports as a whole) around 0.3 per cent of the value shipped. For manufacturing sectors, the number goes up to 0.5 per cent, costs that are around thirty times larger than the interest charge on the value of the goods. One implication of these is that freight costs alone (and the cif/fob ratio) grossly understate the costs of distance. Another is that transport costs have fallen much more through time than suggested by looking at freight charges alone. The share of US imports going by air freight rose from zero to 30 per cent between 1950 and 1998, and containerisation approximately doubled the speed of ocean shipping. Together these give a reduction in shipping time of twenty-six days, equivalent to a shipping cost reduction worth 12–13 per cent of the value of goods traded.

5.2 Remoteness and real income

The previous section made the point that distance matters greatly for economic interactions. How does this feed into the distribution of income across countries? A number of mechanisms might be at work, including the effects of investment flows and technology transfers. Here, to illustrate effects, we concentrate just on the way in which trade flows can generate international income gradients between central and peripheral countries.

The effect of distance on factor prices is easily seen through a simple example. Suppose that half of a firm's costs are intermediate goods, and one-third labour, the remainder being returns to capital. How does the wage that a firm can afford to pay (while just breaking even) depend on the costs it has to bear on shipping its output to final consumers and importing its intermediate inputs? It turns out that a firm that faces 20 per cent transport costs can only afford to pay labour approximately 20 per cent as much as can a firm that faces zero transport costs. As transport costs rise to 30 per cent, the wage the firm can afford to pay drops to 10 per cent, and at 40 per cent transport costs the firm can survive only if it pays its workers nothing. These numbers are based on an example where the cost of capital is the same in the remote country as in the centre. If this cost is higher, then wages in remote countries are depressed even further.

The point of this example is that in remote locations value added gets squeezed in two ways – the firm receives less for its output and pays more for imported equipment and intermediate goods. This means that even quite modest transport costs can have quite a dramatic effect on the wages that firms can afford to pay, and suggests that there will be quite steep 'wage gradients' from central to peripheral locations.

Redding and Venables (2001) measure these wage gradients for a sample 101 countries.[6] Trade data are used to calculate economically correct measures of 'foreign market access' (FMA). This, like a measure of market potential, aggregates expenditure in different countries, with weights inversely proportional to distance and also depending on whether countries share a common border, are islands or are landlocked.[7] Thus, countries close to large foreign export markets have a high-value FMA, while remote countries have low values of this measure.

Figure 5.1 presents the scatterplot of the relationship between this variable and per capita income (both measured in logs, country codes given in the appendix), illustrating a strong positive relationship between the

[6] Wage gradients can be estimated within as well as between countries. Thus, for the United States, Hanson (1998) provides evidence that variation in wages across countries is linked to differential access to markets, even after controlling for a variety of other considerations such as levels of human capital and amenities. For Mexico, Hanson (1996, 1997) finds a regional wage gradient centred on Mexico City prior to trade liberalisation and the partial breakdown of this regional wage gradient after liberalisation as production re-orientated towards the United States.

[7] The relative importance of these factors is found from econometric estimation of some specifications of a gravity model. See Redding and Venables (2001) for details.

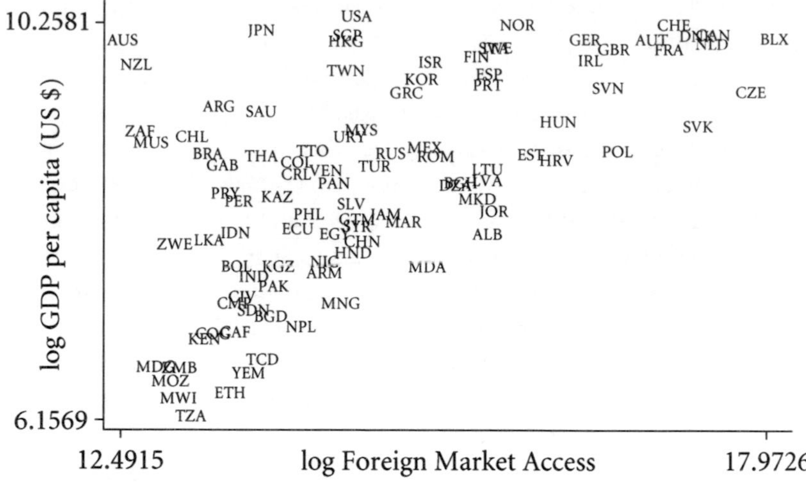

Figure 5.1 GDP per capita and FMA

variables. For example, looking within Europe, there is evidence of a wage gradient from Belgium/Luxembourg (countries with the best foreign market access) through France, Britain, to Spain, Portugal and Greece. Several other points stand out. One is that a number of countries are able to escape the consequence of remoteness from export markets – e.g. Australia, Japan and USA. However, looking at the bottom-right area of the figure, good foreign market access provides a safety net against very low incomes – despite the relatively poor performance of former communist countries.

As noted in the introduction, market access is derived both from proximity to export markets and from access to a large domestic market. Both proximity and scale matter. The scale effect was absent from figure 5.1, but is included in figure 5.2, where the horizontal axis is the sum of foreign market access (FMA) and 'domestic market access' (DMA), a measure of domestic market size adjusted for the area of the country. Combining these effects provides very strong evidence of a wage gradient, indicating the importance of both proximity and scale in determining income levels.

Figures 5.1 and 5.2 just give market access (the penalty of being remote from markets) but in addition 'supplier access' matters. One of the mechanisms by which geographical remoteness depresses wages is the high price of imported equipment and intermediate goods in remote locations. Figure 5.3 presents some direct empirical evidence on the relationship between access to sources of supply and the relative price of these goods. The horizontal axis

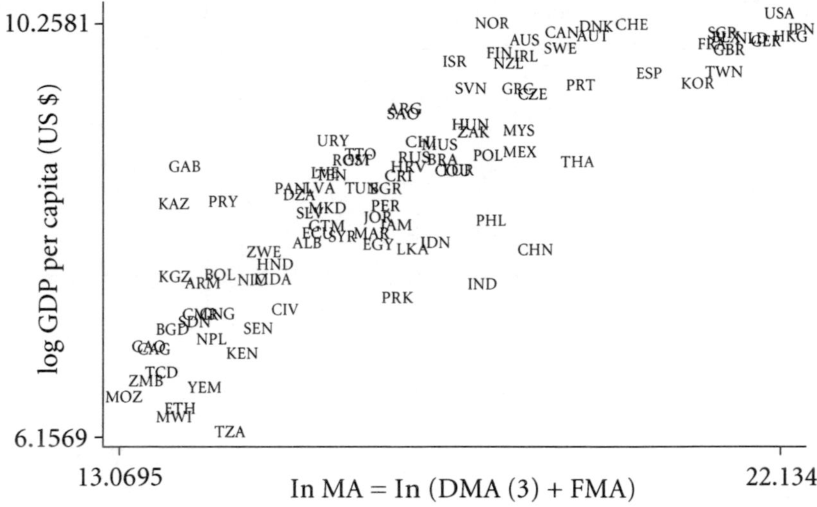

Figure 5.2 GDP per capita and MA = DMA(3) + FMA

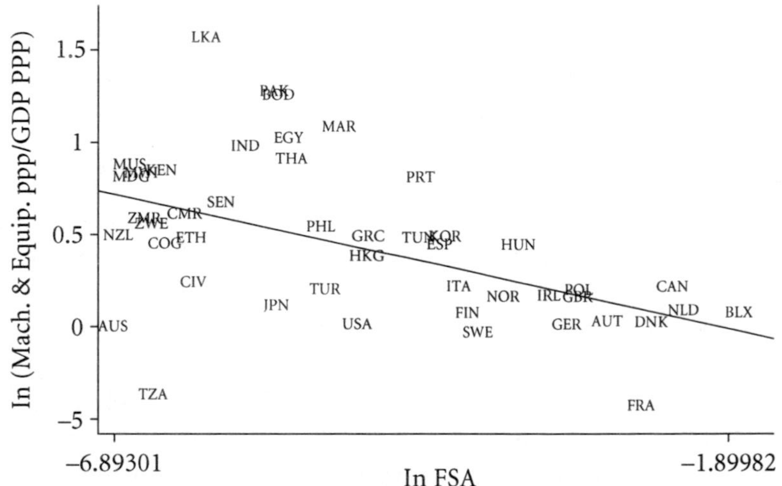

Figure 5.3 Relative price of machinery and equipment and FSA

gives the proper measure of access to foreign suppliers of manufactures (FSA), again derived from trade data, and the vertical axis gives the relative price of machinery and equipment in countries for which data is available. We see a statistically significant negative relationship, confirming that remote countries have to pay higher prices for these goods, and contributing to the squeeze on the wages that firms in these countries can afford to pay.

Table 5.2 *Percentage change in real income from openness*

	Variable			
	1	2	3	4
Country	Access to coast	Loss of island status	Become open	Distance (Central Europe)
Australia		7.3%		
Sri Lanka		7.3%	20.79%	67.4%
Zimbabwe	24.0%		27.7%	
Paraguay	24.0%		25.3%	79.7%
Hungary	24.0%		26.5%	58.3%

Notes:
Actual values for the Sachs and Warner (1995) openness index are 1 in Australia, 0.2321 in Sri Lanka, 0.038 in Hungary, 0.077 in Paraguay, and 0 in Zimbabwe.
Source: Redding and Venables (2000)

5.2.1 *Quantifying the effects*

Per capita incomes depend on additional factors, as well as market and supplier access, and Redding and Venables undertake econometric analysis incorporating a set of other variables. These include measures of endowments and of the quality of institutions, which are important determinants of per capita incomes levels. However, the geographical variables remain highly significant determinants of per capita income levels even once these further variables have been added in.

One way of illustrating the quantitative importance of geography is to undertake a set of hypothetical experiments of the form: suppose we move country 1 to the location of country 2 then, holding other things equal, what would happen to country 1's income? Tables 5.2 and 5.3 report the results of a few experiments of this type. Being landlocked and being an island both have a negative effect on real income, and the first column indicates that the penalty from being landlocked is substantial – removing it would raise income by one-quarter.[8] The cost of island status is smaller, around 7 per cent of GDP (column 2). Column 3 reports a trade policy experiment: changing countries' trade openness (as measured by the Sachs–Warner (1995) openness index) from the 1994 value to the most

[8] The model specification means that the same proportional effect is experienced by all countries.

Table 5.3 *Percentage change in real income from border effects*

Removal of common border	Effect on per capita income	
Germany–Czech Republic	Germany −0.1%	Czech Republic −25.7%
US–Mexico	US −0.5%	Mexico − 27.2%
Zimbabwe–Zambia	Zimbabwe − 0.05%	Zambia − 0.11%

Source: Redding and Venable (2000)

open possible. This too yields extremely large income gains, of around 25 per cent for countries that were, in 1994, quite economically closed. Column 4 reports the experiment of moving a country from its present location to that of Hungary, on the edge of the EU. The dramatic increase in FMA brought about by this change means that, for some of the most remote economies in the sample, income increases by nearly 80 per cent.

Common borders are also important for facilitating trade and improving market access, and table 5.3 quantifies their importance by the hypothetical experiments of closing borders. The effects reported show that smaller countries gain very substantially from access to a large neighbour, as illustrated for Mexico and the Czech Republic. However, two small neighbours, the two African economies, neither of which has large markets or supplies of manufacturers to offer, only experience extremely small border effects. An implication of this is that South–South regional integration schemes yield very limited benefits compared to fuller integration into the world economy as a whole.

5.3 New technologies: the death of distance?

Technical progress has led to substantial reductions in trade costs in the last forty years. Shipping rates and airfreight rates have both fallen, although the decline in these rates ended in the 1960s and 1980s respectively. We have already commented on the cost reductions associated with the speeding up of shipping.

In addition to these changes, the development of information and communications technologies (ICT) has made the transmission of digital information virtually free. These technologies bring great benefits to isolated and distant economies, allowing faster and cheaper exchange of information and ideas. However, it is not clear that they overturn all the economic disadvantages of isolation or lead to the 'death of distance' as suggested by some authors (Cairncross, 2001). In this section we offer a few remarks about the likely implications of these new technologies for isolated and distant economies.

5.3.1 Weightless inputs and outputs

In some activities inputs and outputs can be digitalised – made 'weightless' – and shipped virtually free of charge. These activities can be related to lower wage economies, as recent experience indicates. The highly successful Indian software and IT-enabled services sectors had an output in 2000 of $8 billion with exports of $4 billion. IT-enabled services – call centres ('customer interaction centres'), medical transcriptions, finance and accounting services – had exports to the US of $0.26 billion, predicted to grow to $4 billion by 2005 (*Economist* 5 May 2001). These are substantial sized activities, compared to total Indian exports of $45 billion in 2000, but are less than 1 per cent of total US imports of around $950 billion.[9]

Development of these activities may prove extremely valuable to isolated and distant economies, although a couple of provisos need to be made. First, as activities are codified and digitised, so not only can they be moved costlessly through space, but also they are typically subject to very large productivity increases and price reductions. Thus, the effect of ICT on, say, airline ticketing, has been primarily to replace labour by computer equipment, and only secondarily to allow remaining workers to be employed in India rather than the US or Europe. There is continuing technical progress in these activities so, for example, technology that can capture voice or handwriting will soon make Indian medical transcription obsolete. This suggests that even if more activities become weightless, the share of world expenditure and employment attributable to these activities will remain small – perhaps as little as a few per cent of world GDP.

The second point is that small economies will face intense competition in attracting these activities, as the experience of India already suggests. There is a sense in which 'weightless' activities are the natural comparative

[9] For further discussion of the concept of weightlessness and the implications of new information and communication technologies for economic growth, see Quah (1997, 2001).

advantage of remote economies since these economies have a comparative disadvantage in transport-intensive goods (Venables and Limao, 2002). However, success will require both the telecommunications infrastructure and the skill base to attract investments.

5.3.2 ICT and the costs of remote management

Recent years have seen the growth of both outsourcing and foreign direct investment (FDI), with the associated development of production networks or production chains. FDI has grown faster than either income or trade. The growth of production networks has been studied by a number of researchers. One way to measure their growth is by looking at trade in components, and Yeats (1998) estimates that 30 per cent of world trade in manufactures is now trade in components rather than final products. Hummels, Ishii and Yi (2001) chart trade flows that cross borders multiple times, as when a country imports a component and then re-exports it embodied in some downstream product. They find that (for ten OECD countries) the share of imported value added in exports rose by one-third between 1970 and 1990, reaching 21 per cent of export value.

Both FDI and outsourcing involve, in somewhat different ways, a fragmentation of the structure of the firm, as production is split into geographically and/or organisationally different units. From the international perspective, this fragmentation offers the benefits of being able to move particular stages of the production process to the lowest cost locations – labour-intensive parts to low-wage economies, and so on. However, as well as involving potentially costly shipping of parts and components, it also creates formidable management challenges. Product specification and other information has to be transferred, and production schedules and quality standards have to be monitored. Do new technologies reduce the costs of doing this?

To the extent that pertinent information is 'codifiable', the answer is likely to be yes. The use of ICT for business-to-business trade is well documented, although it is reported often to reduce the number of suppliers a firm uses, rather than increase the number. In mass production of standardised products, designs can be relatively easily codified; where the production process is routine, daily or hourly production runs can be reported and quality data can be monitored.

However, in many activities the pertinent information cannot be codified so easily. There are two sorts of reasons for this. One is the inherent complexity of the activity. For example, frequent design changes and a process of ongoing product design and improvement (involving both marketing and production engineering) may require a level of interaction that – at present – can only be achieved by face-to-face contact. The second reason is to do with the fact that contracts are incomplete, and people on either side of the contract (or in different positions within a single firm) have their own objectives. It is typically expensive or impossible to ensure that their incentives can be shaped to be compatible with meeting the objectives of the firm. While new technologies may reduce the costs of monitoring, it seems unlikely that these problems of incomplete contracts are amenable to a technological fix.

What evidence is there? On the one hand, there is the fact that in recent years there has been a dramatic increase in the outsourcing of activities to specialist suppliers, suggesting that difficulties in writing contracts and monitoring performance have been reduced. On the other hand, a number of empirical studies point to the continuing importance, despite new technologies, of regular face-to-face contact. Thus, Gaspar and Glaeser (1998) argue that telephones are likely to be complements to, not substitutes for, face-to-face contact as they increase the overall amount of business interaction. They suggest that, as a consequence, telephones have historically promoted the development of cities. The evidence on business travel suggests that as electronic communications have increased so too has travel, again indicating the importance of face-to-face contact. Leamer and Stoper (2000) draw the distinction between 'conversational' transactions (that can be done at a distance by ICT) and 'hand-shake' transactions that require face-to-face contact. New technologies allow dispersion of activities that only require 'conversational' transactions, but might also increase the complexity of production and design processes, and hence increase the proportion of activities that require 'hand-shake' communication.

Overall then, it seems that there are some relatively straightforward activities where knowledge can be codified, new technologies will make management from a distance easier, and relocation of the activity to lower-wage regions might be expected. But monitoring, control and information exchange in more complex activities still requires a degree of contact that involves proximity and face-to-face meetings. Perhaps nowhere is this more evident than in design and development of the new technologies themselves.

5.3.3 *The speeding up of production*

New technologies provide radical opportunities for speeding up parts of the overall supply process. There are several ways this can occur. One is simply that basic information – product specifications, orders and invoices – can be transmitted and processed more rapidly. Another is that information about uncertain aspects of the supply process can be discovered and transmitted sooner. For example, retailers' electronic stock control can provide manufacturers with real-time information about sales and hence about changes in fashion and overall expenditure levels. For intermediate goods, improved stock controls and lean production techniques allow manufacturers to detect and identify defects in supplies more rapidly. These changes pose the interesting question: if some elements of the supply process become quicker, what does this do to the marginal value of time saved (or marginal cost of the delay) in other parts of the process? In particular, if one part of the process that takes time is the physical shipment of goods, then will time-saving technical changes encourage firms to move production closer to markets, or allow them to move further away?

There are some reasons to think that the effect might encourage firms to move production closer to markets. The new opportunities created for rapid response can be exploited only if all stages of production are fast. The highly successful Spanish clothing chain, Zara (*Economist*, 19 May 2001) provides an example. It uses real-time sales data, can make a new product line in three weeks (compared to the industry average of nine months) and only commits 15 per cent of production at the start of the season (industry average 60 per cent). It also does almost all its manufacturing (starting with basic fabric dyeing through the full manufacturing process) in house in Spain, with most of the sewing done by 400 local cooperatives (compared to the extensive outsourcing of other firms in the industry).[10]

Just-in-time production techniques provide a further example. New technologies have allowed much-improved stock control and ordering, and a consequent movement of suppliers towards their customers. In a study of the location of suppliers to the US automobile industry, Klier (1999) finds that 70–80 per cent of suppliers are located within one day's

[10] For a formal analysis of the idea that new technologies may encourage firms to move production closer to markets, see Evans and Harrigan (2001).

drive of the assembly plant, although even closer location is limited by the fact that many suppliers serve several assembly plants. He also finds that the concentration of supplier plants around assembly plants has increased since 1980, a timing that he points out is consistent with the introduction of just-in-time production methods. The leader in the application of just-in-time techniques is Toyota, whose independent suppliers are on average only fifty-nine miles away from its assembly plants, to which they make eight deliveries a day. By contrast, General Motors' suppliers in North America are an average of 427 miles away from the plants they serve and make fewer than two deliveries a day. As a result, Toyota and its suppliers maintain inventories that are one-quarter of General Motors' when measured as a percentage of sales (*Fortune*, 8 December 1997).

These examples suggest that, at least in some activities, remote economies may become more marginalised as a consequence of new technologies.

5.3.4 Clustering still matters

Arguments above suggest that new technologies will facilitate the relocation of some activities to lower-wage locations. Other activities may become increasingly locked into established centres. However, for activities that can relocate, clustering is likely to be important. Foreign direct investment projects will tend to go to locations where investors can see that other investors are doing well. Firms will want to move to locations where there is a deep pool of skilled labour and a network of local suppliers. These factors may militate against relocation of these activities to small countries.

Overall then, while it is clear that new technologies will bring many benefits, allowing isolated and remote countries closer contact with the outside world, the 'death of distance' view is misplaced. It is far from clear that new technologies will provide a straightforward development strategy for these countries.

5.4 Conclusions

The review of research in this chapter is partial in its coverage. For example, we have not discussed the implications of smallness for export concentration and for vulnerability, concentrated on the costs of isolation and distance. These factors choke off economic interactions, mean that potential investors can pay only low wages, and reduce real income. New technologies bring benefits, but need further study. Some activities will become more entrenched in existing centres, others will relocate, and the relocation will likely lead to the formation of new clusters.

What are the policy implications of the preceding analysis? We offer just a few points. The first is that infrastructure improvements are important. Changes that reduce isolation will affect prices in the economy, having non-marginal effects that need to be properly evaluated by social cost-benefit analysis. These changes do not necessarily require physical investments. Our discussion of the costs of time in transit point to the importance of port, customs and other frontier delays in deterring investments. The example of Intel's investment in Costa Rica is instructive: Intel went ahead with a $300 million chip facility only after the government of Costa Rica had guaranteed rapid customs clearance of imports, free of bureaucratic and administrative blockages. Similarly, the discussion of shipping costs pointed to the barriers created by ocean-shipping cartels. Competition policy at the international level is needed to break up these cartels.

Second, development strategies need to look carefully at what the comparative advantage of small, distant and isolated economies really is. Traditional analysis points almost exclusively to factor endowments and factor prices, but additional factors need to be taken into account. In addition to looking to their factor endowments and the factor intensity of industries, remote economies should look to 'transport intensity' of industries. Small economies should look to the importance of scale in different sectors, and not just scale within the individual firm, but scale defined to include the size of viable clusters of firms and pools of skilled labour.

Finally, while geography matters, so too do many other factors, including trade policy, institutions and factor endowments. Restrictive trade policy has the effect, like distance, of making a country more economically remote from the rest of the world. Spatial analysis suggests that clustering is important for many activities, indicating that small initial advantages can translate into large differences in outcomes, as 'culmulative causation' drives the growth of the cluster. This highlights the importance of good initial conditions in the business environment.

Appendix 5.1 Countries in figures 5.1, 5.2 and 5.3

ALB	Albania
ARG	Argentina
ARM	Armenia
AUS	Australia
AUT	Austria
BGD	Bangladesh
BGR	Bulgaria
BLX	Belgium/Luxembourg
BOL	Bolivia
BRA	Brazil
CAF	Central African Republic
CAN	Canada
CHE	Switzerland
CHL	Chile
CHN	China
CIV	Côte d'Ivoire
CMR	Cameroon
COG	Congo, Republic of
COL	Colombia
CRI	Costa Rica
CZE	Czech Republic
DEU	Germany
DNK	Denmark
DZA	Algeria
ECU	Ecuador
EGY	Egypt
ESP	Spain
EST	Estonia
ETH	Ethiopia
FIN	Finland
FRA	France
GAB	Gabon
GBR	UK
GRC	Greece
GTM	Guatemala
HKG	Hong Kong
HND	Honduras
HRV	Croatia
HUN	Hungary
IDN	Indonesia
IND	India
IRL	Ireland
ISR	Israel
ITA	Italy
JAM	Jamaica
JOR	Jordan
JPN	Japan
KAZ	Kazakhstan
KEN	Kenya
KGZ	Kyrgyzstan
KOR	Korea, Republic of
LKA	Sri Lanka
LTU	Lithuania
LVA	Latvia
MAR	Morocco
MDA	Moldova
MDG	Madagascar
MEX	Mexico
MKD	Macedonia
MNG	Mongolia
MOZ	Mozambique
MUS	Mauritius
MWI	Malawi
MYS	Malaysia
NIC	Nicaragua
NLD	Netherlands
NOR	Norway
NPL	Nepal
NZL	New Zealand
PAK	Pakistan

PAN Panama
PER Peru
PHL Philippines
POL Poland
PRT Portugal
PRY Paraguay
ROM Romania
RUS Russia
SAU Saudi Arabia
SDN Sudan
SEN Senegal
SGP Singapore
SLV El Salvador
SVK Slovak Republic
SVN Slovenia
SWE Sweden
SYR Syria
TCD Chad
THA Thailand
TTO Trinidad and Tobago
TUN Tunisia
TUR Turkey
TWN Taiwan
TZA Tanzania
URY Uruguay
USA USA
VEN Venezuela
YEM Yemen
ZAP South Mr.
ZMB Zambia
ZWE Zimbabwc

6

The trade performance of small states

ROMAN GRYNBERG AND MOHAMMAD A. RAZZAQUE

6.1 Introduction

Recent years have seen intensifying global integration measured by an unprecedented rise in volume of trade and capital flows and a reduction in barriers to worldwide trade and investment activities. This drive to globalisation received substantial impetus from the successful conclusion of the Uruguay Round of Multilateral Trade Negotiations (MTNs) establishing the WTO, providing specific trade rules and procedures, and promising further liberalisation in the world trade regime. Despite these developments there remain serious concerns that some countries have failed to derive significant benefits from the ongoing process of trade liberalisation and globalisation. This is particularly true for small vulnerable states, which are confronted with a number of overriding problems constraining their economic development and have to depend greatly on international trade to overcome these obstacles.[1] It is now becoming increasingly evident that even in this era of globalisation these countries have not been able to prevent their declining relative importance, or marginalisation, in world trade.

Although small states have attracted a large amount of research and many of them are concerned about the problem of marginalisation, there has been little or no attempt to provide firm evidence of it nor explanation of its causes. In fact, the notion of marginalisation in this literature remains

The views expressed in this chapter are the authors' responsibilities and not necessarily those of the institutions with which they are affiliated.

[1] The most important problems associated with small states are: (1) small size of the domestic market does not allow exploitation of increasing returns to scale in production; (2) small size prevents diversification into a wide range of activities; (3) extremely narrow export base and excessive dependence on foreign trade make them vulnerable to terms of trade shocks and export instability; (4) unfavourable geographical locations make these countries isolated from world economic activities; and (5) many small states are located in regions prone to natural disasters such as cyclones and volcanic activity (Commonwealth Secretariat, 1997).

unclear and is usually associated with the apprehension of losing out from the multilateral trade liberalisation in the global economy.[2] It is against this backdrop that the present chapter defines marginalisation as the declining relative importance in world trade and uses data and statistical tools to investigate the long-term trends in marginalisation of small states. Our focus is on export trade since, given the size of the domestic market, small states are overwhelmingly dependent on exports for their economic growth and development. One important contribution of this chapter is that it makes an attempt to explain the long-term declining share of small states in world merchandise exports, which emphasises the need for diversification of exports and especially expansion of the manufacturing export base in these countries.

The chapter is organised as follows. After this introduction, section 6.2 uses historical time series data to demonstrate how the relative importance of small states has declined both in world merchandise and in commercial services export trade. While section 6.3 summarises the performance of individual countries, section 6.4 argues why marginalisation is a cause for concern, particularly for small states.[3] Section 6.5 provides an empirical analysis of marginalisation of small states in world merchandise exports followed by some discussions on a number of factors that aggravate the process of declining significance. There are some concluding observations in the final section.

6.2 Small states in world trade: volume, growth rate and share

6.2.1 Trade in merchandise goods

Between 1950 and 2000 world exports of merchandise goods grew by more than 100 times: from about US $62 billion to US $6,327 billion (table 6.1). Developed countries registered a 108-fold increase over the half-century while developing economies experienced a rise of 112 times. By these

[2] For example, the Commonwealth Secretariat (1998, p. 19) observes: '[S]mall states are concerned about further marginalisation of their economies as a consequence of the progressive liberalisation of the global economy and acceleration of the economic integration process in North America and Europe.'

[3] Small states in this chapter include all those countries listed in Atkins et al. (2000) and also Jamaica, Lesotho, Namibia and Papua New Guinea but exclude Bhutan. Discussions on the definition of small states can be found in Commonwealth Secretariat (1997).

Table 6.1 *Absolute volume of merchandise exports and imports (in billions of US dollars)*

	1950	1970	1980	1990	1992	1994	1996	1998	1999	2000
					Merchandise exports					
World	61.9	314.6	2,022.4	3,478.2	3,756.1	4,278.9	5,335.3	5,454.4	5,646.7	6,326.5
Developed countries	37.6	225.0	1,285.3	2,489.0	2,686.0	2,949.7	3,598.9	3,703.4	3,769.9	3,984.6
Developing countries	20.4	59.3	586.9	818.8	969.5	1,182.9	1,538.0	1,549.6	1,648.9	2,277.3
LDCs	1.8	5.2	14.2	16.4	16.4	18.1	23.5	24.4	27.6	34.4
Small states	**0.6**	**2.2**	**16.4**	**18.2**	**18.7**	**20.9**	**25.9**	**21.7**	**24.9**	**28.4**
small states without oil	*0.32*	*1.35*	*6.5*	*10.3*	*11.5*	*13.1*	*15.7*	*13.7*	*13.2*	*14.4*
small LDCs	*0.08*	*0.12*	*0.31*	*0.39*	*0.45*	*0.51*	*0.76*	*0.95*	*0.92*	*0.88*
					Merchandise imports					
World	63.7	327.4	2,060.5	3,590.4	3,867.1	4,333.2	5,484.0	5,556.4	5,791.4	6,512
Developed countries	41.7	236.2	1,418.1	2,608.7	2,746.4	2,938.2	3,663.1	3,772.7	3,970.5	4,317
Developing countries	18.4	61.7	493.6	796.2	1,019.5	1,251.8	1,604.3	1,555.9	1,616.4	2,112.0
LDCs	1.5	5.7	22.1	24.6	27.0	27.2	34.7	37.4	38.0	41.0
Small states	**0.7**	**3.5**	**25.1**	**25.4**	**28.2**	**28.1**	**34.6**	**35.4**	**34.6**	**39.0**
less oil-exporters	*0.35*	*2.3*	*10.8*	*13.7*	*15.7*	*17.2*	*20.8*	*21.4*	*22.0*	*24.2*
small LDCs	*0.05*	*0.15*	*0.32*	*0.4*	*0.45*	*0.5*	*0.6*	*0.55*	*0.6*	*0.55*

Note:
Developed, Developing and LDCs are defined as in UNCTAD (2002). Oil-exporting small states are Bahrain, Equatorial Guinea, Gabon and Trinidad and Tobago. Small LDCs are twelve small economies that are also classified as LDCs, Cape Verde, Comoros, Djibouti, Equatorial Guinea, the Gambia, Kiribati, Lesotho, Maldives, Samoa, São Tomé and Principe, Solomon Islands and Vanuatu.

standards, the performance of small states was at best modest as their export receipts increased from US $0.6 billion to US $28.4 billion, i.e. an increase of forty-seven times since 1950. This lacklustre record is matched only by an even worse performance of a mere nineteen-fold increase by the group of least developed countries (LDCs) over the same time.

Table 6.2 provides information on annual average absolute growth of merchandise exports by various country groups. It is estimated that over the period 1950–2000, on average, world exports increased at an annual absolute rate of US $114.2 billion. The comparable figures for LDCs and small states were only US $0.43 and US $0.55 billion respectively. In the 1990s, when global export volumes expanded at an unusually high rate of US $295 billion per annum, with developed and developing countries capturing respectively US $168 and US $127 billion, the exports of two vulnerable groups of LDCs and small states grew by an average of just over US $1 billion each. This, therefore, illustrates how the gains from merchandise export growth in the world economy have largely bypassed these countries. From the figures given in table 6.2 it can be estimated that during 1995–2000 the combined contribution of sixty-nine LDCs and small states to annual average absolute global export growth was only 0.71 per cent.[4] Exclusion of the oil-exporters would slash this share to 0.31 per cent.

As figure 6.1 shows, the growth rates of exports of small states for most periods have been lower than those of the developed and developing countries, thereby causing their relative importance in global export volume to shrink. During the period 1970–2000 world goods exports registered a trend growth rate of 9.17 per cent per annum as compared to 6.72 per cent for small states. In the 1980s and 1990s small states' growth performance was the worst, with a negative growth rate for the 1980s (−1.44 per cent) and then a rate of 3.73 per cent, which is just over half the growth rate achieved by the LDCs, in the 1990s. The volatility in the growth rates of export earnings is consistent with the well-documented experience of economic vulnerability.

The data presented in table 6.1 reveal that almost half of the merchandise exports of thirty-five small states can be attributable to the four oil-rich countries – Bahrain, Equatorial Guinea, Gabon and Trinidad and

[4] There are forty-six LDCs for which data are available, while the corresponding number of small states is thirty-five. However, since twelve small states are also LDCs there is a total of sixty-nine countries in these two groups.

Table 6.2 *Absolute growth of merchandise exports (in billions of US dollars)*

							Average absolute growth	
Country groups	1950–2000	1950–70	1970–2000	1970s	1980s	1990s	1990–4	1995–2000
World	114.2	10.22	192.9	139.92	118.7	294.8	251.46	339.67
Developed countries	77.08	7.94	129	99.93	101.6	167.5	157.23	179.04
Developing countries	37.13	2.28	63.9	49.33	17.12	127.3	94.23	160.63
HPAE	17.62	29.95	35.27	9.78	24.25	67.06	67.22	68.74
Asian Tigers	*10.84*	*16.71*	*21.55*	*5.7*	*18.61*	*35.44*	*38.15*	*33.18*
China	*3.21*	*0.08*	*6.81*	*1.06*	*3.64*	*17.62*	*13.7*	*21.38*
LDCs	**0.43**	**0.13**	**0.61**	**0.65**	**0.07**♣	**1.24**	**0.51**	**1.55**
less oil exporters	*0.34*	*0.11*	*0.47*	*0.58*	*0.05*♣	*1.12*	*0.52*	*1.12*
Small states	**0.55**	**0.07**	**0.75**	**1.14**	**−0.21**♣	**0.82**	**0.66**	**0.87**
less oil exporters	*0.31*	*0.04*	*0.49*	*0.45*	*0.39*	*0.41*	*0.67*	*−0.06*
Small LDCs	*0.016*	*0.009*	*0.03*	*0.019*	*0.011*	*0.018*	*0.03*	*−0.07*

Notes:
(1) The growth of absolute exports as reported in the first six columns is estimated by using a linear trend equation: $X = \alpha + \beta t$, where X stands for exports (in billions of US dollars), α is the intercept, and t is a time trend. The reported figures are estimated βs from different regression equations. (2) All estimated coefficients were statistically significant at least at the 5 per cent level except the ones indicated by ♣. Figures in the last two columns are simple annual average absolute growth. HPAE is the group of high-performing Asian economies, namely, China, Hong Kong, Indonesia, Korea, Malaysia, Singapore, Taiwan and Thailand. Asian Tigers include Hong Kong, Korea, Singapore and Taiwan.

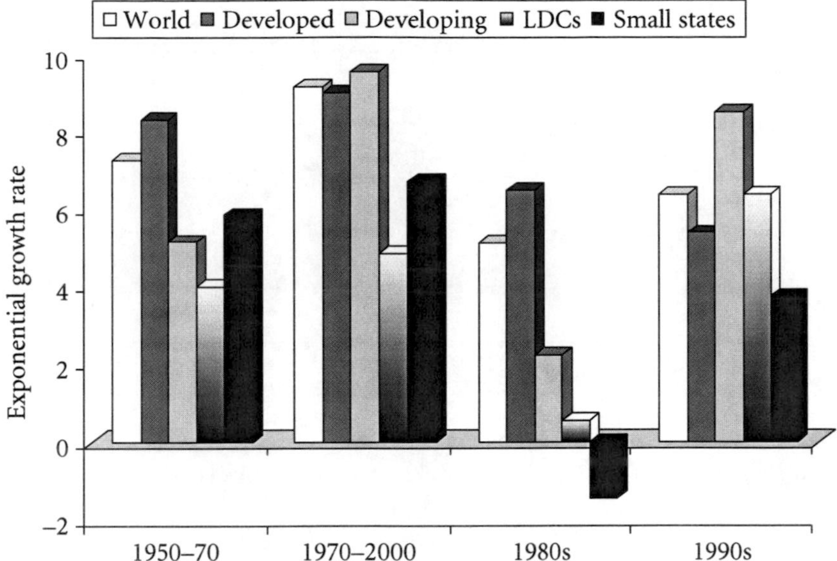

Note: The trend growth rates have been estimated by fitting semi-logarithmic equations to the data.

Source: Authors' estimates based on the data from UNCTAD (2002).

Figure 6.1 Trend growth rates of merchandise exports

Tobago. A close look at the data underlying the table also makes it clear that since 1994 these countries have dominated the growth of small states' merchandise exports, as receipts of others have almost been stagnant. Twelve small states that also belong to the group of LDCs have been the worst performers, recording only an eleven-fold increase in their combined export volume over the corresponding exports in 1950.

Figure 6.2 shows the marginalisation of small states in world merchandise export trade as the combined share of thirty-five small states fell from 1.18 per cent in the mid-1950s to 0.44 per cent in 2000. Excluding the oil-rich small states, the comparable figures are worked out to be respectively 0.68 and 0.23 per cent. The graph representing all small states in figure 6.2 exhibits a sudden jump in 1974 and then portrays a short-lived episode of enhanced but deteriorating share with respect to the secular declining trend of the 1960s. This was due to the export boom of the oil-producing small states following the oil crisis of 1973. By the middle of the 1980s, all small states (including the oil-rich countries) had reversed back to the trend that originated in the early 1960s.

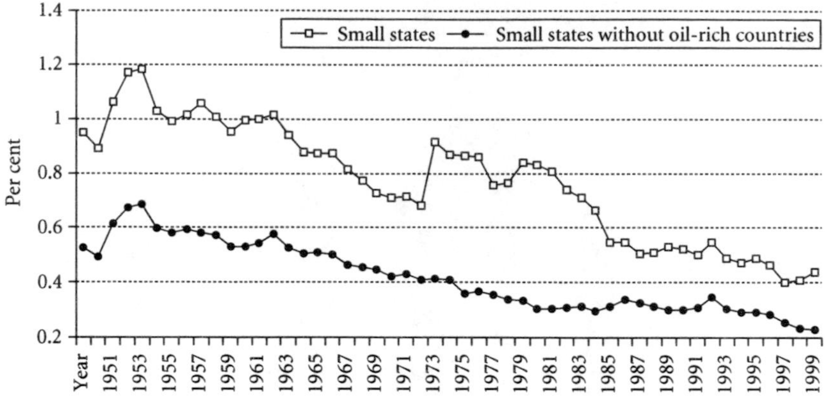

Source: Authors' estimates based on the data from UNCTAD (2002).
Figure 6.2 Share of small states in global merchandise exports: 1950–2000

6.2.2 Exports of commercial services

One of the most significant features of the post-war period of globalisation has been the growing trade in commercial services that include travel, transport, communications, financial and professional services. The value of exports of commercial services now is a quarter of the value of merchandise exports. The rising importance of services trade resulted in the inclusion of the General Agreements on Trade in Services (GATS) in the Uruguay Round of MTNs.

According to the information provided in table 6.3, world exports of commercial services stood at US $1,457 billion in 2000, of which about 72 per cent was accounted for by developed countries. Small states earned US $4.3 billion in 1980, which grew to US $16 billion at the end of 2000. However, about 50 per cent of this absolute growth was due to four countries alone, i.e. Cyprus, Jamaica, Malta and Mauritius, which have a relatively large and well-developed tourism sector.[5]

Table 6.4 provides estimates for the absolute growth of commercial services exports. Between 1980 and 2000 global services exports grew at an annual average rate of about US $63 billion; developed countries experienced a per annum growth of US $44.6 billion and developing countries US $17.5 billion. In contrast, LDCs and small states registered annual

[5] The share of these four countries in small states' manufacturing exports is, however, much lower – about 21 per cent in 2000.

Table 6.3 *Exports of commercial services (in billions of US dollars)*

Country groups	1980	1985	1990	1992	1994	1996	1998	1999	2000
					Exports of commercial services				
World	364.3	381.8	783.2	924.5	1,039.5	1,275.8	1,341.0	1,375.8	1,457.2
Developed countries	277.7	288.9	608.7	708.3	760.8	912.8	974.2	1,006.4	1,046.3
Developing countries	74.0	80.6	153.8	190.4	245.1	310.5	314.0	323.9	360.6
LDCs	2.3	2.4	3.3	3.6	4.3	5.6	5.6	5.9	6.0
Small states	4.3	5.1	9.3	10.8	12.3	13.9	14.5	15.8	16.3
of which major four	1.3	1.5	3.9	4.7	5.4	6.2	6.5	7.1	7.1
small LDCs	0.2	0.2	0.4	0.5	0.6	0.7	0.8	0.9	0.9
					Imports of commercial services				
World	49.0	48.9	100.0	115.1	127.6	154.8	163.3	167.2	177.7
Developed countries	44.0	45.2	100.0	113.7	121.6	144.8	155.4	160.2	166.5
Developing countries	64.1	60.0	100.0	119.3	144.0	182.9	184.1	187.8	208.7
LDCs	75.3	65.2	100.0	111.2	111.2	137.1	144.9	144.9	162.9
Small states	65.7	68.7	100.0	113.4	117.9	137.3	147.8	149.3	158.2
Major four	45.5	45.5	100.0	118.2	131.8	168.2	172.7	177.3	186.4
Small LDCs	59.5	57.1	100.0	121.4	121.4	173.8	197.6	238.1	285.7

Source: Authors' estimates from WTO database. The major four include Cyprus, Jamaica, Malta and Mauritius.

Table 6.4 *Absolute growth of commercial services (in billions of US dollars)*

Country groups	1980–2000	1980s	1990s
World	62.9	32.4	71.1
Developed countries	44.6	26.3	46.0
Developing countries	17.5	5.7	23.9
HPAE	7.7	3.1	9.3
Asian tigers	5.7	2.4	7.0
China	1.4	0.27	2.5
LDCs	**0.22**	**0.07**	**0.32**
Small states	**0.58**	**0.38**	**0.64**
Major four	*0.34*	*0.22*	*0.34*
Small LDCs	*0.04*	*0.012*	*0.061*

absolute growth of US $0.22 and US $0.58 billion respectively. Almost 60 per cent of the growth in small states is attributable to the above-mentioned four countries only. Without these four countries, the combined contribution of LDCs and small states in world growth of commercial services in the 1990s stood at only 0.87 per cent.

The 1980–2000 trend growth rate of services exports for small states is estimated to be just above 7 per cent, which falls short of the growth rates of world, developed and developing country groups (figure 6.3). Therefore, although there had been a steady increase in the volume of service exports of small states, their relative importance actually shrank from 1.18 per cent in 1980 to 1.12 per cent in 2000 (figure 6.4). Figure 6.3 shows that the 1980s was the time when small states enjoyed a higher growth rate than all other country groups. In the following decade, however, small states were outperformed by the developing as well as least developed countries.[6]

6.2.3 *Total export (merchandise plus commercial services) trade*

Since small states have experienced declining shares in both merchandise and services exports, it goes without saying that their significance in the

[6] Figure 6.4 reveals that the relatively superior growth performance of the small states was concentrated only in the early- to mid-1980s, resulting in their rising share. Growth rates in the latter half of the 1980s were actually lower than those for the world, causing relative significance to fall.

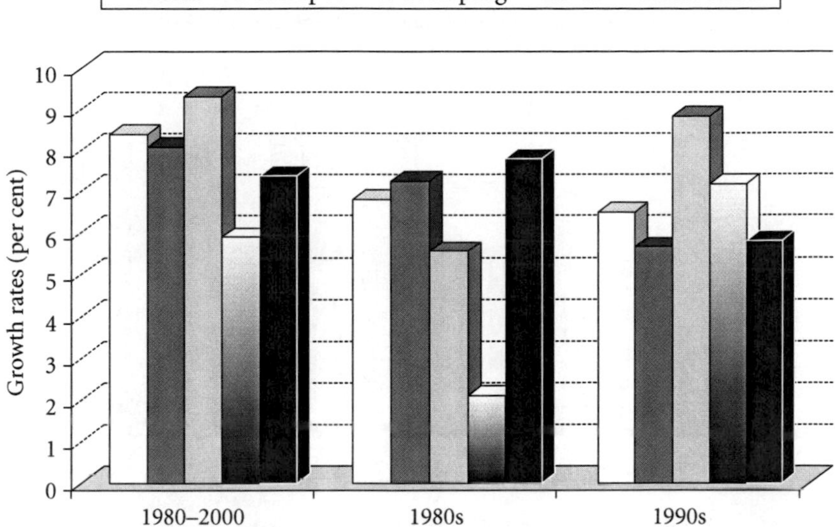

Note: The trend growth rates have been estimated by fitting semi-logarithmic equations to the data.

Figure 6.3 Growth rates of commercial services exports

world's combined exports of merchandise and commercial services has also declined. Table 6.5 gives the volume of export trade of small states along with other country groups, and, based on these figures, in figure 6.5 the share of small states in the combined global exports of merchandise goods and services has been indexed, setting the 1980 share equal to 100. Over time the index has fallen dramatically to reach 62 in 2000, i.e. small states' relative importance in global export trade declined by 38 per cent between 1980 and 2000. Most of this decline took place in the 1980s. While during the early 1990s this trend ceased, by the late 1990s the share had declined by a further 8 percentage points. From the preceding analysis, it should be clear that the deteriorating share or marginalisation of the small states could mostly be explained by their relatively poor performance in merchandise exports.

6.2.4 Total trade transactions

Total trade transactions (i.e. exports and imports of goods and commercial services taken together) of the world economy stood at US $15,749 billion

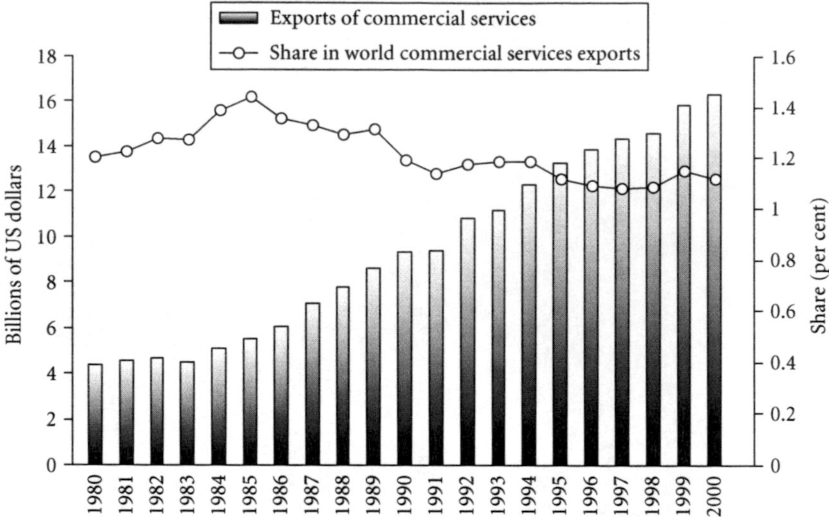

Figure 6.4 Volume and share of small states in exports of commercial services

in 2000, of which two-thirds were attributable to developed countries (table 6.6). During the past twenty years small states' total trade transactions rose at a slower pace than those of developed and developing countries, resulting in a decline in their share from about 1 per cent in 1980 to 0.58 per cent in 2000 (figure 6.6).

6.3 Performance of individual countries

6.3.1 Long-term trends

Countries defined as small states are not homogenous and the performance of individual countries, in fact, differs quite widely. Notwithstanding this dissimilarity, high volatility of exports stands out as the most common characteristic associated with these countries. Graphical plots of aggregate exports, a fundamental aspect of economic vulnerability of individual small states, as depicted in figure 6.7, show that almost all countries have been subject to frequent and, at times, violent fluctuations in their export receipts.[7] This volatility problem arises both in the merchandise goods

[7] Aggregate exports comprise merchandise and commercial services export receipts. Since data on services exports are available since 1980 only, the figure considers 1980–2000.

Table 6.5 *Volume of export trade (merchandise plus commercial services) (US $ billion)*

	1980	1985	1990	1992	1994	1996	1998	1999	2000
World	2,386.7	2,340.4	4,261.4	4,680.6	5,318.4	6,611.1	6,795.4	7,022.5	7,783.7
Developed countries	1,563.0	1,584.1	3,097.7	3,394.3	3,710.5	4,511.7	4,677.6	4,776.3	5,030.9
Developing countries	660.9	575.0	972.6	1,159.9	1,428.0	1,848.5	1,863.6	1,972.8	2,637.9
LDCs	16.9	14.4	19.7	20.0	22.4	29.1	30.0	33.5	40.4
Small states	20.7	23.3	28.0	29.5	33.2	39.8	36.2	40.7	44.7
Small LDCs	*0.5*	*0.5*	*0.8*	*1.0*	*1.2*	*1.6*	*1.6*	*2.0*	*2.0*

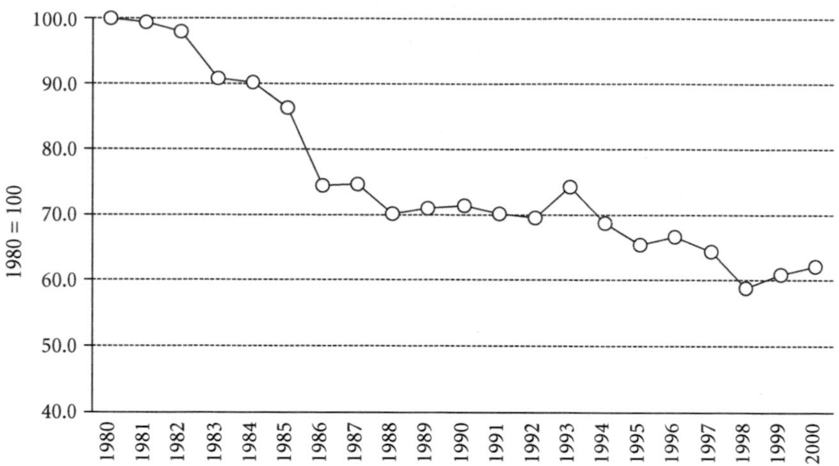

Source: Own computation based on the data from UNCTAD (2002).
Figure 6.5 Declining importance of small states in world export (merchandise plus services) trade

as well as in commercial services exports (see appendices 2 and 3). Dependence on a narrow range of agricultural products that experience either price or exogenous supply shocks on a regular basis is the principal reason for export instability. In the case of commercial services, most small states rely on the tourism sector, which is in turn dependent on such factors as the global political situation which is completely beyond the control of these countries. A close examination of the figures in appendices 2 and 3 reveals that for most individual small states earning instabilities are more prominent in the case of merchandise exports.

Instability of export earnings is also reflected in individual countries' volatile relative significance in world trade, which is depicted in figure 6.8. This figure sketches the evolution of individual countries' share in total world exports by setting their actual shares in 1980 at 1. A value greater than 1 in any of the following years will indicate a rise in the share of the country in question in total world trade, and vice versa. The result indicates that small states, in general, have not been able to improve their share on a long-term basis. For Bahrain, Barbados, Belize, Djibouti, Fiji, Gabon, Gambia, Guyana, Jamaica, São Tomé and Principe, Solomon Islands, Suriname, Tonga, Trinidad and Tobago and Vanuatu there is a clear deteriorating trend in their share of world exports. The figures in appendices 4

Table 6.6 *Total trade transactions of different country groups (US $ billion)*

	1980	1985	1990	1992	1994	1996	1998	1999	2000
World	4,847.6	4,756.1	8,669.7	9,489.4	10,694.9	13,361.6	13,687.3	14,181.2	15,748.8
Developed countries	3,246.6	3,245.0	6,310.0	6,827.0	7,382.9	9,048.9	9,388.4	9,713.5	10,352.6
Developing countries	1,276.3	1,156.1	1,958.9	2,406.1	2,953.6	3,800.5	3,769.5	3,946.3	5,146.7
LDCs	45.7	39.6	53.2	56.9	59.5	76.0	80.3	84.4	95.9
Small states	**50.2**	**45.5**	**60.1**	**65.3**	**69.2**	**83.6**	**81.5**	**85.3**	**94.3**
Small LDCs	*1.96*	*1.81*	*3.04*	*4.12*	*4.13*	*5.41*	*5.43*	*5.68*	*6.21*

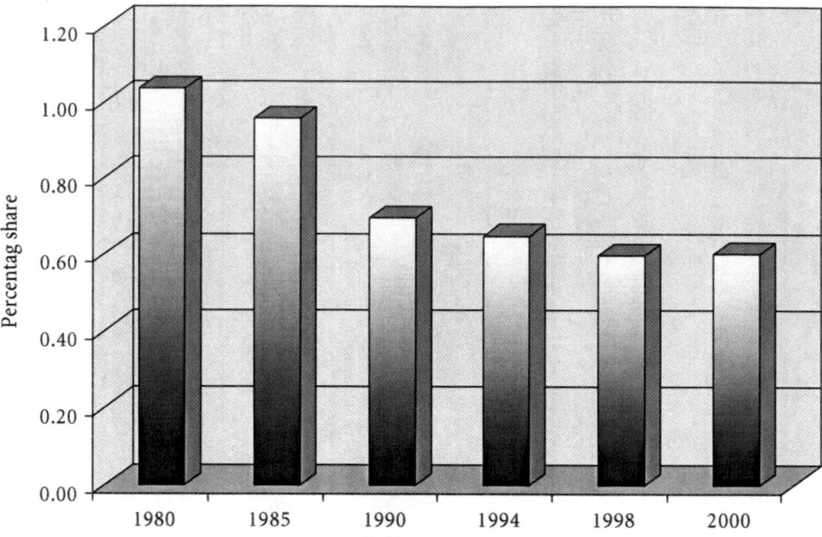

Figure 6.6 Share of small states in world trade transactions

and 5 give similar information disaggregated by merchandise and commercial exports, where it is found that in the case of merchandise exports more small states have experienced relative declines over a long period of time.

As marginalisation is a measure of relative trade performance, a country can only prevent marginalisation if its exports grow at a rate at least as high as that of the world average. Therefore, in order to obtain a long-term view of marginalisation it is essential to compare the trend growth rate of a country's exports with that of the rest of the world. Tables 6.7 and 6.8 present the estimated trend growth rates of individual small states' merchandise and commercial services exports over different periods. Table 6.7 shows that, as against the world growth rate of 9.17 per cent over the period 1970–2000, there are only eight small states (Botswana, Equatorial Guinea, Lesotho, Maldives, Malta, Mauritius, Seychelles and St Vincent and the Grenadines) with a growth rate above the global average.[8] This suggests that the other twenty-seven countries will have shown a long-run tendency of becoming marginalised in merchandise exports. In sharp contrast, in the

[8] Of these countries, some have been resource-rich, such as Botswana, or have commenced from a very low base. Only in the case of Mauritius has there developed a diversified and merchandise export-led growth, which has provided a genuine counter example to the inexorable tendency of small state marginalisation.

Table 6.7 *Growth rates of merchandise exports from individual small states*

Country	1950–2000	1970–2000	1980s	1990s
World	**10.29**	**9.17**	**5.11**	**6.37**
Antigua and Barbuda	7.22	3.92	−6.6	−0.82
Bahrain	8.67	7.49	−5.9	2.9
Barbados	6.40	5.32	−3.2	3.9
Belize	8.38	5.92	−1.7	6.05
Botswana	15.4	14.28	18.6	3.8
Cape Verde	0.95	6.89	6.8	10.8
Comoros	4.73	2.43	2.8	−9.0
Cyprus	8.12	7.89	3.5	1.4
Djibouti	0.59	0.40	8.7	0.7
Dominica	7.58	8.25	15.7	0.5
Equatorial Guinea	2.82	10.57	17.9	24.4
Fiji	7.47	5.92	−0.5	3.0
Gabon	11.9	7.53	−6.7	5.4
Gambia	3.00	−1.41	1.4	−16.9
Grenada	5.00	4.32	7.9	0.5
Guyana	5.14	3.48	−4.2	8.7
Jamaica	6.58	3.94	−1.0	2.1
Kiribati	2.06	−4.38	−2.3	6.2
Lesotho	9.86	11.44	2.2	10.8
Maldives	8.39	12.68	20.8	5.6
Malta	13.5	12.09	6.8	5.9
Mauritius	8.61	10.05	13.0	3.5
Papua New Guinea	11.3	8.08	5.4	3.0
Samoa	1.87	1.20	−1.6	11.3
São Tomé and Principe	0.82	−0.97	−4.2	−7.4
Seychelles	10.2	13.05	6.3	14.1
Solomon Islands	9.50	8.71	1.2	4.5
St Kitts and Nevis	4.12	2.22	3.6	0.6
St Lucia	9.94	8.18	9.9	−8.8
St Vincent & the Grenadines	8.65	9.78	16.3	−5.4
Suriname	7.38	3.39	−1.6	−0.3
Swaziland	10.5	8.38	2.9	5.7
Tonga	4.17	4.71	0.5	−0.8
Trinidad and Tobago	6.71	3.10	−12.6	6.4
Vanuatu	4.40	1.35	−6.7	4.7

Note:
The trend growth rates have been estimated by fitting the usual semi-logarithmic equation to the data.

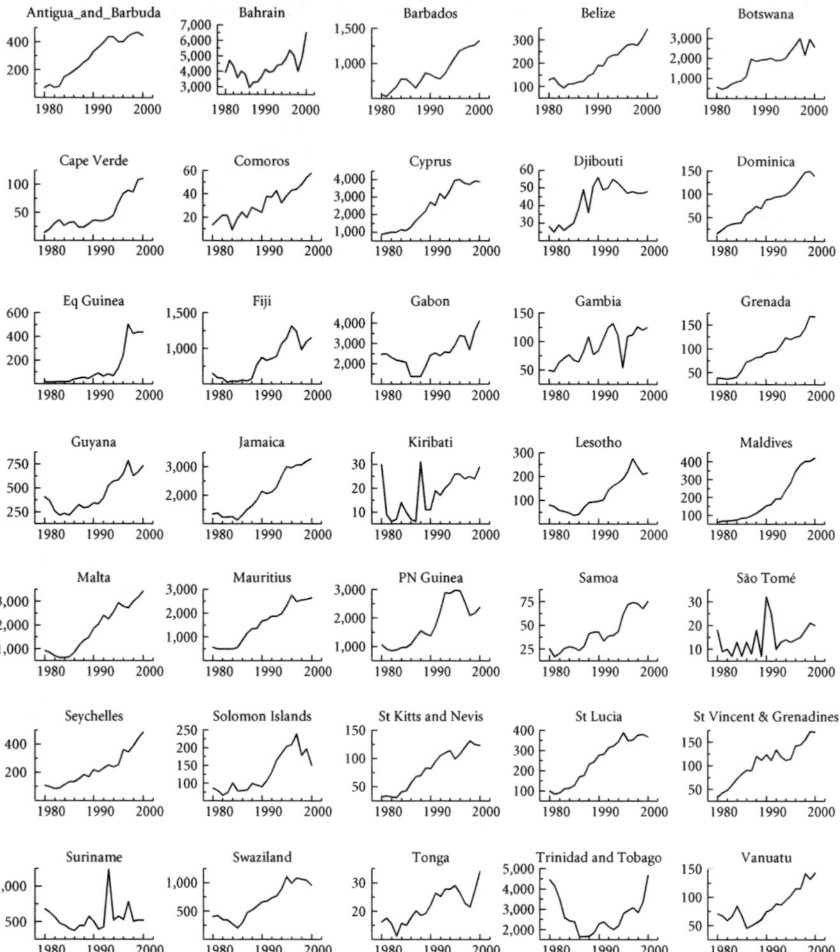

Note: Figures are in millions of US dollars.
Figure 6.7 Total exports (merchandise plus commercial services) of individual small states

case of services exports there are twenty countries that have enjoyed growth rates higher than that of the world during 1980–2000.[9] Therefore, it is the dismal performance of merchandise exports that resulted in the overall poor performance of small states in world trade.

[9] In the following decades of the 1980s and 1990s, these numbers fall slightly to nineteen and seventeen respectively.

Table 6. 8 *Growth rates of commercial services exports*

Country	1980–2000	1980s	1990s
World	**8.4**	**6.8**	**6.5**
Antigua and Barbuda	11.3	21.8	3.19
Bahrain	2.37	11.7	6.55
Barbados	6.32	7.72	6.42
Belize	13.0	14.1	5.00
Botswana	8.34	0.90	6.19
Cape Verde	8.76	3.13	14.2
Comoros	19.4	21.3	17.5
Cyprus	11.7	15.7	5.52
Djibouti	3.86	5.56	−2.62
Dominica	15.7	17.8	11.1
Equatorial Guinea	1.72	1.10	0.29
Fiji	6.73	2.86	3.91
Gabon	1.49	−5.25	−2.30
Gambia	9.47	12.3	7.44
Grenada	11.2	13.5	7.94
Guyana	11.7	17.5	6.40
Jamaica	8.57	9.12	7.86
Kiribati	10.4	2.93	7.20
Lesotho	4.61	0.93	3.41
Maldives	11.1	4.05	13.4
Malta	8.05	6.41	4.66
Mauritius	12.5	11.5	8.60
Papua New Guinea	11.7	8.84	2.24
Samoa	12.7	17.0	7.67
São Tomé and Principe	13.8	7.88	12.4
Seychelles	7.25	8.04	6.68
Solomon Islands	10.5	6.35	10.5
St Kitts and Nevis	12.8	21.5	4.65
St Lucia	11.6	14.2	7.65
St Vincent & the Grenadines	11.1	9.80	11.8
Suriname	−2.61	−16.7	10.6
Swaziland	7.52	7.97	−0.39
Tonga	3.54	4.15	2.91
Trinidad and Tobago	3.31	2.20	6.13
Vanuatu	6.73	−0.34	7.39

Source: Authors' own estimates by fitting semi-logarithmic equation to the data.

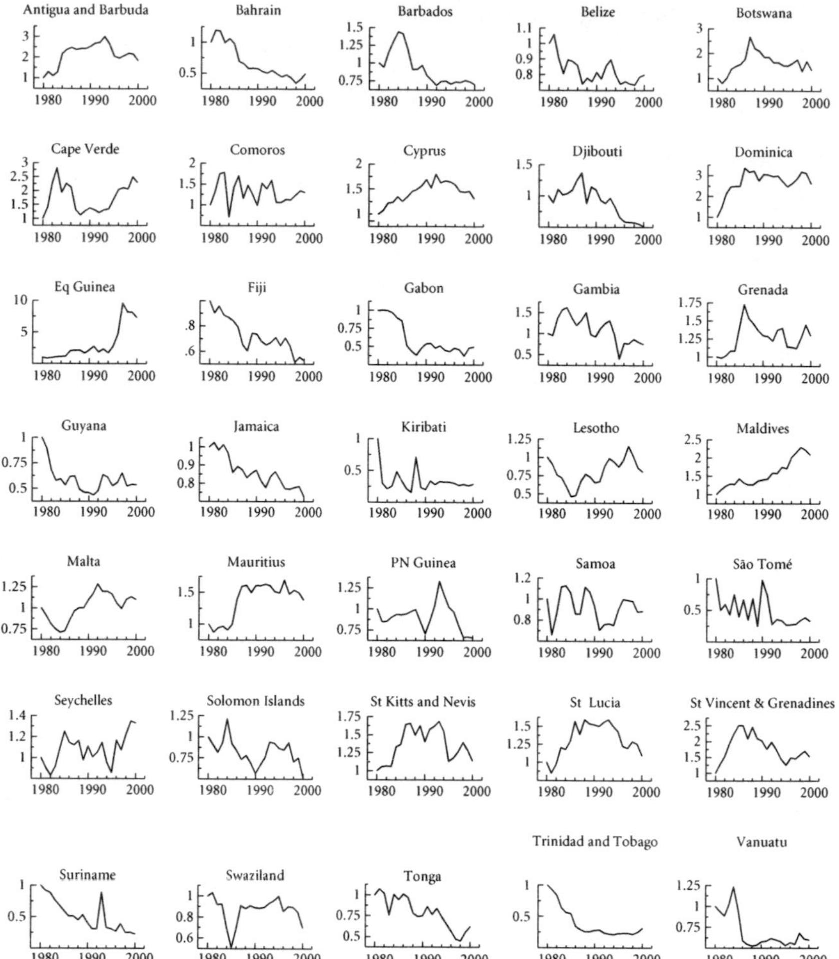

Source: Authors' own estimates.

Figure 6.8 Share of individual small states in global exports of merchandise goods and commercial services (1980 = 1)

It follows from the above that, considering the merchandise exports alone, there are only eight small states that have been able to register positive trend growth in share during the period 1970–2000 (see figure 6.9). But, due to a better performance in the exports of commercial services, the number of small states that prevented marginalisation during 1980–2000 rises to fourteen (see figure 6.10). According to figure 6.9, Botswana is the best performer in merchandise exports among the group of small states, while Kiribati

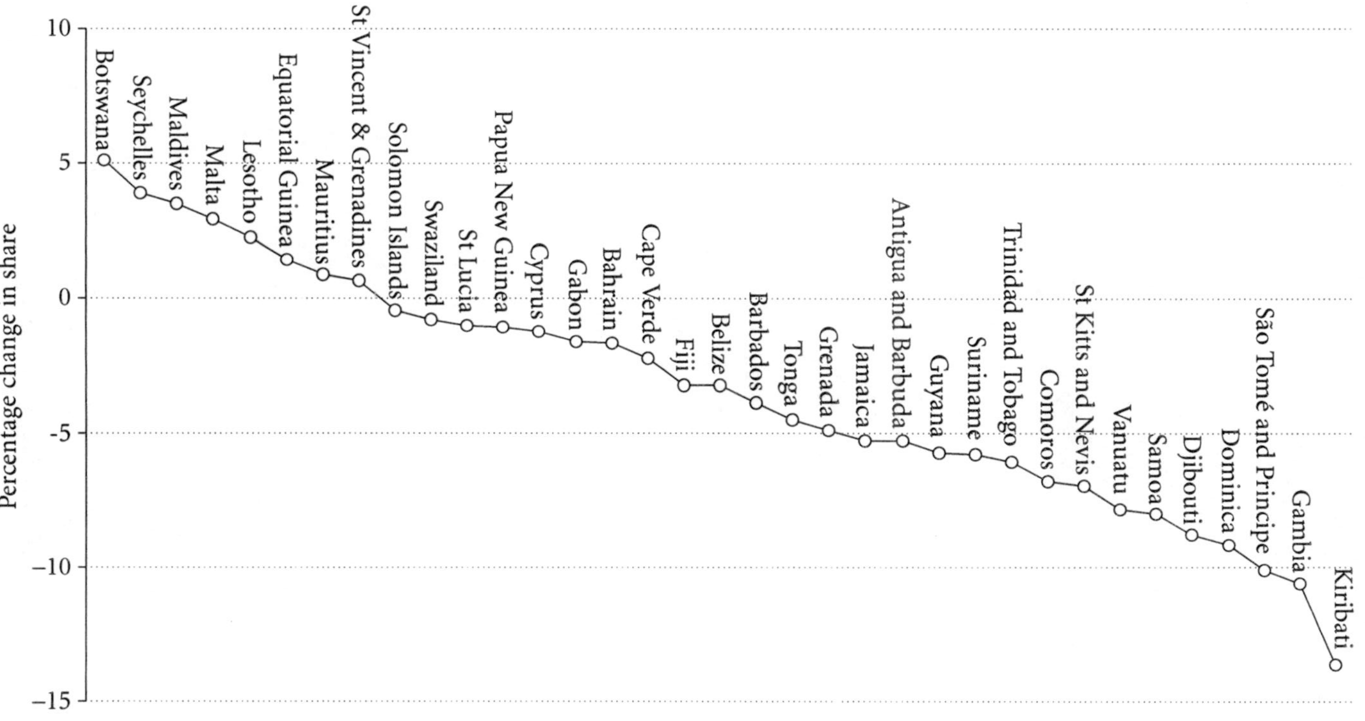

Note: Countries with negative rate of change in share have become marginalised.

Source: Based on authors' own estimates.

Figure 6.9 Marginalisation of individual small states in world merchandise exports, 1970–2000

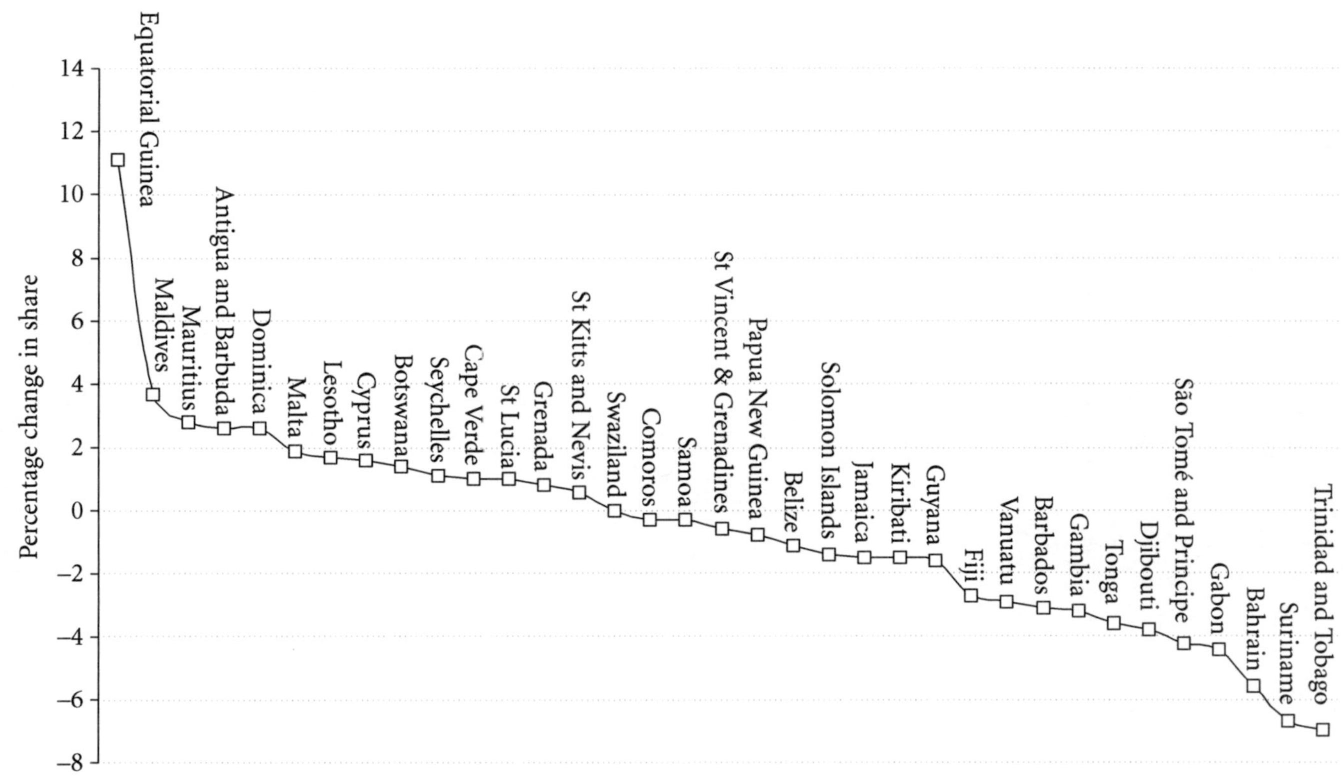

Note: Based on authors' own estimates.

Figure 6.10 Marginalisation of individual small states in total exports (merchandise plus commercial services) 1980–2000

appears to have been the most marginalised. Consideration of total exports (including services), however, changes the relative position, in which case Equatorial Guinea is found to have gained most while Trinidad and Tobago has the highest rate of marginalisation. The relatively good performance of Equatorial Guinea stems from its low base of exports in 1980 (see appendix 2).

6.3.2 *Recent performance of individual countries*

Significant changes in the world trade regime took place in the 1990s with the conclusion of the Uruguay Round of trade negotiations and the subsequent establishment of the WTO. It was thought that by providing clear-cut and fair trade rules the WTO regime would benefit LDCs and vulnerable countries like small states. However, the available evidence shows that the trends in diminishing relative significance of these countries remain uninterrupted. Table 6.9 classifies small states according to whether their individual shares in both the early- and late-1990s increased, decreased or experienced a mixture of both.[10] Considering merchandise exports only, it is observed that almost two-thirds (twenty-two out of thirty-five) of small states saw their average share fall both in 1990–4 and 1995–2000. There are twenty-seven countries (77 per cent) with declining shares in the post-Uruguay Round period. The only two countries that experienced an increase in the share of global merchandised exports throughout the 1990s were Equatorial Guinea and Seychelles.[11]

In the case of commercial services, as shown previously, the performance is much better. As many as thirteen countries (about 37 per cent) increased their shares both in 1990–4 and in 1995–2000. Only eleven countries experienced a decline in their share of world service exports in both halves of the 1990s. However, the number of countries (twenty-one) that have been subject to declining share in the post-Uruguay Round is still comparable to that of merchandise exports. Finally, when merchandise and services exports are considered together there remain only three countries that survived marginalisation in the 1990s. There are twenty-eight countries (80 per cent) that have experienced a reduced share in the late 1990s, nineteen of which experienced decline in both halves of the decade.

[10] The late-1990s (1995–2000) corresponds to the post-Uruguay Round period.

[11] The growth of exports of cocoa beans in the case of Equatorial Guinea and canned tuna in the case of Seychelles resulted in such positive outcomes.

Table 6.9 *A summary of export performance of small states in the 1990s*

Average share increased both in 1990–4 (compared to 1985–90) and in 1995–2000 (compared to 1990–4)	Average share increased in 1990–4 (compared to 1985–90) but fell in 1995–2000	Average share decreased in 1990–4 (compared to 1985–90) but increased in 1995–2000	Average share decreased in 1995–2000 (compared to 1990–4)	Average share fell both in 1990–4 (compared to 1985–90) and in 1995–2000 (compared to 1990–4)
		Merchandise exports		
Equatorial Guinea	Malta	Antigua and Barbuda*	Bahrain	Bahrain
Seychelles	Mauritius*	Cape Verde*	Barbados	Barbados
	Papua New Guinea*	Guyana	Belize	Belize
	Swaziland	Samoa*	Botswana	Botswana
	Tonga*	Trinidad and Tobago*	Comoros	Comoros
			Cyprus	Cyprus
			Djibouti	Djibouti
			Dominica	Dominica
			Fiji	Fiji
			Gabon	Gabon
			Gambia	Gambia
			Grenada	Grenada
			Jamaica	Jamaica
			Kiribati	Kiribati
			Maldives	Maldives
			Malta	São Tomé and Principe
			Mauritius	Solomon Islands
			Papua New Guinea	St Kitts and Nevis
			São Tomé and Principe	

			Solomon Islands	St Lucia
			St Kitts and Nevis	St Vincent and Grenadines
			St Lucia	Suriname
			St Vincent and Grenadines	Vanuatu
			Suriname	
			Swaziland	
			Tonga	
			Vanuatu	
Commercial services				
Comoros	Belize	Cape Verde	Antigua and Barbuda	Antigua and Barbuda
Dominica	Botswana	Jamaica*	Bahamas	Bahamas
Grenada	Cyprus	Suriname*	Bahrain	Bahrain
Kiribati	Fiji*		Barbados	Barbados
Maldives	Gabon*		Belize	Djibouti
Mauritius	Lesotho*		Botswana	Equatorial Guinea
Namibia	Malta*		Cyprus	Gambia
Samoa	Papua New Guinea		Djibouti	Guyana
São Tomé and Principe	St Kitts and Nevis*		Equatorial Guinea	Seychelles
Solomon Islands	Swaziland*		Fiji	Tonga
St Lucia			Gabon	Trinidad and Tobago
St Vincent and Grenadines			Gambia	
Vanuatu			Guyana	
			Lesotho	
			Malta	

Table 6.9 (*cont.*)

Average share increased both in 1990–4 (compared to 1985–90) and in 1995–2000 (compared to 1990–4)	Average share increased in 1990–4 (compared to 1985–90) but fell in 1995–2000	Average share decreased in 1990–4 (compared to 1985–90) but increased in 1995–2000	Average share decreased in 1995–2000 (compared to 1990–4)	Average share fell both in 1990–4 (compared to 1985–90) and in 1995–2000 (compared to 1990–4)
			Papua New Guinea	
			Seychelles	
			St Kitts and Nevis	
			Swaziland	
			Tonga	
			Trinidad and Tobago	
Total exports (merchandise plus services)				
Equatorial Guinea	Antigua and Barbuda	Cape Verde	Antigua and Barbuda	Bahrain
Lesotho	Belize*	Guyana	Bahrain	Barbados
Maldives	Cyprus	Samoa*	Barbados	Botswana
	Malta	Seychelles	Belize	Comoros
	Mauritius		Botswana	Djibouti
	Papua New Guinea*		Comoros	Dominica
	Solomon Islands		Cyprus	Fiji
	St Lucia*		Djibouti	Gabon
	Swaziland		Dominica	Gambia
			Fiji	Grenada
			Gabon	Jamaica
			Gambia	Kiribati

Grenada	São Tomé and Principe
Jamaica	St Kitts and Nevis
Kiribati	St Vincent and Grenadines
Malta	Suriname
Mauritius	Tonga
Papua New Guinea	Trinidad and Tobago
São Tomé and Principe	Vanuatu
Solomon Islands	
St Kitts and Nevis	
St Lucia	
St Vincent and Grenadines	
Suriname	
Swaziland	
Tonga	
Trinidad and Tobago	
Vanuatu	

* indicates that average share was lower than that of 1985–90.

Source: Based on authors' own computation.

How much are the lost exports that result from marginalisation? This may be estimated as the net shifts in exports resulting from the discrepancies between the actual export receipts and the predicted earnings based on countries' share in a previous period. A positive shift is associated with a country's rising share while a negative shift reflects diminishing relative importance or marginalisation. It thus shows: if Antigua and Barbuda, for example, had just maintained its average 1980–5 share in world exports, it should have had an average export receipt of US $327 million in 1995–2000. However, its actual average earnings stood at US $435 million, thus registering a net shift of US $108 million or about 102 per cent of its average 1980–5 exports. Figure 6.11 presents the net shifts in total exports for all small states for 1995–2000 as a percentage of their respective average of 1985–90 exports. It is observed that twenty small states posted net negative shifts whereas fourteen experienced positive changes.[12] For the whole group of small states the net negative shifts were more than 100 per cent of the average exports of 1980–5. In other words, marginalisation has resulted in lost exports to the tune of US $18.19 billion.

Figure 6.12 exhibits the net shifts in total exports for individual small states for 1995–2000 as a percentage of their respective average of 1990–4 exports. It is observed that São Tomé and Principe, Djibouti, Suriname and Gambia experienced negative net shifts in excess of 50 per cent of their average 1990–4 exports. Tonga, Antigua and Barbuda, Papua New Guinea, St Kitts and Nevis, St Lucia, Bahrain, St Vincent and the Grenadines and Fiji are countries that have negative shifts between 20 and 50 per cent of their exports in 1990–4. Only seven small states are found to have enjoyed net positive shifts, of which the gains of Cape Verde and Equatorial Guinea are remarkably high. For the whole group of small states the net shift was found to be negative again and was estimated to be about 15 per cent of their 1990–4 average export earnings. Therefore, in order to prevent marginalisation in the post-Uruguay Round period small states would have required an additional US $4.2 billion worth of exports of merchandise goods and commercial services per annum.

[12] Equatorial Guinea, which had the largest net positive shifts among all small states, is not shown on the graph because of its very large vertical axis value. Equatorial Guinea's net positive shift was computed to be 1,749 per cent of its 1980–5 average export receipts. With a very low base, the country average earnings stood at US $17 million in the early 1980s, rocketing to US $361 million by the end of the 1990s.

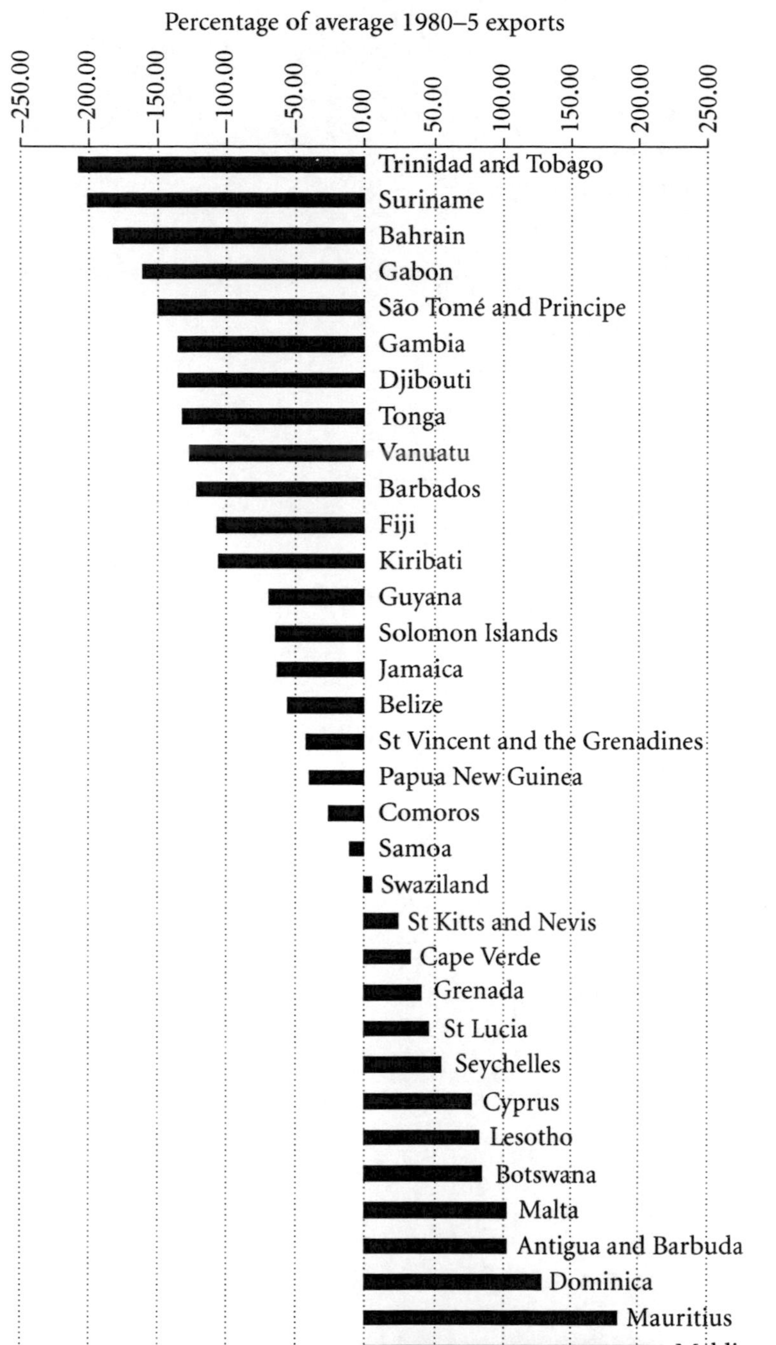

Figure 6.11 Average net shift in exports of small states in 1995–2000 in comparison with 1980–5

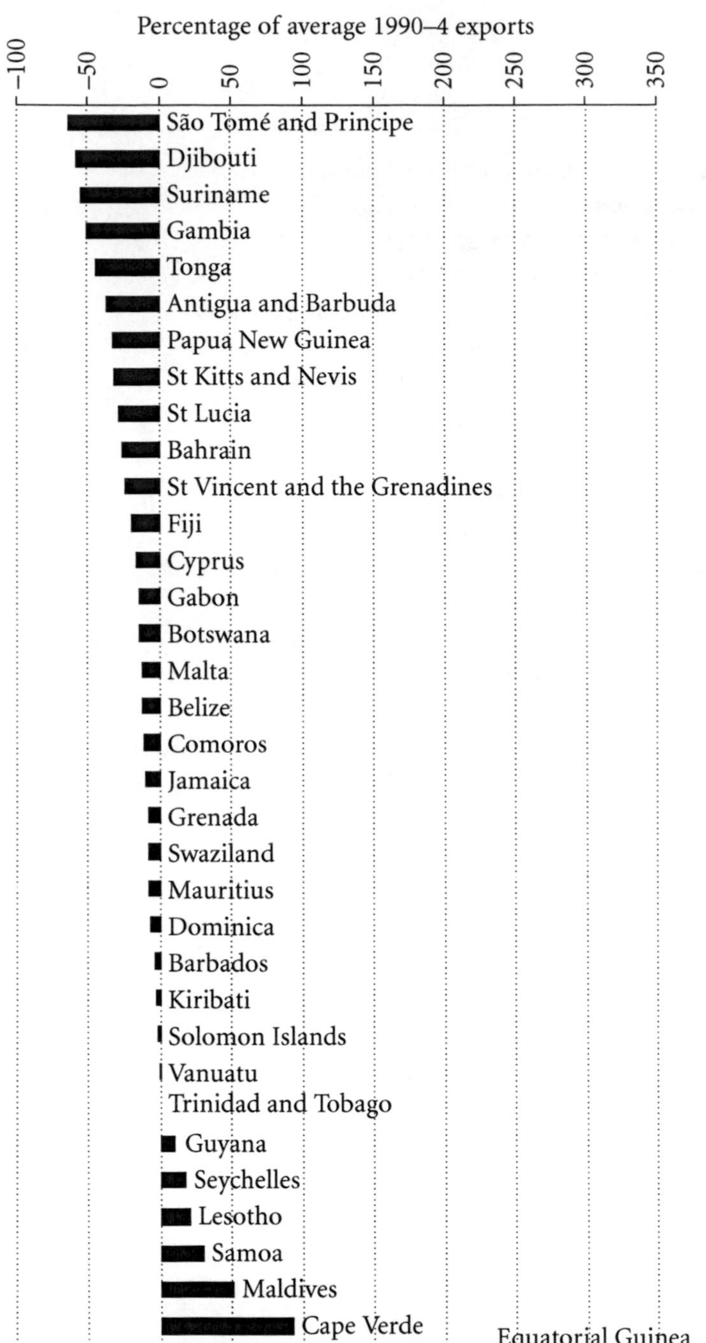

Note: Net shifts are estimated as a percentage of average 1990–4 exports.

Source: Own estimates based on the data from UNCTAD (2002).

Figure 6.12 Average net shift in total exports of small states in 1995–2000 in comparison with 1990–4 exports

6.4 Why is marginalisation of small states a cause for concern?

Marginalisation occurs when the relative importance of a particular country or a group of countries diminishes in world exports or trade. This does not necessarily mean that a declining share is always associated with an absolute fall in export volume. If world exports are expanding rapidly, countries registering modest rates of growth will see their relative share in world trade shrinking. For example, in the 1970s when global merchandise exports grew at about 19 per cent per annum, many countries, including small states, could not prevent marginalisation even when performing at their best compared to any other decade. More importantly, even when a country's share is diminishing in world trade, nothing can be inferred about the resultant welfare implications.[13] However, there are a number reasons for which marginalisation of low-income countries and small states can become a cause for concern.

First, after a high growth period in the 1970s export trade in the world economy expanded at much slower rates of 5.11 and 6.37 per cent per annum respectively in the 1980s and 1990s. Despite these lower rates of growth of global exports, most small states suffered declining shares during 1980–2000. This suggests that export performances of most small states have been poor by the absolute standard of the global average.

More worrying is the fact that for many small states marginalisation often happens to be associated with an absolute fall in export volume. In fact, 31 per cent of the listed small states have seen absolute declines in their exports in the post-Uruguay Round era. This means that a sizeable proportion of the declining share of the group of small states is attributable to negative growth rates of some countries. For these countries, marginalisation is not only about growing more slowly than the rest of the world but also about experiencing falling export revenues.

The difference between declining shares of relatively advanced countries and those of poor and vulnerable small states needs to be understood carefully, since one might argue that falling exports either absolutely or relatively should not be cause for concern for small states, as these are

[13] The welfare implications are much more complicated. First, as mentioned above, a country can have positive export growth associated with falling share in world exports, which means that marginalisation is not always accompanied by declining volume of export receipts. Second, the concept of welfare gains (or losses) is not directly related to export earnings. Exports are needed to finance imports and, consequently, the level of welfare is to be determined by the purchasing power of exports.

common to many developed countries as well. Although a smaller degree of export-orientation and slower growth in the export sector of a country may not be major impediments to its overall economic growth and welfare as long as the non-export sector flourishes, a robust performance of the export sector may prove to be central to the acceleration of the growth process in small states where domestic markets are small either due to low per capita income or due to small size of population or both. Understandably, the Republic of Korea has a much bigger domestic market than that of all small states taken together. Thus, for countries with a large domestic sector the significance of the export sector is not as crucial as for small states. As exports are directed to the world market, low domestic purchasing power or small size of the domestic economy cannot act as a hindrance to the exploitation of the economies of scale in production. Furthermore, in most of these economies market reforms were carried out in the belief that reallocation of resources from non-export sector to export sector would raise total factor productivity growth, contributing to GDP growth. However, since in a large number of small states export sectors either failed to flourish or actually experienced negative growth rates, the growth-promoting role of the export sector has remained unrealised.

The results depicted in figure 6.13 indicate that there is a significant and positive relationship between export growth and overall economic growth in small states. It has been estimated that a 1 per cent rise in export growth rate is associated with 0.4 per cent GDP growth in small states. From this relationship, it is quite straightforward to hypothesise that countries that have experienced rapid marginalisation will have lower GDP growth rates. In figure 6.13 we examine how GDP growth rates are related to growth rates of share of exports in small states over a period of time: 1980–2000. Negative trend growth rates of exports show the marginalisation of a country, while positive rates imply increasing share in world trade. A clear positive relationship is obtained, which suggests that countries that have been able to improve their relative importance in world export trade also enjoy relatively higher GDP growth rates. As most small states have become marginalised over the period 1980–2000, scatter points indicating their share fall on the scale represent negative numbers in figure 6.13.

Finally, it is generally believed that in this era of globalisation if the most vulnerable countries can participate effectively in the world market by

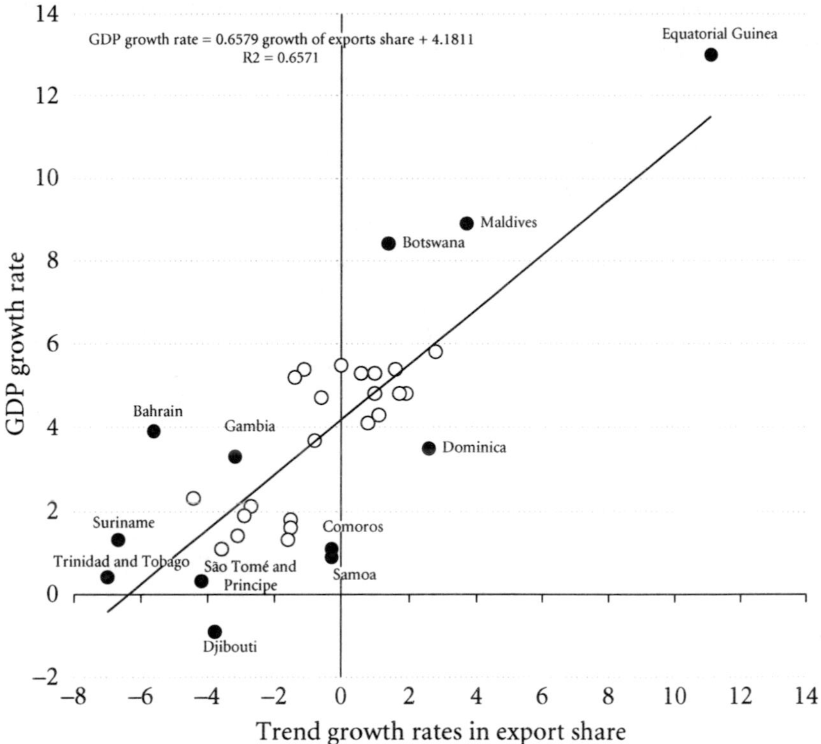

Note: Growth rates of exports share are authors' own estimates based on both merchandise and commercial services exports and correspond to 1980–2000. Except For Equatorial Guinea, GDP growth rates are taken from UNCTAD (2002), which gives the annual average growth for 1980–99. For Equatorial Guinea, the average growth rate of GDP has been taken from Commonwealth Secretariat, *Small States: Economic Review and Basic Statistics* (various issues).

Figure 6.13 Trends in marginalisation and growth of real GDP in small states

enjoying a relatively high growth of their trading volumes, a process of convergence between relatively advanced and underdeveloped countries will be initiated.[14] For this to happen, small states need a larger share of

[14] The 'convergence' hypothesis suggests that income inequalities between countries will diminish as the poorest countries grow more rapidly than the developed ones. Opponents, however, point out that the benefits of globalisation accrue mostly to the developed and more advanced developing countries and it is thus widening the gap between the richest and poorest countries. The evidence provided in this chapter shows that, at least in terms of world export trade, the 'divergence' hypothesis dominates in the comparative analysis of LDCs and small states with developed and advanced developing nations.

foreign capital and technology transferred from the North. Until now this process of accumulation of these key resources for production seems to have been associated with the growth of exports of goods and services. This means that if small states continue to grow at a rate slower than that of developed and relatively advanced developing countries the benefits of globalisation will become even more skewed.

To sum up, a declining share of exports itself is not a cause for concern. However, when world exports are growing slowly, marginalisation of small states is particularly worrying, since these countries have a small export base by an absolute standard. More importantly, many small states are actually being marginalised as a result of an absolute fall in export volume. With an already low export volume, if these countries cannot increase their share in world trade globalisation will contribute to a more skewed distribution of gains from trade.

6.5 Marginalisation in merchandise export trade: a statistical analysis

6.5.1 Understanding marginalisation

The manufacturing export base in most small states is rudimentary and most of these countries have to rely overwhelmingly on agricultural commodities and natural-resource-intensive products for export. As can be seen from figure 6.14, in twenty-five small states (out of a total of thirty-one for which the information is available) primary exports contribute to more than 50 per cent of the receipts from merchandise exports. Only in four countries, i.e. Lesotho, Malta, Mauritius and Swaziland, do we find manufacturing exports significantly greater than primary exports.[15]

Excessive reliance on primary commodities has grave implications for the long-term relative significance of the countries that depend on them. As the income elasticity of demand for agricultural products is low, production of and trade in primary commodities have failed to keep pace with the growth of world trade. In 1980 agricultural products constituted about 16 per cent of world merchandise exports, whereas they now account for

[15] Although Swaziland is shown to have a low primary to manufacturing ratio, agro-based export items such as wood pulp, sugar and other edibles account for about 50 per cent of its exports.

just 7 per cent. This follows the classic Engel's law, which explains the tendency of consumers to spend less on basic food products (or primary commodities) as their incomes rise. Unlike the pattern of the growth in world trade, as small states' merchandise export structures remain dominated by primary commodities there will be a deteriorating trend in the relative importance of these countries in the global trading activities. This process has been exacerbated by the development of new technology and improved productivity growth. While these are beneficial to consumers in general, small states and other commodity-producing countries that continue to rely heavily on primary exports seem to have experienced unfavourable shocks as a result of these developments. The advent of new technologies reduces the intensity of the use of various primary commodities such as metals and agricultural raw materials (World Bank, 1994) and is also responsible for productivity improvement and increased production of many agricultural commodities (Reinhart and Wickham, 1994).

Therefore, the operation of Engel's law (resulting in the diminishing share of agricultural goods in total global consumption expenditure) would guide the effects of technology-induced decline in demand, and the increased supply capacity is translated into depressed prices for agricultural commodities. Empirical evidence, especially since the late 1970s, corroborates this hypothesis. Between 1970 and 1993 real commodity prices more than halved (World Bank, 1994).[16] Then, these prices registered an annual average growth of 6 per cent during 1994–7. This was followed by consecutive declines of 13 and 14.2 per cent respectively in 1998 and 1999 (UNCTAD, 2000). Table 6.10 shows that real prices of seventeen major commodities in 2000 were lower than their corresponding prices in 1980 by 25 per cent or more. For another eight commodities prices fell by more than 50 per cent in 1980–2000. The falling prices of agricultural products have certainly also contributed to the marginalisation of small states.[17]

It needs to be mentioned here that advances in technology and productivity are also taking place in the manufacturing sector. But manufacturing activities provide much more scope for product diversification and innovation, allowing individual countries to specialise in different market niches.

[16] According to World Bank (1994: p. 32), 'the estimated annual loss to developing countries from the fall in commodity prices between 1980 and 1993 reached US $100 billion a year in 1993 – or more than twice the total flow of aid in 1990'.

[17] In fact, the prices of primary commodities have also fallen relative to manufacturing goods, causing terms-of-trade shocks for countries specialising in agricultural products.

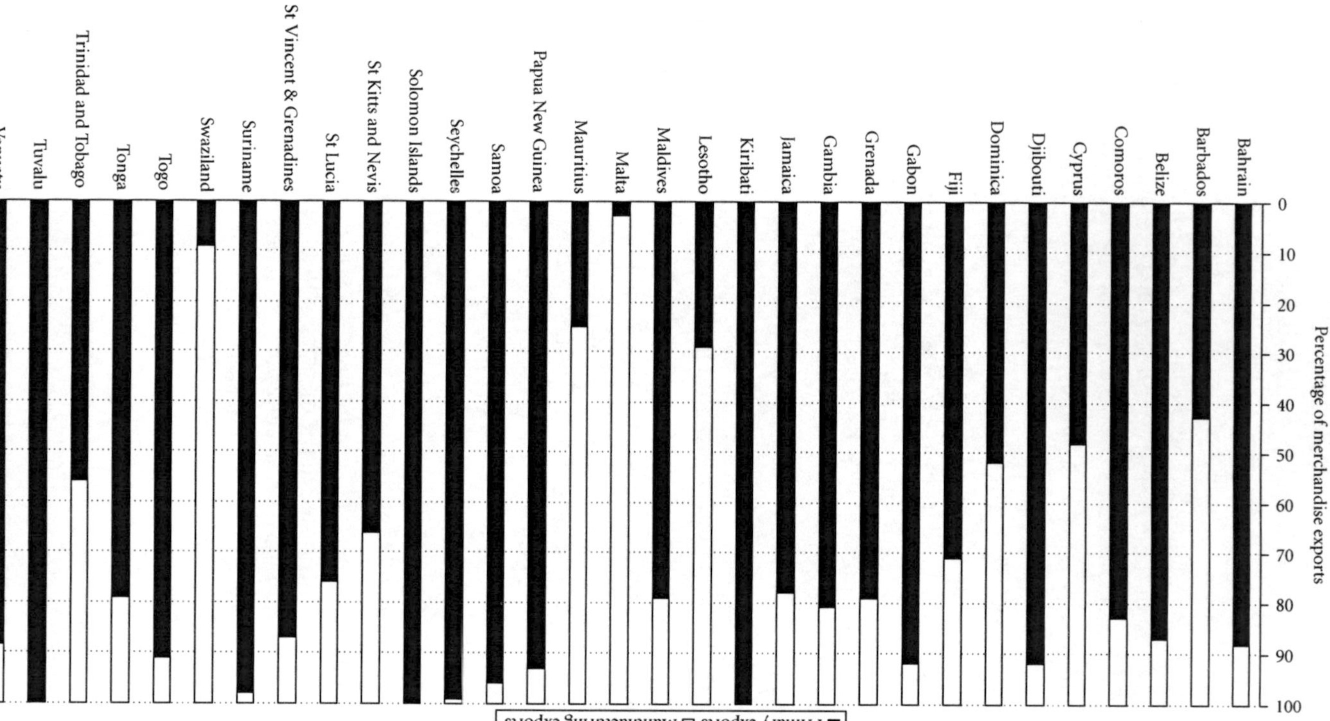

Note: Data have been compiled from UNCTAD (2002), World Bank (2001) and Commonwealth Secretariat (various issues). All data correspond to a year in the late 1990s.

Figure 6.14 Share of primary and manufacturing exports in small states

Table 6.10 *Fall in commodity prices in real terms*

Commodity	Fall in real price in 2000 in comparison to 1980 (%)	Commodity	Fall in real price in 2000 in comparison to 1980 (%)	Commodity	Fall in real price in 2000 in comparison to 1980 (%)
Banana	−4.4	Cotton	−47.6	Coffee	−64.5
Fertiliser	−23.1	Fishmeal	−31.9	Lead	−58.3
Iron ore	−19.5	Groundnut oil	−30.9	Palm oil	−55.8
Tea	−7.5	Maize	−41.6	Rice	−60.9
Aluminium	−27.2	Soybean	−39.0	Rubber	−59.6
Coconut oil	−44.3	Wheat	−45.2	Sugar	−76.6
Copper	−30.9	Cocoa	−71.2	Tin	−73.0

Source: Oxfam estimates from IMF *International Financial Statistics Yearbook.*

Moreover, the income elasticity of demand for manufacturing exports, in general, is higher than for primary commodities, i.e. a given rise in income will result in a proportionately higher expenditure on the former. All this implies that prices of primary commodities relative to those of manufactured goods will have a long-run tendency to deteriorate in the world markets.[18]

The other obvious driving force behind the diminishing share of small states is the rapid rise in trading activities in the world economy itself in the present era of globalisation. In particular, amongst all other categories, trade in high and medium technology-intensive products has registered the most dynamic growth trends in recent times, capturing the largest share of world trade (Commonwealth Secretariat and UNCTAD, 2001) – exports of which are virtually non-existent from small states.[19]

6.5.2 A simple model of marginalisation of small states

The above discussions lead us to perceive the problem of marginalisation of small states in merchandise trade mainly from two perspectives. First, the overriding problem has been the overwhelming dependence on basic primary commodities, many of which have remained dominant since the colonial era. As the demand for these goods is income inelastic by nature, with a rise in world income there will be a natural tendency for primary exporters' share to shrink. That is, other things remaining constant, following Engel's law primary producing countries will show a natural tendency to become marginalised in an expanding global economy. On the other hand, globalisation has resulted in a rapid rise in world trade, mostly dominated by manufactured goods. But due to their inability to transform their export base, small states have not been part of this growth process. Thus, as globalisation accelerates and the same raw materials cross more borders until they are finally processed into manufactured goods, countries confined to the production of raw materials will experience marginalisation. Thus, a simple model of marginalisation of small states can be written in the following way:

$$MAR = f(AGX, GLO) \quad (1)$$

[18] This is usually known as the Singer-Prebisch theory.

[19] According to the Commonwealth Secretariat and UNCTAD (2001), the value of trade in office products now exceeds the value of agricultural trade.

where *MAR*, *AGX* and *GLO* stand respectively for marginalisation (as measured by share of merchandise exports of small states in total global merchandise exports), share of agricultural goods in total global merchandise exports and a measure of globalisation. For this study world exports–GDP ratio will be considered as an indicator of globalisation. According to our hypothesis, one should obtain a positive relationship between *MAR* and *AGX* but an inverse association between *MAR* and *GLO*. Using log-linear transformation and adding an intercept (α) as well as a stochastic error term (ε) the estimating form of (1) becomes:

$$In\ MAR = \alpha + \beta_1\ In\ AGX + \beta_2\ In\ GLO + \varepsilon \qquad (2)$$

6.5.3 Data

The share of small states in world merchandise exports is estimated from the UNCTAD database (UNCTAD, 2001). The share can be calculated for a period of fifty-one years: 1950–2000. Data on world exports of agricultural products have been taken from the Food and Agricultural Organisation (FAO) Yearbook and are available for a maximum of thirty years, thus reducing the sample to thirty years (1970–99). Using this data, the share of agricultural goods in total merchandise exports was calculated. The information on world export–GDP ratio for the whole period 1970–99 is not available from any secondary sources.[20] Therefore, the series of world GDP was constructed by using the IMF index of world GDP volume and using the World Bank estimate of world GDP in 1998.[21]

Figure 6.15 provides graphical plots of the share of agricultural commodities in world merchandise exports and world exports–GDP ratio. In 1970 world exports of agricultural products stood at US $53.5 billion, which by the end of the 1990s had grown to US $442 billion: an eight-fold

[20] The information on world exports is reported in different sources, e.g. IMF, UNCTAD and World Bank. However, the time series on world GDP cannot be obtained from any published database.

[21] According to the World Bank (2000), world GDP in 1998 stood at US $28,445 billion. Using the IMF index of world GDP volume, as given in the International Financial Statistics (IFS), the figures for other years were constructed.

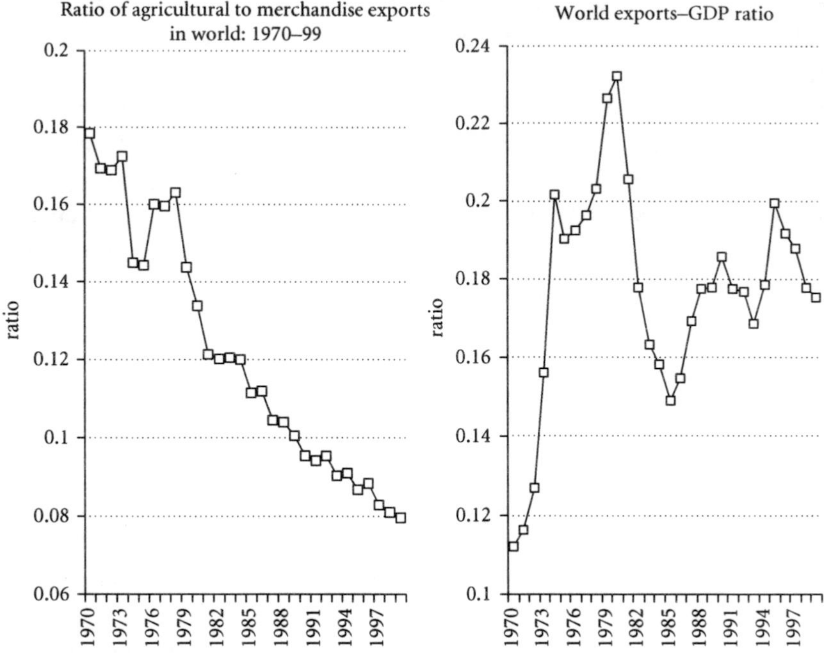

Figure 6.15 Share of agriculture in world exports and world exports–GDP ratio

increase over 1970. During the same period world merchandise exports grew by more than eighteen times despite the fact that even in 1970 the base of overall merchandise exports was about six times higher than that of agricultural exports. As a result, there has been a secular decline in the share of agriculture in total merchandise exports from about 18 per cent at the beginning of the sample to just 8 per cent in the late 1990s, as evident in the left panel of figure 6.15. The world exports–GDP ratio has a rising trend from 1970 to 2000 but it is characterised by wild fluctuations as reflected in the right panel of figure 6.15. In the 1970s world exports–GDP ratio doubled from just over 11 per cent in 1970 to about 23 per cent in 1980 as merchandise exports registered a staggering trend growth rate of 19 per cent per annum. Due to a recession in the world economy, the early 1980s onwards witnessed export growth at much slower rates and even experienced negative growth rates (i.e. decline in absolute exports), which led to a fall in the export ratio. However, from the mid-1980s the trend in world exports–GDP ratio was reversed upward again with some notable fluctuations.

6.5.4 Empirical estimation of the model

Figures 6.16 and 6.17 provide the scatterplots of the dependent and independent variables in model (2). In line with our expectations, a positive relationship between lnMAR and lnAGX (figure 6.16) and an inverse relationship between lnMAR and lnGLO (figure 6.17) are observed. Particularly, the line of the best fit for scatterplots of share of exports and agricultural exports share is fairly strong, as reflected in high R^2. Although these two figures exhibit the bi-variate relationships between the dependent and individual explanatory variables in equation (2), it is important to estimate the model carefully to ascertain that there is a 'genuine' long-run relationship between them.

6.5.4.1 Tests for unit roots and cointegration

The model in equation (2) postulates a long-run relationship between the dependent and explanatory variables based on the time series data. Recent developments in time series econometrics have demonstrated the problem of the Ordinary Least Squares (OLS) regressions in estimating models containing non-stationary variables. A time series is said to be stationary if its mean, variance and auto-covariances are independent of time. There is now compelling evidence that many time series are non-stationary and the use of OLS in estimating regression coefficients may produce spurious results. Under such circumstances the validity of the long-run relationship between the variables in the model may be questioned.[22] In other words, non-stationary time series can produce spurious correlation.[23] In order to avoid this problem it is necessary to consider the integrating properties of the variables and to use an appropriate estimation strategy. Graphical plots of the variables as given in figure 6.18 give a first-hand impression that the variables in our model may be non-stationary on their levels. However, formal tests should be employed in determining the integrating properties of the time series and to distinguish between non-stationary and stationary variables. These tests are known as the unit root tests.

[22] An OLS regression involving non-stationary variables resulting in high R^2 can also be misleading. Moreover, the estimated standard errors and test statistics for '*t*' and '*F*'-tests become non-standard, providing invalid inferences.

[23] One interesting illustration of a spurious relationship is provided by Hendry (1980) who showed a very strong positive relationship between inflation rate and the accumulation of annual rainfall in the United Kingdom.

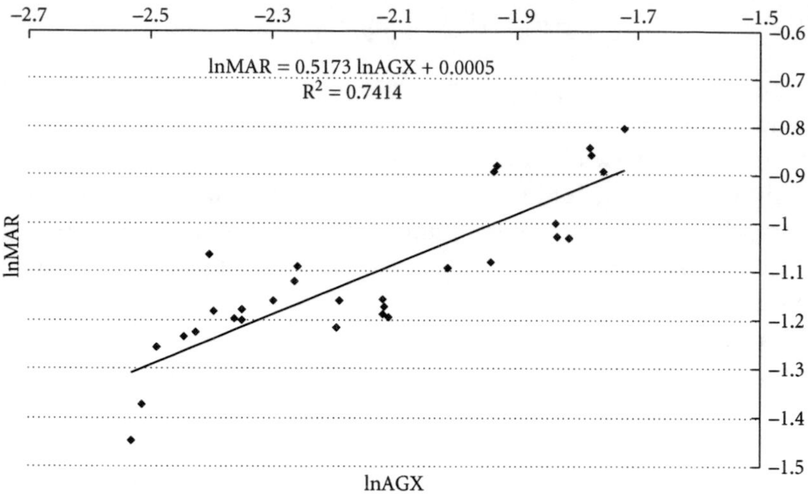

Figure 6.16 Scatterplot of lnMAR and lnAGX

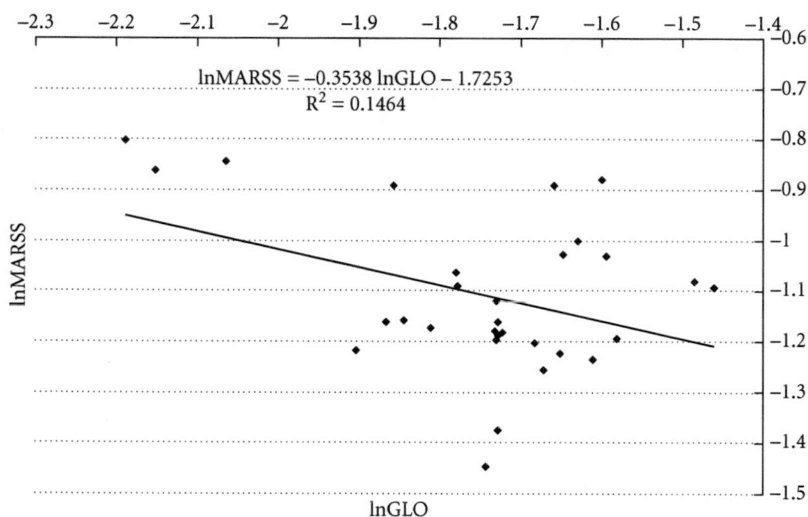

Figure 6.17 Scatterplot of lnMAR and lnGLO

6.5.4.2 Testing the variables for unit roots

First, an '*F*' test of the following form is performed on the variables in the model with the joint restrictions that $\psi = 1$ and $\chi = 0$:

$$\Delta Y_t = \tau + (\psi - 1)Y_{t-1} + \chi T + e_t \qquad (3)$$

where *Y* is the variable under consideration, Δ is first difference operator, subscript '*t*' denotes time period, *T* is the time trend and *e* is the error term. The null hypothesis in this case is that the series is non-stationary (i.e. it contains a unit root) against the alternative of stationary. The F-test values obtained for these series are presented in table 6.11. It can now be seen that the null hypothesis of non-stationary can be rejected for none of the variables as in every case the computed F-statistic falls short of its critical value.

Although the above test indicates the non-stationarity of the variables in our model, the popular methods for testing unit roots are the Dickey–Fuller (DF) and the Augmented Dickey–Fuller (ADF) tests. The DF test for unit root is also based on equation (3) with the null hypothesis of $(\psi - 1) = 0$ (i.e. Y_t is non-stationary) against the alternative of $(\psi - 1) < 0$ (i.e. Y_t is stationary). The Augmented Dickey–Fuller (ADF) test, on the other hand, is a modification of the DF test and involves augmenting equation (3) by lagged values of the dependent variables. This is done to ensure that the error process in the estimating equation is residually uncorrelated. Thus, the ADF version of the test is based on the following equation:

$$\Delta Y_t = \tau + (\psi - 1)Y_{t-1} + \chi T + \delta \Delta Y_{t-1} + e_t \quad (4)$$

The t-ratios on the estimated coefficient of Y_{t-1} in equations (3) and (4) provide the DF and ADF test statistics for the presence of a unit root. In both cases, the estimated t-ratios are non-standard and thus the computed statistics need to be compared with the corresponding critical values in order to make references regarding the stationarity of the variables. It is quite common to find that time series data are non-stationary on their levels but stationary on their first or higher order differences. Following Engle and Granger (1987), a non-stationary series is said to be integrated of order *d*, usually denoted as $\sim I(d)$, if the series can be transformed into a stationary process by differencing it *d* times.

It should be noted that although in equations (3) and (4) the trend term *T* is included, most studies in applied time series econometrics report the DF–ADF test results by including and excluding the trend term separately. When a variable is trended test statistics including the trend term is preferred. In the case of conflicting results, the ADF test is preferred to the DF.

Table 6.12 gives the results of the unit root tests. The DF and ADF test statistics for lnMAR, both with and without the trend term, are smaller than their 95 per cent critical values, suggesting the existence of a unit root

Table 6.11 *Computed F test statistics and critical values*

Variables	Computed F	Critical F	Remark
ln MAR	8.52	10.61	the variable is non-stationary
ln AGX	2.84	10.61	the variable is non-stationary
ln GLO	4.95	10.61	the variable is non-stationary

Note:
In this case the F-test is non-standard and the appropriate critical values are given by Dickey and Fuller (1981) as cited in Maddala (1992).

Table 6.12 *DF and ADF tests for unit roots*

	DF–ADF tests without the trend term		DF–ADF tests including the trend term	
Variables	DF	ADF	DF	ADF
Ln*MAR*	−0.59	−0.51	−1.87	−1.81
ΔIn*MAR*	−5.34*	−4.23*	−5.25*	−4.13*
Ln*AGX*	−0.60	−0.54	−3.08	−3.19
ΔIn*AGX*	−5.65*	−4.35*	−5.54*	−4.27*
Ln*GLO*	−3.34*	−3.98*	−3.06	−3.73*
ΔIn*GLO*	−3.13*	−3.14*	−3.22	−3.29

Notes:
(1) The 95 per cent critical values for DF–ADF tests with and without the trend term are −2.97 and −3.57 respectively. (2) Δ implies first difference of the respective variables. (3) * indicates rejection of the null-hypothesis of non-stationarity at the 95 per cent level of statistical significance.

in the level of the variable.[24] However, when the same tests are performed on the first difference of lnMAR, the null hypothesis of unit root is overwhelmingly rejected at the 95 per cent level. Hence, it can be concluded that lnMAR is non-stationary on its level but stationary on its first differences, or lnMAR is $\sim I(1)$. Similar results are also obtained for lnAGX, as all tests indicate its non-stationarity but stationarity of ΔlnAGX. That is, lnAGX is also $\sim I(1)$. The test results are, however, inconclusive for lnGLO: the DF test with the trend term contradicts the evidence arising out of other tests. Also for ΔlnGLO, DF–ADF tests with and without the trend differ. The

[24] The comparison between test statistics and critical values is made on the basis of their absolute values.

graphical plots of lnGLO and its first difference (ΔlnGLO), as given in figure 6.18, are found not to have any clear trends and hence, based on the evidence of the DF and ADF tests without the trend term, both of them can be regarded as stationary variables. In other words, lnGLO appears to be $\sim I(0)$.[25] Thus the tests seem to suggest that lnMAR and lnAGX are $\sim I(1)$, while lnGLO is $\sim I(0)$.

It needs to be mentioned that low power of the DF–ADF tests is well acknowledged in the literature and the most important problem faced when applying them is their probable poor size and power properties. This is often reflected in the tendency to over-reject the null hypothesis when it is true and under-reject it when it is false (Harris, 1995). This problem is particularly severe in the case of a small sample like ours. Thus Hall (1986) emphasises the importance of the inspection of autocorrelation function and correlogram in determining the integrating properties of the variables with short time length.

Figure 6.18 also provides the correlograms of the level and first differenced variables alongside the graphical plots of the variables.[26] For a non-stationary variable the correlograms die down only slowly whilst for a stationary variable they damp down very quickly (just on the first lag) and then give random movement. It is obvious that the correlograms of lnMAR and lnAGX behave like those of the non-stationary variables, while for ΔlnMAR and ΔlnAGX they provide random movement as is expected for stationary variables. The correlogram of lnGLO is puzzling: it dies down, demonstrating a pattern associated with positive autocorrelation, and then portrays a negative autocorrelation. The correlogram of ΔlnGLO, however, appears to represent a stationary variable. Thus correlograms cannot confirm the order of integration of lnGLO; it can be either an $I(1)$ or an $I(0)$ variable.

6.5.4.3 Estimation strategy

Once it is determined that variables in the model have integrating properties, the only way to infer a long-run relationship is to employ some kind of cointegration technique. There are several cointegration methodologies – the simplest one being the Engle–Granger two-step procedure. The basic idea behind this technique is that if two variables, say, Y_t and X_t, are both

[25] The ADF test with the trend term also supports such a conclusion.

[26] These correlograms are graphical plots of autocorrelation functions of individual variables. The autocorrelation function at lag k, denoted as p_k, is defined as the ratio of covariance at lag k divided by variance, i.e. $p_k = \gamma_k/\gamma_0$. When p_k is plotted against k, the correlogram is obtained.

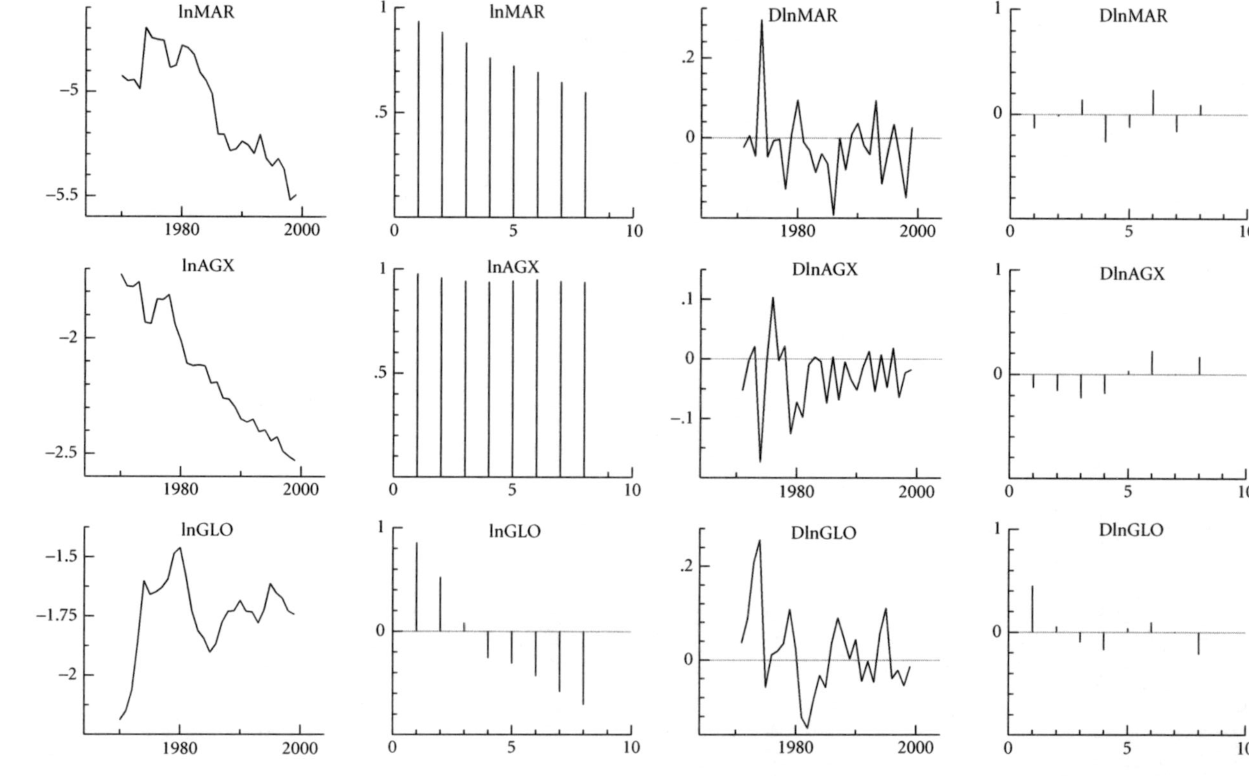

Note: The graphs are produced by using the econometric software PCFiML version 9.0 (Doornik and Hendry, 1997).

Figure 6.18 Plot of variables and their correlograms

$\sim I(d)$, a linear combination of them, such that $V_t = X_t - \theta Y_t$, in general, will also be $\sim I(d)$. Engle and Granger, however, showed that in an exceptional case if the constant θ yields an outcome where $V_t \sim I(d-a)$ and $a > 0$, then X_t and Y_t will be cointegrated. Thus if X_t and Y_t are $\sim I(1)$ they will be cointegrated and have a valid long-run relationship if the residual from the OLS regression of X_t on Y_t is $\sim I(0)$. This is the first step in the Engle–Granger procedure. On the other hand, if the variables are cointegrated there exists an error-correction model (ECM) of that cointegrating relationship, which will then give the short-run dynamics in the second step. Assuming that both Y_t and X_t are $\sim I(1)$ so that ΔY_t and ΔX_t are $\sim I(0)$, the short-run error correction model (ECM) can be represented as:

$$\triangle \ln Y_t = \pi_0 + \sum_{i=0}^{m} \pi_{1i} \triangle \ln X_t + \sum_{i=1}^{n} \pi_{2i} \triangle \ln Y_t + \pi_3 \hat{\nu}_{t-1} + \xi_t$$

where $\hat{\nu}_{t-1}$ is the lagged error from the cointegrating relationship and ξ is the white noise. It is worth noting that the ECM is not a mere regression of the stationary variables, rather it includes ν_{t-1}, the deviation from the long-run relationship. Thus the ECM captures the short-run deviations taking into account long-run information. A valid representation of the ECM will require $0 > \pi_3 \geq -1$. The usual practice with the error-correction modelling is to follow the 'general to specific' methodology by constructing a general model in the beginning and subsequently reducing it to a parsimonious form after dropping all the insignificant variables step by step.

It follows from the above that one could employ the Engle–Granger cointegration procedure to estimate equation (2) and test for a valid long-run relationship. However, since the first step of the Engle–Granger procedure is basically an OLS regression involving non-stationary variables, it yields standard errors that do not provide the basis for valid inferences. Therefore, in estimating equation 2 we cannot be certain about the statistical significance of the individual explanatory variables even when the equation turns out to be a cointegrating relationship.[27] We propose to handle this problem by using the Phillips–Hansen Fully Modified OLS (PHFMOLS) technique (Phillips and Hansen, 1990). The PHFMOLS is a method of an optimal

[27] It might be that only one of the explanatory variables is significant, resulting in a cointegrating relationship, while the other right-hand-side variable does not have any statistically significant influence on the model.

single equation technique, which is asymptotically equivalent to the maximum likelihood procedure. It makes a semi-parametric correction to the OLS estimator to eliminate the dependency on the nuisance parameters and provide standard errors that follow a standard normal distribution asymptotically and thus are valid for drawing inferences. Due to its advantages, the use of PHFMOLS has become quite popular in international trade and macroeconometric modelling.[28]

Yet another problem arising from the estimation of the long-run relationship is that unit root tests of the variables could not confirm the non-stationarity of the lnGLO variable. If lnGLO is indeed stationary on its level, there will be a mixture of $I(1)$ and I(0) variables on the right-hand side of the model, posing the question whether an $I(0)$ regressor can play any role in determining a dependent variable which is $\sim I(1)$. In a study Holden and Perman (1994) considered a model with two $I(1)$ variables and an $I(0)$ variable. The authors tested for the long-run relationship between the two $I(1)$ variables and included the $I(0)$ variable only in the short-run error-correction model. This procedure thus assumes that the $I(0)$ variable does not play a role in the long-run behaviour of the model despite the theoretical justification of including it in the equation. In contrast, Pesaran et al. (2001) have strongly argued that an $I(0)$ variable just like any other $I(1)$ variable can be equally important in the long-run relationship. Pesaran et al. have also devised a strategy which tests the existence of a long-run relationship in the presence of a mixture of $I(0)$ and $I(1)$ variables in the model. For this chapter we will use this test to determine the long-run relationship in equation (2).

6.5.4.4 Test for existence of a long-run relationship

First we apply the Pesaran et al. test to ascertain whether the model in (2) is a cointegrating relationship. This test is based on an OLS estimation of an unrestricted error-correction model, a general specification of which with respect to our model can be written as:

$$\ln MAR_t = \alpha + \Phi_1 \ln MAR_{t-1} + \Phi_2 \ln AGX_{t-1} + \Phi_3 \ln GLO_{t-1} + \sum_{i=1}^{p} \pi_i \Delta \ln MAR_{t-1} + \sum_{i=0}^{g} \pi_2 \Delta \ln AGX_{t-i} + \sum_{i=0}^{g} \pi_3 \Delta \ln GLO_{t-i} + \vartheta_t \quad (5)$$

[28] Amongst others, Athukorala and Riedel (1996), Muscatelli (1995) and Senhadji and Montenegro (1998) have used this technique for modelling trade, whilst Mallick (1999) is an example of the application of the procedure in macroeconometric modelling.

where all the variables are defined as above and the last term on the right-hand side is the white noise. Estimation of (5) in itself is not interesting since the existence of a long-run relationship can only be tested by examining the joint null hypothesis that $\Phi_1 = \Phi_2 = \Phi_3 = 0$ with the help of either a Wald or an F-test. The presence of a long-run relationship requires the rejection of this null. However, the asymptotic distribution of these test statistics is non-standard and Pesaran et al. provide the necessary critical upper (F_U) and lower bound (F_L) values for the tests.[29] The F_U statistics are derived under the assumption that all variables are $\sim I(1)$ and F_L considers all of them to be $\sim I(0)$. If the computed F-statistic (F) – obtained by restricting that $\Phi_1 = \Phi_2 = \Phi_3 = 0$ – is greater than the critical upper value, i.e. $F > F_U$, one can reject the null and conclude that there exists a valid long-run relationship between the variables in the equation. If $F < F_L$, there is no long-run relationship and, finally if $F_L < F < F_U$ the test is inconclusive. Pesaran et al. (p. 2) spell out clearly, '[I]f the computed Wald or F-statistic falls outside the critical value bounds a conclusive inference can be drawn without needing to know whether the underlying regressors are $I(1)$, cointegrated amongst themselves or individually $I(0)$.'

In order to determine the existence of a long-run relationship, equation (3) was run with $p = 1$ and $g = 0$.[30] Initial experiments suggested significant unexplained movement in residuals for 1974 and 1993 and thus the existence of a long-run relationship was tested, including two dummy variables for those two atypical years.[31] The F-test statistic arising out of the Pesaran et al. test was estimated to be 5.01 against its 95 per cent critical upper (F_U) value of 4.85. Since the computed F-statistic exceeds the critical F value, it can be concluded that the variables are cointegrated and consequently there is a valid long-run relationship among the variables in the model. In other words, the share of small states in world total export trade is genuinely influenced by the ratio of global agricultural exports to total exports and by the world exports–GDP ratio.

[29] Pesaran et al. give the critical values for both Wald and F-statistics. In this chapter we will consider only the F-statistics.

[30] Since we have a small sample, overparameterisation of the model can be very problematic in terms of having fewer degrees of freedom. Choice of such lag lengths can be rationalised by the use of annual data.

[31] Had the dummies not been inserted, the residuals would have appeared to be non-normal.

Table 6.13 *PHFMOLS estimates of the long-run relationship*

lnMAR=	-5.15^{***}	$+ 0.42^{***}$ lnAGX	$- 0.18^{**}$ lnGLO	$+ 0.17^{***}$ D74	$+ 0.21^{***}$ D93
(s.e.)	(0.17)	(0.04)	(0.07)	(0.04)	(0.05)
t-ratio	−30.9	9.89	(−2.57)	(4.17)	(3.91)
Adjusted R^2 =	0.85				

Note:
Statistical significance at the 1 and 5 per cent levels is denoted by respectively *** and **. Standard errors (s.e.) of the coefficients are reported inside the parentheses below the estimated coefficients.

6.5.4.5 Estimating the long-run relationship

We now proceed to know the exact nature of the long-run relationship by estimating the model. Since the long-run relationship was tested by inserting two dummy variables, their inclusion may be justified if they are found to be statistically significant in the long-run model. For reasons discussed earlier, the long-run relationship is estimated by the procedure of the Phillips–Hansen Fully Modified OLS (PHFMOLS). The long-run model thus estimated is reported in table 6.13.

The estimated results show that all variables are significant at the conventional level. The coefficient on lnAGX is positively signed as expected. Thus in the long run a 1 per cent fall in the share of agricultural products in world exports reduces small states' share by 0.42 per cent. The sign on lnGLO is negative, which also provides support to our hypothesis. A 1 per cent rise in world exports–GDP ratio reduces the relative importance of small states by 0.18 per cent. Both the dummies also appear to be highly significant at less than the 1 per cent level, justifying their inclusion in the model. The long-run model explains 85 per cent variation in lnMAR.

6.5.4.6 Short-run dynamics

The existence of a long-run relationship would lead to a short-run model, which we model under the framework of the error-correction modelling strategy. The error-correction model regresses the current value of the dependent variables in stationary form onto its own lagged value, current and lagged values of the stationary form of the independent variables and the lagged error term from the cointegrating equation. The general to specific methodology is used to find a parsimonious representation of the relationship. In initial experiments the model was estimated by including the first order lag of the first differences of the dependent and independent variables along with the lagged long-run errors (ECM_{t-1}). Then, most insignificant variables were deleted one by one to give the most parsimonious representation of the short-run model in table 6.14.

In the short run the indicator of globalisation is found to have a significant influence on marginalisation of small states. Like the long-run model, the sign on lnGLO in table 6.14 is negative. Interestingly, however, the short-run model fails to find any significant effect of the global agriculture–total export ratio. In the short-run there may be many other factors that are likely to affect the export performance of small states, which have not been included in the model. This is also reflected in the somewhat low explanatory power of the model as the adjusted R^2 turns out to be only 0.38. The error-correction term is correctly signed and significant, implying that the short-run model converges to long-run relationship. The coefficient on the ECM_{t-1} suggests that it takes just about two-and-a-half years to correct all short run disequilibrium errors.

For diagnostics Godfrey's (1978) LM test for serial correlation, Ramsey's (1969) RESET test for functional form, White's (1980) test for heteroscedasticity and Jarque–Bera's (1987) test for normality of errors are performed. The computed test statistics for serial correlation, functional form and heteroscedasticity follow a chi-square distribution with 1 degree of freedom, while the normality test statistic has a chi-square distribution with 2 degrees of freedom. Since the 95 per cent critical values for $\chi^2(1)$ and $\chi^2(2)$ are 3.84 and 5.99 respectively, on the basis of the computed diagnostic statistics the null hypotheses of no problem of serial correlation, no wrong functional form problem, normality of residuals and homoscedastic distribution of errors cannot be rejected at the 95 per cent level.

In this section an attempt was made to explain the deteriorating trend in the share of exports of small states in terms of agriculture – exports and exports–GDP ratios in the world economy. An examination was made of whether there existed a valid long-run relationship among the variables, as specified in the model. In light of the problems associated with the time series properties of the variables, unit roots and cointegration methodologies were used in the estimation of the equation. The results confirmed a genuine long-run relationship among the variables. In the long run as the share of agriculture in total exports fell and the share of world exports–GDP

Table 6.14 *Short-run error correction model*

$\Delta lnMAR =$	-0.28^{**}	$-0.25^{**}\Delta lnMAR_{t-1}$	$-0.25^{**}\Delta lnGLO_{t-1}$	$+0.16^{***}D93$	$-0.15^{***}D74$	$-0.44^{**}ECM_{t-1}$
(s.e.)	(0.01)	(0.10)	(0.12)	(0.05)	(0.04)	(0.22)
t-ratio	−2.78	−2.55	2.02	3.20	3.78	−2.05

Adjusted $R^2 = 0.38$	$F(5, 20) = 7.67^{***}$
Serial correlation $[\chi^2(1)] = 0.38$	Functional form $[\chi^2(1)] = 0.75$
Normality $[\chi^2(2)] = 1.16$	Heteroscedasticity $[\chi^2(1)] = 0.25$

Note:

*** and ** are for statistical significance at the 1 and 5 per cent levels respectively. The serial correlation test is based on Godfrey's (1978) LM test for serial correlation; functional form on Ramsey's (1969) RESET test; heteroscedasticity on White's (1980) test; and normality of residuals on Jarque–Bera's (1987) test.

rose, small states' share of merchandise exports shrank. The short-run dynamics were modelled following the error-correction methodology where only globalisation was found to affect relative importance of small states. The short-run model explained a relatively small variation in the dependent variable and therefore other exogenous and policy factors might have contributed to the declining importance of small states in the short run.

6.6 Implications for long-term trade and development of small states and concluding remarks

While dependence on primary products and increasing globalisation in the world economy can explain much of the trend in declining significance of small states, there are other factors that aggravate the process either by inhibiting or by not facilitating the desired favourable developments. The long-term trade and development prospects of small states critically hinge upon the interplay of these factors and without addressing them the process of marginalisation cannot be tackled. To conclude this chapter, therefore we provide some discussions on these issues below.

First, as the existing structure of the export sector does not allow small states to take full advantage of high income growth in the world economy one straightforward policy recommendation would call for diversification of their export base by aiming at production and export of manufactured goods. This option has, however, so far been proved to be a very difficult one not only for small states but also for developing countries as a whole. Although most small states have a natural comparative advantage in the production of primary products, many of them in the past pursued an inward-looking import-substitution strategy in order to facilitate the formation of a manufacturing industrial base in the domestic economy. The import-substituting industries developed under a protective regime remained inefficient and, in the face of severe external and internal imbalances which confronted many small states, the policies for trade liberalisation and reforms were carried out. Since the import-substitution regime resulted in policy-induced biases against agriculture, a policy reversal to export-promotion strategy only revived the static comparative advantage of primary commodities. Thus the export structure remained ossified in many states and continued to be dominated by primary commodities, thereby leaving the process of marginalisation uninterrupted.

Second, due to the small size of the domestic market an efficient manufacturing industrial base in small states can only flourish depending on international trade.[32] Small states are, however, frequently confronted by other natural barriers to trade associated with unfavourable geographical characteristics (such as remoteness, isolation and physical dispersion of small pockets of population), which increase the costs of both export and import trade relative to countries with more favourable geographical characteristics. Small states pay higher transportation costs because of geographical locations, small volume of cargo, bulky low-value products (e.g. agricultural commodities) and lack of equivalent return cargo. The figures quoted in Bernal (2001) show that transportation and freight costs for some small states are as high as 30 per cent of export volume compared to only 4 per cent for large states. These excessive costs alone can serve to make small states' exports uncompetitive. There is evidence that a 10 per cent increase in transport costs reduces trade volumes by about 20 per cent (Limão and Venables, 2001). This has some serious consequences for small states as Redding and Venables (2001) show that *ad valorem* transport costs of 20 per cent on both final output and intermediate goods reduce the domestic value added (and thus GDP) by 60 per cent when intermediate goods account for 50 per cent of costs.[33] As excessive transport costs substantially reduce the domestic value added out of the production of export goods dependent on imported inputs, it not only affects international competitiveness but also discourages foreign firms from relocating their production to these countries even when the wages are low.[34]

Third, most small states also suffer from a poor state of physical and social infrastructure (human capital), the development of which is considered to be vital for expanding productive capacities and particularly for exporting the manufactured goods that have witnessed rapid growth in world trade. However, infrastructure development is very expensive and requires long-term investment. Given the current level of income and domestic savings, the development of infrastructure and the level of

[32] Small size of the domestic market does not allow firms to exploit either internal economies of scale (i.e. where unit cost is reduced as the size of the firm gets bigger) or external economies of scale (i.e. where unit cost is influenced by the size of the industry).

[33] This is compared to a country that faces zero transport costs. Redding and Venables revealed that more than 70 per cent of variation in cross-country per capita income could be explained by the geography of access to markets and sources of supply of intermediate inputs.

[34] Note that domestic value added includes, amongst others, profits of the entrepreneurs.

Table 6.15 *Official financial flows (millions of US dollars)*

	Total flows		Total ODA	
Year	Developing countries	Small states	Developing countries	Small states
1975	21,905	982	16,142	865
1980	42,591	1,693	32,460	1,505
1985	41,019	1,730	30,180	1,353
1990	74,122	2,872	56,036	2,427
1995	70,725	1,792	58,706	1,811
1999	79,165	950	50,543	1,076

Source: Authors' estimate from UNCTAD (2001).

domestic investment in many small states will critically depend on the inflow of official development assistance (ODA). The inflow of ODA from the developed countries to small states, however, witnessed a major decline in the 1990s.[35] From the data given in table 6.15 it is found that during the late 1990s the flow of ODA to developing countries and small states declined absolutely. However, while developing countries, on the whole, managed to enjoy increased total financial flows from about US $74 billion in 1990 to about US $79 billion in 1999, small states saw the flow going down by about 67 per cent.

Perhaps the most obvious and important source of financing domestic investment for manufacturing activities is the inflow of foreign direct investment (FDI). During 1990–2000 world FDI inflow grew at a trend rate of 14.2 per cent whereas the comparable rate for small states was computed at 9.57 per cent.[36] Figure 6.19 shows that small states' share in FDI inflow decreased from a high of about 2.5 per cent of total FDI in 1972 to less than 0.5 per cent in 2000, with a clear negative long-term trend persisting.[37]

Fourth, for a long time small states have benefited from the preferential access given to them under various arrangements. The evolving trading system, however, either has reduced the preferential trade margins for these countries or threatens to erode the preferences altogether. For

35 It needs to be mentioned that the flow of ODA to LDCs also declined in the 1990s.

36 For the period 1990–2000 the trend growth rates of FDI inflow into developed and developing countries are estimated to be 13.63 and 15.10 per cent respectively.

37 The estimated trend line indicates a declining trend rate of 4.19 per cent.

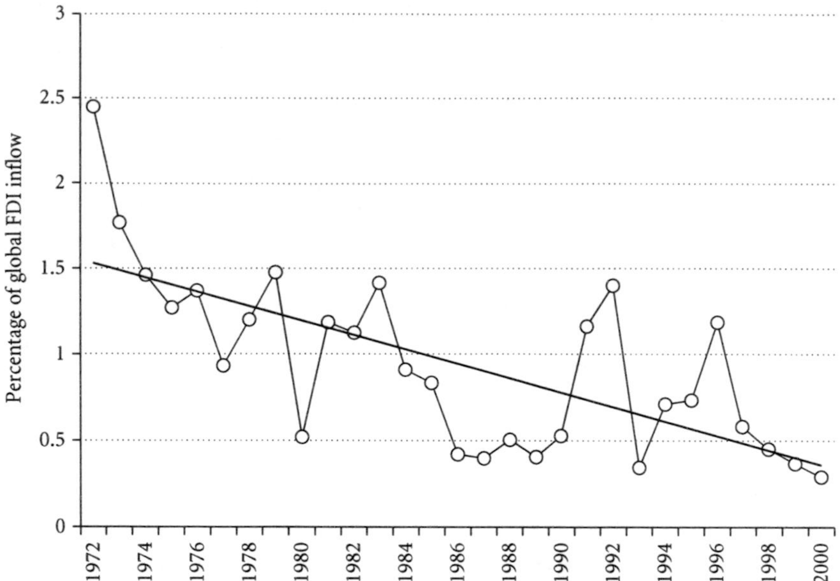

Note: The straight line is the linear trend equation fitted to the data.
Source: Authors' estimates from UNCTAD (2002).
Figure 6.19 Share of small states in global inflow of FDI

example, in the post-Uruguay Round average tariffs on industrial goods stood at only 3.9 per cent, providing a very low margin of preference to the recipient countries. Again, under the Lomé Convention many small states have enjoyed preferential trade margins extended by the EU, which have become incompatible under the WTO regime.[38] WTO compatibility of these provisions will require substantial opening up of the sectors currently protected for the beneficiary countries.[39] As a consequence, the net economic effect of the Uruguay Round trade liberalisation upon the highly trade-preference-dependent economies is found to be negative (Grynberg, 2001). Therefore, it appears that the global trading regime

[38] Grynberg (2001) provides a detailed discussion on this.

[39] Some small states are heavily dependent on various commodity arrangements with the EU. These typically cover exports from small states that would not be competitive in the world market, but are of major economic and social importance to these countries. For example, the Sugar Protocol offers valuable protection to St Kitts and Nevis, where sugar revenue accounts for about 50 per cent of GDP. In light of the problem of WTO incompatibility, these arrangements are being renegotiated and revised, resulting in considerable erosion of trade preferences to small states (Berthelot, 2001).

under the WTO will have further negative consequences on exports and trade of small states.[40]

Last but not least, factors associated with the internal or domestic economy in many small states have adversely affected their export trade. Improper interventions resulting in inefficiencies and leading to wastage of resources, social and political unrest creating a domestic environment hostile to investment and production, inefficient and lengthy bureaucratic procedures along with corruption causing high transaction costs, etc., all act in concert to make the costs of doing business very high, which, in turn, reduces the competitiveness of tradable activities. In fact, the importance of an investment-friendly domestic economy backed by sound macroeconomic management is more crucial in small states as they face some natural disadvantages, which retard investment. Based on the Country Policy and Institutional Assessment (CPIA) of the World Bank, Collier and Dollar (2001) show that, just like the large states, there is a positive relationship between good policy and economic growth. While good governance may not in itself attract investment to locations that are structurally disadvantaged, nevertheless the role of internal factors in export success cannot be overemphasised.

Small states pose a challenge to the international community in the process of globalisation. They point to the fact that increased integration and rising trade and investment in the world economy may not benefit them substantially. The experience of marginalisation in world trade is mainly associated with the inability to diversify exports. Most small states face disadvantages in diversification that stem not only from high unit costs of production but also from a small, narrow and specialised resource base. Between these endowed handicaps and a global policy framework which has emphasised the maintenance of static comparative advantage, diversification into dynamic sectors may initially be of marginal economic viability. Therefore, an important source of funds for diversification must be the international community. Without trade diversification away from traditional exports, globalisation will almost certainly continue to be skewed in favour of those larger states which are better able to respond to market

[40] However, it needs to be noted that while trade preferences have been vital in assisting small economies to diversify production away from traditional monocrops (e.g. in Mauritius), they have at the same time provided incentives not to diversify away from highly preference-dependent exports. Certain quota-dependent preferences such as those which exist for sugar and bananas have provided significant incentives for the continuation of production of particular crops long after the economic necessity for such preferences has disappeared.

signals. While the Bretton Woods institutions have correctly advised small states that establishing a stable and market-friendly policy environment is an absolutely necessary condition to attract the investment needed to assure diversification, this is not a sufficient condition. Only when the international community begins to recognise that market-friendly interventions are necessary to assist small states to diversify their export base will the process of marginalisation be arrested. Failing such a shift in policy, marginalisation will only serve to erode support for globalisation in small states.

Appendix 6.1 *List of small states*

Sl. No.	Country	Remark	Commonwealth member?
1	Antigua and Barbuda		yes
2	**The Bahamas**	**data problem**	yes
3	Bahrain	OIL	
4	Barbados		yes
5	Belize		yes
6	Botswana		yes
7	Cape Verde	LDC	
8	Comoros	LDC	
9	Cyprus		
10	Djibouti	LDC	
11	Dominica		yes
12	Equatorial Guinea	OIL/LDC	
13	Fiji		yes
14	Gabon	OIL	
15	The Gambia	LDC	yes
16	Grenada		yes
17	Guyana		yes
18	Jamaica		yes
19	Kiribati	LDC	yes
20	Lesotho	LDC	yes
21	Maldives	LDC	yes
22	Malta		
23	Mauritius		yes
24	**Namibia**	**data problem**	yes
25	Papua New Guinea		yes
26	Samoa	LDC	yes
27	São Tomé and Principe	LDC	
28	Seychelles		yes
29	Solomon Islands	LDC	yes
30	St Kitts and Nevis		yes
31	St Lucia		yes
32	St Vincent and the Grenadines		yes
33	Suriname		

Appendix 6.1 (*cont.*)

Sl. No.	Country	Remark	Commonwealth member?
34	Swaziland		yes
35	Tonga		yes
36	Trinidad and Tobago	OIL	yes
37	Tuvalu	data not available/LDC	yes
38	Vanuatu	LDC	yes

Note:
The list of small states is taken from Atkin et al. (2001). The Bahamas and Namibia are actually excluded from the data set due to data problems.

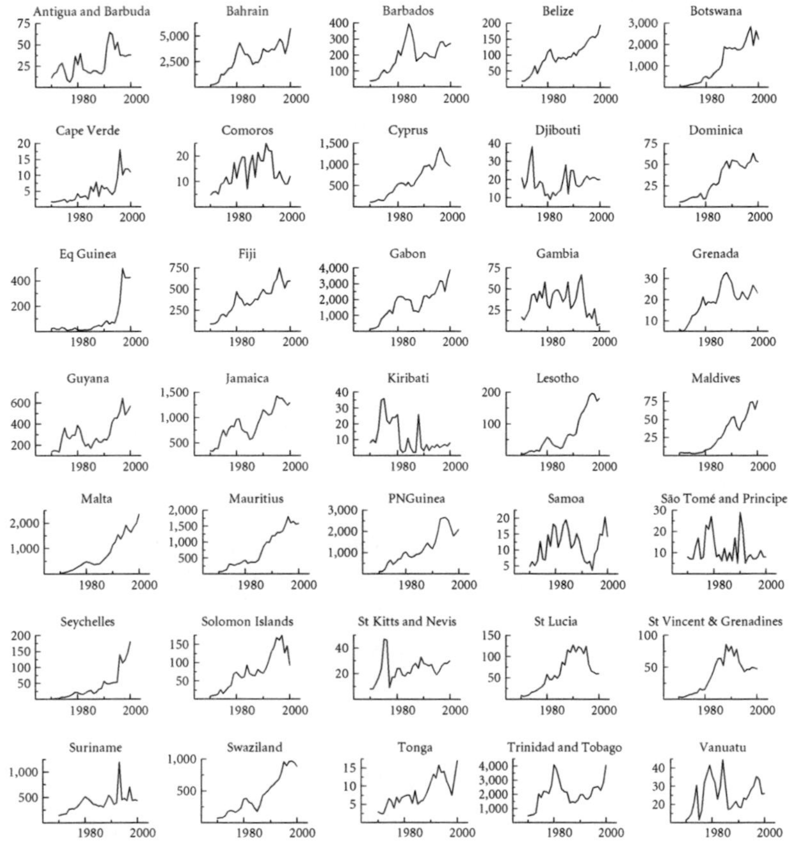

Note: All exports are in millions of US dollars.
Appendix 6.2 Merchandise exports from small states

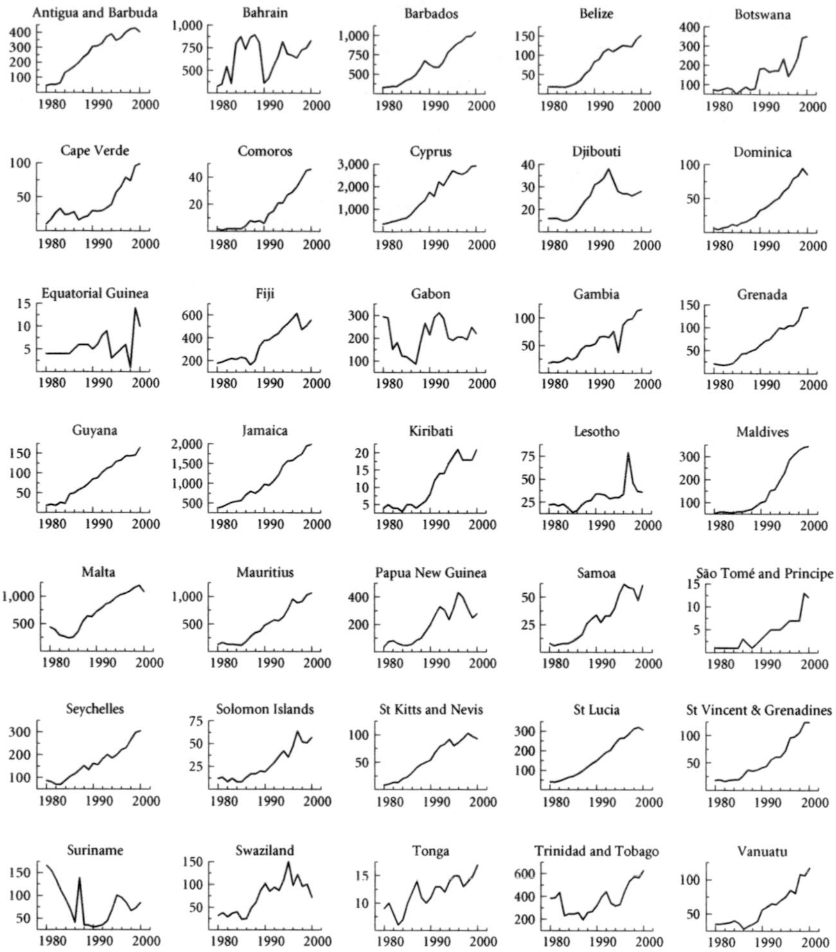

Note: Commercial services exports are given in millions of US dollars.

Appendix 6.3 Commercial services exports from small states

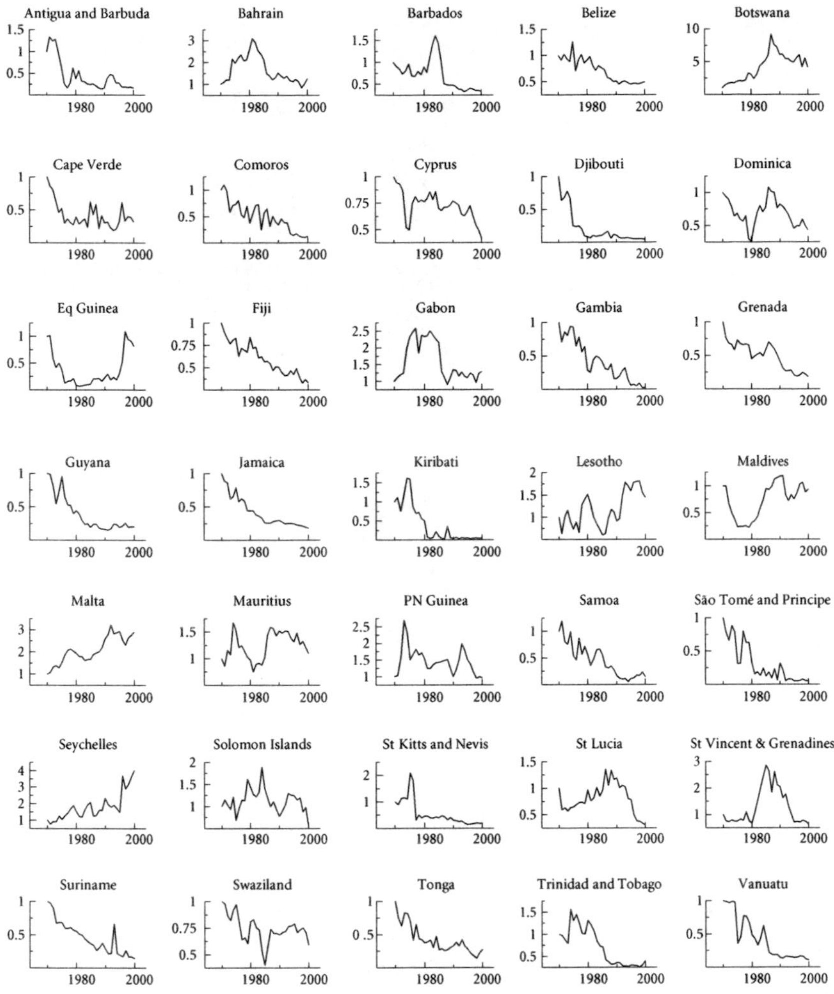

Appendix 6.4 Share of individual small states in world merchandise exports (share in 1970 = 1)

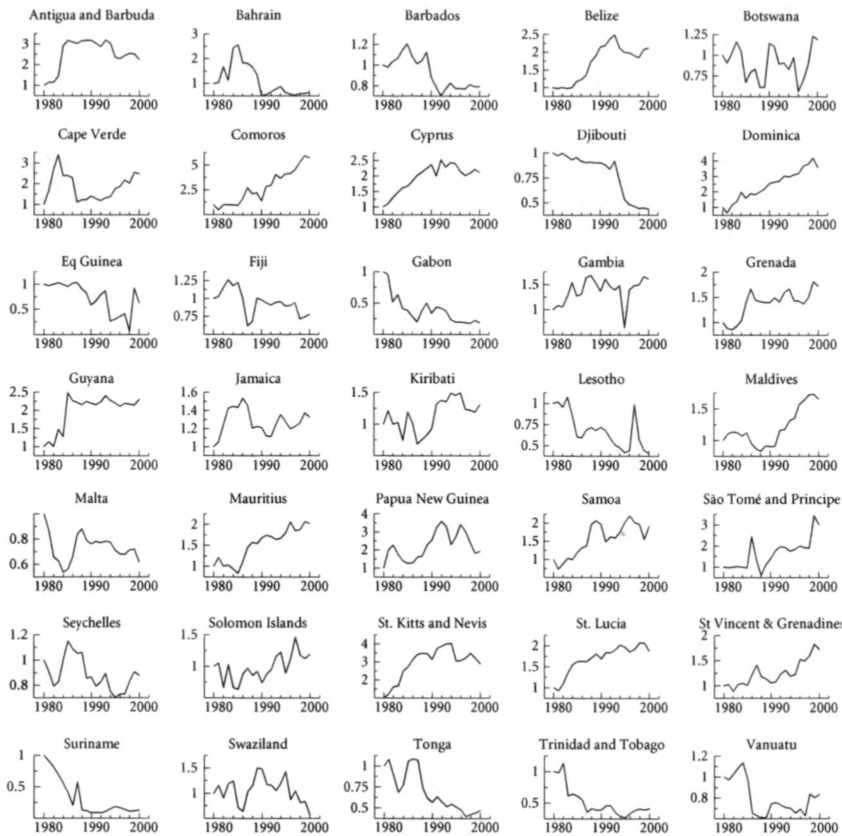

Appendix 6.5 Share of individual small states in world commercial services exports (share in 1980 = 1)

References

Amjadi, A. and Yeats, A. (1995), 'Have Transport Costs Contributed to the Relative Decline of African Exports? Some Preliminary Evidence', *World Bank Policy Research Working Paper*, World Bank, Washington, D.C.

Atkins, J. P., Mazzi, S. and Easter, C. D. (2000), *A Commonwealth Vulnerability Index for Developing Countries: The Position of Small States*, Economic Paper 40, Commonwealth Secretariat, London

Banerjee, A., Dolado, J. J., Galbraith, J. W. and Hendry, D. F. (1993), *Cointegration, Error-Correction and the Econometric Analysis of Non-Stationary Data*, Oxford University Press

Bernal, R. L. (2001), 'Globalisation and Small Developing Economies: Challenges and opportunities', in D. Peretz, R. Faruqi and E. J. Kisanga (eds.), *Small States in the Global Economy*, Commonwealth Secretariat and World Bank

Berthelot, P. (2001), 'Small States in the Lomé Convention and in the New ACP–EU Partnership Agreement: A Commentary', *Small States: Economic Review and Basic Statistics*, vol. 6, Commonwealth Secretariat, London

Bora, B., Grynberg, R. and Razzaque, M. A. (forthcoming), 'Marginalisation of LDCs and Small States in World Trade', EAD Work in Progress Paper, Commonwealth Secretariat, London

Collier, P. and Dollar, D. (2001), 'Aid, Risk and the Special Concerns of Small States', in D. Peretz, R. Faruqi and E. J. Kisanga (eds.), *Small States in the Global Economy*, Commonwealth Secretariat and World Bank

Commonwealth Secretariat (1997), *A Future for Small States: Overcoming Vulnerability*, Report by a Commonwealth Advisory Group

Commonwealth Secretariat/World Bank (2000), *Small States: Meeting Challenges in the Global Economy*, Report of the Commonwealth Secretariat/World Bank Joint Task Force on Small States

Dickey, D. and Fuller, W. A. (1979), 'Distribution of the Estimators for Autoregressive Time Series with a Unit Root', *Journal of American Statistical Association*, vol. 74, pp. 427–33

(1981), 'Likelihood Ratio Statistics for Autoregressive Time Series with a Unit Root', *Econometrica*, vol. 49, pp. 1057–72

Engle, R. F. and Granger, C. W. J. (1987), 'Cointegration and Error-correction: Representation, Estimation and Testing', *Econometrica*, vol. 55, pp. 251–76

Godfrey, L. G. (1978), 'Testing for Higher Order Serial Correlation in Regression Equations when the Regressors Include Lagged Dependent Variables', *Econometrica*, vol. 46, pp. 1293–1301

Grynberg, R. (2001), 'Trade Policy Implications for Small Vulnerable States of the Global Trade Regime Shift', in D. Peretz, R. Faruqi and E. J. Kisanga (eds.), *Small States in the Global Economy*, Commonwealth Secretariat and World Bank

Grynberg, R., Ognistev, V. and Razzaque, M. A. (2002), 'The Cost of Accession to the WTO: A Comparative Assessment of Services Sectoral Commitments by WTO Members and Acceding Countries', EAD Working Paper, Commonwealth Secretariat, London

Gylfason, T. (1999), 'Exports, Inflation and Growth', *World Development*, vol. 27, no. 6, pp. 1031–57

Hall, S. (1986), 'An Application of the Granger and Engle Two-Step Estimation Procedure to United Kingdom Aggregate Wage Data', *Oxford Bulletin of Economics and Statistics*, vol. 48, no. 3, pp. 229–40

Hendry, D. F. (1979), 'Predictive Failure and Econometric Modelling in Macroeconomics: The Transaction Demand for Money', in P. Ormerod (ed.), *Economic Modelling: Current Issues and Problems in Macroeconomic Modelling in the UK and the USA*, London

(1980), 'Econometrics – Alchemy or Science', *Economica*, vol. 47, pp. 387–406

Hughes, A. and Brewster, H. (2002), *Lowering the Threshold: Reducing the Cost and Risk of Private Direct Investment in Least Developed, Small and Vulnerable Economies*, Commonwealth Secretariat, London

International Monetary Fund (2000), *International Financial Statistics Yearbook*, IMF, Washington, D.C.

Jarque, C. M. and Bera, A. K. (1980), 'Efficient Tests for Normality, Homoscedasicity and Serial Independence of Regression Residuals', *Economics Letters*, vol. 6, pp. 255–9

Johansen, S. and Juselius, K. (1990), 'Maximum Likelihood Estimation and Inference on Cointegration with Applications to the Demand for Money', *Oxford Bulletin of Economics and Statistics*, vol. 52, pp. 169–210

Limão, N. and Venables, A. J. (2001), 'Infrastructure, Geographical Disadvantage, Transport Costs, and Trade', *World Bank Economic Review*, vol. 15, pp. 451–79

Maddala, G. (1992), *Introduction to Econometrics*, 2nd edn, Macmillan

Pesaran, M. H, Shin, Yongcheol and Smith, Richard J. (2001), 'Bound Testing Approaches to the Analysis of Level Relationships', *Journal of Applied Econometrics*, special issue in honour of J. D. Sargan on the theme 'Studies in Empirical Macroeconometrics', edited by D. F. Hendry and M. H. Pesaran, pp. 289–326

Ramsey, J. B. (1969), 'Test for Specification Errors in Classical Linear Least Square Regression Analysis', *Journal of the Royal Statistical Society*, pp. 350–71

Redding, S. and Venables, A. J. (2001), 'Economic Geography and International Inequality', paper accessed from http://econ.lse.ac.uk/staff/ajv

Reinhart, C. M. and Wickham, P. (1994), 'Commodity Prices: Cyclical Weakness or Secular Decline?', *IMF Staff Papers*, vol. 41, no. 2, pp. 175–213

UNCTAD (1996), *The Least Developed Countries 1996 Report*, UNCTAD, Geneva

(1997), *The Least Developed Countries 1997 Report*, UNCTAD, Geneva

(1998), *The Least Developed Countries 1998 Report*, UNCTAD, Geneva

(1999), *The Least Developed Countries 1999 Report*, UNCTAD, Geneva

(2001), *World Investment Report 2001: Promoting Linkages*, United Nations, New York and Geneva

(2002), *UNCTAD Handbook of Statistics 2002*, UNCTAD, Geneva

White, H. (1980), 'A Heteroscedasticity Consistent Variance Matrix Estimator and a Direct Test of Heteroscedasticity', *Econometrica*, vol. 48, pp. 817–18

World Bank (1994), *Global Economic Prospects and the Developing Countries 1994*, World Bank, Washington, D.C.

(2000), *World Development Indicators*, CD-Rom, World Bank, Washington, D.C.

7

Small economies and special and differential treatment: strengthening the evidence, countering the fallacies

VIRGINIA HORSCROFT

7.1 Introduction

Small economies present a particular challenge to the multilateral trade regime: will it adjust to arrest their increasing marginalisation in world trade that is undermining their development prospects significantly? This challenge poses the question of whether emerging international trade rules are damaging the trade and development interests of small economies and, if so, whether derogations from those rules can avert such damage. An answer that more favourable treatment offers small economies the potential for a beneficial means of insertion in world markets is incomplete, however, without considering the negotiating context from which trade rules emerge. Whether favourable treatment is likely to result from the interstate bargaining process determining the rules is the more problematic aspect of the challenge small economies pose for the multilateral trading system.

This chapter argues that the peculiar economic characteristics of small economies combine to constrain their potential to benefit from the globalisation of markets under currently agreed trade rules. Though supported by recent empirical evidence, these arguments are contentious[1] and require engaging with contrary views refuting that small size undermines trade competitiveness, that vulnerability to external economic shocks and natural disasters has real economic costs, and that small economies' characteristics are peculiar and worthy of specific responses. The chapter goes on

[1] See Briguglio (1995: 1615–20), Encontre (1999: 265), WTO (1999), UNCTAD (2004a) and Grynberg (2001a: 289–91) for sympathetic reviews of small economies' special concerns, and Srinivasan (1986), Streeten (1993), Easterly and Kraay (2001) and Page and Kleen (2004: 82) for opposing reviews.

to argue that, as the implications of emerging trade rules are realised, the marginalisation of small economies will be exacerbated. Whilst modifying multilateral trade rules is not the only initiative required to address the specific trade and development needs of small economies, it is argued to be vital. The likely economic decline of these states in the absence of favourable treatment will undermine the legitimacy of the multilateral trade regime, particularly its assumption that trade liberalisation on the basis of agreed rules is mutually advantageous. The more significant difficulty, this chapter suggests, is not demonstrating this predicament convincingly but achieving the necessary response as an outcome of trade negotiating processes. Here, the special characteristics of small economies undermine their bargaining power and likelihood of achieving beneficial outcomes from the interstate negotiating processes that determine global trade rules. The chapter concludes that it is not necessarily the case that agreed and emerging international trade rules are beneficial for all states: small economies can make a development case for more favourable treatment.

The economies considered 'small' for the purposes of this chapter are listed in table 7.1, alongside their key economic indicators.[2]

7.2 The costs of being small

When trading internationally in a real world characterised by cross-border transaction costs, size *does* matter. Indeed being small, economically, is a meaningful concept only where transaction costs make national economies distinct entities. Thus, being small is integrally related to remoteness and insularity:[3] a small nation perfectly integrated into a larger contiguous market may not be small economically,[4] but a remote or insular nation facing significant transport costs may be. Once the size of its domestic market matters, the trade predicament of a small economy will be

[2] This chapter does not aim to address the appropriate delineation of small economies; such discussions can be found in Davenport (2001: 1–2), Atkins et al. (2000: 4), Hein (2004), Read (1999: 2–5) and Encontre (2004). The list in table 7.1 is of independent developing states with populations under the standard threshold of 1.5 million, excluding those with GNI per capita above US $9,386 ('high income' in World Bank terminology), but including those above the population threshold identified by the Commonwealth Secretariat as exhibiting similar 'small' characteristics (Botswana, Jamaica, Lesotho, Namibia and Papua New Guinea).

[3] Salmon (2003: 133). [4] Winters and Martins (2004a: 148).

Table 7.1 *Small economies and key economic indicators*

Small economy	Population 2003 ('000s)	Land area (km²)	Total GDP 2003 ($US millions)	World trade share 2000 (%)	UN EVI[a] 2000 (ranking)	Cmwlth CVI[b] 2000 (ranking)	Per capita GNI 2003 ($US)	LDC	SIDS	WTO
Antigua and Barbuda	79	442	757	0.0061	73	8	9,160		✓	✓
Barbados	271	430	2,628	0.0183	82	37	9,270		✓	✓
Belize	259	22,696	928	0.0057	77	22	3,190			✓
Bhutan	874	47,000	645	0.0028	65	20	660	✓		obs
Botswana	1,722	581,730	7,388	0.0350		29	3,430	LLDC		✓
Cape Verde	470	4,033	831	0.0029	16	23	1,490	✓	✓	obs
Comoros	600	2,235	323		24	16	450	✓	✓	
Djibouti	705	23,200	625	0.0032	47	15	910	✓		✓
Dominica	71	751	255	0.0020	18	6	3,360		✓	✓
Equatorial Guinea	494	28,051	2,894		22	7	930	✓		obs
Fiji	835	18,274	2,251	0.0155	80	25	2,360		✓	✓
Gabon	1,344	267,668	5,605	0.0327	39	54	3,580			✓
Gambia	1,421	11,295	386	0.0035	5	10	310	✓		✓
Grenada	105	344	439	0.0034	60	11	3,790		✓	✓
Guinea-Bissau	1,489	36,125	236	0.0011	19		140	✓		✓
Guyana	769	214,969	742	0.0095	34	17	900			✓
Jamaica	2,640	10,990	7,817	0.0506	94	53	2,760		✓	✓
Kiribati	96	726	58		1	4	880	✓	✓	
Lesotho	1,793	30,355	1,135	0.0065	28	31	590	✓		✓
Maldives	293	298	696	0.0058	92	9	2,300	✓	✓	✓
Marshall Islands	53	181	106				2,710		✓	

Table 7.1 (*cont.*)

Small economy	Population 2003 ('000s)	Land area (km^2)	Total GDP 2003 ($US millions)	World trade share 2000 (%)	UN EVI[a] 2000 (ranking)	Cmwlth CVI[b] 2000 (ranking)	Per capita GNI 2003 ($US)	LDC	SIDS	WTO
Mauritius	1,225	2,040	5,225	0.0342	86	47	4,090		✓	✓
Federated States of Micronesia	125	702	241				2,090		✓	
Namibia	2,015	824,292	4,658	0.0263		46	1,870			✓
Nauru	13	21							✓	
Palau	20	459	132				7,500		✓	
Papua New Guinea	5,502	462,840	3,395	0.0301	70	55	510		✓	✓
St Kitts and Nevis	47	261	370	0.0025	37	13	6,880		✓	✓
St Lucia	161	539	693	0.0050	15	18	4,050		✓	✓
St Vincent and the Grenadines	109	388	371	0.0024	32	14	3,300		✓	✓
Samoa	178	2,831	323	0.0012	29	5	1,600	✓	✓	obs
São Tomé and Principe	157	964	54		8	1	320	✓	✓	obs
Seychelles	84	455	720	0.0064	14	21	7,480		✓	obs
Solomon Islands	457	28,896	257	0.0018	27	12	600	✓	✓	✓
Suriname	438	163,265	952	0.0058	59	24	1,990			✓
Swaziland	1,106	17,364	1,845	0.0127	87	19	1,350	LLDC		✓
Timor-Leste	810	14,874	314				430	✓	✓	
Tonga	102	650	163	0.0009	11	3	1,490		✓	obs
Trinidad and Tobago	1,313	5,130	10,201	0.0408	78	62	7,260		✓	✓

Tuvalu	10	26			2			✓	✓	
Vanuatu	210	12,189	283	0.0019	71	2	1,180	✓	✓	obs
Averages				0.3766 *(Sum)*						
Small economies	743	69,268	1,716				2,748			
All least developed countries	14,348	411,629	4,736				310			
All middle income countries	32,151	740,280	64,468				1,920			
High income OECD countries	38,068	1,265,457	1,177,779				29,310			
World	30,152	626,436	174,790				5,500			

LLDC – recognised by the UN as a landlocked developing country, but not as a least developed country (LDC); obs – country has 'Observer' status in the WTO

[a] United Nations 'Economic Vulnerability Index'

[b] Commonwealth Secretariat 'Commonwealth Vulnerability Index'

Source: World Bank (2004), Commonwealth Secretariat (2003), Atkins et al. (2000), WTO (2004), UNCTAD (2003c) and UNCTAD (2004c)

compounded by the importance of economies of scale in production.[5] Where transaction costs impede trade, small economies will have limited opportunities to benefit from globalising markets.

To understand the logic of the predicament facing small developing economies, consider a state with a small domestic market that faces significant trade transaction costs. Its small domestic market arises from its small population and associated low total GDP. Being small contributes to high transport costs via low and infrequent volumes, costs exacerbated by remoteness or insularity.[6] Simple economic models can demonstrate that transport costs can stop trade from being feasible in such scenarios.[7] If limited trade continues, imports of production inputs will bear an excess cost from transport and, where transaction costs prohibit such imports, inputs will be produced domestically at high per unit costs given the small domestic market and consequent inability to exploit economies of scale. Similarly, non-tradable goods like roads and the protection of property rights will be produced domestically at high per unit costs. Wherever higher production and export costs outweigh small states' differential advantages over competitors, even in areas of comparative advantage, their exports will require premium prices in world markets to sell at all.[8]

Comprehensive data have now been compiled substantiating this trade predicament of small economies. Analysis by Winters and Martins (2004a) provides strong evidence that businesses in small states face large and significant cost inflation factors relative to firms in the median state, sufficient to undermine their potential for competitiveness even in areas of comparative advantage.[9] Summary results, presented in table 7.2, indicate that cost inflation factors in micro-states exceed 50 per cent in six of eleven key production inputs, and for small states exceed 30 per cent in five of the inputs, relative to the median state. These detrimental competitiveness implications are captured in the cost inflation factors calculated for representative electronics, garments and tourism businesses (table 7.3): garments manufacturing costs in micro-states are estimated to exceed those in the median state by 36.3 per cent, whilst tourism services costs in small states are estimated to exceed

[5] Winters and Martins (2004a: 8). [6] See Briguglio (1995: 1617).

[7] Winters and Martins (2004a: 3–8); see also Srinivasan (1986: 211).

[8] Winters and Martins (2004a: 1).

[9] Winters and Martins (2004a: 130–47), using various indicators of policy quality, find no evidence that economic policy is worse in small states than in large, and thus reject the hypothesis that the revealed inefficiencies are self-inflicted.

Table 7.2 *Production cost inflation in micro- and small economies*

Area of cost[a]	Micro[b]	Small[c]
Airfreight average	31.8	4.1
Seafreight average	219.6	70.5
Unskilled wages average	60.1	31.6
Semi-Skilled wages average	22.4	12.1
Skilled wages average	38.0	20.3
Telephone marginal costs	98.5	47.2
Electricity marginal costs	93.1	47.0
Water marginal costs	0.0	0.0
Fuel average	53.8	28.3
Personal air travel average	115.7	56.8
Land rent average	−3.5	−17.2

[a] All figures show the percentage deviation of costs from those in the median economy

[b] 'Micro' economy estimates are based on Anguilla (population approximately 12,000)

[c] 'Small' economy estimates are based on Vanuatu (population approximately 200,000)

(source uses 'Very Small' for Vanuatu estimates, and 'Small' for economies the size of Singapore (population approximately 4 million), which well exceeds 'small' in this chapter)

Source: Winters and Martins (2004a: 102–3)

those in the median state by 28.5 per cent. Winters and Martins (2004a: 118–24) illustrate the damaging implications of their findings by calculating the resultant returns to factors of production in the likely scenario that small states are price-takers in world markets, taking import costs as given and receiving the world price for their exports. Using the example of electronic assembly in a micro-state, if infrastructure services costs are also fixed,[10] exports could not be competitive unless capital made losses larger than its profits in the median state or, if capital were remunerated, would not be competitive even if labour earned zero wages. Even in small states, if capital is the residual factor, it must earn near-zero returns if exports in any of the three example industries are to be competitive at world prices (see table 7.4). Winters and Martins (2004a: 119) describe their findings as 'devastating'.

[10] Winters and Martins (2004a: 120) argue that this assumption is reasonable, given that the costs recorded in the dataset approximate general equilibrium results.

Table 7.3 *Cost inflation factors in micro- and small economies*

Industry[a]	Micro[b]	Small[c]
Electronic assembly	36.4	14.3
Clothing	36.3	14.3
Hotels and tourism	57.5	28.5

[a, b, c] See table 7.2

Source: Winters and Martins (2004a: 119)

Table 7.4 *Penalties to value-added in micro- and small economies*

Factor of production bearing penalty[a]	Electronics		Clothing		Tourism	
	Micro[b]	Small[c]	Micro[b]	Small[c]	Micro[b]	Small[c]
All domestic supplies	−38.8	−11.6	−40.1	−12.0	−36.2	−17.4
Value added	−88.0	−29.2	−86.0	−28.6	−71.9	−34.0
Capital	−245.1	−91.8	−263.9	−99.9	−202.1	−98.4
Labour	−175.5	−62.5	−161.0	−57.3	−116.5	−56.6

[a, b, c] See table 7.2

Source: Winters and Martins (2004a: 119)

These data make concrete the substantial economic costs of being small and remote,[11] challenging the argument that being small is not a disadvantage in a globalising world.[12] They also challenge ubiquitous assertions that services are less affected by transport and scale costs in small economies,[13] offering evidence that services exports can be subject to even higher cost inflation factors than goods exports.[14] The findings demonstrate the insufficiency of policy recommendations for small states to specialise in their areas of comparative advantage and trade their way to higher welfare levels. Indeed, argue Winters and Martins (2004b: 4), comparative advantage need not be enough. Small states, like all states, have comparative advantages; what sets them apart is that even if they specialise in these, trade transaction costs and the inherent inefficiencies of small size may prevent trade from being remunerative. Without remunerative returns to

[11] Winters and Martins (2004a: 102). [12] See Page and Kleen (2004: 82) and Read (2004: 368).

[13] See World Bank (2002a: 16) and Page and Kleen (2004: 81–3).

[14] Winters and Martins (2004a: 113–16).

capital, small states will be unable to attract investment; without remunerative returns to labour, human development will be impeded.[15] Rather than being 'extreme',[16] this analysis simply uses new empirical evidence to verify an existing possibility within conventional economic theory. Small states do have comparative advantages, but these need not be 'operational'.[17]

These findings also clarify the types of economic opportunities small states can exploit. Where small economies face world market prices for their exports they are unlikely to be competitive, ruling out the export of generic goods and services. Their export potential is in markets where forms of rent exist or can be created for exploitation. Argues Grynberg (2001a: 292), 'while in other economies these quasi-rents constitute a basis for high profits, in small states they are often a precondition for productive commercial activity as rents are necessary to cover inherently high operating costs'. Examples include scarcity rents in commodity markets, for example Solomon Islands' timber,[18] niche-market rents from location-specific factors like tropical beaches for tourism in the Caribbean and time zones for data processing in Fiji, and niche-market rents from branding as in the cases of Jamaican Rum and Fiji Water.[19] Rents, however, can be transient.[20] Encontre (1999: 261) appraises small economies' experience with niche markets as being typically unsuccessful, characterised by commercial ventures with very short life-spans. Thus, whilst small economies certainly have opportunities to benefit from globalisation, competitiveness requires their productive activities to be limited to those serving specialist markets where shifting rents can be created and exploited, so they are far from having stable foundations for their economic development.

At the same time, small economies have the most to gain from international trade.[21] Their small domestic markets, narrow resource endowments and inability to exploit economies of scale mean the welfare they can attain under autarky is very low indeed.[22] International trade should offer these states the opportunity to overcome their small size and increase their

[15] Winters and Martins (2004a: 119–20). [16] Page and Kleen (2004: 79).

[17] Winters and Martins (2004a: 1).

[18] Grynberg (2001a: 291–3) and Encontre (1999: 267) provide overviews of small economies' rent-based exports.

[19] Competitiveness in most other exports from small states relies on institutions like trade preferences and tax concessions, discussed below.

[20] Armstrong and Read (2002: 2–3) and Grynberg (2001a: 293–5).

[21] Streeten (1993: 198) and Read (1999: 9).

[22] See, for example, Read (2004: 365), Encontre (1999: 268–9) and Burki (2001: 10).

welfare, but this section has argued that nothing in economic theory guarantees that they will be able to operationalise this potential in the presence of significant transaction costs.[23] Their possible marginalisation in the face of globalisation is a pressing concern, particularly because it is they that are most dependent on international trade to improve their economic welfare.[24] Small economies have both limited opportunities to benefit from globalising markets and the most to lose from such marginalisation.[25]

7.3 The costs of vulnerability

Small economies are particularly vulnerable to external shocks from world markets and natural disasters,[26] because of the severe constraints they face in diversifying their production and trade.[27] Thus Atkins et al. (2000: 1) state, 'There is growing international recognition that high economic exposure, remoteness and isolation, and proneness to natural disasters have a debilitating effect on small economies, despite the fact that some of them exhibit relatively high per capita incomes.' Indeed, their vulnerability index ranks twenty-seven small economies among the thirty most vulnerable developing countries.[28] This section will explore the adverse economic impact of vulnerability on small economies.

7.3.1 Vulnerability to external economic shocks

A number of small economies' characteristics make them both highly exposed to external economic shocks and extremely vulnerable to consequent adverse effects. First, the limited production possibilities of their domestic economies make small states highly dependent on trade,[29] with trade accounts typically very open (see figure 7.1).[30] Secondly, their production activities and more so their exports are highly concentrated in a very small number of products (see figure 7.2), Jansen (2004: 14) arguing that small economies' export concentrations are very similar to those in least developed countries (LDCs). Thirdly, small economies' exports are

[23] Winters and Martins (2004a: 3–8). [24] Winters and Martins (2004a: 1–2).

[25] See Grynberg and Razzaque (2003: 30). [26] Atkins et al. (2001: 63).

[27] Briguglio (1995: 1616) and Jansen (2004: 14). Grynberg and Razzaque (2003: 53), Read (1999: 7) and Briguglio (1995: 1616) argue that small economies' typically limited resource endowments exacerbate this lack of diversification.

[28] Atkins et al. (2000: 25–33). [29] Briguglio (1995: 1616).

[30] See also World Bank (2002b: 18).

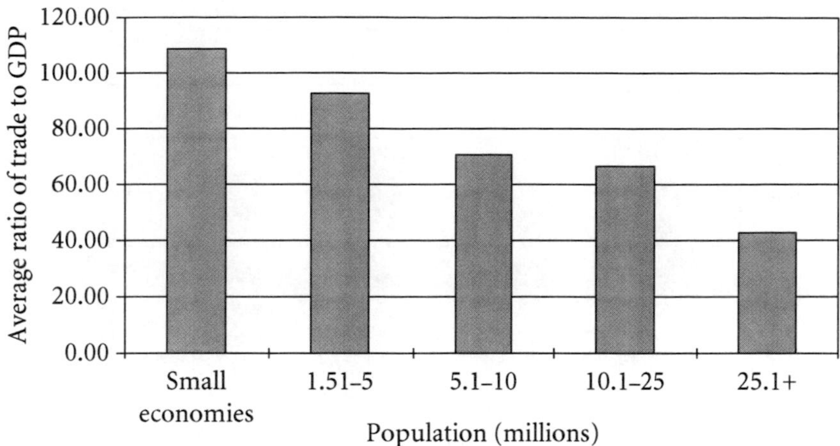

Note: The 'small economies' category refers to those countries listed in table 7.1 for which data were available; the number of observations in each category is 38, 41, 30, 32 and 34 respectively
Source: Jansen (2004) and author's own calculations
Figure 7.1 Openness to trade in small economies

directed to a very limited number of markets.[31] Fourthly, generally the products in which small economies' exports are concentrated are commodities.[32] UNCTAD (2003a: 5) finds that for the subset of small island developing states (SIDS), the average ratio of agricultural trade to GDP is the highest of all country groupings. Finally, and most critically, small economies are unlikely to possess the capacity necessary to mitigate the negative effects of external economic shocks.[33] Not only do they face significant challenges in diversifying their economic activity and export bases,[34] the World Bank (2002b: 18–19) argues small economies have 'a smaller pool of human and institutional resources to draw on to help predict, mitigate, and manage the effects of shocks'. Their small financial systems, with little liquidity and constrained access to international capital, also make it difficult for small states to implement macroeconomic policies to smooth the impact of shocks.[35]

This exposure and vulnerability has a destabilising impact on small economies.[36] Atkins et al. (2000: 5–9) find the income volatility of small

[31] Dehn (2000c: 10, 22), World Bank (2002b: 18), UNCTAD (2003a: 7) and Jansen (2004: 1, 6).
[32] Jansen (2004: 12). [33] Read (2004: 169). [34] Jansen (2004: 6–7, 14).
[35] See World Bank (2001). [36] Auffret (2003a: 4, 7), Jansen (2004: 1) and World Bank (2002b: 21).

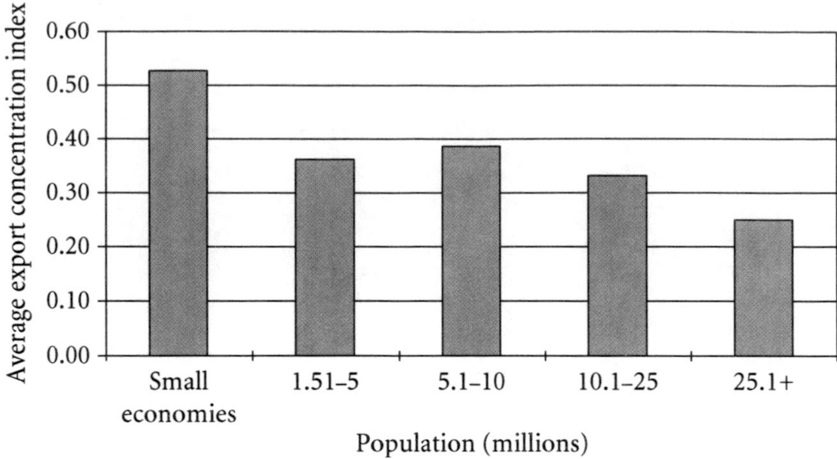

Note: The 'small economies' category refers to those countries listed in table 7.1 for which data were available; the number of observations in each category is 27, 33, 24, 30 and 31 respectively

Source: Jansen (2004) and author's own calculations

Figure 7.2 Export concentration in small economies

states to be the highest in the developing world. Empirical evidence also demonstrates that small states' openness to trade increases the volatility of their output levels and growth rates.[37] Their high export concentrations are found to play a major role in exacerbating the income volatility of small states, through terms-of-trade volatility.[38] Also, extreme concentrations in commodity exports are shown to exacerbate volatility.[39] It is widely recognised that such volatility of income and consumption aggregates *does* matter for economic growth and welfare.[40] Whether or not other characteristics of small economies work to counteract the negative growth impact of volatility[41] makes it no less true that high volatility in key macroeconomic aggregates like income and consumption affects growth negatively.[42] And

[37] Easterly and Kraay (2001: 104), World Bank (2002b: 18) and Jansen (2004: 1, 6).

[38] Jansen (2004: 9–12). [39] Dehn (2000c: 10).

[40] See Jansen (2004: 1), who cites the relevant evidence from the literature, as well as Auffret (2003a: 4, 7), Collier and Dehn (2001: 2), Atkins et al. (2000: 7) and Easterly and Kraay (2001: 104–5). On terms of trade shocks, see Dehn (2000a: 23). On uncertainty and private investment, see the different findings of Dehn (2000b: 3) and Jansen (2004: 3–4).

[41] Easterly and Kraay (2001: 102–8) argue that the negative effect of volatility on growth in small states is offset by the positive effect of their openness to trade on growth, which appears to lead Page and Kleen (2004: 81) to infer that volatility itself does not matter. [42] Read (2004: 169).

as Read (2004: 372) argues, small states' vulnerability to external economic shocks will only *increase* with globalisation and small states' greater integration into world markets.

7.3.2 Vulnerability to natural disasters

The development prospects of small economies are also constrained by the 'multifaceted' welfare effects of natural disasters,[43] to which they are both highly exposed and peculiarly vulnerable. Small states' exposure is geographic, from their typical location within hurricane and cyclone belts, and sometimes seismic activity zones.[44] Small states' vulnerability is socioeconomic, arising from the interaction of a number of their characteristics. First, frequently small size means that natural disasters devastate entire countries, hence aggregate effects are marked relative to large states where these are mitigated by regional variations in the impact on economic activity.[45] Secondly, dependence on agriculture for output and exports increases the economic damage of natural disasters, particularly weather events.[46] Thirdly, small economies' narrow resource bases and undiversified economic activities and exports concentrate risk.[47] Fourthly, their relatively low incomes impede household and state expenditure capacities on preventative measures. Fifthly, inefficient, incomplete or entirely absent insurance markets reduce scope for managing risk.[48]

The exposure and vulnerability of small developing states is evident from the data on natural disasters summarised in table 7.5. Small states are widely recognised as being the most vulnerable to natural disasters because of their exposure, having the highest frequency of natural disasters in the world relative to population or land area.[49] As these states develop, the economic cost of their natural disasters will rise 'exponentially'.[50] That prospect, combined with predicted increases in the frequency and intensity of damaging weather events, leaves SIDS estimated to be facing annual losses from natural disasters exceeding 10 per cent of their GDP by 2050.[51]

43 Charveriat (2000: 10).

44 Charveriat (2000: 47–56), Freeman et al. (2003: 8), Rasmussen (2004: 5), Atkins et al. (2000: 3) and Auffret (2003a: 13).

45 Charveriat (2000: 21, 39).

46 Charveriat (2000: 21).

47 Freeman et al. (2003: 9).

48 Rasmussen (2004: 4), World Bank (2001: 12) and Gurenko and Lester (2004: 3).

49 Rasmussen (2004: 3), Encontre (1999: 262), International Workshop (2004: 2), Atkins et al. (2000: 30), World Bank (2002b: 18) and IMF (2003: 7).

50 Benson and Clay (2003: 76).

51 Freeman et al. (2003: 8).

Table 7.5 *The extreme vulnerability of small economies to natural disasters (1970–2003)*

	Incidence of natural disasters			Population impact of natural disasters	
Country grouping[a]	Number of events[b]	Events/ population (index)	Events/ land Area (index)	Number of events with record of affected persons	Total affected persons (percentage of 2003 population)
Small economies	432	1,229	290	303	67.8
of which: Africa	177	1,051	174	117	93.2
Caribbean/Latin America	96	1,384	697	67	53.2
Pacific	149	1,652	500	110	47.9
SIDS	285	1,495	882	204	46.6
Other least developed countries	1,446	175	126	1,130	109.5
Other developing countries	4,126	74	93	3,130	101.1
Developed countries	1,450	140	84	748	5.4
World	7,454	100	100	5,311	88.6

[a] Only countries with at least one natural disaster during 1970–2003 are included, yielding: 37 small economies of which 13 are in Africa, 11 are in the Caribbean or Latin America, 10 are in the Pacific, and 26 are SIDS; 34 other LDCs; 89 other developing (or transition) countries; and 23 developed countries. Data for country groupings reflect weighted averages of the data for the individual countries therein, calculated on the basis of aggregate group data, rather than reflecting simple averages of individual country data

[b] Only natural disasters involving at least 10 people being killed, at least 100 people being affected, a call for international assistance, or the declaration of a state of emergency are recorded in EM-DAT; 2004 data are excluded because they are preliminary as yet

Source: EM-DAT (2004), World Bank (2004) and UNCTAD (2004c); author's own calculations

Empirical evidence on the economic impacts of natural disasters in small economies indicates the significant challenge to trade and development these pose.[52] Typically, disasters are associated with immediate sharp contractions in output and GDP growth, contractions exacerbated by the share of agriculture in economic activity. External trade balances worsen substantially, from the shocks to exports arising from output shocks and damage to trade infrastructure, and from surges in imports occurring to underpin reconstruction. Current account deficits worsen, sometimes to 'staggering' dimensions.[53] Public finances worsen also, from higher expenditure requirements and a reduced revenue base. Generally, increased foreign aid and official assistance are insufficient to offset these fiscal impacts.[54] As a result of foreign borrowing to fund fiscal and current account deficits, typically external debt to GDP ratios increase. Frequently also, inflation becomes a concern. Although the population proportions affected by natural disasters in small states are relatively low, they reflect significant real costs to the labour force nonetheless. These severe macroeconomic consequences are, of course, in addition to the psychological and social effects of human suffering,[55] the impact of which typically is most acute for the poor.[56]

Furthermore, natural disasters can have significant economic effects on small states beyond the short term. Incomplete reconstruction of damaged capital will necessarily reduce future growth, a growth effect that can emerge from a shortfall or delay in reconstruction financing.[57] Reconstruction may not even be possible, where factor endowments such as coral reefs are destroyed.[58] The redirection of capital from planned projects to reconstruction imposes an opportunity cost on productive capacity and growth, in the likely event that the marginal improvement of reconstructed

[52] For evidence summarised in this paragraph, see Rasmussen (2004: 5–11), Freeman et al. (2003: 11), Charveriat (2000: 15–21, 36–9), Benson et al. (2001: 12–17), ECLAC and IDB (2000: 7–12), World Bank (2002b: 25–7) and IMF (2003: 10–11).

[53] See, in particular, Rasmussen (2004: 8).

[54] Freeman et al. (2003: 14) cite Inter-American Development Bank evidence that an average of 8.6 per cent, and at most 25 per cent of direct disaster costs are covered by international assistance. Dependence on overseas assistance is itself a form of risk exposure, increasingly unwise as real official development assistance declines (Charveriat (2000: 1)).

[55] See especially Charveriat (2000: 10–12).

[56] See, in particular, Freeman et al. (2003: 10) and Charveriat (2000: 26).

[57] Auffret (2003a: 17), ECLAC and IDB (2000: 13–14), IMF (2003: 9) and Charveriat (2000: 13, 22–4).

[58] Charveriat (2000: 23) and ECLAC and IDB (2000: 15).

over pre-disaster capital is less than would have been the rate of return from the planned projects forgone.[59] Moreover, risk reassessments and disaster-induced solvency problems may reduce the investment attractiveness and capacity of vulnerable regions.[60] Damage to educational and health infrastructure, together with household-level effects reducing access to these services, reduce human capital formation – a foundation for future economic growth.[61] Vulnerability to natural disasters also is strongly correlated with income and consumption volatility, with consequent welfare effects.[62] In addition, detrimental long-term effects arise from the increases in poverty typically associated with natural disasters.[63] There is also evidence that worsening public finances go beyond short-term fiscal deficits, to significant reallocations of public resources away from capital expenditure and social sector programmes.[64] Finally, higher external debt increases the future risk exposure of small states, expanding the debt servicing drain on public finances and possibly increasing the risk premiums financiers demand.[65]

These considerations make the argument that natural disasters do not affect long-term economic growth highly improbable.[66] If there has been little empirical evidence of long-term lower economic growth in disaster-prone states, not only is it now emerging,[67] but this is largely the result of there being little empirical work at all on the long-term impacts of natural disasters.[68]

[59] Charveriat (2000: 23).

[60] Auffret (2003a: 28), Freeman et al. (2003: 13) and Charveriat (2000: 23–5).

[61] Freeman et al. (2003: 13), Charveriat (2000: 23) and Encontre (1999: 262).

[62] Rasmussen (2004: 11), Auffret (2003a: 4, 7, 15) and World Bank (2002b: 45).

[63] ECLAC and IDB (2000: 16) and Charveriat (2000: 26).

[64] Benson and Clay (2003: 77, 83). See also ECLAC and IDB (2000: 15), Charveriat (2000: 23), Gurenko and Lester (2004: 3), IMF (2003: 4), Freeman et al. (2003: 13) and evidence of the mirroring of this behaviour by donors in Benson and Clay (2003: 76).

[65] Charveriat (2000: 13, 24), Freeman et al. (2003: 11–13) and ECLAC and IDB (2000: 15).

[66] See Page and Kleen (2004: 79), whose argument to that effect appears to be based on Encontre (1999: 263–4). The latter compares average growth rates with natural disaster incidences in SIDS over two decades, without engaging in statistical analysis to hold other factors constant, to observe only that both high and low growth performers experience both high and low disaster incidences.

[67] See Freeman et al. (2003: 11), Charveriat (2000: 1), ECLAC and IDB (2000: 12–16), Benson et al. (2001: 92) and Auffret (2003b: 28). Benson and Clay (2003: 76) state, 'Disasters, especially when these reoccur frequently, appear to have longer-term consequences for economic growth, development, and poverty reduction.' Similarly Freeman et al. (2003:11) argue, 'The macroeconomic and developmental implications of natural disaster[s] can be both large and long lasting.'

[68] Rasmussen (2004: 11).

Critics contend also that vulnerability to natural disasters is endogenous, implying that policy remedies are readily available to small states at reasonable cost.[69] However, small economies face significant impediments in reducing their vulnerability to natural disasters. The constrained governance capacities of state institutions make problematic the formulation and enforcement of vulnerability-reducing regulations.[70] Continuously shifting vulnerabilities, arising from altered exposure due to climatic changes and from altered vulnerability due to socioeconomic change, exacerbate governance problems by requiring frequent re-evaluations of risks and appropriate preventative measures.[71] Moreover, the costs of preventative measures can be 'inordinately' expensive.[72] Market inefficiencies ensure that disaster insurance, if available at all, is highly volatile and typically requires prohibitively high premiums in small states.[73] Standard policy prescriptions for economic diversification into areas of comparative advantage[74] are of little utility where small size constrains diversification,[75] comparative advantages are held in activities – like agriculture and tourism – particularly vulnerable to natural disasters, and more disaster-resistant activities like manufacturing are uncompetitive. As with external economic shocks, therefore, small economies face substantial obstacles in attempting to reduce their vulnerability to natural disasters.

7.4 The costs of governance

A very important scale economy that small states cannot exploit is governance.[76] Whilst poor governance, in terms of democracy, stability and the rule of law, is not a pressing issue for small states (see table 7.6),[77] policy capacity and the costs of best practice are. The substantial capacity

[69] See Page and Kleen (2004: 79).

[70] On these prescriptions, see Rasmussen (2004: 14) and IMF (2003: 13).

[71] See IPCC (2001) on climate change, in particular for SIDS; and Benson and Clay (2003: 78–80) and Benson et al. (2001: 88) on changing socioeconomic vulnerabilities.

[72] Freeman et al. (2003: 16).

[73] Rasmussen (2004: 12–13), Freeman et al. (2003: 17), World Bank (2001: 9–10) and Auffret (2003b: 13). See also Benson and Clay (2003: 78) and Gurenko and Lester (2004: 2).

[74] See Rasmussen (2004: 14), IMF (2003: 8) and Freeman et al. (2003: 15).

[75] Charveriat (2000: 22).

[76] See Schahczenski (1990) and Braun et al. (2002); see Srinivasan (1986: 211) for an opposing view.

[77] See also Winters and Martins (2004a: 130–47) and Collier and Dollar (2001: 16). On the relationship between good governance and economic success see Burnside and Dollar (1997).

Table 7.6 *2002 governance indicators for small economies*

Governance indicator[a]	Observations[b]	Average[c]
Voice and accountability	40	0.28
Political stability	29	0.32
Government effectiveness	37	−0.17
Regulatory quality	38	−0.22
Rule of law	38	−0.06
Control of corruption	38	−0.09

[a] Estimates range from −2.5 to +2.5, with estimates for the full sample averaging zero

[b] Number of observations varies with missing data

[c] Simple average of estimated scores, none of which are significantly different from zero even at the 10 per cent level

Source: World Bank Institute (2002) and author's own calculations

requirements and costs of implementing international trade agreements[78] are a severe concern for small developing countries, whose human and financial resources are dwarfed by the complex array of international trade disciplines with which they must work.[79] This section will focus on a further relationship between costly governance and trade capacity critical in small states: the way in which state institutions augment the trade capacity of the private sector.

Economies of scale in governance arise from the population-invariant minimum set of responsibilities a state has towards its citizens and with respect to other states, government functions typically exhibiting high fixed and low marginal costs.[80] Governance in small states is thus generally more costly per capita than in large states.[81] Both Murray (1981: 245–7) and Armstrong and Read (2002: 2–3) argue that conventional policy and economic models assume, without making explicit, a minimum state size and administrative resource base which small states fall below. Frequently, these prohibitive costs of adequate governance are mitigated by understaffing

[78] See Finger and Schuler (2002: 501), Michalopoulos (2002: 69) and Armstrong and Read (2002: 16).

[79] On implementation costs, see Finger and Schuler (2002: 501).

[80] Briguglio (1995: 1617), Farrugia (1993: 221), Encontre (1999: 265) and Armstrong and Read (2002: 2).

[81] See Hausmann (2004) for evidence of the poor performance of independent states in the Caribbean relative to their dependent neighbours, and Bertram (2004: 345–50) for similar findings in the Pacific.

among professionals and a reduction in the scope of state responsibilities.[82] Small populations, especially those experiencing skilled labour emigration, present a significant challenge to the recruitment of qualified and experienced officials for public institutions.[83] The result is 'problematic governance capacity': state officials are severely overstretched relative to their responsibilities, and sometimes relative to their skills and experience, whilst even these limited state responsibilities may be inadequate for the needs of the population in the current global context.

Small states' governance constraints affect the trade capacity of their private sectors, especially given the latter's inexperience in international trade and lack of required entrepreneurial skills.[84] For example, if a small state's facilitation of trade is ineffective, consumers and exporters will bear costs arising from inefficient customs, standards and quarantine regulations. States may be unable to facilitate the extremely costly certification systems vital for niche marketing.[85] Government responsibilities may not feasibly extend to the provision of access to overseas market – including regulatory – information to their private sectors,[86] non-rival goods that are otherwise extremely costly to individual entrepreneurs and vital to accessing transitory niches. Small states also may underachieve in negotiating product – especially commodity – pathways, the means by which their private sectors can realise market access abroad.[87]

Their problematic governance capacities make it difficult for small states to reduce trade transaction costs through trade facilitation and to negotiate product pathways for their exports, state activities vital to the trade capacities of their private sectors.

7.5 Characteristics in combination

Thus far, this chapter has presented arguments and evidence regarding the significant economic costs imposed on small states by their size, vulnerability to external economic shocks and natural disasters, and problematic

[82] Farrugia (1993: 222) and Gay (2004: 4).

[83] Briguglio (1995: 1617), Murray (1981: 250–4) and Gay (2004: 15).

[84] See World Bank (2002a: 29) on the entrepreneurial skills base in Pacific Islands.

[85] See Vossenaar (2004: 74–82) on barriers to entry in niche markets; and Saqib (2003: 270–1) on costly certification.

[86] English and de Wulf (2002: 160–2), Wilson (2002: 428) and Grynberg (2001a: 294).

[87] See Wilson (2002: 431–2) on technical barriers to trade, and Malua (2003: 185, 187) and Vossenaar (2004: 79) for case studies.

governance capacities. In each case, it is through a *combination* of many characteristics of small states that these costs are generated.[88] The small size of an economy, for example, is important only in the context of trade transaction costs such as those arising from remoteness and insularity. Small economies are highly vulnerable to external economic shocks where they are open to trade and have undiversified exports. Similarly, their vulnerability to substantial economic damage from natural disasters results from small economies' exposure to such disasters combined with small land areas, large agricultural shares of production and incomplete insurance markets. Finally, small economies' governance capacities are problematic for trade in cases where indivisibilities exist in trade facilitation and skilled human capital is scarce.

It follows that cross-country econometric analyses regressing economic growth on any one characteristic – distances to major markets, population sizes, numbers of natural disasters, and so forth – may not yield significant results. Large contiguous states with great distances between capitals will offset the detrimental effects of distance for small insular states. Small states integrated and contiguous with regional markets will offset the detrimental effects of small domestic markets for small remote states. Large developed states experiencing many natural disasters will offset the detrimental growth impacts of natural disasters on developing countries with small land areas. Because it is combinations of characteristics that engender disadvantages, it is erroneous to treat these characteristics as being separable for analytical purposes.[89] For the same reason, it is mistaken to argue as Srinivasan (1986: 217) does that small economies do not face a special predicament because, 'Many of the problems allegedly faced by small economies are . . . not peculiar to them', a position echoed by Page and Kleen (2004: 80). Instead, since it is the combination of many characteristics of small economies that yields the significant economic costs that undermine their trade prospects, states exhibiting those multiple characteristics have a strong case for special consideration. The interaction of characteristics deriving from small size, vulnerability and governance capacity impedes the potential of small economies to integrate into globalising markets on a competitive basis, and thereby mitigate the constraint on their development posed by size.

[88] See also Salmon (2002: 4) on this point.

[89] For an example of such an approach, see Page and Kleen (2004: 80).

7.6 The limits of regionalism

The standard recommendation for small states to mitigate the deleterious effects of their small size, vulnerability and governance capacities is regionalism.[90] Thus, for example, the integration of small economies in regional markets is argued to overcome the limits of small domestic markets and the constraints on their exploiting economies of scale.[91] Regional cooperation is meant to mitigate small states' vulnerability to natural disasters, particularly regarding the costs of preventative actions and the capacity to absorb damage. Regional government is proffered as a solution to indivisibilities in governance via the exploitation of scale economies and the regional provision of public goods and infrastructure.[92] As Murray (1981: 247) argues, small states are to be 'scaled up' to suit existing 'doctrines of effective administration'. In the extreme, small states are recommended to cease to be states.[93] Consequently, the existence of the opportunity for regional integration is argued to make persistent small size an endogenous characteristic, a policy choice for which small states should bear the costs.

It is beyond contention that regionalism has much to offer small economies. It is also readily apparent that small states have recognised these advantages and forged various regional groupings incorporating, to different degrees, integrated markets, natural disaster cooperation, and elements of regional governance.[94] However, there are strict limitations on the extent to which regionalism can *solve* the trade predicaments of small economies.

First, full market integration among a region of small economies will not necessarily make those states better off, or more able to compete in global markets. The most obvious reason is trade diversion, with economic models demonstrating that the integration of a group of small economies may reduce their aggregate welfare.[95] Empirical analysis also calls into question the degree to which geographical regions of small states can be assumed to be regions in economic terms. Bertram (2004: 345, 352), for example, provides evidence that the small economies of the Pacific do not form an economic region, and cites similar evidence for geographic regions elsewhere.[96] Eliminating trade barriers, even achieving regulatory

[90] See Streeten (1993: 197). [91] Hausmann (2004) and Streeten (1993: 197–8).
[92] Streeten (1993: 197) and Schiff and Andriamananjara (1998: 2–3).
[93] See Srinivasan (1986: 211). [94] See, for example, South Pacific Forum Secretariat (2001).
[95] Schiff (1996: 11, 32), Read (1999: 15) and World Bank (2002a: 10–11).
[96] See also Encontre (1999: 265).

harmonisation, will not necessarily eliminate trade transaction costs and forge a large single market in any of the main geographic regions where small economies are concentrated. Substantial transaction costs will persist from remoteness and insularity; aggregating populations not only yields numbers still small in global terms but misleadingly implies a single domestic market. On this basis, the World Bank (2002a: 7–8) criticises regional integration among Pacific Islands because it will yield a still small 'aggregate' market dispersed over hundreds of islands with extremely high intra-regional transport costs, and virtually identical patterns of economic activity and comparative advantage.

Secondly, regional cooperation is unlikely to alleviate fully the economic costs of vulnerability to natural disasters. Small states are already cooperating to enhance their capacity to provide public goods such as early warning systems, cooperation which could increase to encompass risk pooling.[97] The degree of risk covariance within regions, however, together with their relatively low income levels throughout, must constrain the potential of regionalism to enhance coping strategies. Moreover, the extremely similar patterns of economic activity and exports within regions of small states suggest that mitigating vulnerability through diversification at a regional level will be problematic. Additionally, the most significant limitations on disaster insurance appear to arise not from inadequate regional cooperation but from weaknesses in global reinsurance markets.[98]

Thirdly, regional government is not a complete solution for governance problems in small states. It offers, and is being utilised for, substantial economies of scale in policy development and in negotiations with states outside the region.[99] However, the dispersion of regional populations among remote insular land areas inhibits the potential for efficient regional provision of public goods and infrastructure. Additionally, the recruitment problems posed by small populations and skilled labour emigration are mitigated – not eliminated – at the regional level.

This section contends not that regionalism does not offer opportunities for small states to mitigate the costs imposed by their economic size, vulnerability and governance capacities, but that these opportunities are limited. Small economies' predicaments cannot be eliminated entirely by

[97] World Bank (2001: 13).

[98] See Freeman et al. (2003: 17), Rasmussen (2004: 10) and World Bank (2001: 10).

[99] Winters and Martins (2004a: 148), Schiff and Andriamananjara (1998: 2, 29) and South Pacific Forum Secretariat (2001: 507–9).

regional integration, and it is thus mistaken to attribute this predicament to the policy choices of those states.

With the advantages of regionalism qualified, policy prescriptions shift to global integration for small states,[100] implying that small states' disadvantages arise from their lack of integration into the global economy.[101] By any measure of trade exposure, the degree of global integration of small economies is not deficient nor – as the next sections will demonstrate – will more integration necessarily benefit small states facing inherent challenges to their competitiveness. Instead, what small economies require is a more beneficial means of insertion into international markets than they currently experience.

7.7 Being ill-equipped to benefit from globalisation

The foregoing sections have explored small economies' peculiar disadvantages in their potential to exploit opportunities arising from globalisation. These constraints on their global competitiveness are persistent, to varying degrees, and condition an expectation of small economies' increasing marginalisation in world trade and declining development prospects. This expectation is not radical, with Winters and Martins (2004a: 2) arguing that, in the absence of mitigating policies by the international community, small economies will become worse off as the world economy globalises. Encontre (1999: 269) adds that most SIDS are likely to gain 'little benefit' from the process of multilateral trade liberalisation,[102] with UNCTAD's Officer-in-Charge (2004a: v) arguing that SIDS' intrinsic disadvantages mean they will be 'unable to seize these [globalisation] opportunities unless certain special measures to compensate their disadvantages are granted to them by their development partners'. Grynberg and Razzaque (2003: 52–3) demonstrate that small economies are already being marginalised in world trade flows, while Braun et al. (2002) provide evidence of the declining relative economic performance of newly independent states, such as small economies, largely as a result of the associated decline in the size of their secure market access which the existence of sovereignty – even with open trade policies – necessarily

[100] World Bank (2002a: 10) and Schiff (2002: 18).

[101] See Page and Kleen (2004: 43).

[102] The other exception he notes is any SIDS that are able to enhance the global competitiveness of their merchandise exports, which the earlier cited evidence regarding business costs in small economies would appear to make unlikely.

implies.[103] Bertram (2004: 344) finds similar evidence for small independent states in the Pacific, as well as for the whole group of SIDS.

This argument is not about the past growth performance of small economies, and their ensuing current levels of per capita income. Nothing in the argument is invalidated by evidence that small economies are not currently the world's lowest per capita income group, or have not suffered the world's lowest growth rates in recent years.[104] As the data in table 7.7 indicate, the recent historical growth performance of small economies has exceeded that of LDCs. Beyond the averages, it is important to recognise that the relatively better performance of some small economies masks the poor growth record and current low per capita income levels of others. In particular, sixteen of the forty-one small economies considered in this chapter are LDCs (representing one third of LDCs),[105] and a further two are landlocked developing countries. Briguglio (1995: 1615) cautions that per capita income data conceal the reality of small economies' threatened economic viability, and Read (2004: 365) argues that, 'Globalization represents a particularly significant threat to the continued survival of many successful small island states as independent entities given the greater susceptibility of their economies to changes in the international system.' However, relatively good past economic performance has led some analysts to argue that it is difficult for small economies to 'make a development case' for special and differential treatment.[106] As Winters and Martins (2004a: 1) argue, that reasoning is invalid because it is based on historical data only,

> . . . ignoring the question of [whether] small countries are likely to be able to respond to the changes brought about by globalisation and the ability of small countries to respond to present and future changes in the global trading system. For small states the policy issue is not past performance but rather whether they are well positioned, given the globalisation of trade, to capitalise and achieve growth rates similar to those achieved in the past.

The validity of a future expectation cannot not be judged on the basis of historical data.

[103] See also Hausmann (2004). Additionally, World Bank (2002b: 2–3) data indicate the declining average growth rate of GDP in Pacific Islands since the 1970s, to a point of virtual stagnation.

[104] See Easterly and Kraay (2001: 97–8) and Page and Kleen (2004: 80–2) in particular, but also Read (2004: 368).

[105] Note also that of these, UNCTAD (2004b: 5) regards seven as 'regressing' economies, and a further four as 'slow-growth' economies.

[106] Page and Kleen (2004: 82).

Table 7.7 *Average annual GDP growth (1990–2000)*

Country grouping[a]	GDP growth rate (%)	Per capita GDP growth rate (%)
Small economies[b]	3.6	1.9
All least developed countries	3.6	1.1
All developing countries	4.8	3.0
Developed market economies	2.4	1.7

[a] The definition of country groupings is given in UNCTAD (2003c: x)
[b] Simple average, excluding Nauru, Palau and Timor-Leste due to missing data
Source: UNCTAD (2003c) and author's own calculations

This historical economic performance of small economies occurred in the context of their particular mode of insertion into specific market structures in the global economy in that period. By contrast, expectations about future economic performance must account for recent and imminent changes in the global economy and multilateral trading system, altering both that mode of insertion and the structures of particular markets of interest to small economies. A relevant global economic change, for example, is the declining real value of aid and declining share of it accruing to small economies typically heavily reliant on it.[107] A relevant change within the multilateral trading system would exist if, for example, the selection of markets being liberalised and distortions dismantled were detrimental to the export competitiveness of small economies. Analysts have typically assumed that there must exist advantages of small size – asserting greater social cohesion, bureaucratic flexibility, less popular resistance to change, greater solidarity, fewer vested interests, a disproportionately strong international voice and freedom from interference by major powers[108] – sufficient to offset small economies' lack of international competitiveness. These advantages, if they exist, need have had no such strong offsetting effects on competitiveness if, instead, the relatively good average growth performance of small economies has arisen from their historically favourable means of insertion in the global economy.

[107] Based on data in UNCTAD (2003c); see also Grynberg (2001b: 330) and Briguglio (1995: 1622) and Collier and Dollar (2001: 23) on higher per capita aid receipts in small states than in large.

[108] Streeten (1993: 199–200), Srinivasan (1986: 211, 214), WTO (2002: 11) and Armstrong and Read (2002: 8).

7.8 Being vulnerable to harm from globalisation

Thus far, this chapter has explored why small economies are poorly positioned to exploit the opportunities emerging from globalisation. Equally critical is the threat that further globalisation of markets according to currently agreed multilateral trade rules will damage the economic welfare of small economies. Underpinning this threat is the dependence of most small states on trade preferences for the feasibility of their key exports to major markets in developed countries.[109] Tariff preferences are already eroding as a consequence of multilateral trade liberalisation and the proliferation of free trade agreements.[110] In compliance with WTO dispute rulings, small economies also face the imminent modification or dismantling of especially favourable subsidy preference schemes for their commodities.[111] This section will show how preferential access to markets in developed countries has been vital to the economic performance of small states, how vulnerable these states are to preference erosion, and the gravity of the economic consequences of their loss of preferences.

Small economies enjoy a considerable degree of preferential access to the markets of their former colonial and major regional powers, particularly for the tropical commodities that colonial rule structured as their comparative advantages. Small economies' access to preferential arrangements is summarised in table 7.8.[112] The value of these preferences to small economies has been substantial, flowing through terms-of-trade gains, greater export values and volumes, higher GDP, greater employment especially in rural areas, a degree of stability in 'farm gate' prices, higher household incomes, and increased government revenue.[113] Reviewing the

[109] Grynberg (2001a: 274–9). [110] Schiff (2002: 14).

[111] See Oxfam (2004: 2–3) on WTO disputes and the EU sugar regime, Mitchell (2004: 34, 38) on catalysts for change in the US sugar regime, and Laurent (forthcoming: 2–9) on WTO disputes and the EU banana regime. Note that this chapter will use 'tariff preferences' to refer to preference schemes based on simple tariff concessions, and 'subsidy preferences' to refer to preference schemes based on tariff-free quota access to subsidised markets abroad.

[112] See Panagariya (2002: 1419–21) on ACP–EU schemes, and Ozden and Sharma (2004: 5–6) for an overview of the CBI. Note that in the absence of specific preferential schemes, non-LDC small economies must rely on Generalised System of Preferences (GSP) schemes. The smaller preferential margins available under GSP than under ACP–EU arrangements, for example, is suggested by Tangermann (2000: 21). See also Grynberg (2001a: 279).

[113] See UNCTAD (2003a: 18) on the substantial benefits; Ozden and Sharma (2004: 12) on accruing preference rents; Subramanian (2003a: 2) on terms-of-trade and export gains; Armstrong and Read (2002: 8) on export multiplier effects; Choraria (2004: 13–14) for value-chain

literature on the impact of preferences, Alexandraki and Lankes (2004: 6–7) argue that preferences have enhanced market access relative to the counter-factual of no preferences, encouraged export-driven economic development and provided valuable transfers to small economies. UNCTAD (2003a: 7) argues that preferential margins have been sufficient to compensate for the inherent lack of competitiveness of the exports of small – in particular island – economies. Alexandraki and Lankes (2004: 24) calculate that, among non-LDC developing countries, eleven of the twelve states receiving the highest total preference margins for their exports are small economies.[114] These data dispel assumptions that middle-income status alone is sufficient to avert the problems of adjusting to liberalising markets. The findings, reproduced in table 7.9, indicate clearly the size and importance of trade preferences, with preference margins adding almost a quarter or more to the value of exports for the top six of these small economies. For sugar, for example, small economies account for nearly 93 per cent of the total ACP sugar quota volume in the EU market, and hold another tenth of that volume again from US sugar quotas.[115]

Small economies' extreme vulnerability to significant economic damage from the loss of preferences arises from the highly preference-dependent structure of their exports and production. This dependence is characterised by the concentration of their exports in a very small number of commodities, the directing of those commodities to a limited range of markets, costs of production that market – rather than preferential – prices would not cover, and a lack of competitiveness in entering alternative productive activities and export markets.[116] Thus Alexandraki and Lankes (2004: 5–6, 11) conclude that preference erosion is a significant source of vulnerability for countries with deep preferential access to major developed country markets, an undiversified export base concentrated in commodities enjoying preferential access, and high export concentration in those markets where preferences are set to decline. Exemplifying export

analyses, Laurent (forthcoming: 13) and Melville (2003: 105) on rural multiplier and development effects; and Romalis (2003: 10–12) for discussion of the large, significant growth benefits of preferential access.

114 Note also that small economies are among the LDCs facing the highest losses from preference erosion (Subramanian (2003a: 12)); see also Tangermann (2000: 16).

115 Author's own calculations based on data in Mitchell (2004: 31, 39).

116 UNCTAD (2003a: 7) argues that these trade patterns for SIDS are similar to those of LDCs.

Table 7.8 *The major preferential trade arrangements of small economies*

Small economy	EU		US			Canada		Japan	Australia & New Zealand
by region	Cotonou	EBA	CBI	AGOA	GSP–LDC	CARIBCAN	GSP–LDC	GSP–LDC	SPARTECA
Africa									
Botswana	✓			✓					
Cape Verde	✓	✓		✓	✓		✓	✓	
Comoros	✓	✓			✓		✓		
Djibouti	✓	✓		✓	✓		✓		
Equatorial Guinea	✓	✓			✓		✓	✓	
Gabon	✓			✓					
Gambia	✓	✓		✓	✓		✓	✓	
Guinea-Bissau	✓	✓		✓	✓		✓	✓	
Lesotho	✓	✓		✓	✓		✓	✓	
Mauritius	✓			✓					
Namibia	✓			✓					
São Tomé and Principe	✓	✓		✓	✓		✓	✓	
Seychelles	✓			✓					
Swaziland	✓			✓					
Asia									✓
Bhutan		✓			✓		✓	✓	
Maldives		✓					✓	✓	
Timor-Leste									
Caribbean and Latin America									
Antigua and Barbuda	✓		✓			✓			
Barbados	✓		✓			✓			

Belize	✓		✓		✓			
Dominica	✓		✓		✓			
Grenada	✓		✓		✓			
Guyana	✓		✓		✓			
Jamaica	✓		✓		✓			
St Kitts and Nevis	✓		✓		✓			
St Lucia	✓		✓		✓			
St Vincent and the Grenadines	✓		✓		✓			
Suriname	✓							
Trinidad and Tobago			✓		✓			
Pacific	✓							
Fiji	✓							✓
Kiribati	✓	✓		✓		✓	✓	✓
Marshall Islands	✓							✓
Federated States of Micronesia	✓							✓
Nauru	✓							✓
Palau	✓							
Papua New Guinea	✓							✓
Samoa	✓	✓		✓		✓	✓	✓
Solomon Islands	✓	✓				✓	✓	✓
Tonga	✓							✓
Tuvalu	✓	✓		✓		✓	✓	✓
Vanuatu	✓	✓		✓		✓	✓	✓

Source: EC (2004a), EC (2004b), USTR (2004a), USTR (2004b), USTR (2004c), Trade Point (2005), Government of Canada (2002), Ministry of Foreign Affairs (2004) and Pacific Islands Forum Secretariat (1998)

Table 7.9 *Preference margins by product for most vulnerable middle-income countries*

Country	Total preference margin	Percentage of preference margin accounted for by preferences for:			
		Sugar	Bananas	Garments[a]	Other
Mauritius	39.9	84	0	13	3
St Lucia	32.9	0	94	2	4
Belize	29.3	47	23	0	30
St Kitts and Nevis	28.7	94	0	0	6
Guyana	24.2	95	0	1	4
Fiji	24.1	96	0	1	2[b]
Dominica	15.9	0	97	0	3
Seychelles	12.2	0	0	0	100
Jamaica	9.7	67	8	7	18
St Vincent and the Grenadines	9.4	0	89	0	11
Albania	8.9	0	0	48	52
Swaziland	8.2	97	0	1	2
Middle-income countries[c]	4.9	42	19	12	27

[a] Garments includes textiles and clothing
[b] Discrepancy in original source
[c] Average for 76 middle-income developing countries, weighted by margin
Source: Alexandraki and Lankes (2004: 24)

concentrations, preferential beef exports account for 98 per cent of Botswana's agricultural exports to the EU, with equivalent figures of 97 per cent for bananas from St Vincent and the Grenadines and 83 per cent for sugar from Mauritius.[117]

The economic damage that will ensue for small economies that lose their historically vital preferential access to major markets is estimated to be substantial. Alexandraki and Lankes (2004: 25) estimate that eleven of the twelve worst affected middle-income developing countries will be small economies, with estimated losses shown in table 7.10. Sugar and banana

[117] Data from Tangermann (2000: 10); see also Mitchell (2004: 19) for data on sugar export concentration.

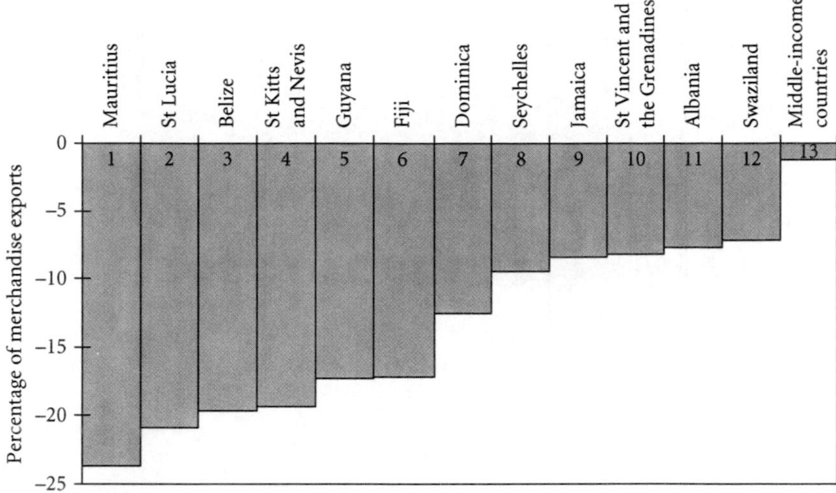

Source: Alexandraki and Lankes (2004: 25)

Figure 7.3 Losses from preference erosion as a percentage of merchandise exports

preferences are the main source of vulnerability.[118] For a 40 per cent reduction in preference margins, losses of a fifth to nearly a quarter of total exports are estimated for the most vulnerable small economies, as depicted in figure 7.3 (assuming a supply elasticity of 1.5). Even with a zero supply elasticity, the losses from a 40 per cent reduction in preference margins as a share of exports, GDP and government revenue, are substantial for these small economies (see table 7.10).[119] Guyana stands to lose the equivalent of over 5 per cent of GDP, Mauritius nearly 25 per cent of government revenue. Overall Alexandraki and Lankes (2004: 8, 26) argue that preference erosion is most acute for SIDS, and that aggregate losses are several

[118] To what extent this vulnerability might be mitigated in the short term by Economic Partnership Agreements, if these preserve aspects of current preferential arrangements (Schiff (2002: 15–17), is yet to be seen; but preferential prices will anyway fall as EU reforms to the relevant parts of the Common Agricultural Policy (CAP) commence.

[119] Note also that these findings exclude the effects of preference erosion in minor ACP–EU schemes (beef, veal and rum), and in markets outside Canada, the EU, Japan and the US. Thus, the results miss the impact of eroding Australian and New Zealand preferences on Pacific Islands, and the impact of the withdrawal of Multi-Fibre Agreement (MFA) quotas on small economies (Alexandraki and Lankes (2004: 6, 10, 18)). Ozden and Sharma (2004: 3), for example, find that the withdrawal of MFA quotas would be the equivalent of virtually eliminating the benefits of the CBI to garments industries in the Caribbean.

Table 7.10 *Macroeconomic losses from preference erosion in most vulnerable middle-income countries*

	Loss as a % of goods exports			Losses assuming zero supply elasticity (e = 0)			
Country	e = 1.5	e = 1.0	e = 1.0	Absolute ($US millions)	% of goods & services exports	% of GDP	% of government revenue
Mauritius	−23.7	−19.6	−11.5	−201	−7.2	−4.4	−24.4
St Lucia	−20.9	−17.2	−9.8	−4	−1.1	−0.6	−1.9
Belize	−19.6	−16.1	−9.1	−18	−4.1	−2.1	−8.0
St Kitts and Nevis	−19.3	−15.9	−8.9	−3	−1.8	−0.8	−1.9
Guyana	−17.3	−14.2	−7.9	−41	−6.2	−5.8	−17.7
Fiji	−17.2	−14.0	−7.8	−41	−3.8	−2.2	−9.1
Dominica	−12.6	−10.2	−5.5	−2	−1.9	−0.9	−2.3
Seychelles	−9.5	−7.7	−4.2	−10	−1.9	−1.6	−3.7
Jamaica	−8.4	−6.8	−3.5	−46	−1.4	−0.6	−2.2
St Vincent and the Grenadines	−8.2	−6.6	−3.4	−5	−2.7	−1.3	−4.3
Albania	−7.7	−6.3	−3.3	−10	−1.2	−0.2	−1.0
Swaziland	−7.2	−5.8	−3.0	−21	−1.8	−1.6	−5.8

Source: Alexandraki and Lankes (2004: 25–6)

times larger for middle-income developing countries than for LDCs. Among LDCs, Subramanian (2003a: 9–10, 13–14) makes similar findings: small economies are among those with the highest preference dependence, poised to lose most from preference erosion.

In light of the above, it is clear that multilateral trade liberalisation in agriculture will not necessarily make small economies better off. They are significant beneficiaries of current market distortions, will suffer absolute welfare losses when these distortions are dismantled, and have little potential to diversify into economic activities in which their exports will be competitive.[120] UNCTAD (2003a: 16–18, 32) demonstrates that under all feasible scenarios for agricultural liberalisation in the Doha Round, SIDS will suffer absolute welfare losses. Of these, Mauritius, Jamaica and Fiji will suffer the largest losses. Only if general agricultural liberalisation is augmented by providing SIDS with tariff-free access for *all* of their commodity exports to *all* major developed country markets will they be better off.

The foregoing does not preclude the validity of findings that preference schemes, particularly interventions in EU and US commodity markets related to subsidy preferences, are grossly market distorting and enormously wasteful to operate.[121] For recipients, such schemes may impose a significant administrative burden,[122] impede the efficient allocation of productive resources,[123] and act as a disincentive to trade liberalisation including through recipients' reluctance to participate in reciprocal trade negotiations.[124] Their persistence may well be driven more by the vested interests of producers, processors and distributors in developed countries, than by the trade interests of declared recipients.[125] Furthermore, preferences may have benefited their donors by reducing developing country pressure to free markets in their export interests.[126] That their

[120] See Grynberg and Razzaque (2003: 52) on the absolute welfare loss to preference dependent states caused by the Uruguay Round; and Mattoo and Subramanian (2004: 3) for a discussion of the ambivalence of small states to further trade liberalisation.

[121] See Mitchell (2004: 18), Borrell (1999: 8) and Oxfam (2004: 1).

[122] See Panagariya (2002: 1429–30) and Keck and Low (2004: 11–12).

[123] Subramanian (2003a: 2), Page and Kleen (2004: 26) and Levantis et al. (2003: 1).

[124] See Ozden and Reinhardt (2003: 20–1), Panagariya (2002: 1416), Keck and Low (2004: 13–14), Alexandraki and Lankes (2004: 5), Kennes (2000: 99) and Brock and McGee (2004: 15).

[125] See Watkins (2004: 20–5), Subramanian (2003a: 2), Borrell (1999: 13, 19), Ozden and Sharma (2004: 12) and Anderson (2004: 6).

[126] See Watkins (2004: 41), Panagariya (2002: 1430), Page and Kleen (2004: 41), Levantis et al. (2003: 1) and Subramanian (2003a: 2).

existence is lamented does not mean that removing preferential schemes will be any less damaging to small economies, however.[127] Simply because preference-dependent states are few and would lose only a fraction of what global welfare would gain from liberalisation[128] does not make that loss any less detrimental to the development prospects of small economies.

For preference-dependent states, the alternative policy to pursuing extended preferences is 'adjustment', a term implying that there exists an alternative sustainable development path. Yet, for the reasons outlined earlier, small economies may lack both the potential for competitiveness in exports historically benefiting from preferences and the robust macroeconomic situations to absorb the impact of collapsing industries.[129] Small economies also face significant competitiveness constraints in entering new economic activities and non-preferential markets, arising from combinations of characteristics associated with their small size, vulnerability to external economic shocks and natural disasters, and governance capacity.[130] Certainly, preferences have encouraged small economies to maintain industries which are inefficient by best-practice standards, thus inhibiting their incentives to shift to patterns of production and trade that are sustainable in the absence of preferences.[131] This chapter argues that, at least in the near future, the feasibility of alternative employments for these production resources should not be assumed automatically.

Salmon (2002: 11) offers a necessary caution against the kind of reasoning that consists in affirming ex post facto that providing preferences was not legitimate for small economies since they have performed well, when their good performance has arisen precisely from those preferences. Small economies have benefited substantially from preferential access to subsidised markets in the developed world, yet their economies are now precariously positioned as these market-distorting subsidies are reduced and non-LDC small economies are set to lose preferential access.[132] Transfers, equivalent to previous preference

[127] Levantis et al. (2003: 2) make a similar argument.

[128] See Mitchell (2004: 26–7) and Panagariya (2002: 1426).

[129] See Alexandraki and Lankes (2004: 5) on factors affecting states' capacities to manage preference losses.

[130] UNCTAD (2003b: 20), for example, demonstrates this predicament with respect to the Windward Islands.

[131] Page and Kleen (2004: 28).

[132] Grynberg (2001a: 279).

rents,[133] need not have equivalent effects if channelled through donors' aid administrations according to their development priorities.[134] Even direct financial transfers[135] would not necessarily engender the same macroeconomic outcomes:[136] what small economies lose with preferences is the feasibility of engaging in productive export activities at remunerative prices, with concomitant gains in foreign exchange, employment and stability of trade and transport patterns. Adequate compensation would therefore involve funding the economic transition to equivalently remunerative export industries, including possibly persistent subsidies to make comparative advantages operational in the near future. A more palatable alternative to donors, discussed earlier, might be the extension of tariff-free access for all exports from all small economies into all developed country markets. Otherwise, globalisation along the lines of currently agreed multilateral trade rules will make small economies worse off, making a strong development case for more favourable treatment for small economies.

7.9 Small economies' predicament as a trade concern

At the core of the present economic predicament of small economies is trade: small economies rely on trade to enhance their development prospects beyond the constraints of small size, yet face severe limitations on their potential for competitiveness in world markets. Moreover, their predicament is a relevant concern for trade negotiations; a failure to address it is a threat to the legitimacy of the multilateral trade regime.[137] This is not to say that appropriate modifications of trade agreements will be sufficient to alleviate small economies' development problems, nor that other international forums and organisations will not prove vital to this effort.[138] The UNCTAD, World Bank, IMF and Commonwealth Secretariat, as well as bilateral and NGO donors, can play, and in many

[133] These are advocated because they make explicit the aid transfer to recipients previously occurring through preferences, without imposing the global welfare losses of the market interventions underpinning those preferences. See Mitchell (2004: 27), Borrell (1999: 8, 17), Page and Kleen (2004: 11, 14, 16, 63), Fowler and Fokker (2004: 34–5) and Kennes (2000: 103).

[134] Page and Kleen (2004: 65, 91); for an example of this intention, see EC (2005: 6).

[135] Alexandraki and Lankes (2004: 27) argue that targeting such transfers would be straightforward.

[136] See, for example, the modelling of different compensation scenarios in Levantis et al. (2003: 6–8).

[137] Grynberg (2001a: 305) and Keck and Low (2004: 8).

[138] Page and Kleen (2004: 70) and Grynberg (2001b: 339).

cases already are playing, critical roles.[139] But this does not make multilateral, regional and bilateral trade negotiations any less relevant to the predicament of small economies.[140]

Four specific avenues through which current trade negotiations affect the development prospects of small economies are noteworthy here. First, agreed and impending multilateral trade rules threaten to erode or dismantle the preferential access on the basis of which small economies have participated successfully in world markets in the past. Secondly, the selective liberalisation of global markets under multilateral rules omits markets of particular relevance to small economies, notably semi-skilled and unskilled labour services. Thirdly, elements of agreed multilateral trade rules constrain the policy space available to small states – or the international community – to improve their development prospects. Examples include proscriptions preventing small states – whether from their own resources or international assistance – from offering investment incentives to export industries[141] or subsidising transport services. Fourthly, small states are especially disadvantaged in their capacity to challenge the abuse of trade rules by other states; accommodating this weakness in the redesign of rules and the allocation of technical assistance could prove valuable.[142]

Given the importance of trade regimes to the development prospects of small economies, it is often asserted that small economies should embrace multilateral trade rules with greater vigour.[143] Such arguments conflate free trade with currently agreed multilateral trade rules. The integration of small economies into an idealised global free market is very different from the insertion of small economies into world markets on the terms of currently agreed trade rules. Emerging from a process of interstate negotiation

[139] See, for example, UNCTAD (2004a), World Bank (2003), IMF (2003) and Commonwealth Secretariat (2003).

[140] It is, for example, mistaken to argue as Page and Kleen (2004: 43) do that because trade does not necessarily lead to development, the readjustment of trade rules is not necessarily relevant to the promotion of development.

[141] See English and de Wulf (2002: 164–9) and Grynberg (2001a: 272, 298).

[142] See Wilson (2002: 428–31) on non-tariff barriers to trade; and Davenport (2001: 10) on the importance of protecting small states from anti-dumping and countervailing measures. Protecting small economies from parallel trade-related abuses is also important: see, for example, the OECD's 'Harmful Tax Initiative' which incorporates a protectionist intent in its 'unfair' tax competition provisions, threatening the viability of financial services industries with demonstrated probity in small economies (see Grynberg et al. (2003: 2–6, 10–12, 19–23), Armstrong and Read (2002: 21) and Read (2004: 371)).

[143] See Burki (2001: 9–10), Kennes (2000: 9) and World Bank (2002a: 3).

and bargaining, trade rules are widely recognised as being biased in favour of the economic interests of major powers.[144] Negotiated rules come with no guarantee of being beneficial to the welfare of any one participant. When small economies 'integrate into the global economy' by becoming subject to multilateral trade rules, the markets of export interest to them and into which they are inserted are not necessarily those that are free, nor will their participation in negotiations necessarily change that.[145] Thus, for example, small economies are bound by intellectual property rules defined by developed countries in the WTO,[146] but their semi-skilled and unskilled labour cannot move freely into industrialised markets.[147] In a later section, this chapter will address the suggestion that the value to small economies of multilateral rules *per se* overrides whatever terms those rules might contain.[148]

7.10 The feasibility of favourable treatment for small economies

This chapter has brought together evidence that small economies face substantial challenges to competitive participation in world markets, in support of the contention that the trade of small economies requires more favourable treatment if they are to avoid the imminent prospect of marginalisation.[149] This section will argue that such favourable treatment is feasible, and furthermore that it would impose a negligible financial cost on the international community. The only significant cost would be ideological; as Winters and Martins (2004a: 149) argue, attaining the favourable treatment that small economies require would necessitate 'conscious policy-shifts in the major capitals'.

If small economies were to be accorded duty- and quota-free access for all of their exports in major markets,[150] derogations from WTO rules would be required. It is the current WTO-incompatibility of this necessary discrimination among developing countries that has enabled larger or more

[144] See Finger and Winters (2002: 53–5) on exclusion of the interests of the weak; Ozden and Reinhardt (2003: 5) and Oyejide (2002: 505–6) on the structural biases in GSP schemes, and Freund (2003: 5, 23) on biases in trade agreements between unequal powers.

[145] See Ozden and Reinhardt (2003: 3) for the opposite assumption of effective bargaining power.

[146] See Subramanian (2003b: 169–72).

[147] Chanda (2002: 307).

[148] Page and Kleen (2004: 82). See also Armstrong and Read (2002: 11) for a discussion of small states and trade rules as public goods.

[149] Grynberg and Razzaque (2003: 1).

[150] See Hoekman et al. (2003: 10, 19) for equity arguments in support of this inclusion; see also Mattoo and Subramanian (2004).

competitive developing countries to challenge successfully the existing preferences accorded to small economies.[151] The life of tariff preferences is of course finite, their value eroding with multilateral liberalisation, but even finite preferences would provide small economies with a necessary reprieve. WTO rules could also be adjusted to benefit small economies in areas such as the feasibility of their access to and retaliatory measures under dispute settlement,[152] the extent of their benefits from technical assistance programmes,[153] and the achievement of a degree of rule-ordering of their accession processes.[154]

In addition to tariff-free access for their exports, small economies would benefit from amendments to specific WTO agreements that are unduly prejudicial to their interests.[155] Exemptions from subsidies disciplines, for example, are necessary to allow state interventions to overcome market failures which are undermining particular trade opportunities for small economies.[156] Whilst it is not feasible for small economies to use domestic resources to subsidise their way out of their pervasive cost disadvantages, exemptions from subsidies disciplines would also avert the WTO-incompatibility of subsidies for the trade of small economies that are sourced internationally. Alongside free market access for their exports, Winters and Martins (2004a: 149) argue that such international subsidisation of small economies' trade is one of the few possible policy responses that could sustain small economies' participation in world markets. A second example is that small economies require long transition periods for the implementation of WTO disciplines, the extreme costs and complexity of which are beyond the current resources, capacity and development interests of small states.[157] In place of a fixed transition period, compliance could be required only once state institutions and resources – including any forthcoming technical assistance – are sufficient for implementation to be effective. A final example is provided by current fisheries negotiations. It is vital to the interests of small coastal states that derogations prevent new

[151] Successful challenges that some developed countries are using as levers to direct small states into reciprocal trade agreements in order to preserve something of their current preferential access. [152] Delich (2002: 76–8). [153] Mattoo and Subramanian (2004: 6).

[154] On accession, see Grynberg (2001a: 307), Grynberg (2001b: 333–4) and Langhammer and Lücke (2000).

[155] For a broader framework within which these specific suggestions could fit, see ICTSD (2003) or Keck and Low (2004). [156] Davenport (2001: 10).

[157] Hoekman et al. (2003: 5, 16) and Finger and Schuler (2002: 493, 501); see also Rodrik (2002: 8–9) and Page and Kleen (2004: 56).

rules from reducing their revenue from fisheries access fees and associated development assistance, impeding their efforts to domesticate their fisheries industries, and disallowing their support to artisanal fisheries activities.[158]

Incorporating specific derogations from particular rules to target the needs of certain categories of states has extensive precedent in the WTO.[159] Without overarching recognition of the special circumstances of small economies such as that provided by the Doha Declaration and Small Economies Work Program (SEWP),[160] however, it will prove harder for small states to leverage such derogations in specific negotiating groups. And without overarching tariff preferences or international subsidisation of small economies' trade as the foundation of the international response to the trade predicament of small economies, rule derogations will amount to little more than piecemeal concessions lacking the potential to tackle that predicament effectively.

In pursuing the recognition of their interests in multilateral trade negotiations, small economies encounter opposition even at a conceptual level. Non-discrimination and reciprocity are described as the 'pillars' of the WTO,[161] which rule derogations for some states are accused of undermining.[162] Yet, as Keck and Low (2004: 3) state, 'The battle to establish the principle that a set of uniform multilateral rights and obligations among a deeply diverse set of nations could not serve the best interests of all parties was won a long time ago.' What appears to be particularly threatening to proponents of the doctrine that trade liberalisation necessarily advantages all, is the prospect of rule derogations for small economies based on the argument that small states otherwise would not benefit from globalisation.[163] Apart from conflating current multilateral rules with free trade, this attitude also supposes faith in free trade to be hopelessly fragile if favourable treatment for small economies, explicable and justifiable *within* economic models of comparative advantage, can undermine it. Still, critics argue that special and differential treatment can only be temporary, if 'equal treatment' is to remain a core principle of the WTO,[164] supposedly invalidating the claims of small economies because their small size, remoteness and exposure to

[158] For the details of how fisheries negotiations affect small states, see Grynberg (2003: 69–72) and also Vossenaar (2004: 67).

[159] See Davenport (2001: 4–5) and Grynberg (2001a) for examples of such derogations.

[160] See WTO (2001: 7–8) and also Tulloch (2001).

[161] Freund (2003: 2).

[162] Ozden and Reinhardt (2003: 4).

[163] See Page and Kleen (2004: 79–80).

[164] Page and Kleen (2004: 46, 77).

natural disasters are permanent. But, favourable treatment of small economies' trade is not expected to alter fixed features like small size, large distances to markets and frequent natural disasters.[165] Such features merely act as identifiers of likely candidates for assistance. Instead, more favourable treatment is intended to alleviate the *effects* that combinations of the characteristics of small economies have on their trade competitiveness. These effects are persistent, but aspects of them may reduce in intensity in the medium term in specific cases, for example if transport costs decline significantly, or if complete and competitive disaster insurance markets develop.

It has been suggested that special and differential treatment, in as far as it detracts from the systemic value of consistent rules, injures the interests of weak participants like small states in the multilateral trade regime.[166] However, one cannot extrapolate from the idea that international rules are a public good the argument that small administrations can gain particular benefit from implementing them, without accounting for the cost that complex and often inappropriate disciplines impose. The systemic value of the trade regime to all members could reasonably be expected to be sufficient to absorb the negligible cost of rule derogations for a group of states accounting in aggregate for only a fraction of 1 per cent of world trade.[167] If the rules are inappropriate for small economies, negotiating derogations within the framework of the trade regime supports their interests. The marginal nature of small economies in the world trading system makes incredible claims that more favourable treatment of them would impose significant financial costs on others.[168] UNCTAD (2003a: 19) demonstrates for agriculture that free access for the exports of SIDS would have virtually no effect on the welfare of other developing countries; Winters and Martins (2004a: 150) argue that the costs to the international community of subsidising all exports from small states would be 'perfectly manageable'.[169] The cost to the legitimacy of the international trade regime if it does not adjust to accommodate the trade predicament of small economies may be more substantial, however.[170] The further marginalisation of small economies in world trade will expose the insincerity of the rhetoric of mutually advantageous negotiated trade liberalisation.

[165] For the contrary position, see Page and Kleen (2004: 15, 46, 80).

[166] See Page and Kleen (2004: 7–8, 81). [167] See Grynberg and Razzaque (2003: 11).

[168] See Breckenridge (2002: 11).

[169] See also Davenport (2001: 1, 17–18) and Stevens (2002: 25–6).

[170] Stevens (2002: 1) and Drahos (2004: 9–10).

7.11 Small states, negotiating weaknesses

Possessing a good case for favourable treatment in trade negotiations is important, but the value of a good argument arises not of itself but from its contribution to the bargaining power of the states concerned. What weakens small states' prospects of attaining special and differential treatment in multilateral negotiations are their substantial disadvantages in other aspects of bargaining power. Most critically, small economies lack market power, and thus the potential to make credible threats impelling others to negotiate with them.[171] Their intelligence networks, gathering and analysing information about their trade performance and economic interests, also are weak from the extremely constrained research capacities of their bureaucracies and also of the relatively small firms implied by their small market sizes. If market power and intelligence networks are the most important elements of bargaining power, the prospects of small states attaining more favourable trade treatment as a negotiated outcome are bleak.

In an attempt to mitigate this weakness, small states have utilised their enrolment power to form coalitions among the collection of states that share small, vulnerable or island characteristics. The coalition does not benefit from greater bargaining power through market size, since the aggregated market of members is still insignificant in global terms. But this coalition has utilised the support of international organisations well, its intelligence networks have been strengthened by the pooling of state and regional administrative resources, and its cohesiveness has strengthened the voice of these states in multilateral negotiations. Cohesion and voice, however, have depended crucially on the inclusion in the coalition of states whose larger populations or economic success lead opponents to question the deservedness of special treatment.[172] But these inclusions are vital to the negotiating power of the group. Cohesion depends on including all states perceiving themselves and perceived by the group as small; splitting traditional regions of small states by excluding Papua New Guinea or Jamaica on the basis of population, or Barbados or Trinidad and Tobago on the basis of per capita income, would be extremely costly to group cohesion.[173] Voice depends on including strong states to lead the group; excluding Mauritius, Jamaica or

[171] On elements of bargaining power see Drahos (2004: 6–8) and also Mattoo and Subramanian (2004: 3). [172] Davenport (2001: 1) and Hein (2004 : 6–7) discuss this point.

[173] See Narlikar (2003: 2, 27–9, 183), including the critical statement: 'Stability of allies is a crucial asset for the weak.'

Barbados on grounds of size or success would cost the group historical leaders, links to information networks in other coalitions, and states with strong economic interests in the SEWP.[174] If membership were fixed exactly by small population or lower-middle income thresholds, the bargaining power of the coalition would dissipate: critics could be satisfied that no anomalies remained, but equally would no longer have to engage with the group's demands.[175]

This discussion of the negotiating process from which multilateral trade rules emerge should temper suggestions that the continued presence – rather than exit – of small states in the WTO indicates that they must derive a net benefit from its agreements.[176] WTO negotiations involve an unrolling of 'consensus', starting with the most powerful economies and progressively incorporating other major players and coalitions until it reaches the periphery – populated by small states – by which time the 'consensus' is a foregone conclusion.[177] Furthermore, the governance capabilities of small states are so constrained that they have little capacity even to assess the implications for their development prospects of the many alternative proposals coming forward. Thus, for small states in multilateral negotiations, concepts like informed choice and cost-benefit analysis are somewhat irrelevant.[178] To a limited extent, it is appropriate to characterise international trade rules – for example, liberalisation commitments – as public goods negotiated with the resources of major powers and upon which small states can free ride.[179] It is equally feasible, however, that rules determined in the absence of input from small states will prove adverse to their interests, with an alternative characterisation of the process being of small states getting damaged in the crossfire of negotiations between major powers.[180]

7.12 Conclusion

This chapter has presented evidence that the globalisation of markets under existing and emerging multilateral trade rules will damage the trade and development interests of small economies. Arresting their further

[174] See Narlikar (2003: 16, 183).

[175] See Encontre (2004: 92, 98) and Hein (2004: 12–13, 20) for emphasis on the need to define group membership strictly.

[176] Page and Kleen (2004: 43, 82).

[177] See Narlikar (2003: 37), Drahos (2004: 11, 17) and Brock and McGee (2004: 9).

[178] On this point see Drahos (2004: 4–10), and also Finger and Winters (2002: 55).

[179] Armstrong and Read (2002: 15–16); see also Page and Kleen (2004: 82) and Narlikar (2003: 37).

[180] Grynberg (2001b: 334), Grynberg (2003: 70) and Watkins (2004: 16–17).

marginalisation in world trade is not a simple matter of domestic economic 'adjustment' towards productive activities and trade patterns that are sustainable in globalised markets. Instead, characteristics of small economies, centring around their size, vulnerability and governance capacity, combine to yield significant cost disadvantages large enough to undermine substantially these states' capacities to participate in trade on a remunerative basis, even in areas of comparative advantage. Where small economies cannot obtain premium prices for their products abroad, their exports will struggle to be feasible. Any diminished trading success will only compound the deleterious effects of small size on their economic welfare, with increasing marginalisation in world trade being the last thing that small economies can afford.

This chapter has also shown that preferential access to major developed country markets has contributed to the relatively good historical income and growth performances of small economies, preferences that are now being eroded or dismantled. As Armstrong and Read (2002: 19) conclude, 'Strict adherence to axiomatic multilateralism and the creation of a level playing-field for international trade is therefore likely to deprive small states of many niche opportunities by removing marginal but critically important sources of protection which contribute to their growth success.' At the same time, the significant challenges to their competitiveness posed by their small size, vulnerability and constrained governance make it extremely difficult for small economies to take advantage of new opportunities emerging from the globalisation of markets.

At the current juncture of international trade negotiations, small economies are precariously positioned: certain to lose from the greater liberalisation of markets for their key exports, they lack the bargaining power to achieve more favourable treatment and greater trade-related assistance that might forestall otherwise disquieting economic prospects in the near future. Among the necessary international responses, multilateral trade rules can be adjusted to accommodate the concerns of small economies, but whether major powers will be willing to negotiate this adjustment, and thereby support the legitimacy of the international trade regime, is less certain.

References

Alexandraki, K. and H. P. Lankes (2004): *The Impact of Preference Erosion on Middle-Income Developiong Countries.* IMF Working Paper 169. Washington, D.C.: International Monetary Fund

Anderson, K. (2004): *The Challenge of Reducing Subsidies and Trade Barriers.* World Bank Policy Research Working Paper 3415. Washington, D.C.: World Bank

Armstrong, H. W. and R. Read (2002): *The Importance of Being Unimportant: The Political Economy of Trade and Growth in Small States.* Lancaster: University of Lancaster

Atkins, J. P., S. Mazzi and C. D. Easter (2000): *A Commonwealth Vulnerability Index for Developing Countries: The Position of Small States.* London: Commonwealth Secretariat

(2001): 'Small States: A Composite Vulnerability Index', in *Small States in the Global Economy*, ed. D. Peretz, R. Faruqi and E. J. Kisanga. London: Commonwealth Secretariat, 53–92

Auffret, P. (2003a): *Catastrophe Insurance Market in the Caribbean Region: Market Failures and Recommendations for Public Sector Interventions.* World Bank Policy Research Working Paper 2963. Washington, D.C.: World Bank

(2003b): *High Consumption Volatility: The Impact of Natural Disasters?* World Bank Policy Research Working Paper 2962. Washington, D.C.: World Bank

Benson, C. and E. Clay (2003): *Economic and Financial Impacts of Natural Disasters: An Assessment of Their Effects and Options for Mitigation: Synthesis Report.* London: Overseas Development Institute

Benson, C., E. Clay, F. V. Michael and A. W. Robertson (2001): *Dominica: Natural Disasters and Economic Development in a Small Island State.* Disaster Risk Management Working Paper 2. Washington, D.C.: World Bank

Bertram, G. (2004): 'On the Convergence of Small Island Economies with Their Metropolitan Patrons', *World Development*, 32, 343–64

Borrell, B. (1999): *Bananas: Straightening out Bent Ideas on Trade as Aid.* Canberra and Sydney: Centre for International Economics

Braun, M., R. Hausmann and L. Pritchett (2002): *The Proliferation of Sovereigns: Are There Lessons for Integration?* Harvard University, Kennedy School of Government at Harvard University and Kennedy School of Government at Harvard University/Center for Global Development

Breckenridge, A. (2002): *Developing an Issues-Based Approach to Special and Differential Treatment.* Paper presented to the Trade and Integration Network, Third Meeting, 19–20 March 2002. Washington, D.C.: Inter-American Development Bank

Briguglio, L. (1995): 'Small Island Developing States and Their Economic Vulnerabilities', *World Development*, 23, 1615–32

Brock, K., and R. McGee (2004): *Mapping Trade Policy: Understanding the Challenges of Civil Society Participation.* IDS Working Paper 225. Brighton: Institute of Development Studies

Burki, S. J. (2001): 'Integrating Small States in a Fast-Changing Global Economy', in *Small States in the Global Economy*, ed. D. Peretz, R. Faruqi and E. J. Kisanga. London: Commonwealth Secretariat, 7–10

Burnside, C. and D. Dollar (1997): *Aid, Policies, and Growth.* World Bank Policy Research Working Paper 1777. Washington, D.C.: World Bank

Chanda, R. (2002): 'Movement of Natural Persons and the GATS: Major Trade Policy Impediments', in *Development, Trade, and the WTO: A Handbook*, ed. B. Hoekman, A. Mattoo and P. English. Washington, D.C.: World Bank, 304–14

Charveriat, C. (2000): *Natural Disasters in Latin America and the Caribbean: An Overview of Risk.* Research Department Working Paper 434. Washington, D.C.: Inter-American Development Bank

Choraria, J. (2004): *A Note on Commodity Value Chains Compression – Coffee, Cocoa and Sugar.* London: Commonwealth Secretariat

Collier, P. and J. Dehn (2001): *Aid, Shocks, and Growth.* World Bank Policy Research Working Paper 2688. Washington, D.C.: World Bank

Collier, P. and D. Dollar (2001): 'Aid, Risk and the Special Concerns of Small States', in *Small States in the Global Economy*, ed. D. Peretz, R. Faruqi and E. J. Kisanga. London: Commonwealth Secretariat, 11–38

Commonwealth Secretariat (2003): *Small States: Economic Review and Basic Statistics.* London: Commonwealth Secretariat

Davenport, M. (2001): *A Study of Alternative Special and Differential Arrangements for Small Economies.* London: Commonwealth Secretariat

Dehn, J. (2000a): *Commodity Price Uncertainty and Shocks: Implications for Economic Growth.* Working Paper 10. Oxford: Centre for the Study of African Economies

(2000b): *Commodity Price Uncertainty in Developing Countries.* Working Paper 11. Oxford: Centre for the Study of African Economies

(2000c): *Private Investment in Developing Countries: The Effects of Commodity Shocks and Uncertainty.* Working Paper 12. Oxford: Centre for the Study of African Economies

Delich, V. (2002): 'Developing Countries and the WTO Dispute Settlement Mechanism', in *Development, Trade, and the WTO: A Handbook*, ed. B. Hoekman, A. Mattoo and P. English. Washington, D.C.: World Bank, 71–80

Drahos, P. (2004): *When the Weak Bargain with the Strong: Negotiations in the WTO.* Canberra: Australian National University

Easterly, W. and A. Kraay (2001): 'Small States, Small Problems? Income, Growth and Volatility in Small States', in *Small States in the Global Economy*, ed. D. Peretz, R. Faruqi and E. J. Kisanga. London: Commonwealth Secretariat, 93–116

EC (2004a): 'ACP–EU Agreement', Brussels: Europa – European Commission. 18 February 2005: http://europa.eu.int/comm/development/body/cotonou/index_en.htm

EC (2004b): 'Generalised System of Preferences', Brussels: Europa – European Commission. 18 February 2005: http://europa.eu.int/comm/trade/issues/global/gsp/eba/ug.htm

(2005): *Action Plan on Accompanying Measures for Sugar Protocol Countries Affected by the Reform of the EU Sugar Regime*. Commission Staff Working Paper SEC(2005)61. Brussels: European Commission

ECLAC and IDB (2000): *A Matter of Development: How to Reduce Vulnerability in the Face of Natural Disasters*. Mexico and Washington, D.C.: Economic Commission for Latin America and the Caribbean / Inter-American Development Bank

EM-DAT (2004): 'EM-DAT: The OFDA/CRED International Disaster Database', Brussels: Université Catholique de Louvain. 18 February 2005: www.em-dat.net

Encontre, P. (1999): 'The Vulnerability and Resilience of Small Island Developing States in the Context of Globalization', *Natural Resources Forum*, 23, 261–70

(2004): 'SIDS as a Category: Adopting Criteria Would Enhance Credibility', in *Is a Special Treatment of Small Island Developing States Possible?*, ed. UNCTAD. UNCTAD/LDC/2004/1. New York and Geneva: United Nations Conference on Trade and Development, 91–102

English, P. and L. de Wulf (2002): 'Export Development Policies and Institutions', in *Development, Trade, and the WTO: A Handbook*, ed. B. Hoekman, A. Mattoo and P. English. Washington, D.C.: World Bank, 160–70

Farrugia, C. (1993): 'The Special Working Environment of Senior Administrators in Small States', *World Development*, 21, 221–6

Finger, J. M. and P. Schuler (2002): 'Implementation of WTO Commitments: The Development Challenge', in *Development, Trade, and the WTO: A Handbook*, ed. B. Hoekman, A. Mattoo and P. English. Washington, D.C.: World Bank, 493–503

Finger, J. M., and L. A. Winters (2002): 'Reciprocity in the WTO', in *Development, Trade, and the WTO: A Handbook*, ed. B. Hoekman, A. Mattoo and P. English. Washington, D.C.: World Bank, 50–60

Fowler, P., and R. Fokker (2004): *A Sweet Future? The Potential for EU Sugar Reform to Contribute to Poverty Reduction in Southern Africa*. Washington, D.C.: Oxfam International

Freeman, P. K., M. Keen and M. Mani (2003): *Dealing with Increased Risk of Natural Disasters: Challenges and Options*. IMF Working Paper 197. Washington, D.C.: International Monetary Fund

Freund, C. (2003): *Reciprocity in Free Trade Agreements*. World Bank Policy Research Working Paper 3061. Washington, D.C.: World Bank

Gay, D. (2004): *How Economies Participate in the WTO: Vanuatu's Suspended WTO Accession*. Paper prepared for the Institute for International Business, Economics and Law. Adelaide: University of Adelaide

Government of Canada (2002): 'Improving Access for the Products of the Least Developed Countries (LDCs) to the Canadian Market', Ottowa: Government of Canada. 18 February 2005: http://www.dfait-maeci.gc.ca/tna-nac/2ldc-dis02-en.asp

Grynberg, R. (2001a): 'Trade Policy Implications for Small Vulnerable States of the Global Trade Regime Shift', in *Small States in the Global Economy*, ed. D. Peretz, R. Faruqi and E. J. Kisanga. London: Commonwealth Secretariat, 267–328

(2001b): 'The Pacific Island States and the WTO: Towards a Post-Seattle Agenda for Small Vulnerable States', in *Small States in the Global Economy*, ed. D. Peretz, R. Faruqi and E. J. Kisanga. London: Commonwealth Secretariat, 329–42

(2003): 'WTO Fisheries Subsidies Negotiations: Implications for Fisheries Access Arrangements and Sustainable Management', in *Fisheries Issues in WTO and ACP–EU Trade Negotiations*, ed. R. Grynberg. London: Commonwealth Secretariat, 59–82

Grynberg, R. and M. A. Razzaque (2003): *The Trade Performance of Small States*. London: Commonwealth Secretariat

Grynberg, R., S. Silva and J. Y. Remy (2003): *Plurilateral Financial Standards and Their Regulation: The Experience of Small Developing States*. London: Commonwealth Secretariat

Gurenko, E. and R. Lester (2004): *Rapid Onset Natural Disasters: The Role of Financing in Effective Risk Management*. World Bank Policy Research Working Paper 3278. Washington, D.C.: World Bank

Hausmann, R. (2004): *Sovereignty and Prosperity: The Challenges of Small States*. Paper presented to the World Bank Small States Forum, 3 October 2004. Washington, D.C.: World Bank

Hein, P. (2004): 'Small Island Developing States: Origin of the Category and Definition Issues', in *Is a Special Treatment of Small Island Developing States Possible?*, ed. UNCTAD. UNCTAD/LDC/2004/1. New York and Geneva: United Nations Conference on Trade and Development, 1–22

Hoekman, B., C. Michalopoulos and L. A. Winters (2003): *More Favorable and Differential Treatment of Developing Countries: Towards a New Approach in the WTO*. World Bank Policy Research Working Paper 3107. Washington, D.C.: World Bank

ICTSD (2003): *'Spaces for Development Policy': Revisiting Special and Differential Treatment*. Paper prepared for the joint ICTSD–GP International Dialogue 'Making Special and Differential Treatment More Effective and Responsive to Development Needs', 6–7 May 2003. Geneva: International Centre for Trade and Sustainable Development

IMF (2003): *Fund Assistance for Countries Facing Exogenous Shocks*. Washington, D.C.: International Monetary Fund

International Workshop (2004): 'Report on the International Workshop on Economic Vulnerability and Resilience of Small States', 1–3 March 2004. Malta: Commonwealth Secretariat, Economics Department of the University of Malta, Islands and Small States Institute at the Foundation for International Studies of the University of Malta

IPCC (2001): 'Climate Change 2001: The Scientific Basis and Climate Change: Impacts, Adaptation, and Vulnerability: Summary for Policymakers', Geneva: Intergovernmental Panel on Climate Change. 2 February 2005: www.ipcc.ch

Jansen, M. (2004): *Income Volatility in Small and Developing Economies: Export Concentration Matters.* WTO Discussion Paper 3. Geneva: World Trade Organization

Keck, A., and P. Low (2004): *Special and Differential Treatment in the WTO: Why, When and How?* WTO Staff Working Paper [ERSD-2004–03]. Geneva: World Trade Organization

Kennes, W. (2000): *Small Developing Countries and Global Markets: Competing in the Big League.* Basingstoke: Macmillan Press

Langhammer, R. J. and M. Lücke (2000): *WTO Negotiations and Accession Issues for Vulnerable Economies.* Kiel Working Paper 990. Kiel: Kiel Institute of World Economics

Laurent, E. (forthcoming): 'Small States in the Banana Dispute: And the Environment for Bananas from the Eastern Caribbean Countries, Following the Implementation of the Reforms of the European Union's Banana Market', London: Commonwealth Secretariat

Levantis, T., F. Jotzo and V. Tulpule (2003): *Ending of EU Sugar Trade Preferences: Potential Consequences for Fiji.* ABARE Current Issues 03.2. Canberra: Australian Bureau of Agricultural and Resource Economics

Malua, M. B. (2003): 'Case Study: The Pacific Islands', in *Turning Losses into Gains: SIDS and Multilateral Trade Liberalisation in Agriculture*, ed. UNCTAD. UNCTAD/DITC/TNCD/2003/1. New York and Geneva: United Nations Conference on Trade and Development, 171–204

Mattoo, A., and A. Subramanian (2004): *The WTO and the Poorest Countries: The Stark Reality.* IMF Working Paper 81. Washington, D.C.: International Monetary Fund

Melville, G. (2003): 'Case Study: The Windward Islands', in *Turning Losses into Gains: SIDS and Multilateral Trade Liberalisation in Agriculture*, ed. UNCTAD. UNCTAD/DITC/TNCD/2003/1. New York and Geneva: United Nations Conference on Trade and Development, 97–126

Michalopoulos, C. (2002): 'WTO Accession', in *Development, Trade, and the WTO: A Handbook*, ed. B. Hoekman, A. Mattoo and P. English. Washington, D.C.: World Bank, 61–70

Ministry of Foreign Affairs (2004): 'Beneficiaries of Japan's GSP', Tokyo: Ministry of Foreign Affairs of Japan. 18 February 2005: http://www.mofa.go.jp/policy/economy/gsp/benef.html

Mitchell, D. (2004): *Sugar Policies: Opportunities for Change.* World Bank Policy Research Working Paper 3222. Washington, D.C.: World Bank

Murray, D. J. (1981): 'Microstates: Public Administration for the Small and Beautiful', *Public Administration and Development*, 1, 245–56

Narlikar, A. (2003): *International Trade and Developing Countries: Bargaining Coalitions in the GATT and WTO.* London: Routledge

Oxfam (2004): *An End to EU Sugar Dumping? Implications of the Interim WTO Panel Ruling in the Dispute against EU Sugar Policies Brought by Brazil, Thailand, and Australia.* Washington, D.C.: Oxfam International

Oyejide, T. A. (2002): 'Special and Differential Treatment', in *Development, Trade, and the WTO: A Handbook*, ed. B. Hoekman, A. Mattoo and P. English. Washington, D.C.: World Bank, 504–8

Ozden, C. and E. Reinhardt (2003): *The Perversity of Preferences: GSP and Developing Country Trade Policies, 1976–2000.* World Bank Policy Research Working Paper 2955. Washington, D.C.: World Bank

Ozden, C. and G. Sharma (2004): *Price Effects of Preferential Market Access: The Caribbean Basic Initiative and the Apparel Sector.* World Bank Policy Research Working Paper 3244. Washington, D.C.: World Bank

Pacific Islands Forum Secretariat (1998): 'SPARTECA: What is SPARTECA?', Suva: Pacific Islands Forum Secretariat. 18 February 2005: http://www.forumsec.org.fj/docs/SPARTECA/Sec1.htm

Page, S., and P. Kleen (2004): *Special and Differential Treatment of Developing Countries in the World Trade Organization.* London: Overseas Development Institute

Panagariya, A. (2002): 'EU Preferential Trade Arrangements and Developing Countries', *The World Economy*, 25, 1415–32

Rasmussen, T. N. (2004): *Macroeconomic Implications of Natural Disasters in the Caribbean.* IMF Working Paper 224. Washington, D.C.: International Monetary Fund

Read, R. (1999): *The Case for Special and Differential Treatment of Small Island Developing States (SIDS) under the WTO.* Lancaster: University of Lancaster

(2004): 'The Implications of Increasing Globalization and Regionalism for the Economic Growth of Small Island States', *World Development*, 32, 365

Rodrik, D. (2002): 'Trade Policy Reform as Institutional Reform', in *Development, Trade, and the WTO: A Handbook*, ed. B. Hoekman, A. Mattoo and P. English. Washington, D.C.: World Bank, 3–10

Romalis, J. (2003): *Would Rich Country Trade Preferences Help Poor Countries Grow? Evidence from the Generalized System of Preferences.* Chicago: University of Chicago

Salmon, J.-M. (2002): 'The Treatment of Small and Vulnerable Island Economies in the EPA Negotiations', Université des Antilles et de la Guyane

(2003): 'Case Study: The Indian Ocean Islands', in *Turning Losses into Gains: SIDS and Multilateral Trade Liberalisation in Agriculture*, ed. UNCTAD. UNCTAD/DITC/TNCD/2003/1. New York and Geneva: United Nations Conference on Trade and Development, 127–69

Saqib, M. (2003): 'Technical Barriers to Trade and the Role of Indian Standard-Setting Institutions', in *India and the WTO*, ed. A. Mattoo and R. M. Stern. Washington, D.C.: World Bank and Oxford University Press, 269–98

Schahczenski, J. J. (1990): 'Development Administration in the Small Developing State: A Review', *Public Administration and Development*, 10, 69–80

Schiff, M. (1996): *Small Is Beautiful: Preferential Trade Agreements and the Impact of Country Size, Market Share, Efficiency, and Trade Policy.* World Bank Policy Research Working Paper 1668. Washington, D.C.: World Bank

(2002): *Regional Integration and Development in Small States.* World Bank Policy Research Working Paper 2797. Washington, D.C.: World Bank

Schiff, M. and S. Andriamananjara (1998): *Regional Groupings among Microstates.* World Bank Policy Research Working Paper 1922. Washington, D.C.: World Bank

South Pacific Forum Secretariat (2001): 'Sharing Capacity: The Pacific Experience with Regional Co-operation and Integration', in *Small States in the Global Economy*, ed. D. Peretz, R. Faruqi and E. J. Kisanga. London: Commonwealth Secretariat, 507–31

Srinivasan, T. N. (1986): 'The Costs and Benefits of Being a Small, Remote, Island, Landlocked, or Ministrate Economy', *World Bank Research Observer*, 1, 205–18

Stevens, C. (2002): *The Future of Special and Differential Treatment (SDT) for Developing Countries in the WTO.* IDS Working Paper 163. Brighton: Institute of Development Studies

Streeten, P. (1993): 'The Special Problems of Small Countries', *World Development*, 21, 197–202

Subramanian, A. (2003a): *Financing of Losses from Preference Erosion.* WT/TF/COH/14 Communication from the IMF, 14 February. Geneva: World Trade Organization

(2003b): 'India as User and Creator of Intellectual Property: The Challenges Post-Doha', in *India and the WTO*, ed. A. Mattoo and R. M. Stern. Washington, D.C. and Oxford: World Bank and Oxford University Press, 169–95

Tangermann, S. (2000): *The Cotonou Agreement and the Value of Preferences in Agricultural Markets for the African ACP.* Paper prepared for UNCTAD. Gottingen: Institute of Agricultural Economics

Trade Point (2005): 'Trade Agreements: Caribcan', Port of Spain: Trade Point. 18 February 2005: http://www.tradetnt.com/caribcan.shtml

Tulloch, P. (2001): 'Small Economies in the WTO', in *Small States in the Global Economy*, ed. D. Peretz, R. Faruqi and E. J. Kisanga. London: Commonwealth Secretariat, 257–66

UNCTAD (2003a): *Turning Losses into Gains: SIDS and Multilateral Trade Liberalisation in Agriculture.* UNCTAD/DITC/TNCD/2003/1. New York and Geneva: United Nations Conference on Trade and Development

(2003b): *Major Developments and Recent Trends in International Banana Marketing Structures.* UNCTAD/DTIC/COM/2003/1. New York and Geneva: United Nations Conference on Trade and Development

(2003c): *UNCTAD Handbook of Statistics.* TD/STAT.28. New York and Geneva: United Nations Conference on Trade and Development

(2004a): *Is a Special Treatment of Small Island Developing States Possible?* UNCTAD/LDC/2004/1. New York and Geneva: United Nations Conference on Trade and Development

(2004b): *The Least Developed Countries Report 2004.* UNCTAD/LDC/2004. New York and Geneva: United Nations Conference on Trade and Development

(2004c): *Development and Globalization: Facts and Figures.* UNCTAD/GDS/CSIR/2004/1. New York and Geneva: United Nations Conference on Trade and Development

USTR (2004a): 'Caribbean Basin Initiative', Washington, D.C.: Office of the United States Trade Representative. 18 February 2005: http://www.ustr.gov/Trade_Development/Preference _Programs/CBI/Section_Index.html

(2004b): *2004 Comprehensive Report on US Trade and Investment Policy toward Sub-Saharan Africa and Implementation of the African Growth and Opportunity Act.* Washington, D.C.: Office of the United States Trade Representative

(2004c): 'Addendum (to US Generalized System of Preferences Guidebook)', Washington, D.C.: Office of the United States Trade Representative. 18 February 2005: http://www.ustr. gov/assets/Trade_Development/Preference_Programs/GSP/asset_upload_file90_5432.pdf

Vossenaar, R. (2004): 'Trade and the Environment: An Important Relationship for SIDS', in *Is a Special Treatment of Small Island Developing States Possible?*, ed. UNCTAD. UNCTAD/LDC/2004/1. New York and Geneva: United Nations Conference on Trade and Development, 57–90

Watkins, K. (2004): *Dumping on the World: How EU Sugar Policies Hurt Poor Countries.* Washington, D.C.: Oxfam International

Wilson, J. S. (2002): 'Standards, Regulation, and Trade: WTO Rules and Developing Country Concerns', in *Development, Trade, and the WTO: A Handbook*, ed. B. Hoekman, A. Mattoo and P. English. Washington, D.C.: World Bank, 428–38

Winters, L. A. and P. M. G. Martins (2004a): *Beautiful but Costly: Business Costs in Small Remote Economies.* London: Commonwealth Secretariat

(2004b): *When Comparative Advantage Doesn't Matter: Business Costs in Small Economies.* London: Commonwealth Secretariat

World Bank (2001): *Catastrophe Risk Management: Using Alternative Risk Financing and Insurance Pooling Mechanisms.* Washington, D.C.: World Bank

(2002a): *Pacific Islands Regional Economic Report: Embarking on a Global Voyage: Trade Liberalization and Complementary Reforms in the Pacific.* Washington, D.C.: World Bank

(2002b): *Caribbean Economic Overview 2002: Macroeconomic Volatility, Household Vulnerability, and Institutional and Policy Responses.* Washington, D.C.: World Bank

(2003): 'World Bank and IMF Announce Plans to Support Developing Countries with Trade-Related Adjustment Needs in the WTO Round', News Release 2004/62/S. Washington, D.C.: World Bank. 20 January 2005: http:// web.worldbank.org/WBSITE/EXTERNAL/NEWS/0,,contentMDK:20124989~menuPK:34463~pagePK:64003015~piPK:64003012~theSitePK:4607,00.html

(2004): 'World Development Indicators Database', Washington, D.C.: World Bank. 31 January 2005: http://www.esds.ac.uk

World Bank Institute (2002): 'Governance Research Indicators Dataset', Washington, D.C.: World Bank. 2 February 2005: http://www.worldbank.org/wbi/governance/govdata2002/index.html

WTO (1999): *Proposals for Addressing Concerns on Marginalization of Certain Small Economies.* WT/GC/W/361, 12 October 1999. Geneva: World Trade Organization

(2001): *Ministerial Declaration: Adopted on 14 November 2001.* WT/MIN(01)/DEC/1, 20 November 2001. Geneva: World Trade Organization

(2002): *Small Economies: A Literature Review: Note by the Secretariat.* WT/COMTD/SE/W/4, 23 July 2002. Geneva: World Trade Organization

(2004): 'Members and Observers', Geneva: World Trade Organization. 1 February 2005: http://www.wto.org/english/thewto_e/whatis_e/tif_e/org6_e.htm88

PART II

WTO and small economies

8

Small vulnerable economy issues and the WTO

ROMAN GRYNBERG AND JAN YVES REMY

8.1 Introduction

Since the second Ministerial Conference of the WTO[1] held in Geneva in 1998 there has been an attempt by small, vulnerable economies (SVEs)[2] to achieve some measure of recognition of the particular problems that confront them in the process of globalisation. At the failed Seattle Ministerial Conference the establishment of a work programme for small economies was agreed to by Members[3] but as the draft text was not accepted it was left until the fourth session in Doha before a small economies work programme was agreed.[4]

The views expressed are those of the authors and not necessarily those of the Commonwealth Secretariat.

[1] Ministerial Declaration, Second Session, Ministerial Conference of the World Trade Organization WT/MIN(98)/DEC/1, 25 May 1998 (98-2149), Geneva, 18 and 20 May 1998, adopted on 20 May 1998, para. 6:

> We remain deeply concerned over the marginalization of least-developed countries and certain small economies, and recognize the urgent need to address this issue which has been compounded by the chronic foreign debt problem facing many of them.

[2] The authors are keenly aware that there is a substantial difference between small *states* and small economies. Small economies include the self-selected group of WTO Members which includes countries as large as Sri Lanka, Cuba and Bolivia which are not necessarily small states. Small economies often do not face the constraints imposed by very small administrative capacity to implement the WTO agreements. Employing the World Bank/Commonwealth criteria of a population of 1.5 million would have excluded these larger countries. The WTO mandates and nomenclature refer to small economies but the problems addressed in this chapter refer to the problems of small states, which are usually more vulnerable and have vastly different problems, both economically and administratively, than some of the larger 'small economies' that are members of the small economies group at the WTO. For the purposes of this chapter, reference to small states, as distinct from small economies, will be to small, vulnerable economies.

[3] The later versions of the draft text of the Seattle Ministerial Declaration contained no square brackets in the section pertaining to small economies but the draft ministerial declaration was not endorsed by WTO Members.

[4] Ministerial Declaration, Fourth Session, Ministerial Conference of the World Trade Organization, WT/MIN(01)/DEC/1, 20 November 2001 (01-5859), Doha, 9–14 November 2001, adopted on 14 November 2001, para. 35:

This chapter addresses several issues pertaining to the apparent contradiction in the wording of the work programme agreed to at Doha, which on the one hand mandates Members to frame responses to trade concerns of small, vulnerable economies, but on the other prohibits the creation of a sub-category of states. The relevant paragraph of the Ministerial Declaration was a political compromise between the small economy proponents of the WTO work programme, and developed countries which insisted on the definitional caveat. It has created a conundrum of sorts for negotiators, as it seems impossible to target responses to the concerns of a group that is yet to be defined or recognised because WTO Members have consistently refused to recognise SVEs as a distinct category. While the creation of a WTO sub-category of Members is explicitly prohibited in the work programme, this does not nullify the right of any WTO Member or group of Members to make a proposal during negotiations that includes such a group of countries.

The chapter seeks to review the concerns and specificities of small states, thereby highlighting the peculiarities and natural disadvantages that inhibit the ability of SVEs to thrive, and at times survive, in the multilateral trading context. It then considers the implicit definitions and other sub-categorisations relating to smallness already existing in various WTO agreements as well as in its administrative practice. The chapter argues that small states have many characteristics that are similar to, but sufficiently distinct from, those of least developed countries (the only formally recognised group in the WTO) which warrant special treatment of them in the WTO.[5] The chapter however argues that such special treatment can begin only with a definition, which it goes some way in advancing. Lastly, the authors briefly examine the discussions currently taking place in WTO sessions pursuant to the work programme, which underscores the intense

We agree to a work programme, under the auspices of the General Council, to examine issues relating to the trade of small economies. The objective of this work is to frame responses to the trade-related issues identified for the fuller integration of small, vulnerable economies into the multilateral trading system, and not to create a sub-category of WTO Members. The General Council shall review the work programme and make recommendations for action to the Fifth Session of the Ministerial Conference.

[5] The category of least developed country is defined by the UN's Economic and Social Commission and is external to the WTO. The category of developing country is determined in the WTO by self-election, which has meant that until very recently high-income countries such as South Korea, Israel and Singapore have chosen to define themselves as developing countries.

discomfort that some WTO Members may feel with the creation of new categories. However, irrespective of this stated uneasiness, the chapter argues that they have already done so during the Uruguay Round and must do so implicitly or explicitly if they are to address the legitimate trade concerns of small, vulnerable states.

8.2 Small states, globalisation and the WTO

Prior to any discussion of the definitional issue, the first question that must be answered is why SVEs require particular attention in the WTO. SVEs comprise small states and small island states which in particular suffer from a combination of inherited and inherent characteristics that impede their ability to integrate into the global economy. These characteristics include smallness, physical isolation from markets, dispersion of small pockets of populations and a small and highly specialised human and physical resource base. These together raise the operating cost structure of small economies and render market adjustment more difficult. The high cost structure that has traditionally been associated with these economies has meant that many have predicated their export trade upon products or services where the export price includes either market or institutionalised quasi-rents, as few other activities have proven viable for these very small producers. These market-based quasi-rents have been based on either short temporary booms which have facilitated resource extractive activities and created transitory rents or short-term niche markets. The institutional sources of quasi-rent have stemmed from either trade preferences, tax concessions or sovereignty-based activities.

Historically SVEs have become dependent upon these forms of export-oriented activities primarily because few other exports ever developed. Merchandise exports in particular have been based on high rates of trade preference resulting from high most-favoured nation (MFN) tariffs, or preference donors have created quota-based systems such as the Sugar and Banana Protocols. It is these particularly distortive trade measures that are most beneficial to SVEs because they offer guaranteed access under quota for what are often small volumes that would otherwise not be traded. In so doing, these measures have addressed the marketing constraints faced by SVEs.

Over the years since the creation of the WTO, these high rates of trade preference along with the tariff quotas have been diminished by a series of disputes and ongoing negotiations that have shaken the foundation of SVEs. These include:

i) The Banana Dispute which has not only caused a major restructuring in the Caribbean and parts of Africa but is forcing a complete realignment of trade regimes throughout the ACP regions and necessitating reciprocity in the ACP–EU trade relationship.
ii) The Sugar Dispute between Brazil/Australia/Thailand and the EU over subsidies in the EU sugar regime will force similar adjustment in at least twelve small ACP states that have been substantial beneficiaries of the Sugar Protocol of the Cotonou Agreement.
iii) The Thailand–Philippines/EU mediation over margins of preference for canned tuna has further eroded the competitive position of a number of small states, including Mauritius, Papua New Guinea, Fiji and Seychelles.
iv) The Fisheries Subsidies negotiations threaten to undermine the revenue of small coastal developing states which are highly dependent upon fisheries access arrangements.
v) The full implementation of the provisions of the Agreement on Subsidies and Countervailing Measures (ASCM) will by 2008 undermine the ability of many small developing countries to use their current range of export incentives in the Export Processing Zones.

Nonetheless, the economic adjustments and loss of quasi-rents in export-oriented activities brought by these changes in the WTO are not the only cause for concern. In addition, the OECD's Harmful Tax Initiative has served to undermine the development of offshore finance centres located predominantly in small states which have used this sector to diversify away from the highly trade-preference dependent activities. Thus the international trade policy shift that has occurred in recent years has served to thoroughly undermine the export sector of small states.

In fact, no other group of developing countries, including least developed countries (LDCs), has been obliged to undertake such wide-ranging adjustments necessitated by the last decade of globalisation. This is the reason for the particular problems of small states which, in the WTO context, include:

i) Loss of trade preferences stemming from MFN liberalisation and WTO disputes.

ii) Application of rules, including the ASCM, in a manner that does not recognise the inherent economic characteristics of small states.
iii) Implementation of complex and burdensome WTO obligations which are beyond the scope of small states with very small administrations.

8.3 WTO precedents on sub-categorisation of Members, including small economies

WTO provisions have created a number of sub-categories of Members and, in the process, have set precedents that may be useful for present purposes. These usually constitute provisions on special and differential treatment for small Members or small suppliers, although it is noteworthy that preferential treatment is not given in all cases. For instance, small Members pay proportionately higher contributions to the WTO budget than larger Members. This has been justified from the earliest days of the GATT 1947 by the cost to the Organisation of providing services to Members.

MFN treatment and non-discrimination between its Members are among the most basic principles of the WTO. However, there is an increasing amount of trade being carried out on the basis of exceptions to these basic rules and which allow for differentiation among Members. For instance, there are provisions permitting free-trade areas and customs unions or preferences for developing countries and LDCs. Tulloch has also drawn attention to the fact that special characteristics, interests and concerns of various groups of countries, other than developing countries or least-developed countries, are recognised and accommodated in some of the WTO Agreements.[6]

LDCs constitute the only sub-category of WTO Members that is clearly agreed to and defined. The WTO has agreed that the LDCs are those countries designated as such by the United Nations, and which are Members of WTO. As this grouping is clearly defined, LDCs are specifically referred to and granted special and differential treatment in many WTO Agreements, including the Decision on Measures in Favour of Least-Developed Countries appended to the Final Act of the Uruguay Round.

[6] Peter Tulloch, 'Small Economies in the WTO' in David Peretz, Rumman Faruqui and Eliawony J. Kisanga (eds.), *Small States in the Global Economy*, Commonwealth Secretariat and World Bank, 2001, p. 258.

Apart from these references to LDCs, the WTO also recognises other sub-groupings within the broader category of developing countries. This has often been done either explicitly or implicitly through the creation of *de minimis* thresholds that in effect distinguish small states and often entitle them to special and/or preferential treatment. This is reflected in the following WTO Agreements and practices:

(a) The Agreement on Agriculture and its related Decision contain special provisions for net food-importing developing countries.[7] Article 6:2 also contains special provisions for low-income or resource-poor producers in developing countries, which are aimed at encouraging diversification away from growing illicit narcotic crops.[8]

(b) The ASCM also grants developing countries with a per capita GNP below US $1,000 the same treatment as least developed countries in respect of export subsidies.[9] Other developing countries are granted a transitional period to phase out their export subsidies on non-agricultural products, unless they have reached export competitiveness in particular products. Furthermore, the Agreement defines export competitiveness to exist if a developing country Member's exports of the product in question have reached a share of at least 3.25 per cent in world trade in the relevant period.[10] The Agreement also provides for the termination of any countervailing duty investigations as soon as the authorities determine that the volume of subsidised imports represents less than 4 per cent of the total imports of the like product in the importing Member concerned.[11] Significantly, at the Doha Ministerial Conference, while explicitly rejecting the creation of a new category of small states, another *de minimis* threshold was established for defining the conditions under which developing country Members may obtain an extension of the rights to use prohibited export subsidies.[12]

[7] Agreement on Agriculture, Article 16. [8] Agreement on Agriculture, Article 6.2.

[9] Agreement on Subsidies and Countervailing Measures, Article 3 and Annex VII.

[10] Agreement on Subsidies and Countervailing Measures, Article 27.6.

[11] Agreement on Subsidies and Countervailing Measures, Article 27.10.

[12] Procedures for extensions under Article 27.4 for certain developing country members, G/SCM/39, 20 November 2001. The provisions state:

> Programmes eligible for extension pursuant to these procedures, and for which members shall therefore grant extensions for calendar year 2003 as referred to in 1(c), are export subsidy programmes (i) in the form of full or partial exemptions from import duties and internal taxes, (ii) which were in existence not later than 1 September 2001, and (iii) which

(c) The Agreement on Implementation of Article VI of GATT 1994 provides that the volume of dumped imports shall normally be regarded as negligible if the volume of dumped imports from a particular country is found to account for less than 3 per cent of imports of the like product in the importing Member, unless the countries which individually account for less than 3 per cent of the imports of the like product in the importing Member collectively account for more than 7 per cent of imports of the like product in the importing Member.[13] The Agreement also provides that due account shall be taken of any difficulties experienced by interested parties, in particular small companies, in supplying information.[14]

(d) The Agreement on Safeguards lays down that safeguard measures shall not be applied against a product originating in a developing country Member as long as its share of imports of the product concerned in the importing Member does not exceed 3 per cent, provided that the developing country Members with less than 3 per cent import share collectively account for no more than 9 per cent of the total imports of the product concerned.[15]

(e) The Agreement on Textiles and Clothing lays down meaningful improvement in access for exports of Members that are subject to restriction and account for 1.2 per cent or less of the total volume of restrictions applied by the importing Member concerned.[16] Special and differential treatment provisions under the Agreement apply to Members whose total volume of textile and clothing exports is small in comparison with the total volume of exports of other Members and who account for a small percentage of total imports of that product into the importing Members.[17] Furthermore, special consideration is to be given to wool products from wool-producing country Members whose economy and textiles and clothing trade are dependent on the wool sector, whose total textile and clothing exports consist almost

are provided by developing country members (iv) whose share of world merchandise export trade was not greater than 0.10 per cent, (v) whose total Gross National Income ('GNI') for the year 2000 as published by the World Bank was at or below US$ 20 billion, (vi) and who are otherwise eligible to request an extension pursuant to Article 27.4, and (vii) in respect of which these procedures are followed.

[13] Agreement on Implementation of Article VI of GATT, Article 5:8.

[14] Agreement on Implementation of Article VI of GATT, Article 6.

[15] Agreement on Safeguards, Article 9.

[16] Agreement on Textiles and Clothing, Article 2.

[17] Article 6:6(a).

exclusively of wool products, and whose volume of textile and clothing trade is comparatively small in the markets of the importing Member.[18]

(f) In the Doha Declaration dealing with Technical Cooperation and Capacity Building, Ministers agreed that priority shall be accorded to small, vulnerable and transitional economies, as well as Members and Observers without representation in Geneva.[19] Members with a relatively small share of world trade are subject to less frequent review of their trade regime under the Trade Policy Review Mechanism.[20]

(g) The rules setting contributions to the WTO budget, drawn up under Article VII of the Agreement establishing the Organisation, provide that each Member's contribution is a function of its share of world trade. However, these rules provide that Members with less than 0.015 per cent of world trade pay a minimum contribution of 0.015 per cent of the budget (this figure has been modified on a number of occasions in the past and was reduced from 0.03 per cent from the budget year 2000).

8.4 A small matter of definition

While WTO members have been emphatic in their opposition to the creation of a separate category of SVEs and have frequently restated their support for the principles of non-discrimination, they have nonetheless systematically created at least seven *de minimis* thresholds in various agreements and administrative arrangements, which reveals a preference for rules dependent upon the size of the particular Member. As mentioned above, the difficulty arises because the mandate undertaken by WTO Members is to 'frame responses to the trade-related issues identified for the fuller integration of small, vulnerable economies into the multilateral trading system'. Clearly such responses, if they are to involve any derogation from, or alteration of, existing WTO rules, by definition will require WTO Members to differentiate between those Members to which the derogation or alteration of obligations applies and those outside that group. However, because WTO Members went on to say that they would not create a new sub-category of WTO Members, the Doha mandate creates an impossible conundrum for policy-makers and negotiators.

[18] Article 6:6(b).

[19] Ministerial Declaration WT/MIN(01)/DEC/1, 20 November 2001, para. 38.

[20] GATT 1994, Annex 3 Trade Policy Review Mechanism, para. C(ii).

In fact, should WTO Members desire it, the task of defining SVEs is far from impossible. Quite inadvertently, WTO Members may have in fact created a defined, albeit imperfect, category of 'vulnerable' states. The ECOSOC definition of an LDC, the only category of WTO Members officially recognised, is defined by resort to three criteria, one of which is the UN Economic Vulnerability Index (EVI). If a country's rating on the EVI is greater than 31 then it is deemed to be vulnerable. If it is greater than 36 then a country is deemed to be highly vulnerable. In order to be an LDC, a country must rank above 36. Unfortunately only 128 UN Members have been classified on the EVI. The first 96 countries on the list in Appendix 8.2 of this chapter would qualify as 'vulnerable' using this criterion. However, one limitation of the list is that, while EVIs have been calculated for 128 countries, it does not include all WTO Members and acceding countries, notably transition economies.

For expository purposes, one could use a trade criterion of 0.05 per cent of world trade for measuring 'smallness'. This threshold would categorise some eighty-six WTO Members as small. In total these eighty-six states account for 1.5 per cent of world trade and if the trade of least developed countries is subtracted then the total amount of world trade potentially affected by the WTO recognising small economies, as a group, is a mere 1.1 per cent (see Appendix 8.2).

Unfortunately, if individual thresholds are chosen there are some anomalies that would be created. This is because at least five countries, namely Cyprus, Malta, Iceland, Singapore and Liechtenstein, are either small or vulnerable economies. This could be resolved, however, if EU members are excluded on the basis that any criteria would be restricted to developing countries. In this way, Cyprus, Malta and Liechtenstein would be excluded. In addition, if one uses both filters, i.e. 'small' and 'vulnerable', Iceland and Singapore would also be excluded.[21] Notably, the Doha Ministerial mandate uses both these terms in its language.

This raises the question of the choice of thresholds for the definition of small. There is little doubt that the threshold chosen for expository purposes is *ad hoc* in nature. There is and can be no legitimate theoretical explanation for the choice of 0.05 per cent as a threshold except for the purely practical consideration that it excludes the most egregious

[21] It should be noted that the UN has not classified Iceland on the vulnerability index and if it were included then, given its dependence on a very narrow range of exports, it may also have an EVI classification above 31.

anomalies, something that would be necessary in order to satisfy WTO Members that a trade advantage were not being offered to high-income developed countries. In defence of such an *ad hoc* approach to the definition of small, one need look no further than WTO practice itself, as WTO Members in the past have never provided a justification for the particular choice of *de minimis* thresholds in any of the WTO Agreements.

For the moment, this definitional debate could be largely academic because, as will be seen below, the demands currently being made by SVEs in WTO negotiations may not as yet require a formal definition *per se.* However, the emerging situation and debate suggest that it may soon be necessary for proponents of a definition to develop at least the contours of a working definition in order to address more specifically the economic and trade concerns of Members. Significantly, given the precedence above, there are a host of possible definitions and approaches to the issue that can be employed depending upon the circumstances.

8.5 Small economy issues in the dedicated sessions of the WTO

Discussions concerning small economies in the WTO have taken place in four dedicated sessions of the Committee on Trade and Development (CTD). This Committee was entrusted with the task of ensuring compliance with, and completion of, the Doha mandate regarding small economies.[22]

The dedicated sessions have shown the small economies' representatives to be the agenda-setters, as they have taken the lead in initiating and steering discussions thus far. In particular, a grouping of SVEs[23] has submitted papers and tabled various proposals specific to their circumstances. In their first paper, the SVEs underscore the characteristics that make them vulnerable, and the implications that these characteristics have on their trade and development.[24] In sessions of the CTD, SVE representatives have also

[22] See the Framework and Procedures of the Work Programme given to the CTD on 1 March by the General Council, at WT/L/447. This requires the CTD *inter alia* to conduct these discussions in scheduled Dedicated Sessions; to report regularly to the General Council, which has overall responsibility for ensuring that responses to the trade-related concerns identified in these Dedicated Sessions are arrived at; and where necessary to work with the other relevant subsidiary bodies of the WTO. The WTO Secretariat is also instructed to provide relevant information and factual analysis to inform discussions taking place in these Dedicated Sessions.

[23] These include Barbados, Belize, Bolivia, Cuba, Dominican Republic, El Salvador, Fiji Islands, Guatemala, Haiti, Honduras, Jamaica, Mauritius, Nicaragua, Papua New Guinea, Paraguay, Saint Lucia, Solomon Islands, Sri Lanka and Trinidad and Tobago.

[24] See WT/COMTD/SE//Rev 1*, 3 May 2002.

recounted their day-to-day hardships in trying to operate in a multilateral trading context. Although the developed countries have been generally supportive of these papers and have encouraged the sharing of individual experiences, they have at times raised the definitional issue, with the wearying precaution that the mandate clearly restricts sub-categorisation of the kind that SVEs appear interested in.[25]

The actual proposals tabled by SVEs thus far address concerns of smaller economies generally, and are relatively modest in scope.[26] They are expressly intended to complement others submitted in specific negotiating groups. Their coverage is both procedural and substantive in nature, and proposals are aimed generally at improving administrative procedures for SVEs, as well as refashioning current rules to better suit and accommodate their needs. Developed countries have in general been amenable to the former, but as regards the rule-based proposals, they have indicated discomfort with the idea of changing rules to address the need of a sub-category of WTO Members.[27] Many SVEs have however indicated their intention to present, and have proposals accepted as, a packaged and all-inclusive deal.

Not surprisingly, one of the proposals made seeks to retain the margins of preferences for small-economy exports. However, this has led to some contention within the small economies camp, and in particular concern from the likes of some Latin American countries, who self-define as small economies, and who would want existing preferences extended to all small economies. A number of the proponents of the proposal, however, feel that such a blanket application to all self-professed small economies would have the effect of diluting any advantage or benefit to SVEs. This would be an area where a definition could be helpful.

Less contentious were proposals on Article XXIV and Regional Trading Arrangements, which seek to ensure non-reciprocity in regional trade agreements between developed and small economies. Small economies

[25] See in this regard, minutes of the Dedicated Sessions, available at WT/COMTD/SE/M/1, 2, 3 and 4.

[26] The proponents of this submission were Barbados, Belize, Bolivia, Dominican Republic, Guatemala, Honduras, Mauritius and Sri Lanka. See WT/COMTD/SE/W/3 for the entire exposition of these proposals and the backgrounds informing them.

[27] The general response to these proposals has been encouraging and supportive, with a few pointed questions being asked in particular by the developing countries in dedicated sessions. Notably, the US has tendered a written questionnaire to the proposal's proponents, in which they have sought clarification and further information on the proposals. The full version of the questions posed by the United States and the responses received from the proponents of the proposal are available at WT/COMTD/SE/W/7.

have proposed that sufficient space for policy development specific to their needs be retained in the WTO, and that developed countries do not require concessions in negotiations that are inconsistent with development, financial and trade needs of smaller economies.

Most proposals are aimed at improving how the rules of various WTO Agreements work and affect small economies. One such proposal regarding the ASCM seeks to ensure that small economies are not made subject to the provisions of paragraph 1(a) of Article 3 of the ASCM requiring phasing out of fiscal incentives. The proposal further provides that the rules and procedures of the Agreement be modified for small economies. However, developed countries have generally not seen the need for such special treatment of smaller economies, arguing that current procedures are working well, and that any special consideration would encourage sub-categorisation of the kind prohibited under the mandate. Other more administrative proposals which call for the explicit recognition of the right of small economies to designate regional bodies as their 'competent authorities' for the purposes of that Agreement have been more generally supported by developed countries, with some instances of voluntary pledges for the provision of technical assistance. A similar proposal in the context of the SPS and TBT Agreements has likewise been welcomed, and developed countries have been generally supportive of any requests for technical assistance in the establishment of joint and/or shared missions for current non-resident Members.

Proposals for the revision of some rules in the Safeguards Agreement for small economies – including those relating to the definition of domestic industry, serious injury, investigations, reporting requirements, causation and the non-attribution principle, the right of compensation and/or retaliation – were not embraced by developed countries who drew attention to the fact that Article XIX of the Agreement already catered for developing countries. The proponents have however responded that the rules of the Safeguards Agreement entail cumbersome administrative procedures which would need to be simplified for smaller economies.

There have also been proposals for developed countries to assist small economies in complying with their obligations under the SPS and TBT Agreements through (1) use of the former's technology and technical facilities on preferential and non-commercial terms, preferably free of costs, and (2) appropriate flexibility for small economies in dealing with timeframes and notifications requirements. Developed countries again have reacted to these proposals negatively by suggesting that technical regulation was also a problem for them, and smaller economies could focus instead on the notification requirements of these Agreements. Some developed countries have even suggested the increased use of electronic technology, for example in accessing such notifications. According to smaller economies however, the plight of the developed countries was not comparable to that of smaller developing ones, and flexibility needed to be incorporated into the time-frame and notification requirements.

Proposals on the dispute settlement body were met with comments from developing countries that many of the issues raised were already being discussed in the context of Special and Differential Treatment in Dispute Settlement Understanding negotiations. The proponents expressed their awareness and intention to participate concurrently in these discussions as well. On issues of graduation and accession of small economies from LDC status, there is general agreement that these issues would have to be considered to develop acceptable guidelines and procedure for small economies.

The proponents of all of these proposals attempted to make them the basis of recommendations to the General Council,[28] as required under the mandate. However, lack of consensus, particularly by developed countries, on the suitability and workability of some proposals, and on the issue of how to prevent the creation of a two-tier system of rights and obligations within the WTO, prevented the forwarding of these proposals.

8.6 Conclusion

The present discussions in the WTO underscore the discomfort among developed countries with the idea of explicitly recognising a sub-category of smaller economies, and further SVEs. However, it is hard to surmise how execution of the mandate in paragraph 35, requiring the framing of trade-related responses to problems of smaller vulnerable economies, can occur without the logical first step of defining and clarifying what a small, vulnerable economy is. The existence of clear precedents in the text and practice of the WTO exposes the possibility and indeed desirability of doing so, once the requisite political will exists. In order for small states within the WTO to gain any measure of success in current trade negotiations, they must first and foremost achieve recognition as a separate sub-grouping within the membership of the WTO.

[28] This request is contained in the Communication found at WT/COMTD/SE/W/8.

Appendix 8.1 *Table of other negotiating proposals made or to be made in favour of small developing states in the WTO*

Subject area/relevant WTO Agreement	Background	Content of proposal
Fisheries Subsidies (ASCM, including Article XVI GATT, GATT 1994: GATT Agreement on Subsidies and Countervailing Measures Article 1, Article 3.1, Article 27, Article 6, Annex VII)	SVEs have relatively high dependence on domestic and export fisheries. Large exporting countries seeking negotiations of fisheries subsidies on basis that subsidies have harmful effect on sustainable fish catches. SVEs fisheries interests extend to the following main areas: revenue generation from access fees, domestic and foreign fishers operating for export in the EEZ and territorial sea, artisan fisheries within their territorial sea.	Ensure that Article 1 of the ASCM is clarified explicitly to exclude certain types of assistance from definition of subsidy (including access fees and development assistance, fiscal incentives to domestication and fisheries development, artisanal fisheries).
TRIPs (Article 67)	Due to limited capacity, many SVEs are unable to implement complex rules and procedures in TRIPs. Article 67 of TRIPs makes provision for developed countries to assist with such implementation, upon request. However, SVEs often have problems even identifying their needs to make such requests, and do not have the ability to implement this agreement.	Explicit recognition that SVEs may designate regional body as competent authority for implementation of the TRIPs Agreement. This should be assisted by developed countries through the provision of technical and financial assistance.
Regional Trade Arrangements (RTAs) (in particular, Article		Provisions in Article XXIV to be interpreted to incorporate

XXIV and Enabling Clause, para. 3, Understanding on the Interpretation of Article XXIV GATT 1994)		incomplete reciprocity for SVEs as contained in Enabling Clause. In particular, to incorporate notion of **flexibility** in 'substantially all trade' in Article XXIV: 8 to accommodate asymmetric liberalisation between developing countries with less than average of 0.05 per cent of world merchandise export (in last five years) and developed countries, suitable to the circumstances of SVEs. Flexibility to entail: 1) Asymmetry in timetabling of tariff reduction and elimination during transitional periods; 2) Any FTAs involving SVEs and developed countries (as referred to above) should be an 'exceptional' case and the 'reasonable length of time' is to be twenty-five years.
Trade preferences (Part IV of GATT 1994 and Enabling Clause)	SVEs are particularly trade preference dependent. The erosion of trade preferences jeopardises the future of SVEs in critical areas such as agriculture and manufacturing. Current WTO negotiations and rules threaten these arrangements.	'Grandfathering' of existing margins of trade preferences for products and small economies accounting for less than 3.25 per cent of world trade.

Appendix 8.1 (*cont.*)

Subject area/relevant WTO Agreement	Background	Content of proposal
Agreement on Subsidies and Countervailing Measures (ASCM) (Article XVI GATT 1994, ASCM Article 27, Annex VII, Doha Ministerial Declaration (c))	SVEs suffer from diseconomies of scale caused by the combined effect of their small size and physical isolation which together necessitate compensatory measures to offset these inherent cost disadvantages. Moreover, without these compensatory measures SVEs will be unable to attract investment. WTO provisions 'recognize that subsidies may play an important role in economic development programs of developing country members' and provide flexibility for certain developing countries in the application of subsidies. The Agreement does not grant the necessary flexibility to SVEs. Moreover, existing fiscal incentives are required to be phased out under current WTO rules.	SVEs **shall be granted** a **permanent** exemption from the provisions of paragraph 1(a) of Article 3 (ASCM). SVEs should be allowed the provision of subsidies to reduce the costs of marketing exports of non-agricultural products (including export promotion and advisory services), including handling, upgrading and other processing costs of international transport and freight. SVEs should be allowed to provide internal transport and freight charges on export shipments, provided or mandated by governments on terms more favourable than for domestic

		shipments for non-agricultural products. **Fall-back position** Provision to permit SVEs to maintain export subsidies on products for which the ratio between CIF and FOB is greater than . . .
Agreement on Agriculture (Article 9)	SVEs suffer from diseconomies of scale caused by the combined effect of their small size and physical isolation which necessitate compensatory measures to offset these inherent cost disadvantages. Moreover, without these compensatory measures SVEs will be unable to attract investment. WTO provisions 'recognize that subsidies may play an important role in economic development programs of developing country members' and flexibility for certain developing countries in the application of subsidies. The Agreement does not grant the necessary flexibility to SVEs. Existing fiscal incentives are required to be phased out under current WTO rules.	Permanent exemption from the reduction commitments in Article 9 in the Agreement on Agriculture. **Fall-back position** Indefinite extension of the right to maintain the export subsidies described in Article 9(d) and (e) of the Agreement on Agriculture for SVEs.

Appendix 8.2 *Total trade in goods and services sorted by average percentage share 1998–2000*

Total trade in goods and services (US $ million)	1998	1999	2000	average 1998–2000	average 1998–2000 share (%)	2000 share (%)
1 United States	1,995,459	2,140,380	2,472,460	2,202,766.33	15.42	15.9397
2 Germany	1,218,840	1,234,558	1,254,113	1,235,837.33	8.65	8.0851
3 Japan	798,199	858,549	986,299	881,015.50	6.17	6.3586
4 United Kingdom	768,695	785,237	825,536	793,155.93	5.55	5.3221
5 France	731,704	727,349	732,608	730,553.77	5.11	4.7230
6 Italy	579,021	562,534	582,028	574,527.63	4.02	3.7523
7 Canada	495,867	542,234	611,711	549,937.23	3.85	3.9436
8 Netherlands	470,123	478,530	498,210	482,287.47	3.38	3.2119
9 Hong Kong, China	421,225	414,030	480,701	438,651.93	3.07	3.0990
10 China	370,790	410,582	529,792	437,054.73	3.06	3.4155
11 Belgium	348,938	350,891	369,704	356,511.06	2.50	2.3834
12 Spain	320,745	338,836	351,379	336,986.63	2.36	2.2653
13 Korea, Rep. of	271,556	314,496	397,768	327,940.23	2.30	2.5644
14 Mexico	266,941	304,037	371,196	314,058.00	2.20	2.3931
15 Taipei, Chinese	249,946	267,659	326,699	281,434.67	1.97	2.1062
16 Singapore	242,905	262,601	314,723	273,409.57	1.91	2.0290
17 Switzerland	227,374	224,514	227,770	226,552.40	1.59	1.4684
18 Sweden	192,021	201,625	203,029	198,891.60	1.39	1.3089
19 Austria	186,779	192,644	192,737	190,719.97	1.34	1.2426
20 Malaysia	150,633	171,972	206,268	176,291.13	1.23	1.3298
21 Ireland	177,698	154,761	166,780	166,412.80	1.16	1.0752
22 *Russian Fed.*	161,701	137,624	178,007	159,110.67	1.11	1.1476
23 Australia	149,809	156,840	168,397	158,348.67	1.11	1.0856

24	Denmark	122,920	132,072	141,222	132,071.20	0.92	0.9104
25	Thailand	114,216	127,543	153,201	131,653.27	0.92	0.9877
26	Brazil	131,701	117,513	135,585	128,266.33	0.90	0.8741
27	India	104,162	113,484	135,728	117,791.47	0.82	0.8750
28	Norway	107,252	109,576	124,058	113,628.80	0.80	0.7998
29	Indonesia	98,397	97,629	125,587	107,204.33	0.75	0.8096
30	Turkey	109,261	93,734	112,557	105,184.00	0.74	0.7256
31	*Saudi Arabia*	79,745	91,292	121,052	97,363.37	0.68	0.7804
32	Poland	95,059	90,360	103,368	96,262.33	0.67	0.6664
33	Finland	88,571	86,083	92,189	88,947.67	0.62	0.5943
34	Portugal	78,805	79,802	79,092	79,233.00	0.55	0.5099
35	Israel	67,768	76,919	91,433	78,706.37	0.55	0.5895
36	Philippines	76,572	75,732	77,673	76,658.87	0.54	0.5007
37	United Arab Emirates	67,950	70,100	79,701	72,583.77	0.51	0.5138
38	Czech Rep.	67,449	66,978	73,113	69,179.83	0.48	0.4714
39	South Africa	66,972	63,614	69,247	66,610.93	0.47	0.4464
40	Argentina	69,339	60,067	63,246	64,217.40	0.45	0.4077
41	Hungary	53,811	55,677	63,849	57,778.93	0.40	0.4116
42	Greece	41,026	60,336	70,741	57,367.60	0.40	0.4561
43	Luxembourg	43,203	48,099	52,062	47,787.95	0.33	0.3356
44	Venezuela	38,898	38,720	53,649	43,755.67	0.31	0.3459
45	Chile	40,285	37,228	43,059	40,190.67	0.28	0.2776
46	Egypt	32,738	35,636	39,291	35,888.33	0.25	0.2533
47	*Ukraine*	36,449	32,295	37,055	35,266.33	0.25	0.2389
48	New Zealand	31,701	34,354	35,050	33,702.00	0.24	0.2260
49	Colombia	30,648	27,180	29,941	29,256.17	0.20	0.1930
50	*Viet Nam*	25,473	27,641	34,475	29,196.33	0.20	0.2223
51	Nigeria	23,120	25,754	37,125	28,666.10	0.20	0.2393
52	Slovak Rep.	28,338	25,210	28,685	27,410.77	0.19	0.1849

Appendix 8.2 (*cont.*)

Total trade in goods and services (US $ million)	1998	1999	2000	average 1998–2000	average 1998–2000 share (%)	2000 share (%)
53 *Algeria*	22,114	24,781	34,119	27,004.43	0.19	0.2200
54 Kuwait	23,071	24,148	31,619	26,279.33	0.18	0.2038
55 Romania	22,259	21,197	26,132	23,196.00	0.16	0.1685
56 Slovenia	22,516	21,906	22,071	22,164.27	0.16	0.1423
57 Morocco	20,646	21,806	22,438	21,629.77	0.15	0.1447
58 Pakistan	21,031	20,351	22,030	21,137.33	0.15	0.1420
59 Croatia	19,210	17,909	18,262	18,460.07	0.13	0.1177
60 Dominican Rep.	16,298	17,169	19,697	17,721.50	0.12	0.1270
61 Tunisia	17,327	17,763	17,624	17,571.50	0.12	0.1136
62 Peru	17,949	16,477	18,048	17,491.33	0.12	0.1164
63 *Kazakhstan*	14,601	13,670	19,259	15,843.43	0.11	0.1242
64 Panama	16,947	14,785	15,767	15,832.93	0.11	0.1016
65 Bangladesh	13,273	14,578	16,259	14,703.23	0.10	0.1048
66 Costa Rica	13,903	15,342	14,732	14,659.10	0.10	0.0950
67 *Belarus*	15,203	13,039	15,721	14,654.10	0.10	0.1013
68 Oman	12,645	13,273	17,696	14,538.07	0.10	0.1141
69 Sri Lanka	12,341	12,290	14,430	13,020.10	0.09	0.0930
70 Bulgaria	11,932	12,321	14,614	12,955.50	0.09	0.0942
71 *Libyan Arab Jamahiriya*	13,137	11,624	13,607	12,789.10	0.09	0.0877
72 Qatar	8,823	10,360	13,687	10,956.77	0.08	0.0882
73 Angola	8,141	10,614	13,652	10,802.10	0.08	0.0880
74 Ecuador	11,624	9,441	10,885	10,649.97	0.07	0.0702
75 Lithuania	11,354	9,528	10,912	10,598.03	0.07	0.0703

76	*Syrian Arab Rep.*	9,183	10,227	11,818	10,409.33	0.07	0.0762
77	Cuba	8,982	9,589	10,495	9,688.67	0.07	0.0677
78	Bahrain	7,946	9,005	11,587	9,512.27	0.07	0.0747
79	Estonia	8,786	8,098	9,735	8,872.87	0.06	0.0628
80	Côte d'Ivoire	9,434	9,293	7,649	8,791.87	0.06	0.0493
81	Guatemala	8,442	8,419	9,361	8,740.87	0.06	0.0603
82	Jordan	8,605	8,298	9,037	8,646.33	0.06	0.0583
83	Macau, China	7,995	8,158	9,453	8,535.37	0.06	0.0609
84	*Lebanon*	8,946	8,119	8,369	8,478.00	0.06	0.0540
85	Cyprus	8,323	8,333	8,575	8,410.37	0.06	0.0553
86	El Salvador	7,524	7,822	9,242	8,195.80	0.06	0.0596
87	Uruguay	8,571	7,472	7,877	7,973.07	0.06	0.0508
88	Jamaica	7,358	7,420	7,851	7,543.13	0.05	0.0506
89	Paraguay	8,645	6,732	6,241	7,205.97	0.05	0.0402
90	*Uzbekistan*	6,817	6,347	7,594	6,919.10	0.05	0.0490
91	Latvia	6,973	6,454	7,077	6,834.67	0.05	0.0456
92	Malta	6,165	6,611	7,507	6,760.77	0.05	0.0484
93	Trinidad and Tobago	6,066	6,414	7,506	6,661.73	0.05	0.0484
94	Iceland	5,993	6,174	6,368	6,178.40	0.04	0.0411
95	Zimbabwe	5,679	5,896	6,644	6,073.07	0.04	0.0428
96	Kenya	6,309	5,706	6,184	6,066.20	0.04	0.0399
97	Ghana	5,963	6,264	5,657	5,961.17	0.04	0.0365
98	*Yemen*	4,574	5,411	7,510	5,831.80	0.04	0.0484
99	Honduras	5,187	5,227	5,714	5,376.13	0.04	0.0368
100	Mauritius	5,219	5,446	5,312	5,325.63	0.04	0.0342
101	Brunei Darussalam	4,748	5,383	5,740	5,290.57	0.04	0.0370
102	*Bosnia and Herzegovina*	4,979	5,467	5,412	5,285.87	0.04	0.0349
103	Botswana	4,801	5,525	5,435	5,253.37	0.04	0.0350
104	*Bahamas*	4,556	4,881	5,613	5,016.50	0.04	0.0362

Appendix 8.2 (*cont.*)

Total trade in goods and services (US $ million)	1998	1999	2000	average 1998–2000	average 1998–2000 share (%)	2000 share (%)
105 Gabon	4,245	4,511	5,066	4,607.20	0.03	0.0327
106 Cameroon	4,154	4,727	4,889	4,589.97	0.03	0.0315
107 Myanmar	4,477	4,206	4,762	4,481.87	0.03	0.0307
108 Papua New Guinea	3,963	3,975	4,669	4,202.50	0.03	0.0301
109 Namibia	3,493	3,625	4,087	3,735.00	0.03	0.0263
110 *Azerbaijan*	3,414	3,171	4,107	3,564.03	0.02	0.0265
111 Congo	2,656	3,384	4,576	3,538.60	0.02	0.0295
112 *TFYR Macedonia*	3,433	3,337	3,824	3,531.33	0.02	0.0247
113 Bolivia	3,522	3,269	3,498	3,429.53	0.02	0.0226
114 Tanzania, United Rep. of	3,373	3,298	3,290	3,320.53	0.02	0.0212
115 Senegal	3,047	3,171	2,982	3,066.60	0.02	0.0192
116 *Sudan*	2,542	2,387	3,829	2,919.47	0.02	0.0247
117 Nicaragua	2,447	2,819	2,888	2,718.13	0.02	0.0186
118 Barbados	2,595	2,695	2,832	2,707.17	0.02	0.0183
119 *Nepal*	2,343	2,763	2,967	2,690.87	0.02	0.0191
120 *Cambodia*	2,243	2,511	3,248	2,667.20	0.02	0.0209
121 Uganda	2,581	2,524	2,574	2,559.67	0.02	0.0166
122 Congo, Dem. Rep. of	2,609	2,176	2,053	2,279.33	0.02	0.0132
123 Swaziland	2,387	2,197	1,973	2,185.93	0.02	0.0127
124 Zambia	2,173	2,046	2,177	2,132.03	0.01	0.0140
125 Fiji	1,846	2,060	2,405	2,103.83	0.01	0.0155
126 Madagascar	1,821	1,953	2,530	2,101.40	0.01	0.0163
127 Mozambique	1,663	2,061	2,174	1,965.73	0.01	0.0140

128	Georgia	1,983	1,634	1,852	1,823.13	0.01	0.0119
129	Albania	1,222	1,618	2,168	1,669.20	0.01	0.0140
130	Moldova, Rep. of	2,013	1,383	1,602	1,666.10	0.01	0.0103
131	Haiti	1,488	1,650	1,692	1,609.93	0.01	0.0109
132	Guinea	1,605	1,533	1,568	1,568.80	0.01	0.0101
133	*Tajikistan*	1,392	1,429	1,879	1,566.90	0.01	0.0121
134	Mali	1,512	1,630	1,546	1,562.93	0.01	0.0100
135	Guyana	1,485	1,414	1,471	1,456.80	0.01	0.0095
136	*Armenia*	1,344	1,281	1,484	1,369.67	0.01	0.0096
137	Kyrgyz Rep.	1,521	1,222	1,215	1,319.33	0.01	0.0078
138	Benin	1,305	1,425	1,215	1,314.90	0.01	0.0078
139	Mongolia	1,204	1,178	1,410	1,264.13	0.01	0.0091
140	Togo	1,188	1,065	1,361	1,204.77	0.01	0.0088
141	Malawi	1,238	1,267	1,083	1,195.87	0.01	0.0070
142	*Lao People's Dem. Rep.*	1,057	1,016	1,217	1,096.63	0.01	0.0078
143	Lesotho	1,156	1,035	1,016	1,069.00	0.01	0.0065
144	Burkina Faso	1,150	1,009	883	1,014.07	0.01	0.0057
145	Antigua and Barbuda	952	997	947	965.47	0.01	0.0061
146	*Seychelles*	880	977	994	950.00	0.01	0.0064
147	Suriname	968	849	907	907.97	0.01	0.0058
148	Maldives	833	892	904	876.40	0.01	0.0058
149	St Lucia	799	821	782	800.43	0.01	0.0050
150	Belize	693	791	882	788.53	0.01	0.0057
151	Mauritania	831	748	781	786.77	0.01	0.0050
152	Chad	800	752	765	772.17	0.01	0.0049
153	Niger	768	656	639	687.80	0.00	0.0041
154	Gambia	558	524	550	544.13	0.00	0.0035
155	Grenada	409	478	530	471.90	0.00	0.0034
156	Djibouti	434	464	495	464.10	0.00	0.0032

Appendix 8.2 (*cont.*)

Total trade in goods and services (US $ million)	1998	1999	2000	average 1998–2000	average 1998–2000 share (%)	2000 share (%)
157 *Cape Verde*	411	469	447	442.30	0.00	0.0029
158 Rwanda	430	455	434	440.03	0.00	0.0028
159 Central African Republic	443	398	411	417.23	0.00	0.0026
160 St Vincent and the Grenadines	400	412	375	395.63	0.00	0.0024
161 *Bhutan*	332	371	436	379.50	0.00	0.0028
162 Solomon Islands	407	411	273	363.97	0.00	0.0018
163 St Kitts and Nevis	336	358	391	361.70	0.00	0.0025
164 Dominica	300	326	312	312.93	0.00	0.0020
165 *Vanuatu*	261	255	294	270.30	0.00	0.0019
166 Burundi	230	178	193	200.40	0.00	0.0012
167 *Samoa*	204	200	187	196.83	0.00	0.0012
168 Sierra Leone	166	150	238	184.70	0.00	0.0015
169 Guinea-Bissau	92	135	171	132.83	0.00	0.0011
170 *Tonga*	123	124	145	130.73	0.00	0.0009
171 *Federal Rep. of Yugoslavia*	–	–	–	–	–	–
172 *Andorra*	–	–	–	–	–	–
173 Liechtenstein	–	–	–	–	–	–
Total	13,441,042	13,905,731	15,511,380	14,286,051.25	100.0000	100.0000

Source: World Trade Organization, statistics used for calculation of budget contributions. The countries in italics are those currently acceding to the World Trade Organization.

Appendix 8.3 *United Nations Economic Vulnerability Index Sorted by vulnerability*

S.No.	Country name	EVI
1	Kiribati	74.32
2	Tuvalu	73.68
3	Chad	64.41
4	Liberia	63.62
5	Gambia	61.83
6	Cambodia	61.00
7	Saudi Arabia	60.01
8	São Tomé and Principe	59.07
9	Niger	58.98
10	Benin	58.68
11	Tonga	58.63
12	Nigeria	58.41
13	Somalia	58.04
14	Seychelles	57.02
15	Saint Lucia	56.99
16	Cape Verde	56.98
17	Uganda	56.52
18	Dominica	56.05
19	Guinea-Bissau	55.91
20	Rwanda	55.85
21	Qatar	55.84
22	Equatorial Guinea	55.81
23	United Arab Emirates	55.55
24	Comoros	55.36
25	Angola	55.19
26	Libyan Arab Jamahiriya	54.01
27	Solomon Islands	53.93
28	Lesotho	53.11
29	Samoa	52.45
30	Dem. Rep. of the Congo	51.89
31	Zambia	51.82
32	Saint Vincent & the Grenadines	51.65
33	Burundi	51.55
34	Guyana	51.41
35	Brunei Darussalam	51.07
36	Syrian Arab Republic	51.04
37	Saint Kitts and Nevis	50.26

Appendix 8.3 (*cont.*)

S.No.	Country name	EVI
38	Iran (Islamic Rep. of)	50.00
39	Gabon	49.96
40	Myanmar	49.82
41	Mongolia	49.73
42	Yemen	49.54
43	Oman	49.05
44	Mali	48.41
45	Bahrain	48.15
46	Congo (Rep. of)	46.90
47	Djibouti	46.60
48	Sierra Leone	46.30
49	Guinea	45.77
50	Laos	45.65
51	Haiti	45.61
52	Dominican Rep.	45.54
53	Bahamas	45.37
54	Togo	45.30
55	Afghanistan	44.89
56	Burkina Faso	44.58
57	Ethiopia	44.58
58	Sudan	44.45
59	Suriname	44.28
60	Grenada	43.67
61	Nicaragua	43.16
62	Ghana	43.13
63	Paraguay	43.05
64	Central African Rep.	42.43
65	Bhutan	42.27
66	Lebanon	41.90
67	Malawi	41.57
68	Cuba	41.50
69	Mauritania	41.42
70	Papua New Guinea	41.40
71	Vanuatu	41.31
72	Algeria	41.30
73	Antigua and Barbuda	41.20
74	Tunisia	41.08
75	Zimbabwe	40.94

Appendix 8.3 (*cont.*)

S.No.	Country name	EVI
76	Senegal	40.86
77	Belize	40.47
78	Trinidad and Tobago	39.03
79	Malta	38.98
80	Fiji Islands	37.39
81	Mozambique	37.36
82	Barbados	36.54
83	Nepal	36.37
84	Tanzania (Utd Rep. of)	36.23
85	Honduras	35.73
86	Mauritius	35.21
87	Swaziland	35.02
88	Morocco	33.82
89	Venezuela	33.79
90	Côte d'Ivoire	32.81
91	Dem. P. Rep. of Korea	32.31
92	Maldives	32.18
93	Cameroon	31.59
94	Jamaica	31.18
95	Singapore	31.02
96	Viet Nam	31.02
97	Cyprus	29.87
98	Ecuador	29.40
99	Panama	28.89
100	El Salvador	28.36
101	Kenya	27.75
102	Jordan	27.70
103	Bolivia	27.24
104	Eritrea	27.06
105	Madagascar	26.75
106	Sri Lanka	26.18
107	Peru	26.13
108	Guatemala	25.99
109	Chile	25.09
110	Philippines	25.00
111	Egypt	24.85
112	Colombia	24.28
113	Uruguay	24.09

Appendix 8.3 (*cont.*)

S.No.	Country name	EVI
114	Costa Rica	23.99
115	Bangladesh	23.77
116	Israel	23.35
117	South Africa	22.43
118	Pakistan	22.21
119	Turkey	19.33
120	Thailand	17.92
121	Indonesia	17.38
122	Malaysia	16.55
123	Korea (Rep. of)	16.09
124	Mexico	15.47
125	Argentina	15.22
126	Brazil	15.20
127	India	12.20
128	China	4.18

Source: United Nations Economic and Social Council.

9

Special and differential treatment for small developing economies

RICHARD L. BERNAL

9.1 Introduction

The international community has recognised that there are significant differences between countries at different levels of development. It is for this reason that it formally acknowledges developed countries, developing countries and least developed countries (LDCs). It was recognised that in a multilateral trading system with a standard set of rules the developing countries and LDCs would be at a disadvantage relative to the developed countries. It was also deemed desirable that the economic growth/development and structural adjustment of developing countries and LDCs should be promoted by special and differential treatment (SDT). In a multilateral trading system with such wide differences among countries, special and differential treatment is a necessity and is therefore one of the fundamental principles of the World Trade Organization agreements. It has the same validity as the most favoured nation principle and is not a derogation to be applied to some countries on a temporary basis.

Up to the present time the international community has proceeded on the basis of different levels of development. However, in addition to differences in levels of development there are substantial differences in size among economies. Small developing economies (SDEs) are a sub-set of developing countries. The SDEs are a specific type of developing country whose stability, adjustment and growth are constrained by both level of

This is a revised edition of a paper presented at the Conference on Special and Differential Treatment for Small Developing Economies, Inter-American Development Bank, Montego Bay, Jamaica, 15 December 2003 and the First Meeting of the Steering Committee of 'Global Trade and Financial Architecture', Oxford, England, 24 January 2005.

The views expressed in this chapter are those of the author and not those of the Caribbean Regional Negotiating Machinery.

development and small size. Small size is an additional constraint, which distinguishes small developing economies from the genre of developing economies as a whole. The existing SDT provisions suffer from many inadequacies and do not consciously take account of small size in their design. Therefore the provisions, which give expression to the principle of special and differential treatment for developing countries, need to be revised and refined to take specific account of the issues, which arise from small size.

This chapter explains why small developing economies must be afforded special and differential treatment, identifies the characteristics of SDEs, outlines specific measures of SDT which are appropriate for these economies and establishes the direct relationship between the characteristics and the SDT measures. Section 9.2 explains why SDEs should be afforded SDT and how this is beneficial to them and the international community. Having done this, section 9.3 reviews the evolution and status of SDT and finds that there is an unresolved debate about the efficacy of SDT. Section 9.4 then examines the issues in this debate, concluding that there is a need to establish more clearly the link between the characteristics of developing countries and the existing SDT measures. The characteristics of SDEs are outlined in section 9.5 and the implications of the features for the functioning of SDEs are examined in the next section. Against this background, specific SDT measures appropriate for SDEs are set out in section 9.7. How these SDT measures address the characteristics of SDEs is explained in the following section. That leaves the question of the identification of SDEs, which is treated in the penultimate section. The conclusions are stated in the final section.

9.2 Why SDT for small developing economies?

Small developing economies should be afforded special and differential treatment for at least four reasons, which are important not only to these economies but also to the international community.

1. Small developing economies have structural and institutional characteristics, which affect the process of economic growth, constrain the attainment of economies of scale and scope, increase their vulnerability to external events and limit their capacity for adjustment. These characteristics are sufficient to identify small developing economies as a subset of the genre of economy commonly referred to as developing

economies. Given the high degree of openness of small developing economies and their supply-side constraints, external developments have a very significant effect on their economic growth and the stability of income. The terms and conditions under which these economies participate in the world economy and their internal economic management are the critical determinants of the economic progress and capacity for adjustment in SDEs. External arrangements and internal policy must be complementary because both are necessary but not sufficient conditions for economic development. The benefits of sound economic management can only be realised if international economic arrangements do not frustrate these efforts, e.g. by protectionist barriers to export markets. SDT for SDEs must allow adequate 'policy space' as the type of policies appropriate for these economies will of necessity differ from those suitable for developed economies. Therefore, the disciplines applicable to the trade policy of these economies must be different from that applicable to the developed countries. The recognition of this for developing countries as a whole is part of the rationale for SDT.[1]

2. The availability of SDT is of considerable importance to small developing economies because of the critical influence of external trade on the growth and economic development of these economies. The significance to the international community of SDT for these economies derives from the large number of small states and the fact that their non-participation would prevent the emergence of a truly seamless world economy, leaving the multilateral trading system with less than complete membership. In addition, to the extent that SDT promotes the growth of import capacity and export production, this serves to expand world trade to the benefit of all trading nations. It is therefore in the interest of the developed countries to facilitate the integration of small developing countries into the world economy in ways that encourage their growth.
3. The political significance of this issue derives from the fact that the majority of states in the world are small. There are eighty-nine countries that have a population of less than 5 million, forty-nine have fewer than 1.5 million people, and twenty-eight have fewer than 500,000 people.[2] Indeed, the number of countries has increased

[1] Constantine Michalopoulos, *Developing Countries in the WTO* (London: Palgrave, 2001) p. 36.

[2] *A Future for Small States. Overcoming Vulnerability* (London: Commonwealth Secretariat, 1997) p. 8–10.

significantly in recent decades. At the time of World War I, there were sixty-two independent countries, by 1946 that number had risen to seventy-four and currently there are over 200. The number of small states has also increased and is likely to increase in the future, as there is a trend towards the fragmentation of states as witnessed in recent years in Eastern Europe and Africa.

4. Increasingly developed countries have balked at permitting SDT because several developing countries have demonstrated the capacity to compete effectively with developed countries in price and quality in an increasing range of goods and services. They have argued that developing countries do not need SDT and that granting it to them would undermine free trade to the detriment of all. However, small developing economies as a whole constitute an infinitesimal fraction of world trade and therefore SDT for them would not distort multilateral free trade. The eighty-six smallest economies, most of which are small developing economies, account for only 1.5 per cent of world trade and such a minute percentage could not disrupt the operation of the multilateral trading system.[3]

9.3 Evolution and status of special and differential treatment

Differentiated treatment is a well-established concept and practice in multilateral, regional and bilateral trade agreements. The rationale for differentiated treatment has been based on the recognition of differences in the level of development among trading partners and has as its objective the promotion of growth and development of the less developed partners. Differentiated treatment had its origin in the colonial trade arrangement and the principle has continued in various forms in agreements between countries at different levels of development. The dissolution of colonial regimes ushered in an era in which the international community accepted the responsibility to assist in reducing the desperate and persistent poverty of a considerable share of mankind. The prevailing view was that poverty reduction required economic development and that trade could be the 'engine of growth'. The procreative power of trade could be enhanced by preferential access to markets in developed countries and the nurturing of

[3] Roman Grynberg and Jan Yves Remy, 'Small Vulnerable Economy Issues and the WTO' in *Small States. Economic Review and Basic Statistics*, vol. 8, p. 28.

export capacity through protection from full or immediate exposure to international competition. This philosophy of trade-led development continues to inform differentiated treatment in the form of permanent or temporary non-reciprocity, which is embodied in several trade agreements between developed countries and small developing countries: for example, the Lomé Convention and its successor the Cotonou Agreement, the Caribbean Basin Economic Recovery Act, CARIBCAN and the Andean Trade Preferences Act.

Small developing economies have been among groups of developing countries that have been afforded SDT in a variety of forms of trade agreements. Special and differential treatment in the WTO agreements assumes particular importance for small developing economies because all other trade agreements have to be compatible with the WTO. Negotiations on SDT for SDEs must therefore be an integral component of the WTO process because these economies more than any other group of countries need a rules-based multilateral trading system. It is in their vital interest that rule-making be conducted within a multilateral framework in which decision-making is by consensus. In this type of arrangement small countries, because of their numbers, have more influence as compared with their limited leverage in bilateral negotiations with larger countries.[4]

Differentiated treatment became a part of the rules of the multilateral trading system when the concept was introduced into the General Agreement on Tariffs and Trade (GATT). Although the initial premise underlying GATT (1947) was parity of obligations between all trading nations, differentiated treatment for developing countries was acknowledged as a complementary principle. This took the form of preferential treatment for developing countries, in the form of preferential access to developed country markets through tariff preferences, and exemptions from GATT rules. In 1965, the special status of the developing country in the multilateral trading system was established with the adoption of a new Part IV of the GATT, which embodied what was termed 'special and differential treatment'. This treatment was defined as non-reciprocity for developing countries. Preferential access to developed country markets such as the preferential tariffs under the Generalized System of Preferences

[4] Richard L. Bernal, 'Small Developing Countries and the Multilateral Trade System. A Caribbean Perspective' in *Commonwealth Finance Ministers Reference Book* (London: Henley Media Group for the Commonwealth Secretariat, September 2004).

derive from the waiver in 1971 from Article I (MFN obligation) of the GATT. In 1979 the Enabling Clause gave the 1971 waiver permanent status but also indicated that SDT is not a permanent right.

Developing countries suffered a reversal on SDT during the Uruguay Round when they agreed to the concept of a 'single undertaking'. This was in keeping with a gradual but resolute shift in the attitude of developed countries towards SDT for developing countries other than the 'least developed countries'. There is a school of thought that SDT should be targeted to the least developed countries because there is no dispute about their need for assistance in integrating into the international trade system and that a process of graduation should be established for the more advanced developing countries.[5] The change began in the 1980s, reflecting a congruence of factors including:

(1) A change in the thinking in the economics profession about the role of trade in economic development and the respective roles of the state and the market. This coincided with the rise to prominence of the private-sector-led, market-forces approach to development and structural adjustment both in academic circles and in the international financial institutions. By the 1990s the so-called 'Washington Consensus' had become the dominant paradigm with many ardent exponents in developing countries.

(2) A few developing countries had emerged from the pack and proved to be competitive with developed countries in a range of goods and services, including manufactured goods, which until then had been the traditional preserve of developed countries. Developed countries became increasingly reluctant to maintain SDT for all developing countries because the advanced developing countries such as the newly industrialised countries, especially the 'Asian Tigers', would be beneficiaries. These countries, it was felt, were sufficiently competitive to assume stronger disciplines than the rest of the developing countries. The developed countries faced the dilemma that they could not eliminate SDT or the category of developing country from the WTO agreements. This prompted the developed countries to pursue a strategy of pushing to confine SDT to the LDCs and calling for the graduation of the

[5] Constantine Michalopoulos, *The Role of Special and Differential Treatment for Developing Countries in GATT and the World Trade Organization*, Working Paper No. 2147 (Washington D.C.: World Bank, 1999).

most advanced of the developing countries. EU Trade Commissioner Mandelson has warned that 'advanced developing countries must be aware that they cannot be granted the same advantages and privileges as weak and vulnerable countries'.[6] This attitude is quite understandable given some of the countries that are entitled to benefit from SDT: for example, the World Bank's *Global Economic Prospects 2005* makes reference to 'large developing countries' including China, Russia and India.[7]

(3) Developing countries relinquished some aspects of SDT either because they were pressured or in some cases of their own volition. An example of relinquishing existing SDT under duress was when, starting with Korea, Argentina and Brazil, several developing countries gave up their rights under Article XVIII:B,[8] which under certain circumstances permits the imposition of quantitative restrictions or tariff surcharges for balance-of-payments adjustment purposes. Another example of foregoing SDT provisions is the fact that only one least developed country maintains balance-of-payments restrictions invoked under Article XVIII(B).[9]

(4) There has been less use of some SDT provisions than expected. For example, only twenty-five developing countries availed themselves of the opportunity to notify to the WTO exemptions under the Agreement on Agriculture, including investment subsidies, agricultural input subsidies and domestic support to encourage diversification from cultivation of narcotic crops.[10] The underutilisation of SDT is not necessarily an indication of lack of interest or the inappropriateness of SDT provisions but is a result of severely constrained institutional capacity, paucity of financial resources and conditionality of lending and policy advice by multilateral financial institutions.[11]

[6] Speech by EU Trade Commissioner Peter Mandelson, ACP Ministerial Meeting, Brussels, 1 December 2004.

[7] *Global Economic Prospects. Trade, Regionalism and Development. 2005* (Washington D.C.: World Bank, 2005) p. 3.

[8] Murray Gibbs, *Special and Differential Treatment in the Context of Globalisation* (Geneva: UNCTAD, 1998) p. 5.

[9] Amar Breckenridge, 'Developing an Issues-Based Approach to Special and Differential Treatment', Paper presented at the Inter-American Development Bank, Third Meeting of the Integration and Trade Network, 19–20 March 2002.

[10] Anwarul Hoda, *Special and Differential Treatment in Agricultural Negotiations*, Working Paper No. 100 (New Delhi: Indian Council for Research on International Economic Relations, May 2003) p. 9.

[11] Francis Mangeni, 'Strengthening Special and Differential Treatment in the WTO Agreements', ICTSD Resource Paper No. 4 (2003).

(5) Some developing countries began to evince doubt about the benefits of SDT. The 'earlier paradigm did not enjoy a consensus even among developing countries, it was viewed as ideological baggage from the past by some, or as a crutch which developing countries no longer needed and which was actually hindering their competitiveness'.[12] The view that SDT had been adverse for developing countries is in part attributable to what Whalley describes as 'the installation of meritocratic trade officials in a number of developing countries'.[13]

(6) There was a growing recognition among an increasing number of both developing and developed countries that developing countries would benefit more from improved market access and elimination or substantial reductions in subsidies and domestic support in the agriculture sectors of the developed countries than in what appeared to be the futile attempts to extract concessions from the quagmire of SDT. It is in this milieu that a number of developing countries took a strategy decision to focus their efforts in areas of negotiation other than SDT.

The concerns in developing countries about the reduced role of SDT were assuaged by the much-heralded benefits of the Uruguay Round for the global economy and in particular developing countries. Quantitative estimates of the impact of the Round varied,[14] with the most frequently cited estimates by GATT and the OECD. The GATT study forecasted an increase of $230 billion (1992 dollars) in world GDP by 2005 and world trade was predicted to grow by 12.4 per cent or $745 billion.[15] According to the OECD report, world GDP would rise by $274 billion (1992 dollars) by 2002.[16] Estimates of the impact of the Uruguay Round on developing countries ranged from $13 billion to $125 billion per annum in increased income in 1992 dollars. Several studies made the startling prediction that the gains accruing to developing countries, measured as a percentage of GDP, would exceed the benefits to be realised by industrial countries.[17]

[12] Murray Gibbs, *Special and Differential Treatment in the Context of Globalisation* (Geneva: UNCTAD, 1998) p. 4.

[13] John Whalley, 'Special and Differential Treatment in the Millennium Round', *The World Economy*, vol. 22, issue 8 (November 1999) p. 1089.

[14] For a comprehensive review of the impact of the Uruguay Round see Jeffrey Schott, *The Uruguay Round. An Assessment* (Washington D.C.: Institute of International Economics, 1994) pp. 16–18.

[15] 'Economy-wide Effects of the Uruguay Round'. GATT Background Paper (Geneva, 1993).

[16] *Assessing the Effects of the Uruguay Round* (Paris: Organisation for Economic Cooperation and Development, 1993).

However, by the time of the WTO Ministerial meeting in Seattle the majority of developing countries felt they had not realised the gains they had anticipated and SDT assumed prominence in their negotiating demands.[18]

The Ministerial Declaration of the WTO meeting in Doha in 2001 states that 'provisions for special and differential treatment are an integral part of the WTO agreements' and mandates a review of SDT provisions with the objective of 'strengthening them and making them more precise, effective and operational'. Subsequently developing countries have made numerous proposals, of which eighty-eight are being carefully studied. Up to the time of writing there has not been agreement on even one proposal of economic substance.

Special and differential treatment is embodied in the WTO agreements[19] in 147 provisions, of which 107 were adopted at the conclusion of the Uruguay Round, and 22 apply only to least-developed member countries. These measures are incorporated in the Multilateral Agreement on Trade in Goods, the General Agreement on Trade in Services (GATS), the Agreement on Trade-Related Aspects of Intellectual Property (TRIPS), the Understanding on Rules and Procedures governing the Settlement of Disputes (DSU), and in several Ministerial Decisions. There are twelve provisions in four agreements and one decision, which are aimed at increasing the trade opportunities of developing country members. There are forty-nine provisions under which WTO members should safeguard the interest of developing countries. In addition, there are thirty provisions that permit flexibility of commitments, of action and use of policy instruments. However, measures to promote trade opportunities and safeguards are for the most part best endeavours, which are not enforceable and have not been fully implemented.

[17] Thomas Hertel, Will Martin, Koji Yanagishima and Retina Dimaranan, 'Liberalising Manufacturers Trade in a Changing World Economy' (pp. 183–215), Glenn W. Harrison, Thomas F. Rutherford and David G. Tarr, 'Quantifying the Uruguay Round' (pp. 216–52) and Joseph F. Francois, Bradley McDonald and Hakan Nordstrom, 'The Uruguay Round: A Numerically Based Qualitative Assessment' (pp. 253–91) in Will Martin and L. Alan Winters (eds.), *The Uruguay Round and the Developing Countries* (Cambridge: Cambridge University Press, 1996).

[18] Richard L. Bernal, 'Sleepless in Seattle: The WTO Ministerial of 1999', *Social and Economic Studies*, vol. 48, no. 3 (September 1999) pp. 61–84.

[19] 'Implementation of Special and Differential Treatment Provisions in WTO Agreements and Decisions', World Trade Organisation, Committee on Trade and Development, WT/COMTD/W/77, 25 October 2000, pp. 3–4.

9.4 Debate over the efficacy of SDT

Special and differential treatment for developing countries has been a controversial topic since it was first broached in the 1950s. There has been a vigorous debate on the rationale for, and the efficacy of, SDT. At the theoretical level there are two contending views that differ, almost diametrically, on the conditions in which trade will promote growth and economic development. At one end of the spectrum of views are the advocates of free trade and at the other are those that argue that the free trade model is not sufficiently realistic to explain the reality of international trade and certainly not the trade of developing countries. At the empirical level there has been a dispute about whether statistical data supports conclusions on positive or negative impacts of SDT on developing countries. The critics of SDT for developing countries state that SDT has not worked and that it cannot work.

1. The neo-classical theory of international trade is the basis for the advocacy of free trade as the approach to trade, which ensures that all participating countries derive benefit. Every country has a comparative advantage in some good or service and trade on this basis will generate growth and maximise consumer welfare.[20] International trade on the basis of comparative advantage as determined by their different factor endowments[21] is supposed to be best for individual countries and the world economy as a whole. The paradigm referred to by its proponents as 'the pure theory of international trade'[22] is what Hirschman[23] has termed 'monoeconomics' as its prescriptions are the same for all economies.

The assumptions of the neo-classical approach are very restrictive and bear little relationship to reality. The policy prescriptions have elicited scepticism and prompted alternative views about the role of trade in economic development, employing models which more accurately reflect the

[20] Paul A. Samuelson, 'The Gains from International Trade', *Canadian Journal of Economics and Political Science*, vol. 5 (May 1939).

[21] Eli Hecksher, 'The Effects of Foreign Trade on the Distribution of Income' (1919) in H. Ellis and L. Metzler (eds.), *Readings in International Trade* (Homewood: Richard D. Irwin, 1950) and Bertil Ohlin, *International and Inter-regional Trade* (Cambridge, Mass.: Harvard University Press, 1933).

[22] Murray C. Kemp, *The Pure Theory of International Trade and Investment* (Englewoods Cliffs: Prentice-Hall, 1969).

[23] Albert Hirschman, *Essays in Trespassing: Economics to Politics and Beyond* (Cambridge: Cambridge University Press, 1983) chapter 1.

reality of developing countries. The divergence between the assumptions underpinning this theory of international trade and reality has forced even one of the most avid proponents of free trade, Bhagwati, to concede that 'if markets do not work well, or are absent or incomplete, then the invisible hand may point in the wrong direction: free trade cannot then be asserted to be the best policy'.[24]

During the 1950s and 1960s the virtues of international trade for economic development were extolled by Viner,[25] Harberler[26] and Craincross[27] but elicited vigorous criticism from several perspectives. It was claimed that the history of the now developed countries was a vindication of free trade policies, with the experience of Britain,[28] Italy[29] and the US[30] in the nineteenth century cited as evidence. The experience of developing countries was in contrast to the predictions, prompting different explanations. Nurske[31] pointed to the lagging demand for primary products and the enclave nature of export industries was also put forward.[32] By far the most telling comments highlighted the deteriorating terms of trade between manufactured goods and primary products. Prebisch[33] and Singer[34] identified the problem of developing country trade as inherent in the structure of the world capitalist system, the international division of labour and the deformed economic structure of developing countries. The developed/industrialised countries which form the core export manufactured goods and the developing countries

[24] Jagdish Bhagwati, *Free Trade Today* (Princeton: Princeton University Press, 2002) p. 12.

[25] Jacob Viner, *International Trade and Economic Development* (Glencoe: Free Press, 1952).

[26] Gottfried Harberler, *International Trade and Economic Development* (Cairo: National Bank, 1959).

[27] A. K. Craincross, 'International Trade and Economic Development', *Kyklos*, vol. 13, no. 4 (1960) and 'International Trade and Economic Development', *Economica*, vol. 28, no. 3 (August 1961).

[28] Phyllis Deane and W. A. Cole, *British Economic Growth* (Cambridge: Cambridge University Press, 2nd edn, 1969).

[29] Robert M. Stern, *Foreign Trade and Economic Growth in Italy* (New York: Praeger, 1967).

[30] Douglas V. North, *The Economic Growth of the United States, 1790–1860* (New York: Prentice-Hall, 1961).

[31] Ragnar Nurske, 'Patterns of Trade and Development' in *Problems of Capital Formation in Underdeveloped Countries and Patterns of Trade and Development* (Oxford: Oxford University Press, 1967).

[32] Jonathon V. Levin, *The Export Economies* (Cambridge, Mass.: Harvard University Press, 1960).

[33] Raul Prebisch, *The Economic Development of Latin America and its Principal Problems* (New York: United Nations Economic Commission for Latin America, 1950) and 'Commercial Policy in the Underdeveloped Countries', *American Economic Review* (May 1959).

[34] H. W. Singer, 'The Distribution of Gains Between Investing and Borrowing Countries', *American Economic Review*, vol. II, no. 2 (May 1950).

export primary products from the periphery. The core derives a disproportionate share of the gains from international trade because of differences in the income and price elasticities of demand for primary products and manufactured goods and differences in technology, industrial organisation and the operation of labour markets, which are part of the structure of the core–periphery system. Lewis[35] argued that in a dual-sector economy with labour surplus, low productivity in the subsistence sector is the critical factor whatever the demand conditions. Myrdal[36] also focuses on low productivity which is caused by the structure of underdeveloped countries that generate a predominance of 'backward effects' (which are growth retarding) over 'spread effects' (which are growth stimulating).

The disadvantaged position of developing countries gained credence because the majority of empirical studies provided support in the form of evidence of the long-term deterioration in the terms of trade of primary products, which were the export mainstay of the developing countries. There was deterioration in the relative real prices of non-oil commodities throughout the twentieth century.[37]

Recent developments in trade theory, which incorporate imperfect competition and increasing economies of scale,[38] cast further doubt on neoclassical trade theory but do not resolve the dispute over trade and growth. Ocampo's survey of the literature concludes that new trade theories do not justify protectionism or laissez-faire industrial policy nor do they substantiate an automatic connection between liberalisation and productivity. Indeed, 'they indicate that trade liberalization should be coupled with an active industrial policy, particularly in sectors subject to significant economies of scale'.[39]

[35] W. Arthur Lewis, 'Economic Development with Unlimited Supplies of Labour', *Manchester School of Economics and Social Studies*, vol. 24, no. 2 (May 1954).

[36] Gunnar Myrdal, *An International Economy, Problems and Prospects* (New York: Harper & Row, 1956) and *Economic Theory and Under-Developed Regions* (London: Methuen, 1965).

[37] Matthias Lutz, 'The Effects of Volatility in the Terms of Trade on Output Growth', *World Development*, vol. 22 (1994) pp. 1959–75.

[38] Paul Krugman, 'Increasing Returns, Imperfect Competition and the Positive Theory of International Trade' in *Handbook of International Economics*, vol. 3 (New York: Elsevier-North-Holland, 1995) pp. 1243–77.

[39] Jose Antonio Ocampo, 'New Theories of International Trade and Trade Policy in Developing Countries' in Manuel R. Agosin and Diana Tussie (eds.), *Trade and Growth: New Dilemmas in Trade Policy* (New York: St Martin's Press, 1993) pp. 121–41.

2. Based on the neo-classical theory of international trade, it is asserted that trade liberalisation can and does increase economic growth. This proposition is the position advocated by developed countries: for example, an OECD publication states: 'Exposure to international trade is a powerful stimulus to efficiency. Efficiency in turn, contributes to economic growth and rising incomes.' The report goes on to claim that in 'the last decade, countries that have been more open have achieved double the annual average growth than others'.[40] This claim is supported by empirical studies, which purport to show an association between policies of openness such as trade liberalisation and higher rates of economic growth.[41] One of the implications is that inadequate or delayed trade liberalisation reduces the growth of developing countries. In keeping with this view, many governments in developing countries misguidedly avail themselves of certain SDT measures which retard the realisation of their growth potential.

The empiricism of most of the studies that support the liberalisation-cum-growth dictum exhibits serious weaknesses. A comprehensive survey of the literature concludes that there is 'little evidence that open trade policies, which lower tariffs and non-tariff barriers to trade, are significantly associated with economic growth'.[42] The real issue is the quality of domestic policy as shown by the fact that developing countries with sound policies achieve efficiency, international competitiveness and growth and are able to take advantage of open trade regimes. Rodrik has suggested that macroeconomic stability, human resources, investment and good

[40] *Open Markets Matter: The Benefits of Trade and Investment Liberalization* (Paris: Organization for Economic Cooperation and Development, 1998) p. 10.

[41] Bela Belassa, 'Economic Development in Small Countries', *Acta Oeconomica*, vol. 37, no. 3–4 (1986) pp. 325–40, David Dollar, 'Outward Oriented Development Economies Really Do Grow More Rapidly: Evidence from 95 LDCs, 1976–1985', *Economic and Cultural Change*, vol. 40, no. 3 (April 1992) pp. 523–44, Jeffrey Sachs and A. Warner, 'Economic Reform and the Process of Global Integration', *Brookings Papers on Economic Activity*, no. 1 (1995) pp. 1–95, Sabastian Edwards, 'Openness, Productivity and Growth: What Do We Really Know?', *Economic Journal*, vol. 108 (1998) pp. 383–98, Jacob A. Frankel and D. Romer, 'Does Trade Cause Growth?', *American Economic Review*, vol. 89 (1999) pp. 379–99 and David Dollar and Aart Kraay, *Growth is Good for the Poor* (World Bank: Development Research Group, 2000).

[42] Francisco Rodriquez and Dani Rodrik, *Trade Policy and Economic Growth: A Skeptic's Guide to the Cross-National Evidence*, NBER Working Paper 7081 (Cambridge: National Bureau of Economic Research, April 1999). For similar findings see A. Harrison and G. Hanson, 'Who Gains from Trade Reform? Some Remaining Puzzles', *Journal of Development Economics*, vol. 59 (1999) pp. 125–54.

governance should be the focus of developing countries seeking enhanced economic growth.[43] Even the Asian Tigers[44] or newly industrialised countries, which are often cited as examples of the success of outward-oriented policies, on closer examination reveal that their strategies involved selective import liberalisation over an extended period.[45] The causality is not that the economy is opened and then economic growth follows. That there is no automaticity in this sequence is evident in the numerous instances of developing countries that have liberalised their trade regimes with disastrous consequences, providing ample material for anti-globalisation and anti-free trade advocates.

3. If trade liberalisation is the best way to stimulate the expansion of trade and promote growth, any policy that deviates from this will produce second-best results and is therefore harmful. Reference is made to the fact that the majority of developing countries have not achieved the kinds of growth rates warranted for economic development and poverty reduction despite the existence of extensive special and differential treatment. More specifically, preferential market access has not prompted export expansion and thereby not promoted economic growth. Nor have infant industries graduated into competitive export industries despite extended periods of protection from the full brunt of competition from imports. Indeed, it is the competition from imports which will either eliminate industries that are not viable or force them to become sufficiently efficient to survive. The conclusion of this line of reasoning is the abolition of provisions which are intended to nurture infant industries. This amounts to what Chang calls 'kicking away the ladder', which was a key element in the development of the now developed countries.[46]

It is ironic that the developed countries that never tire of exhorting developing countries to relinquish SDT for reciprocal trade have quietly

[43] Dani Rodrik, *The New Global Economy and Developing Countries: Making Openness Work* (Washington, D.C.: Overseas Development Council, 1999).

[44] The Asian Tigers are frequently cited as examples of the stimulating effect of openness on growth. This much-heralded 'success' has been questioned, e.g. Paul Krugman, 'The Myth of the Asia Miracle', *Foreign Affairs*, vol. 73, no. 6 (1994) pp. 62–78.

[45] Alice H. Amsden, 'Trade Policy and Economic Performance in South Korea' in Manuel R. Agosin and Diana Tussie (eds.), *Trade and Growth: New Dilemmas in Trade Policy* (New York: St Martin's Press, 1993) pp. 187–214 and Robert Wade, *Governing the Market. Economic Theory and the Role of Government in East Asian Industrialization* (Princeton: Princeton University Press, 1990) pp. 113–58.

[46] Ha-Joon Chang, *Kicking Away the Ladder: Development Strategy in Historical Perspectives* (London: Anthem Press, 2002).

continued to deploy an array of protectionist barriers, especially against imports from developing countries. In addition, the extensive system of subsidies, domestic support and export subsidies in the agriculture sector of developed countries, most notably in the US, the EU and Japan, is tantamount to unilaterally appointed SDT. The double standard goes even further when the governments in the developed countries maintain special programmes for vulnerable producers in their national markets. They operate programmes for small and medium-size firms, family-owned farms and disadvantaged regions. These involve finance at below-market rates, technical assistance and reserving a part of the market in government procurement. The practice of SDT at home does not diminish the virulence of their opposition to SDT for developing countries in the multilateral trading system.

While there is substance to the statement that developing countries have not grown as expected or desired despite SDT, it is also grossly inaccurate because it is based on an incomplete analysis of the international trade environment in which developing countries have operated. The evaluation of the performance of the trade of developing countries must include the harmful policies of developed countries starting with the $311 billion of subsidies lavished on agriculture in the OECD countries in 2001, an amount that exceeds the GDP of Sub-Saharan Africa and is six times total foreign aid.[47] Tariff peaks stymie developing country exports; for example 60 per cent of imports from developing countries entering Canada, the EU, Japan and the US were subject to tariff peaks.[48] There is also tariff escalation, non-tariff barriers, quotas, sanitary and phyto-sanitary measures, and a host of other protectionist policies and trade-distorting practices such as dumping. Ironically, what these policies amount to is special and differential treatment granted unilaterally to themselves by the developed countries. It is very problematic to assess the efficacy of SDT for developing countries because most of the measures are best-endeavour commitments couched in hortatory language but are not specific and definitely not enforceable. Even more disappointing is the new trend for developed countries to offer technical assistance as the answer to demands for SDT. It creates the invidious position that obviously it is a gesture that developing countries cannot refuse but in reality it is more of a placebo than a lasting solution.

[47] *Human Development Report 2003* (New York: United Nations Development Programme, 2003) p. 155.

[48] *Human Development Report 2003* (New York: United Nations Development Programme, 2003) p. 156.

4. It has frequently been said that SDT in the form of non-reciprocity has produced perverse trade policy choices in developing countries. Specifically, it has encouraged them to be protectionist, delaying trade liberalisation[49] as long as they can get away with it. This is the natural course of action because there is no obligation to reciprocate, prompting some to speak of the 'perversity of preferences'[50] of schemes such as the Generalized System of Preferences (GSP). The existence of SDT is purported to 'discourage effective efforts to integrate into the world economy' and 'merely exacerbates the difficulties of pursuing satisfactory policies' and 'should be phased out as soon as possible'.[51] This kind of attribution is too superficial because it overlooks the motivations for deferring trade liberalisation which are present in every country whether it enjoys SDT or not. The common motivations emanate from the desire to preserve market position by minimising competition from imports and garner economic rents and higher profits.

What has not been definitively established in the debate on the efficacy of SDT is how each measure of SDT is directly related to a specific aspect of developing countries. This is partly due to the wide range of countries covered by the existing outmoded nomenclature of developing country and least developed country. It is extremely difficult to identify a typical developing country or a feature that is common to all developing countries to the same extent. Not all developing countries exhibit all the features and problems ascribed to the category.

Some countries, by virtue of not being classified as developed or industrialised, are still counted among the so-called developing countries. These advanced developing countries have proven themselves to be internationally competitive, industrialised and large enough not to be price-takers in a wide and growing range of goods and services. In this context, the call for SDT for SDEs will not succeed unless (a) these countries can be identified as a separate genre of economy, not developed, nor least developed, but a sub-set of developing countries having characteristics which derive from

[49] Robert E. Hudec, *Developing Countries in the GATT Legal System* (London: Gower, 1987).

[50] Caglar Ozden and Eric Reinhardt, *The Perversity of Preferences: The Generalized System of Preferences and Developing Country Trade Policies, 1976–2000.* Policy Research Working Paper No. 2955 (Washington, D.C.: World Bank, 2003).

[51] J. Michael Finger and L. Alan Winters, 'What can the WTO do for Developing Countries?' in Anne Krueger (ed.), *The WTO as an International Organization* (Chicago: University of Chicago, 1998) p. 390.

being developing and from being small; (b) the need for SDT is established based on the characteristics of SDEs and the implications for their functioning, growth, development and structural transformation; (c) each and every type of measure of SDT proposed for SDEs is shown to be directly related to and addressing a specific characteristic and/or aspect of the functioning of SDEs. The next section is therefore devoted to identifying and describing the characteristics of small developing economies.

9.5 Characteristics of small developing economies

Small developing economies have certain characteristics,[52] such as a high degree of openness, limited diversity in economic activity, export-concentration on one to three products, significant dependency on trade taxes, and small size of firms. Some developing countries and least developed countries in general may exhibit some of the characteristics listed as defining small developing economies. This has led some to argue that many of the problems attributed to small developing economies are not unique to them or can be addressed by appropriate policy measures and therefore smallness does not differentiate economies.[53] Careful analysis reveals, however, that the characteristics, which are common to different types of developing countries, differ by degree between the different types of developing countries. Therefore what sets small developing economies apart and defines them as a distinct genre of developing country is the combination of characteristics and the degree or extent of these characteristics.

9.5.1 Acute vulnerability

The high degree of openness and the concentration in a few export products, particularly some primary products and agricultural commodities whose prices and demand are subject to fluctuations in world markets, make small developing economies vulnerable to external economic events. Substantial dependence on external sources of economic growth makes small developing countries acutely vulnerable to exogenous shocks. The

[52] There is a view that small countries are so heterogeneous that they do not exhibit uniform characteristics and do not behave in the same way in similar circumstances. See Peter J. Lloyd, *International Trade Problems of Small Nations* (Durham, N.C.: Duke University Press, 1968).

[53] T. N. Srinivasan, 'The Costs and Benefits of Being a Small, Island, Landlocked, or Ministate Economy', *World Bank Research Observer*, vol. 1, no. 2 (1986).

exposure of small developing economies to real shocks is much greater than in larger economies, which are usually more diversified in structure and exports. Gonzales regards vulnerability as such a critical aspect that he speaks of small vulnerable transitional developing states as a distinct category of economy.[54] The WTO Ministerial Declaration of Doha makes reference to the objective of identifying trade-related issues for the fuller integration of 'small, vulnerable economies' into the multilateral trading system.[55]

Economic vulnerability can be a feature of an economy of any size and level of development, but it is compounded by small size, a high degree of openness, narrow export concentration, susceptibility to natural disasters, remoteness and insularity. Small developing economies have structural features that make them more vulnerable to external shocks.[56] Indeed, acute vulnerability is a feature that is unique to small developing economies, differentiating them from other types of economies that may share characteristics such as openness, weak adjustment capacity and limited institutional capacity.

The characteristic of small developing economies that most differentiates them from other developing countries is acute vulnerability. This is a condition which arises from a high degree of openness compounded by a high degree of export concentration and export market concentration. Export concentration is not unique to small developing economies; it is a feature of several developing countries and is particularly common among the least developed countries. However, concentration on a few exports, concomitant with small size of productive units and a disarticulated adjustment capacity, gives export concentration an importance in small developing economies beyond that of other developing countries.

9.5.1.1 High degree of openness

External transactions are large in relation to total economic activity, as indicated by the high ratio of trade to GDP. There is heavy reliance on external trade because of a narrow range of resources and the inability to

[54] Anthony Gonzales, 'Policy Implications of Smallness as a Factor in the Lomé, FTAA and WTO Negotiations', Caribbean RNM/IDB Regional Technical Cooperation Project No. ATN/JF/SF-6158-RG, September 2000.

[55] WTO Ministerial Declaration, Doha, 9–14 November 2001, WT/MIN (01)/DEC/1, 20 November 2001, paragraph 35, p. 8.

[56] 'Small and Relatively Less Developed Economies and Western Hemisphere Integration', OAS/Ser.W/XIII.7 (Washington, D.C.: Organization of American States, September 1996).

support certain types of production, given the small scale of the market. Economic openness is measured by imports and exports of goods and services as a percentage of GDP. A high degree of openness is not peculiar to small developing economies, as the growth of interdependence and the increase of international transactions relative to national production have resulted in all economies showing increased levels of openness. For many developed countries, a high degree of openness is typical; however, the implications of this are very different compared to small developing countries. A high level of openness coexists in most small developing economies with extreme export concentration and internationally uncompetitive production, resulting in vulnerability. In contrast, a high degree of openness in developed economies is indicative of their integration in the global economy and their ability to compete in global markets.

9.5.1.2 Export concentration

The limited range of economic activity in small developing economies is reflected in concentration on one to three exports accompanied, in the majority of cases, by a relatively high reliance on primary commodities. In extreme cases, one export, often a primary product or tourism, accounts for nearly all exports. Empirical analyses have detected a positive and statistically significant relationship between export concentration and export instability[57] and, through its effects on terms of trade, volatility has a major effect on income volatility.[58] The terms of trade volatility is 30 per cent higher for small developing economies than for other developing countries.[59]

9.5.1.3 Export market concentration

In many small developing economies export concentration is accompanied by export market concentration, i.e. dependence on one or two export markets. For example, in the 1990s, Britain absorbed Dominica's bananas when that product accounted for 90 per cent of total exports.

[57] J. Love, 'Commodity Concentration and Export Earnings Instability: A Shift from Cross-section to Time Series Analysis', *Journal of Development Economics*, vol. 24 (1986) pp. 239–48.

[58] Marion Jansen, 'Income Volatility in Small and Developing Countries', WTO Discussion Paper (December 2004) p. 5.

[59] M. Ayhan Kose and Eswar S. Prasad, 'Thinking Big', *Finance and Development*, vol. 39, no. 4 (December 2002).

9.5.1.4 Export marketing monopoly

The effect of export market concentration is particularly detrimental to economic development if the export marketing is controlled by a single multinational corporation.[60] This is frequently the case, in part because of the very small export volume, for example the export of bananas and sugar from the Caribbean. Even where an export is handled by several multinational corporations, the transactions constitute intra-firm trade[61] and not the arm's-length international trade of economics textbooks. For a long time the world bauxite trade was conducted on the basis of intra-firm transfers[62] and there was no genuine world market in operation.

9.5.1.5 Acuteness

The extent of vulnerability of an economy can be measured by a 'vulnerability index': for example the index constructed by Atkins, Mazzi and Easter[63] incorporates economic exposure, susceptibility to environmental events and remoteness and insularity. Gonzales uses income volatility, growth resilience and preference dependence.[64] Different vulnerability indices have been formulated differing in which variables are included and the methodology of weighting. Despite differences, all vulnerability indices reveal a relationship between vulnerability and size, with the smallest countries being the most vulnerable. Atkins et al. found that twenty-eight of the thirty most vulnerable were small developing economies.[65] A Commonwealth Secretariat/World Bank study has shown that of 111 developing countries, twenty-six of the twenty-eight most vulnerable were small countries and

[60] George Beckford, *Persistent Poverty. Underdevelopment in Plantation Economies of the Third World* (Oxford: Oxford University Press, 1972).

[61] Gerald K. Helleiner, *Intra-Firm Trade and the Developing Countries* (London: Macmillan, 1981).

[62] Norman Girvan, *Corporate Imperialism: Conflict and Expropriation: Transnational Corporations and Economic Nationalism in the Third World* (New York: Monthly Review Press, 1976).

[63] Lino Briguglio, 'Small Island Developing States and their Economic Vulnerabilities', *World Development*, vol. 23, no. 9 (1995) pp. 1615–32, and Jonathan P. Atkins, Sonia Mazzi and Christopher D. Easter, 'Small States: A Composite Vulnerability Index' in David Peretz, Rumman Faruqi and Eliawony J. Kisanga (eds.), *Small States in the Global Economy* (London: Commonwealth Secretariat, 2001) pp. 53–92.

[64] Anthony Gonzales, 'Policy Implications of Smallness as a Factor in the Lomé, FTAA and WTO Negotiations', Caribbean RNM/IDB Regional Technical Cooperation Project No. ATN/JF/SF-6158-RG, September 2000.

[65] Jonathan P. Atkins, Sonia Mazzi and Christopher D. Easter, 'Small States: A Composite Vulnerability Index' in David Peretz, Rumman Faruqi and Eliawony J. Kisanga (eds.), *Small States in the Global Economy* (London: Commonwealth Secretariat, 2001) p. 63.

that the least vulnerable economies were all large countries.[66] Argentina, Brazil, Canada and the United States have vulnerability indices of 0.2 or less while the ten smallest countries range from 0.59 to 0.84.[67]

9.5.2 Imperfect markets

The small size of markets in small developing economies results in market structures which are characterised by substantial imperfections. These derive from the limited number of participants, and in many cases there are monopolies and oligopolies. Even where there are a large number of producers or traders, one or a few firms effectively dominate the operation of markets both in the financial as well as in the real sector. Market imperfections, of one kind or another, are to be found in economies of all types, but in small developing economies these imperfections are particularly perverse. For example, monopolies in small developing economies are especially inefficient because the market is so small that there is little prospect of competition and they suffer from the lack of economies of scale.

9.5.3 Small size of firms

Firms from small countries are small by comparison with multinational corporations and firms in large economies. Small firms are at a disadvantage in the global marketplace because they cannot realise economies of scale, are not attractive business partners, and cannot spend significant funds on marketing, research and development. The difference in the size of total sales of the largest national firms is a good indicator of the enormous gap between firms competing in the global marketplace. The total sales of General Motors are 328 times larger than those of the largest nationally owned firm in the SDEs of the English-speaking Caribbean. Sales and employment of some multinational corporations are larger than the GDP and population of many small developing economies. Given the minute size of even the largest firms in small developing economies, they in essence constitute micro-enterprises by global standards and this remains the case even when they merge within regional integration schemes among such economies.

[66] 'Small States: Meeting Challenges in the Global Economy', Interim Report of the Commonwealth Secretariat/World Bank Joint Taskforce on Small States, October 1999, p. 13.

[67] Lino Briguglio, 'Small Island Developing States and their Economic Vulnerabilities', *World Development*, vol. 23, no. 9 (1995) pp. 1615–32.

9.5.4 Dependence on trade taxes

There is a high dependence on trade taxes as a percentage of government revenue in small developing economies. Trade taxes account for more than one-half of government revenue in St Lucia, Belize and the Bahamas, and over one-third of government revenue in Guatemala and the Dominican Republic. The extreme dependence on trade taxes as a source of fiscal revenue accounts for the resolute and persistent resistance of governments in small countries to contemplate tariff reductions. This, rather than protection of local industry, has delayed or blocked trade liberalisation in small developing economies. Ironically, more costly imports due to high tariffs result in high input costs, which reduce the international competitiveness of exports of goods and services. This in many instances, however, is justified by the need to control import demand for balance-of-payments purposes.

9.5.5 Limited institutional capacity

Small developing economies have very limited institutional capacity and this has a number of implications which increase the cost of goods and services provided by the state, which in turn increase the cost of production in the private sector. In many instances the government cannot sustain specialised services, with the result that they are either not available or have to be imported. Even where the state has the capacity to supply certain goods and services, these tend to be high cost because of the absence of economies of scale and the indivisibility of certain public service functions.

9.6 Implications of small size

There is no direct correlation between size and economic growth[68] and level of development. This is evident in the fact that many countries which are small in terms of standard indicators such as population, land area and GDP are ranked favourably according to levels of GDP per capita and the UN's Human Development Index. Nevertheless, small size has

[68] Chris Milner and T. Westaway, 'Country Size and the Medium-Term Growth Process: Some Cross-Country Evidence', *World Development*, vol. 21, no. 2 (1993) pp. 203–11, and H. W. Armstrong and R. Read, 'Trade and Growth in Small States: The Impact of Global Trade Liberalization', *World Economy*, vol. 21, issue 4 (June 1998) pp. 563–85.

implications for the international trade of these countries. These implications include:

9.6.1 *Volatility*

Small developing economies have traditionally experienced pronounced economic volatility because:

(a) Acute vulnerability is especially severe when export earnings depend on products which are prone to instability such as primary products[69] or goods whose market access depends on voluntary preferential arrangements in developed countries. This instability is heightened when exports depend on a few external markets, because exports are exposed to fluctuations in demand and price, and changes in market access policy in importing countries. It has been suggested that many small economies can reduce export instability by shifting to services, particularly tourism and financial services. The change in export composition toward the service industry has not always been accompanied by reduced instability in export earnings.[70]

(b) One of the peculiarities of small developing countries, particularly small islands, is the fragility of their ecologies, the prevalence of natural disasters and their susceptibility to environmental damage from natural disasters. Natural disasters have been a recurring factor in the volatility of small developing economies. The World Bank has estimated that the impact of a natural disaster on a small economy and its financial sector can be far more devastating than it is on a large economy, where the damage is relatively localised. For example, the damage to Jamaica from Hurricane Gilbert in 1988 amounted to about 33 per cent of GDP, damage to Antigua from Hurricanes Luis and Marilyn in 1995 amounted to about 66 per cent of GDP, and Montserrat suffered losses totalling 500 per cent of GDP from Hurricane Hugo in 1989. In comparison, the damage to the United States from Hurricane Andrew in 1992, while much larger in absolute financial terms, amounted to only 0.2 per cent of GDP.

[69] On the instability of primary product export earnings see *Global Economic Prospects and the Developing Countries 1994* (Washington, D.C.: World Bank, 1994) chapter 2.

[70] Ransford Palmer, 'Export Earnings, Instability, and Economic Growth, 1957 to 1986' in David L. McKee (ed.), *External Linkages in Small Economies* (Westport: Praeger, 1994) pp. 31–4.

(c) Small developing economies exhibit a very high reliance on foreign capital inflows in the form of private direct foreign investment and development aid. The average of the ratio of the volume of capital flows to GDP is larger in small developing economies than in other developing countries and the ratio of foreign aid to GDP is about 20 per cent, double that of other developing countries.[71] Foreign aid flows are subject to considerable fluctuations from year to year because they are allocated according to the political priorities of donor governments. The evidence for the last twenty years reveals that small developing economies are at a disadvantage in attracting direct foreign investment compared to larger developing countries. This is in part due to the perception that smaller countries are riskier investment environments. Even when they have sound economic policies and the macroeconomic fundamentals are good, small developing countries are rated 29 per cent more risky.[72]

Volatility is a feature of developing countries which export primary products, particularly agricultural commodities and minerals, and which experience fluctuations in capital flows. Volatility is costly because of its adverse impact on financial intermediation, exchange rates, inflation, income distribution, resource allocation, productivity and investment.[73] Income volatility has a strong negative effect on economic growth in developing countries[74] and adversely affects investment.[75]

Small developing economies experience higher levels of volatility than other economies, indicating that small size is related to volatility. Empirical studies have documented greater volatility of output[76] and real

[71] M. Ayhan Kose and Eswar Prasad, 'Thinking Big', *Finance and Development*, vol. 39, no. 4 (December 2002).

[72] Paul Collier and David Dollar, 'Aid, Risk and the Special Concerns of Small States', Development Research Group, World Bank, February 1999.

[73] *Overcoming Volatility: Economic and Social Progress in Latin America, 1995 Report* (Washington, D.C.: Inter-American Development Bank, 1995) pp. 194–5.

[74] William Easterly and Aart Kraay, 'Small States, Small Problems? Income, Growth and Volatility in Small States', *World Development*, vol. 28, no. 11 (2000) pp. 2013–27, and Garey Remy and Valerie A. Remy, 'Cross-country Evidence on the Link between Volatility and Growth', *American Economic Review*, vol. 86 (1995) pp. 1138–51.

[75] J. Aizenmann and N. Marion, 'Volatility and Investment: Interpreting Evidence from Developing Countries', *Economica*, vol. 66 (1999) pp. 157–81.

[76] Garey Ramey and Valery A. Ramey, 'Cross-country Evidence on the Link between Volatility and Growth', *American Economic Review*, vol. 86 (1995) pp. 1138–51.

per capita income[77] in small economies, and income volatility increases the smaller the economy.[78] Estimates by the World Bank and Commonwealth Secretariat show that 'the standard deviation of annual real per capita growth is about 25 per cent higher'.[79] Small developing economies experience difficulty in sustaining economic growth and they may, as Looney argues, be incapable of sustaining economic growth.[80] During the period 1980–98 only twenty-four of fifty-three small island countries achieved growth and the 'average per capita growth rate was negative'.[81]

9.6.2 Sub-optimal resource use, allocation and mobilisation

Small markets are imperfect markets and this has several implications for resource use, allocation and mobilisation:

(a) Small markets are not competitive business environments even with a large number of firms because a very limited number of participants achieve dominance and hence there is an oligopoly or a monopoly. These market situations reduce the efficiency with which firms operate and lead to distortions in resource use. The lack of market-driven competition leads to inefficiency and higher costs, as firms are not driven by the dynamics of competition to optimise efficiency and introduce new technology and improved production systems. A firm's international competitiveness depends on its capacity to innovate continually in production techniques and products. The national market conditions in which the company operates are a significant variable in its drive to develop its competitive advantages.

(b) The small size and skewed structure of the market inhibits the ability of small developing economies to garner resources from external

[77] William Easterly and Aart Kraay, 'Small States, Small Problems? Income, Growth and Volatility in Small States', *World Development*, vol. 28, no. 11 (2000) pp. 2013–27.

[78] Marion Jansen, 'Income Volatility in Small Developing Economies. Export Concentration Matters', WTO Discussion Paper (December 2004).

[79] 'Small States, Meeting Challenges in the Global Economy', Interim Report of the Commonwealth Secretariat/World Bank Joint Taskforce on Small States, October 1999, p. 13.

[80] Robert E. Looney, 'Economic Characteristics Associated with Size: Development Problems Confronting Smaller Third World States', *Singapore Economic Review*, vol. 37, no. 2 (October 1992) pp. 1–19.

[81] *Human Development Report 2003* (New York: United Nations Development Programme, 2003) p. 72.

sources, in particular private foreign investment. Investors often are unaware of opportunities in small developing economies or do not consider them to be worthwhile as investment locations because of the limited size of the national market. Further, investment in export sectors tends to be biased in favour of larger economies, even when these economies are low-income and less developed.

(c) The high import content of production and consumption, undiversified economic structure and the lack of competitive markets in small developing economies mean that there are rigidities in resource allocation. This makes the adjustment process more difficult and, of necessity, slower than the adjustment process in larger, more developed economies.

(d) Small firms and farms are unable to sustain a consistent supply in volume and quality in both the local and export markets, and this results in their elimination from the market even where they are competitive in price and acceptable in quality on most occasions. For example, the tourism sector often imports food products which are produced locally because supply is not consistent.[82]

(e) International competitiveness and efficiency is sub-optimal because labour productivity can never be at its maximum as small developing economies cannot provide opportunities for specialisation. In these circumstances, highly skilled personnel function as generalists, which reduces their productivity. This inherent trend is compounded by the migration of a significant proportion of university-trained persons seeking jobs suited to their type and level of training. In some situations a highly specialist person, e.g. a neurosurgeon, may not be able to find sufficient work in an economy of 500,000 or fewer people. Small developing economies such as Fiji, Haiti, Jamaica and Trinidad and Tobago have more than 60 per cent of their highly skilled population living abroad and the figure reaches 83 per cent in the case of Guyana. The comparable data for large developing economies – Brazil, China, India, Indonesia and Thailand – are less than 3.2 per cent.[83]

[82] Rebecca Torres and Janet Henshall Momsen, 'Challenges and Potential for Linking Tourism and Agriculture to Achieve Pro-Poor Tourism Objectives', *Progress in Development Studies*, vol. 4, no. 4 (October 2004) pp. 294–318.

[83] Jean-Christophe Dumont and Georges Lemaitre, *Counting Immigrants and Expatriates in OECD Countries: A New Perspective* (Paris: OECD, 2005) p. 14.

9.6.3 *Constrained international competitiveness*

It is firms not countries that conduct international trade. Firms in small developing economies are small by global standards, although they may be very large by local standards. Such firms are constrained by a business environment which is less conducive to attaining international competitiveness than those of large developing countries or developed countries where economies of scale can be realised without involvement in export activity and firms can benefit from modern infrastructure, large markets and enterprise cluster. Even in developed countries small firms find it more difficult than large firms to overcome the difficulties of breaking into export markets and undertaking foreign investment. The result is that less than 0.2 per cent of small firms have multinational operations.[84] Despite these difficulties, some firms in small developing economies have attained international competitiveness,[85] established worldwide brands and become multinational enterprises.

(a) Small developing economies have severe constraints on their material and labour inputs, both in amount and variety, because of their limited land areas, narrow resource bases and small populations. These constraints prevent the attainment of economies of scale for a wide range of products and lead to high unit costs of production, especially in manufacturing.[86] Small market size also tends to cause high costs because there is often a lack of competition, and in many instances the markets are oligopolistic or controlled by monopolies.

Firms in small economies, especially small developing economies,[87] are at a major disadvantage compared to large firms in the global context. These small firms cannot attain either internal economies of scale[88] (where

[84] Zoltan J. Acs, Randall Morck, J. Myles Shaver and Bernard Yeong, 'The Internationalization of Small and Medium-Sized Enterprises' in Zoltan J. Acs and Bernard Yeong (eds.), *Small and Medium-Sized Enterprises in the Global Economy* (Ann Arbor: University of Michigan Press, 1999) p. 52.

[85] Ganesh Wignarja, Marlon Lezama and David Joiner, *Small States in Transition: From Vulnerability to Competitiveness* (London: Commonwealth Secretariat, 2004).

[86] Donald B. Keesing, 'Population and Industrial Development: Some Evidence from Trade Patterns', *American Economic Review*, vol. 58, no. 3 (1968) pp. 448–55.

[87] Firms in small developing economies are discussed in Alvin G. Wint, *Managing Towards International Competitiveness: Cases and Lessons from the Caribbean* (Kingston: Ian Randle Publishers, 1997), and Alvin G. Wint, *Competitiveness in Small Developing Economies: Insights from the Caribbean* (Kingston: University of the West Indies Press, 2003).

[88] The cost disadvantages suffered by small firms result from the lack of economies of scale, higher costs of inputs and higher transportation costs. See L. Alan Winters and Pedro M. G. Martins,

unit cost is influenced by the size of firm) or external economies of scale (where unit cost depends on the size of the industry, but not necessarily on the size of any one firm). A small economy and, by extension, small industries (including export sectors) are unlikely to foster the competitive dynamics necessary for firms in small economies to achieve competitive advantage. Competitive advantage in the sense in which Porter[89] uses the term is more likely to occur when the economy is a developed one and is large enough to sustain 'clusters' of firms connected through vertical and horizontal relationships and where there are networks[90] of related and supporting industries. A firm working with world-class local suppliers can benefit from cross-fertilisation opportunities and overcome information asymmetries. Related industries can also be an important source of innovations and can provide strategic alliances and joint ventures.

Firms in small developing countries also have severe difficulties in attaining 'economies of scope', i.e. economies obtained by a firm using its existing resources, skills and technologies to create new products and/or services for export. Exposure to global competition requires small firms to invest heavily just to survive in their national market, and more so in order to export. Larger firms are better able to generate new products and sources from existing organisations and networks. Very large firms, such as multinational corporations, operate internationally in ways that are very different from small firms.

The disabilities constraining small firms increase the smaller the developing economy in which they operate. Firms in micro-developing economies face higher costs than other small developing economies.[91]

(b) A small developing economy is an aggregation of firms which are small in the world market and therefore 'price-takers', i.e. exercising no influence on world market prices for goods, services and assets. Inputs,

'Beautiful but Costly: Business Costs in Small Economies' (a study prepared for the Commonwealth Secretariat and the United Nations Conference on Trade and Development, 2004). For the opposing view see Boris Blazic-Metzner and Helen Hughes, 'Growth Experience of Small Countries' in B. Jalan (ed.), *Problems and Policies in Small Economies* (New York: St Martin's Press, 1982) pp. 85–102.

89 Michael E. Porter, *The Competitive Advantage of Nations* (New York: Free Press, 1990) pp. 71–3.

90 Christopher A. Bartlett and Sumantra Ghoshal, *Managing Across Borders* (Boston: Harvard Business School Press, 1989).

91 Alan L. Winters and Pedro M. G. Martins, 'Beautiful but Costly: Business Costs in Small Economies' (a study prepared for the Commonwealth Secretariat and the United Nations Conference on Trade and Development, 2004).

including imports, cost firms in small economies more than large firms, thereby making firms in small economies relatively less efficient.

Small developing economies pay higher transportation costs[92] because of the relatively small volume of cargo, small cargo units and the need for bulk breaking. Small economies pay an average of 10 per cent of the value of merchandise exports as freight costs, compared to a 4.5 per cent worldwide average and 8.3 per cent for developing countries.[93] Small developing economies spend more on freight costs as a percentage of imports than large countries. The world average is roughly 5.25 per cent whereas the SDEs of the Caribbean pay between 9 and 13 per cent.[94]

The public sector and government expenditure in small developing economies accounts for a larger share of GDP[95] than in larger countries. This is a reflection of the indivisibility of public administration structures, the lack of economies of scale in the provision of public goods and the execution of certain functions which every country, no matter how small, has to carry out, e.g. a head of state, a parliament, a police force, etc. The growth of the public sector has also been due in part to attempts to compensate for the absence of the private sector in certain economic activities, as well as the inability of firms in small developing economies to finance large infrastructure projects either in the narrow local capital market or in international financial markets.

The small size of the market and the prevalence of small firms make it difficult for small economies to attract private foreign investment and joint venture partnerships even when the policy regime and economic fundamentals are better than competing locations. The result is that both the public sector and the private sector composed of small firms pay higher interest rates and other costs, which serve to increase the costs of production. Small firms and farms find it more difficult than larger entities to meet the cost of compliance with international standards. For example, in

[92] Dennis Pantin, *The Economics of Sustainable Development in Small Caribbean Islands* (Mona, Jamaica: Centre for Environment and Development, University of the West Indies, 1994) p. 16.

[93] *A Future for Small States: Overcoming Vulnerability* (London: Commonwealth Secretariat, 1997) p. 29, and M. Ayhan Kose and Eswar S. Prasad, 'Thinking Big', *Finance and Development*, vol. 39, no. 4 (December 2002).

[94] *UNCTAD Review of Maritime Transport, 1997* (Geneva: UNCTAD, 1997).

[95] Robert E. Looney, 'Profiles of Small Lesser Developed Economies', *Canadian Journal of Development Studies*, vol. 10, no. 1 (1989) pp. 21–37, Michael Howard, *Public Finance in Small Open Economies. The Caribbean Experience* (Westport: Praeger, 1992), and Alberto Alesina and Enrico Spolaore, *The Size of Nations* (Cambridge, Mass.: MIT Press, 2003) chapter 10.

developing countries enterprise size is the key variable in the ability to comply with sanitary and phyto-sanitary measures in developed country markets.[96]

9.6.4 Disarticulated adjustment capacity

The high import content of production and consumption and the rigidity inherent in the undiversified economic structure of small developing economies severely hamper resource allocation, which makes the adjustment process more difficult and slower than in larger economies. In many situations, adjustment requires resource creation as well as resource allocation. The undiversified economic structure of small developing economies causes the adjustment process to be more difficult, larger relative to GDP and of necessity slower than in larger countries.[97]

There is a high degree of openness in small developing economies, one of the consequences of which is that movements in the price of imports dominate the overall domestic price level. The prices of non-traded goods also tend to adjust rapidly through the impact of foreign prices on wages and other costs. Exchange rate charges do not have the desired effect on the balance of payments because of low import and export price elasticities.

Stabilisation policy must be designed specifically for small developing countries, taking cognisance of the structure of markets and the nature of their operations. The uncompetitive nature of these markets, particularly where monopolies and oligopolies exist, and the limited number and type of institutions make resource utilisation and allocation more problematic than in large developed economies. These types of market situations are characterised by rigidities which make the adjustment process more time-consuming, and which diminish the efficacy of conventional policy measures such as open market operations and recalibration of economy-wide prices such as the exchange rate. Furthermore, structural adjustment, like stabilisation, is a more difficult process in small developing economies because the inherent rigidities in the structure and operation of markets complicate the process of resource reallocation. The nature of these small

[96] 'Food Safety and Agricultural Health Standards. Challenges and Opportunities for Developing Country Exports', World Bank Report No. 31207, 10 January 2005, p. 62.

[97] Gerald K. Helleiner, 'Why Small Countries Worry: Neglected Issues in Current Analyses of the Benefits and Costs of Small Countries of Integrating with Large Ones', *World Economy*, vol. 19, no. 6 (November 1996) pp. 759–63.

markets also restricts the ability of private-sector entities and the government to mobilise additional resources, both within these economies and from external sources.

Small developing economies have structural features that need to be changed (where feasible) if these economies are to cope with the rapid and profound changes associated with globalisation. Adjustment will not suffice to enable these economies to manage the changes in the global economy successfully since adjustment implies marginal and incremental modification to an economic structure which is fundamentally sound and conducive to sustainable economic growth. Economic transformation goes beyond the resource utilisation, reallocation and mobilisation intrinsic in stabilisation and structural adjustment to incorporate resource creation over the medium to long term. Transformation in the current and future global economy will entail the ability of small developing economies to facilitate the rapid and frictionless international mobility of goods, services, finance, capital and technology which is the essence of a seamless global economy.

9.7 Special and differential treatment for small developing economies

The design of measures to address the characteristics and interests of small developing economies should not be limited to measures which avoid putting these economies at a disadvantage, nor should it be confined to best-endeavour commitments to promote trade opportunities and safeguard the interests of these economies. For example, Article IV of the GATS specifies measures aimed at increasing the participation of developing countries in the global trade in services, through specific commitments in relation to strengthening the efficiency, capacity and competitiveness of their domestic services. It also requires developed member countries to facilitate the access of developing country service suppliers to information related to market access.

9.7.1 Guiding principles

The overall goal of special and differential treatment applicable to small developing economies is the promotion of economic development, which entails a quantitative dimension, i.e. growth, and a qualitative dimension, i.e. structural transformation, and therefore must be guided by the following principles:

(1) The measures must be precise and enforceable and not merely best-endeavour commitments.
(2) Those provisions dealing with the disabilities in the process of development should be subject to periodic review and renegotiation where appropriate.
(3) The provisions which address the problems arising from small size must be long term and should be renewable.
(4) Sectors or products which are clearly recognised to be internationally competitive should be exempt from SDT.
(5) Where a SDE produces a large enough share of world production of a commodity it should not be entitled to SDT for that commodity.
(6) Provisions must take account of the differences in the size of firms involved in international trade, bearing in mind that firms from small developing economies are micro-enterprises by global standards.
(7) Given the structural and institutional limitations on the capacity for economic management, SDEs must have the maximum degree of freedom to pursue development policies.

9.7.2 Specific measures

The classification of SDT measures used by the WTO is not as helpful as it could be because the categories are too broad and consequently it does not allow the connection between the provision and the issue it is intended to address to be lucidly established. The categories employed by the WTO are increasing trade opportunities of developing countries, safeguarding the interests of developing countries, flexibility of commitments, transitional time periods and technical assistance. In order to overcome the limitations of the WTO classification and improve the specificity of the measures and elucidate the link with how they help SDEs, nine types of measures are proposed and illustrations are provided where pertinent. The examples provided are not intended to be an exhaustive list of existing SDT measures as such a cataloguing exercise has already been completed by the WTO.

9.7.2.1 Differentiated obligations

Trade between developed countries and small developing economies should be governed by the principle of less than full reciprocity. There would be reciprocity in some subjects and in some sectors and products but SDEs would undertake commitments to the extent consistent with their capacity for adjustment, level of development and their administrative and institutional capabilities for implementation. Developed countries would maintain existing preferential market access for as long as possible and seek to create trade opportunities by more favourable market access for goods and services from SDEs through specific measures on an issue-by-issue basis and, where appropriate, on a product-by-product basis.

Consideration could be given to the inclusion of an 'enabling clause' for small developing economies, which would allow for the differential application of rules in the levels of obligation for small developing economies within the developing country framework.

9.7.2.2 Asymmetrically phased implementation

Given the small size of firms, the small scale of production and limited size of the market, small developing economies will require a longer period of adjustment than developed economies. Hence, there must be asymmetrically phased implementation of rules and disciplines, permitting a longer adjustment period for small developing economies. For example, in agricultural trade, particularly food items, small developing economies should be allowed the flexibility to implement their commitments to reduction of protection and domestic support over a longer period than the implementation period prescribed for larger economies.

Provision for such differentiated phase-in schedules was included in both the Agreement on Textiles and Clothing (ATC) and the TRIPs Agreement. In the ATC, small suppliers were allowed longer phase-out periods for the Multi-Fiber Agreement (MFA) as well as greater flexibility in growth rates, etc. Under the TRIPs Agreement, developing countries and LDCs were allowed the longest phase-in period for implementation of their obligations.

The weakness of the current provisions which allow longer implementation periods is that they are not related to any measure of implementation capacity, the cost of implementation or any evaluation of if and when implementation has been accomplished or to what extent further work is required and how long a period would be needed. These deficiencies have to be remedied in a revision of implementation and adjustment periods.

9.7.2.3 Exemptions from commitments in certain areas

Given the vast disparities in size, the extremely small size of some economies and the human, financial and institutional costs involved in implementing the trade agreements, small developing economies should be permitted some exemptions. This would not only address the question of disparities, but also avoid delays which may occur because SDEs, despite their best efforts, are unlikely to meet certain requirements and timetables. For example, if, as is likely, exports subsidies are outlawed, smaller economies should be exempt from this requirement. Exemptions should also be considered for standardising technical requirements through national organisations and participation in international standardisation processes where these have no applicability because of lack of production or importation or exports. Where complete exemptions are not feasible, *de minimis* provisions would be helpful.

An example of this type of measure is the provision which exempts developing countries from the disciplines in some types of export subsidies. This type of provision should be included in other aspects of the WTO agreements. For example, in government procurement agreements the very small developing economies should have their government procurement markets exempt from coverage given their very small size.

9.7.2.4 Flexibility in application and adherence of disciplines under prescribed circumstances

Small developing economies are highly open economies and are therefore more susceptible to balance-of-payments problems. This is particularly the case for small developing countries where balance-of-payment deficits tend to be persistent because of their structural origins. The balance-of-payment provisions such as those provided in Articles XII and XVIII:B of the GATT are not confined to any particular type of country but all members may avail themselves of the right to resort to these provisions under the circumstances prescribed. Because of the vulnerability of small developing economies to balance-of-payments problems, these provisions should be made more applicable to them by permitting additional facilities to enable them to (a) maintain sufficient flexibility in their tariff structure to be able to grant the tariff protection required for the establishment of a particular industry, and (b) apply quantitative restrictions for balance-of-payments purposes which take full account of the continued high level of demand for imports likely to be generated by their programmes of economic development.

9.7.2.5 Temporary suspension of obligations in prescribed circumstances

Small developing countries should be allowed to suspend their obligations in certain specified circumstances, for periods of up to one year, starting with six months in the first instance. Situations that would trigger the right to suspend certain obligations could include natural disasters and the sudden and substantial collapse in earnings of one of the principal exports, defined to be over a prescribed percentage of total exports over the previous five years. Small island developing states in particular are prone to natural disasters, causing devastation and necessitating an extended period of national reconstruction, particularly in agriculture. For example, a hurricane that hits Florida does not affect the rest of the United States but when this happens to a small island such as one of those in the Caribbean, the entire country is damaged. The experience of small developing economies dependent on one or two primary products or sensitive services, e.g. tourism, reveals that the devastating impact that the events such as natural disasters have on the fortunes of a single commodity can be both in the short and the long run.

9.7.2.6 Development promoting policy

There should be a shift in the focus of SDT from exempting developing countries from having to fulfil certain obligations to measures which proactively promote economic development. The forgoing of obligations has not always been helpful to the adjustment and development of developing countries. It has resulted in the postponement of adjustment to the detriment of economic development, international competitiveness and the diversification of exports. Prolonged adjustment periods can be as harmful to development as adjustment that is too short. Development promoting SDT would furnish governments in small developing economies with the policy flexibility which they need, while not relying on governments in developed countries to honour the hortatory language of 'best-endeavour' clauses. This emphasis on policy space for developing countries rather than developed countries making exceptions may have the advantage of arousing less opposition in developed countries to SDT.

Special and differential measures which stimulate development by stimulating investment, enhancing international competitiveness and promoting export production and diversification can take the form of:

(a) preferential access to the markets of developed countries. Market access is critical to stimulating market forces which can produce trade-led growth. Developed countries can promote this in small developing economies by (i) establishing or maintaining preferential market access arrangements, (ii) reducing protectionism in their markets, (iii) a liberal dispensation on regional trade agreements among small developing economies, (iv) more liberal provisions on Mode 4 of services, the movement of natural persons, and (v) accepting measures for small developing economies for which other economies are not eligible, e.g. geographical indications.
(b) allowing governments in small developing economies the policy space to promote development by means not open to all members of the WTO because these economies are characterised by serious market imperfections or market failures. This could entail the implementation of existing SDT, which allows use of some subsidies, investment incentives, waiving the principle of national treatment for firms which are small by global standards or for exporters whose share of world trade in a particular product is below a certain level.
(c) affording the right to use a 'positive list' approach in deciding which products are to undertake tariff reductions, particularly in agriculture.[98] The principle of non-reciprocity as expressed, for example, in Article XIX(2) of the GATS allows 'appropriate flexibility' for developing countries, including 'opening fewer sectors, liberalizing fewer types of transactions, progressively extending market access in line with their development situation'.
(d) allowing more latitude in rules of origin so that they do not negate preferential market access but serve instead to stimulate development. Relaxation of rules of origin has boosted apparel production in countries benefiting from the Caribbean Basin Economic Recovery Act and the African Growth and Opportunity Act.

[98] Manuela Tortora, 'Special and Differential Treatment and Development Issues in the Multilateral Trade Negotiations: The Skeleton in the Closet' (Geneva: UNCTAD, January 2003), UNCTAD/WEB/CDP/ BKGD/16, p. 14.

(e) permitting a more generous approach to safeguards for small developing economies.

9.7.2.7 Technical assistance and training

The need for technical assistance to the small developing economies is widely accepted; however, it is not a panacea nor should it be a placebo. This issue requires some fresh thinking as the institutional capacity is so constrained in most small countries that there is a need for technical assistance to identify technical assistance needs. Technical assistance should focus on:

(a) promoting the development of adequate institutional capacity by training technicians to improve the implementation of the international trade agreements. The costs of implementing the commitments in the Uruguay Round turned out to be enormous relative to the resources of the developing countries;[99]
(b) assisting small developing economies in fulfilling their obligations assumed in international agreements, in particular commitments under the WTO;
(c) supporting the efforts of SDEs to prepare technically for negotiations, attending meetings and maintaining representation at the WTO in Geneva;
(d) contributing to efforts by small developing economies to undertake the structural, institutional and legislative adjustment necessary to stimulate and sustain economic development.

Technical assistance is provided for in the WTO in fourteen provisions across six agreements and one ministerial decision. The major difficulty has been ensuring that these provisions are given practical effect and that the presently inadequate funding is substantially increased.

9.7.2.8 Enabling access to mediation

The Understanding on Rules and Procedures governing the Settlement of Disputes (DSU) is currently under review in light of the experiences of the

[99] Michael J. Finger and P. Schuler, *The Implementation of the Uruguay Round Commitments: The Development Challenge*, Policy Research Working Paper No. 2215 (Washington, D.C.: World Bank, 2000).

past few years. The problems which have been identified in the operations of the Dispute Settlement Mechanism (DSM) include:

(a) the limited capability of small developing countries to make use of the mechanism because of their inadequate expertise and institutional capacity to implement panel findings;
(b) the high cost and administrative difficulties of using the dispute settlement mechanism.

There are provisions in the DSU which grant technical assistance to developing countries. These need to be extended to small developing economies and made more effective for these countries. The cost entailed and the difficulties experienced by the countries of the English-speaking Caribbean in the banana dispute between the US and Latin American banana exporting countries and the EU illustrates the problems which small developing countries face in attempting to utilise the DSM.

9.7.2.9 Development funding for implementation and trade capacity-building

The cost of implementation of commitments in the WTO can be very substantial for small developing countries, particularly in the short run, and can amount to a significant share of development assistance.[100]

The current concept of trade capacity-building must be redimensioned to include building trade capacity in both the private and the public sectors. While this may not form part of a trade agreement, the measures of SDT should include not only those expressed in the rules but also financing to ensure that capacity created or enhanced by technical assistance is put on a sustainable basis. Measures of SDT in some cases cannot come to fruition without being complemented by development funding. Development funding for capacity-building should take account of financing for industry and product adjustment, compensation for the loss of preferences, the cost of implementation, improving international competitiveness and strengthening negotiating capacity.

The opportunities created by trade liberalisation can only come to fruition if there is investment, but in the case of small developing

[100] Sheila Page and Peter Kleen, 'Special and Differential Treatment of Developing Countries in the World Trade Organization', First draft, Overseas Development Institute, August 2004, p. 36.

economies not all of this will materialise in the form of private investment and hence there is a role for development financing. The financing facility does not have to be part of the WTO; in fact it would be more appropriate to locate it in a multilateral institution specialising in development financing. Hoekman[101] suggests that a levy of 0.25 on imports of OECD countries would generate $10 billion for support to developing countries. The World Bank and the WTO should collaborate on establishing an adequately funded trade capacity-building and adjustment facility to address this issue. Collaboration between multilateral institutions and bilateral agencies must strive for coherence in policies of trade capacity-building and strengthen cooperation to rationalise resource use and avoid duplication in programming.

9.8 How SDT addresses the characteristics and problems of SDEs

There has been a failure clearly to identify and articulate the direct link between the structural characteristics and institutional features of developing economies and SDT measures, both actual and proposed. The failure to establish how SDT measures are directly related to specific aspects of developing economies and therefore how they have a beneficial effect on trade and development has led to a critique of the concept of SDT and its efficacy. Indeed, SDT is now widely regarded as an attempt by developing countries to gain an unfair advantage in international trade arrangements and an unjustified ploy to avoid reciprocity.

This section explains the direct link between each measure of SDT and the specific structural characteristics and institutional features of small developing economies. The nine types of special and differential treatment suggested in this chapter are aimed at directly addressing the characteristics and problems of small developing economies. The links between the SDT measures and the characteristics and problems of small developing economies which they are intended to address are set out in table 9.1. In some cases more than one measure may be related to a single characteristic of SDEs.

[101] Bernard Hoekman, 'Operationalizing the Concept of Policy Space in the WTO: Beyond Special and Differential Treatment', Policy Brief No. 4, The William Davidson Institute, University of Michigan, July 2004, p. 13.

Table 9.1 *Relationship between characteristics of small developing economies and special and differential treatment measures*

Features	Measures								
	Different obligations	Asymmetrically phased implementation	Exemptions	Flexibility	Temporary suspension	Development promotion	Technical Assistance	Mediation	Development fund
Acute vulnerability				X	X	X			X
Imperfect markets	X		X			X			
Small size of firms	X	X	X			X	X		X
Dependence on trade taxes	X	X	X		X	X			X
Limited institutional capacity	X	X	X				X	X	X
Volatility				X	X				
Sub-optimal use of resources	X					X			X
Lack of international competitiveness	X	X	X			X	X		X
Disarticulated adjustment capacity		X	X		X	X	X		X

9.9 Identification of small developing economies

Neo-classical trade theory assumes that international trade takes place between countries in an environment of perfect competition, and trade occurs because of differences in comparative advantage, which in turn derive from differences in resource endowment or technology. In this paradigm the effects of size of country and size of firm are not taken into account. However, in reality, size has important implications. Economies of scale, the size of a country and the size of a firm are important considerations because large firms can achieve economies of scale and market dominance (including oligopoly and even monopoly) which put small firms at a disadvantage. While the discipline of economics has not dealt adequately with the question of small size, the effect of small size has however been recognised in national economic policy, as all countries have policies specifically designed to promote the viability of small businesses and small farms. This tenet of conventional national policy needs to be applied to the global economy and be recognised in the rules of international trade agreements, given the disparities in size among firms and countries. More generally, small and/or vulnerable participants (both firms and households) in national economies are afforded appropriate treatment by compensatory policy measures. These compensatory measures are fiscal transfers, technical assistance and enabling programmes, e.g. subsidies or low-cost finance or rules which discriminate in their favour, such as quotas or prevention of market dominance by larger firms. In the world economy there is no multilateral entity which provides fiscal transfers to small and/or vulnerable countries and firms. Therefore measures must be included in the rules governing the multilateral trading system to ensure that the vulnerable survive, adjust and develop.

Small economies as a distinctive genre of economy attracted the interest of academics in the 1960s. Subsequently, several technical studies of a policy-oriented nature have been carried out on small economies and, in particular, small island states by the Commonwealth Secretariat, the World Bank, UNCTAD, the Organisation of American States and the Free Trade Area of the Americas (FTAA) Working Group on Small Economies. There is a general consensus in these studies that small economies have characteristics which distinguish them as a particular genre of economy and that these features are constraints on their capacity for trade and development. The first meaningful attempt to grapple with the concerns of small developing countries in a trade agreement was the Free Trade Area of the Americas process.[102] Since its inception in the mid-1990s the FTAA negotiations have included a Working Group on Small Economies. The issue finally emerged in the World Trade Organisation when the Declaration of the Ministerial meeting in Doha in November 2001 mandated a Work Programme on Small Economies.[103]

While the WTO Agreement does not recognise small developing economies as a distinct category, it explicitly recognises that there are different types of economies and that economies other than developed economies require rules and disciplines which are specifically designed to take account of their relative disabilities and promote their development. The preamble of the WTO Agreement recognises that there is a need for positive efforts designed to ensure that developing countries 'secure a share in the growth in international trade commensurate with the needs of the economic development'. The Uruguay Round Agreements include provisions for developing member countries and there are some concessions to the least developed countries, Net Food Importing Countries, countries 'below $1,000 per capita' and narcotic economies.

There is no single definition of a small developing economy, undoubtedly because size is a relative concept. Definitions based on quantitative criteria vary considerably because they employ different criteria and select different cut-off points. The most frequently used criteria have been size of population, size of land area and value of Gross Domestic Product or some combination of these. As for population, Gutierrez proposed a range of 8–12 million,[104] Kuznets[105] and Streeten[106] selected an upper limit of 10 million, Chenery and Syrquin[107] and Lloyd and Sundram[108] used 5 million.

[102] Richard L. Bernal, 'The Integration of Small Economies in the Free Trade Area of the Americas', *Policy Papers on the Americas*, vol. IX, study 1 (Washington, D.C.: Center for Strategic and International Studies, February 1998).

[103] The work programme has the caveat 'not to create a sub-category of WTO Members'. WTO Ministerial Declaration, Doha, 9–14 November 2001, WT/MIN (01)/DEC/1, 20 November 2001, paragraph 35.

[104] Mario A. Gutierrez, 'Is Small Beautiful for Economic Integration?', *Journal of World Trade Law*, vol. 30, no. 4 (1996).

[105] Simon Kuznets, 'Economic Growth of Small Nations' in E. A. G. Robinson (ed.), *Economic Consequences of Size on Nations* (London: Macmillan, 1960) p. 5.

[106] Paul Streeten, 'The Special Problems of Small Countries', *World Development*, vol. 21, no. 2 (1993) p. 197.

[107] Hollis Chenery and M. Syrquin, *Patterns of Development, 1950–1970* (Oxford: Oxford University Press, 1975).

[108] Peter Lloyd and R. M. Sundram, 'Characteristics of Small Economies' in B. Jalan (ed.), *Problems and Policies of Small Economies* (New York: St Martin's Press, 1982).

Armstrong and Read[109] suggested 3 million and a figure of 1.5 million has been employed by the Commonwealth Secretariat/World Bank Joint Task Force,[110] while a report from the United Nations Development Programme (UNDP) speaks of countries with small populations as those with fewer than 40 million.[111] A study by the United Nations Economic Commission for Latin America and the Caribbean (ECLAC) opted for GDP and selected a ceiling of $15 billion, while Kennes[112] chose a cut-off point of $10 billion in GNP. The problem with using GDP or population is that small is a relative concept, hence both figures have to be revised over time. This dilemma is illustrated by the Commonwealth Secretariat's research, which used a population of 1 million in 1985 but by 1997 had revised the cut-off point to 1.5 million. Demas[113] combined a population of 5 million or less and less than 20,000 square miles of usable land. Bernal[114] applied three criteria without selecting absolute limits and compared data for the thirty-four countries participating in the negotiations for a Free Trade Area of the Americas. A clear bunching of countries emerged at one end on the continuum, all exhibiting smallness in the three criteria. Davenport[115] has proposed the use of the share of world trade and calculates that at a cut-off point of 0.02 per cent thirty-six countries would be small.

Various international organisations classify countries into categories according to selected indicators for operational and analytical purposes. The classifications used by international organisations mainly relate to per capita income levels, indicators of development status, and some selected concept of 'size'. While the main classification criterion used by

[109] H. W. Armstrong and R. Read, 'Western European Micro-States and EU Autonomous Regions: The Advantages of Size and Sovereignty', *World Development*, vol. 23, no. 8 (1998) pp. 1229–45.

[110] Commonwealth Secretariat/World Bank Joint Task Force, 'Making Small States: Meeting Challenges in the Global Economy'. Report of the Commonwealth Secretariat – World Bank Joint Task Force on Small States (2000).

[111] *Human Development Report 2003* (New York: United Nations Development Programme, 2004) p. 72.

[112] Walter Kennes, *Small Developing Countries and Global Markets. Competing in the Big League* (London: Macmillan Press, 2000) p. 7.

[113] William Demas, *The Economics of Development of Small Countries with Special Reference to the Caribbean* (Montreal: McGill University, 1965) p. 2.

[114] Richard L. Bernal, 'The Integration of Small Economies into the Free Trade Area of the Americas', *Policy Papers on the Americas*, vol. IX, study 1 (Washington, D.C.: Center for Strategic and International Studies, February 1998).

[115] Michael Davenport, *A Study of Alternative Special and Differential Arrangements for Small Economies* (London: Commonwealth Secretariat, December 2001).

institutions such as the International Monetary Fund (IMF), the World Bank and the United Nations for establishing country categories is the level of per capita income, these institutions also classify countries by aggregate income levels, the types of goods exported (e.g. fuels, non-fuel primary products, manufactures or services) and fiscal structure.

The definition of what is a small developing economy[116] is an issue which can be resolved technically and should not be allowed to delay substantive discussions. An appropriate definition can be derived, based on one or more criteria – population, land area and GDP – and could be arrived at by consensus. As in any categorisation there will be debate about those countries that are just above or below the line of demarcation. Although the dilemma of where exactly to draw the line can be resolved technically, it does introduce a discretionary element into the exercise, which sceptics and opponents have capitalised on to frustrate the identification of small developing economies. This can be resolved by negotiation or by techniques such as 'self-selection' which has been applied for development status under the GATT system and now under the WTO. Indeed, there is no official definition of 'developing country' in the WTO, as status is by self-definition by member countries but is not automatically granted when negotiating accession to the WTO.

9.10 The way forward

The resolution of the deadlock on maintaining and/or strengthening SDT is for the membership of the WTO to accept and to acknowledge that there are differences in size and level of development among countries, and consequently that they have different capabilities which must be addressed by differentiated treatment. This is allowed by and provided for in the WTO, based on two complementary principles, namely the most favoured nation principle and the principle of special and more favoured treatment. Obviously there will be rules that are shared by all and there will be special rules for those disadvantaged by size, level of development or both. The reality is that there are two kinds of SDT in operation: that which is provided by multilateral consent to developing countries, including LDCs,

[116] The absence of a formal definition of small developing economy does not invalidate the justification for SDT. As in the case of developing countries, the lack of a consensus on a formal definition did not prevent the application of SDT to these economies. The design and application of SDT to SDEs does not therefore require a formal definition if the WTO extends the right of self-definition.

and deviations which the developed countries have unilaterally abrogated to themselves. When developed countries violate the rules and spirit of free trade within the multilateral trading system codified in the WTO this is tantamount to unilateral SDT for the more developed.

9.10.1 Differentiated treatment

Nearly all multilateral institutions when dealing with economic issues have recognised the diversity of economies and the necessity of differentiation in order to calibrate their policies to the specific needs of different types of economies. Rather than adopt the typologies employed by other institutions such as the IMF, World Bank and United Nations, the membership of the WTO must formulate a classification of countries based on trade-related criteria. The use of per capita incomes is fraught with problems, which are well known and need not be rehashed here. It would not make for appropriate SDT to apply the proposal of the International Food and Agriculture Trade Policy Council[117] that there should be three groups of countries that should be eligible for SDT: (a) least developed countries, i.e. with per capita incomes of less than $900; (b) lower middle-income developing countries, i.e. with income per capita of between $901 and $3,035; and (c) upper middle-income developing countries, i.e. with income per capita of between $3,035 and $9,385. Such a classification is open to all the disadvantages of using per capita income as a proxy for development and the failure to recognise structural characteristics of developing countries, in particular small size. Size is not the only structural feature which warrants consideration, but it is a factor which affects a significant number of developing countries and is likely to become more significant as globalisation proceeds. However, addressing the concerns of small developing economies is a challenge which can be accommodated by the multilateral trading system because collectively they account for such a minute share of world trade.

The most appropriate classification of members of the WTO involves four types of economies:

(a) developed economies, i.e. OECD member states and by self-definition;
(b) developing economies, i.e. with a per capita income of over $1,000 and which are outside the range of small developing economies. Some of

[117] 'A New Approach to Special and Differential Treatment', International Food and Agriculture Trade Policy Council, Position Paper no. 13, 15 September 2004, p. 2.

the economies in this category could be reclassified as developed by mutual agreement after review of agreed-upon economic criteria;

(c) small developing economies, i.e. over $1,000 in per capita income and smallness based on a combination of criteria of population, land area, GDP and vulnerability;

(d) least developed economies, i.e. with a per capita income of less than $1,000 and which could graduate to the status of developing economy or small developing economy.

Least developed economies and both types of developing economies would be eligible for Special and Differential Treatment but each of these three types of economies would have a different package of measures designed specifically for that particular type of economy. The packages would have some measures common to all and some unique elements. Some measures common to all eligible economies would be given specificity for each type of economy by variations in degree, duration and implementation schedule.

9.10.2 Implementation, adjustment and graduation

SDT should be subject to periodic reviews, the objectives of which are to (a) permit adjustment to the respective SDT packages, (b) allow for graduation, and (c) evaluate the extent to which the developed countries are adhering to their SDT commitments.

Improved economic development is a realisable possibility for the majority of developing countries if they can overcome some of the structural and institutional features which currently inhibit their development. The existence of these impediments is the basis justifying specific SDT measures and therefore, to the extent that there has been structural and institutional transformation, an economy's need for SDT could change over time. There should be periodic reviews of SDT allowing for the possibility of adjustment to some components in the package for each type of economy. Any adjustment recommended by the periodic reviews would require decision by consensus. Countries as they develop may graduate from one category to another and indeed may even become ineligible for SDT by attaining the status of a developed country. At the same time, developed country implementation of SDT measures should be evaluated, and if they failed to comply with their commitments they should be subject to payment of compensation and retaliation through the Dispute Settlement Mechanism.

SDT designed, implemented, reviewed and adjusted in the manner proposed in this chapter would make developed countries more readily agreeable to SDT provisions because of periodic review of adjustments to SDT as needs change and even of graduation. Developing countries would be assured that enforceable reviews would prevent or at least considerably reduce the incidence of developed countries' repeated postponements of implementation and serial renewals of exemptions. The enforceability of SDT measures would imbue developing countries with a positive disposition towards trade liberalisation, as they would have the assurance that their development was being meaningfully addressed through SDT. This in turn would induce them to engage in the full agenda of issues before the WTO and to contemplate new subjects, confident that their characteristics and concerns would be taken into account in the new SDT provisions.

9.11 Conclusions

It is now time to recognise formally that there are four different types of economies, namely developed, developing, small developing and least developed. All economies cannot be treated identically, i.e. there cannot be a single set of rules. There must be differences in the rules and their application to take account of the differences in types of economies. All multilateral economic institutions acknowledge these two facts and specifically the WTO recognises three kinds of economies and provides for special and more favourable treatment, commonly referred to as special and differential treatment (SDT). The three-country typology of the WTO is hopelessly outdated and is now a major obstacle to the negotiations of the Doha Development Agenda. The developed countries have resisted further SDT measures and have even tried to eliminate existing SDT because of their unwillingness to extend this type of treatment to the advanced developing countries. The deadlock can be broken by a four-economy typology in which classification is based on sound economic criteria encompassing the dominant features of reality, differences in size and level of development. Four types of economies should be recognised, namely developed, developing, small developing and least developed. The latter three would be eligible for SDT, with a specific package of measures for each category of economy. The packages would be a mix of measures common to all, unique to one type of economy and different in degree and implementation schedule.

The approach recommended is good politics and even better economics.

10

A study of alternative special and differential arrangements for small economies

MICHAEL DAVENPORT

10.1 Introduction

The difficulties faced by the small states (SS) in fully integrating into the world trading system are well documented. They include the problems created by transport costs together with the other costs associated with isolation and/or insularity and the absence of economies of scale and of scope associated with a small domestic market.[1] However, suggestions that the SS should receive a certain Special and Differential Treatment (SDT), modelled on, though not necessarily identical to, that enjoyed by the Least Developed Countries (LDCs), have not been broadly accepted, despite the obvious fact that, almost by definition, the SS are of little importance in world trade. *Ex ante* one would not anticipate a major distortion of trading patterns, for example through trade diversion, by giving producers each with a contribution to world trade measured in hundredths of one percentage point special treatment as regards market access or as regards compliance with WTO disciplines. Nor would the loss in tariff revenue appear, *ex ante*, to be large. This chapter looks at the possibilities of SDT based on de minimis thresholds, both in terms of preferential market access and WTO disciplines, though clearly more can be said of a quantitative nature as regards the first of these. As regards the former, it will look at the threats of trade diversion to the LDCs and other developing countries, and losses

I should like to acknowledge the support of the Economic Affairs Division of the Commonwealth Secretariat, and in particular that of Dr Roman Grynberg who proposed the study, and Miho Shirotori of UNCTAD for comments on an earlier draft. Particular thanks are due to Graham Johnstone whose skills enormously eased the computing burden.

The study was financed jointly by the Commonwealth Secretariat and UNCTAD.

[1] See for example Briguglio (1995), Commonwealth Secretariat (1997), Grynberg (forthcoming), Read (1998).

in tariff revenue that would be implied by extending preferential treatment to the SS.

10.2 Background

The WTO at present formally recognises the group of Least Developed Countries (LDCs) defined by the UN Economic and Social Committee. This means that those small states which fall within the LDC list are eligible for Special and Differential Treatment (SDT) under certain WTO agreements. Of the UN Committee on Sustainable Development list of forty-four small states, only seven countries are on the LDC list (see Appendix 10.1). The CS–WB Joint Task Force list of small vulnerable states (SVSs) also included Jamaica, Lesotho, Namibia and Papua New Guinea, of which only the second is an LDC. The non-LDC small states generally receive the much more limited standard SDT which is more restricted than that available to the LDCs, whether in the form of preferential tariff regimes or derogations from WTO disciplines. One of the reasons for the restricted nature of the SDT for 'other' developing countries may be that access to this group is through self-selection.

Even were the SVSs to seek limited recognition – perhaps only to reduce the cost of WTO membership or that of the disputes settlement procedure – there is a clear need for an unambiguous definition of a small vulnerable state.[2] But both the standard and the special Generalised System of Preferences (GSP) schemes remain an important component – perhaps still the most important component despite the erosion of tariff preferences through successive trade rounds – of the SDT accorded to the developing countries. The SS have argued for special access preferences parallel to those of the LDCs. Yet defining a new group of countries for special SDT appears to create major problems for other WTO Members. However, for market access another approach to the special GSP issue, which would obviate the need for contentious lists of deserving beneficiaries, is both coherent and feasible. This would be through the extension of de minimis provisions, already well established in the WTO trade agreements, to preferential market access so that countries with exports below a certain share

[2] For example, the presence on the UN list of a number of high-income small states – Bahrain, Cyprus, Estonia and Malta – may militate against the chances of the group as a whole being recognised as meriting some SDT.

of world trade, presumably determined on the basis of an average over a past period, would be allowed tariff-free access to all markets and derogation from most or all non-tariff restrictions such as quotas.

The basic reasoning in favour of preferential access for the SS is that

- it would be of help to small states who experience major difficulties in participating in the trading system. In particular it would be of benefit in terms of overcoming the disadvantage of the diseconomies of scale;
- below a certain percentage level of world trade, depending on the number of beneficiaries involved, there may be little or no threat to the interests of other countries (though, as with any preferential scheme, individual, particularly small, producers might suffer). Once the trade flow rose above the threshold and gave cause for concern about trade diversion, the preference would automatically be rescinded;
- and, similarly depending on the number of beneficiaries, the loss in tariff revenue for the importing countries is likely to be limited.

But SDT based on de minimis criteria need not be limited to market access issues. Already the LDCs receive SDT as regards a number of WTO disciplines. This chapter will examine the extent that the SS might also receive special treatment as regards WTO rules on the basis of the size of their shares in trade measured in the aggregate or with respect to particular categories of product.

The de minimis rules would cover all developing country (non-OECD) exporters, but it is likely that the small states would benefit disproportionately because of the small size of their export flows, even typically of their principal export products. Whether such an approach is practicable on the basis of aggregate trade flows – in which case share in world trade might become the basis for a definition of small states – or trade flows at some narrower customs classification can only be determined through an examination of the data.

Whether the goal is to define a new group of small states for which a particular range of SDT instruments is warranted, or whether the small states were to demand the same SDT as that enjoyed by the LDCs, the definition of small states has proved both conceptually difficult and politically fraught. Self-election is unlikely to be an approach acceptable as the basis for a new range of SDT instruments or inclusion within the SDT currently available to the LDCs. The Commonwealth Secretariat initially adopted a purely demographic criterion with a population cut-off of 1 million, later increased to 1.5 million and then stretched to include some countries with considerably larger populations but other characteristics similar to small countries.[3] However, a definition based solely or largely on non-economic criteria would be difficult to defend as appropriate for SDT in a WTO context, particularly if small but high-income developing countries were to qualify.

Disagreements about SDT for small states in various multilateral fora helped to trigger a study by a group jointly established by the Commonwealth Secretariat and the World Bank. Small states were defined as countries with a population of 1.5 million or less. In addition, four somewhat larger states – Jamaica, Lesotho, Namibia and Papua New Guinea – were included in the small state category on the grounds that they share many of the physical and economic characteristics of small states. An Index of Output Volatility was used as the basis for establishing a composite vulnerability index. First, using a sample of small states and other developing countries, regression analysis was used to explain output volatility in terms of specified economic and environmental causes of instability. The variables which were found significant were a country's openness, as measured by export dependence (exports of goods and non-factor services as a percentage of GDP); its lack of diversification, measured by the UNCTAD diversification index; and its susceptibility to natural disasters, measured by the proportion of the population affected by such events estimated over a relatively long period of time. Second, the model so developed was used to predict individual vulnerability scores for all countries for which data were available. These vulnerability scores form the Composite Vulnerability Index.

Under the GATT, the notion that developing countries should enjoy special and differential treatment (SDT) was an outcome of the Tokyo Round and became enshrined in the Enabling Clause of the GATT in 1979. The scope of SDT became both more extensive and more complex in the Uruguay Round. However, in only one of the Agreements, that on Subsidies, is either the term 'developing country' or the term 'least developed country' defined. In that case the least developed are either included on the list prepared by the UN or within a group of twenty additional developing countries with per capita incomes of under $1,000 per annum. Otherwise developing countries are self-elected in the WTO, while the least developed are defined by the UN Economic and Social Committee (ECOSOC).

[3] Commonwealth Secretariat (1997).

The WTO does recognise the issue of smallness. For example, in the Agreement on Antidumping de minimis provisions specifically exempt small producers from antidumping action. The Agreement on Clothing and Textiles also makes special provision for small producers. In terms of fees for WTO membership smallness is also recognised, though in the opposite direction since a new member must pay a minimum fee based on 0.015 per cent of total WTO member trade (which represents a considerable burden for certain Pacific island states).[4]

There is no technical reason why SDT – including tariff preferences – could not be enhanced for other groups of economies, whether defined in terms of size, as islands or as landlocked, or in terms of measures of vulnerability. In a proposal tabled at the ongoing negotiations in agriculture, a group of small island developing states (SIDS) – comprising Dominica, Mauritius, St Kitts and Nevis, St Vincent and the Grenadines and Trinidad and Tobago – argued that SIDS-specific characteristics, including smallness and remoteness, result in diseconomies of scale and scope and high input and transport costs, and these have constrained their effective participation in international agricultural trade.[5] *Inter alia*, they proposed that the SIDS be provided with security of access for one or two commodities which they are able to produce on a commercial basis, that non-reciprocal preferential tariff rates be improved, that the 'substantially all trade' provision of GATT Article XXIV on customs unions should not apply in the case of SIDS, that SIDS be allocated increases in minimum access tariff rate quotas and that SIDS be exempted from further reduction commitments on support and protection.

However, efforts by small states to have the WTO recognise them as a distinct group with specific SDT have foundered on resistance by other WTO Members. Other developing countries, in particular the LDCs, could see recognition of the small states as a threat to their own SDT through the erosion of tariff preferences, through the increased difficulties of obtaining special treatment in the future if the beneficiaries are more numerous and through the dilution of limited technical assistance budgets. Developed countries have tended to resist the proliferation of special interest groups on the grounds that preferential access can give rise to surges of imports and threats to their own producers. Also, among the developed countries,

[4] The minimum equivalent for UN membership is 0.003 per cent of GDP.

[5] WTO (2000).

there has been resistance to the use of SDT on the grounds that it can lead the beneficiaries to avoid the hard economic choices necessary to assure the competitiveness of their exports and their own development. This latter argument ignores the evidence that SS face inherent cost structures that, regardless of all plausible domestic actions on rents and inefficiencies, will inevitably prevent them competing in world export markets without significant margins of preference.

10.3 The use of 'objective' variables

Arguments about the particular economic disadvantages of small states have been dismissed as special pleading and counter-examples, such as Singapore, Estonia and Liechtenstein, have been suggested. Secondly, small states may have low shares in world trade – but in particular goods these shares can be relatively high, for example the Bahamas and Jamaica in rum and Mauritius, Fiji and Guyana in cane sugar. Thus a blanket argument that trade diversion away from other developing or developed countries would not result from granting the equivalent trade preferences to those given the LDCs may be hard to sustain.[6] However, the proposal that tariff preferences be given to any developing country on the basis of its low level of exports, relative to world trade or the importing country's overall imports, uncomplicated by arguments about vulnerability or the low level of development of the exporter, is more difficult to resist. These tariff preferences could extend to all merchandise exports of the country in question or be confined to those exports in which the share (in world trade or in the importing country's market) was below a particular threshold.[7]

This section examines the possibility of using 'objective' variables, i.e. those based solely on patterns of merchandise trade, as criteria for SDT. First, consider the use of the share in world merchandise trade as a measure of a country's trading significance: a very small share in world trade implies that granting that country SDT is likely to have a minimal impact on the importing country's domestic producers and a minimal trade diversion effect on other exporters. As Figure 10.1 (and the more complete data given in Appendix 10.2) shows, there is some overlap in the share of world trade between all five sets of countries and notably between small states (using

[6] See UNCTAD/Commonwealth Secretariat (2001) for a discussion of trade diversion in the context of improving GSP for LDCs, particularly in the context of EBA. [7] Ibid., p. 5

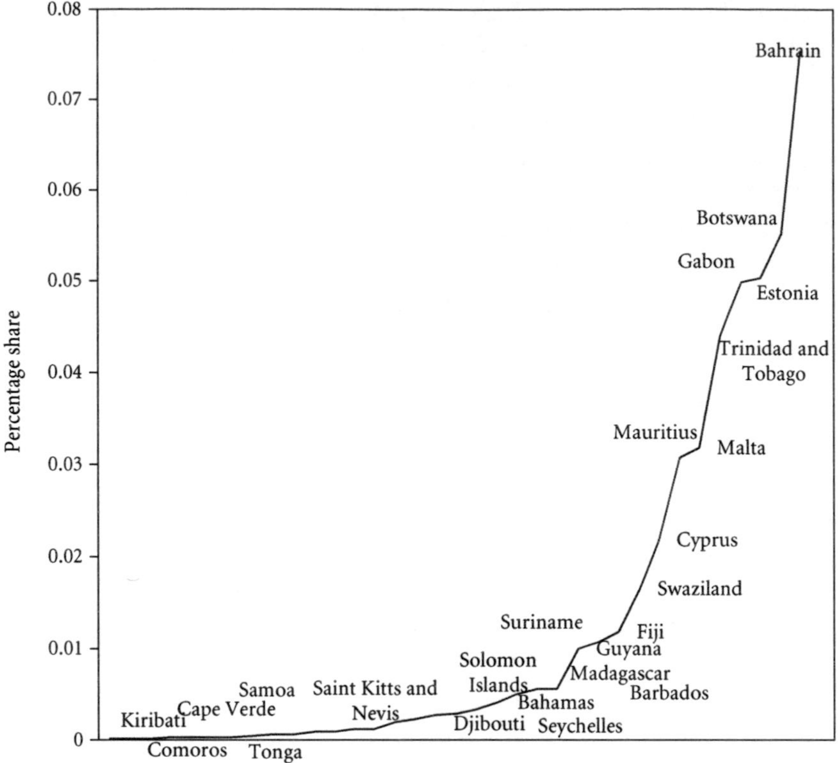

Figure 10.1 Share in world trade (1998–9), selected small states

the original CS–WB list, i.e. excluding Jamaica, Lesotho, Namibia and Papua New Guinea), the LDCs (the ECOSOC list excluding those classified as small states) and other developing countries. It is true that, if one were to take the same threshold as was used in calculations of membership dues to the WTO, that is 0.03 per cent of world trade, most of the small island states in the Caribbean and the Commonwealth would be included.[8] But Trinidad and Tobago, Botswana, Mauritius and Gabon would be excluded, as well as Malta, Estonia and Bahrain (see table 4 in Appendix 10.2).[9] Among non-LDC developing countries, Nicaragua, Panama, the Lebanon,

[8] The WTO minimum level of membership dues was based on 0.03 per cent of trade of WTO members. It is now based on 0.015 per cent. Our data refer to the UN estimates of world trade – including non-members of the WTO.

[9] Note that only twelve SS were included in the cluster and discriminant analysis. The available data for thirty-four SS are given in table 4 in Appendix 10.2.

the Dominican Republic, Paraguay, Bolivia, El Salvador, Jamaica, Namibia, Honduras and the Congo (Kinshasa), plus seven countries in transition, would be included. If the criterion were changed to 0.02 per cent of world trade, only the first five of these non-LDC developing countries and six countries in transition would qualify. But the same small states – plus Cyprus – would fail to qualify.

This raises the question of whether the addition of a number of other variables might refine the grouping of SS, and perhaps also those of the LDCs, 'other' developing countries and so on. The obvious statistical technique is cluster analysis. This technique is in keeping with the spirit of the study: the data should determine which countries should be grouped together, not prior considerations about vulnerability, underdevelopment or other sources of relative weakness.

The variables selected on which to examine the presence of clusters of like countries were constrained by data limitations. Eventually, in addition to the country's share in world trade, variables were chosen to measure export earnings volatility, the concentration of exports and the share of trade (exports plus imports of goods and services) in GDP. Other variables could be suggested but, even among those chosen, there are major gaps, especially among the small countries and notably among the new island states in the Pacific (see Appendix 10.2). Of the 184 countries in the total sample, a full set of data was available for only 95 countries. (If cluster analysis were to be used actually to group countries for determining SDT it would be necessary to fill in the missing data or select new variables; the purpose here is simply suggestive.)

Clearly more work could be done in the selection of variables, use of alternative clustering techniques and filling in missing data points.[10] The cluster analysis was only intended to indicate similarities and dissimilarities among groups of countries on the basis of a limited number of trade variables. However, the analysis was pursued through a different approach, that of discriminant analysis. This starts from the opposite perspective. The same five independent variables are combined into weighted linear functions which best separate (or technically maximise the distance between) the groups of SS, LDCs, 'other' developing countries, countries in transition and high-income countries.

[10] For example, alternative measures of distance between clusters could be tried. Only squared Euclidean distance was used here.

Some interesting results did emerge. There was a tendency for the outliers, e.g. China for its size and Malaysia for its share of trade in GDP, to break off and form separate clusters of one or two states. There was no clear separation of the rich countries or the countries in transition. However, the SS and the LDCs consistently ended up in the same cluster. This is not surprising if the mean values of the variables used are compared (see table 10.1). The averages for the share in world trade and for export volatility are the same for the SS and the LDCs. In terms of export concentration the SS show more concentration than the LDCs on the basis of the index but less on the basis of the number of products measure. Only in terms of trade as a share of GDP are they at opposite ends of the spectrum. More detailed results are given in Appendix 10.2.

In the first analysis twelve out of thirteen small states were correctly classified, as were all the LDCs and thirty-two out of thirty-six other developing countries. The only misclassified small state was Trinidad and Tobago which was classified as 'other developing'. Of the other developing countries, Nicaragua and Jamaica were misclassified as small states and Malaysia and China as developed countries. Except for the case of China which is clearly *sui generis*, these errors are unsurprising. Only eleven out of seventeen countries in transition and thirteen out of twenty-three high-income countries were correctly identified. The former set of errors is also understandable, given that countries in transition are as much politically as economically defined. As regards the high-income countries, Iceland was classified as a small state, Greece, Kuwait, Portugal, Finland and Ireland as developing countries, and New Zealand, Israel, Norway and Denmark as countries in transition.

The results of the cluster and the discriminant analysis are interesting when considered together. The discriminant analysis clearly established that the SS were a separately identifiable group – with only one exception – on the basis of the five trade-related variables, i.e. share of world trade, volatility of merchandise export earnings, concentration of exports (two measures) and share of trade in GDP. The cluster analysis, on the other hand, strongly suggested that in terms of the same variables, the LDCs and the SS have a great deal in common. Indeed the only variable in which they differ substantially is the share of trade in GDP – which did most of the work in distinguishing the two groups in the discriminant analysis. More work in this area might yield interesting insights, though it is doubtful that such statistical manipulations will themselves yield a taxonomy acceptable

Table 10.1 *Selected export variables*

	share of world trade, 1996	export volatility 1970–98	export concentration index, 1998	export concentration, no. of products, 1998	trade share in GDP, %
small states					
average	0.013	0.46	0.46	64	125.2
minimum	0.000	0.10	0.09	6	42.3
maximum	0.075	0.97	0.82	204	238.0
LDCs (excl. small states)					
average	0.013	0.44	0.34	49	54.3
minimum	0.000	0.10	0.27	20	20.8
maximum	0.076	1.70	0.45	78	134.9
other developing countries					
average	0.369	0.37	0.31	162	72.0
minimum	0.004	0.06	0.07	29	16.3
maximum	3.173	0.85	0.79	232	183.0
countries in transition					
average	0.189	0.21	0.16	182	88.3
minimum	0.003	0.06	0.06	75	30.1
maximum	1.543	0.61	0.31	228	143.9
high-income countries (excl. small states)					
average	2.707	0.17	0.17	216	73.7
minimum	0.035	0.02	0.05	86	19.4
maximum	12.239	0.48	0.66	236	284.6

Note:
for definitions of the variables see Appendix 10.2

for determining which countries qualify for any particular SDT. But further work might reinforce the conclusions of this section. In terms of objective variables, unrelated to controversial concepts, which are sometimes suspected of being self-serving, such as 'vulnerability' or 'underdevelopment', or even, 'disadvantage', the SS are similar to the LDCs – they cluster together – though, when the variables are given different weights, they clearly constitute a separate and well-defined group.

However, for practical considerations of SDT based on the de minimis principle, the share in world trade may, for the time being, be the most politically down-to-earth solution. To recap, a maximum share of 0.02 per cent of world trade (i.e. trade of WTO members) would, on the basis of 1996 data, exclude Trinidad, Botswana and Gabon among the SS. It would include Lesotho among LDCs and Nicaragua, Panama and the Lebanon among 'other' developing countries. It might be argued that, given that the criterion for admission into this group is essentially the smallness of the country and its negligible impact on world trade, a few additional members is of limited importance in economic terms.

As regards the use of the de minimis principle in the granting of SDT in terms of preferential market access, there is a question about whether it could be used to qualify a country for 'special' or LDC or some other improved treatment under a country's GSP. GSP schemes are not WTO-negotiated but are 'concessions' on the part of each donor, i.e. importing country, and subject to the unilaterally determined rules of that country. That however does not preclude the use of an overall world trade share de minimis criterion in those rules. If SDT under the de minimis rule were part of a WTO agreement then the lack of predictability associated with the current GSP would be significantly lessened. Another approach would be through de minimis rules at a low level of product disaggregation. This is examined in the next section but one.

One element of SDT as regards WTO disciplines that might be extended on the basis of the de minimis share of world trade is likely to be security from contingent protection. The aggressive pursuit of anti-subsidy violations, to include for example EPZs, now appears a priority among certain developed countries. Article 27 of the 1995 GATT allows for time extensions for LDCs and twenty other developing countries for their compliance with the Agreement on Subsidies. These extensions were further prolonged at the Doha Ministerial Meeting. They could be extended indefinitely to countries meeting the de minimis criterion. After all, an SS government is limited in the extent to which it can subsidise an export, and, in any event, these exports will be minor in terms of world trade in the good in question. A new safeguard clause to protect domestic suppliers of the goods in question against import surges, both defined in terms of the change in share of domestic consumption satisfied by the SS producer and clearly related to the derogation, might be necessary. Similar derogations on de minimis grounds from anti-dumping are also feasible though, perhaps, more difficult to defend on the grounds that the smallness of the country in which a firm is based does not preclude that firm from engaging in dumping, though it must make it less likely given that the home market will provide limited opportunities for cross-subsidisation. The third of the contingent protection devices sanctioned by the GATT is safeguards action. The Safeguards Agreement already has a de minimis clause: '[s]afeguards measures shall not be applied against a product originating in a developing country Member as long as its share of imports . . . does not exceed 3 per cent, provided that developing country Members with less than 3 per cent import share collectively account for not more than 9 per cent of total imports of the product concerned'.[11] Except in the event that the second condition applies or the safeguards action was being applied at a different level of product disaggregation to that used for the SDT, safeguards actions against a small state would be precluded by a de minimis rule of 3 per cent or less. However, to guard against these possibilities, it would make sense to include security from safeguards actions as part of the SDT, with the coverage defined by the de minimis rule at a broad level of disaggregation, say the two-digit level. There are, no doubt, other areas where the de minimis principle might be appropriate to justify a measure of SDT as regards WTO disciplines. In the next round there are likely to be a number of new areas where special treatment of LDCs or other groups of developing countries is granted, and in some or all of these there may be a role for the de minimis principle.

10.4 Analysis by sector

The de minimis principle is applicable at any level for which the appropriate statistics are available. The most telling of the arguments against the de minimis principle – that a country might have a small share in

[11] GATT Secretariat (1994), p. 320.

overall world trade but could still be a threat to domestic producers in particular sectors – can be largely countered by applying the principle at a more disaggregated level. For purposes of SDT outside of market access, there is a case for examining trade variables at a sectoral level. For example, a share in apparel trade of below a certain threshold could mean an accelerated timetable for the removal of MFA quotas. A share in world agricultural trade below a certain threshold could qualify for exemption from all quantitative restrictions on market access. Such an approach merits further study. This section will concentrate on the agricultural sector.

The Uruguay Round Agreement on Agriculture (AoA) provides SDT to developing countries through such devices as favourable thresholds and longer implementation periods under the three 'pillars' of agricultural protection, market access, domestic support and export competition policies. These elements of SDT apply to developing countries across the board. LDCs, however, have a more extensive package of SDT which exempts them from making reduction commitments under the three pillars. The question arises whether the same or similar LDC SDT might be given to developing countries whose share in world trade in all agricultural products – or in particular sub-groups – is below a certain threshold.

In the continuing WTO negotiations on agriculture, many SS have pointed out that 'implementation of the AoA suggests that many small developing countries lack the technical, institutional and infrastructural capacity to take advantage of the limited market opportunities that have emerged from the global trading system'.[12] In this context, several small countries have made proposals in the current agricultural negotiations where the de minimis principle could be relevant. For example, Swaziland has proposed, *inter alia*, that small developing countries be guaranteed against any disadvantage from new SDT granted to other developing countries.[13] This suggestion could largely be met through SDT based on de minimis rules. The adverse trade diversion effects from, say, the EU's new EBA or other improvements in access provided to LDC producers could be largely pre-empted by granting the excluded countries tariff and quota-free access under carefully selected de minimis rules. Again it should be stressed

[12] G/AG/NG/W/100. See www.wto.org for proposals in ongoing agricultural negotiations. For a summary of the proposals put to the Agricultural Committee, see Shirotori (2001).

[13] G/AG/NG/W/95.

that, if preferences under the de minimis rule were agreed under the WTO, the non-predictability associated with the current autonomous preferences would be reduced.

Agricultural trade is more affected by protection in the developed countries than is trade in other primary products or manufactures – other than apparel. Protection in agriculture is complicated by the widespread use of seasonal restrictions, specific duties and TRQs (tariff rate quotas) as well as the extremely high and trade-distorting support to domestic farmers and export subsidies in developed economies. There is also residual protection in the form of reference prices, minimum entry prices and variable levies. If the de minimis principle were adopted to reduce or eliminate tariff protection for marginal exporters, protection through other barriers to market access should be eradicated lest the same degree of protection is sustained through other instruments.

In the current WTO negotiations on agriculture a number of proposals have been made on which the findings of this report have some bearing. A number of countries have proposed greater tariff reductions and the elimination of quantitative restrictions on products of interest to the developing countries, while others have emphasised liberalisation of trade in tropical products. SDT based on the de minimis principle would not substitute for, but could complement, a broader liberalisation of trade through deeper than average tariff cuts in products of special concern to the developing countries. The same de minimis rules might apply to SDT in the form of derogations from WTO rules in agriculture, such as on subsidies or on SPS regulations, to the extent that it is technically feasible to have different rules applicable in, say, the meat sector from those in the cereals sector.

Consider first the use of share in world trade in agriculture as the criterion for the application of the de minimis principle to determine the beneficiaries of SDT in any of these areas. To cover all the SS the threshold would have to be relatively high at 0.15 per cent (see Figure 10.2). However, such a threshold would mean that a large number of non-SS developing countries, of which a minority are LDCs, would also qualify. If the threshold were set at 0.06 per cent, seven SS would be excluded (see Figure 10.2) and sixty-three non-SS developing countries would be included, of which nine would be LDCs. An alternative, more finely tuned, approach is the application of the de minimis principle at the chapter (two-digit) level.

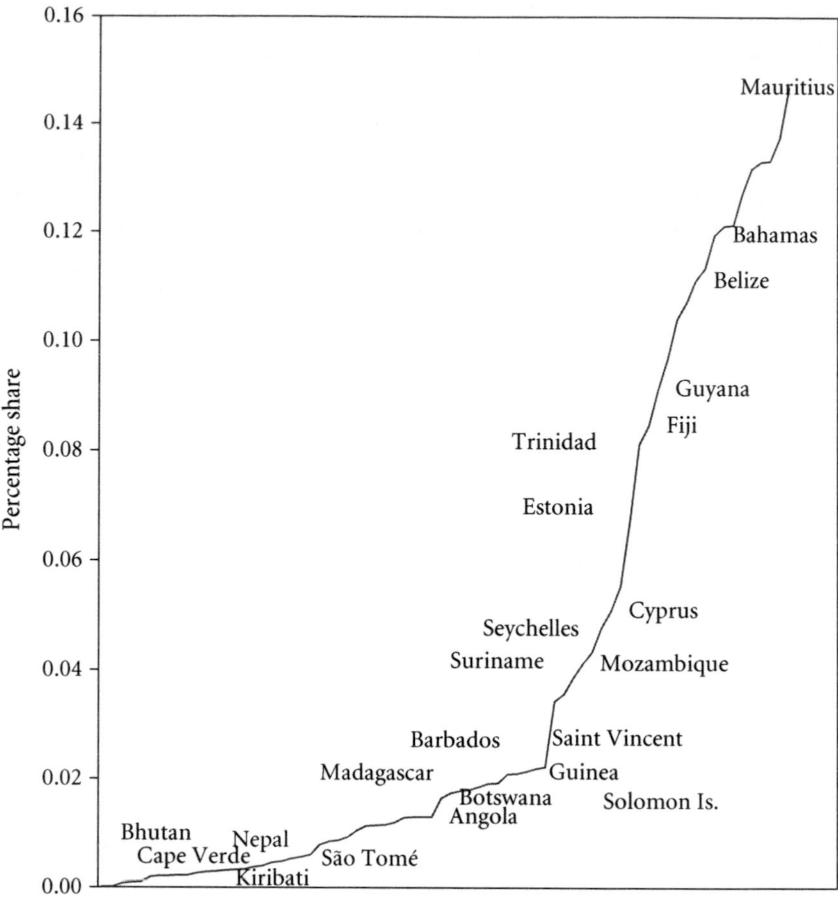

Figure 10.2 Share in world agricultural trade (1998–9), selected small states

The share of agricultural trade covered by alternative de minimis thresholds applied at the chapter level for different groups of countries is shown in table 1 in Appendix 10.3. For details of the database for world trade, see Appendix 10.4.[14] Thus if the 0.3 per cent threshold were applied to agricultural chapters, an average of 73.5 per cent of SS agricultural exports would

[14] It was found necessary to impose, as a secondary condition for inclusion in the analysis though not necessarily in the scheme were it to be implemented, a minimum percentage of the exporting country's total exports in order to exclude the huge number of very small trade flows which might in many cases have arisen from the return of an import order, re-exports or errors in customs classification. This was set at 0.5 per cent.

be covered. This would equate to 27 per cent of total exports. Twenty-nine small states would find that more than 90 per cent of their agricultural exports benefited.[15] Whether the de minimis rule was used for SDT for preferential market access or for relief from WTO disciplines, it would be significant. The principal SS beneficiaries of this rule are shown in table 1 in Appendix 10.3.

Table 2 in Appendix 10.3 looks at the major beneficiaries of a 0.3 or a 0.5 per cent de minimis rule among other developing countries. On average, 53 per cent of LDC agricultural exports would be covered – though many of these already benefit from tariff- and quota-free access to the largest developed country markets. Only seven 'other' developing countries and seven countries in transition would find that more than 50 per cent of their agricultural exports were covered by a 0.3 per cent rule, and in most cases – Nicaragua and Georgia are exceptions – agricultural exports are a small component of total exports. The benefits of the rule would then be heavily concentrated among small state agricultural exports.

The results also have some bearing on the vexed issue of tariff rate quotas (TRQs). Some developed countries, including the United States, are pressing for the gradual elimination of TRQs in favour of a tariff-only regime. Others (Turkey, India) argue for their eventual abolition and, in the meantime, for expanded quotas and reduced in-quota tariff rates. Abolishing TRQs would result in more liberal trade only if tariffs were significantly reduced. And unless this were the case, exporting countries currently with TRQs have no incentive to agree to their abolition.

It would be undesirable if any imports from countries benefiting from tariff preferences on the basis of the de minimis principle were included in unchanged TRQs. That would mean that any expansion of trade resulting from the new preferences (trade creation) would be entirely or largely offset by reductions in imports from other suppliers (trade diversion). Imports from the new beneficiary countries should either be totally separate from existing TRQs or the TRQs should be increased to ensure that some expansion in exports is not precluded. From the viewpoint of economic efficiency, allocating TRQs to particular countries is 'second best' to a global allocation. Also, on balance, imports under the de minimis principle would be best excluded from TRQs and the issue of

[15] Note that throughout the de minimis analysis, forty-five SS have been included, one more than in the CS–WB list. The additional country is Eritrea.

de minimis imports kept separate from the TRQ debate. However, it could be argued that the SIDS proposal to allocate certain increases in TRQs with zero in-quota rates to small island developing countries would cause minimal distortion since the amount of trade involved would be small.[16] It is also true that TRQs have been largely 'captured' by large exporters.

Thus one approach would be to provide country-specific TRQs with zero tariffs to countries from whom imports in a base year were less than some minimum share of total imports, with the TRQs equal to those imports (in volume terms) but with an added fixed percentage, say 20 per cent, to allow for expansion on the basis of the tariff preference. Table 3 in Appendix 10.3 shows the coverage by a 3 per cent de minimis rule of small states' exports to the EU at the eight-digit level. If TRQs were set to cover all this trade, only 1.5 per cent of EU imports of agricultural goods would be affected, plus any increase in imports that might be allowed for and encouraged by the establishment of these preferences.

10.5 Line-by-line analysis

If the use of variables relating to merchandise trade in the aggregate does not yield an acceptable set of criteria for determining which countries should be eligible for trade preferences, an alternative might be to give trade preferences line by line according to the exporting country's weight in world imports. To some extent this idea has already been put into practice. The EU's standard GSP scheme includes a number of provisions that limit the preferential treatment for individual countries. The so-called 'graduation mechanism' leads to the preferences being phased out for specific sectors of countries on the basis of a development index (based on income per capita and the level of exports of manufactured products) and a specialisation index (based on the ratio between the country's share of total EU imports and that country's share of EU imports in the sector in question). However, if the imports from a given country in a specific sector exceeded 25 per cent of all imports in the EU from all beneficiary countries in that sector during the year 1992, exports from that country in that sector do not benefit from GSP treatment whatever its level of development. This

[16] G/AG/NG/W/97.

provision is commonly known as the 'lion's share clause'. Likewise the graduation mechanism does not apply to countries whose exports to the EU in a given sector did not exceed 2 per cent of all beneficiary countries' exports to the EU in that sector. This exception is known as the 'minimal share clause'.[17]

In examining who would benefit from special tariff preferences – say completely tariff- and quota-free access to developed country markets – based solely on the smallness of their exports relative to total world imports of that product group, world imports from developing countries were analysed at the six-digit Harmonised Sytem (HS) level.[18] The OECD countries and non-sovereign states were excluded from the analysis, thus preserving the principle of preferential treatment for developing countries, while the loss in tariff revenues is significantly reduced.

A number of alternative threshold levels of a country's share in world imports, 2 per cent, 3 per cent and 4 per cent, were tried. Only trade flows equal to at least 0.5 per cent of the country's total exports to the world were included. The data set used is described in Appendix 10.4.[19] The 3 per cent rule implies a coverage of 3.6 per cent of all imports (including from OECD countries). The loss of tariff revenue would be considerably less than this because tariff-free products, either through zero MFN or GSP rates, are also included here. The likely costs in tariff revenue lost to the EU are discussed below.

The summary results are presented in table 4 in Appendix 10.3 with country details in table 5 in the same appendix. With the 3 per cent threshold, the small states find that 74 per cent of their exports (unweighted average across countries) are covered, which equates to 65 per cent of world imports from these countries. Over 90 per cent of the exports of fifteen of these countries satisfy the de minimis criterion, while for one of these countries – Nauru – only 16 per cent of its exports qualify, while for the Seychelles only 25 per cent of exports are covered. Other SS where the share of covered exports is low include Suriname, Guyana, the

[17] These provisions, originally in the 2000–2 EU GSP scheme, have been retained in the 2002–4 scheme.

[18] The six-digit level is the most disaggregated classification adopted in common by all users of the Harmonised System. A number of additional digits may be added by a country's statistical office or customs department but these are country-specific and have no value for aggregating or comparing trade flows across countries.

[19] The Eurostat CD-ROM, *Intra and Extra EU Trade*, was used.

Marshall Islands and the Bahamas. Among the LDCs, on average 62 per cent of exports are covered, thirteen out of the thirty-two have more than 75 per cent of their exports covered but five – Malawi, Bangladesh, Congo (DR), Mali and Mauritania – have less than 25 per cent of their exports covered. In the cases of the last two of these, less than 10 per cent are covered.

On the other hand, among 'other developing' countries, two – Oman and Congo – have over 90 per cent of their exports covered, and another five – Syria, Cambodia, Nicaragua, Lebanon and Namibia – have all but 75 per cent covered. Of the countries in transition, Turkmenistan, Azerbaijan, Armenia, Tajikistan and Georgia have over 75 per cent of their exports covered while the Russian Federation has barely 1 per cent covered. Among the higher income group, only Brunei has over half of its exports covered, but those consist of tariff-free petroleum.

Whether countries outside the SS or LDC categories receiving SDT benefits on the basis of a de minimis rule is considered appropriate, an unfortunate anomaly or simply 'the luck of the draw' is largely a matter of judgement. Of course, on many of the lines involved the MFN or at least the standard GSP tariff may already be zero. Such lines dominate the exports of Armenia (diamonds) and Congo, Syria, Azerbaijan, Georgia and Turkmenistan (petroleum and petroleum products). But the principal export of Oman, Cambodia, Lesotho and Nicaragua is, in each case, apparel, while Namibia exports a variety of fish, both of which are 'sensitive' products in most developed country markets.

The main reason for the low coverage of the exports of certain countries by the de minimis thresholds is that in those countries exports are dominated by one or two products and for those products they supply over the threshold percentage of world imports. In order to examine in greater detail the implications of implementing a de minimis rule, the major exports of the countries with low coverage under the 3 per cent threshold were examined. Table 6 in Appendix 10.3 shows the principal exports of these countries and their shares in world trade. For many of the lines in question – gold (Guyana), tankers (Marshall Islands), boats and planes (Bahamas), phosphates (Nauru) – the relevant MFN tariff in many import jurisdictions, including the EU and the US, is zero. All these countries are members of the ACP group and all of the listed products currently enter the EU duty-free under the Cotonou Agreement with the single exception of frozen rock lobsters (Bahamas) for which the 12.5 per cent MFN tariff is reduced to 4.3 per cent for ACP exporters. Of course in other jurisdictions, in particular the US which is the major destination for Caribbean exports or Australia and Japan for Pacific island exports, the relevant tariffs are not necessarily zero.

With or without SDT arrangements for the exports of small states, the prospects for the ACP countries are particularly sensitive to the negotiations on the aftermath of the Lomé Conventions. For non-LDCs, the Cotonou Agreement envisages either the establishment of reciprocal preferential trade arrangements between non-LDC ACP countries, either singly or in regional groupings, or standard GSP treatment. In the latter case the Seychelles would not qualify for better than standard GSP access for its tuna exports, even if a 3 per cent de minimis criterion for preferential market access were agreed. A de minimis rule for most ACP states would enable them to enter the negotiations in a much stronger position. Clearly, in general, the gains to individual countries associated with market access preferences based on the de minimis principle would depend on the extent to which each country's export products qualify, and for those that do not, the details of any changes in the trade regimes in force that might accompany the introduction of the de minimis principle.

Turning to the commodities with the highest coverage under a 3 per cent de minimis rule, 85 per cent of the total coverage of all merchandise exports of the developing countries is accounted for by the fifty six-digit lines listed in the last column of table 7 in Appendix 10.3. It is immediately clear that a large share of this trade is both free of tariffs and non-tariff barriers in most importing countries, including the largest importers, the US and the EU. Such goods include petroleum and other energy products (including propane, natural gas and electricity), metals and minerals and their alloys (including gold, aluminium, iron ore and diamonds), most unprocessed commodities (including wood, cotton and coffee), many mechanical and electronic products (including circuits and cathodes, data processing equipment, radio equipment), medical instruments, jewellery and medicaments.[20] Not all these goods are imported duty-free everywhere but most of them are in the major industrialised country markets as well as in many developing countries.

[20] The substantial exports of vehicles and vehicle parts recorded for a number of SS, in particular the Pacific Islands, is presumably mostly the repatriation of private vehicles by expatriates.

In many developed countries the relevant GSP tariff will be zero even though the MFN tariff is significant. Here the loss associated with missing out on the de minimis criterion may be less serious. However, the GSP schemes are not in general highly utilised, whether by reason of demanding, often unrealistic, rules of origin, ignorance of the availability of the preferential margin or, simply, because the opportunity costs of meeting the bureaucratic requirements for participation in the relevant scheme may be such as to discourage exporters from pursuing the opportunity.[21]

The lines where there are both significant tariffs (and often non-tariff barriers as well) are those involving apparel of all sorts, footwear, travel goods, shellfish and bananas. In most developed countries trade in apparel is still tightly controlled by the system of quotas agreed under the Multi-Fibre Arrangement derogation from WTO rules due to end in 2005. There are also tariffs, generally at high rates, levied on almost all clothing imports by the developed countries. Clothing, footwear and travel goods continue to attract high rates of duty in the largest developed countries – MFN rates of around 7 to 10 per cent with reduced GSP rates and zero LDC rates (except for clothing in the US). The US imports frozen shrimps and bananas tariff-free but the EU has MFN rates of 12 per cent and 16 per cent respectively. EU imports of ACP shrimps are tariff-free and the rate on GSP shrimps is 4.2 per cent. ACP and LDC bananas are imported tariff-free – subject to complex licensing and quota arrangements which have been declared non-WTO compliant and thus are due to change – and GSP imports (with certain exclusions) pay 16 per cent duty. Thus in the case of bananas the major potential gainers from the de minimis rule – St Lucia, Dominica, St Vincent and Belize – already benefit from tariff-free access, unconstrained by quotas, to their main markets in the EU and the US.

These products account only for about 13 per cent of world imports covered by the de minimis 3 per cent rule. But they are the goods where trade

[21] Facilitating the utilisation of the special GSP would clearly be of considerable value to existing beneficiary countries (LDCs, with, in the EU's case, ACPs) and to any new beneficiaries under the de minimis scheme. The most important deterrent to using the schemes is probably the rules of origin. The small volumes of trade involved suggest that these could be easily liberalised if not abolished. The anti-surge clause in the EU EBA scheme, and similar provisions elsewhere, could be used to prevent the large-scale 're-sourcing' of goods from other producers to benefit from tariff-free access. Secondly, much could be done to reduce information gaps and bureaucratic hurdles.

barriers are significant and therefore tariff- and quota-free access would mean a significant preference for the countries that benefited under a de minimis rule. Table 8 in Appendix 10.3 looks more closely at the main beneficiaries of the principal non-tariff-free products covered by the 3 per cent rule. It shows the share in their total exports of the qualifying products in question.

The small states and the LDCs are well represented among the major beneficiaries. Table 8 also emphasises the major role that would be played by so-called 'sensitive' products, in particular apparel and footwear, among the qualifying trade flows. There is a scattering of gains for Eastern European and CIS member states. In many cases the SS and LDCs already benefit from tariff-free entry into the EU (as ACP members or LDCs) and US markets (as LDCs or under the CBI or under the nascent AGOA). Under the de minimis rule they would now face competition from new beneficiaries. One effect in apparel trade would be to redistribute tariff-free entry into the EU from the major beneficiaries of EBA and ACP status, including Bangladesh and Mauritius, to countries that have hitherto had to contend with the limited preference margin in the standard EU GSP, including Cambodia, Sri Lanka, Macedonia, Laos and Viet Nam. In the case of the US, imports of garments, currently excluded from the US GSP scheme, from Eastern Europe and South Asia – and notably Mauritius – would benefit at the expense of those from Mexico and the Caribbean.

There will be, of course, trade diversion and trade-offs. The existing US, EU and other major preferential schemes which go beyond the standard developing country GSP, such as EBA, ACP, CBI and AGOA, are directed at different groups and cover different products. For example, what the ACP states lose through new competition in the EU they may stand to gain on the US market. Even the gains to the CBI beneficiaries on the US market would be significant since at present the CBI preferences are hedged about with exacting rules of origin, such as limiting preferences to goods made with US fabrics. Overall, as long as world demand schedules are not totally price-inelastic, overall trade creation will outstrip trade diversion.

The opposite side of the coin is presented in table 9 in Appendix 10.3 – those countries which are most likely to suffer from increased competition from the beneficiaries of the de minimis rule. The figures are based on maximalist assumptions:

- there is no increase in overall world trade in the relevant products, i.e. no trade creation, despite the introduction of zero tariffs and elimination of NTBs for qualifying exporters, and
- all the countries benefiting from the 3 per cent de minimis rule increase their exports of the covered products to 3 per cent, and
- all the most vulnerable countries share in trade diversion in proportion to their existing market share.

Both the first two assumptions are extreme. The second is demonstrably so since all the product lines listed are already tariff- and NTB-free for the ACP states and LDCs on the EU market and for some countries and lines on the US market while their export shares on these markets remain, in many cases, very small.[22] Clearly the tariff preferences do not fully compensate for other factors behind lack of competitiveness. Nevertheless table 9 still gives an indication of where the problems of trade diversion might be most significant.

Table 9 shows the result of the level of dependency of certain countries on exports of those goods whose trade flows will be most affected by a de minimis principle. The third column gives the share of world trade already taken (in 1999) by the countries which would benefit under the 3 per cent rule. The fifth column shows the maximum share of world trade which these countries could command – and still be eligible for SDT under the 3 per cent de minimis rule. The most vulnerable countries to this new preference scheme will experience a fall in total merchandise exports depending on the level of trade diversion and the share in total country exports of the product in question. Under the assumption that all supplying countries lose exports in proportion to their share of the world market, the figures in the final columns of the table show the maximum impact on total exports of each of the cited countries.

It appears that the major trade diversion problems – at least given the assumptions – would come in cotton jerseys, shrimps and men's cotton trousers. In clothing the MFA distorts world markets but most of the smaller exporters are not quota-constrained. In travel goods China would experience the greatest impact but given the scale and diversity of

[22] Because all the main beneficiaries of the de minimis rule applied to bananas are ACP states with zero tariffs on their predominant markets, the EU and US, bananas have been omitted from table 9.

China's exports it would not appear to create a major problem. In clothing a number of different countries would suffer from the increased competition from a de minimis rule. Honduras – which is vulnerable in a number of lines – Tunisia, Bangladesh and the Dominican Republic are potentially the most at risk, though, interestingly, Bangladesh is one of the major beneficiaries in men's cotton trousers. As an LDC, Bangladesh already has tariff- and quota-free access to the EU market, though on the US market clothing exporters are given no special LDC preferences and, as a result, Bangladesh would be vulnerable on that market. Duty-free access for aluminium exports would be some threat to the UAE, Russia and South Africa though the potential losses in exports are modest.

Finally table 10 in Appendix 10.3 looks at the cost to the importing country in terms of lost tariff revenue. The EU was taken as an example. The impact of the 3 per cent de minimis rule on customs duty receipts from the sixteen principal tariff lines was estimated by applying the appropriate GSP rate for all qualifying countries, i.e. all developing countries except the ACP states, the LDCs and Myanmar and North Korea. These lines make up some 85 per cent of total world trade covered by the 3 per cent rule. The overall loss was calculated as ECU 526 million on average in 1998/99. This compares with actual customs receipts by the EU of an average ECU 11.9 billion over the two years. The cost of implementing the de minimis scheme for these sixteen products would then be 4.4 per cent of total customs revenues. These products cover about 85 per cent of the total covered imports of the EU but, at the same time, they include clothing and footwear from most of the major suppliers. These have much higher than average tariffs. True, some of the imports would have entered at the MFN rate owing to rules of origin and other obstacles to using the GSP but, on the other hand, no adjustment is made for lower tariff rates for countries with which the EU has preferential trade arrangements, such as most of North Africa. On balance it seems unlikely that the customs loss would be more than 5 or 6 per cent. Since customs revenues in any event have been declining as a source of public revenue with the gradual erosion of MFN tariffs and a rapidly expanding network of Preferential Trade Agreements, from a public revenue viewpoint the significance of a de minimis scheme is minor.

10.6 Conclusions

This study has covered a lot of ground, albeit without going into some of the issues raised in as much detail as one would have liked. The task was to undertake a preliminary investigation of the possible role of the de minimis principle in the granting of SDT as regards both market access and WTO disciplines to the small states. Those states' own proposals for SDT have not been well received by other developing countries or by the developed world. However, the argument for applying the de minimis principle is self-evident: granting SDT to countries with a very small share of world trade – and which, largely because of that, have difficulties in integrating into the world trading system – could be of major help to them but will have little impact on world trade flows or the overall impact of WTO disciplines. In the general area of market access, preferences – which could cover exemption from all quantitative import restrictions as well as tariff preferences – could be based on the application of the de minimis principle at alternative levels of trade disaggregation. The argument that trade will be minimally distorted carries most weight when the finest level of disaggregation of world trade data, i.e. HS six-digit codes, are used.

Simulating the effects of applying de minimis rules was both technically more complex and intellectually more provocative than had been expected. In general the conclusions as regard the feasibility of the de minimis approach are largely positive:

- The de minimis criteria at different levels of trade focus well on the SS. Even taking a maximum overall share in merchandise trade of 0.02 will include all but eight of the World Bank list of forty-four small vulnerable states (and among those eight, Cyprus, Malta, Estonia and Bahrain feature) while only eleven countries neither on the list nor LDCs are included. Inevitably the results are not as tidy as one might have wished. If the de minimis threshold is set high enough to cover a predetermined group of SS, other countries will slip in under the threshold. This is true whether the threshold is set as a share of total world merchandise trade or as the share of trade in a six-digit HS tariff line – given that world trade cannot be defined at any finer level of disaggregation. The question is how much does that matter – if the impact of other trade flows or of derogations as regards WTO disciplines is going to be minimal.

- Discriminant functions based on share in world trade, volatility of export earnings, concentration of exports and share of trade in GDP separate out the small states even more precisely. Though the exercise was weakened by missing data problems, the discriminant analysis did show that the SS were a clearly identifiable group of countries, while the cluster analysis showed that, apart from their much higher dependence on trade, they were in other objective respects very akin to the LDCs.
- In the agricultural area, where subsidies are an important issue and the LDCs and other states with a per capita income of less than US $1,000 have a longer period of adjustment to the WTO rules, de minimis criteria based on share of world trade in a particular section, for example meat or fish or dairy goods or vegetable oils, might be appropriate for extending derogations from WTO disciplines. The sectoral level might also be most appropriate for the granting of freedom from the threat of countervailing, antidumping or safeguards actions for those suppliers with below a certain share in world trade in a two-digit product group.
- As for TRQs, which are being much discussed in the current agricultural negotiations in Geneva, a system based on the de minimis principle, applied by an individual importing jurisdiction – the EU is used as an example – is feasible. If TRQs were set to cover all EU imports for countries supplying less than 3 per cent of all eight-digit tariff lines, only 1.5 per cent of EU imports of agricultural goods would be affected, plus any increase in imports that might be allowed for and encouraged by the establishment of these preferences.
- De minimis rules could also tackle the concerns of the developing countries about the diversion of trade associated with the new initiatives of the developed countries (including the EU, the US, Japan and Canada) in expanding their LDC GSP schemes. Trade diversion will result from newly formed or deepened free-trade areas, such as is envisaged by the Cotonou Agreement and in the Free Trade Area of the Americas. One way of protecting small producers, who may be the most vulnerable to trade diversion, is through complementing these initiatives with preference schemes based on the de minimis principle.
- For market access, tariff preferences based on the finest feasible level of disaggregation, the six-digit level, would minimise trade diversion and the economic damage to domestic and foreign suppliers.

Appendix 10.1

Table 1 *List of small states recognised by the CS–WB Task Force*[a]

	Population, '000s	Landlocked or island ACP state	On ECOSOC list of LDCs
Antigua and Barbuda	65	yes	no
Bahamas	268	yes	no
Bahrain	535	no	no
Barbados	260	yes	no
Belize	204	no	no
Bhutan	759	yes	yes
Botswana	1,401	yes	no
Cape Verde	370	yes	yes
Comoros	607	yes	yes
Cook Islands	20	yes	no
Cyprus	726	no	no
Djibouti	557	no	yes
Dominica	71	yes	no
Equatorial Guinea	379	no	yes
Estonia	1,450	no	no
Fiji	758	yes	no
Gabon	1,248	no	no
Gambia	1,042	no	yes
Grenada	92	yes	no
Guinea-Bissau	1,161	no	yes
Guyana	816	no	no
Kiribati	78	yes	yes
Maldives	236	no	yes
Malta	361	no	no
Marshall Islands	62	yes	no
Mauritius	1,091	yes	no
Micronesia, Fed. States of	113	yes	no
Nauru	11	yes	no
Niue	2	yes	no
Palau	19	yes	no
Qatar	742	no	no
Samoa	167	yes	yes
São Tomé and Principe	127	yes	yes
Seychelles	72	yes	no
Solomon Islands	354	yes	yes
St Kitts and Nevis	42	yes	no
St Lucia	139	yes	no

Table 1 (*cont.*)

	Population, '000s	Landlocked or island ACP state	On ECOSOC list of LDCs
St Vincent & Grenadines	11	yes	no
Suriname	414	no	no
Swaziland	809	yes	no
Tonga	93	yes	no
Trinidad and Tobago	1,278	yes	no
Tuvalu	11	yes	yes
Vanuatu	161	yes	yes

[a] Certain newly independent countries have been added to the original list. These are the Cook Islands, the Marshall Islands, the Federation of Micronesia, Nauru, Niue, Palau, Tuvalu and Vanuatu.

Appendix 10.2 Cluster and discriminant analysis

The following variables were used:

- share in overall world trade, average 1996–8[23]
- a measure of export earnings volatility: the coefficient of variation of merchandise export earnings about their trend between 1970 and 1998 (calculated by the author on the basis of World Bank data)
- the Hirschmann index of the concentration of exports (1997)[24, 25]
- the number of products exported at the three-digit SITC, revision 2, level where the value of exports is greater than US $100,000 or represents at least 0.3 per cent of the country's total exports[26]
- the share of trade (imports plus exports of goods and services) in GDP (1997).[27]

23 Taken from UNCTAD (2001a).

24 See UNCTAD (2001a), table 4.5 and notes for the source of the data and a definition of the index.

25 The export concentration index takes values between 0 (minimum concentration) and 1 (maximum concentration). It is calculated using the formula, $Ex_{i} = \sqrt{[\Sigma x_i/X]^2} / \sqrt{[1/n]}$, where x_i/X is the share of product i in total exports, X, the summation is carried out over all i, from 1 to n, and n equals 239, the number of products at the three-digit SITC, revision two, level.

26 Taken from UNCTAD (2001a)

27 Taken from World Bank (2001).

The cluster analysis method chosen used squared Euclidean distance to measure dissimilarity between unweighted pair-group centroids. The *centroid* of a cluster is the average point in the multidimensional space defined by the dimensions. In a sense, it is the *centre of gravity* for the respective cluster. In this method, the distance between two clusters is determined as the difference between centroids.[28, 29] There are a large number of other clustering methodologies, but time precluded a full investigation, and, in any event, it is unlikely that the results would have been radically different.

Various analyses were carried out. For example, where the OECD countries were excluded and a breakdown into five clusters was specified with a view to comparing the results with the groups, SS, LDC, 'other' developing, transition and high income,[30] most of the small states, LDCs, Central American countries and the Asian CIS member states, together with Albania, Syria and Algeria, were put in one cluster. The second cluster was made up of most other developing countries and most European countries in transition. The third group consisted of just Malta and Bahrain – small but diverse exporters. The fourth and fifth clusters were made up of Malaysia (abnormally high share of trade in GDP) and China (large and very diverse in exports) respectively. When the number of clusters was specified at four, Malaysia and China were grouped together and when three clusters were specified, the small states, LDCs and smaller other developing countries made up one cluster, the larger other developing countries a second and Malaysia and China the third. Even at the two-cluster level, Malaysia and China were put together in one cluster and the rest of the developing world in another. The technical statistics on the cluster analysis are available from the author.

The results differed little whether the OECD countries were included and/or the countries in transition excluded. Essentially with no prespecified weighting of the variables, the analysis starts with the outliers breaking off into separate clusters, either individually or as pairs. There were clear indications that the smaller and poorer developing countries are 'different'

[28] Sokal and Sneath (1967) use the abbreviation *UPGMC* to refer to this method as *unweighted pair-group method using the centroid average.* Euclidean distance is given by the formula, distance $(x,y) = \{\Sigma_i (x_i - y_i)^2\}$, where x_i and y_i are the values of variable i in clusters x and y respectively. [29] Everitt (1980) and Sokal and Sneath (1967).

[30] Here the high-income group consists of five countries/territories: Brunei, Hong Kong, Israel, Kuwait and Singapore.

from the other developing and richer transition countries, but the differences were less – in terms of squared Euclidean distance between cluster centroids – than between either group and Malta and Bahrain together or Malaysia or China separately. With a lot more 'data mining' along these lines but with additional variables, alternative clustering techniques[31] and, probably, fewer missing data points, a more convincing taxonomy would certainly result. But whether, without the use of 'prejudgemental' variables like real *per capita* income or output volatility, one could end up with a grouping with a claim to serve as the basis for SDT is doubtful.

Discriminant analysis starts from the opposite perspective. The same five independent variables are combined into $(n-1)$ weighted linear functions that maximise the distance between the n groups. Again there are a number of different techniques, using different combinations of distance measures (in our case squared Euclidean distance), measures of group centrality (in our case centroids) and techniques for agglomeration or division (in our case agglomeration). The value of each function for each observation is called its discriminant score. Each set of scores is used to predict the group to which the observation (country) belongs. A statistic, Wilk's Lambda, measures the proportion of the variance between the groups that the set of functions do *not* explain. This statistic follows an F-distribution and only when an independent variable contributes significantly – 5 per cent was used here – to the explanation of the between-group variance is it included.

The first of the analyses divided the developing world into five groups:

- small states (the World Bank list),
- LDCs (the ECOSOC list less any small states),
- other developing countries, i.e. claiming that status at the WTO, except for
- countries in transition, the former communist Central European and East European countries, and those included among the
- high-income countries, as classified by the World Bank.

The list of countries in each group is given in table 4.

[31] Including monotonic transformations of the existing variables. The technique used here is not invariant to such transformations as standardisation.

Table 1 *Discriminant analysis: summary results with five groups*

	Predicted group membership					
	small states	LDCs	other developing	transition	high income	total
small states	11	0	1	0	0	12
LDCs	0	7	0	0	0	7
other developing	2	0	32	0	2	36
transition	0	1	4	11	1	17
high income	1	0	5	4	13	23

Table 2 *Discriminant analysis: summary results with four groups*

	Predicted group membership				
	small states	LDCs	other developing	high income	total
small states	11	0	1	0	12
LDCs	0	6	1	0	7
other developing	2	1	34	7	44
high income	0	0	3	29	32

The data were analysed in three different ways: first, all the five groups were included; secondly, the countries in transition group was eliminated with those countries being split into high-income and developing countries using the World Bank classification; and finally, both the countries in transition and the high-income countries were excluded, leaving just the three sets of developing countries.

In the first analysis four variables contributed to the discriminant functions at the 5 per cent significance level – the number of products, the volatility of export earnings, trade as a percentage of GDP and the percentage of world trade. The Hirschmann concentration index reduced Wilk's Lambda from 0.172 to 0.149 (raising the explained variance from 83 per cent to 85 per cent) but that was not statistically significant, presumably because a large part of its explanatory power was shared by the number of products variable.

In the second exercise, the transition countries were excluded as a group and were reallocated into other developing or high income according to whether they were applicants for EU membership or not.[32] Again Trinidad was misallocated as other developing. Among LDCs Tanzania was put in the other developing group. Jamaica and Nicaragua were again classed as small states, but Colombia, Indonesia, Thailand and India as high income. Albania was classed as an LDC, Romania as other developing, Russia as developed and Iceland and Kuwait again as small states.

Table 3 *Discriminant analysis: summary results with three groups*

	Predicted group membership			
	small states	LDCs	other developing	Total
small states	11	0	1	12
LDCs	0	6	1	7
other developing	2	0	34	36

Finally, when the developed and countries in transition are excluded from the analysis, Tanzania, Trinidad and Estonia (still included as a small state) are classified as other developing and Nicaragua and Jamaica as small states.

These results are encouraging, though more work could be clearly done towards an 'objective' identification of trade disadvantage through the inclusion of other variables in cluster or, particularly, discriminant analysis. Whether such statistical exercises could ever yield a taxonomy accepted for SDT must remain doubtful, even if they are based on only trade variables. As the definitions of groups of countries become more complex and more difficult to interpret – as inevitably discriminant functions are – they will encounter increased resistance from countries who are excluded or simply believe in a simple and comprehensive international trade regime.

[32] This is clearly an arbitrary and arguable criterion. But the aim of this section of the chapter is essentially experimental. Clearly there is scope for a lot more analysis in this area.

Table 4 *Country data used in cluster and discriminant analysis*

	share of world trade 1996/98	export earnings volatility 1980–99	export concentration 1996/98	number of products 1996/98	% share of trade in GDP 1996
Small states					
São Tomé and Principe	0.0002	0.58	n.a.	n.a.	117.6
Comoros	0.0002	0.39	n.a.	n.a.	64.5
Kiribati	0.0002	0.68	n.a.	n.a.	n.a.
Cape Verde	0.0002	0.59	n.a.	n.a.	87.9
Samoa	0.0002	0.43	n.a.	n.a.	n.a.
Tonga	0.0003	0.31	n.a.	n.a.	n.a.
Gambia	0.0003	0.41	n.a.	n.a.	143.0
Grenada	0.0004	0.22	0.37	15	110.0
Guinea-Bissau	0.0006	0.75	n.a.	n.a.	42.3
Saint Kitts and Nevis	0.0006	0.38	0.63	11	122.7
Saint Vincent/Grenadines	0.0009	0.55	0.43	25	116.5
Dominica	0.0009	0.67	0.55	18	109.7
Antigua and Barbuda	0.0012	0.51	n.a.	n.a.	n.a.
Saint Lucia	0.0012	0.63	0.62	17	137.6
Bhutan	0.0019	0.10	n.a.	n.a.	77.7
Seychelles	0.0023	0.56	0.82	6	136.2
Djibouti	0.0028	0.79	n.a.	n.a.	99.4
Belize	0.0029	0.32	0.42	18	94.3
Solomon Islands	0.0034	0.72	n.a.	n.a.	n.a.
Bahamas	0.0040	0.36	n.a.	n.a.	n.a.
Barbados	0.0050	0.50	0.19	69	n.a.
Equatorial Guinea	0.0057	0.97	n.a.	n.a.	238.0

Guyana	0.0100	0.27	n.a.	n.a.	206.7
Suriname	0.0108	0.17	0.58	52	n.a.
Fiji	0.0118	0.47	n.a.	n.a.	118.4
Swaziland	0.0166	0.38	n.a.	n.a.	174.0
Cyprus	0.0218	0.33	0.16	103	n.a.
Mauritius	0.0308	0.28	0.32	93	129.2
Malta	0.0319	0.18	0.51	101	186.7
Trinidad and Tobago	0.0439	0.45	0.32	128	94.8
Estonia	0.0498	n.a.	0.09	204	145.7
Gabon	0.0503	0.38	0.81	65	96.1
Botswana	0.0551	0.52	n.a.	n.a.	86.6
Bahrain	0.0754	0.27	0.54	98	193.6
average	**0.0128**	**0.46**	**0.46**	**64**	**125.2**
minimum	**0.0002**	**0.10**	**0.09**	**6**	**42.3**
maximum	**0.0754**	**0.97**	**0.82**	**204**	**238.0**
LDCs (excluding small state LDCs)					
Sierra Leone	0.0005	0.33	n.a.	n.a.	49.5
Burundi	0.0012	0.44	n.a.	n.a.	20.8
Rwanda	0.0013	0.47	n.a.	n.a.	32.0
Chad	0.0020	0.52	n.a.	n.a.	49.0
Haiti	0.0021	0.42	0.27	32	35.4
Mozambique	0.0032	0.35	0.40	62	62.3
Somalia	0.0034	0.42	n.a.	n.a.	n.a.
Niger	0.0050	0.10	n.a.	n.a.	40.4
Central African Republic	0.0051	0.36	0.44	20	38.7
Burkina Faso	0.0053	1.08	n.a.	n.a.	41.7

Table 4 (*cont.*)

	share of world trade 1996/98	export earnings volatility 1980–99	export concentration 1996/98	number of products 1996/98	% share of trade in GDP 1996
Madagascar	0.0056	0.18	0.27	65	46.3
Togo	0.0058	0.38	n.a.	n.a.	70.6
Lao People's Dem. Rep.	0.0060	0.46	n.a.	n.a.	n.a.
Dem. Rep. of the Congo	0.0067	0.45	n.a.	n.a.	50.0
Benin	0.0075	0.68	n.a.	n.a.	58.9
Nepal	0.0076	0.36	0.45	36	58.0
Liberia	0.0093	0.27	n.a.	n.a.	n.a.
Lesotho	0.0036	0.41	n.a.	n.a.	142.0
Mauritania	0.0096	0.25	n.a.	n.a.	84.2
Mali	0.0096	0.24	n.a.	n.a.	53.9
Ethiopia	0.0099	0.31	n.a.	n.a.	40.5
Malawi	0.0099	0.46	n.a.	n.a.	56.9
Uganda	0.0103	0.34	n.a.	n.a.	35.0
Sudan	0.0118	0.25	0.33	20	n.a.
Cambodia	0.0130	1.70	n.a.	n.a.	68.8
Utd Rep. of Tanzania	0.0132	0.25	0.27	76	57.7
Guinea	0.0159	0.38	n.a.	n.a.	38.1
Zambia	0.0178	0.22	n.a.	n.a.	73.7
Senegal	0.0194	0.44	n.a.	n.a.	71.5
Yemen	0.0451	0.60	n.a.	n.a.	67.6
Bangladesh	0.0689	0.83	0.30	78	30.0
Angola	0.0757	0.21	n.a.	n.a.	134.9
average	**0.0134**	**0.44**	**0.34**	**49**	**54.3**

minimum	**0.0005**	**0.10**	**0.27**	**20**	**20.8**
maximum	**0.0757**	**1.70**	**0.45**	**78**	**134.9**
Other developing countries					
Nicaragua	0.0120	0.34	0.26	83	84.4
Panama	0.0130	0.44	0.32	82	n.a.
Lebanon	0.0146	0.23	n.a.	n.a.	69.3
Dominican Republic	0.0153	0.30	0.79	100	96.3
Paraguay	0.0195	0.55	0.40	96	46.5
Bolivia	0.0209	0.21	0.21	85	49.0
El Salvador	0.0223	0.31	0.30	145	54.7
Jamaica	0.0247	0.19	0.53	79	127.1
Namibia	0.0251	0.06	n.a.	n.a.	116.2
Honduras	0.0264	0.47	0.39	118	88.3
Congo	0.0276	0.57	n.a.	n.a.	163.2
Ghana	0.0330	0.42	n.a.	n.a.	59.5
Jordan	0.0332	0.68	n.a.	n.a.	135.2
Cameroon	0.0365	0.52	0.37	91	44.7
Kenya	0.0371	0.33	0.26	155	69.8
Papua New Guinea	0.0402	0.50	n.a.	n.a.	109.0
Guatemala	0.0407	0.20	0.25	162	40.4
Zimbabwe	0.0447	0.44	0.27	182	72.7
Uruguay	0.0489	0.35	0.18	160	42.4
Egypt	0.0645	0.19	0.28	159	46.1
Syrian Arab Republic	0.0671	0.55	0.57	109	73.7
Côte d'Ivoire	0.0810	0.20	n.a.	n.a.	78.9
Costa Rica	0.0828	0.85	0.22	166	91.9
Sri Lanka	0.0835	0.15	n.a.	n.a.	78.9

Table 4 (*cont.*)

	share of world trade 1996/98	export earnings volatility 1980–99	export concentration 1996/98	number of products 1996/98	% share of trade in GDP 1996
Ecuador	0.0876	0.21	0.36	172	53.9
Tunisia	0.1031	0.68	0.21	180	85.3
Peru	0.1104	0.28	0.23	181	28.3
Oman	0.1250	0.68	0.74	147	n.a.
Morocco	0.1299	0.69	0.18	152	55.5
Viet Nam	0.1559	0.47	n.a.	n.a.	100.0
Pakistan	0.1628	0.22	0.23	143	37.5
Libyan Arab Jamahiriya	0.1706	0.41	0.77	29	n.a.
Colombia	0.2027	0.12	0.26	199	34.0
Algeria	0.2346	0.31	0.56	86	54.8
Chile	0.2895	0.25	0.30	207	58.4
Nigeria	0.2915	0.30	n.a.	n.a.	75.6
Iran, Islamic Rep. of	0.3728	0.26	n.a.	n.a.	n.a.
Venezuela	0.3814	0.28	0.57	165	57.9
Turkey	0.4622	0.49	0.10	223	49.0
Argentina	0.4622	0.40	0.14	221	18.1
Philippines	0.4714	0.45	0.37	204	89.8
South Africa	0.5313	0.21	0.16	227	n.a.
India	0.6140	0.13	0.12	222	27.1
Brazil	0.9308	0.33	0.09	222	16.3
Indonesia	0.9382	0.17	0.16	215	52.3
Thailand	1.0293	0.24	0.09	220	84.4
Saudi Arabia	1.0735	0.35	0.74	167	73.4

Malaysia	1.4121	0.45	0.19	226	183.0
Mexico	1.9198	0.45	0.12	229	62.8
Korea, Republic of	2.4463	0.65	0.15	221	68.7
China	3.1730	0.34	0.07	232	39.9
average	**0.3692**	**0.37**	**0.31**	**162**	**72.0**
minimum	**0.0036**	**0.06**	**0.07**	**29**	**16.3**
maximum	**3.1730**	**0.85**	**0.79**	**232**	**183.0**
Countries in transition					
Albania	0.0034	0.45	0.20	75	54.8
Georgia	0.0039	0.33	n.a.	n.a.	30.1
Armenia	0.0046	0.21	0.24	93	78.8
Kyrgyzstan	0.0101	0.13	0.17	137	87.3
Azerbaijan	0.0121	0.20	n.a.	n.a.	62.3
Moldova, Rep. of	0.0173	0.11	0.31	117	131.2
Former Yug. Rep. of Macedonia	0.0231	0.07	0.13	150	78.1
Latvia	0.0300	0.11	0.16	191	109.9
Lithuania	0.0669	0.16	0.12	212	116.5
Croatia	0.0811	0.07	0.12	207	95.5
Uzbekistan	0.0852	0.61	n.a.	n.a.	n.a.
Bulgaria	0.0901	0.06	0.09	211	122.7
Kazakhstan	0.1088	0.20	0.30	181	71.3
Belarus	0.1224	0.41	n.a.	n.a.	100.4
Romania	0.1521	0.40	0.12	203	65.1
Slovenia	0.1577	0.06	0.11	211	109.5
Slovakia	0.1701	0.18	0.11	210	128.1

Table 4 (*cont.*)

	share of world trade 1996/98	export earnings volatility 1980–99	export concentration 1996/98	number of products 1996/98	% share of trade in GDP 1996
Ukraine	0.2524	0.18	n.a.	n.a.	93.9
Hungary	0.3204	0.18	0.10	215	78.8
Czech Republic	0.4375	0.17	0.06	228	143.9
Poland	0.4765	0.19	0.07	227	52.5
Russian Federation	1.5427	0.10	0.25	227	44.2
average	**0.1895**	**0.21**	**0.16**	**182**	**88.3**
minimum	**0.0034**	**0.06**	**0.06**	**75**	**30.1**
maximum	**1.5427**	**0.61**	**0.31**	**228**	**143.9**
High-income countries (exc. small states)					
Iceland	0.0348	0.13	0.38	86	72.1
Greece	0.1658	0.14	0.10	216	39.2
Kuwait	0.2344	0.48	0.66	148	92.6
New Zealand	0.2487	0.08	0.17	209	56.6
Israel	0.4098	0.20	0.27	200	77.8
Portugal	0.4369	0.23	0.12	222	69.2
United Arab Emirates	0.5184	0.32	n.a.	n.a.	n.a.
Finland	0.7364	0.33	0.20	222	67.4
Norway	0.8448	0.12	0.35	218	72.6
Denmark	0.8840	0.08	0.08	226	65.9
Ireland	1.0162	0.43	0.18	221	137.5
Austria	1.0922	0.05	0.07	n.a.	82.2

Australia	1.0988	0.02	0.14	233	40.0
Switzerland	1.3737	0.12	0.12	221	67.9
Sweden	1.5457	0.11	0.14	230	73.2
Spain	1.9344	0.14	0.12	233	50.1
Singapore	2.2060	0.39	0.23	225	n.a.
Belgium–Luxembourg	3.1820	0.05	0.10	236	n.a.
China, Hong Kong SAR	3.3271	0.21	0.17	175	284.6
Netherlands	3.6227	0.05	0.07	235	100.9
Canada	3.8639	0.06	0.13	235	75.3
Italy	4.5161	0.19	0.05	234	48.2
United Kingdom	5.0057	0.12	0.07	236	59.9
France	5.4179	0.11	0.07	236	45.4
Japan	7.4768	0.18	0.13	225	19.4
Germany	9.6672	0.04	0.09	236	47.2
United States	12.2389	0.09	0.08	235	24.7
average	**2.7074**	**0.17**	**0.17**	**216**	**73.7**
minimum	**0.0348**	**0.02**	**0.05**	**86**	**19.4**
maximum	**12.2389**	**0.48**	**0.66**	**236**	**284.6**

Note:
Where data for only two or fewer factors were available, the country was excluded from the analysis.

Appendix 10.3 Results of line-by-line de minimis analysis

Table 1 *Small state beneficiaries from de minimis rule (0.3 or 0.5 per cent world trade) applied to agriculture at two-digit level*

	Exports			max. share of world imports: 0.3 %			max. share of world imports: 0.5 %		
					% share covered of			% share covered of	
	agric. $ '000	total $ '000	agric. as % total	no. chapters covered	agr. expts	total expts	no. chapters covered	agr. expts	total expts
Small states									
Bhutan	155	1,652	9.4	2	100.0	9.4	2	100.0	9.4
Comoros	8,310	19,172	43.3	2	100.0	43.3	2	100.0	43.3
Cook Islands	898	5,298	16.9	5	100.0	16.9	5	100.0	16.9
Guinea-Bissau	8,082	30,323	26.7	3	100.0	26.7	3	100.0	26.7
Kiribati	6,199	6,444	96.2	1	100.0	96.2	1	100.0	96.2
Niue	188	664	28.3	3	100.0	28.3	3	100.0	28.3
Tuvalu	28	1,483	1.9	1	100.0	1.9	1	100.0	1.9
Micronesia, FS	42,003	52,485	80.0	2	100.0	80.0	2	100.0	80.0
Tonga	15,034	17,170	87.6	8	99.6	87.2	8	99.6	87.2
São Tomé	9,250	14,418	64.2	3	99.5	63.8	3	99.5	63.8
Solomon Is.	59,505	111,832	53.2	6	99.3	52.8	6	99.3	52.8
Marshall Is.	29,611	40,437	73.2	2	99.3	72.7	2	99.3	72.7
St Lucia	62,320	88,636	70.3	4	99.1	69.7	4	99.1	69.7
Vanuatu	26,415	33,476	78.9	4	98.9	78.0	4	98.9	78.0
Saint Vincent	60,653	203,016	29.9	6	98.7	29.5	6	98.7	29.5
Grenada	22,409	41,037	54.6	7	98.6	53.8	7	98.6	53.8
Dominica	36,872	90,147	40.9	5	98.5	40.3	5	98.5	40.3

Palau	20,816	38,172	54.5	2	98.3	53.6	2	98.3	53.6
Equatorial Guinea	54,302	674,659	8.0	2	98.2	7.9	2	98.2	7.9
Maldives	33,390	146,113	22.9	3	97.7	22.3	3	97.7	22.3
Gambia	30,323	88,832	34.1	3	97.5	33.3	3	97.5	33.3
Antigua	7,567	19,315	39.2	8	96.2	37.7	8	96.2	37.7
Botswana	46,734	441,564	10.6	1	95.1	10.1	1	95.1	10.1
Suriname	101,082	574,716	17.6	3	95.1	16.7	3	95.1	16.7
St Kitts	10,825	48,265	22.4	2	95.0	21.3	2	95.0	21.3
Samoa	11,423	49,764	23.0	5	94.8	21.8	5	94.8	21.8
Eritrea	1,943	10,095	19.2	3	94.5	18.2	3	94.5	18.2
Cape Verde	1,966	20,743	9.5	1	92.6	8.8	1	92.6	8.8
Djibouti	2,478	44,503	5.6	4	87.9	4.9	4	87.9	4.9
Nauru	1,331	29,163	4.6	2	73.9	3.4	2	73.9	3.4
Estonia	192,432	2,938,907	6.5	3	66.7	4.4	3	66.7	4.4
Cyprus	144,365	797,341	18.1	5	55.1	10.0	6	89.4	16.2
Barbados	63,002	199,045	31.7	7	50.5	16.0	8	95.9	30.3
Trinidad	230,672	2,563,756	9.0	2	48.7	4.4	4	77.9	7.0
Belize	315,227	356,346	88.5	5	31.6	27.9	6	83.5	73.9
Fiji	240,425	595,399	40.4	7	28.8	11.6	7	28.8	11.6
Seychelles	135,850	148,368	91.6	2	24.5	22.4	2	24.5	22.4
Bahamas	339,055	830,498	40.8	1	22.8	9.3	1	22.8	9.3
Swaziland	123,002	139,004	88.5	3	20.4	18.1	3	20.4	18.1
Guyana	259,082	544,867	47.5	2	19.8	9.4	3	43.8	20.8
Mauritius	416,936	1,623,513	25.7	1	10.0	2.6	2	20.2	5.2
Bahrain	6,324	1,528,823	0.4	0	0.0	0.0	0	0.0	0.0
Gabon	17,238	3,298,542	0.5	0	0.0	0.0	0	0.0	0.0
Malta	16,122	1,789,395	0.9	0	0.0	0.0	0	0.0	0.0
Qatar	1,028	6,058,264	0.0	0	0.0	0.0	0	0.0	0.0

Table 1 (*cont.*)

	Exports			max. share of world imports: 0.3 %			max. share of world imports: 0.5 %		
					% share covered of			% share covered of	
	agric. $ '000	total $ '000	agric. as % total	no. chapters covered	agr. expts	total expts	no. chapters covered	agr. expts	total expts
Average			**35.5**	**3.1**	**73.5**	**27.4**	**3.3**	**77.4**	**29.1**
No. with share >90%					**29**			**29**	
No. with share >75%					**30**			**34**	
No. with share <25%					**8**			**7**	

Table 2 *Other principal beneficiaries from de minimis rule (0.3 or 0.5 per cent world trade) applied to agriculture at two-digit level (only countries with over 50 per cent of agricultural exports covered by the rule are individually cited)*

	exports			max. share of world imports: 0.3 %			max. share of world imports: 0.5 %		
					% share covered of			% share covered of	
	agric. $ '000	total $ '000	agric. as % total	no. chapters covered	agr. expts	total expts	no. chapters covered	agr. expts	total expts
LDCs									
Lesotho	399	15,926	2.5	1	100.0	2.5	1	100.0	2.5
Somalia	9,524	11,611	82.0	4	99.7	81.8	3	20.1	16.5
Rwanda	32,193	42,349	76.0	3	99.3	75.5	3	99.3	75.5
Afghanistan	20,142	59,750	33.7	4	98.8	33.3	4	98.8	33.3
Mozambique	116,698	231,035	50.5	6	98.2	49.6	5	95.7	48.3
Burkina Faso	32,677	140,762	23.2	4	97.9	22.7	4	97.9	22.7
Togo	54,702	231,668	23.6	6	94.7	22.4	6	94.7	22.4
Haiti	34,027	336,217	10.1	5	93.5	9.5	5	93.5	9.5
Benin	26,505	153,461	17.3	4	91.3	15.8	4	91.3	15.8
Cent. Afr. Rep.	13,524	208,545	6.5	3	90.1	5.8	3	90.1	5.8
Sierra Leone	6,371	79,906	8.0	3	87.5	7.0	3	87.5	7.0
Guinea	51,161	728,280	7.0	3	86.7	6.1	3	86.7	6.1
Congo, DR	52,662	1,194,832	4.4	1	77.8	3.4	1	77.8	3.4
Yemen	36,503	1,920,024	1.9	1	75.9	1.4	1	75.9	1.4
Nepal	8,879	385,205	2.3	2	71.9	1.7	2	71.9	1.7
Angola	36,950	4,774,590	0.8	1	65.1	0.5	1	65.1	0.5
Madagascar	343,843	747,815	46.0	8	60.9	28.0	8	60.9	28.0
Zambia	59,409	567,601	10.5	4	58.8	6.2	5	89.7	9.4

Table 2 (*cont.*)

	exports			max. share of world imports: 0.3 %			max. share of world imports: 0.5 %		
					% share covered of			% share covered of	
	agric. $ '000	total $ '000	agric. as % total	no. chapters covered	agr. expts	tota l expts	no. chapters covered	agr. expts	total expts
average (all LDCs)			**31.7**	**2.8**	**53.1**	**13.9**	**3.0**	**58.6**	**16.1**
No. with share >90%					**6**			**6**	
No. with share >75%					**14**			**16**	
No. with share <25%					**13**			**11**	
Other developing countries									
Korea, DPR	102,386	854,163	12.0	3	96.8	11.6	3	96.8	11.6
Oman	40,541	5,364,417	0.8	1	84.4	0.6	1	84.4	0.6
Congo	29,925	1,820,687	1.6	2	82.7	1.4	2	82.7	1.4
Lebanon	50,559	489,892	10.3	6	78.4	8.1	6	78.4	8.1
Cambodia	24,709	1,186,370	2.1	1	70.0	1.5	1	70.0	1.5
Jordan	24,191	451,293	5.4	3	69.8	3.7	2	51.8	2.8
Nicaragua	433,076	803,675	53.9	9	55.0	29.6	10	62.2	33.5
average (all other dev'g c'tries)			**22.6**	**1.9**	**17.3**	**3.1**	**2.4**	**22.0**	**4.3**
No. with share >90%					**0**			**0**	
No. with share >75%					**0**			**0**	
No. with share <25%					**16**			**11**	
Countries in transition									
Armenia	17,639	147,300	12.0	4	97.4	11.7	4	97.4	11.7
Georgia	70,477	318,783	22.1	7	96.1	21.2	7	96.1	21.2
Tajikistan	31,321	259,511	12.1	5	90.8	11.0	6	96.5	11.7

Mongolia	24,358	369,488	6.6	3	88.5	5.8	3	88.5	5.8
Azerbaijan	77,446	662,730	11.7	4	83.8	9.8	4	83.8	9.8
Albania	25,655	256,073	10.0	5	82.7	8.3	5	82.7	8.3
Uzbekistan	142,000	1,424,079	10.0	4	80.4	8.0	4	80.4	8.0
Lithuania	322,426	2,775,181	11.6	6	52.1	6.1	6	52.1	6.1
average (all countries in transition)			**11.5**	**3.1**	**44.0**	**5.7**	**3.5**	**53.9**	**7.6**
No. with share >90%					**2**			**4**	
No. with share >75%					**7**			**10**	
No. with share <25%					**8**			**6**	

Table 3 *Coverage of 3 per cent de minimis rule, eight-digit tariff lines in agriculture (HS sections 01–24), EU imports (1998–9)*

	Number of 8-digit tariff lines	Covered exports, ECU '000	Percent. total exports
Solomon Is.	9	29,886	93.0
São Tomé Principe	13	8,335	80.8
St Vincent	10	31,000	71.7
Guinea-Bissau	20	6,391	68.9
St Lucia	6	51,313	67.4
Dominica	8	22,648	57.2
Barbados	7	25,531	31.4
Belize	17	56,563	30.3
Kiribati	6	538	29.9
Antigua	14	1,116	22.4
Maldives	4	13,581	21.5
St Kitts & Nevis	3	8,768	21.4
Djibouti	22	1,205	19.8
Vanuatu	7	2,684	15.3
Cape Verde	19	1,582	15.1
Gambia	14	12,559	14.5
Suriname	7	30,913	11.7
Grenada	11	2,614	9.9
Western Samoa	2	828	9.0
Seychelles	10	7,821	7.7
Swaziland	17	12,094	7.2
Tonga	5	361	6.5
Cyprus	15	19,664	6.2

Cook Is., Tokelau Is., Niue	9	308	5.4
Micronesia, FS	2	505	4.6
Fiji	3	5,835	2.7
Equatorial Guinea	2	7,279	2.3
Nauru	2	21	2.2
Trinidad & Tobago	3	27,079	2.0
Marshall Islands	1	108	1.6
Comoros	1	106	1.3
Estonia	5	14,405	0.9
Tuvalu	4	48	0.9
Bhutan	3	18	0.8
Botswana	3	1,863	0.8
Guyana	3	1,599	0.6
Bahamas	2	1,966	0.5
Gabon	2	7,205	0.4
Mauritius	1	2,826	0.2
Malta	1	1,119	0.1
Bahrain	1	409	0.1
Palau	0	0	0.0
Qatar	0	0	0.0
Total	294	420,686	1.5[a]

[a] Percentage of total EU 1998–9 imports of agricultural products (HS sections 1–24)

Table 4 *Summary results of de minimis analysis: shares of world imports covered by country group (six-digit HS products groups, 1999, $ '000 and per cent)*

Maximum share in world imports %	2.0	3.0	4.0
Small states (45)			
av. no. of products lines covered	15.8	16.5	16.8
av. share expts. covered	64.9	74.0	77.4
no. with share > 90%	11	15	17
no. with share > 75%	20	26	28
no. with share < 25 %	4	1	0
share of world impts. covered	43.3	64.8	67.7
LDCs (exc. small states) (33)			
av. no. of products lines covered	10.6	11.6	12.3
av. share expts. covered	50.4	62.1	71.0
no. with share > 90%	4	4	7
no. with share > 75%	11	14	19
no. with share < 25 %	11	5	2
share of world impts. covered	31.3	54.7	66.5
Other developing countries (54)			
av. no. of products lines covered	9.5	11.6	13.1
av. share expts. covered	24.3	31.4	36.9
no. with share > 90%	0	2	3
no. with share > 75%	3	5	9
no. with share < 25%	34	24	20
share of world impts. covered	5.3	7.9	9.7

Countries in transition (24)			
av. no. of products lines covered	19.7	22.7	24.1
av. share expts. covered	41.1	48.8	53.5
no. with share > 90%	0	0	2
no. with share > 75%	3	5	6
no. with share < 25%	7	6	4
share of world impts. covered	11.9	15.2	17.0
High-income countries (exc. small states) (5)			
av. no. of products lines covered	0.4	0.6	0.8
av. share expts. covered	12.9	16.7	36.2
no. with share > 90%	0	0	1
no. with share > 75%	0	0	1
no. with share < 25 %	4	4	3
share of world impts. covered	3.1	8.3	16.3
All countries (161)			
av. no. of products lines covered	12.9	14.5	15.5
av. share expts. covered	43.3	51.8	57.7
no. with share > 90%	15	21	30
no. with share > 75%	37	50	63
no. with share < 20%	60	40	29
share of world impts. from non-OECD covered	6.9	10.5	13.2
share of total world impts. (incl. OECD)	2.3	3.6	4.5

Table 5 *Results of de minimis analysis: shares of world imports covered by country group (six-digit HS products groups, 1999, $ '000 and per cent, ranked by share covered under 3 per cent rule)*

		de minimis share								
		2.0			3.0			4.0		
	total exports, $ '000	no. of lines covered	exports covered, $ '000	% total exports covered	no. of lines covered	exports covered, $ '000	% total exports covered	no. of lines covered	exports covered, $ '000	% total exports covered
Small states										
Niue	664	17	664	100.0	17	664	100.0	17	664	100.0
Tuvalu	1,483	24	1,483	100.0	24	1,483	100.0	24	1,483	100.0
Bhutan	1,652	30	1,652	100.0	30	1,652	100.0	30	1,652	100.0
Botswana	441,564	4	90,104	20.4	5	430,187	97.4	5	430,187	97.4
Guinea-Bissau	30,323	13	29,502	97.3	13	29,502	97.3	13	29,502	97.3
Palau	38,172	13	24,511	64.2	14	37,035	97.0	14	37,035	97.0
Kiribati	6,444	9	6,233	96.7	9	6,233	96.7	9	6,233	96.7
Cook Islands	5,298	18	5,072	95.7	18	5,072	95.7	18	5,072	95.7
Tonga	17,170	17	16,095	93.7	18	16,370	95.3	18	16,370	95.3
Gambia	88,832	10	67,219	75.7	11	86,388	94.2	11	83,688	94.2
São Tomé	14,418	21	13,582	94.2	21	13,582	94.2	21	13,582	94.2
Cape Verde	20,743	15	19,375	93.4	15	19,375	93.4	15	19,375	93.4
Djibouti	44,503	11	41,484	93.2	11	41,484	93.2	11	41,484	93.2
Maldives	146,113	17	123,016	84.2	18	134,480	92.0	18	134,480	92.0
St Kitts and Nevis	48,265	17	44,045	91.3	17	44,045	91.3	17	44,045	91.3
Swaziland	139,004	10	23,394	16.8	12	124,377	89.5	12	124,377	89.5
Eritrea	10,095	21	8,983	89.0	21	8,983	89.0	21	8,983	89.0

St Lucia	88,636	18	78,329	88.4	18	78,329	88.4	18	78,329	88.4
Samoa	49,764	9	42,761	85.9	9	42,761	85.9	10	45,282	91.0
St Vincent	203,016	13	118,367	58.3	14	173,487	85.5	14	173,487	85.5
Bahrain	1,528,823	15	1,015,798	66.4	18	1,273,569	83.3	19	1,290,014	84.4
Dominica	90,147	21	69,626	77.2	22	74,124	82.2	22	74,124	82.2
Equatorial Guinea	674,659	6	539,456	80.0	7	546,899	81.1	8	586,490	86.9
Antigua	19,315	32	15,555	80.5	32	15,555	80.5	32	15,555	80.5
Malta	1,789,395	24	1,41,4856	79.1	24	1,414,856	79.1	24	1,414,856	79.1
Qatar	6,058,264	4	343,376	5.7	7	4,703,572	77.6	8	4,803,452	79.3
Barbados	199,045	31	148,942	74.8	31	148,942	74.8	31	148,942	74.8
Solomon Is.	111,832	10	31,315	28.0	12	82,261	73.6	12	82,261	73.6
Belize	356,346	19	235,976	66.2	20	240,038	67.4	21	257,876	72.4
Mauritius	1,623,513	15	639,662	39.4	20	1,047,964	64.5	20	1,047,964	64.5
Trinidad	2,563,756	8	1,425,586	55.6	10	1,487,557	58.0	12	1,521,175	59.3
Gabon	3,298,542	1	1,848,381	56.0	2	1,870,452	56.7	2	1,870,452	56.7
Comoros	19,172	16	10,554	55.0	16	10,554	55.0	16	10,554	55.0
Vanuatu	33,476	14	18,329	54.8	14	18,329	54.8	14	18,329	54.8
Micronesia, FS	52,485	10	28,574	54.4	10	28,574	54.4	10	28,574	54.4
Cyprus	797,341	25	420,508	52.7	26	432,062	54.2	27	438,661	55.0
Fiji	595,399	34	295,730	49.7	36	319,031	53.6	37	474,358	79.7
Grenada	41,037	14	21,913	53.4	14	21,913	53.4	14	21,913	53.4
Estonia	2,938,907	23	1,275,133	43.4	23	1,275,133	43.4	26	1,491,023	50.7
Suriname	574,716	11	227,547	39.6	11	227,547	39.6	11	227,547	39.6
Guyana	544,867	13	207,073	38.0	14	212,215	38.9	16	352,432	64.7
Marshall Is.	40,437	5	14,936	36.9	5	14,936	36.9	5	14,936	36.9
Bahamas	830,498	14	261,719	31.5	16	277,799	33.4	16	277,799	33.4
Seychelles	148,368	13	37,169	25.1	13	37,169	25.1	13	37,169	25.1
Nauru	29,163	7	4,615	15.8	7	4,615	15.8	8	27,875	95.6

Table 5 (*cont.*)

		de minimis share								
		2.0			3.0			4.0		
	total exports, $ '000	no. of lines covered	exports covered, $ '000	% total exports covered	no. of lines covered	exports covered, $ '000	% total exports covered	no. of lines covered	exports covered, $ '000	% total exports covered
LCDs										
Lesotho	15,926	5	15,683	98.5	5	15,683	98.5	5	15,683	98.5
Burundi	62,551	5	60,924	97.4	5	60,924	97.4	5	60,924	97.4
Central African Rep.	208,545	6	202,305	97.0	6	202,305	97.0	6	202,305	97.0
Yemen	1,920,024	2	1,859,838	96.9	2	1,859,838	96.9	2	1,859,838	96.9
Burkina Faso	140,762	6	112,618	80.0	8	126,594	89.9	8	126,594	89.9
Lao PDR	235,326	34	207,768	88.3	34	207,768	88.3	34	207,768	88.3
Angola	4,774,590	1	87,255	1.8	2	4,151,284	86.9	3	4,697,845	98.4
Rwanda	42,349	9	36,159	85.4	10	36,696	86.7	10	36,696	86.7
Chad	101,585	2	86,746	85.4	2	86,746	85.4	2	86,746	85.4
Sierra Leone	79,906	15	67,840	84.9	15	67,840	84.9	15	67,840	84.9
Tanzania, Utd Rep.	441,072	24	356,686	80.9	25	361,135	81.9	26	373,655	84.7
Mozambique	231,035	26	180,901	78.3	27	183,631	79.5	27	183,631	79.5
Benin	153,461	7	8,573	5.6	9	121,249	79.0	9	121,249	79.0
Haiti	336,217	23	240,656	71.6	27	261,274	77.7	27	261,274	77.7
Ethiopia	335,069	5	26,011	7.8	7	249,146	74.4	9	256,501	76.6
Afghanistan	59,750	8	13,242	22.2	11	42,558	71.2	11	42,558	71.2
Sudan	479,394	8	316,416	66.0	9	338,223	70.6	10	349,104	72.8
Togo	231,668	10	138,742	59.9	13	162,402	70.1	14	178,833	77.2

Madagascar	747,815	25	490,215	65.6	25	490,215	65.6	25	490,215	65.6
Liberia	598,111	8	359,468	60.1	9	390,880	65.4	10	527,209	88.1
Niger	293,324	5	168,135	57.3	5	168,135	57.3	5	168,135	57.3
Myanmar	1,080,187	27	554,713	51.4	29	614,399	56.9	29	614,399	56.9
Zambia	567,601	11	108,788	19.2	13	304,335	53.6	15	320,240	56.4
Senegal	514,168	14	241,201	46.9	14	241,201	46.9	15	289,158	56.2
Guinea	728,280	13	337,678	46.4	13	337,678	46.4	13	337,678	46.4
Nepal	385,205	22	166,110	43.1	22	166,110	43.1	22	166,110	43.1
Somalia	11,611	12	3,522	30.3	12	3,522	30.3	12	3,522	30.3
Uganda	427,612	8	82,192	19.2	10	108,029	25.3	11	399,833	93.5
Malawi	503,079	12	85,500	17.0	13	119,970	23.8	14	124,724	24.8
Bangladesh	4,912,592	7	365,257	7.4	10	746,599	15.2	14	1,805,653	36.8
Congo, DR	1,194,832	4	179,899	15.1	4	179,899	15.1	4	179,899	15.1
Mali	238,439	7	19,574	8.2	7	19,574	8.2	9	218,475	91.6
Mauritania	582,618	3	38,799	6.7	3	38,799	6.7	5	327,439	56.2
Other developing countries										
Oman	5,364,417	3	194,574	3.6	4	5,056,862	94.3	4	5,056,862	94.3
Congo	1,820,687	9	1,636,076	89.9	10	1,657,410	91.0	10	1,657,410	91.0
Syrian AR	2,867,613	6	2,382,211	83.1	7	2,537,635	88.5	8	2,560,271	89.3
Cambodia	1,186,370	27	937,686	79.0	27	937,686	79.0	29	957,787	80.7
Nicaragua	803,675	20	600,527	74.7	22	629,849	78.4	22	629,849	78.4
Lebanon	489,892	19	320,583	65.4	22	366,692	74.9	23	378,790	77.3
Namibia	535,415	12	315,567	58.9	13	399,647	74.6	14	406,142	75.9
Bolivia	944,354	18	458,807	48.6	20	588,809	62.4	23	736,886	78.0
Cameroon	1,889,290	8	1,035,160	54.8	9	1,142,296	60.5	10	1,220,385	64.6
Egypt	4,133,097	17	2,348,224	56.8	21	2,471,592	59.8	22	2,638,504	63.8
Papua New Guinea	1,975,562	6	1,092,380	55.3	7	1,122,399	56.8	7	1,122,399	56.8

Table 5 (*cont.*)

		de minimis share								
		2.0			3.0			4.0		
	total exports, $ '000	no. of lines covered	exports covered, $ '000	% total exports covered	no. of lines covered	exports covered, $ '000	% total exports covered	no. of lines covered	exports covered, $ '000	% total exports covered
Countries in transition										
Turkmenistan	458,148	12	270,645	59.1	13	410,486	89.6	14	418,440	91.3
Azerbaijan	662,730	9	576,106	86.9	11	592,753	89.4	12	596,800	90.1
Armenia	147,300	15	126,877	86.1	17	128,778	87.4	17	128,778	87.4
Tajikistan	259,511	17	224,101	86.4	18	225,422	86.9	18	225,422	86.9
Georgia	318,783	28	226,754	71.1	32	265,785	83.4	34	274,481	86.1
Albania	256,073	26	114,640	44.8	29	184,472	72.0	29	184,472	72.0
Kyrgyzstan	306,223	15	207,330	67.7	15	207,330	67.7	16	256,988	83.9
Moldova, Rep.	640,062	30	228,287	35.7	37	392,143	61.3	38	397,626	62.1
Macedonia, FYR	870,447	40	450,398	51.7	42	520,505	59.8	43	570,795	65.6
Bosnia/Herzegovina	500,287	34	246,708	49.3	36	265,686	53.1	36	265,686	53.1
Kazakhstan	4,950,620	12	2,165,032	43.7	17	2,560,959	51.7	21	2,798,031	56.5
Latvia	2,340,537	15	697,262	29.8	18	1,186,625	50.7	20	1,331,258	56.9

Table 6 *Principal exports of small states with lowest coverage by 3 per cent de minimis rule (1999, $ '000 and %)*

HS code	short description	exports $'000	share of country exports, %	share of world imports, %	covered by 3% rule
Suriname					
281810	artificial corundum	322,147	56.1	93.8	no
710811	gold (powder etc.)	47,734	8.3	32.3	no
270820	pitch coke	46,100	8.0	69.2	no
030612	frozen lobsters	38,449	6.7	16.3	no
080290	nuts, other	27,610	4.8	7.6	no
750890	articles of nickel	19,895	3.5	10.7	no
711100	silver, gold/platinum-clad	10,641	1.9	55.3	no
030378	frozen hake	9,637	1.7	5.1	no
Guyana					
170111	raw cane sugar	135,244	24.8	26.3	no
710812	gold	118,278	21.7	5.2	no
260600	aluminium ores, concentrates	91,662	16.8	0.6	yes
100620	husked or brown rice	51,491	9.5	7.8	no
Marshall Is.					
030343	frozen skipjack etc.	24,571	60.8	4.8	no
890120	tankers	8,349	20.6	0.4	yes
030342	frozen yellowfin tuna	3,484	8.6	0.0	yes

Table 6 (*cont.*)

HS code	short description	exports $'000	share of country exports, %	share of world imports, %	covered by 3% rule
Bahamas					
220840	rum and taffia	254,208	30.6	49.4	no
890392	motorboats and yachts	115,143	13.9	5.0	no
880230	light aeroplanes	85,931	10.3	0.5	yes
030611	frozen rock lobster etc.	73,770	8.9	11.2	no
271000	petroleum oils	61,547	7.4	0.1	yes
390311	primary polystyrene	39,865	4.8	4.8	no
Seychelles					
160414	tuna, skipjack etc.	100,764	67.9	19.6	no
030343	frozen skipjack	6,012	4.1	0.3	yes
030342	frozen yellowfin	5,746	3.9	0.0	yes
030420	frozen fillets	4,967	3.3	0.8	yes
030349	other frozen tuna	4,630	3.1	0.0	yes
Nauru					
251010	phosphates	23,260	79.8	4.5	no
290243	p-xylene	1,512	5.2	0.1	yes
290321	chloroethylene	1,318	4.5	0.0	yes

Table 7 *Principal exports of all developing countries covered by 3 per cent de minimis rule (1999, six-digit classification)*

HS code	short description	share total covered exports, %	cumulative share covered, %
270900	petroleum, crude	31.4	31.4
271000	petroleum, other	9.6	41.0
847330	vehicle parts	6.3	47.3
854213	semiconductor circuits	2.7	50.0
710812	gold	2.0	52.0
090111	coffee	1.9	53.8
611020	cotton jerseys etc.	1.6	55.4
854230	integrated circuits	1.5	56.9
620342	cotton men's trousers	1.4	58.2
870323	motor cars	1.3	59.5
847160	data-processing units	1.3	60.8
710239	diamonds	1.2	62.0
610910	cotton t-shirts etc.	1.2	63.2
854219	integrated circuits	1.2	64.4
852990	radio parts	1.1	65.5
620462	cotton women's trousers	1.1	66.6
847170	data-processing units	1.0	67.7
520100	cotton	1.0	68.7
710231	diamonds	1.0	69.7
620520	cotton men's shirts	1.0	70.6
440710	coniferous wood	1.0	71.6
030613	frozen shrimps	0.9	72.5
640399	footwear, leather uppers	0.8	73.3
300490	medicaments	0.7	74.1
852520	radio parts	0.7	74.8

Table 7 (*cont.*)

HS code	short description	share total covered exports, %	cumulative share covered, %
880240	aircraft	0.7	75.5
611030	jerseys, man-made fibres	0.6	76.1
854240	integrated circuits	0.6	76.7
880230	aircraft	0.6	77.3
760120	aluminium alloys	0.6	77.9
711319	jewellery	0.6	78.4
740311	copper cathodes	0.5	79.0
170111	raw cane sugar	0.5	79.5
870899	vehicle parts	0.5	80.0
760110	aluminium	0.5	80.5
854430	ignition sets	0.4	80.9
080300	bananas	0.4	81.3
610510	cotton men's shirts	0.4	81.6
260111	iron ores	0.3	82.0
420292	travel bags etc.	0.3	82.3
271112	propane, liquefied	0.3	82.6
271121	natural gas	0.3	82.9
870322	motor cars	0.3	83.2
621210	brassières	0.3	83.5
611010	wool jerseys etc.	0.3	83.7
850440	static converters	0.3	84.0
901890	medical instruments	0.3	84.3
271600	electrical energy	0.3	84.5
620640	w's shirts, man-made fibres	0.2	84.8

Table 8 *Share of major beneficiaries' total exports of principal non-zero tariff lines covered by 3 per cent de minimis rule*

HS code	short description	country and share expts. covered, %		country and share expts. covered, %		country and share expts. covered, %		country and share expts. covered, %		country and share expts. covered, %	
030613	frozen shrimps	Mozambique	35.2	Madagascar	12.3	Myanmar	9.2	Belize	8.9	Senegal	8.1
080300	bananas	St Lucia	60.8	Dominica	25.6	St Vincent	15.6	Belize	10.4	Cameroon	5.7
420292	travel bags etc.	Sri Lanka	2.0	Viet Nam	1.8	Myanmar	0.6	Philippines	0.5		
610510	men's cotton shirts	Palau	25.7	Mauritius	4.5	Micronesia, FS	4.1	Haiti	3.0	Myanmar	2.8
610910	cotton t-shirts etc.	Haiti	37.9	Mauritius	11.8	Jamaica	6.9	Dominican Republic	4.4	Cambodia	3.7
611010	jerseys, wool	Madagascar	10.0	Mauritius	5.0	Mongolia	2.1	Jamaica	2.1	Tunisia	1.5
611020	cotton jerseys etc.	Cambodia	11.5	Palau	11.3	Fiji	5.7	Guatemala	5.4	Mauritius	5.3
611030	jerseys, man-made fabric	Cambodia	12.9	Lao PDR	10.0	Myanmar	4.6	Sri Lanka	3.3	Morocco	2.0
61	**total chapter 61**	**Cambodia**	**15.9**	**Maldives**	**14.9**	**Nicaragua**	**10.8**				
620342	men's cotton trousers	Maldives	9.0	Cambodia	8.4	Nicaragua	7.8	Nepal	6.3	Bangladesh	4.5
620462	women's cotton trousers	Cape Verde	10.1	Macedonia, FYR	6.8	Mauritius	6.8	Nepal	6.7	Nicaragua	4.9
620520	men's cotton suits	Macedonia, FYR	3.0	Sri Lanka	2.0	Lithuania	1.3	Cyprus	1.2	Bulgaria	1.1
620640	women's blouses, man-made fabric	Haiti	2.7	St Lucia	2.3	Barbados	1.8	Sri Lanka	1.7	Morocco	1.4

Table 8 (*cont.*)

HS code	short description	country and share expts. covered, %		country and share expts. covered, %		country and share expts. covered, %		country and share expts. covered, %		country and share expts. covered, %	
621210	brassières	Tuvalu	7.0	Cape Verde	6.2	Bosnia/ Herzegovina	3.6	Romania	3.1	Sierra Leone	2.3
62	**total chapter 62**	**Bahrain**	**11.6**	**Somalia**	**5.5**	**Tajikistan**	**2.9**				
640399	footwear, leather uppers	Tajikistan	43.4	Bosnia/ Herzegovina	10.1	Bahrain	8.6	Yugoslavia	7.1	Ghana	6.1
760120	alum. alloys, unwrought	Sierra Leone	16.5	Cyprus	6.2	South Africa	3.1	Korea, DPR	2.2	Argentina	2.1
760110	aluminium, unwrought	Slovenia	1.4	Brazil	0.7	Argentina	0.6	Uruguay	0.6	Venezuela	0.6

Table 9 *Impact on other exporters of full utilisation of 3 per cent de minimis rule*

HS Code	short description	world share of covered imports, %	no. of countries covered	possible share of world trade %	Fall in total exports of most vulnerable developing countries, %					
030613	frozen shrimps	16.7	73	100.0	Ecuador	11.3	Bangladesh	5.0	Viet Nam	3.7
080300	bananas	10.7	25	75.0	Ecuador	17.8	Panama	10.8	Costa Rica	8.9
420292	travel bags etc.	6.8	5	15.0	China	0.1				
610510	men's cotton shirts	17.1	40	100.0	Hong Kong	1.2	China	0.4	Botswana	0.0
610910	cotton t-shirts etc.	20.1	85	84.9	Honduras	5.7	Hong Kong	1.0	India	0.6
611010	jerseys, wool	9.9	29	87.0	Bangladesh	5.5	Hong Kong	1.5	China	0.6
611020	jerseys, cotton	23.7	72	100.0	Honduras	10.7	El Salvador	8.3		
611030	jerseys, man-made fabrics	10.1	53	100.0	Honduras	3.7	Pakistan	3.0	Peru	1.6
620342	men's cotton trousers	18.5	89	100.0	Dominican Rep.	8.1	Tunisia	7.0	Bangladesh	5.8
620462	women's cotton trousers	20.3	55	100.0	Tunisia	4.1	Hong Kong	1.5	China	0.4
620520	men's cotton suits	22.7	58	100.0	Bangladesh	7.0	Hong Kong	1.0	India	1.0
620640	women's blouses, man-made fabric	12.3	15	45.0	Romania	0.5	Morocco	0.5	Hong Kong	0.2
621210	brassières	10.7	37	100.0	Honduras	3.5	Dominican Rep.	3.3	Tunisia	1.9
640399	footwear, leather uppers	9.0	45	100.0	Viet Nam	4.9	Brazil	2.0	China	1.8
760120	alum. alloys, unwrought	6.2	24	72.0	UAE	1.6	Russian Fed.	0.9	Botswana	0.0
760110	aluminium, unwrought	10.3	26	78.0	Russian Fed.	4.1	South Africa	1.9		

Table 10 *Estimated revenue loss to EU of giving tariff-free access on existing quantities of imports for principal tariff lines covered by 3 per cent de minimis rule (ECU million and %)*

HS Code	short description	principal EU GSP tariff rate	EU imports excl. ACP and LDC, av. 1998–99, ECU '000	Tariff loss, ECU '000
030613	frozen shrimps	4.2	5,527	232
080300	bananas	16.0	21,132	3,381
420292	travel bags etc.	3.3	735	24
610510	men's cotton shirts	10.2	5,374	548
610910	cotton t-shirts etc.	10.2	210,871	21,509
611010	jerseys, wool	10.2	212,410	21,666
611020	cotton jerseys etc.	10.2	346,136	35,306
611030	jerseys, man-made fabric	10.2	362,281	36,953
620342	men's cotton trousers	10.8	631,689	68,222
620462	women's cotton trousers	10.8	1,097,174	118,495
620520	men's cotton suits	10.8	981,327	105,983
620640	women's blouses, man-made fabric	10.8	378,704	40,900
621210	brassières	5.5	811	45
640399	footwear, leather uppers	5.6	530,215	29,692
760110	aluminium, unwrought	6.0	428,717	25,723
760120	alum. alloys, unwrought	6.0	287,129	17,228
	Totals		5,500,232	525,907

Appendix 10.4 Notes on data sources

The purpose was to base the calculations of the impact of the de minimis principle on as comprehensive a database as possible. There is apparently no readily available database of exports by all countries at any level of disaggregation, whether using the SITC or HS system. Clearly the HS system is to be preferred as this permits the examination of tariff and NTB barriers (though these are typically based on the HS eight-digit or higher classification). The six-digit classification is the maximum disaggregation which is common to all countries using the HS system.

Not all countries report their exports by destination and to have relied on those that do so would have meant that a large number of small countries – the focus of the study – would have been excluded. Thus the database had to be constructed on the basis of UN Statistics Division–UNCTAD reported imports by country source. The number of 'reporter' countries has been increasing. For the year 1999 sixty-six countries reported, including all the OECD and many large developing countries.[33] The reported imports by source were then aggregated over the roughly 50,000 HS six-digit product lines.

The intention had been to use two years' average: 1998 and 1999 were selected since our source of data, the UNCTAD TRAINS database, does not yet cover the year 2000.[34] (The other UN database, PC-TAS, which has data for 2000, was discarded because certain data refers to customs unions, e.g. SACU, and are not available for the members independently.) However, it was found that 1998 import data for at least one country, Tuvalu, had not yet been incorporated in the system. Secondly, the data for 1999 was more complete because there were more reporter countries for that year. Comparing the two years, for 1998 our aggregated data accounted for 61.6 per cent of total world imports (the sum of total imports which is reported by all UN member countries). For 1999 it accounted for 68.1 per cent. If the de minimis principle were to be implemented, an average of two or three years would be appropriate, though a prior exercise to minimise missing data would be desirable through a drive to promote the number of reporter countries.

The main source of the shortfall in the disaggregated data relative to the total of reported world imports is the fact that not all shipments are identified by country of origin. This could lead to bias if small shipments are more likely to be unidentified by source country and small shipments tend to come from a particular group of countries, who might plausibly be the SS. This would lead to a relative underreporting of imports from the SS and a greater probability that their export lines would meet the de minimis criteria. Whether this leads to a serious bias could only be investigated by examining the procedures of customs officials in different countries. However, if the de minimis principle were accepted it would be necessary to ensure an improved recording of sources of imports.

[33] The following were the largest countries not to report: Bangladesh, Egypt, India, Iran, Pakistan, the Philippines, Saudi Arabia and Ukraine.

[34] The TRAINS database is on imports at the most detailed level of the Harmonized System, i.e. the six-digit level, obtained directly from the reporter countries or indirectly through the Latin American Integration Association (LAIA), the European Union (EU), the Inter-American Development Bank (IDB), the Board for the Cartagena Agreement (JUNAC), the World Trade Organization (WTO) and the United Nations Statistical Division (UNSD). For details see UNCTAD (2001b).

Of course, the calculations are based on import data, when it might seem more logical to base the de minimis rules on shares in world exports. It will be many years before all small states – and even some big ones – report exports at the six-digit level. If share in world exports is indeed the appropriate criterion, there may be a small bias in the calculations if the exports of particular countries are characterised by a larger or smaller than average cif mark-up. Since many small states are remote and the percentage cif mark-up on their exports may be above that of the world for the same products, using import data may discriminate against those countries in terms of meeting the de minimis criterion.

Another source of bias, again probably small, might have crept in if in fact there were a pattern of non-reporting countries importing more or less from the small states or any other group of countries than the world as a whole does. This, of course, is difficult to assess since we do not have data on the pattern of imports of the non-reporters.

Bibliography

Briguglio, L. (1995), 'Small Island Developing States and their Economic Vulnerabilities', *World Development*, vol. 23, no. 9

Commonwealth Advisor Group (1997), *A Future for Small States: Overcoming Vulnerability*, London: Commonwealth Secretariat

Commonwealth Secretariat, World Bank (2000), *Small States: Meeting Challenges in the Global Economy*, Report of the Commonwealth Secretariat/World Bank Joint Task Force on Small States, London, Washington D.C.

Everitt, Brian (1980), *Cluster Analysis*, New York: Halsted Press

GATT Secretariat (1994), *The Results of the Uruguay Round of Multilateral Trade Negotiations: The Legal Texts*, Geneva

Grynberg, Roman (forthcoming), *A Theory of Trade and Development of Small Vulnerable States*

Read, Robert (1988), 'A Comparison of the Performance of the Different Micro-States and between Micro-States and Larger Countries', *World Development*, vol. 26, no. 4

Shirotori, Miho (2001), *WTO Negotiations on Agriculture: Negotiating Issues in the Second Phase*, UNCTAD, May

Sokal, R. R., and Sneath, P. H. A. (1963), *Principles of Numerical Taxonomy*, San Francisco: Freeman

South Pacific Forum (2001), 'Options for a Definition of Small Vulnerable States', paper prepared for the meeting of the Second Inter-Governmental Organisation Meeting of Small Island States, London, March 22–23

UNCTAD (1998), 'Ways and Means of Enhancing the Utilization of Trade Preferences by Developing Countries, in particular LDCs, as well as further ways of Expanding Preferences', Trade and Development Board, TD/B/COMESA.1/20, Geneva, 21 July

UNCTAD (2001a), *Handbook of Statistics, 2000*, Geneva and New York

UNCTAD (2001b), *A User Manual for TRAINS (Trade Analysis and Information System)*, Geneva

UNCTAD/Commonwealth Secretariat (2001), *Duty and Quota Free Market Access for LDCs: An Analysis of Quad Initiatives*, London, Geneva

United Nations (1998a), 'Development of a Vulnerability Index for Small States', Report to the Secretary General, Draft, New York

(1998b), 'How to Include an Index of Vulnerability in the Criteria for Identifying the LDCs?', Draft, CDP12.98/WG3/3, New York, 8 September

WTO (2000), Negotiations on Agriculture, 'Proposals by Small, Island Developing States', G/AG/NG/W/97

World Bank (2001), *World Development Indicators*, Washington D.C.

PART III

WTO dispute settlement

11

Small states in the banana dispute: implications of EU reforms for Eastern Caribbean islands and lessons for the future

EDWIN LAURENT

11.1 Introduction

The high-profile and long-running transatlantic dispute over the European Union's banana import regime was widely perceived as a straightforward fracas between the EU on the one hand and the US and Latin American exporters on the other. In reality however, it involved a diverse mix of participants, including some of the world's smallest states, which had a decisive bearing on the evolution of the regime. Among the most determined and active were Caribbean exporters, led by the tiny Windward Islands.[1] This study examines their performance, the implications for them of the outcome of the dispute and the lessons to be learnt, amongst the most intriguing of which is that their size does not automatically preclude small states from actually being more than passive onlookers in the processes of international decision-making that determine their future.

11.1.1 What was the dispute?

The trigger that precipitated the 'banana war' was the approach to the unification of the European Communities markets from 1 January 1993. Prior to this, the various Member States had operated their own import arrangements for bananas, in some cases applying a variety of tariff and quota restrictions. At one extreme was Germany with no import restrictions and at the other Spain, which effectively reserved its entire domestic market for bananas from the Canary Islands. Between these extremes were the range of

[1] The Windward Islands grouping consists of the Commonwealth of Dominica, Grenada, St Lucia and St Vincent and the Grenadines.

import systems operated by the individual Member States. France maintained import duty and a virtual ban on bananas from Latin America though it provided import quotas for the bananas from francophone exporters in Africa. The UK permitted virtually unrestricted access for bananas from the African, Caribbean and Pacific Group (ACP) with a quota for Latin American bananas. Table 11.1 shows the import patterns prior to and since the Single Market.

With consumption growing and already close to 4 million tonnes and average prices well in excess of those on the world market, the EU market was a particularly attractive prize both for exporting nations and for marketing companies. The members of both groups therefore were evidently anxious to increase the volume of their banana sales to Europe. But the very cause of the attractive prices, the widespread import regulation, also limited import volumes and the scope for exporters and banana companies to win increased sales. All the major companies and exporting states lobbied in European capitals for whichever post-Single-Market regulatory arrangement they envisaged would, according to their circumstances, safeguard their existing volumes, prices and profit margins and/or permit their expanded exports.

In the years before the Single Market, suppliers could roughly be categorised into two interest groups: one which sought to prevent any change to the rules that would reduce their volumes and returns and the other that wanted some considerable progress in liberalisation, which would permit the expansion of their sales.

11.1.2 Why was there a problem?

An underlying complication in the EU banana market was the substantial differential in the production and shipping costs of its various suppliers. The large and highly capitalised plantations of Central and South America benefit from favourable climatic and other conditions such as vast expanses of suitable flat land with deep fertile soils and, most especially, economies of scale in production and shipping. These plantations, which in general enjoy low unit labour and related costs, are able get their bananas to Europe at substantially lower cost than those produced by the ACP or the overseas European producers like the Canary Islands, Martinique and Guadeloupe.

By contrast, production costs in the Windward Islands are high due to a variety of factors, including their hilly and difficult terrain, the small size of

Table 11.1 *Supplies of bananas to the EU 15, 1990–2002 (thousand tonnes)*

	1990	1991	1992	1993	1994	1995	1996	1997	1998	1999	2000	2001	2002
EU DOM	737	699	706	644	585	658	685	811	786	729	782	767	n/a
ACP	622	596	680	748	727	764	800	693	655	676	756	730	726
Of which:													
Carib. ACP*	384	342	384	374	328	340	362	295.4	273	278	288	207	185
Ivory Coast	95	116	144	161	149	160	181	166	158	193	200	218	211
Cameroon	78	115	110	147	158	165	167	157	155	161	205	216	230
Dominican Rep.	4	10	39	62	86	75	61	49	56	42	60	86	97
Dollar	2,363	2,641	2,731	2,560	2,450	2,405	2,470	2,462	2,426	2,522	2,543	2,561	2,611
Of which:													
Colombia	421	518	533	452	511	557	653	569	541	552	617	644	665
Costa Rica	643	608	520	565	727	564	604	603	640	663	656	634	686
Ecuador	381	646	745	651	612	632	686	738	569	697	691	702	829
Panama	649	591	601	569	427	416	311	358	417	422	389	347	307
Total	3,722	3,936	4,117	3,951	3,762	3,827	3,955	3,966	3,867	3,927	4,081	4,059	

* Traditional suppliers

Source: European Commission, DG Agriculture.

the severely under-capitalised, family-owned and operated farms (averaging less than 5 acres), unfavourable rainfall patterns and limited availability of arable land, all of which combine to preclude their ability to benefit from economies of scale. This competitive disadvantage is compounded by susceptibility to storms and hurricanes and a wage and social cost structure that is significantly more burdensome than the average for the Latin American plantations.

Table 11.2 shows the differential costs in 1999 among a sample of producers.

It is evident that, being so much cheaper, 'dollar' bananas (as the Latin American bananas are popularly known) would, unless impeded by regulation, quickly be able to supplant European and most ACP bananas on the EU market. To prevent this happening and to permit European bananas and those from the ACP (linked from 1975 by the Lomé Convention to the EC) to be sold, various national tariff and non-tariff barriers were introduced. In order to prevent circumvention of the restrictions through re-export of 'dollar' bananas from those EC members with liberal import regimes to the more restrictive, derogations from the rules requiring free circulation of goods were invoked for bananas by the UK, France, Spain, Portugal, Italy and Greece. The protective arrangements were enshrined in the Lomé Conventions in which the EC undertook to ensure that none of the twelve traditional ACP suppliers[2] would be placed in a disadvantaged position.

11.1.3 Prelude to battle

The approach of the 1993 Single Market was seen as a threat by the ACP banana suppliers. The derogations permitting their key importers, the UK, France and Italy, to block 'dollar' bananas being re-exported from another Member State would come to an end and the national regimes were all set to be dismantled and replaced by a unified import regime. Their fear was that a liberal regime would so dilute their effective preference that they would not be able to compete with bananas from Latin America. On the other hand, producers in these countries and the companies that marketed

[2] The traditional suppliers as listed in the ACP–EU Convention of Lomé were Belize, Cameroon, Cape Verde, Commonwealth of Dominica, Grenada, Ivory Coast, Jamaica, Madagascar, St Lucia, St Vincent and the Grenadines, Somalia and Suriname.

Table 11.2 *Average 1999 fob prices of a sample of suppliers (US $ per tonne)*

Ecuador	235
Belize	419
Jamaica	558
Suriname	636
Dominica	547
St Vincent	500
St Lucia	498

Sources: FAO Year Book and Windwards Islands Banana Development Company (WIBDECO)

their fruit, principally Chiquita, Dole, Del Monté and Noboa, were keen for a more liberal regime permitting greater access for 'dollar' bananas.

The first of the battles of the 'banana war' was therefore over the nature of the unified regime. The EC had a bound import duty rate in the GATT of 20 per cent but, given the price differentials, it was clear that such a tariff on its own would be insufficient to permit continued access for the ACP. Some European producer interests initially favoured a reference price mechanism[3] or simply a commitment to provide a subsidy that would compensate the producers for any declines in price. The Windward Islands, with their overwhelming dependence on banana exports, were particularly determined to ensure that any new system would permit the continued marketing of their bananas on a viable basis. They were wary of an arrangement that would rely exclusively on a direct subsidy since, among other things, they were unsure of the required long-term commitment in Europe for such considerable financial support to the ACP. The alluring option of campaigning for the retention of the distinct national regimes was dismissed as impractical in the single market context.

The Caribbean exporters committed themselves quite early to becoming actively involved in the search for a new banana regime. Their aim was to ensure that, even with the disappearance of the national regimes, the 1993

[3] A minimum selling price for bananas would be set which would be sufficiently high to permit the higher-cost European and ACP bananas to be marketed profitably; however, this would not have assured them of being able to market their bananas since marketing companies would have preferred to handle the lower-cost bananas on which they would now make greatly increased profit. This alternative was dismissed in the early stages.

European Single Market and its Common Organisation of the Market (COM) would deliver the equivalent security of access and remunerative prices upon which they had hitherto relied.

In the first phase of the banana dispute, the run-up to the Single Market, the main protagonists were Latin American exporters and some of the international companies, particularly Chiquita, that campaigned for a liberalised market in which there would be an end to quantitative import restrictions even if a flat tariff was retained. Such was the confidence in this camp that some gambled heavily on the expectation of being able to export more bananas to Europe. Chiquita bought six custom-built refrigerated banana ships to add to its existing fleet and increased its investment in Latin American plantations. So widespread was the expectation among banana companies that Geest, which had been marketing only Windward Island bananas, bought a plantation in Costa Rica.

Nonetheless, even in the face of such confident and powerful opposition, the Caribbean traditional suppliers were quite determined and insisted to European Member States and the Commission that it would not be acceptable to abandon their treaty commitments under the Lomé Convention, which had assured them that their exports would not be placed in a worse position than they were currently or had been in the past.[4] Using the indices of economic dependence, they stressed the calamitous economic, social and political consequences of the loss of their banana industry for which there were no short-term alternatives. Their message was clearly and consistently articulated by diplomatic representatives of the Windward Islands but significantly also by senior political figures, including their Prime Ministers, who were quite visible and vocal campaigners in Brussels and other European capitals.

11.1.3.1 The first phase of the banana wars

From the outset, the three small islands of Dominica, St Lucia and St Vincent and the Grenadines were at the centre of the coalition that was seeking to ensure that the COM would effectively limit imports of 'dollar bananas' so as to ensure a tight market and high enough prices. The coalition included Caribbean and other ACP suppliers, the Caribbean Banana

[4] Protocol V of the Fourth ACP–EC Convention of Lomé stipulated that 'In respect of its banana exports to the Community markets, no ACP State shall be placed, as regards access to its traditional markets, in a less favourable position than in the past or at present.'

Exporters Association (CBEA), Geest Plc, Fyffes Plc and eventually the French marketing companies and producer interests in the overseas Departments. The coalition's wide-ranging campaign recognised that securing a favourable position in the Council of Ministers would require convincing public opinion and enlisting the support of various groups including the Commission, the EU Parliament, National Governments and Parliaments, NGOs, church groups and journalists among others. Recognising that EU banana trade policy would not be made in isolation, the 'coalition' targeted important third parties that were exerting pressure on Europe for liberal reform. Hence, there was a very active campaign in Washington focusing principally on the Congress. As well, direct though limited contact was maintained with Latin American supplying states and the multinational companies themselves in the hope of at least tempering their opposition to a restrictive regime. It was the threat and danger posed to the Windward Islands that provided the moral legitimacy and rationale for the campaign. Its most public aim was to ensure that the EU would honour its obligations to these islands, who, given the nature of their production on small family-run farms and their lack of alternatives, would suffer disastrous economic and social consequences should they lose bananas. In addition, they also were to a large extent the 'face' of the campaign. The safeguarding of the banana industry became their top foreign policy objective, hence their representatives sought out or even created opportunities to promote and advance their case. Despite the fact that by 1992 the Windward Islands accounted for only 7.6 per cent of the EU banana imports, in the perception of the public (particularly in the UK), a key policy question to be addressed was how the trade in their bananas would be safeguarded.

In the end the COM, enshrined in EC Regulation 404 of 1993, was an attempt to translate the existing national regimes into a unified system. It awarded quotas for Latin American bananas totalling 2.2 million tonnes and each ACP traditional exporter was assigned a maximum tonnage within an autonomous quota for the ACP. There was no price support for the ACP though the European suppliers were subsidised up to predetermined maximum volumes per region. In an attempt to unify the market further and provide an inducement for traders to handle the more costly ACP and European bananas, a system popularly referred to as the 'B' licence system gave them a share of the import licences for 'dollar' bananas according to the volume of ACP or European bananas that they marketed.

11.1.3.2 The early challenges

This system was challenged from the outset; five Latin American countries (Colombia, Costa Rica, Guatemala, Nicaragua and Venezuela) initiated a Panel complaint against the quota system in 1993. Following negotiations with the Commission, all except Guatemala withdrew their complaint and, the following year, signed the Banana Framework Agreement (BFA) that gave them fixed country quotas and the consequent potentially lucrative power to control their exports to Europe.

The 1994 BFA itself did not end the dispute since it excluded one of the WTO complainants, Guatemala, which could still pursue the dispute. Instead it introduced a new issue of contention, the BFA itself. Then Ecuador, Honduras and Panama which had previously rejected the quotas offered to them under the BFA acceded to the GATT and promptly joined Guatemala in their complaint. Protesting their opposition to the BFA's restrictions and ceilings on their exports, they claimed privately that the Commission had not treated them fairly in the allocations. Quite ominously, the international companies saw the BFA as a threat to their operations in Latin America. The award of quotas to the exporting countries handed their governments considerable potential power. They could have a real say in the export to Europe since operators wishing to export bananas could now be subjected to conditions and the prior approval of these countries' authorities. Some of the BFA countries, in particular Colombia, used the arrangement to promote local marketing companies and, along with Costa Rica, sought to impose export levies.

The ACP was becoming more active in the dispute with a prominent role for the Caribbean as the Ambassador of the three Windward Islands began presiding over the ACP Working Group on bananas. ACP participation in the Dispute process was organised, a legal consortium was engaged and a legal defence of the contested provisions prepared. The processes were managed by the ACP Banana Working Group Chairman in full collaboration with national representatives. For the Panel Hearing two of the ACP legal advisers were included on the delegation of St Lucia, but they were expelled by the Panel on the grounds that they were not full-time employees of the government. This prompted the leader of the delegation to walk out in protest at what he asserted was an inequitable ruling essentially disempowering small states that could not afford to retain the required specialists on a permanent basis and had to rely on outside expertise to assist in the presentation of their case before the Panel. Denying them that ability would have entrenched their disadvantage in disputes as they presented and advanced their case.

This ruling by the Panel would have been appealed by St Lucia and the Caribbean but, as third parties, they could not introduce independent grounds of appeal. Even if the Appellate Body did not explicitly overturn the contentious ruling, by reaffirming the sovereign right of countries to determine the composition of delegations to its meeting, it in effect implied its dissent with the Panel's ruling. As a result, subsequent WTO practice has been that Parties to disputes have been able to engage outside experts. This facility has since been used in many instances by Members. Indeed, the WTO Advisory Law Centre was subsequently created in recognition of that capacity gap in developing countries that was so dramatically demonstrated by this incident in 1997.

11.1.4 Resolution of the dispute and subsequent reforms

Following the successful challenge in the WTO to the regime, in an attempt to conform to the rules, the EU introduced a new system on 1 January 1999[5] that abandoned the 'B' licences and country-specific quotas for the non-substantial suppliers that were BFA signatories, Nicaragua and Venezuela and the individual ACP traditional suppliers. From 1999 the latter were assigned a quota of 857,000 tonnes for the group as a whole. The MFN quota remained at 2.553 million tonnes but with shares to the four 'substantial' suppliers, Colombia, Costa Rica, Ecuador and Panama, according to their 1994–6 exports and the remaining 9.43 per cent (240,748 tonnes) of the quota reserved for the 'others' category of suppliers. The in-quota tariff rate for MFN suppliers was 75 Euro and a prohibitive 737 Euro for out-of-quota imports. No duty was levied on ACP imports within the group's quota as well as any which were imported within the 240,748 tonne 'others' category. Additional imports would attract a prohibitive duty of 537 Euro per tonne. The Caribbean and the ACP were able neither to overcome the high out-of-quota tariff nor to compete within the MFN quota

[5] The EC implementation measures are contained in the following regulations: (i) EC Regulation No. 1637/1998 amending the contested parent EC Regulation No. 404/1993 which established the Common Organisation of the Market in bananas, (ii) EC Regulation No. 2362 of 1998 which laid down the detailed rules for operationalising Regulation 404 of 1993. Both of the EC 1998 Regulations 1637 and 2362 were applied from 1 January 1999.

despite getting in duty free and, as a result, their exports were virtually limited to the ACP quota. The inability of the ACP to compete even on the basis of duty-free entry demonstrates that effective access is secured not simply by exemption from import duty but rather by the adequacy of the preferential margin and the possible existence of other protective mechanisms or structures.

The new system was again challenged, this time by Ecuador which claimed that the EC had still not complied with the Panel's decisions.

The earlier defeat in the WTO was compounded by the US imposition of US $191 million worth of trade sanctions against the EU, which more than anything else completely changed the attitude of Member States. With the dispute costing their exporters, they were determined to end it and directed the Commission accordingly. The latter intensified its negotiations with the United States Trade Representative (USTR) and some headway was made, reaching agreement that the quota system would be retained, with licences issued on a historical basis. Very soon, however, talks floundered, with the main sticking point over the share of licences for newcomers: the EU and Ecuador wanted 20 per cent and the US, 3.5 per cent.

To get around the impasse, the Commission began work on a potentially chaotic 'first come, first served' (FCFS) system for the award of import permits, which would have been disastrous for the Caribbean. But even more damaging to them would have been the alternative single tariff. The US though would not accept FCFS, insisting on a historically based system for the determination of licence eligibility.

11.1.5 The breakthrough

Secret negotiations between the two sides had nonetheless been proceeding simultaneously and, in a surprise announcement on 11 April 2001, the Commission and the US Trade Representative jointly confirmed that agreement was reached to end the dispute. Ecuador, the winner of the last Panel, was incensed that a deal was struck without its involvement and threatened to initiate new proceedings in the WTO. To avert this, a new set of discussions with Ecuador was quickly initiated and formally concluded on 30 April 2001 with an agreement that left intact most of the US/EU deal but made some minor changes to the proposed implementation.

11.1.6 The Agreement

The Agreements with the US and Ecuador were reflected in a new set of import rules enshrined in a Commission Regulation adopted on 2 May 2001 to operate in two phases. The first lasted from 1 July 2001 to 31 December 2001, in which the quantitative limitations and tariffs were unchanged. The licensing system was adjusted. The significant feature of the system is that only 'operators', i.e. persons or registered companies or agents who had, during a specified reference period, imported bananas into the EU, are eligible for import licences and hence they determine the source from which bananas are imported.

The US ended its sanctions and, along with Ecuador, agreed to support the application in the WTO for a waiver for the Cotonou Partnership Agreement. Once 100,000 tonnes were transferred from the ACP quota to the MFN quota and a GATT Article XIII waiver was obtained for the ACP quota (done at Doha, 14 November 2001), Phase II could begin on 1 January 2002.

11.1.7 Impact of the changes

The regulatory changes since the early 1990s have had a fundamental impact on shaping the character of the EU banana market, through determining the origins and levels of supply and hence prices. In addition, the requirement that, to be saleable, banana imports must be covered by scarce licences has generated valuable 'quota rent' that is earned by the licence holder. The extent to which this is shared with other participants along the production/supply chain varies according to the differing circumstances, including their relative bargaining strengths.

The changes in regulation, by permitting larger volumes of cheaper 'dollar' banana imports into the UK, caused a decline in prices. Selling prices for Windward bananas fell by 10 per cent from their level at the start of the Single Market whilst 'dollar' banana prices were more or less unchanged. The Windward Island farmers are not only affected by the price drop but even more by the loss of the *de facto* subsidy which they had enjoyed under the 'B' licensing system that ended in 2000.

Simultaneously, with the price declines, the import patterns were changing not only between the ACP and 'dollar' suppliers but also among ACP

Table 11.3 *Nominal and real retail prices of bananas in the UK, 1990–2003*

	Retail prices of bananas £/kg	Real prices (1990 = 100)
1990	1.14	100
1991	1.19	98.4
1992	1.06	84.7
1993	0.96	75.4
1994	0.94	72.2
1995	0.80	59.4
1996	0.89	64.5
1997	1.00	70.2
1998	1.04	70.6
1999	1.02	68.2
2000	0.99	64.2
2001	1.08	68.9
2002	1.02	64.1
Jan–Mar 2002	1.09	
Jan–Mar 2003	0.90	

Source: Fyffes 1992–2003, ONS 1990–1; real prices calculated by NERA[6]

suppliers. As shown in figure 11.1, the traditional Caribbean suppliers were losing out to West Africa and the Dominican Republic whilst Ecuador was expanding as Panama and Honduras went into decline. The subsidised EU producers have been able to maintain their supply levels.

Although the Windward Islands, through their marketing company WIBDECO, controlled sufficient import licences to be able to handle their exports, production was declining sharply. The cause was principally the reduction in the number of farmers and the abandonment of farms. Figure 11.2 shows the declining number of growers in the Windward Islands falling from 24,100 in 1993 to 7,300 in 2001.

The consequences of such a decline on rural employment and income were massive since there was no sufficient productive activity to replace bananas fully. In his 2002 study of agricultural performance in the Eastern Caribbean, Gary Melville found great official enthusiasm for diversification but overall the production and export performance of non-traditional agri-

6 'Banana exports from the Caribbean since 1992'. Report by National Economic Research Associates (NERA), June 2003, London.

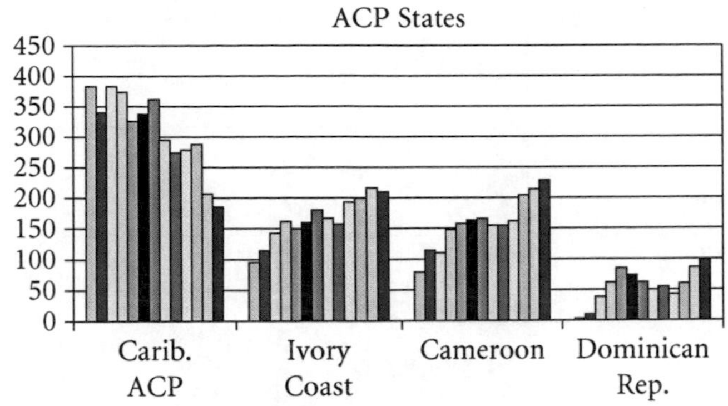

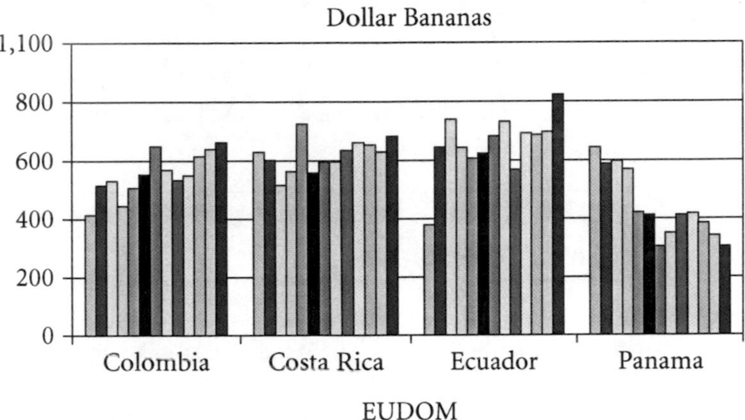

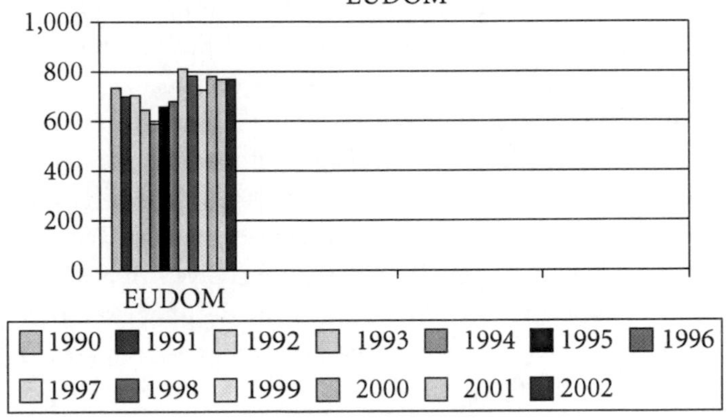

Note: Ivory Coast, Cameroon, and the Caribbean ACP supplier, Belize, exported above their traditional quotas between 1994 and 1998

Source: DG Agriculture

Figure 11.1 Supplies of bananas to the EU 15, 1990–2002 (thousand tonnes)

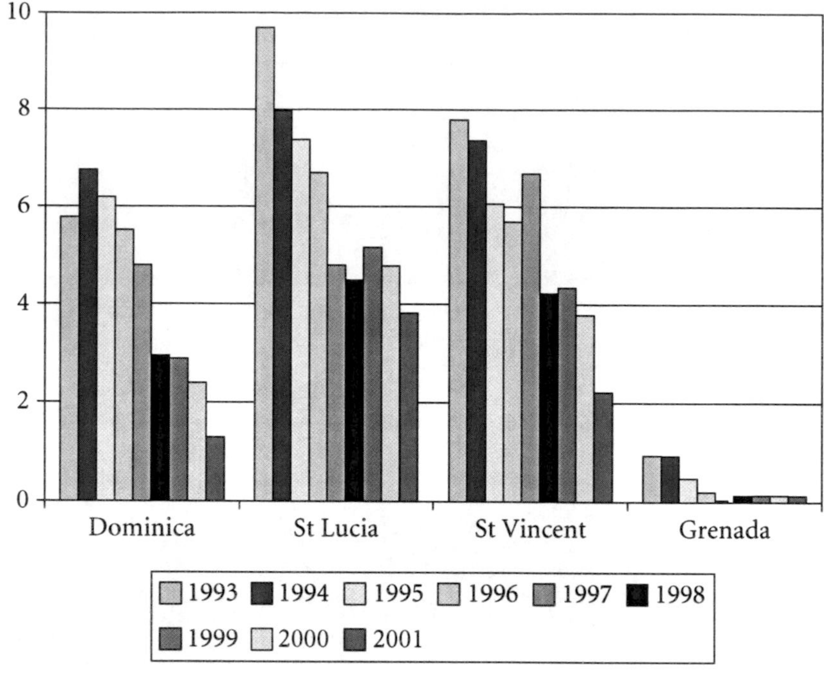

Source: WIBDECO

Figure 11.2 Number of active growers in the Windward Islands, 1993–2001('000)

culture was erratic. This he attributed in part to unfavourable climatic conditions, including natural disasters, a variety of production problems and difficulties in meeting the phytosanitary requirements in export markets.[7]

It was not only the loss of direct and indirect employment (at the ports, in transportation, production of packaging materials, etc.) which resulted from the decline in banana production but also the loss of national income due to declining export earnings from banana exports. Table 11.4 shows what has been happening in US dollar terms. Given that no account has been taken of inflation, the full impact of the declines on those countries which are heavily reliant on banana exports would be even greater than initially suggested by the figures.

The economic consequences of such a massive loss of earnings by a sector whose income rapidly circulated within the rural and national

[7] 'Situational Analysis of the Agriculture Sector of the OECS member countries'. Gary Melville, FAO Capacity Building Project, December 2002.

Table 11.4 *Export values (fob) (US $ million)*

	Windward Islands							
Year	Dominica	St Lucia	St Vincent	Grenada	Total	Jamaica	Belize	Suriname
1991	32	60	34	4	130	49	7	10
1992	32	72	40	3	147	40	10	10
1993	26	55	25	2	107	36	12	11
1994	24	49	17	–	92	46	15	11
1995	18	52	25	2	97	46	22	8
1996	18	52	22	1	93	45	29	9
1997	18	37	16	–	71	45	26	24
1998	15	37	22	–	74	36	25	15
1999	15	34	20	–	69	29	27	21
2000	12	28	19	–	59	23	–	–
2001	8	16	13	–	36	–	–	–
2002	–	–	–	–	45	–	–	–

Source: WIBDECO (Windward Islands 1992–2002), FAO Yearbooks vols. 47, 50, and 53. Values for Jamaica, Belize and Suriname for 1999 and 2000 are from NERA

economies were quite catastrophic. In May, the ACP Ministerial spokesman Julian Hunte, addressing the twenty-eight ACP–EU Council of Ministers 2003 stated, 'Dominica, one of the most vulnerable suppliers, has been so damaged by the falling prices and resultant export volumes, that its economy is literally on the verge of collapse. It had to have recourse to the IMF but a turnabout would only be possible if the country can again begin to earn sufficient foreign exchange.'

11.1.8 2004 – Enlargement

In May 2004, ten new members acceded to the Union and, in keeping with its WTO commitments to MFN suppliers and the new Member States themselves, the EU increased the 'dollar' quota. It was generally agreed that this should be related to historical import levels. Writing in *Eurofruit Magazine* of May 2003, Jessica Greniez indicated however that it is not simple to arrive at actual levels of imports and alluded to the 'incoherence of certain customs data supplied by the candidate countries'. One cause of difficulty was that a sizeable portion of these countries' banana imports had actually been re-exported from the EU, hence the danger of double counting. Over-estimation could have destabilised the market because, if the quota was set too high, too many licences would be awarded, resulting in excessive imports that would have driven down prices even further. In addition, there could have been the possibility that effective demand for bananas in the ten new Member States would decline once the latter joined the EU since their banana imports would face an import tariff that would make them more expensive.

11.1.9 How is the Caribbean adapting?

The changes that have been taking place result in lower prices to farmers who face greater competition and uncertainty. The islands are therefore forced by circumstances to adapt. At the domestic level serious efforts are being made to secure the structural adjustment of the industry. Attempts to increase productivity rely on investment in irrigation, feeder roads and improved farming practices and standards. In the Windward Islands, the management of the industry has been privatised and opened up to competition. Previously, national growers' associations controlled the bulk purchase and distribution to farmers of certain inputs and managed banana collection and export. The aim of all of these measures has been to promote efficiency and to lower costs.

In a situation of declining real prices, it is perceived as essential that farmers' share of the final price is not further reduced. The Windward Islands and Jamaica have been involved in the actual import and marketing of their bananas in Europe. Their marketing companies though are under pressure to continue to cut costs and to maximise returns. The Windward Islands have been introducing specific measures to safeguard their position in a weakening market. They have been developing contractual arrangements with supermarkets that permit their bananas to be sent from the ripening rooms straight to the supermarkets; in some cases the bananas are actually pre-packed on the farms in the islands for the supermarkets. The Windward Islands have also begun producing organic bananas (still at minimal levels) and ensuring that more of their banana production qualifies for 'fair trade' certification and bears that label when marketed. The retail prices of organic and of 'fair trade' bananas are higher than for the others, hence these niche markets offer a more favourable return to the farmers.

Particularly in these islands with their production on small, independent, family-owned and operated farms, conducive environmental factors and considerations and marketing being in the hands of various farmers' associations, there is considerable potential for further expansion of the use of the 'fair trade' label. Despite the much higher cost and labour required for the production of organic bananas, there seems to be considerable long-term benefit to be gained by the small Caribbean suppliers from committing more resources to expanding their share of this small but growing and lucrative niche market.

11.2 Subsequent challenges

There can be little doubt that small developing economies cannot indefinitely defy the logic of the marketplace since their ability to export is dependent on the policies of other players in the global trading system. In this case, the EU and indeed other prospective importers have their own range of commitments for tariff reduction and broader trade liberalisation goals. Therefore the Windward Islands can only continue trade in the long term if they manage to produce and supply competitively, whether it is bananas or any other products. These islands, with growing populations and facing irreversible declines in employment and income from bananas, must find new sources of productive activity in which they can be internationally competitive. Ultimately, this would be the only prospect for these countries in a liberalised environment in which effective preferences have disappeared. But they require time for orderly transition if they are to be able to make the necessary adjustments.

11.2.1 2006 – Abolition of the quota system

The next challenge for Caribbean bananas will come with the proposed dismantling of the tariff rate quota system and its replacement by a flat tariff scheduled for 1 January 2006.

Given the differences between costs of production in the Windward Islands and the most competitive 'dollar' suppliers, unless the tariff is sufficiently high, the former will not be able to find buyers for their bananas. As has already been shown in table 11.2, there is a massive gap between the various suppliers, with Ecuador for instance able to export at less than half the prices of most Caribbean fruit. Their cost disadvantage is compounded by their substantially higher unit freight charges due to their small volumes. There is no doubt that the large low-cost producers benefit from liberalisation. However, unless some means to trade are provided for the small vulnerable suppliers, who have no immediate alternative, then contrary to the very principles of the WTO, only some countries, the already more competitive, will benefit from liberalisation. Adequate support (possibly preferential) arrangements are required by the small suppliers if they are to export successfully rather than being further marginalised in the global trading system.

In order then for the tariff alone to provide the possibility of the Caribbean banana being marketable, the rates have to be at a level that might well be considered too high by some MFN suppliers.

According to the agreement reached at Doha, the EC would, upon request, enter into consultations over the tariff level with any interested Member. The talks between the Commission and the nine Latin American suppliers began in late 2004.[8] The Latin American suppliers have the right to take the issue to arbitration if they are not satisfied with the proposed level. If ultimately no agreement is arrived at, the WTO waiver for Cotonou will cease to apply to bananas from 1 January 2006. It is ironic that it is the ACP which will be at risk if the EU and the Latins cannot reach agreement!

Whilst the Caribbean needs a high tariff under the 2006 flat tariff regime in order that its bananas, which should enter duty free, will be competitive, the Latin American producers resist that. Those that are relatively higher cost are concerned that they could be displaced by the more competitive ACP suppliers (West African and Dominican Republic), which will enjoy a price advantage over them. The lowest-cost Latin Americans, such as Ecuador, fear that a high tariff will increase prices and dampen demand, hence their exports would decrease. Also the margins of their trading companies such as Noboa would be eroded. Ideas have been circulated that a solution would be to place a ceiling on the volume of ACP bananas which will be eligible for duty-free entry. This could partially appease the Latin Americans but will cause problems of its own for the ACP. Essentially if this duty-free quota is available to all the ACP, there will be intensive competition among the suppliers since the more competitive who have the capacity to expand production will invariably do so up to the point where the quota will be oversubscribed by further imports. Of course, disruption can be avoided by retaining the licensing system.

[8] Annex to WTO decision on the waiver for EC–ACP Partnership Agreement – 14 November 2001, Doha.

11.2.2 2008 – End of the Cotonou trade preferences

By 2008, the current Cotonou trade preferences are to expire. Whatever replaces them will be determined by the current negotiations between the ACP and the EU for new Economic Partnership Agreements (EPAs). However, the effectiveness of access will depend not only on the nature of the preferences secured but also on the import system in place at the time which will impact on market prices and security.

11.3 Lessons to be learned

11.3.1 Implications of the banana challenge for other commodity protocols and preferences

With the largely successful challenge in the WTO to the Banana Protocol, concerns have been expressed within the ACP regarding possible consequent vulnerability of the other commodity Protocols. Is it that politically and legally they are no longer inviolable, or are their provisions for quantitative allocations fundamentally flawed? However, the methods of allocation of volumes to the ACP vary among the Protocols. In the case of bananas, it was initially the guaranteed share of the tariff rate quotas to the individual traditional suppliers then later to the ACP as a group. (This violated the provisions of GATT Article 13.) In the case of sugar, however, the EC purchased set quantities at negotiated prices. With respect to beef and veal, it has fixed upper limits on the volumes of ACP imports that will enter at reduced duty.

What the Protocols ultimately provide for the ACP is the prospect of marketing specified volumes of the covered products on a remunerative basis. However, the instruments and their legal and regulatory arrangements are all fundamentally different. Consequently, the fact that some of the provisions of the Banana Protocol fell foul of WTO rules does not signify that the other Protocols, which share the same objectives but are based on differing trading and regulatory arrangements, would be in similar legal jeopardy in the WTO. Though the successful challenge in the WTO to the Banana Protocol does not directly imply legal vulnerability of the other protocols, their ACP beneficiaries nonetheless need to be concerned. The WTO Panel did not question the underlying aims of the Banana Protocol but, by rejecting the quota arrangements and the licensing system used by the EC to give effect to its objectives, it clearly established that the instruments used by Members to implement their bilateral treaty obligations must conform to WTO rules.[9] The EU had a definite and unambiguous obligation to the twelve ACP traditional suppliers to ensure that they would not be 'worse off than in the past or at present'. The Panel rejected the arrangements for giving effect to that commitment but did not indicate any acceptable alternative and feasible means of achieving the same objective. Indeed none has so far been found.

The other Commodity Protocols can therefore be challenged not necessarily directly but through the instruments used to give them effect. Already, Australia, Brazil and Thailand have formally challenged certain aspects of the sugar regime that are essential for the trade in ACP sugar on a remunerative basis. The complainants formulated their case on their perceptions of the precise vulnerabilities and violations of the specific Protocol or its beneficiary mechanism rather than those aspects challenged in the banana case, but which might not have been relevant.

Linked to the potential legal vulnerability of the Protocols exposed by the banana challenge is the perception that they have ceased to be sacrosanct. It is no longer 'politically incorrect' to challenge provisions of the ACP–EC Agreement. Although the Commission conducted a spirited defence before the Panel, the EU clearly lost the will to continue to defend the contentious provisions of Protocol V. When the first opportunity arose to dispense with its obligations, the EC sought in the negotiations for the 2000 Partnership Agreement with the ACP (Cotonou) to exclude all market access commitments from the Banana Protocol. The ACP was though able finally to secure a commitment from the EC, albeit one that was weaker and less clear than its predecessor.[10] The history of the banana dispute suggests

[9] The final remarks 8.3 of the Report of the Panel – EC Regime for the Importation, Sale and Distribution of Bananas, 22 May 1997, reads, 'From a substantive perspective, the fundamental principles of the WTO and WTO rules are designed to foster the development of countries, not impede it. Having heard the arguments of a large number of Members interested in this case and having worked through a complex set of claims under several WTO agreements, we conclude that the system is flexible enough to allow, through WTO-consistent trade and non-trade measures, appropriate policy responses in the wide variety of circumstances across countries, including countries that are currently heavily dependent on the production and commercialization of bananas.'

[10] 'The Community agrees to examine and where necessary take measures aimed at ensuring the continued viability of their banana export industries and the continuing outlet for their bananas on the Community Market.' Protocol V, Article I, ACP–EU Partnership Agreement, Cotonou, 23 May 2000.

that the commitment of the EC to the Commodity Protocols, should they encounter serious difficulties in the WTO, cannot be taken for granted.

11.3.2 Strategy and tactics

It is in the areas of campaign planning and management methodology that the most important lessons for the defence of the other Commodity Protocols can be learnt from the banana 'wars'. These lessons include:

- **Having an inclusive, coherent and well co-ordinated coalition.** ACP–EU banana exporters (States and producers associations), their marketing companies and other allies such as NGOs cooperated and pooled resources to take on the massive task of influencing opinion in the EU as a whole.
- **The need for clearly articulated and simply expressed goals.** In order to get the range of politicians, NGOs, journalists and other non-technical supporters to advance the 'case' for the Caribbean and ACP banana and to sway public opinion, the argumentation was kept simple even if the underlying issues were highly complex and technical.
- **Public relations are vital.** Being at a major disadvantage to the 'opposition' in terms of conventional negotiating and commercial power it was essential to win over public opinion through a massive and effective campaign. Whilst there is natural public sympathy for the underdog, retaining support requires having a competently articulated, sound and morally justifiable case.
- **There must be a redefinition of the parameters of the debate.** If the public is to become engaged, it is necessary to move beyond the technical questions and consideration of the case for the particular Commodity Protocol simply in terms of conformity of the Protocol's provision and instruments with WTO rules. Rather, the debate needs to be expanded to include more fundamental issues including development considerations, equity and the desirability and right of all countries to participate on a sustainable basis in the global trading system. It must of course be emphasised that the technical legal debate over compatibility needs, in any event, simultaneously to be competently and vigorously pursued. The defence requires high visibility and sophistication in the negotiations.
- **It is necessary to canvass all key targets.** Just as the 'banana coalition' targeted very broadly its lobbying, negotiations and canvassing way

beyond immediately responsible Commission officials, the defence of the other Protocols will have to do likewise. The banana targets included the Commission at all levels, all EU Member States, the US Government and Congress, the Latin American banana exporters, the international community, NGOs, journalists and others.

- **Defence is costly.** A tremendous amount of financial, political and intellectual resources have to be committed.

11.3.3 Other systemic lessons

There are a number of broad systemic lessons to be learnt from the banana dispute that transcend its product and geographic context and are applicable to international trade negotiations by small states.

The first is that small size and consequent lack of commercial and political power do not, on their own, preclude countries from exercising influence over international decision-making and events that impact on their vital national interests. However, they need to understand their real national interests and then define them in the form of clear, readily articulated and comprehensible objectives to which combined national effort can be devoted in a coherent and consistent manner. For small developing countries lacking political and commercial power as well as visibility and influence on the international stage, the share of total resources that they need to invest to win international support would be considerable. Therefore if they are to have real influence, small states are obliged to concentrate their efforts on achieving their priority goals. The conventional approach of giving more or less equal attention to the international advancement of the full range of perceived national goals and interests is beyond the capacity of small states whose efforts would be dissipated in the pursuit of a broad agenda. It might seem counter-intuitive, but small states can actually achieve greater concrete results with ruthless prioritisation of their goals and concentrating their forces on the most important, even if this precludes the direct pursuit of less vital aims. This insistence on the need to focus on priority concerns must not be confused with a simplistic concentration on a single goal or a narrow policy agenda. Rather, small states have to be active participants in the multilateral system with an interest in and voice on more than the issues of immediate concern to them if they are to have the ability to exert real influence on any issues, including those which are of vital concern. The 'secret' is that they themselves must neither lose sight of the key issues in their fight to advance their national interests, nor so deflect resources to peripheral pursuits as to prejudice the attainment of their priority goals.

It is a truism that the stronger the international opposition to the particular goal/s the greater the commitment of resources and effort that will be needed. Changing the positions of governments and of major institutions generally requires more than the formulation and presentation of valid arguments. The frequently encountered unwillingness of negotiators to concede, even when faced with irrefutable arguments, could be for a number of reasons, including a resistance to change already endorsed decisions or positions (sometimes bureaucratic inertia). Also, it is generally the case that the interlocutors are not the real decision-makers but are instructed or influenced by superiors and other entities such as national Parliaments, public opinion or even third countries, international institutions or the business community. When presented with conflicting but convincing arguments, the technical or ministerial representatives who engage in international negotiations would of course be expected to seek adjustment to their brief or national position. However, when they face representatives of weak and relatively uninfluential states, they might not feel the necessity to undertake the negotiations with and/or persuasion of their superiors, Parliaments, business and other interests groups required in order to be able to accept the position which the weak states have successfully championed in their negotiations but which conflicts with their original national or institutional mandates or interests.

Small states, seeking through lobbying and negotiation to change the position of more powerful countries, need not only to convince their interlocutors at the negotiating table, but, having determined all the actual locations of decision-making authority and sources of influence, to seek to win these over as well. The targets then are not just the interlocutors but others within the hierarchy who could even include subordinates who have delegated authority, which the latter might, for whatever reason, be unwilling to override. To be successful, the small states will have to engage all required targets within the vertical and horizontal planes of authority.

Whilst such a broad strategy will invariably be demanding, unless all those with influence are either won over or neutralised, any which are not can subsequently seek to block or undo the outcome being sought by the small state/s.

The historical association of many small states with major powers can sometimes result in an over-reliance and trust in international goodwill and the expectation that friendly developed countries will secure their interests. Whilst there is considerable evidence in the banana dispute of such principled commitment, it would be uncertain in the long term or when the small states' aims conflict with the national interests or priorities of their 'benefactors'. Hence, small states must appreciate their ultimate responsibility for achieving through their own domestic and international action the outcomes that they desire, whether or not that entails mobilising support and working with allies.

Securing international change can be very demanding and is likely to be proportionately difficult for small developing countries. Hence, in order to be able to commit the required resources, they need to mobilise effectively and engage all their national capacity. Their political, diplomatic, business, NGO, academic and other emissaries who will articulate and advance the identified goals must be very well briefed and present persuasive, consistent and coherent arguments. Senior Ministers and even Heads of Government can be enlisted to use their influence and the opportunities that arise or are deliberately created for interaction with and persuading of decision-makers in target countries and institutions. During the 1990s, given the overwhelming importance of the issue to their economies, advancing their interests in the banana dispute was the overriding foreign policy objective of the Windward Islands. That objective to a large extent defined their policy stance towards the various members of the EU, to Latin America, the US and also in multilateral spheres such as the Organisation of American States and the UN.

In their pursuit of favourable decision-making at an international level, small states will be able to obtain leverage through working with allies and benefiting from the support of friendly countries and institutions. However, actually securing the desired objectives will require effective preparation of positions and arguments and skilful negotiation by the countries' representatives. Hence it is essential that small countries field skilled and dedicated tacticians and negotiators who can actually win debates and change the views even of the experienced and trained negotiators and representatives of the developed countries and the multilateral institutions. The methods to ensure that capacity will be long term and entail a combination of training, careful recruitment, development and retention.

11.4 Conclusion

The aim of the small Caribbean traditional banana suppliers at the start of the 1990s was simply to secure continued access to the EU banana market on a viable basis. They wanted the changes to the regulatory system to be sufficiently benign to ensure adequate preferential margins and high enough market prices. The islands also understood that they would need to restructure their banana industries drastically to reduce costs of production substantially and to make the industry more competitive. Simultaneously the agricultural sector and wider economy would need to be restructured to create new sources of income and employment.

Despite their small size and lack of power in the traditional commercial and political sense, these islands through commitment and perseverance were able, along with their allies and supporters, to ensure that the banana import regime retained its preferential character and that the market continued to be regulated so that prices remained substantially above world market levels. The problem however is that, despite advances in efficiency reflected in reduced costs and improved quality, the differential between the competitive Latin American producers and the Caribbean producers remains wide. Whilst these islands have achieved a considerable measure of success in the battle over the regulation of the system, they have been losing market share, with their exports falling drastically. In the Windward Islands for instance, the drop was from 274,000 tonnes in 1992 to 99,000 tonnes by 2002.[11] This loss of banana production has not been significantly replaced by other productive activity. The result has been an increase in unemployment and sharp declines in foreign earnings.

If these islands are to avoid the complete loss of the market before alternative productive activities have been developed, they will need through diplomatic and other means to seek to ensure that the changes to the market over the next few years and beyond preserve the required favourable and preferential access terms essential to their ability to dispose of their bananas in Europe. For their long-term economic stability and growth, it will be essential that continued attention be paid to minimising costs of production at all levels in order to reduce as much as possible the cost handicap which they face. Most importantly, renewed commitment and effort will need to be put into diversification, possibly to include

[11] Source: Windwards Islands Banana Development Company (WIBDECO).

organic and 'fair trade' bananas as well as new lines of agricultural and non-agricultural production and services. To be successful, diversification will require that the introduction of viable new crops is initially alongside bananas. An attempt immediately and simply to displace bananas with another crop is unlikely to have any chance of success, though the process of identifying, testing and introducing new lines must be completed in the time remaining when some measure of rural income and employment stability is still provided by the banana industry.

12

Impact of changes in the European Union's policy for banana imports on the Eastern Caribbean Region (1992–2002)

CLAUDIUS PREVILLE

12.1 Introduction

Ever since the demise of sugar as a major export crop from the Windward Islands[1] to the United Kingdom in the 1950s, bananas have assumed prominence as the only viable export alternative. Yet, the viability of exporting Windward Islands bananas to the United Kingdom has been directly linked to the preferential market access that they enjoy, i.e. tariff- and quota-free market access. Preferential market access for bananas to the European Community (EC) had in fact been secured for all African, Caribbean and Pacific (ACP) countries since the signing of the Treaty of Rome in 1957.[2] At the signing of the Treaty of Rome, EC Member States had agreed that a tariff and, optionally, a quota would apply with respect to other banana imports. In practice, these sources of other banana imports were largely a few countries in Central and Latin America, from where a number of United States based transnational corporations (TNCs) operated,[3] the so-called *dollar zone* countries.[4] A notable exception to the generally agreed scheme of granting preferential market access was found in Germany, where, under a special protocol annexed to the Treaty of Rome, Germany had secured the right to import nearly all its bananas from dollar zone sources free of duty and taxes. Germany had won the right to this

[1] The Windward Islands are St Lucia, St Vincent and the Grenadines, Grenada and Dominica.

[2] Although it should be noted that at the signing of the Treaty of Rome, most of the countries which subsequently became ACP members were colonies of an EU member.

[3] Chiquita Brands International Inc. (Chiquita), Dole Food Company (Dole) and Fresh Del Monte Produce (Del Monte).

[4] The dollar zone countries include Colombia, Costa Rica, Dominican Republic, Ecuador, Guatemala, Honduras, Mexico, Nicaragua and Panama.

special protocol given that it was the largest single consumer of bananas in Europe at the time, and that it had traditionally sourced all its imports from the dollar zone.

Essentially, EC members found themselves implementing two banana import policies that were in fact diametrically opposed to each other, and this would become the major point of contention when the Single European Market (SEM) was implemented in 1993. There was a threefold basis for granting preferential market access to ACP countries. First, since they were all colonies or ex-colonies of an EC member at the time, it was viewed as a mechanism through which their economic development could be facilitated. Second, there existed little diversity in their exports, making them extremely vulnerable as single commodity dependent economies. Third, the traditional production, marketing and distribution processes they utilised did not allow them to enjoy economies of scale, causing their costs to be relatively high. However, in the dollar zone countries the converse obtained. All of these countries had attained independence several centuries prior, and their production systems were characterised by large-scale capital-intensive plantation technology. Coupled with vertically integrated systems of shipping, marketing and distribution, bananas from dollar zone countries are relatively cheap to produce, market and distribute in the EC.[5]

This study is concerned with the impact of implementing the various changes in the European Union (EU) banana import policy on the Eastern Caribbean economies, notably those of the Windward Islands, over the 1992–2002 period, and the remainder of the chapter is structured as follows. First, the economic importance of bananas to the Eastern Caribbean is discussed and it is shown that the commodity has made a major contribution to gross domestic product (GDP), the current account of the balance of payments (BOP) and employment in the early 1990s. The social importance of the banana industry is then discussed, and it is argued that the benefits of economic prosperity were passed onto ordinary farmers and their families, resulting in relatively low poverty rates and a more equitable division of wealth. The proceedings against the EU banana regime in the WTO are discussed in some detail, identifying who the main protagonists were and what their underlying motive had

[5] See Preville (2002: 114–17) for a discussion of the banana commodity chains through which Caribbean and dollar zone bananas are produced, shipped, marketed and distributed.

been. The EU's response to the WTO ruling is discussed in terms of the various modifications that have been proposed and implemented with regard to its banana import regime. The extent of the decline of the Eastern Caribbean's banana industry since the creation of the SEM in 1993 is analysed. It is argued that despite preferential market access enjoyed by these countries, a combination of declining returns, the uncertainty that prevailed since the creation of the single market and the subsequent WTO ruling have been the major causes of the industry's decline. The impact of a declining banana industry on the income of producers is then brought out, showing that the revenue of regional producers has declined by approximately 60 per cent since the WTO ruling and has resulted in greater impoverishment of the region as a whole. The extent to which the decline in the region's banana industry might have affected the Organisation of Eastern Caribbean States (OECS) economy as a whole, given their common currency and monetary policy as set by the Eastern Caribbean Central Bank (ECCB), is examined. Next, there is discussion of the economic and social outlook for the region under complete liberalisation in 2006. It draws upon a model of strategic behaviour developed in Preville (2002) and an economic outlook prepared by the World Bank in 2002. Finally, some concluding remarks are presented.

12.2 Economic importance of banana exports in the Eastern Caribbean

The economic importance of bananas to the Eastern Caribbean producers can be directly measured using three indicators: their contribution to real GDP, employment and the current account of the BOP.[6] Let us examine each of these in some detail.

12.2.1 Contribution to real GDP

In 1991, bananas accounted for slightly more than 20 per cent of Dominica's GDP, 7 per cent of St Vincent's GDP and 6.3 per cent of St Lucia's GDP, in real terms (table 12.1). Although in all of these islands the

[6] Bananas are also thought to have an *indirect* contribution to fiscal revenue. However, this aspect is not discussed here since it is not easily quantifiable, given that neither imported inputs nor exports are taxed.

Table 12.1 *Percentage contribution of bananas to real GDP*

	1991	1992	1993	1994	1995
St Lucia	6.3	8.2	7.1	5.3	5.7
St Vincent	7.0	9.9	6.1	1.7	3.7
Grenada	n/a	n/a	n/a	n/a	n/a
Dominica	20.3	20.1	19.7	18.2	16.0

Source: Pantin et al. (1999: 26)

Table 12.2 *Banana output as a percentage of agriculture GDP*

	1991	1992	1993	1994	1995
St Lucia	30.6	26.0	27.5	34.6	33.0
St Vincent	40.1	57.0	38.7	18.7	26.0
Grenada	n/a	n/a	n/a	n/a	n/a
Dominica	31.4	36.2	34.2	27.2	22.8

Source: Pantin et al. (1999: 26)

trend has been for some diversification away from bananas, in 1995 they nevertheless accounted for 16 per cent of Dominica's real GDP.[7]

Yet, these figures somewhat understate the real importance of bananas to the agricultural sector in these islands. Banana production accounted for no less than one fifth and as high as nearly two thirds of all agricultural production in St Lucia, St Vincent and Dominica during the 1991–5 period (table 12.2).

12.2.2 Contribution to employment

Not surprisingly, the substantial contribution of banana production to agriculture GDP is also captured by a strong employment effect in these economies. The employment effect is measured in terms of active growers[8] in the banana industry as well as projected direct and indirect labour effects. Table 12.3 shows that in the early to mid-1990s, there were no less

[7] The contribution of bananas to Grenada's economy is rather small and estimated at only 1 to 2 per cent.

[8] An active grower is defined as a farmer who owns land and actively cultivates bananas on it for the purpose of international trade in a particular calendar year.

Table 12.3 *Active growers in the Windward Islands banana industry*

	1992	1993	1994	1995	1996
St Lucia	9,500	9,663	8,011	7,379	6,677
St Vincent	8,000	7,800	7,375	6,139	5,667
Grenada	600	869	897	450	150
Dominica	6,550	5,779	6,763	6,218	5,471
Total	24,650	24,111	23,046	20,186	17,965

Source: WIBDECO (2003)

than 20,000 active growers in the Windward Islands banana industry and those growers were relatively evenly distributed among these islands, with the exception of Grenada.

Moreover, in terms of direct employment, it is estimated that in 1992 the Windward Islands banana industry employed approximately 56,000 workers, of whom more than 20,000 were employed in both St Lucia and St Vincent, and no less than 10,000 were employed in Dominica.[9] Considering that in 1992 the combined labour force of these islands was approximately 190,000 and that nearly 20 per cent of the labour force was unemployed, then effectively the regional banana industry accounted for more than one quarter of its employment. We shall discuss the indirect employment effects under the section on social importance of the banana industry below; however, let us first examine an important macroeconomic contribution – the contribution of banana exports to the stability of the current account of the BOP.

12.2.3 Contribution to the current account of the BOP

A first measure of the importance of bananas to the stability of the current account of the BOP is its contribution to merchandise exports (table 12.4). It is seen that for the major banana exporting islands, the commodity accounted for about half of their merchandise exports in the early 1990s, with a tendency for a decline towards the mid-1990s.

Yet, a better appreciation of the contribution of bananas to the current account of the BOP is captured by its overall effect on foreign exchange inflows. This is captured by examining the share of banana exports as a percentage of exports of goods and non-factor services, as a percentage of

[9] Based on data obtained from WIBDECO in September 2003.

Table 12.4 *Banana exports as a percentage of exports of goods*

	1991	1992	1993	1994	1995
St Lucia	48.0	53.8	41.3	42.9	41.4
St Vincent	49.6	47.5	40.2	30.2	39.8
Grenada	13.6	12.4	7.9	9.1	8.7
Dominica	53.7	55.3	50.0	44.3	36.5

Source: Pantin et al. (1999: 26)

exports of goods, non-factor services and remittances, and as a percentage of exports of goods, non-factor services, remittances and foreign direct investment, respectively. Let us examine each of these in greater detail. When exports of goods and non-factor services are considered, there is a distinctive decline in the contribution of bananas to the current account of the BOP with respect to St Lucia and, to a lesser extent, St Vincent (table 12.5).

Among the major sub-sectors within services, St Lucia's tourism sector is the most significant while that of Dominica is largely under-developed. This largely explains the observed differences that non-factor services make where the current account of the BOP is concerned.

As might be expected, when private remittances are introduced the contribution of bananas to the BOP typically declines for all countries, but not as drastically as was the case when only goods and non-factor services were considered (table 12.6). This is because the flow of remittances is relatively small in comparison with exports of non-factor services. A notable exception appears to be the case of St Lucia in 1993, when that ratio actually increased considerably to 48.4 per cent, reflecting a net outflow of remittances from the country to the rest of the world.

Finally, the effect of introducing foreign direct investment is to reduce the importance of the contribution of bananas to the current account of the BOP further, and that effect appears to have been strongest for St Vincent.

In addition to the importance of bananas for the economies of the Windward Islands, they are also important to the regional economy of the Eastern Caribbean on the whole, where a single currency, the Eastern Caribbean Dollar (ECD), issued and monitored by the Eastern Caribbean Central Bank (ECCB), has been in effect for nearly three decades. By the mid-1990s, bananas contributed 26 per cent of the merchandise exports of

Table 12.5 *Banana exports as a percentage of exports of goods and non-factor services*

	1991	1992	1993	1994
St Lucia	28.0	30.5	25.4	22.3
St Vincent	46.6	42.4	34.1	23.9
Grenada	6.8	4.8	2.7	2.7
Dominica	51.3	48.0	37.6	36.9

Source: Pantin et al. (1999: 27)

Table 12.6 *Banana exports as a percentage of exports of goods, non-factor services and private remittances*

	1991	1992	1993	1994
St Lucia	26.0	28.4	48.4	21.0
St Vincent	39.9	36.9	28.5	19.5
Grenada	5.2	3.8	2.2	2.2
Dominica	42.4	40.5	30.7	29.8

Source: Pantin et al. (1999: 27)

the regional economy and 7 per cent of regional exports of goods and non-factor services. Therefore, while banana exports are extremely important for stability of the current account of the BOP of the Windward Islands economies, their importance for the regional currency union is significantly less.

12.3 Social importance of banana exports in the Eastern Caribbean

Bananas play an extremely important role in the social stability of the economies of the major exporting countries in the Eastern Caribbean. Such social importance derives from the process through which Windward Islands bananas are produced for exports. In addition to the direct employment generated by the region's banana industry, there is a considerable indirect employment effect, which manifests itself through the number of persons resident in growers' and workers' households.

In the Windward Islands, it is estimated that 98,127 persons were resident in banana growers' households and a further 141,021 persons were resident in banana workers' households in 1992.[10] Therefore, although the region's banana industry directly employed only 56,428 persons in 1992, when its indirect employment effects are considered approximately 240,000 persons benefited from the industry in one way or another by being part of a grower or worker household. Consequently, there has been a progressive division of wealth in these societies, with a considerable multiplier effect.

The gender dimension is also important for understanding the social importance of banana production in the Windward Islands. A study by Babb (1998) reveals that 50 per cent of the households in Dominica are female headed, and corresponding figures for Grenada, St Vincent and St Lucia are 45 per cent, 44 per cent and 43 per cent respectively. This implies that any deterioration of the banana industry in these countries adversely impacts upon the welfare of women and the children for whom they are responsible.

12.4 WTO proceedings against the EU banana regime

As indicated in the introduction, at the signing of the Treaty of Rome in 1957 the EC authorised two banana import policies. Simultaneously, it allowed Germany to import virtually all its bananas from Latin America duty and tax free, and Britain, France, Spain and Portugal to import unlimited quantities of bananas from ACP countries duty and tax free. Banana imports from any other source were subjected to duty and tax. As such, when the time came for implementation of the Single European Market (SEM), EU Member States had to adopt a common policy on banana imports with respect to all sources of supply. The EU members that previously owned ACP colonies (Britain, France, Spain and Portugal) argued that bananas from these countries should continue to enjoy preferential access and enter the EU duty and tax free. Contemporaneously, the EU members that previously had little or no colonial interests among ACP countries (Germany, Belgium, Luxembourg, Netherlands, Ireland) argued that bananas from Latin America should be allowed duty- and tax-free entry into the EU.

Effective demand for bananas in the EU is essentially fixed, given that the commodity is both price- and income-inelastic. Additionally, the *perceived*

[10] Pantin et al. (1999: 31). Additionally, indirect employment covers port, transport and packaging workers.

cost of producing Latin American bananas is significantly lower than that of producing ACP bananas, and, whereas smallholder farms in ACP countries are already operating at capacity limit, large-scale Latin American plantations typically operate with capacity reserves.[11] Therefore, any decision to liberalise the EU banana trade fully, i.e. to grant duty- and tax-free market access to *all* exporting countries, would have been tantamount to eliminating Caribbean ACP supplies from the market and substituting Latin American supplies for these. With the preceding in mind, and given the EU's need to protect its own domestic producers, it opted for an import regime that largely preserved the existing pattern of trade where ACP countries were concerned, while all bananas imported from Latin America were subjected to a quota and a tariff. Germany was adversely affected by this policy since it continued to import bananas from Latin America, which were now subjected to a tariff. (Hence the seeds of disunity were allowed to take root.)

Consequently, the EU banana regime was challenged on several fronts. First, it was challenged in the ECJ by Germany, Denmark and the Benelux countries on the grounds that it would not fulfil the objectives of the single market. Second, some Latin American countries initiated a GATT panel to investigate the legality of the banana import policies of several EU members before the SEM, and another to investigate the legality of the new banana import policy under the SEM. Both these GATT panels ruled that the banana import policies did not conform with GATT law, particularly Article I which requires most favoured nation (MFN) treatment for all GATT members. Third, under the influence of the world's largest banana TNC, the United States initiated an investigation of the EU banana import policy under Section 301 of its 1974 Trade Act. Fourth, the United States along with several countries in Latin America initiated a WTO Panel to investigate the EU banana import policy, which ultimately led to its defeat. In this section we shall only examine the WTO Panel investigation and ruling in detail.[12] (See Preville (2002, 137–42) for a thorough discussion of the first three of these.)

[11] Let us put this point into proper perspective. The reader will appreciate that only one country in Latin America, Ecuador, is capable of supplying the entire EU market at approximately one third of the cost of ACP supplies, and still possess sufficient reserves to meet the demand of a country the size of New York city! By contrast, even if the EU bought every single banana grown in the ACP countries, its demand would be only approximately one-third exhausted.

[12] This section draws heavily upon the author's earlier work (Preville, 2002).

Joint and individual requests for consultations with the European Communities on its banana import regime were made by the United States, Ecuador, Guatemala, Honduras and Mexico (Complaining Parties) on 5 February 1996. In addition to the import regime established under EEC Regulation 404/93, consultations were also meant to address subsequent legislation, regulations and administrative processes related to it. These consultations did not result in a mutually satisfactory outcome, hence on 11 April 1996 the Complaining Parties made a request for establishment of a Panel. The Panel's terms of reference included examining violations under the GATT, the Agreement on Import Licensing Procedures, the Agreement on Agriculture, the GATS, and the Agreement on Trade Related Investment Measures (WTO, 1997a: 1).

In its defence, the EU deplored the manner in which the Panel had been established, questioning the adequacy of consultations[13] as well as the clarity of the issue[14] under dispute. However, the Complaining Parties countered that their action was consistent with Article 4.7 of the DSU, which provides for establishment of a Panel sixty days after the start of consultations (WTO, 1997a: 3–7). Additionally, the EU questioned the legitimacy of the US interests in the claim that was being pursued, since there was no banana trade between those countries. The US argued in turn that it had a significant commercial interest since two of its firms, Chiquita and Dole, had played a major role in developing the EU's banana market in the past. Moreover, the US argued that under Article XXIII of the GATT, dispute settlement action could be initiated by any Member if, in its view, one Member's action was inconsistent with another's interests (WTO, 1997a: 8–9).

Not surprisingly, the Panel ruled against the EU, concluding that certain aspects of its regime were inconsistent with its obligations under Articles I:1, III:4, X:3 and XIII:1 of the GATT,[15] Article 1.2 of the Licensing

[13] The EU argued that only the barest outline of complaints had been presented during consultations, and that Complaining Parties had not exhausted the possibility of reaching a mutually satisfactory solution as foreseen under Article 4.3 of the DSU (WTO, 1997a: paras. II.2, II.5).

[14] Specifically, the EU argued that at the consultations stage of dispute settlement the responding party should be given as clear a picture as possible of the case against it. It said it had prepared several questions for consideration of the Complaining Parties and had been in the process of preparing relevant responses to questions submitted by them when they announced a decision to establish a panel. Moreover, the request for establishment of a panel did not identify the specific measure at issue, but merely cited 'the regime' (WTO, 1997a: paras. II.3, II.9).

[15] These articles deal with the most favoured nation (MFN) treatment requirement of trade in goods. Specifically, Article I:1 deals with non-discriminatory tariff treatment; and Article XIII:1 deals with quota restrictions on sources of supply.

Agreement and Articles II and XVII of the GATS.[16] Additionally, it recommended that the Dispute Settlement Body request the EU to modify its banana regime, to make it conform with its obligations under the GATT, the Licensing Agreement and the GATS (WTO, 1997a: para. 9.1–9.2). The EU appealed the Panel's ruling both on certain issues of law and on some of the legal interpretations developed by the Panel. Specifically, the EU again took issue with the right of the US to advance claims under the GATT and the manner in which the Panel had been established (WTO, 1997b: paras. 15–18). Additionally, where the legal interpretations of the Panel were concerned, the EU brought many issues into question, taking them in turn under the categories of measures affecting trade in goods and services.

The Appellate Body largely upheld the findings of the Panel. In particular, it upheld the Panel's conclusion that the US had a right to bring a claim in the dispute and that the establishment of the Panel was consistent with requirements under Article 6.2 of the DSU (WTO, 1997b: para. 255a–b). Additionally, it upheld the conclusion of the Panel that the Agreement on Agriculture did not permit the EU to act in a manner inconsistent with its obligations under Article XIII of the GATT 1994; and that the allocation of shares of the tariff quota was not consistent with Article XIII:1 of the GATT 1994 (WTO, 1997b: para. 255d–e).

12.5 Changes to the EU regime for banana imports prior to and since the WTO ruling

In its ruling against the EU banana regime, the second GATT Panel instigated by the Latin Americans (mentioned above) had found both the import regime and the procedure through which the EU extended preferential market access to the ACP countries, i.e. the Lomé Convention, to be in contravention of GATT law (GATT, 1994: paras. 169–70), and mandated the EU to bring its import policy into compliance. With the support of ACP countries, the EU was able to prevent the GATT Council from adopting the panel report. Yet, realising that if these Latin American countries initiated a WTO Panel to investigate the EU banana import policy it would most likely be defeated, the EU proposed to create its first Framework Agreement with the Latin Americans.

[16] These are the GATS non-discrimination clauses, which require that WTO members accord all 'services' and 'service suppliers' similar treatment, regardless of the mode of supply of such services.

Under the proposed Framework Agreement, the Complaining Parties would be allocated certain shares of the import quota based on past performance, and the quota would be increased annually by an autonomous amount. In addition to guaranteeing market shares for these countries, the EU agreed to expand the tariff quota annually and reduce the in-quota tariff to ECU 75 per metric tonne (European Council, 1998: Article 18). But the Latin American countries were divided on the matter, in terms of both the size of the quota and their individual shares, rendering the agreement unstable. Notably, Ecuador, Guatemala, Honduras and Panama objected to the agreement, while Costa Rica, Colombia, Nicaragua and Venezuela accepted it (European Commission, 1994: 11–12). Nevertheless, the EU had ensured that the Framework Agreement was agreed to by the US as part of the completion of negotiations under the Uruguay Round.[17] Additionally, the GATT Council agreed to grant the EU a waiver of Article I.1, thus allowing the EU to give preferential treatment to the goods originating from the ACP countries (European Commission, 1995: 16).

Since 1999, the EU has modified its banana regime several times and the evidence suggests that most of these modifications have taken into consideration the need for WTO compatibility. This is reflected in the sheer number of Commission Regulations that have been passed to modify the original Regulation 404/93. In introducing Commission Regulation 2374 in 2000, while the EU stated that the regulation was being adopted with a view to ensure uninterrupted supplies and trade with the partner countries, it carefully stated that subsequent measures might be introduced with a view to 'complying with the international commitments entered into by the Community within the World Trade Organization'.[18] Moreover, the regulations introduced in 2001 gave even greater recognition to the WTO rulings. Council Regulation 216 of 2001 clearly states that it takes due account 'of the conclusions of the special group set up under the dispute settlement system of the World Trade Organization (WTO)'.[19] It further sets out the size of the tariff quotas, which is based on a projection of *effective* demand for bananas in the EU as of 2001, structured as follows:

[17] As the EU explains, although the Framework Agreement was subjected to 'criticism both inside and outside the Community', it nevertheless formed 'an integral part of the Uruguay Round as signed in April in Marakesh'. (European Commission, 1994: 12). The US was one of the signatories.

[18] See European Commission (2000).

[19] See European Commission (2001a).

(a) a tariff quota of 2,200,000 tonnes net weight, called 'quota A';
(b) an additional tariff quota of 353,000 tonnes net weight, called 'quota B';
(c) an autonomous tariff quota of 850,000 tonnes net weight, called 'quota C'.

In this revised regime, imports under tariff quotas 'A' and 'B' are subjected to a customs duty of €75 per tonne, while those under quota 'C' are subjected to a customs duty of €300 per tonne. Additionally, the EU grants ACP countries a tariff preference of €300 per tonne, consistent with its obligations to the ACP countries.[20]

The last significant changes that have since been made to the tariff quotas were introduced in December 2001 under Commission Regulation 2587 and, according to the EU, the changes introduced 'shall apply to imports of fresh products falling within CN code 08030019 until the entry into force, no later than 1 January 2006, of the rate of the common customs tariff for those products established under the procedure provided for in Article XXVIII of the General Agreement on Tariffs and Trade'.[21] In other words, these rules will apply until 31 December 2005. The notable change to the tariff quotas are: quota 'B' has increased to 453,000 tonnes; while quota 'C' has reduced to 750,000 tonnes. ACP countries continue to enjoy a tariff preference of €300 per tonne and zero duty on imports.[22] Additionally, 'traditional importers' have been redefined to refer specifically to primary importers, and the share of licences awarded to non-traditional importers has increased from 3.5 per cent to 11 per cent. Subsequent regulations passed by the Commission with respect to bananas have not altered the sizes of the quotas, or the applicable tariffs, but have modified rules for their allocation to specific countries within the set categories.[23]

12.6 Extent of decline of the Eastern Caribbean region's banana industry

Let us now examine the extent to which the Windward Islands banana industry has actually declined since the implementation of the SEM in 1993 (internal liberalisation) and particularly following the WTO ruling in 1997. Decline of the industry is measured in terms of reduction in production,

[20] Ibid., p. 3. [21] See European Commission (2001b).
[22] Ibid., pp. 14–15. This effectively grants the ACP countries duty-free market access.
[23] See, for instance, European Commission (2002) and (2003).

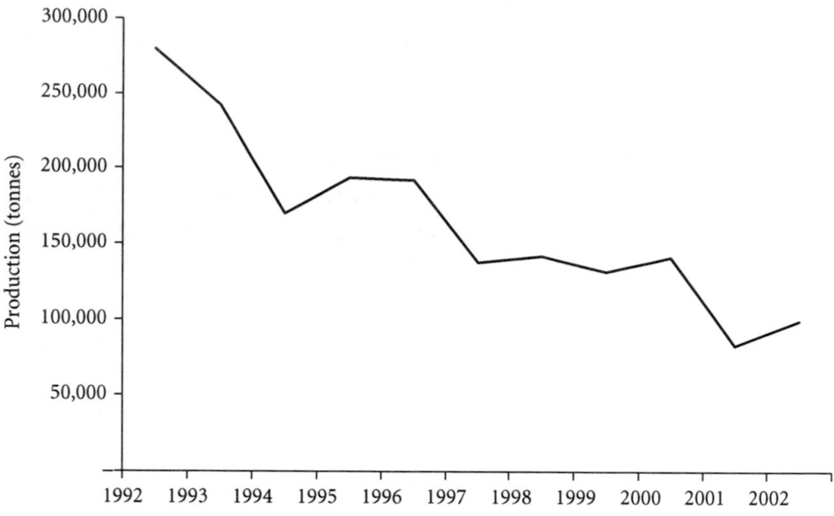

Source: Author's construction based on data from WIBDECO (2003)
Figure 12.1 Extent of decline of Windward Islands banana production

exports[24] and employment, respectively. Figure 12.1 shows that Windward Islands banana production has declined from 279,812 tonnes in 1992 to a mere 99,089 tonnes in 2002, or by approximately 65 per cent over that period.

Not surprisingly, the rate of decline in Windward Islands banana production was most severe in the 1992–4 and 1996–2001 periods, corresponding to the periods of implementation of the SEM and the protracted WTO dispute and its settlement, respectively. The uncertainty over whether or not the Windward Islands would continue to enjoy preferential market access in the EU when the SEM was implemented resulted in a decline in production of approximately 39 per cent. However, once these countries were assured of continued preferential market access, there was an initial recovery in production over the 1994–6 period (figure 12.1). Additionally, as we have seen, by late 1995 it had become clear that the United States, along with several major banana-producing countries in

[24] With very minor exceptions, practically all bananas produced in the Windward Islands are for export and so the production and export trends are similar. Moreover, where there are exceptions, such differences between production and export are statistically insignificant at the 1 per cent level.

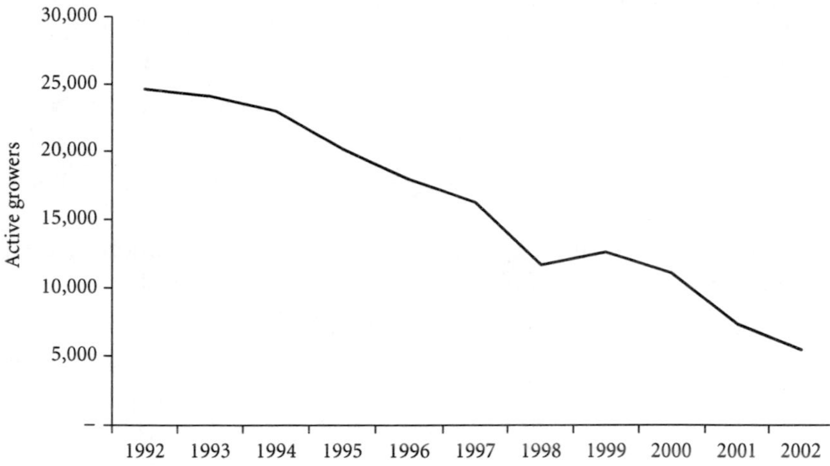

Source: Author's construction based on data from WIBDECO (2003)
Figure 12.2 Extent of decline in active growers of Windward Islands bananas

Latin America, intended to establish a WTO Panel for investigation of the legality of EU banana import policy. Since it is well known that the EU banana import policy favours the Windward Islands, their producers were aware that any finding of the WTO Panel against the EU would essentially be a finding against their interest. Moreover, these producers had every reason to believe that the WTO Panel would rule against the EU in light of the fact that two previous GATT Panels had found EU banana import policy to contravene GATT law. Consequently, coupled with declining returns, there was a secular decline in Windward Islands banana production over the 1996–2002 period, with the industry's output contracting by 57 per cent.

The extent of decline of the regional banana industry is also captured by the trend in active growers (figure 12.2), which shows that the number of active growers in the Windward Islands has declined from 24,650 to 5,475 over the 1992–2002 period, or by approximately 78 per cent.

The decline in the number of active growers of Windward Islands bananas follows the trend in decline in production, but with a much steeper gradient. Implementation of the SEM does not appear to have been a cause for great concern among growers, in light of the fact that slightly less than 7 per cent of them actually exited the industry over the 1992–4 period. However, the protracted WTO dispute, which culminated in an adverse ruling against the EU, coupled with changes in the regime since the WTO ruling, have been seen as major causes for concern among growers since 1995. The number of active growers declined by approximately 29 per cent over the 1994–7 period, and by approximately 66 per cent over the 1997–2002 period. While the WTO Panel was looking into the banana dispute, anxiety and uncertainty among growers resulted in a significant number of them exiting the industry. However, once the WTO Panel had ruled against the EU there was no need for further speculation and hence there was a massive exodus of growers out of the banana industry. In fact, within the first year following the WTO ruling, the number of active growers had declined by approximately 28 per cent relative to their 1997 level, before stabilising somewhat for the next two years.

So to summarise, since the implementation of the SEM the Windward Islands banana industry has contracted significantly in real terms, whether industry decline is measured in terms of reduction in production and exports, or active growers. Output of the Windward Islands banana industry has shrunk by 65 per cent, and the industry has lost 78 per cent of its active growers since 1992. In both cases, most of that decline took place during the period under which the WTO Panel was investigating the EU banana import policy and subsequently when that Panel had ruled against the EU, and since the EU's implementation of modified regimes.

12.7 Impact of industry decline on the Windward Islands export revenue

The statistically significant contraction of the Windward Islands banana industry is expected to have had a profound adverse impact on the region's revenue from banana exports, and figure 12.3 confirms such expectation.

Revenue obtained from exports of Windward Islands bananas declined from ECD 376.2 million in 1992 to ECD 117.7 million in 2002, or by approximately 69 per cent. Implementation of the SEM resulted in significant revenue losses of 42 per cent during the 1992–4 period; however, even more significant revenue losses of up to 60 per cent were incurred during

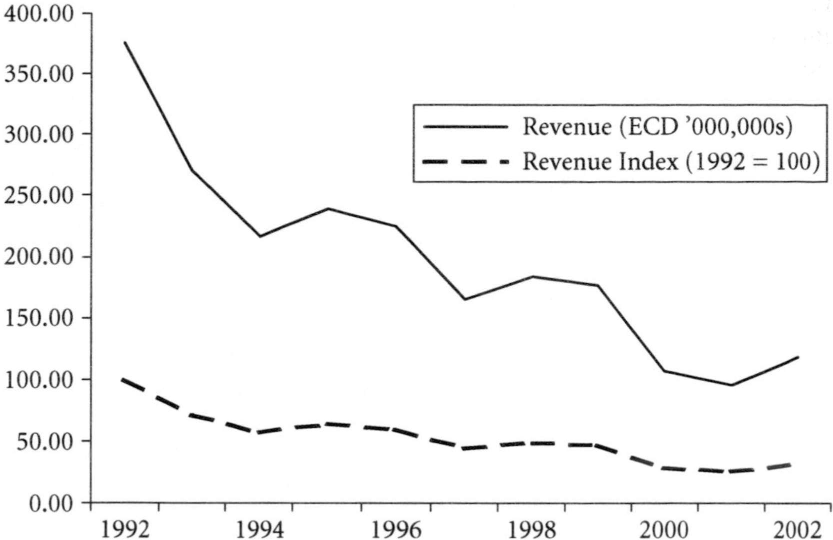

Source: Author's construction based on data from WIBDECO (2003)

Figure 12.3 Impact of declining banana industry on regional export revenue

the 1995–2001 period of the WTO dispute, its settlement and the EU's implementation of alternative banana import policies.

Whereas all of the Windward Islands banana industries have been adversely affected by the SEM and changes in the EU banana import policy since the WTO ruling, individual countries' export revenues have been affected to varying degrees. Figure 12.4 shows that in absolute terms, St Lucia appears to have been most severely affected by developments in the EU banana import policy since 1992, with its export revenue falling from ECD 185 million to ECD 59 million over the 1992–2002 period.

Absolute declines in banana export revenue were also substantial for St Vincent, falling from ECD 101 million to ECD 39 million, and for Dominica, falling from ECD 82 million to ECD 20 million, over the 1992–2002 period (figure 12.4). Grenada had never been a major exporter of bananas in the Eastern Caribbean region. Yet, even there it is clear that for the period since the WTO ruling (1997–2002) its industry has further declined to the extent that export revenue has remained below ECD 1 million. In fact in relative terms, export revenue from Grenada's banana industry has contracted the most since 1992 (see figure 12.5), even after controlling for an export ban that was

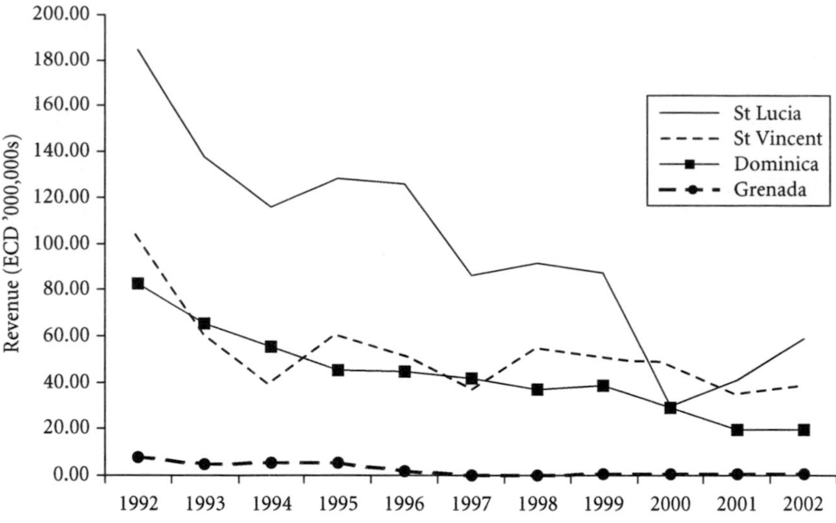

Source: Author's construction based on data from WIBDECO (2003)
Figure 12.4 Banana export revenue decline in individual countries

imposed by WIBDECO in 1997, resulting in no exports from Grenada that year.[25]

In relative terms, where the other Windward Islands were concerned, Dominica appears to have been most adversely affected since 1992, losing 78 per cent of its export revenue over the 1992–2002 period, followed by St Lucia, 68 per cent, and St Vincent, 62 per cent (figure 12.5). Additionally, the rates of decline in export revenue were highest for St Lucia and St Vincent, with Dominica's being the most gradual.

In summary, the substantial decline in output of the Windward Islands banana industry is expected to have adversely impacted economic growth and increased unemployment. (The unemployment effect is quantified below.) Additionally, export revenues of all countries have declined considerably, suggesting possible deterioration in their BOP positions given that

[25] Grenada resumed exports in November 1998. It must be noted though, that the overall decline in Grenada's banana industry cannot be attributed exclusively to external circumstances, i.e. implementation of the SEM by the EU in 1993 and the ruling on illegality of the EU's banana import policy by the WTO in 1997. Grenada had long been diversifying its agricultural production away from bananas and is a major producer of nutmeg and spices, but the WTO ruling does appear to have caused it to take decisive action to exit the industry.

Source: Author's construction based on data from WIBDECO (2003)
Figure 12.5 Rate of banana export revenue decline in individual countries

they have not developed alternative industries to compensate for revenue shortfalls from banana exports. Let us therefore discuss the impact of this decline on the individual economies and the OECS region.

12.8 Impact of industry decline on individual countries and the OECS region

Let us now discuss the extent to which industry decline has adversely affected these countries in the contexts of their growth rates, overall contributions to the current account of the BOP and unemployment.

12.8.1 Impact of industrial decline on economic growth

Economic growth has been sluggish in St Lucia and Dominica, averaging 2 per cent, and somewhat more buoyant in Grenada, averaging over 5 per cent, and St Vincent, averaging over 4 per cent over the 1995–2000 period. Additionally, it would appear that for Dominica and to a lesser extent St Lucia, growth in agriculture GDP influences the overall direction of economic growth (figure 12.6). In Dominica, the significant contraction of the

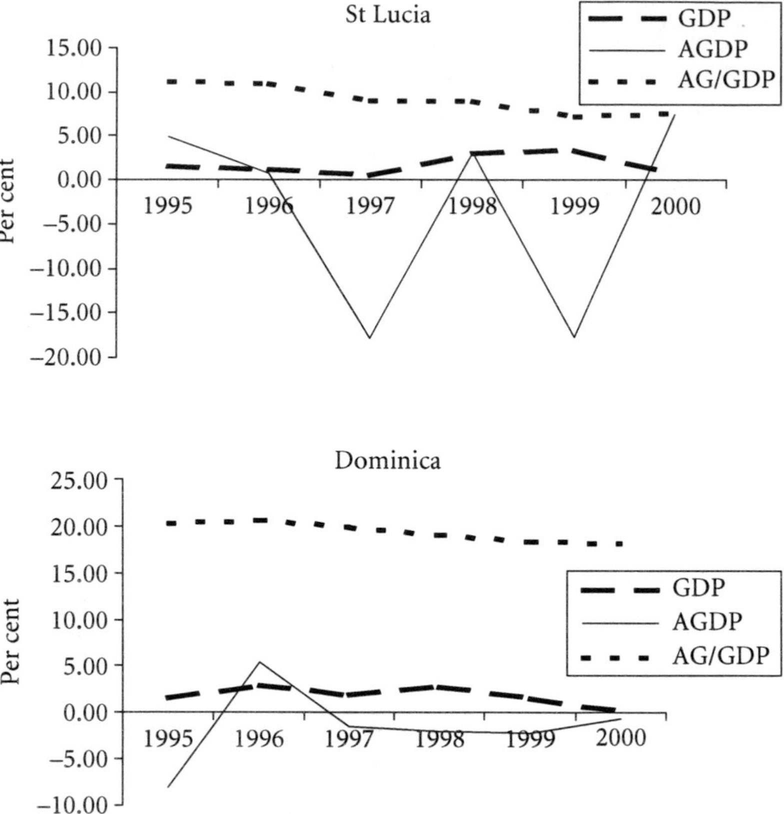

Source: Author's construction based on data from ECCB (2002, 2001)
Figure 12.6 Growth in GDP, Agriculture GDP (AGDP) and Agriculture's share of GDP (AG/GDP) in St Lucia and Dominica

agricultural sector in 1995 (−8.1 per cent) resulted in slim growth that year (1.6 per cent); however, recovery of the agriculture sector in the following year (5.5 per cent) resulted in nearly twice the growth rate of the previous year (3.1 per cent). Subsequently, there has been a tendency for Dominica's agriculture sector to contract at an average rate of −1.6 per cent over the 1997–2000 period, and this has been mirrored by a modest 1.6 per cent growth of GDP on average. Growth of St Lucia's agriculture GDP over the 1995–2000 period has been characterised by significant contractions, followed by brief periods of modest recovery, and growth of the economy typically follows that trend. Growth of St Lucia's agriculture sector averaged 2.9 per cent over the 1995–6 period and this was mirrored by a 1.5 per cent growth of GDP. The significant contraction of the agriculture sector in 1997 (−17.8 per cent) resulted in a stagnant economy with growth of less than 1 per cent. Subsequently, the recovery of the agriculture sector in 1998 (3.1 per cent) coincided with the recovery of the economy (3.1 per cent), and when the agriculture sector experienced its next major contraction in 1999 (−17.6 per cent) St Lucia's economy returned to stagnation one year later.

The major reason why the performance of St Lucia's agriculture sector in 1999 did not immediately impact economic growth as in 1997 is linked to increased diversification of the economy, with agriculture accounting for a decreasing share of GDP, falling from 11.1 per cent in 1996 to 7.2 per cent in 1999. In Dominica on the other hand, agriculture's share of GDP has changed very little over the same period and remains at more than 18 per cent in 2000 (figure 12.6).

Conversely, for Grenada, and to a lesser extent St Vincent, growth in agriculture GDP appears to have a much less significant impact on the overall direction of economic growth (figure 12.7).

St Vincent's agriculture sector experienced a record growth of 42 per cent in 1995 and this translated to economic growth of slightly more than 8 per cent that year, with agriculture's share of GDP at slightly less than 16 per cent. Subsequently, the significant contraction of St Vincent's agriculture sector over the 1996–7 period of −9.7 per cent on average had an adverse impact on the economy, which grew at 2.1 per cent on average. The recovery of St Vincent's agriculture in 1998 (8.3 per cent) did result in a significant improvement in economic growth (5.8 per cent); however, since 1999 the performance of the agriculture sector appears to have had a noticeably weaker impact on economic growth. St Vincent's economy is gradually becoming more diversified, with agriculture's share of GDP falling from 15.6 per cent in 1995 to 11.5 per cent in 1999. Therefore, while developments in agriculture continue to impact overall growth, the tendency is for the extent of this influence to diminish over time.

Grenada's economy has shown the most resilience to developments in the agriculture sector and the tendency has been for an improvement in such resilience over time. In 1995 the nearly 7 per cent growth of Grenada's agriculture sector was accompanied by a slightly more than 3 per cent growth of GDP. However, when the agriculture sector contracted by nearly 8 per cent the following year, GDP growth declined only perceptibly, remaining at slightly less than 3 per cent. Subsequent developments in

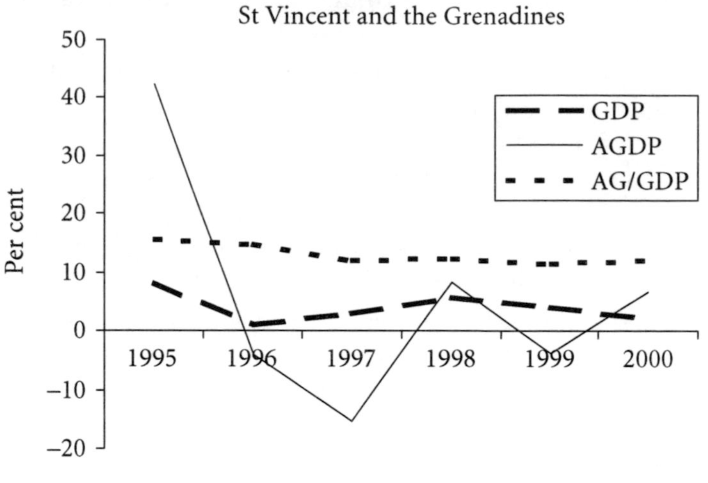

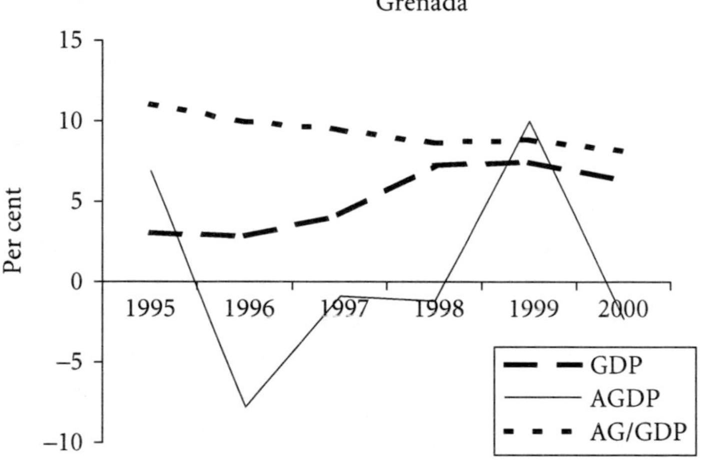

Source: Author's construction based on data from ECCB (2002, 2001)

Figure 12.7 Growth in GDP, Agriculture GDP (AGDP) and Agriculture's share of GDP (AG/GDP) in St Vincent and Grenada

Grenada's agriculture sector over the 1997–2000 period appear to have had little impact on its economic growth, which averaged 6.4 per cent. The explanation for Grenada's growth performance is linked to greater diversification of its economy away from agriculture over time, with agriculture accounting for only 8.2 per cent of its GDP in 2000 (figure 12.7).

So to summarise, the performance of the agriculture sector impacts to varying degrees on economic growth among the Windward Islands, with Dominica being the most vulnerable and Grenada the least. The extent of vulnerability of growth to the performance of agriculture depends on agriculture's contribution to GDP – as agriculture's share of GDP declines, overall economic growth is less susceptible to developments in the agriculture sector. Therefore, while developments in the EU regime for banana imports since the SEM was implemented have adversely affected economic growth of all countries, it has been Dominica's growth that has been worst hit, followed by St Lucia and St Vincent, while Grenada's economic growth appears to have been immune to developments in EU banana import policy. Let us now examine the impact of developments in EU banana import policy on the BOP positions of these countries.

12.8.2 Impact on the current account of the BOP

Another indicator of the extent to which contraction of the banana industry is expected to have had an adverse impact on individual economies and the regional Eastern Caribbean economy is its contribution to reducing the deficit (or increasing the surplus) on the current account of the BOP. In the Eastern Caribbean context, the major components of the current account to consider are goods and services, particularly the extent to which banana exports contribute to total exports of goods and non-factor services. Figure 12.8 shows that over the 1994–2000 period, the general tendency was for a decrease in the share of bananas in the export of goods from the Windward Islands, although that trend was less distinct for St Lucia and St Vincent, which show alternating periods of increase and decrease. Over that period bananas accounted for the maximum share of St Lucia's exports of goods in 1996 (54 per cent), followed by 1999 (53 per cent), but had declined considerably to only 20 per cent in 2000. St Vincent's maximum occurred in 1998 (41 per cent) and had declined to 34 per cent in 2000, while for Dominica, its ratio of banana exports to exports of goods follows a secular decline from 43 per cent in 1994 to 22 per cent in 2000.[26]

Moreover, when exports of goods and non-factor services are considered, it appears that the importance of the contribution of bananas to

[26] In the case of Grenada, its share of bananas in exports of goods had diminished to less than 1 per cent since 1997, while Dominica's trend suggests increased agricultural diversification.

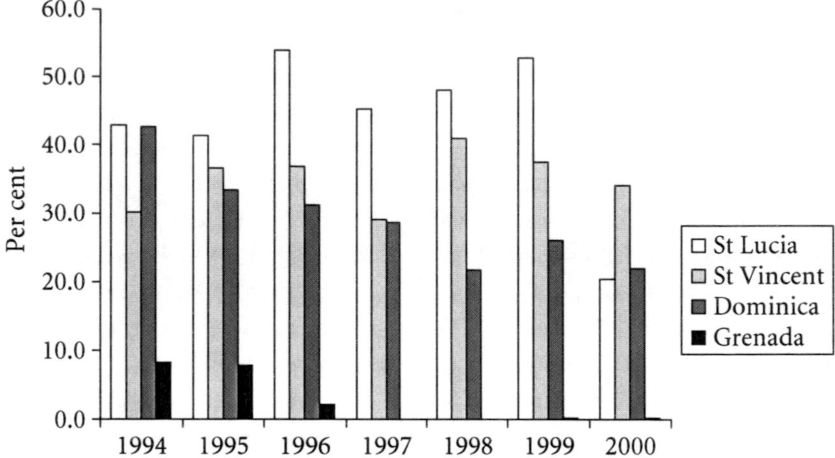

Source: Author's construction based on data from ECCB (2002, 2001)

Figure 12.8 Contribution of bananas to exports of goods

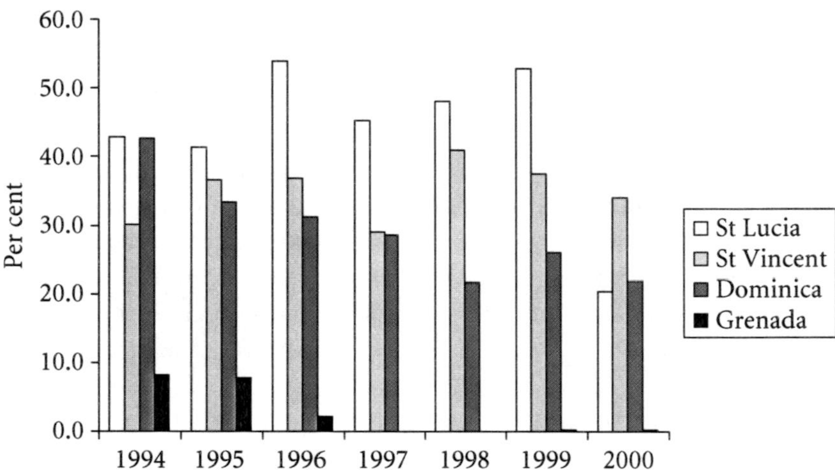

Source: Author's construction based on data from ECCB (2002, 2001)

Figure 12.9 Contribution of bananas to exports of goods and non-factor services

stability of the current account of the BOP has diminished over time (figure 12.9). The contribution of bananas as a percentage of exports of goods and non-factor services for Dominica (the least diversified economy of the Windward Islands) declined from 20.4 per cent in 1994 to 7.8 per cent in 2000; for St Vincent and St Lucia, the contribution of

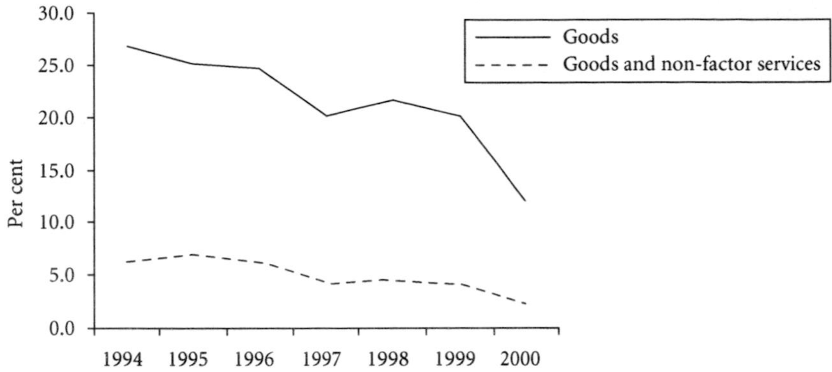

Source: Author's construction based on data from ECCB (2002, 2001)
Figure 12.10 Contribution of bananas to the stability of the current account of the BOP within the Eastern Caribbean Currency Union

bananas to exports of goods and non-factor services declined from 13.1 per cent and 12.7 per cent in 1994 to 9.9 per cent and 2.9 per cent in 2000, respectively.[27]

At the regional level within the Eastern Caribbean Currency Union, the contribution of bananas to the stability of the current account of the balance of payments has also diminished significantly over time (figure 12.10).

In 1994 bananas contributed 26.8 per cent of the value of exports of goods from the Eastern Caribbean Currency Union area. However, after following a secular declining trend over the 1994–2000 period, this figure had diminished to only 12.1 per cent in 2000. Moreover, when the commodity's contribution to exports of goods and non-factor services is analysed, an even more pronounced trend emerges – its contribution is seen to diminish from 6.3 per cent in 1994 to a mere 2.5 per cent in 2000.

12.8.3 Impact on (un)employment

We discussed earlier the extent of decline of the Windward Islands banana industry as measured by the decline in the number of active growers. Quantification of the exact contribution to regional unemployment rates

[27] It has been noted above that since 1997 bananas accounted for less than 1 per cent of Grenada's export of goods. Therefore, when non-factor services are included, the importance of bananas to Grenada's economy becomes barely discernible.

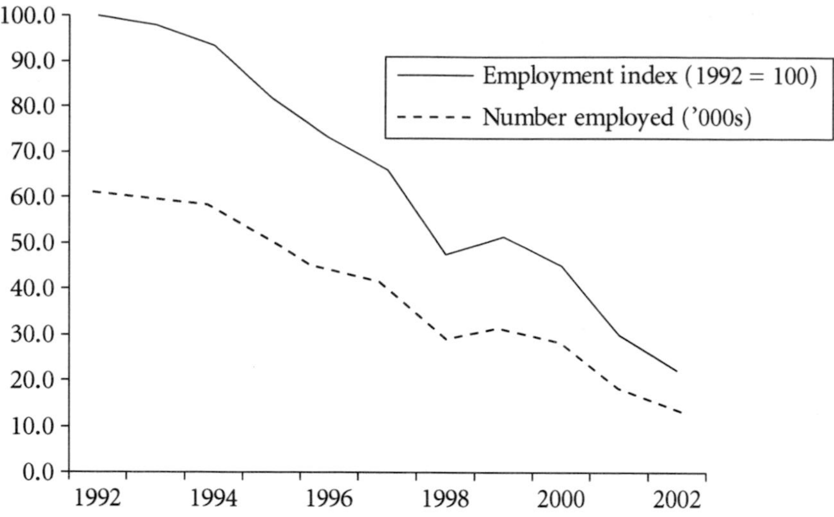

Source: Author's construction based on data from ECCB (2002, 2001)
Figure 12.11 Changes in the number of persons employed in the regional banana industry and an index of employment

that have arisen from contraction of the banana industry is difficult for two reasons. First, unemployment data series covering the period 1992–2002 are not available for most of the Windward Islands. Second, the number of persons employed by a grower depends on the availability of surplus labour, as well as family relations.[28] However, based on a number of studies that have been conducted on the region's banana industry, a crude estimate of the mean number of workers employed per active grower has been found to be 2.49.[29] Using that estimate of the mean (and assuming it remained unchanged over the 1992–2002 period), a data series of the approximate number of persons directly employed by the banana industry has been estimated. Figure 12.11 shows absolute changes in the number of persons employed by the regional banana industry, along with an employment index.

[28] On a typical smallholder banana farm in the Windward Islands, it is quite common to find that most of the workers are either family members or close friends of family members. It is quite rare that workers on a smallholder farm have no relationship whatsoever with the owner (grower).

[29] These studies include: a survey conducted by Cargill Technical Services (1998) on St Lucia, a study performed by Addy (1999) for the International Labour Organization (ILO), and a study conducted by Pantin et al. (1999) for WINFA, CPDC and Oxfam Caribbean.

It is seen that the approximate number of persons employed in the regional banana industry has declined considerably from 61,379 in 1992 to 13,633 in 2002, i.e. approximately 86 per cent of the labour force within the banana industry was made unemployed over the 1992–2002 period. With an estimate of 20 per cent of the labour force of the Windward Islands employed in the banana industry in 1992, the contraction in the regional banana industry has contributed approximately 17 per cent of the region's unemployment. Moreover, the real challenge appears to be that most of this unemployment is *structural* in nature. The typical banana farmer has only primary education and is over forty years old; therefore, the possibilities for absorbing the labour released in another sector of the economy are extremely slim. This is particularly important in light of the fact that most of the economic diversification (and growth) that has been taking place throughout the region has been in the services sector and that sector requires a highly skilled labour force.

So to summarise, from the preceding analysis four conclusions can be arrived at. First, at the regional level very little (and declining) significance can be attached to the contribution of bananas towards the stability of the current account of the BOP, particularly when both goods and non-factor services are taken into account. Second, for the banana exporting countries, although its contribution remains extremely important where exports of goods are concerned, when non-factor services are also taken into account the contribution of bananas to stability of the current account of the BOP appears not to be that significant. Third, the most significant impact of changes to the EU banana import policy over the 1992–2002 period on the Eastern Caribbean region has been increased *structural* unemployment. Fourth, though not easy to establish a statistically significant relationship, growth in the agriculture sector contributes positively to growth of GDP.

12.9 Economic and social outlook for the OECS economies (2004–2006)

So far, we have seen that the banana industry in the Windward Islands has undergone extensive contraction since the implementation of the SEM, and that most of this contraction has actually taken place since the commencement of the WTO dispute, including the prelude to this battle, i.e. the instigation of a Section 301 procedure under the United States Trade Act of 1974 in 1994 by the United States Trade Representative. Since 1992, the regional banana industry has contracted by approximately 65 per cent, falling from an output of 279,812 tonnes in 1992 to a mere 99,089 tonnes in 2002. Moreover, in the process the number of active growers in the regional banana industry has declined by approximately 78 per cent during the 1992–2002 period, falling from 24,650 to 5,475 growers. With an estimated 2.49 persons being directly employed for every grower in the regional banana industry, this implies that approximately 47,746 persons were made unemployed (and most of whom possibly still are) since the onset of the SEM in 1992.

Yet, analysis of the classical macroeconomic indicators (growth and the BOP) suggests, at the very best, weak causal links between the extent of decline of the regional banana industry and deterioration of such indicators. No definitive causal links could be established between growth of the agriculture sector and growth of real GDP. However, the empirical evidence suggests that the growth rates of economies that are least diversified (with agriculture accounting for a significant share of GDP) have been adversely affected the most. Additionally, when the contribution of bananas to the stability of the current account of the BOP is analysed, that ratio has declined significantly over the 1994–2000 period, especially when exports of both goods and non-factor services are taken into account. In the meantime, the EU is set to implement two major changes to its banana import policy over the 2004–2006 period. First, the EU will be required to expand its tariff-quota in May 2004, in order to accommodate ten accession (new) members. Second, following from the protracted and acrimonious WTO banana dispute, the EU has proposed to dismantle its tariff-quota completely and replace it with a tariff in 2006. With the preceding analysis in mind, what therefore might these policy changes imply, in terms of an economic and social outlook for the individual banana exporting countries and the regional OECS economy? Let us briefly discuss.

12.9.1 Economic outlook

The World Bank projected that growth rates in the developing countries might reach 3.9 per cent and 4.7 per cent in 2003 and 2004, respectively, with the Latin America and Caribbean regions projected to grow at much slower rates of 1.8 per cent and 3.7 per cent.[30] Assuming these rates are representative for the region as a whole, then the smaller Eastern Caribbean economies can achieve growth rates of up to 5 per cent and 6 per cent, in 2003 and 2004, respectively. For the less diversified of the Windward Islands, growth rates of 2.5 per cent and 3.5 per cent might be more realistic for 2003 and 2004, respectively. However, the changes in the policy regime proposed by the EU over the 2004–2006 period are likely to impact these growth rates adversely and increase *structural* unemployment.

Expansion of the tariff-quota in May 2004 can adversely impact export revenue, if the EU underestimates the current level of banana re-exports from its members to these accession countries.[31] Additionally, given that accession members will be required to pay a 20 per cent tariff on all imports and that their income levels are significantly lower than existing EU members, *effective* demand is likely to decline. Yet, once the quota has been set, regardless of effective demand, TNCs operating from the *dollar zone* can engage in a strategic game, i.e. continue to fill the quota in order to force market prices downwards. Any substantial decline in market prices over a protracted period will cause Eastern Caribbean growers to exit production, with resulting increases in *structural* unemployment.

Liberalisation, i.e. elimination of the tariff-quota system and its replacement with a tariff in 2006, will result in cessation of banana production in the Eastern Caribbean, which in turn will result in deterioration of its BOP position, economic growth, and substantial increase in *structural* unemployment. The US-based TNCs that dominate the EU banana market have a history of engaging in anti-competitive behaviour once an opportunity presents itself (see Preville (2002: 61–7) for a discussion of this). The oversupply situation that existed in the EU prior to creating the SEM is the most recent instance of such behaviour. Preville (2002: 263–83) has developed an oligopoly model of the EU banana market, in which it is assumed that firms are engaged in Cournot-Nash behaviour for setting quantities, while each of the dominant TNCs command some degree of market power based on branding and oligopolistic interdependence is strong. He then simulates a game that dominant TNCs are likely to play under liberalisation (based

[30] See the World Bank Group, 'World Bank sees sluggish economic outlook, calls for progress on trade issues that will help developing countries', *News Release No.* 2003/151/S, 11 December 2002.

[31] There is some evidence that banana re-exports from EU members to several of the accession members constitutes a significant component of their total imports. However, more research needs to be done to quantify it accurately.

on observed empirical evidence), which ultimately eliminates the Eastern Caribbean countries from the market while reducing the welfare of EU consumers and increasing monopoly power and profits for TNCs.

12.9.2 Social outlook

We have seen that the banana production process in the Eastern Caribbean relies strongly on family members and close friends for its labour supply. Additionally, the indirect employment effects, though not easily quantifiable, are considerable – approximately four persons reside in each grower's household and a further three persons reside in each worker's household. Considering that most of the unemployment created within the banana sector is structural in nature, it implies increased poverty for all growers, workers and their households. The policy change that will be made necessary in order to accommodate accession members in 2004 is not likely to worsen social conditions within the Eastern Caribbean, given that their current quota levels will continue to be assured.[32] However, the policy change that the EU has proposed to implement from 2006 is likely to have catastrophic implications for the region's poverty, given that it will *substantially* increase structural unemployment, when the few remaining banana growers cease production. Further research will need to be conducted in order to estimate the extent of increase in regional poverty as a consequence of this proposed policy change.

12.10 Conclusions

The objective of this study has been to analyse the impact of implementation of the various changes in the EU market for banana imports on the Eastern Caribbean region over the 1992–2002 period, and to suggest how further modifications that are scheduled to be made to EU banana import policy over the 2004–2006 period might affect the situation. Since 1992 there have been three distinct sets of banana import policy changes: first, the creation of the common organisation of the market in bananas under the implementation of the SEM with Regulation 404 of 1993; second, the

[32] The impact of expanding the tariff-quota to accommodate EU accession members in 2004 on the Eastern Caribbean's poverty is likely to be negligible only if it does not result in further structural unemployment. If the quota size is accurately estimated, then there should be a very negligible adverse impact on market prices and export revenue.

creation of a framework agreement between the EU and a few countries in Latin America as a consequence of a second GATT Panel ruling against the EU banana import policy in 1994; third, the implementation of a number of changes to the original banana import policy introduced under Regulation 404 of 1993 since a WTO Panel ruling against the EU banana import policy in 1997.

Overwhelmingly, the empirical evidence has shown that the implementation of various changes to the EU policy for banana imports since 1992 has significantly adversely impacted on the economies of the Eastern Caribbean, particularly those that export bananas, i.e. the Windward Islands. The most visible and directly quantifiable indicator of this impact has been significant increases in structural unemployment. Active growers in the regional banana industry declined by approximately 78 per cent over the period 1992–2002, falling from 24,650 to 5,475, and this translates to a contraction in the labour force employed in the banana sector by approximately 86 per cent. Yet another directly quantifiable indicator of the extent of decline of the region's banana industry is the contraction in production, with real output falling from 279,812 tonnes in 1992 to 99,089 tonnes in 2002, or approximately 65 per cent. In both these cases, most of the contraction has taken place since the instigation of WTO action against the EU banana import policy.

Additionally, though it remains difficult to establish statistically significant relationships between economic growth and growth of the agriculture sector on the one hand, and the impact of declining export revenue on the current account of the BOP, on the other hand, the empirical evidence leads to two conclusions. First, the growth trend of most of these countries is influenced by the trend in agriculture growth, although the more diversified the production base the less susceptible is economic growth to growth of agriculture. Second, banana exports make a significant contribution to reducing the deficit on the current account of the BOP, although when non-factor services are also taken into account, the extent of that contribution significantly declines.

The likely long-run consequence of liberalising the EU banana trade has both economic and social dimensions and the social dimensions seem to be more important. Increased structural unemployment leads to increased poverty and can lead to increased societal instability. In the face of such adversity, crime and the lure of illicit drugs become alternative industries for the poor and indigent.

References

Addy, D. (1999) 'Restructuring and the Loss of Preferences: Labor Challenges for the Caribbean Banana Industry', *ILO Caribbean Studies and Working Papers, No. 1*

Babb, C. (1998) 'Gender, Women and Poverty in the Windward Islands', UNIFEM, UNDP (March)

Cargill Technical Services Limited (1998) 'Socio Economic Impact of Banana Restructuring in St Lucia', vol. 1 (November)

ECCB (2001) 'Balance of Payments for Year Ending December 2001', Basseterre, St Kitts (December)

ECCB (2002) 'Report and Statement of Accounts for Financial Year 1 April 2001 to 31 March 2002', Basseterre, St Kitts (28 June)

European Commission (1994) 'Report on the EC Banana Regime', Brussels: VI/5671/94 (July)

European Commission (1995) 'Report on the Operation of the Banana Regime', Brussels: SEC (95) 1565 Final (11 October)

European Commission (2000) 'Commission Regulation (EC) No. 2374/2000 on imports of bananas under the tariff quotas and of traditional ACP bananas for 2001', *Official Journal of the European Communities*, L 275 (26 October)

European Commission (2001a) 'Commission Regulation (EC) No. 216/2001 amending Regulation 404/93 on the common organization of the market in bananas', *Official Journal of the European Communities*, L 31 (29 January)

European Commission (2001b) 'Commission Regulation (EC) No. 2587/2001 amending Regulation (EEC) No. 404/93 on the common organization of the market in bananas', *Official Journal of the European Communities*, L 345 (19 December)

European Commission (2002) 'Commission Regulation (EC) No. 349/2002 amending Regulation (EC) No. 896/2001 laying down detailed rules for applying Council Regulation (EEC) No. 404/93 as regards the arrangements for importing bananas into the Community', *Official Journal of the European Communities*, L 55 (25 February)

European Commission (2003) 'Commission Regulation (EC) No. 1439/2003 amending Regulation (EC) No. 896/2001 laying down detailed rules for applying Council Regulation (EEC) No. 404/93 as regards the arrangements for importing bananas into the Community', *Official Journal of the European Communities*, L 204 (12 August)

European Council (1998) 'Council Regulation (EC) No. 1637/98 of 20 July 1998 amending Regulation (EEC) No. 404/93 on the Common Organization of the Market in Bananas', *Official Journal of the European Communities*, L 210

GATT (1994) 'EEC – Import Regime for Bananas: Report of the Panel', DS38/R (18 January)

Pantin, D., W. Sandiford and M. Henry (1999) 'Cake, Mama Coca Or? Alternative Facing the Caribbean Banana Industry in the Light of the April 1999 World Trade Organization (WTO) Ruling on the European Union's (EU) Banana Regime', commissioned by WINFA, CPDC and Oxfam Caribbean (20 September)

Preville, C. (2002) *Trade Liberalization under Imperfect Competition. An Analysis of the European Union's Market for Banana Imports.* Maastricht: Shaker Publishing BV

WIBDECO (2003) 'Computer data files', Director of Technical Services

World Bank Group (2002) 'World Bank sees sluggish economic outlook, calls for progress on trade issues that will help developing countries', *News Release No.* 2003/151/S, 11 December

WTO (1997a) *Report of the Panel* in 'European Communities – Regime for the Importation, Sale and Distribution of Bananas' – WT/DS27/ECU (May)

WTO (1997b) *Report of the Appellate Body* in 'European Communities – Regime for the Importation, Sale and Distribution of Bananas – AB-1997-3', WT/DS27/AB/R (September)

13

Jamaica and the case in the WTO against the European Communities regime for the importation, sale and distribution of bananas, 1992–2001

MARCIA THOMAS

13.1 Background

The banana is the most widely consumed fruit in the European Union (EU). The Member States of the Union provided stable markets for bananas from the African, Caribbean and Pacific (ACP) Group of States and Latin America for many years. Bananas are an important export product for a number of small Caribbean countries which are members of the Caribbean Community (CARICOM). They are one of the three primary export crops in Jamaica, the others being sugar and coffee. Currently, the banana is Jamaica's third most important export crop.

For Jamaica, bananas have been one of the major export crops since 1869 following their introduction as part of the ongoing effort to diversify the economy out of its dependence on sugar production. Banana cultivation was dominated by small farmers as it required little investment outlay and generated a steady income, thus contributing to poverty alleviation. Owen Jefferson in his book *The Post-War Development of Jamaica* points out that by 1890, bananas had replaced sugar as the leading export crop and in 1930 accounted for 57 per cent of total exports from Jamaica. Jefferson also points out that banana production collapsed in the 1940s due to the ravages of Panama disease which cannot be treated. Exports were also severely restricted during the Second World War due to the lack of shipping capacity. Thereafter, bananas never regained the position as Jamaica's major export crop although production levels rose significantly during the 1950s and '60s. The production levels of the 1950s and '60s, up

'European Communities' is the name still used for the members of the European Union in the context of the WTO and in international trade matters.

to 200,000 tonnes between 1965 and 1966, were never again achieved in succeeding decades. From 1974 to 1984, exports began to decline, varying from a high of 78,807 tonnes in 1977 to a dramatic low of 11,100 tonnes in 1984. From 1985, the industry began a slow recovery until the entire crop was destroyed by Hurricane Gilbert in September 1988. Thereafter, the effort to revitalise and restructure the industry begun in 1984 had to be restarted. Export levels rose to 76,723 tonnes in 1992 when the banana dispute began.

In spite of the fluctuations in the fortunes of the industry over the years, bananas have continued to be among the major export crops in Jamaica and a primary source of income and employment in Jamaica's eastern parishes of St Mary, St Thomas and Portland. There is also significant production in the parishes of St James and Clarendon.

Jamaica and other Caribbean countries have had preferential access to the market of the United Kingdom under the system of Commonwealth Preferences for many years pre-dating 1975. Jamaican bananas up to the 1950s had a dominant share of the UK market. The main competitor was Cameroon, and, later, the Windward Islands. Latin American bananas (dollar bananas) were basically kept out of the UK market. A negligible quota was allocated to dollar bananas. Owen Jefferson states that the Latin quota for the UK market was 4,000 tonnes per year.

The United Kingdom became a member of the European Economic Community (EEC) in January 1972 and accepted the Common Agricultural Policy (CAP) of the Community. From 1975, the preferential market access granted to former colonies became a contractual trade and aid arrangement between the African, Caribbean and Pacific Group of States (ACP) and the European Community under successive Lomé Conventions. Protocol 5 of the Lomé Conventions on Bananas stated that 'no ACP State shall be placed, as regards access to its traditional markets, in a less favourable situation than in the past or at present'. Jamaica and other ACP states were allocated quotas to export bananas to the Community duty free. Jamaica was allocated a quota of 105,000 tonnes for the UK market. The preferential market access and facilities such as STABEX, the compensatory finance scheme for the stabilisation of export earnings, provided under the Lomé Conventions, were of vital importance to the banana industry in Jamaica. It should be noted that STABEX was terminated with the Lomé IV Convention in 2000.

The completion of the European Single Market in 1992[1] allowed larger quantities of Latin American bananas to enter the UK market in that year. With the introduction of the Common Organisation of the Market (COM)[2] for bananas (EC Regulation 404/93), which entered into force on 26 February 1993 and became applicable on 1 July 1993, Latin American banana producers and the American-owned multinational corporations (MNCs, primarily Chiquita and Dole), which produce and distribute Latin American bananas, began their efforts to gain a firmer foothold in the wider European market. The Latin Americans and the MNCs were opposed to the quota restrictions and other measures applied under the COM (Regulation 404/93) to regulate the European market for bananas. The Latin Americans, for some time, were also concerned about the preferential access accorded to ACP states under the Lomé Conventions.

Latin American countries are among the world's largest producers of bananas. Ecuador is the world's principal exporter of bananas, exporting approximately 3.8 million tonnes per annum, and is currently the major exporter to the European Union,[3] exporting an average of 1.2 million tonnes per annum. Of the Latin American countries, Mexico was the relative newcomer to the banana trade in the EU market and, until the 1990s, had not exported significant quantities of bananas to the European Union. It was Mexico's ambition to secure a share of the market for its expanded banana production.

Under the Lomé Conventions (1975–2000), the markets of the United Kingdom and France were mainly supplied on preferential terms with bananas from the ACP states (their former colonies). The British market was supplied with bananas from Jamaica, the Leeward and Windward Islands, Belize and Suriname. Since 1992, Jamaica's exports to the UK have ranged from a high of 81,433 tonnes (1996) to a low of 42,026 tonnes (2001).

The French market was supplied with fruit from French West Africa – primarily Cameroon and Côte d'Ivoire – and their overseas Departments in the Caribbean – Martinique and Guadeloupe. The markets of Germany, the Netherlands and some other European countries, including the newer members of the Union, Sweden, Finland and Austria, were predominantly

[1] In 1992, the completion of the Single Market facilitated the free flow of goods and services, including bananas, within the EU.

[2] The COM is part of the administrative arrangements of the CAP of the EU and aims to harmonise the separate national systems which existed prior to membership of the Union.

[3] From 5th Edition Ecuador Exports – CORPE/Banco del Pacifico.

supplied with bananas by the Latin American countries without quota restrictions prior to 1993. Germany had a free market in bananas and the other countries had a tariff of 20 per cent. Countries such as Spain, Portugal and Greece had quantitative restrictions (quotas) to protect domestic banana production in their territories of the Canary Islands, Madeira, the Azores and Crete. Portugal was also importing bananas from Cape Verde, and Italy was offering concessions to Somalia.[4] Some members of the European Union, such as Germany and the Netherlands, were openly opposed to the COM with its quota restrictions. Within the Union, there were only five Member States – UK, France, Spain, Portugal and Greece – which supported the 1993 COM for bananas.

In 1993, there were several challenges to the COM (EC Regulation 404/93) in the European Court of Justice by Germany and other EU Members.[5] Germany, supported by the Netherlands and Belgium, sought an injunction in the European Court to suspend Regulation 404/93 on the ground that it would severely damage the banana trade in that country. The Court rejected the petition. In spite of these internal challenges, the EU membership, as a whole, could not ignore their contractual obligations to ACP states.

The USA, which became a key player in the banana dispute under the WTO, does not itself produce bananas for export, but, as previously indicated, US-owned MNCs produce and export bananas from Latin America. Therefore, the USA claimed interest in the context of services (the WTO General Agreement on Trade in Services (GATS)). In examining the USA's involvement in the banana dispute, the relationship between the MNCs and the Republican and the Democratic Parties should also be considered. It was the view that President Bill Clinton felt obliged to pursue this case in the WTO because of the financial contributions which were made to the Democratic Party.

In the pre-WTO period, the European Commission and the Members of the European Communities had not used the Article XXV provision of GATT 1947 to seek a waiver from the most favoured nation (MFN) principle (GATT Article I) and other relevant provisions of the GATT for the trade provisions of the Lomé Conventions. It was felt that the Lomé

[4] David Raboy et al., *The EC Banana Regime and the GATT Draft Final Act 1993.*

[5] See judgments of the Court of Justice of the European Union 1993, 1994, 1995, 1997 (Cases C280/93, C-68/95 and T-252/97).

Conventions were given legitimacy under Part IV – Trade and Development – of the GATT 1947, which allowed developed countries to assist developing countries, whether individually or as a group. The Lomé concessions were also bound in the Communities' GATT/Uruguay Round Schedule of Concessions.

13.2 The GATT Banana Panels 1992–1994[6]

In early 1993, a group of Latin American countries – Nicaragua, Costa Rica, Colombia, Guatemala and Venezuela – requested that GATT Contracting Parties establish a panel to determine whether the European Communities' new Regime for the Importation, Sale and Distribution of Bananas (EC Regulation 404/93), scheduled to be implemented on 1 July 1993 and which preserved a share of the market for ACP states, was consistent with the rules of the 1947 General Agreement on Tariffs and Trade (GATT). The group had requested consultations with the EC in late 1992.

The Panel, in fact, was established to examine the banana regime in existence prior to 1993 as the European Commission argued that it could not agree to the examination of its new regime, which was not as yet in effect.

With the establishment of this first banana panel, the ACP states, including Jamaica and other Caribbean banana-producing countries, became third parties to the dispute so as to be able to protect their interest. At this point not all members of CARICOM were parties to the GATT. Countries, such as St Lucia, acceded to the GATT because of the challenge to bananas on which their economies depended. St Lucia, Dominica and St Vincent and the Grenadines became GATT Contracting Parties in 1993. Jamaica had been a GATT Contracting Party since 1963.

The Panel ruled that quantitative restrictions applied by Spain, France, Italy, Portugal and the United Kingdom were inconsistent with GATT rules (particularly Article XI – elimination of quantitative restrictions) and so was the preferential market access accorded to ACP states under the Banana Protocol (Protocol 5) of Lomé IV. The ACP preferential access was found to be in violation of GATT Article I, the MFN principle. The Panel recommended that the European Commission should either make its regime conform to GATT rules or should seek a waiver from GATT rules under GATT Article XXV. The European Commission, Member States of the

[6] GATT Activity Reports 1993, 1994, 1995.

Union and ACP states opposed the panel ruling. The ruling had, in fact, raised questions about the legitimacy of non-reciprocal preferential arrangements between developed and developing countries.

The panel report was not adopted as, under the GATT, Contracting Parties could block the adoption of the reports. Therefore, the European Commission, the Members of the Communities and the ACP countries prevented the adoption of the panel report.

In June 1993, a second GATT Panel was established to consider the EC's new banana regime (EC Regulation 404/93). The Panel was requested by the same group of Latin American countries which had requested the first panel.

In early 1994, the Panel, in its report, ruled that the EC's new banana regime was also inconsistent with GATT rules in several provisions including its tariff quota restrictions. Again, it pointed out that the preferential access to the EC market accorded to ACP states was inconsistent with the MFN principles of GATT Article I. The EC was again requested to make its banana regime consistent with GATT rules. The adoption of the panel report was again blocked.

In April 1994, the European Commission and the Members of the European Communities entered into an agreement (the Framework Agreement on Bananas) with four of the original five Latin American countries which were complainants in the two banana panels. These countries were Colombia, Costa Rica, Nicaragua and Venezuela. The countries became known as the Banana Framework Agreement (BFA) countries. Guatemala did not enter into this agreement. Under the BFA, the countries involved were given access to the EC market under mutually agreed terms, which included a commitment not to pursue adoption of the panel reports. The Agreement became part of the EC's Uruguay Round (UR) Schedule of Concessions. It entered into force on 1 January 1995 – and remained applicable until 2002.

Guatemala and other Latin American banana producers – Mexico, Honduras, Ecuador and Panama – remained opposed to the EC's banana regime which they continued to view as discriminatory and inimical to their interest. They were deeply concerned that the panel reports had not been adopted and that the banana problem had not been resolved during the UR negotiations.[7] Mexico, Honduras, Ecuador, Panama and the United

[7] The EC was reluctant to negotiate on the liberalisation of bananas and other agricultural products covered by the Lomé Convention and its own CAP (John Croome, *Reshaping the World Trading System*).

States had followed the proceedings of the two banana panels with keen interest. The USA was acting to protect the interest of its multinational companies, Dole and Chiquita.

To give legitimacy to the trade provisions of the Lomé IV Convention and particularly the Banana Protocol, the EC and ACP states formally requested a waiver from GATT Article I (the MFN principle) in November 1994. This was in keeping with the recommendations of the two GATT Panels. GATT Contracting Parties granted the waiver in December 1994. This waiver enabled the European Communities to continue granting non-reciprocal preferential market access to the ACP states. The waiver did not, however, mean that other countries could not take dispute settlement action against the European Communities. In fact, the USA and Guatemala reserved their rights in this matter.

Guatemala, Ecuador, Honduras, Mexico and Panama[8] continued to urge the EC to find a solution to the banana problem, pointing out that the 1993 banana regime imposed quantitative restrictions on all members of the Communities whereas previously only five countries had restrictions.

13.3 The banana dispute in the WTO

With the end of the Uruguay Round Negotiations in 1994, the World Trade Organization (WTO) was established in January 1995 and superseded the GATT. The UR also introduced a formal dispute settlement mechanism within the WTO governed by the Understanding on Rules and Procedures Governing the Settlement of Disputes, commonly known as the Dispute Settlement Understanding (DSU). Under the provisions of the DSU, it now required a consensus not to adopt panel reports (the negative consensus). This rule virtually guaranteed the adoption of WTO panel reports, as it was highly unlikely that the party in whose interest the panel had ruled would join such a consensus. The DSU also introduced an appeal body, the Appellate Body.

Under the new terms of dispute settlement, in October 1995, three of the Latin American Complainants – Guatemala, Honduras and Mexico – and the United States requested consultations with the European Commission

[8] Although Panama has followed the banana dispute with keen interest and is a major supplier of bananas, that country did not formally become a complainant or even request third party status in the banana panels. Panama however did participate in certain consultations.

on its Regime for the Importation, Sale and Distribution of Bananas (EC Regulation 404 of July 1993).

Not much progress towards a solution was made in the consultations. In May 1996, the Complainants, now including Ecuador, requested the establishment of a panel to determine the consistency of the Regime with provisions of the GATT and other WTO Agreements. The ACP banana-producing countries (Jamaica, Belize, the banana-producing OECS States,[9] Suriname, Dominican Republic, Ghana, Cameroon and Côte d'Ivoire), as well as the BFA countries (Colombia, Costa Rica, Nicaragua and Venezuela) and others (Canada, Japan, India and the Philippines), sought third party status in the dispute. Countries like Canada and Japan had primarily systemic interest in the dispute, as against 'substantial trade interest'.[10] The ACP countries sought an enhanced third party status.

Under Article 10 of the DSU, a third party to a dispute has only a limited level of participation. The DSU makes provisions for a dispute to have co-complainants but not co-respondents and only recognises the rights of parties to a dispute. Jamaica and other ACP states felt that the production and export of bananas, and the preservation of their preferential access to the market of the European Communities, was of such importance to them that they had a right to be accorded more than the limited Article 10 participation of the DSU.[11] The ACP countries, in fact, felt that they had substantial trade interests in the dispute.

At the meeting of the DSB on 8 May 1996, Jamaica, claiming substantial trade interest, requested enhanced third party status. Acting on behalf of the ACP countries, at the first administrative meeting of the Panel which addressed procedural issues, Jamaica restated the request, asking that the ACP countries be accorded enhanced third party rights in the following manner:

1. to be present at all meetings of the Panel;
2. to present written submissions at all meetings of the Panel;
3. to present their point of view;
4. to receive copies of all documents.

[9] Organization of Eastern Caribbean States (OECS) – St Kitts/Nevis, St Lucia, St Vincent and the Grenadines, Dominica, Grenada, Antigua and Barbuda.

[10] Substantial interests include not only trade interests but also systemic interests.

[11] Under Article 10 of the DSU, third parties have an opportunity to be heard by the Panel, to make a written submission, and to receive submissions.

Based on the ACP's request and following consultations with the parties, all third parties were granted a certain enhanced level of participation in the panel proceedings. They were, in addition to the usual Article 10 provisions, permitted to observe the main proceedings of the Panel, and to make a brief statement at the second meeting.

Although obtaining legal assistance from Professor Friedl Weiss of the WTO,[12] as provided to developing countries under the DSU (Article 27.2), the ACP also found it necessary to employ international trade lawyers from France, USA and Ireland to prepare their panel submissions and to present their case. There was controversy surrounding this within the ACP and later in the Panel. Should the hired lawyers speak on behalf of the ACP states, or should the Permanent Representatives of the ACP states speak, with the lawyers acting only as advisers? Eventually the lawyers, including Mr Christopher Palin (USA) and Mr Phillip Lee (Ireland), representing primarily the Caribbean interest, were accredited to the delegations of ACP states. Palin and Lee were accredited to the delegation of St Lucia. The European Commission's Legal Adviser, Mr Pieter Kuijper, and his team represented the Commission. The USA had its own legal representatives out of the Office of the US Trade Representative (USTR), and the Latin Americans drew on their own expertise, utilising the services of legal advisers provided by the WTO, including Professor Ernst Ulrich Petersman.

At the first substantive session of the Panel, the USA and others questioned the presence of the ACP's international trade lawyers in the room, particularly Palin and Lee. The Panel, following consultations with the parties, reminded both parties and third parties that only members of governments, including the European Commission, and international civil servants should attend panel meetings. The lawyers contracted by the Caribbean countries withdrew. The USA, by its actions, had challenged the right of ACP states, particularly the Caribbean states, to constitute their own delegations. This became an extremely controversial issue. It should be noted that in July 1997 when the Appellate Body met to hear the EC's appeal, in a procedural ruling on a request from St Lucia, the Body allowed

[12] The WTO legal experts could only act in an advisory capacity and were only available on a part-time basis. The WTO has very few legal advisers available to developing countries. In fact, a group of countries has established in Geneva an Advisory Centre on WTO Law to provide training and legal assistance to developing countries.

the participation of private lawyers, stating that, after hearing the legal arguments from both sides, it was their opinion that it is for 'a WTO Member to decide who should represent it as members of its delegation in an oral hearing of the Appellate Body'. During the procedural stage, the standing (*locus standi*) of the USA in the dispute was also questioned without effect.

The ACP states, in their first submission to the Panel, supported the EC's effort to establish the legitimacy of the banana regime and the rights of ACP states under the Lomé Convention. The ACP also stressed the importance of bananas to the economies of ACP states. For the Caribbean, it was argued that the economies of entire countries were dependent on the export of bananas. For Jamaica, it was stated that certain parishes depended on banana cultivation for income and employment. The destruction of the banana industry through the end of preferential access would be devastating to the countries, particularly those of the Eastern Caribbean. It was felt that the Panel should not take a purely legalistic approach to the dispute but should consider also the economic and social implications, particularly for the small and vulnerable Caribbean states.

The Panel issued its report in May 1997 and, as in the GATT panels, ruled that the EC's banana regime was inconsistent with provisions of the GATT 1994 and other WTO agreements. The Panel recommended that the EC make its regime consistent with WTO rules.

The panel report was not adopted as the EC appealed the ruling, as allowed under Article 16.4 of the DSU. This dispute was subsequently to become a real test of the mettle of the WTO Dispute Settlement Mechanism. It should be noted, however, that the Canada/Brazil dispute on measures affecting the export of civilian aircrafts and possibly others have now tested the mechanism even further.

The Appellate Body, with a few adjustments, upheld the ruling of the Panel. On 25 September 1997, the DSB adopted the Reports of the Panel and the Appellate Body. The EC was required to review and amend its banana import regime to make it WTO consistent by 1 January 1999, a period of fifteen months. An Arbitrator appointed by the Director General set this date in December 1997. The ACP countries argued that, under the Fourth Lomé Convention, the European Communities had a contractual obligation to maintain preferential market access for ACP states at remunerative prices.

13.4 Jamaica and other Caribbean countries seeking to protect their interests

To protect their interest throughout the panel process and to contribute to the development of a new banana regime as required by the Panel, there were extensive consultations between CARICOM Ministers and other officials, and the parties to the dispute. There were missions to lobby US Government officials, visits to the Latin American countries, particularly Ecuador, and regular meetings with UK and EC officials. Jamaica played a very active role in this process, chairing, through the Permanent Mission, the ACP Group in Geneva and leading various missions. The local Banana Export Company (BECO) was also very active, as was Jamaica's Embassy in Washington, D.C., the Jamaica Marketing Company (JAMCO), the High Commission in London and the Jamaican Embassy in Brussels.

Jamaican embassies and high commissions were working with the groups of Caribbean ambassadors in the principal capitals, and with the ACP Banana Working Group and the ACP Secretariat in Brussels. The Caribbean Banana Exporters Association (CBEA), a grouping of British and Irish companies and others with interest in the production, export and distribution of Caribbean bananas in London, was also very active in the consultative and lobbying process.

In April 1999, CARICOM[13] Heads of Government established the CARICOM ad hoc Group of Experts on Bananas mandated to coordinate the region's strategy-building with regard to the banana dispute. The Group had several meetings during 1999 and held consultations with high-level officials of the EC, Ecuador and the Office of the USTR. In December 1999, the Caribbean countries submitted to the EU a set of specific proposals for a two-tiered tariff rate quota regime based on a pre-1993 reference period. This proposal was contained in a letter to the EC and USTR signed by Prime Minister Edison James of Dominica, lead Prime Minister on banana issues. The USA indicated support for this Caribbean proposal.

During 1998, the USA had itself proposed a non-restrictive tariff system to replace the tariff rate quotas (TRQs). The tariff on Latin American bananas would have to be significantly higher than the existing 75 Euros per tonne. ACP bananas would continue to enter the EC market duty free,

[13] The CARICOM Secretariat played an important role in the banana dispute from the very beginning. The Assistant Secretary-General, Byron Blake, attended Panel proceedings and initiated and participated in consultations.

thus maintaining their preferential access. For the USA, if any TRQ system were to be acceptable, it would have to conform to the requirements of Article XIII of GATT 1994.

The Caribbean's consultations with the USA were viewed with suspicion by the EC and it was necessary for Caribbean countries to assure the EC that their efforts were aimed at seeking a mutually acceptable solution and, in this spirit, the region had been consulting with all parties to the dispute.

13.5 Testing the WTO dispute settlement mechanism

In July 1998, it was announced that the EC had designed a new banana import regime (EC Regulation 1637/98). Even before the Regime was tabled in the WTO's Dispute Settlement Body (DSB), there was opposition from the complainants who claimed that the regime was still WTO inconsistent. In October 1998, the EC produced Regulation 2362/98 concerning the administration of import licences for bananas under Regulation 404/93. Both Regulations were denounced by the complainants, particularly Ecuador. In August, Ecuador requested consultations with the EC and expressed the view that the matter should be settled under Article 21.5 of the DSU, which provides for the reconvening of the Panel to determine the WTO consistency of the new implementation measure.

There were threats from the USA to impose unilateral trade sanctions against members of the European Community under its domestic 1974 Trade Act (Section 301). In fact, in November 1998, the USA made a unilateral determination under Section 306 of its 1974 Trade Act that the EC's measures failed to implement the WTO recommendations. The USA proceeded to impose *ad valorem* duties of 100 per cent on selected goods from the European Union. This measure should have taken effect in January 1999. This led the European Commission on 25 November 1998 to request dispute settlement consultations with the USA regarding the Section 301 procedure of the US Trade Act 1974. This Panel was established on 2 March 1999 and Jamaica was among those countries which sought third party status. The Panel generated a lot of interest in and outside the WTO as there had long been serious concern about the USA's custom of resorting to unilateral trade measures, particularly through the extraterritorial application of its domestic legislation.

In December 1998, Ecuador formally requested the re-convening of the original WTO Panel under Article 21.5 to determine the WTO consistency of the EC's measures (i.e. Regulations 1637/98 and 2362/98) to implement the rulings contained in the panel reports adopted in September 1997. Earlier in December 1998, the EC had requested the establishment of a panel under Article 21.5 of the DSU with the mandate to find that its implementation measures must be presumed to conform to WTO rules unless their conformity had been duly challenged under appropriate DSB procedures. The EC's request was again a controversial one as this kind of respondent-initiated request was not foreseen in the dispute settlement mechanism. The EC on its own initiative was requesting the establishment of a panel which would practically make a de facto interpretation of Article 21.5. The interpretation of articles in WTO Agreements under Article IX.2 of the Agreement Establishing the WTO (Marrakesh Agreement) was the sole responsibility of WTO Members. The Panels requested by Ecuador and the EC were established by the DSB on 12 January 1999.

In January 1999, the USA sought under Article 22.2 of the DSU to obtain official WTO authorisation of its unilateral sanctions imposed on EU products in December 1999. The US sought to remove duty concessions on trade in goods from the EU valued at US $520 million and to impose duties of 100 per cent. The USA argued that Article 22.2 gave it the right to resort independently to sanctions within twenty days after the reasonable implementation period (fifteen months) had expired. The USA had conveniently omitted to note that under Article 21.5 of the DSU, it was the Panel which had to determine that the new implementation measure was still WTO inconsistent. At this point, the Panels requested by both the EC and Ecuador under Article 21.5 still had not met. The USA had not requested such a panel.

The USA's request for authority to impose sanctions under Article 22.2 was included on the agenda of the DSB meeting scheduled for 25 January 1999. At this meeting there was an extraordinary development. When the agenda was to be adopted, the delegations of St Lucia and Dominica objected to the inclusion of the item concerning the USA's request for authorisation. The DSB found itself in a procedural dilemma, there was no consensus on the adoption of the agenda and the meeting was suspended to allow time for consultations. The action of St Lucia and Dominica supported by the European Communities and Côte d'Ivoire was very controversial. It raised the very sensitive issue of whether a member could block the adoption of the entire agenda and the implications of such action for the future of the WTO and its work. In other international fora such as the

United Nations, the adoption of the agenda is an important issue for developing countries. As Members looked on with concern, and some would use the word consternation, the action of Dominica and St Lucia received a lot of press coverage. Their action did demonstrate, however, that the consensus rule could be used by small developing countries to further their interests.

The meeting of the DSB resumed on 28 January 1999 (and continued on 29 January and 1 February) with the disputed item still on the agenda. The Chairman's decision to retain the item on the agenda after inconclusive consultations was also very controversial. The Chairman had decided to retain the item because, in his view, the Rules of Procedure should not modify the rights and obligations of Members under WTO Agreements and should not be so interpreted as to block meetings in cases where a Member has a specific right to request a specific decision unless there was a consensus against such a request. However, the representative of St Lucia indicated that, in the spirit of compromise, the delegation wished to move forward with the agenda.

On the interpretation of Article 21.5 and Article 22, there was the important question of precedence: which came first, Article 21.5 to determine compliance or Article 22 to impose sanctions, or did the two work together? This became the subject of intense debate in the WTO. Many WTO Members, including Jamaica, felt that sanctions under Article 22 could not be imposed until a determination of non-compliance had been made under Article 21.5.

In fact, by correspondence dated 21 January 1999, the EC submitted to the General Council a request for the adoption of an authoritative interpretation under Article IX.2 of the Marrakesh Agreement of Articles 3.7, 21.5, 22.2, 22.6, 22.7 and 23 of the DSU. The General Council considered the request in February 1999. Many Members supported the EC's view that recourse to retaliation under Article 22 of the DSU is sequential and should come into effect after a determination under Article 21.5 of non-compliance. This was seen as an important safeguard for the multilateral trading system. It was decided that the matter should be referred to the Review of the DSU taking place in the DSB.

Jamaica, in its statement in the General Council, pointed out the importance of the matter which addressed the effective functioning of the DSB and the multilateral trading system. Jamaica supported the view that an objective determination of non-compliance of the implementing measure was necessary before the DSB could authorise any Member to impose sanctions under Article 22. Jamaica reiterated its position that where existing rules are clear they should be upheld and where ambiguities exist they should be clarified. Jamaica also expressed the view that unilateral action by a Member is contrary to the spirit of decision-making on a multilateral consensual basis. Jamaica further felt that the General Council had the authority under Article IX.2 of the Marrakesh Agreement to deliberate on the interpretation of the articles to offer guidance to the DSB. The interpretation, in Jamaica's view, should not have been referred to the DSU Review but should have been addressed expeditiously in the General Council and the DSB in order to make progress in the banana dispute. The General Council's 15 February 1999 meeting was inconclusive.

The EC objected to the level of nullification and impairment of benefits claimed by the USA in its request to apply sanctions and requested arbitration under Article 22.6 of the DSU. On 29 January 1999, when the DSB resumed its meeting begun on 25 January, the original panel was requested to arbitrate in the matter. The USA's unilateral sanctions were scheduled to take effect on 3 March 1999 before any arbitration process established under Article 22 could complete its work and, in fact, before it could determine the level of sanctions which should be imposed. The EC, at the beginning of March, requested a full meeting of the General Council of the WTO (the principal body of the WTO when Ministerial meetings are not in session) to discuss what it viewed as a development which had serious implications for all WTO Members and for the WTO dispute settlement mechanism.

In April 1999, the Arbitrators and the Article 21.5 Panels submitted their reports simultaneously to the parties. The Arbitrators under Articles 22.6 and 22.7 of the DSU had decided to authorise the USA to suspend concessions to the EC to the amount of US $191.4 million per year. The Article 21.5 Panel requested by Ecuador ruled that aspects of the EC's import regime for bananas were inconsistent with the EC's obligations under specific Articles of GATT 1994 and GATS. The Panel recommended that the EC be requested to bring its new implementation measures into conformity with WTO rules.

The Article 21.5 Panel requested by the EC, after hearing arguments from the European Commission, the sole party, and third parties Jamaica, India and Japan, did not offer a formal finding. The case raised the question of whether the original respondent in a dispute could invoke Article 21.5 to determine the WTO consistency of its implementing measure. Japan and India participated as third parties because of their systemic interest. Japan pointed out the anomalies in the panel proceeding – the fact that the complainants did not participate, which made it difficult for the Panel to fulfil its mandate to make an objective assessment under the DSU – and it was not, in Japan's view, the function of the Panel to make a presumption of innocence. Japan held the view that failure to utilise properly Article 21.5 procedures was a serious violation of the dispute settlement procedures. India focused on the relationship between Articles 21.5 and 22. India felt that a determination of non-compliance had to be made multilaterally in accordance with Article 21.5 before there could be resort to Article 22 measures. For India, recourse to Article 21.5, in the manner demonstrated by the EC, was a fundamental right available to all Members of WTO in the dispute settlement system. Jamaica, as an original third party, supported the EC's analysis of Article 23 of the DSU. However, Jamaica felt that an assessment of Articles 21.5 and 22 of the DSU was not within the Panel's terms of reference. The Panel did not rule out the possibility of Article 21.5 being used by a respondent on its own initiative to obtain a determination of the WTO consistency of its implementing measure.

Returning to the sanctions issue, on 11 May 1999 the EC requested the DSB to establish a panel to consider the US decision, effective 3 March 1999, to impose sanctions in the form of import duties on US $520 million per year of EU products. On 16 June 1999, the DSB established a panel on US Import Measures on Certain Products from the European Communities. Jamaica, Dominica and St Lucia were among the countries requesting third party status. In its report issued on 17 July 1999, the Panel ruled that US unilateral action in imposing sanctions violated specific articles of the DSU and GATT 1994. The Panel recommended that the USA be required to conform to its obligations under the WTO Agreements.

In this 'sanctions' dispute, both the EC and the USA in September 1999 appealed certain issues of law in the panel report and certain legal interpretations developed by the Panel. Jamaica and other CARICOM Members maintained their third party status at the appellate level. The Appellate Body, while reversing other rulings of the Panel, upheld its ruling that the USA's action of 3 March was no longer in existence and, therefore, made no recommendations to the DSB. The Appellate Body, however, also upheld the ruling that the 3 March measure was not consistent with Article 21.5 of the DSU.

The inconsistency of the EU's Regulations 1637/98 and 2362/98 having been established by the Article 21.5 panel process, the EC was required promptly to make its banana regime WTO consistent. This did not curtail the request for dispute settlement procedures. Ecuador was now looking at Article 22 of the DSU with the objective of imposing sanctions against the EU. In November 1999, Ecuador requested authorisation by the DSB to suspend concessions or other obligations under the TRIPS (intellectual property), GATS (services) and GATT 1994 (goods) Agreements to the amount of US $450 million. However, Ecuador had to admit that the withdrawal of concessions in the goods sector would not be practicable or effective. Ecuador, as a country dependent on imports, was more likely to be negatively affected than the EC. Ecuador would therefore focus on the GATS (services) and the TRIPS (intellectual property) Agreements. On 19 November 1999, the EC requested arbitration under Article 22.6 of the DSU because, among other things, as with the USA's earlier request, the EC viewed the amount of the concession to be suspended as excessive.

In its decision circulated on 24 March 2000, the Arbitrators concluded that Ecuador's request had not fully followed the principles and procedures of Article 22.3 of the DSU and that the level of suspension requested by Ecuador exceeded the level of nullification and impairment it had experienced from the failure of the EC to bring its banana regime into WTO compliance. The Arbitrators suggested that Ecuador submit another request for authorisation of suspension of concessions and other obligations consistent with its conclusions, which included: that Ecuador obtain authorisation to suspend concessions or other obligations to a level not exceeding US $201.6 million per year; that these concessions be obtained under GATT 1994 concerning certain categories of goods; under GATS with respect to wholesale trade in services; and, if necessary, under the TRIPS Agreement with respect to copyright and related rights, geographical indications and industrial design. In reality, the panel ruling made it difficult under TRIPS to suspend concessions. The international nature of intellectual property rights and the number of agents involved make it difficult for a country to impose sanctions without infringing the rights of others. Ecuador's resort to Article 22 of the DSU is an indication of the procedural difficulties a developing country, in a dispute with a developed country, could have in imposing sanctions.

Hereafter, the banana dispute took another turn in the WTO, impacting on waiver procedures in the Council for Trade in Goods. In 1999, the ACP and EU concluded negotiations for a twenty-year partnership agreement as a successor to the Fourth Lomé Convention. The trade provisions in the new agreement were transitional and the Banana Protocol was redrafted to focus on technical assistance. After eight years, the ACP and EU would complete negotiations to establish a new WTO-compatible trading relationship. A waiver was required under Article IX of the Agreement establishing the WTO (the Marrakesh Agreement) from the MFN principle (Article I) of GATT 1994 for the new ACP/EU Partnership Agreement's transitional trade provisions. In fact, Lomé IV and its waiver had expired in February 2000. Following informal consultations with WTO Members, including the complainants in the banana dispute, the EC and ACP formally introduced the waiver request in the WTO Council for Trade in Goods on 5 April 2000. However, the complainants in the banana dispute indicated that the documentation accompanying the waiver request could not be regarded as complete without the EC's new WTO-compatible banana regime. As a result of this impasse in the Council for Trade in Goods, consideration of the waiver request could not commence. The trade aspects of the Cotonou Agreement (the Partnership Agreement was signed in Cotonou, Benin, on 23 June 2000) could not be legitimised by a WTO waiver.

In the meantime, the EC and other interested parties were continuing the quest for a WTO-consistent Regime for the Importation, Sale and Distribution of Bananas. The EC was required under the DSU (Article 22.6) to report regularly to the DSB on progress to implement the recommendations of the Panel. At every DSB meeting at which the EC filed an implementation report, usually indicating that it had still been unable to finalise a WTO-compatible regime, the complainants took the opportunity to accuse the EC of making little effort to comply with the Panels' recommendations. The complainants and their allies felt that the EC's action, or rather inaction, was a threat to the DSU and, indeed, to the entire multilateral trading system. As EU Members began to feel the effects of the sanctions, the European Commission found itself under severe pressure from all sides, from within the membership of the European Union, from the complainants and other interested parties in Latin America, including the BFA countries and Panama, and from the ACP which felt that the EC was not doing enough to protect its interest.

13.6 The quest for a WTO-consistent banana regime

The European Commission continued to have intensive consultations with the interested parties in a bid to find a compromise which would lead to a new banana regime acceptable to all parties and consistent with WTO rules. The ACP states were working hard to try to preserve their small share of the Communities' market while the Latin Americans and the US companies were negotiating aggressively to increase their share of the market. At the same time, all were concerned that increased supplies of bananas would adversely affect the prices in the market. A further difficulty for ACP states, which preferred a tariff rate quota (TRQ) system based on a historical reference period and a licensing system, was that by this time (May 2000), there were at least ten EU Member States which were showing a preference for a tariff only system. France and Spain were not in favour of such a system. The UK's position was ambiguous.

In November 1999, the European Commission had proposed a new regime. This was a two-stage approach: a tariff only system accompanied by a tariff preference for ACP states. There would be a transitional period of TRQs, which would end on 31 December 2005, and a tariff only system would be introduced on 1 January 2006. This tariff would be implemented based on GATT Article XXVIII negotiations (modification of concessions). However, after nearly six months of intense consultations, this system still had not fully found favour with the complainants. Frustrated, the EC began to look again at a 'First Come, First Served' (FCFS) system which it had previously considered. An FCFS system was viewed as a lottery in which access to duty concessions would be determined at the time of the customs declaration, i.e. the order of priority for access to quotas would be determined by the date of the presentation of the import request.

Caribbean banana producers were definitely not in favour of the FCFS system. They had submitted their own proposal in December 1999 and, for them, a transitional period of ten years with a TRQ system managed by licence allocation and based on a historical reference period (pre-1993) was essential. This system provided predictability, certainty and security of access for small states, like Jamaica and her CARICOM partners, to the EU market. Caribbean countries were becoming increasingly concerned about the direction the banana dispute was taking and the implications for them of certain solutions of which there were several.

In August 2000, representatives of Costa Rica, Colombia, Ecuador, Honduras, Guatemala, Mexico, Venezuela, Nicaragua and Panama meeting in Panama City decided to take a unified position in opposing the European Communities' most recent proposals for a new banana regime which in their view still favoured ACP countries and continued to be discriminatory.

An urgent meeting of Caribbean banana-exporting countries was convened in New York on 7 September 2000 to review recent developments and prepare for consultations in Quito and Washington, D.C. There was consensus at this meeting that an FCFS system would be seriously damaging to the Caribbean. It was also noted that the system which found greatest favour with all parties, a system of TRQs with licences based on a historical reference period, was technically not WTO consistent and would require a waiver. There was also disagreement among the parties over the details of this TRQ system. The meeting felt that the Caribbean had to try to get the main parties (USA and EU) to resume negotiations.

The Latin American Group of Colombia, Costa Rica, Guatemala, Honduras, Nicaragua, Panama and Venezuela, meeting in Panama City in October 2000, rejected the FCFS system and indicated a willingness to support the Caribbean's December 1999 proposal. It will be recalled that the USA had also supported the Caribbean proposal as a basis for negotiations. There was little support for the FCFS system.

However, a report out of Brussels (Dow Jones) in December 2000 indicated that the European Agriculture Ministers meeting on 19 December 2000 adopted regulations for the EC's new banana import regime. EC Trade Commissioner Pascal Lamy was quoted as saying that the new WTO-compatible regulations would mark the end of the banana dispute and the lifting of the nearly US $200 million worth of sanctions imposed by the USA. The report indicated that the new rules would grant traditional suppliers of bananas access to 83 per cent of the total quota of 2.4 million tonnes, while non-traditional suppliers would have the remaining 17 per cent. According to this report, under the new regime the EC would allow bananas to be imported through licences distributed on the basis of past trade between 1994 and 1996. There would be three import quotas with different tariffs until 2006, when a tariff only system would take effect. The Dow Jones report also pointed out that the EC–Ecuador deal would increase the import volumes from Latin America by 100,000 tonnes to 353,000 tonnes – in line with the EC–US Agreement – and would improve market access to traditional and non-traditional importers from Ecuador.

The adoption of the new banana regime in December 2000 by EU Agriculture Ministers clearly demonstrated that, while Caribbean and Latin American banana producers were expressing their objections to the EC's FCFS proposal, the EC was continuing negotiations with the USA and Ecuador. Together they had agreed on the framework for a new banana regime based on the FCFS proposal. The EC informed the DSB in January 2001 that it was modifying the banana regime, paving the way for rapid implementation of a WTO-compatible regime based on the FCFS system.

At the meeting of the CARICOM Council for Trade and Economic Development (COTED) held on 11–12 January 2001, Trade Ministers issued a statement stating that the EC's FCFS proposal was totally inconsistent with the EU's commitment under the Cotonou Agreement and would lead to the total destruction of the Caribbean banana industry with resultant severe economic and social damage and dislocation. The Ministers called on the EU and USA to resume negotiations to find a satisfactory compromise. The Caribbean's position was also made clear at the WTO's DSB meeting restating their preference for a historically based quota system. At COTED, CARICOM Ministers had established a working group on the development of the Caribbean banana industry. The working group was scheduled to meet in Barbados in February and would seek to develop a technical position and strategy for a lobby campaign focusing on Washington, D.C., London and Brussels.

In the meantime, a rivalry had developed between the two American companies involved in the dispute, Chiquita and Dole. Dole had found ways to improve its position in Europe while Chiquita, inflexible in its position, was floundering, claiming that the protracted banana dispute had led to a reduction of its share of the market and consequently to a reduction in its profits. It was being reported in January 2001 that Chiquita was contemplating filing for bankruptcy protection and filing a lawsuit against the EC. It was further reported that Chiquita, in January, sued the European Commission for damages amounting to Euro 564 million. The Commission, from reports, was hoping that Chiquita's weakening position would lead the USA, at the negotiating table, willingly to take a more flexible position.

The Caribbean's lobbying efforts saw, among other things, letters being sent to US President George Bush and to the President of the EU Council.

The FCFS system[14] was scheduled to be implemented on 1 April 2001, but given the unpopularity of the system, the EC agreed to delay its implementation while efforts were made through negotiations with the USA to find an alternative system.

Another factor in the search for a WTO-consistent banana regime became the European Communities' ambition to achieve the launch of a new round of comprehensive multilateral trade negotiations in the WTO. It became important that the EC prove its commitment to the multilateral trading system and its respect for the dispute settlement mechanism. There was, therefore, a renewed willingness to work out its differences on trade issues with the USA.

On 11 April 2001, it was announced that the European Commission and the United States had reached agreement on a proposal based on tariff rate quotas, with licences to be based on a reference period (1994–6). A specific quota (Quota C) was reserved for ACP states and the quota system would be transitional until December 2005, after which a tariff only system would be implemented. This new regime, with similar elements to the EC's previous proposals, would take effect on 1 July 2001, at which time the US sanctions would end. The new regime would require a waiver in the WTO from not only Article I of GATT 1994 but also Article XIII (administration of quantitative restrictions (QRs)). The proposal was greeted with cautious optimism in the Caribbean and elsewhere as details were not available. Ecuador was not happy.

Officials of the European Commission and the Government of Ecuador held consultations, after which it was announced, on 30 April 2001, that an understanding had been reached. This understanding, it was reported, recognised Ecuador's rights as a principal supplier of bananas to the EC and gave Ecuador increased market access. It was also compatible with the agreement reached with the USA.

13.7 The new banana regime (EC Regulation 896/2001)

The new banana regime was implemented by EC Regulation 896/2001 adopted on 7 May 2001. This Regulation sets out the management system for the Tariff Rate Quotas (TRQs). The reference period used was the three-year period 1994–6, which was the most recent period for which the Commission had reliable data on primary imports. Traditional operators

[14] EC Doc. Com(2000) 621 final, 4 October 2000.

Table 13.1 *Phase I: 1 July – 31 December 2001*[15]

TRQs tonnage	Non-preferential tariff	ACP tariff
A. 2,200,000	75 Euros per tonne	Duty free
B. 353,000	75 Euros per tonne	Duty free
C. 857,000	300 Euros per tonne	Duty free

Table 13.2 *Phase II: 1 January 2002–31 December 2005*

TRQs tonnage	Non-preferential tariff	ACP tariff
A. 2,200,000	75 Euros	Duty free
B. 453,000	75 Euros	Duty free
C. 758,000	no access	Duty free

were required to apply by 11 May 2001 to be allocated licences under TRQs A, B and C, based on their exports during the reference period. ACP banana-exporting countries shared the specific C quota of 857,000 tonnes.

The TRQs were to be made available as follows: 83 per cent to traditional operators; 17 per cent to non-traditional operators. The regime would be implemented in two phases from 1 July 2001 to 31 December 2005 as shown in tables 13.1 and 13.2.

In the second phase, the ACP quota would be reduced to 758,000 tonnes, a reduction of 100,000 tonnes.

Following the implementation of this new banana regime, the USA would end its sanctions. The USA and Ecuador would also support the EC's request in the WTO Council for Trade in Goods for a waiver for the trade aspects of the ACP/EU Cotonou Agreement and a waiver from Article XIII of GATT 1994 for the banana regime.

13.8 The banana dispute and the negotiations for a new Partnership Agreement between the ACP and the EU (the Cotonou Agreement)

In 1990, the Fourth ACP/EU Lomé Convention (Lomé IV) with its Commodity Protocols, including the Banana Protocol, was negotiated for

[15] Taken from the *Commonwealth Trade Hot Topics*, Issue No. 3, 11 April 2001. The deal by Ambassador Edwin Laurent ended the Banana War.

a period of ten years. On the recommendation of the second Banana Panel in 1993, a waiver from the MFN principle of Article I of GATT was sought and was granted in December 1994.

The Lomé IV Convention was scheduled to expire in February 2000. It was agreed that a new agreement would be negotiated to replace it. The negotiations for the ACP/EU Partnership Agreement commenced in September 1998.

From the very outset, the European Commission made it clear that ultimately the trade arrangements with the ACP had to become WTO compatible. Since the signing of Lomé IV in 1990, there had been many developments in the international trading environment and in the European Communities, which set the scene for the negotiations between the ACP and the EU. These developments included:

- The introduction in 1992 of the Single Market and the Common Organization of the Market which allowed for the free circulation of Latin American bananas within all Member States of the European Community, including the United Kingdom.
- The creation of the European Union when the Maastricht Treaty entered into force in November 1993.
- The initiation of the first banana dispute in the GATT in 1992 and the second in 1993.
- The establishment of the World Trade Organization (WTO) in January 1995.
- The enlargement of the European Union in 1995 when Austria, Finland and Sweden became members. These members had no colonial obligations.
- The publication by the European Commission in 1996 of its Green Paper on relations between the European Union and the ACP on the eve of the twenty-first century. The paper examined critically the trade preferences, taking account of WTO rules.
- The initiation in 1996 of the first banana dispute under the new dispute settlement rules of the WTO.
- The application for membership of the European Union by a new group of countries mainly from Eastern Europe.
- The need to reform the EC's Common Agricultural Policy resulting from WTO obligations, the further enlargement of the EU and internal EU pressures for reform.

- From as early as 1996, the call for expanding the WTO Work Programme to include new issues such as investment, competition policy, government procurement and trade facilitation.
- After 1998, the campaign to launch an expanded round of multilateral trade negotiations in the WTO. The WTO Agreements on Agriculture and Services (GATS) mandated the launch of negotiations to liberalise trade in agriculture and services further by 2000 (the so-called built-in agenda). The EC and the EU Member States became aggressive proponents of a new round of trade negotiations which would incorporate agriculture and services.[16]
- Since 1998, the involvement of CARICOM countries in the negotiations for the Free Trade Area of the Americas (FTAA), which is intended to be a reciprocal preferential arrangement. The Lomé Convention included a provision which stated that any concessions negotiated with other developed countries should also be accorded to the members of the EU (Declaration XXXI of the Cotonou Agreement).
- The decision of many developed countries, including Members of the EU, to review their overseas development aid policies and, as a result, to focus their foreign aid on the least developed countries (LDCs) or on those developing countries within their regional sphere of influence.
- During the 1990s, the acceleration of globalisation driven by the phenomenal progress in technology, particularly in telecommunications.

It was in this atmosphere of change and realignment that the new ACP/EU Partnership Agreement was negotiated over a period of eighteen months.

The European Commission and Members of the European Union held the view that the twenty-five-year relationship between the EU and the ACP under successive Lomé Conventions had not achieved its development objectives. In fact, the share of ACP countries in trade with the EU had been declining. The Commission and Members of the EU felt that the new agreement with the ACP had to take account of and reflect the global realties if an environment attractive to foreign investors was to be created in the ACP states. To accomplish this, there had to be recognition that non-reciprocal trade preferences now under attack in the WTO in the protracted banana dispute had had limited success and now had to be reviewed in the context of WTO rules. In other words, they had to be made WTO compatible.

[16] The new round of trade negotiations covering a wider range of issues would aid EC negotiating strategies in agriculture and would support the reform of the CAP.

The ACP states, at the start of the negotiations with the EU, felt strongly that the non-reciprocal preferences continued to play an important role in their trading relationship with the EU. They pointed to other problems, such as lack of technical capacity, indebtedness and supply side constraints, which had prevented ACP states from taking full advantage of the trade and economic provisions of the Lomé Conventions.

The Honourable Billie Miller, Deputy Prime Minister and Minister of Foreign Affairs of Barbados, in her role of President in Office of the ACP Council of Ministers at the launch of the ACP/EU negotiations in September 1998, said that ACP states, while accepting that negotiations would be overlaid by the notion of WTO compatibility, called for the application of WTO rules on the basis of flexibility that would make them compatible with the basic objective of development. The ACP, in her view, needed a reasonable transition period within which to adjust. However, the long-term objective of free trade that was being promoted, she pointed out in her address, could only be valid when 'free trade' became synonymous with 'fair trade'.

As indicated, the Banana Dispute might not have been the central issue dictating that the trade arrangements to be negotiated between the ACP and EU would have to change to ones which would be WTO compatible, but it highlighted the difficulties faced by the non-reciprocal preferential arrangements in the WTO system and the precarious nature of their continued existence in that system. Both developed and developing members of the WTO were pointing to these preferential arrangements as discriminatory and injurious to their interests. Further challenges to aspects of the common organisation of the EU market to which the commodity protocols were linked appeared to be inevitable.

The ACP/EU Partnership Agreement was signed in Cotonou, Benin, on 23 June 2000 and became known as the Cotonou Agreement. Under the Cotonou trade arrangements, new WTO-compatible trade arrangements (free-trade arrangements) are to be negotiated during a preparatory period extending up to 2008. The objective will be to liberalise trade between ACP states and the EU during a transition period of at least twelve years. The negotiations commenced in September 2002.

The trade arrangements of the Cotonou Agreement required a waiver from Article I of GATT 1994. These arrangements, during the preparatory period, continued, to a large extent, the trade arrangements of the Lomé IV Convention. Changes had been made to the Banana Protocol (Protocol 5) to shift the focus from market access. However, the acquisition of a waiver for the entire trade package was still a necessity.

13.9 The request for a waiver in the WTO's Council for Trade in Goods

The EC, with Tanzania and Jamaica, on behalf of the ACP, submitted the request for a waiver on 5 April 2000 for the trade aspects of the Cotonou Agreement required under Article IX of the Agreement Establishing the WTO.

Formal consideration of the waiver request could not commence in the WTO Council for Trade in Goods (CTG) as banana-producing countries of South and Central America (Honduras, Guatemala, Costa Rica, Panama, Colombia, Ecuador and Paraguay) objected on the ground that the complete text of the Cotonou Agreement had to be translated into the three WTO languages (English, French and Spanish). The Permanent Representative of Uruguay was then chairing the CTG. Later, the translated documentation provided was still considered inadequate by the group of dissident South and Central American countries which were now demanding that the European Commission table the specific details of the preferences to be granted to the ACP states under the new banana regime. Without this document, these countries claimed that they were not in a position to make a judgement on the true nature of the banana regime, which they saw as part of the trade aspects of the Cotonou Agreement. They were adamant that the details of the banana regime were essential if they were to be able to protect their rights.

When the new Chairman of the CTG, the Permanent Representative of Hungary, took office in March 2001, it was nearly a year after the waiver request was tabled in the Council and consideration of it had not begun. The ACP countries, including Jamaica, viewed the intransigence of the group of Latin American countries as an attempt to block the waiver process and to hold the Partnership Agreement and the ACP countries hostage in order to achieve a settlement in the banana dispute. The United States, itself providing preferential market access to developing countries under the Caribbean Basin Initiative and the Andean Pact Agreement, on the basis of its systemic interest, was trying to take a constructive approach to finding a solution to the waiver impasse in the CTG.

To address the demand for more documentation, the EC, in March 2001, tabled its new banana regime, contained in EC Council Regulation No. 216/2001 of 29 January 2001, which aimed to implement the Commission's FCFS proposal. But still, this did not satisfy the South and Central American banana producers. They continued to obstruct examination of the waiver request. In any case, there was strong opposition to the EC's proposal, including from Jamaica and other ACP states.

In April 2001, the EC presented to the Council the elements of the agreement reached with the USA and Ecuador which would later be contained in EC Regulation 896/2001. The latest Agreement between the EC and the USA and Ecuador was notified to the WTO Dispute Settlement Body as a mutually agreed solution to the banana dispute. With this new regime, the EC, in June 2001, submitted to the CTG a second waiver request from Article XIII of GATT 1994 to cover the TRQ allocations to the ACP (i.e. for the Transitional Regime for the EC's Autonomous Tariff Rate Quotas on Imports of Bananas). In arriving at an agreement with the EC on the new banana regime, the USA and Ecuador had agreed to support the EC's requests for the two waivers.

At the meeting of the CTG on 5 July 2001, the EC's second waiver request was on the table but so was an amendment proposed by Ecuador. Panama, Honduras, Guatemala and Costa Rica continued to be obstructive and argued that the EC's two waiver requests should be considered separately as they addressed different articles of GATT 1994. Panama, Honduras and Guatemala reiterated their view that EC preferences were injurious to their trade interest. In their opinion, the documentation presented by the EC was still inadequate. They insisted that requirements of Article 1 of the Understanding in Respect of Waivers of Obligations under GATT 1994 had not been met. Interestingly, the Latin American countries were receiving support from members of the Association of South East Asian Nations (ASEAN), such as the Philippines and Thailand. These countries were eager to have consultations with the EC concerning market access for products of interest to them, including canned tuna.

By October 2001, the 4th WTO Ministerial Conference to be held in Doha, Qatar, on 9–13 November 2001, was fast approaching and the banana issue was not fully resolved. The consideration of the waivers for the trade aspects of the Cotonou Agreement and the banana regime continued to be held hostage by Latin American countries in the CTG.

In frustration, Jamaica and other ACP countries wanted to see the waiver issue resolved at the Doha Ministerial Conference.

13.10 Breaking the waiver deadlock at the Doha Ministerial Conference

The ACP Group met in Brussels from 3 to 6 November 2001 in preparation for the WTO Doha Ministerial Conference. The coordinator of the ACP Group in Geneva, the Permanent Representative of Gabon, reported on the waiver exercise in Geneva over nearly eighteen frustrating months. The Members of the ACP felt strongly that action had to be taken to secure the waiver. It was made clear that the waiver for the Cotonou Agreement, which was important to all ACP countries, had to be one of the gains from Doha. A way had to be found to have consideration of the waiver placed on the agenda of the conference in spite of some procedural difficulties.[17]

At Doha, it was decided that the ACP would join forces with the African Group and the Least Developed Countries (LDCs) as membership overlapped and this collaboration would strengthen the position of these developing countries. At the first business session of the Conference, the ACP/Africa/LDC Group crossed their first hurdle by gaining approval for the new item, 'ACP/EC Request for a Waiver for the New Partnership Agreement', to be placed on the agenda. The Latin American countries appeared to have been caught off guard by this ACP manoeuvre. The ACP/Africa/LDC Group made it clear that they would not be able to join consensus on a new round of multilateral trade negotiations, if, among other things, progress was not made on the matter of the waiver.

Thereafter, intense negotiations ensued, involving the EC, ACP, the Latin Americans and the interested ASEAN countries. The CARICOM countries, including Jamaica, St Lucia, Belize and the representative of the Caribbean Regional Negotiating Machinery (CRNM), participated in these negotiations. However, progress depended on the deals brokered in consultations between the EC and the Latin Americans, and ultimately, between the EC and the Philippines and Thailand.

[17] The Rules of Procedure for the Ministerial Conference stated that Members should propose items for the agenda six weeks before the opening of the Conference and any additional item was to be proposed under 'Other Business' at the opening of the session with the agreement of the Conference.

The ACP/Africa/LDC Group was not certain that the waivers had been secured until the morning of 14 November 2001 (the Doha Ministerial Conference should have ended on 13 November 2001 but was extended well into 14 November). Once agreement had been reached, as a procedural matter, the working party for consideration of the waiver request and the Council for Trade in Goods had to be convened to approve the draft waiver decisions. At the final plenary of the Ministerial Conference, Ministers approved the decision granting a waiver from Article I of GATT 1994 until 31 December 2007 for the ACP–EU Partnership Agreement (Annex IV) and the decision granting a waiver from paragraphs 1 and 2 of Article XIII of GATT 1994 for the Transitional Regime for the EC's Autonomous Tariff Rate Quotas on Imports of Bananas (Annex V). This latter decision provides a waiver for the period 1 January 2002 to 31 December 2005 with respect to the EC's separate tariff quota of 750,000 tonnes for bananas of ACP origin.

While these waiver decisions address the legal status of the trade aspects of the Cotonou Agreement and the banana regime in the WTO, they do not prevent a WTO Member from requesting consultations with the EC on difficulties which may arise from implementation of the tariff rate quotas, the inconsistent application of TRQs for ACP bananas, or from resort to dispute settlement proceedings if rights are deemed to be affected. However, the adoption of the waiver decisions at the 4th WTO Ministerial Conference formally brought an end to the banana dispute which had dragged on for nearly ten painful years for Jamaica and other banana-producing countries of CARICOM and the ACP.

13.11 The impact of the banana dispute on Jamaica's banana industry

In the disputes in the GATT and WTO, Jamaica, with its CARICOM partners, spent nearly ten years and considerable resources in the struggle to preserve the non-reciprocal preferential access for bananas to the market of the European Union and, specifically, the United Kingdom.

In over 100 years, the banana industry in Jamaica, with preferential market access and assistance from the UK Government and the European Community, had survived the ravages of hurricanes, the export slump of the Second World War, outbreaks of Panama and Leaf Spot diseases, and competition from new entrants to the market of the United Kingdom, including the Windward Islands in the 1950s. As previously indicated, Latin American bananas, in any significant quantities, were kept out of the UK market until 1992.

It is interesting to note that Owen Jefferson in his 1972 publication *The Post-War Development of Jamaica*, referring to the dominance of small farmers in banana production in Jamaica, stated that 'while this pattern ensures a wide spread of the income generated it poses problems for the future competitiveness of the industry which would assume even more importance if the sheltered market were removed'.

As the banana dispute progressed and intensified in 1996, the question was whether, this time, the Jamaican banana industry could survive the challenge in the WTO to the EC's regime for bananas (in effect, the removal of the sheltered market). The dispute caused the Government of Jamaica to re-examine its policies governing the trade in bananas and brought into focus the whole issue of Jamaica's dependence on preferential market access for its agricultural products.

Prior to 1984, the production of bananas for export was dominated by small to medium-sized farmers occupying 3 to 25 acres of land in several parishes, but primarily in the eastern parishes of St Thomas, St Mary and Portland. Yields per acre were low and the cost of production was high. Jamaica's small farmers were at a disadvantage when compared to the large banana producers in Latin America and Africa. After the decline in production and exports in 1984,[18] the number of small farmers in bananas began to decline in spite of efforts to assist them. The decision was then taken to encourage consolidation into larger farms of 1,000 acres or more to achieve improved yields per acre and better quality of the fruit as well as to improve efficiency in operations and to reduce the cost of production.

Almost a decade later in 1993, when the first panel was established in the GATT, over 1,000 small farmers remained in banana production for export. By the end of 2001, it was estimated that fewer than 200 small farmers remained in banana production for export. The number of small farmers declined dramatically over the period 1993–2001 because their operations

[18] In 1984, banana exports decreased by 52 per cent to 11,100 tonnes and net revenue decreased by 45 per cent. This was the smallest quantity of bananas ever exported. The sharp decline was attributed to unusually cold weather conditions, rationalisation of the industry, shortage of rice leading to increased local demand for bananas, leaf spot disease and requirements for higher quality standards in the UK market leading to a large quantity of rejected fruit. (Source: *Social and Economic Survey of Jamaica*, PIOJ, 1984.)

were increasingly uneconomical due to their high costs of production. Also, with the liberalisation of the EU market commencing in 1992, these small farmers were increasingly unable to achieve the high product standards required in the EU market and thus to compete against fruit from Latin America.

Bananas imported into the EU had to attain a standard of no less than 85 per cent Percentage Unit Within Specification (PUWS), with the ideal being 90 per cent. Over the years, the EC had instituted more stringent sanitary and phyto-sanitary (SPS) measures in addition to technical regulations. Currently, banana producers are required to keep detailed records of their production methods and preparation procedures for export. Upon request, it must be possible to trace a particular shipment of bananas back to its source of origin and to identify production methods and preparation procedures. For example, a farmer must be able to identify the type of fertilisers and chemicals used on his banana crop over the production period. All these requirements for standards and traceability presented a great challenge to small farmers as well as to the larger producers.

With the larger quantities of bananas entering the EU market from Latin America and elsewhere, prices began to decline. Between 1996 and 2002, prices for bananas imported into the UK moved from £615 per tonne to £420 per tonne. At the same time, the prices of inputs (fertilisers, sprays and other chemicals) were increasing. With profit margins declining, small farmers, already high-cost producers, had even less incentive to produce bananas for export. Many small farmers began to concentrate more fully on producing fruit for the domestic market or turned to producing other crops such as plantains. Exports from small farmers declined in 2000 to 8,228 tonnes. This declined further to 3,936 tonnes in 2001 and to 1,993 tonnes in 2002.

By 2001, nearly 90 per cent of the fruit exported from Jamaica came from three large estates, St Mary, Eastern and Victoria. The fruit produced on these estates largely met the grade in quality (nearly 90 per cent PUWS). However, even relying heavily on technology, reducing the cost of production remained a challenge. In comparison to Latin American producers, even an estate of 1,000 acres in a small developing country such as Jamaica cannot achieve the same level of production, efficiency and productivity of a larger operation in South and Central America. A Latin American banana producer can obtain yields of over 20 tonnes per acre. A Jamaican estate yields on average about 7–8 tonnes per acre. In Latin America, one box of bananas is produced at a cost of US $2–5.00. In Jamaica, the same box of bananas is produced at US $10.50–12.00, more than twice the Latin American price.

During the period of the banana dispute, Jamaica's banana exports declined from a high in 1996 of 87,433 tonnes to 43,000 tonnes in 2001 and 39,896 tonnes in 2002. Foreign exchange earnings declined by over 50 per cent during the same period. In 1996, Jamaica earned US $45 million and in 2001 and 2002 earnings declined to US $18.7 million and US $17.6 million respectively. Jamaica's quota resulting from the new EC banana regime now stands at about 70,000 tonnes as the ACP quota for 2002–5 was reduced and Jamaica's production levels have been low.

With the end of the dispute, the waiver for the Transitional Regime for the EC's Autonomous Tariff Rate Quotas on Imports of Bananas extends up to December 2005. During this period, preferential access to the EU market based on quotas will be maintained, but, thereafter, a tariff only system will be implemented. The objective of those producing bananas for export in Jamaica will be to increase production; improve and maintain the quality of the fruit; meet SPS and other environmental standards; improve efficiency; reduce transport and operational costs; and, generally, reduce the overall costs of production in order to become more competitive in the EU market.

However, to reduce the costs of production, these banana producers also face the challenge of addressing praedial larceny (theft of fruit), security costs and maintenance costs for essential activities such as spraying to control the Black Sigatoka disease which still poses a threat to bananas in Jamaica. A further challenge will also be the price of bananas in the EU market because as larger quantities of bananas enter the market, the price is further reduced.

The Banana Export Company (BECO) has indicated that barring serious natural or man-made disasters, Jamaica has the potential to increase its exports to 60,000 tonnes in the transition period. However, in September 2002, one of the larger banana farms, Victoria in western Jamaica, ceased operation, putting 300 employees out of work. This, however, is viewed as part of the effort to rationalise the industry. BECO is continuing work to reduce the costs of production, to increase efficiency and to encourage the introduction and maintenance of international standards for farm operations in adherence to ISO 9000 and ISO 14000 standards.

As stated earlier, small and medium-sized banana producers are focusing their attention on the domestic market where, currently, prices are competitive and there is increasing demand for fruit for domestic consumption, use in the tourist industry, and for commercial use in the making of banana chips. It is roughly estimated that, all things being equal, a farmer with about 10 acres of land under cultivation solely to supply the domestic market could earn a gross income of about J $3,000,000 (US $50,000) per annum. While this income does not compensate fully for income from export production, there appears to be a future for banana producers in the domestic market. However, there is a warning that small farmers will have to improve and maintain their farming practices. Producing for the domestic market does not mean that farmers can become neglectful and fail to maintain standards of crop management, particularly in disease control. Poor and inefficient farming practices will lead to reduction in production and income, will threaten neighbouring farms, and thus the survival of the banana industry.

The EU-funded Banana Support Programme is assisting small and medium-sized farmers in traditional banana growing areas in St Mary, St Thomas, Portland, St James and Clarendon to improve banana production and to diversify their production into non-traditional crops for both the domestic and export markets. In addition, efforts are being made by the Ministry of Agriculture and its Rural Agricultural Development Authority (RADA) to introduce ginger into parishes like St Mary and St Thomas. Jamaican ginger has been highly sought after in the international market, but, as with other products, cost of production presents a problem. As a result, emphasis is being placed on the promotion of crop care management in an effort to reduce the cost of production and regain and expand market share. As some communities in the traditional banana parishes have been seriously affected by the decline in banana production for export, it is felt that diversification will contribute to poverty alleviation.

Banana producers are seriously looking also at the development of value-added products from the fruit and the entire plant for both the domestic and export markets which can generate higher incomes and increased employment. It is felt in many quarters that the survival of the banana industry in Jamaica will depend on the ability to develop and to identify and introduce new, marketable by-products. This requires investment in research and development, and proper market research and analysis during the transition period. The Jamaica Business Development Centre is working presently with the support of the industry to identify, develop and promote value-added products from the banana plant.

In summary, the decline in banana exports and the number of small and medium-sized farmers producing fruit for export cannot be entirely attributed to the results of the dispute in the WTO. However, the banana dispute undermined the security of the EU market for fruit from Jamaica and other Caribbean banana-producing countries. It also phased out various incentives that were available to Jamaican banana exporters under the EC's banana regime. The reality is that, over the years, banana production has been affected by the liberalisation of the EU market commencing with the Common Organization of the Market in 1992; the introduction of higher standards for the fruit dating back to the mid-1980s; reduction in price due to over-supply; high production costs; labour problems; inconsistent disease control; and inclement weather conditions. All these pre-existing problems and the erosion of the preferential market access resulting from the dispute have further exposed the fragility of the banana industry in Jamaica. The Government of Jamaica, while still focusing on the production of bananas for export and the domestic market, is advocating diversification into by-products and other export crops.

In 2006 there will be further liberalisation of the market for bananas in the European Union, not only because the new EC banana regime will give way to a tariff only regime after 2005, but also because of the current negotiations in agriculture in the WTO. The WTO Agreement on Agriculture mandated that negotiations to liberalise trade in agriculture further should commence in 2000. At the 4th WTO Ministerial Conference held in Doha in November 2001, agriculture was incorporated into the expanded Doha negotiating agenda. A primary objective in the agriculture negotiations is the further reduction of tariff levels on all agricultural products. The goal of members of the CAIRNS Group,[19] of which several Latin American banana-producing countries are members, is to achieve a significant

[19] This is a group of major producers of agricultural products which includes Argentina, Australia, Brazil, Bolivia, Canada, Chile, Colombia, Costa Rica, Guatemala, Hungary, Indonesia, Malaysia, Paraguay, Philippines, New Zealand, South Africa, Thailand and Uruguay. These countries are seeking extensive liberalisation of trade in agriculture.

reduction of the EC's existing bound tariffs on agricultural products of interest to them. In the GATT Uruguay Round, the EC bound its tariff on bananas at 650 ECUS (Euros) per tonne, while the current applied tariff for non-ACP banana exports is 75 Euros per tonne. Latin American banana producers will want the EC to bind its tariff for bananas close to or below the existing applied tariff rate. It is important for Jamaica and its CARICOM partners that, in these negotiations, the EC is able to bind the tariff rate at a level that continues to provide ACP countries with meaningful preferential access. A tariff bound at too low a rate and offering little flexibility will not allow countries like Jamaica to compete in the EU market and will deliver yet another severe blow to the banana industry in Jamaica and other CARICOM countries.

In the agriculture negotiations, the EC and ACP have proposed the adoption of the Uruguay Round approach for the reduction of tariffs. This approach is more flexible and will result in more moderate tariff reductions. The EC has proposed an overall average tariff reduction on imports of 36 per cent. Other WTO Members, such as the members of the CAIRNS Group, have proposed the use of the Swiss Formula, a mathematical equation, which would result in more significant tariff reductions than that proposed by the EC. These issues remain to be resolved in the WTO agriculture negotiations scheduled to conclude in December 2004.

The survival of Jamaica's banana exports from 2006 onwards will depend greatly on the tariff rate emerging from the WTO negotiations and the subsequent tariff regime for non-ACP states to be implemented by the European Commission for an enlarged European Union of twenty-five Members. Survival will also depend on the industry's ability to reduce the costs of production, improve efficiency, achieve consistently higher yields, and to maintain high quality standards for export. Price stability in the EU market will also be a very important issue if profit margins are to be maintained, giving banana exporters an incentive to continue in production for export. In the current economic climate, Jamaica cannot afford, in the short to medium term, to lose the foreign exchange earned from the export of bananas or to jeopardise the economic and social stability of rural communities, particularly in eastern parishes, further. However, the extreme vulnerability of this industry is a stark reality and the survival of exports from 2006 will continue to be a major challenge for the government and the industry.

Reference sources

GATT/WTO Reports in the Banana Dispute

GATT Panels Reports

(GATT)DS 32/R (1993)	EC – Regime for the Importation, Sale and Distribution of Bananas Report of the Panel
(GATT)DS 38/R (1994)	EC – Regime for the Importation, Sale and Distribution of Bananas Report of the Panel

WTO Panel/Appellate Body Reports

WT/DS27/R/GTM (22 May 1997) (separate reports were issued for all parties)	EC – Regime for the Importation, Sale and Distribution of Bananas Report of the Panel
WT/DS27/AB/R (9 September 1997)	EC – Regime for the Importation, Sale and Distribution of Bananas Report of the Appellate Body
WT/DS27/RW/ECU (12 April 1999)	EC – Regime for the Importation, Sale and Distribution of Bananas: Recourse to Article 21.5 by Ecuador Report of the Panel
WT/DS27/RW/EEC (12 April 1999)	EC – Regime for the Importation, Sale and Distribution of Bananas: Recourse to Article 21.5 by the European Communities Report of the Panel
WT/DS27/ARB/USA (9 April 1999) (Request by USA for Authorisation of Suspension of Concessions)	EC – Regime for the Importation, Sale and Distribution of Bananas: Recourse to Arbitration by the European Communities under Article 22.6 of the DSU Decision by the Arbitrators
WT/DS152/R (22 December 1999)	US – Section 301–310 of the Trade Act of 1974 Report of the Panel

WT/DS27/ARB/ECU (24 March 2000) (Request by Ecuador for Authorisation of Suspension of Concession)	EC – Regime for the Importation, Sale and Distribution of Bananas: Recourse to Arbitration by the European Communities Decision by the Arbitrators
WT/DS165/R (17 July 2000)	US – Import Measures on Certain Products from the European Communities Report of the Panel
WT/DS165AB/R (11 December 2000)	US – Import Measures on Certain Products from the European Communities Report of the Appellate Body

Organisations, etc.

Ministry of Agriculture
Rural Agricultural Development Agency (RADA)
Banana Board
All Island Banana Growers Association
Banana Export Company (BECO)
Planning Institute of Jamaica
Jamaica Business Development Centre
Ministry of Foreign Affairs and Foreign Trade
Permanent Mission of Jamaica to the Office of the United Nations, its Specialised Agencies and other International Organizations at Geneva
Embassy of Jamaica, Brussels
Delegation of the European Commission, Jamaica
European Commission

14

WTO complaints by Australia and Brazil regarding the EU sugar regime

STEPHEN J. ORAVA AND CAROL C. GEORGE

14.1 Introduction

On 27 September 2002, the Governments of Australia and Brazil (the 'Complainants') filed requests for consultations with the European Communities (EC) alleging that the structure of its sugar market violates its obligations under certain agreements of the World Trade Organisation (WTO). If the Complainants are successful in their challenge, the EC may find itself obligated to change the nature of its sugar market in order to bring it into compliance with WTO obligations. Such changes could result in a significant reduction in price supports from which domestic and certain African, Caribbean and Pacific (ACP) suppliers benefit.

14.2 The EU Common Market Organisation for sugar

14.2.1 General structure

The EU's Common Market Organisation (CMO) for sugar has the following five principal features:

- production quota scheme
- guaranteed price and intervention mechanism
- export refund programme
- production levies
- preferential import programme.

14.2.2 Quota scheme

Under the CMO, processors are required to pay growers a guaranteed minimum beet price, and the EC will pay producers a fixed 'intervention price' for a certain quantity (quota) of refined white sugar per EC Member State. National quotas are allocated to individual sugar-producing factories. There are two types of quota, A and B, the main difference being the level of the production levies applied to them. Only 'quota sugar' can be sold in the EC; sugar produced in excess of quota ('C-sugar') must be exported without any export refund. Thus, the quota system acts as a limitation on the supply of sugar on the EC sugar market.

14.2.3 Prices

Quota sugar in excess of EC consumption is eligible for price support through the intervention mechanism and export refunds. The 'intervention price' is the price at which the EC is prepared (and obligated) to buy white quota sugar. The intervention price therefore acts as a guaranteed minimum price. It is fixed annually by the EC Council of Ministers of Agriculture based on a proposal by the Commission. Producers may either sell their surplus quota sugar to an Intervention Agency at the fixed price, or they may export it and obtain a refund of the difference between the EC intervention price and the world market price. Producers pay a levy on the production of quota sugar to cover the cost of refunding these losses.

Raw sugar and 'basic beet' and cane prices are derived from the intervention price. The basic beet price guaranteed to the farmers is about 58 per cent of the intervention price, while processors receive 42 per cent, plus the difference between the higher EC market prices and the intervention price.

14.2.4 Export and production refunds

Under the export refund programme, surplus quota sugar and preferential sugar are exported with the support of export refunds. Losses incurred on the world market are recouped by receipt of export refunds paid out of production levy proceeds. The Commission manages this programme by deciding weekly on the refund rates based on offers made by sugar traders and taking into account the world price of sugar and the total quantity of sugar that might qualify for refunds during the marketing season. Approved export refunds will never exceed the maximum export refund, which is equal to the intervention price (plus storage and shipping costs) minus the export price obtained on the world market.

In addition, the EC makes available to domestic chemical and pharmaceutical producers 'production refunds' in connection with their use of highly priced sugar products as raw materials. The production refund level is derived from the average of the awarded export refunds and is fixed on a quarterly basis.

14.2.5 Production levies

The EC charges producers 'production levies' that are intended to recover from the sugar industry the cost of the export refunds and production refunds. Thus, the export refund support system is 'self-financing' and therefore, arguably, not a direct subsidy from the EC. The levies are paid by the sugar producers who reclaim 58 per cent of the levy from the farmers by a discount on the beet price.

Each Member State has a national Paying Agency and Intervention Agency that collects the production levies, pays the export refunds and buys the sugar at the intervention price, should it be offered to them. In practice, there has only been one intervention purchase (by a German Intervention Agency in the mid-eighties). Apparently, the option of exporting surplus quota sugar with the support of export refunds is more attractive than selling the sugar to an Intervention Agency.

14.2.6 Preferential import programme

The UK has historically imported large quantities of raw cane sugar from ACP countries for refining in the UK. When the UK joined the EC, provision for importation of sugar from the ACP countries was incorporated into the 1975 EC/ACP (IVth Lomé) Convention and embodied in the CMO. This protected the interests of the UK refiners and supplying countries, and ensured that supply channels were not disrupted. Under the Eighth Protocol (Sugar Protocol) to the Convention, the EC guarantees that it will buy annually a fixed quantity of white sugar equivalents from the ACP countries for an indefinite period. These imports are exempt from import duties. India was also added to the list of countries for preferential treatment. This imported sugar is referred to as 'preferential sugar'.

Prices to be paid for preferential sugar are negotiated annually between the EC and the ACP countries. Under the Sugar Protocol, the price is to be 'within the price range obtaining in the Community, taking into account all relevant economic factors'. In practice, the price for ACP raw cane sugar has always been equivalent to the intervention price for EU-produced raw sugar, and the guaranteed price of white sugar has been equivalent to the derived intervention price in the UK. The EC guarantees that price and is prepared to buy through the Intervention Agencies in case no other buyer is prepared to buy at the guaranteed price (which has never happened). In practice, therefore, the ACP countries receive the same guaranteed price as Community sugar producers.

14.3 Basis for WTO complaints

The Complainants present two main claims: first, that the EC has provided export subsidies in excess of its WTO commitments, and second, that the provision of a guaranteed intervention price is a violation of the national treatment obligation in that it is available only to EC producers. Little elaboration is provided in the request for consultations, and we can only surmise that the following is the approach that Brazil and Australia will pursue in potential dispute settlement proceedings.

14.3.1 Export subsidies in excess of commitments

The Complainants assert that under the CMO for sugar the EC is, in two regards, providing export subsidies for sugar that exceed the reduction commitment levels set out in its Schedule. First, they claim that the *CMO for sugar, its intervention price system and regulatory mechanism*, taken as a whole, enable producers to export C-sugar at prices below the total cost of production. They argue that by guaranteeing a high domestic price for A-quota and B-quota sugar, the EC is subsidising exports of non-quota C-sugar on the world market, in excess of its reduction commitments.

Secondly, they claim that the *export refunds* provided to producers in relation to surplus A-quota and B-quota sugar are export subsidies in excess of the export subsidy reduction commitments of the EC. In support of these assertions, they cite certain provisions of the WTO Agreement on Agriculture, the Agreement on Subsidies and Countervailing Measures ('SCM Agreement') and the GATT 1994.

14.3.1.1 SCM Agreement

Without demonstrating that the measures at issue are export subsidies, or subsidies at all, the Claimants cite Articles 3.1 and 3.2 of the SCM Agreement, which prohibit subsidies that are contingent upon export performance. A footnote to Article 3.1(a) makes clear that factual, as opposed to legal, contingency may suffice.[1] Importantly, however, Article 3.1 is expressly subject to the provisions of the Agriculture Agreement, which apply to agricultural products, including sugar, by reason of Article 2 and Annex I on Product Coverage. The Agriculture Agreement therefore supersedes the prohibition on export subsidies under the SCM Agreement.

The Complainants also contend that the alleged export subsidies are not exempt from challenge under Article 3 of the SCM Agreement, by reason of the 'Peace Clause' in Article 13(c) of the Agriculture Agreement. This clause imposes restraints on countervailing duty actions against export subsidies and exempts them from actions under Articles 3, 5 or 6 of the SCM Agreement during the implementation period, which expired at the end of 2003. Brazil claims that the Peace Clause does not apply because the alleged export subsidies do not 'conform fully to the provisions of Part V of the Agriculture Agreement', based on the level of subsidies exceeding scheduled commitments.

14.3.1.2 Agriculture Agreement

In the WTO Agreement on Agriculture, Members have undertaken to *reduce* export subsidies and, further, that they will not provide export subsidies except in accordance with the Agreement and the commitments as specified in each Member's Schedule.[2] Article 8 is the basic foundation for the Claimants' main claim.

14.3.1.2.1 Definition The Agriculture Agreement does not define 'subsidy'. Article 1 of the SCM Agreement, which defines 'subsidy' for the purposes of *that* agreement, deems a subsidy to exist if there is any form of

[1] 'This standard is met when the facts demonstrate that the granting of a subsidy, without having been made legally contingent upon export performance, is in fact tied to actual or anticipated exportation or export earnings. The mere fact that a subsidy is granted to enterprises which export shall not for that reason alone be considered to be an export subsidy within the meaning of this provision.'

[2] Agreement on Agriculture, Article 8: 'Each Member undertakes not to provide export subsidies otherwise than in conformity with this Agreement and with the commitments as specified in that Member's Schedule.'

income or price support (Article 1(a)(2)) and a benefit is thereby conferred. If Article 1 of the SCM Agreement applies to these claims, the first question is whether the CMO on sugar, or the export refund, even if they amount to price support, confer a benefit. If so, and they are therefore 'subsidies', are they 'export' subsidies?

'Export subsidies' are defined in Article 1(e) of the Agriculture Agreement as 'subsidies contingent on export performance, including the export subsidies listed in Article 9 of this Agreement'. This corresponds generally to the description of the prohibited subsidies in SCM Article 3.1, except that it includes no sub-text in relation to legal or factual contingency. Although that provision may be subordinated to the Agriculture Agreement, it is possible that a WTO panel might seek to harmonise the agreements in regard to the definition, thus adopting the standard of actual or anticipated contingency as a means of determining whether export subsidies exist.

With respect to the system as a whole, neither Brazil nor Australia identify precisely which element of the 'intervention price system' is the benefit conferred, or how the alleged subsidisation of C-sugar is contingent upon export performance. From one perspective, the EC has never, with the exception of one incident, provided any intervention payment to producers, and EC market prices sustain themselves. This is not a government payment scheme: consumers pay the high prices. Neither is it clear that the industry-financed export refund, which *is* contingent upon export, is a benefit conferred by the government. Taken in isolation, the export refund regime may be interpreted as not price support at all, but a voluntary insurance fund to cover losses incurred by the industry.

14.3.1.2.2 Export subsidies subject to reduction Certain types of export subsidies are positively identified, in Article 9.1 of the Agriculture Agreement, as being subject to reduction commitments. These are largely *direct* export subsidies, which are considered to cause the most distortion. The Claimants point to those export subsidies defined in sub-paragraphs (a) and (c) of Article 9.1.[3]

[3] Agriculture Agreement, Article 9.1(a) and (c):
'1. The following export subsidies are subject to reduction commitments under this Agreement:
(a) the provision by governments or their agencies of direct subsidies, including payments-in-kind, to a firm, to an industry, to producers of an agricultural product, to a cooperative or other

Article 3.3 of the Agriculture Agreement states that a Member cannot provide these types of export subsidies in regard to any agricultural products or groups of products that are not specified in Section II of Part IV of the Member's Schedule. It may only provide Article 9.1 export subsidies in relation to those particular agricultural products/groups of products set out in its Schedule, and only to the extent of the budgetary outlay and quantity commitment levels specified therein.

14.3.1.2.3 Non-circumvention of export subsidy commitments Article 10 of the Agriculture Agreement requires that 'other' export subsidies, those not listed in Article 9.1, shall not be applied in such a way as to circumvent the export subsidy commitments. The fact that the Complainants rely on this provision implies that they may wish to demonstrate that the CMO in sugar amounts to another type of export subsidy, perhaps not as well defined as those listed in Article 9.1, that allegedly circumvents the commitments of the EC. This view is supported by the fact that they have also cited provisions of Article XVI of GATT 1994, which contains references, in paragraphs 3 and 4, to the concept of indirect subsidisation. Those provisions also denounce the notion that any subsidy should result in a WTO Member having more than an equitable share in the world export trade in the subsidised product.

Most of the relevant obligations in Article XVI of GATT 1994 have been elaborated upon in the SCM Agreement, but WTO dispute settlement panels are still obliged to apply them along with the Uruguay Round agreements, including the SCM Agreement, whenever such application is possible and does not raise a conflict.

14.3.1.3 Conclusion

The success of the claim, that export subsidies have been applied in excess of commitments of the EC, will depend on a persuasive argument that the overall effect of domestic price support, exports of surplus quota sugar with refunds, and exports of C-sugar should be considered together and

association of such producers, or to a marketing board, contingent on export performance;

. . .

(c) payments on the export of an agricultural product that are financed by virtue of governmental action, whether or not a charge on the public account is involved, including payments that are financed from the proceeds of a levy imposed on the agricultural product concerned or on an agricultural product from which the exported product is derived;'

that the cumulative effect is a form of indirect subsidisation that is not in keeping with the spirit of the Agreement. To support this claim, the concept of export subsidies subject to reduction in the Agriculture Agreement will have to be construed much more broadly than the express provisions appear to dictate. Notably, the other factors in play in the system, the special safeguard measures keeping out non-preferential sugar imports and preferential arrangements with the ACP countries, have *not* been directly challenged by Brazil and Australia in these requests.

14.3.2 Intervention price constitutes a national treatment violation

The second main argument put forward by the Complainants is that the guarantee of a fixed Intervention Price for in-quota sugar sold in the EC is a violation of Article III of the GATT, because it is only available to EC producers, thus affording imported products less favourable treatment. Article III of the GATT has been considered at length in the history of the GATT and the WTO and extensive analysis would be necessary to assess thoroughly whether there is legal foundation to this claim. Whatever its technical merits, however, the claim is of little practical importance, given that almost all non-preferential sugar imports are excluded from the EC market by 140 per cent tariffs. The only significant imports are those imported on a preferential basis, which enter free of tariffs and receive what is in effect the guaranteed intervention price. In the absence of a challenge against tariffs, non-tariff barriers and MFN, Brazil and Australia will benefit little from a national treatment claim.

14.4 Policy arguments in support of complaints

The policy arguments in favour of the complaints by Australia and Brazil are persuasive from both a trade and a development perspective. From a trade policy perspective, principles embodied in the WTO and other trade agreements disfavour the use of subsidies as an instrument of trade policy, particularly where they are directly related to exports. The basis for this relates to the distortions that such subsidies cause in otherwise competitive markets. In this case, EU export-contingent subsidies for sugar are alleged to be the cause of substantial declines in the world market price for sugar to levels below the cost of production for the most efficient producers. Such distortions and the inefficiencies that they cause are the basis for the prohibitions on export subsidies in trade agreements.

In addition to basic trade policy objections to the EU's sugar regime, substantial development-based objections have been raised, both by WTO Members and by non-governmental organisations (NGOs). For example, Oxfam prepared a briefing paper on 'The Great EU Sugar Scam', in which it set forth its unequivocal views on the cover:

> European consumers and taxpayers are paying to destroy livelihoods in developing countries. Under the Common Agricultural Policy (CAP), the EU has emerged as the world's largest exporter of white sugar. Subsidies and tariffs generate vast profits for big sugar processors and large farmers – and vast surpluses that are dumped on world markets. Smallholder farmers and agricultural labourers in poor countries suffer the consequences. Oxfam is calling for an immediate end to EU sugar exports and improved market access for the poorest countries.

As discussed below, however, certain ACP countries rely heavily on the EU regime to support their economy. Oxfam considers that those benefits accruing to certain ACP countries are unjustified, however, because 'almost 80 per cent of the benefits accrue to just five of them – Mauritius, Fiji, Guyana, Swaziland and Jamaica – none of which are least developed countries'. It also argues that the preferential access accorded to these ACP countries has:

- 'limited the opportunity for these ACP countries to add value to their commodity exports and create their own white sugar brands' and
- 'led several countries to have a high degree of dependence on exports of raw sugar cane'.

Essentially, other WTO Members and certain NGOs consider that sacrificing the interests of certain developing ACP countries, at least in the short term, is acceptable in order to improve the situation for a larger group of developing and least developed countries that are not benefiting under the current EU regime. It is obvious that Australia and Brazil support their WTO complaints because it is in the interests of their sugar producers and exporters, but they have not paired this self-interest with any proposals about how to address the adverse consequences, whether intended or unintended, on a number of ACP countries. Certain NGOs similarly ignore or otherwise marginalise the interests of these ACP countries by failing to understand the magnitude of the irreversible damage that would be caused.

It would appear warranted for the Complainants and interested NGOs to evaluate how to address the specific consequences of succeeding in a WTO challenge prior to moving forward and to present proposals now for addressing the potentially catastrophic effects of a successful WTO case on a number of ACP countries.

14.5 Impact on ACP countries

For certain ACP countries, the consequences of a successful case that results in the removal or substantial lowering of the guaranteed price for the purchase of ACP raw cane sugar could be catastrophic in the short term. For example, as reported by the EC's Court of Auditors, Mauritius benefits the most out of all ACP countries in the preferential structure of the EC regime. Approximately 95 per cent of all 1998 sales were conducted under the EC's Sugar Protocol. A substantial decline in the prices guaranteed to raw sugar cane originating in Mauritius, in favour of cheaper exports from Australia and Brazil, would have disastrous effects on the local economy and societal welfare generally.

More generally, the benefits of the EU's preferential sugar regime are estimated at Euro 500 million per year compared to the earnings available on the world market. Most of the benefits of the sugar regime accrue to only a few developing countries, including Fiji, Guyana, Jamaica, Mauritius and Swaziland. Thus, the impact on these countries of a successful challenge by Australia and Brazil would be to destroy their primary source of income.

Although it may be the case that these five economies, as well as several other developing and least developed ACP countries, focus too narrowly on a single crop, the type of systemic changes necessary to transform their economies will take decades. The effects of the reforms in the EU market, however, are likely to be immediate and catastrophic.

14.6 Third party participation in WTO proceedings

Based on the significant adverse effects described above, those ACP countries that are also WTO Members may determine that it is in their interests to participate directly in the WTO case. Because the countries would essentially be supporting the EC's defence of the case, their role would be limited to joining in consultations, if permitted, and participating as a third party in any dispute panel and/or Appellate Body proceedings.

14.6.1 Joining consultations

Article 4.11 of the Understanding on Rules and Procedures Governing the Settlement of Disputes (DSU) provides for the participation of third party countries in consultations. In general, for a WTO Member to participate in consultations in the dispute involving the EU sugar regime, it must:

(1) consider that it has a substantial trade interest in the consultations between the EU and the Complainants;
(2) notify the EU, the Complainants, and the WTO's Dispute Settlement Body (DSB) by 11 October 2002; and
(3) ensure that the EU agrees that the third country's claim of substantial interest is 'well founded' and informs the DSB accordingly.

The previous section on the impact of a successful case appears to provide ample support for certain ACP countries to satisfy the above conditions for consultations. As a legal matter, the only condition effectively outside the control of these countries is the final condition of obtaining the EU's consent for the countries to join consultations.

In the past, WTO Members have refused to grant this consent, although only in unusual and highly controversial cases and/or where the countries denied consent were supporting the complainants. For example, as part of the lengthy dispute settlement proceedings challenging the EU's banana regime, the EU requested WTO consultations regarding the US approach to retaliation following an adverse panel and Appellate Body decision, the so-called 'carousel'.[4] The United States refused to allow Australia, the Dominican Republic, Jamaica, Japan and St Lucia to join consultations, relying on the discretion accorded to the defending Member under DSU Article 4.11 and on its view that such countries did not have a substantial trade interest in the dispute. The EU was especially critical of the US action and thus is unlikely to refuse requests from the ACP countries, especially as they are supportive of its defence.

[4] See, e.g., United States – Section 306 of the Trade Act of 1974 and Amendments thereto, WT/DS200.

Therefore, the first step for ACP countries that would be adversely affected by a successful challenge to the EU sugar regime or that would otherwise be affected by any reform to such regime is to request immediately to join consultations under DSU Article 4.11.

14.6.2 Third-party participation before a panel and/or the Appellate Body

Assuming consultations fail to resolve the dispute and the Complainants decide to request the establishment of a WTO dispute settlement panel, ACP countries may decide to participate in the panel proceedings as a third party. DSU Article 10.2 enables third-party WTO Members to notify the DSB and participate in the proceedings where they have a substantial interest in the matter before the panel. Unlike in consultations, DSU Article 10.2 does not accord any discretion to the defending Member(s) or the Complainants to prevent other WTO Members from participating in the proceedings as third parties. Thus, ACP countries that may be adversely affected by a successful challenge to the EU sugar regime have the right, as WTO Members, to participate in the panel proceedings. A similar right exists if a panel's findings are appealed to the Appellate Body.

14.7 Conclusion

Australia and Brazil have initiated the first formal step in WTO dispute settlement proceedings by requesting consultations with the EC regarding its sugar regime. The precise nature of the Complainants' claims remains unclear, although they clearly target the EC's mechanisms for ensuring relatively higher prices for EU-origin sugar beets and for preferential imports of raw cane sugar. If the Complainants are successful, the EC may decide to reform its sugar regime in a manner that reduces or eliminates the price supports for the purchase of preferential imports of raw cane sugar. Such a result would be catastrophic for certain ACP countries that rely almost exclusively on the EC market for sales of their raw cane sugar.

Although the Complainants and certain NGOs have voiced strong opposition to the EU sugar regime on trade and development grounds, they have not shown sufficient concern about the effects of reforms on those developing and least developed ACP countries that rely on the regime almost exclusively to support their countries. Certainly, the benefits to reforming the EU sugar regime for the Complainants and other producing countries should be balanced against the significant and irreversible harm that may be caused to certain ACP countries. The focus moving forward should be on achieving such a balance through comprehensive negotiations in the context of the Doha Development Agenda among all interested parties rather than on a resource-intensive WTO dispute on the technical details of the EU regime.

15

Reform of EU export subsidies on sugar: the legal and economic implications for the ACP countries

ROMAN GRYNBERG, CHRIS MILNER, WYN MORGAN AND EVIOUS ZGOVU

15.1 Introduction

ACP countries have preferential terms of access for their sugar exports to the EU. The Sugar Protocol of the Lomé Agreement gives (indefinite) duty-free access for agreed quantities of sugar at guaranteed (protected domestic EU) prices to specific ACP Protocol countries.[1] This results in these ACP countries receiving prices for their sugar exports to the EU that are in excess of those on the world market, and a corresponding transfer of income that embodies a significant element of rent or 'aid'.

In September 2002, Australia and Brazil filed complaints and requests for consultations with the EU at the WTO, concerning the nature of the EU's sugar market. The complaint is that the volume of EU subsidised exports of sugar exceeds the levels the EU had committed itself to under the Uruguay Round Agreements. If this challenge at the WTO leads to reforms of the EU sugar policies, then this may lead to reductions in protected EU import prices and therefore in turn to reductions in the level of income transfer to the ACP Protocol exporters. Reduced rents or 'aid' to these relatively sugar-dependent ACP exporters may have serious macroeconomic implications, in terms of incomes, employment, the balance of payments and tax revenue.

15.2 The EU sugar regime

The production of beet sugar in the EU is limited under the Common Agricultural Policy (CAP) by the imposition of country-specific quotas that

[1] In addition to this 'preferential sugar', there are 'special preferential sugar' imports.

form part of an overall EU quota limit. Quotas apply to the finished refined product (white sugar) but implicitly constrain production of the raw beet. Each Member State is allocated a quota by the Council of Ministers, which it then distributes to processors according to its own national rules.

The quotas themselves are further subdivided into three parts, 'A', 'B' and 'C' quotas. In essence, 'A' and 'B' are the main quotas and differ only in the level of the levy imposed on producers. 'A' attracts a fixed levy of 2 per cent of the intervention price while 'B' producers face a variable levy of up to 37.5 per cent of intervention price, dependent upon the cost of export refunds. A further storage cost levy, used to pay back producers for storage costs, is charged on all sales bar those into intervention. C-quota sugar is not eligible for intervention buying and is thus exported without subsidy and sold at the world market price.

The intervention price is set by the Council and this, along with the storage cost levy, creates a floor price for sugar in the EU. Clearly prices do not always equate to this but will move between this minimum level and the threshold price level (the price at which imports enter the EU) and possibly higher. When production is at a level that threatens the floor price, the Commission buys surplus sugar into intervention from A- and B-quota production. However, given the export arrangements, intervention rarely occurs.

Guaranteed prices for refined sugar are set annually and are then translated into minimum beet prices for producers. Refiners therefore must pay beet producers 58 per cent of the intervention price as a minimum, while processors receive 42 per cent of the intervention price.

The sugar regime has specific provisions for both the export and import of sugar. Exports can be of two types of sugar – surplus quota sugar and C-sugar. The former is exported onto world markets with the aid of export refunds. Such refunds are necessary to ensure that the sugar refiners can actually export, the refunds making up the difference between the (high) internal EU price and the (lower) world market price. The value of these subsidies varies each year depending on the relative level of prices in the two markets, while the final level of export refunds will determine the level of the levy imposed on B-quota sugar. C-sugar is exported without support and as such is sold at the going world market price.

As with all products covered by the CAP, there is a common tariff imposed on all non-EU imports that is set at a level higher than the internal guaranteed price to protect domestic producers.

Table 15.1 *ACP export quotas in tonnes (1998–9)*

Barbados	50,312.4
Belize	40,348.8
Congo	10,186.1
Côte d'Ivoire	10,186.1
Fiji	165,348.3
Guyana	159,410.1
Jamaica	118,696.0
Madagascar	10,760.0
Malawi	20,824.4
Mauritius	491,030.5
St Kitts & Nevis	15,590.9
Swaziland	117,844.5
Tanzania	10,186.1
Trinidad & Tobago	43,751.0
Zambia	0.0
Zimbabwe	30,224.8
Total	1,294,700.0

Source: ACP (http://www.acpsugar.org/acpstats1.htm)

There is, however, an exception to this arrangement and that is the provision for preferential imports from ACP countries. Under the Lomé (now Cotonou) Convention, the EU agrees to buy a pre-determined, but fixed, volume of imports from a range of countries which are exempt from the duties normally applied to imports and which are purchased at a price that is roughly equivalent to the EU's internal intervention price. The vast majority of such 'preferential' sugar flows to the UK for refining.

The Uruguay Round (UR) Agreement covered agricultural products for the first time. For the sugar sector, the emphasis was placed on reducing distortions to trade, either via import restrictions or through export subsidies. In the case of the EU, the system of a guaranteed minimum import price based on a variable levy had to be replaced with fixed import tariffs.

The new policy had to be introduced in mid-1995 and the EU was further tasked with reducing the fixed tariff by 20 per cent in relation to the 1986–8 base period, over the six-year period of 1995/6 to 2000/1. In effect this meant that the import tariff on white sugar was introduced at 507 ECU/tonne in 1995/6 and had to be reduced gradually to 419 ECU/tonne by 2000/1. However, there is a 'Special Safeguard Clause' that allows the EU to impose an additional tariff if the import price falls below 90 per cent of a so-called trigger price of 531 ECU/tonne.

More significantly for the EU, the UR Agreement required its policy on export subsidies and volumes to be altered. In 2000/1, the volume of subsidised exports had to be some 21 per cent lower than the base period of 1986/7–1988/9, while the total expenditure on export subsidies had to be 36 per cent lower than the same base period.

15.2.1 Implications of the sugar regime

The principles of the EU sugar market regime are illustrated in figure 15.1, with production of sugar divided into A- and B-quotas and C-production. The production of A-sugar is paid the guaranteed price P_A, and the production of B-sugar the price P_B, whereas the production of C-sugar is paid the prevailing world market price P_w. The prices of A- and B-sugar are linked to the intervention price (P^I) by charging the production of A-sugar a levy of 2 per cent and the production of B-sugar a maximum levy of 37.5 per cent.[2] Domestic consumption of sugar in the EU (Q_1) is given by the intersection of the intervention price (P^I) and the demand curve (D). Excess supplies of A- and B-sugar (A + B − Q) are exported to the world market at the price P_w, the costs of exports (equal to the shaded area c + d) being covered by the revenue from levies on A- and B-production (equal to the shaded area a + b + c). The provision of export support through levies on production might be viewed as cross-subsidisation of exports, and incompatible with the regulations of the WTO. Certainly the provision for B-sugar is subject to reduction commitments according to the WTO Agreement.

If the scale of the supported exports in the international market is relatively large then one may for some purposes wish to distinguish between the actual world price (P_w) and a post-reform world price ($P^I{}_w$). Reduced exports by the EU, both of those eligible for export support and those not (because of reduced incentives to produce for a protected market), may reduce world supply sufficiently to shift the world price upwards.

The implications of the Sugar Protocol arrangements for the sugar export earnings of the respective ACP countries are illustrated in figure 15.2. On the

[2] If necessary, a supplementary levy can be applied to cover losses caused by the disposal of Community production in excess of internal consumption.

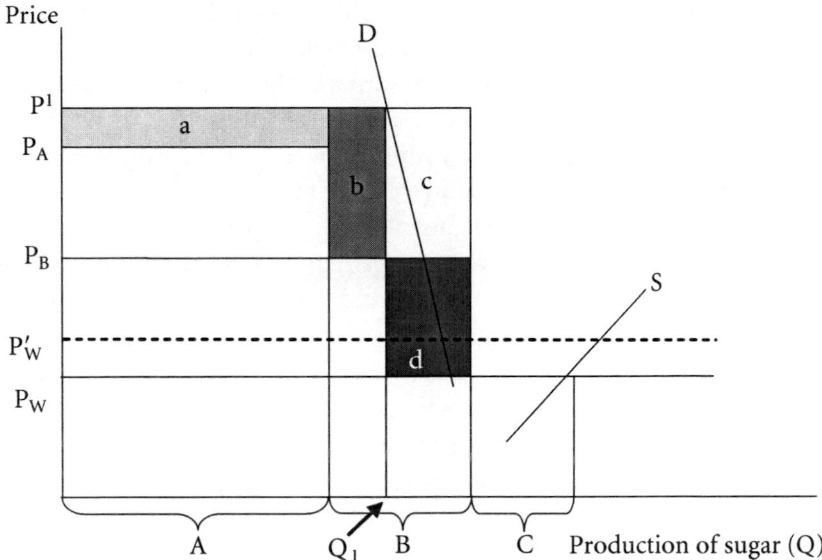

Figure 15.1 EU sugar scheme

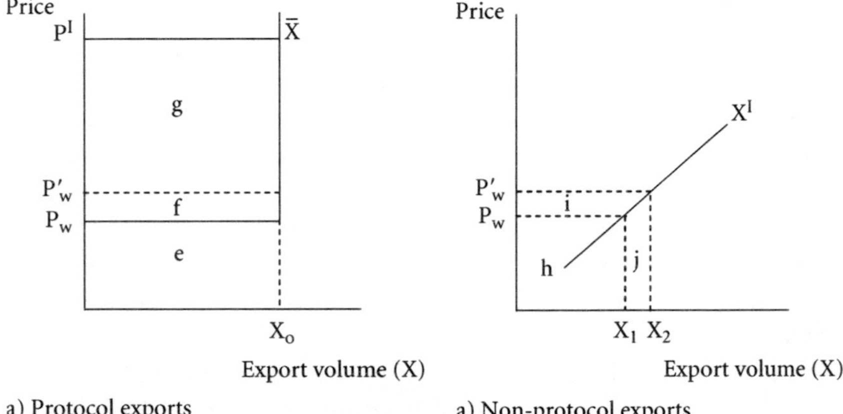

a) Protocol exports a) Non-protocol exports

Figure 15.2 Export revenues and income transfers for Sugar Protocol countries

quota set for Protocol exports (part a) of figure 15.2, the price received by the ACP exports can be approximated by P^I.

The total revenue for an export quota of X_o is given by the area (e + f + g). When compared with the prevailing world price (P_w), this constitutes an additional income transfer of area (f + g). If the world price is variant with the scale of these EU imports from ACP countries (an equivalent amount of which can be re-exported at world prices by the EU), then this income transfer is a reasonable approximation for valuing the rent accruing to the ACP exporters. In the case of wider reforms of the EU's sugar regime, one might anticipate a rise in the world price of sugar (e.g. to P^{I}_{w}), in which case the total rent transfer associated with the Sugar Protocol would be better viewed as being equivalent to the area g in figure 15.2.

In part b of the figure we recognise that the protocol exporters may generate sugar export earnings from exporting (volume X_1 in figure 15.2) beyond their protocol quotas, but at world prices. The export earnings at the prevailing world price are represented by area h. Again, any reforms of the EU regime that raised the world price to P^{I}_{w} would increase export earnings on non-protocol exports to non-EU destinations to (h + i + j). The net effect of EU sugar reforms that reduced the EU import (or intervention) price to P^{I}_{w} would therefore reduce the export earnings of the protocol exporters by (g − i − j).

15.3 Impact of current EU sugar regime on Sugar Protocol countries

The methodology employed is based on figure 15.2. We initially base the estimates on the annual average (2001) International Sugar Agreement (ISA) daily price (19.04 US cents/kg) to proxy the world price (P_w) and the average unit value of ACP exports to EU adjusted uniformally for annual (2001) average c.i.f. on London daily price (2.42 US cents/kg) to represent the EU intervention price (P^{I}).

At this stage (i.e. without reform to the EU regime) it is assumed that the world price of sugar is unaffected by the ACP trade. The results of this decomposition of the value of ACP sugar exports to the EU are reported in table 15.2.[3]

The first two columns of table 15.2 report on the value and volume of sugar exports to the EU in 2001 of the protocol exporters. Note that we report here on all the quota-owning countries under the Sugar Protocol, some of which (St Kitts, Suriname and Uganda) did not export any sugar to the EU in 2001.

The estimated value of the total income transfer component of the total sugar export earnings (of all the protocol countries in 2001) to the EU is $490.2 million (2001 prices). This is equivalent to just under 60 per cent of

[3] For earlier but comparable estimates of the transfer see McDonald (1996).

Table 15.2 *Estimates of current income transfer (2001)*

	Value of sugar exports to EU (in US $ million)	Volume of sugar exports to EU (in tonnes)	Total income transfer to ACP exporters[1] (US $'000, 2001 prices)	Share of total transfer (%)
Barbados	27.2	51,488	16,150.7	3.3
Belize	24.9	47,070	14,798.8	3.0
Congo, Rep.	1.1	2,050	660.1	0.1
Côte d'Ivoire	5.5	10,400	3,268.2	0.7
Fiji	82.1	155,386	48,754.2	9.9
Guyana	102.5	193,945	60,879.4	12.4
Jamaica	78.1	147,720	46,399.3	9.5
Kenya	2	3,789	1,186.9	0.2
Madagascar	8.3	15,731	4,924.1	1.0
Malawi	20.6	39,051	12,219.7	2.5
Mauritius	304.2	575,421	18,0714.7	36.9
St Kitts	0	0	0	0
Suriname	0	0	0	0
Swaziland	94.9	179,510	56,377.2	11.5
Tanzania	7.5	14,105	4,473.1	0.9
Trinidad & Tobago	24.7	46,699	14,678.4	3.0
Uganda	0	0	0	0
Zambia	8.1	15,395	4,796.2	1.0
Zimbabwe	33.5	63,434	19,887.1	4.1
Total	825.2	1,561,194	490,167.8	100

(1) Based on unit value of actual imports of ACP exporters to EU, adjusted for c.i.f. Alternative estimates based on the negotiated import price under the Sugar Protocol were also made.

the total value of these countries' sugar exports to the EU. Mauritius receives the largest share (36.9 per cent), and Mauritius plus Fiji, Guyana, Jamaica and Swaziland receive about 80 per cent of the total transfer. This concentration indicates that any EU sugar reform which lowers the EU import price to the ACP protocol exporters will have very uneven adjustment implications across the countries involved.

The transfer is expressed relative to the current value of total sugar exports and those to the EU, and of total exports, in table 15.3. Given the uniform treatment of protocol exporters by the EU and that (not surprisingly) all these countries only export to the EU under the protocol provisions, the total transfer constitutes a very uniform share of the value of protocol exporters' sugar exports to the EU. For every dollar's worth of sugar exports to the EU, the EU pays about 60 cents over the current world price of raw sugar. Alternatively viewed, each dollar's worth of sugar exported to the EU would only generate about 40 cents if sold at the world price. Thus the greater the relative share of sugar exports to the EU in total sugar exports, the more that the ratio in the second column of table 15.3 tends towards that in the first column. Thus, Barbados exports sugar only to the EU and the share of the transfer in total sugar exports is the same as it is in sugar exports to the EU (59.4 per cent). Similarly Kenya, Mauritius, Jamaica, Guyana, Tanzania and Trinidad and Tobago export sugar predominantly to the EU only. By contrast, for several of the African economies (e.g. Congo, Côte d'Ivoire, Zambia and Zimbabwe), the greater importance of sugar exports to non-EU markets reduces the importance of the transfer relative to total sugar exports.

How important the transfer is in total exports depends upon the size and degree of diversification of a country's exports. For many of the countries the transfer is small relative to total exports. For some, however, it is moderately important (nearly 4 per cent for Jamaica and Malawi), for others rather important (up to nearly 10 per cent for Barbados, Belize, Fiji and Swaziland), and for some it is extremely important (over 10 per cent for Guyana and Mauritius). In table 15.4, we express the total current transfer in per capita terms (total transfer divided by total population) and as a percentage of GDP (total transfer divided by GDP) for each country.

The transfer per capita figures show a very marked variation, depending on the allocation of the transfer across countries and on the size of countries in population terms. For some of the African economies, the transfer translates into a negligible per capita transfer. Consider Kenya, Congo (Rep.), Côte d'Ivoire, Madagascar, Tanzania and Zambia for whom the transfer is

Table 15.3 *Current income transfer relative to trade levels*

	Transfer as % of the value of:		
	Sugar exports to EU	Total sugar exports	Total exports
Barbados	59.4	59.4	7.1
Belize	59.4	43.5	8.9
Congo, Rep.	60.0	6.7	0.0
Côte d'Ivoire	59.4	24.9	0.1
Fiji	59.4	48.8	8.6
Guyana	59.4	53.6	12.7
Jamaica	59.4	58.1	3.8
Kenya	59.3	59.3	0.1
Madagascar	59.3	51.8	0.5
Malawi	59.3	45.4	3.9
Mauritius	59.4	57.2	11.9
St Kitts	–	–	0.0
Suriname	–	–	0.0
Swaziland	59.4	35.4	7.0
Tanzania	59.6	59.6	0.6
Trinidad & Tobago	59.4	53.4	0.3
Uganda	–	–	0.0
Zambia	59.2	15.8	0.6
Zimbabwe	59.4	26.3	1.1
Protocol total	59.4	47.3	2.1

equivalent to less than a dollar per person. By contrast, for some of the small economies the transfer is rather substantial in per capita terms, being over 50 dollars per person for instance for Swaziland, Fiji, Belize and Guyana. In the case of Mauritius, it is equivalent to 150 dollars per Mauritian.

What these absolute amounts per capita translate into in relative terms depends on average incomes (GDP per head) in each country. We can gauge this from the transfer to GDP values in the second column of table 15.4, since this is the same as the transfer per head as a ratio of the GDP per head. Thus, for instance, elimination of the current transfer would (in accounting terms) lower per capita GDP in Madagascar by 0.1 per cent and in Fiji by 2.9 per cent. In relative terms, therefore, a dollar's worth of transfer implies a larger increase in per capita income the poorer the country. Thus, although the transfer per capita is three times larger in absolute terms

Table 15.4 *Current income transfer to relative domestic and per capita income*

	Transfer per capita ($)	Transfer as % of GDP
Barbados	60.2	0.6
Belize	59.9	1.9
Congo, Rep.	0.2	0.0
Côte d'Ivoire	0.2	0.0
Fiji	59.2	2.9
Guyana	79.4	8.7
Jamaica	17.2	0.6
Kenya	0.0	0.0
Madagascar	0.3	0.1
Malawi	1.2	0.7
Mauritius	150.6	4.0
St Kitts	–	–
Suriname	–	–
Swaziland	51.3	4.3
Tanzania	0.1	0.0
Trinidad & Tobago	11.3	0.2
Uganda	–	–
Zambia	0.5	0.1
Zimbabwe	1.6	0.2
Protocol total	3.0	0.6

for Mauritius than Swaziland, its elimination would lower GDP per head more in Swaziland (by 4.3 per cent) than in Mauritius (by 4.0 per cent).

The transfer is most important in relative income terms for Guyana, where the transfer represents 8.7 per cent of GDP. Indeed, the particularly sensitive countries might be viewed as all those where the transfer to GDP constitutes more than 1 per cent of GDP, namely Belize, Fiji, Guyana, Mauritius and Swaziland.

15.4 The impact of EU policy regime on EU and world prices

15.4.1 The impact of an import tariff

Before the Uruguay Round of the GATT was agreed, the EU operated a system of support prices protected by a variable import levy (VIL). The level of the VIL changes with world prices and is simply the difference between the threshold price and the world price. Under this arrangement, the guaranteed internal price in the EU, set by policy-makers, is insulated from movements in world prices such that if world prices fall, the VIL will increase and vice versa.

Under the UR agreement, the VIL was replaced with a fixed rate tariff that was to be reduced over a six-year period. By moving to this system, the EU was no longer able to insulate its domestic price from world price movements and thus it was less able to 'protect' it. Thus, if world prices were to fall, the price at which imports entered the EU would also fall and vice versa. As the tariff is reduced, the relationship between world and EU prices becomes closer until the point where, after complete removal of the tariff, the prices equate. The impact on world markets is to see the level of imports into the EU rise.

15.4.2 The impact of a unit export refund

Export subsidies are used to provide exporters with a per-unit payment to allow them to sell their exports onto the world market when domestic prices are supported to a level above world prices. If the domestic guaranteed price is fixed then the unit export refund will vary with world prices. As the guaranteed price is reduced then, *ceteris paribus*, the unit export refund is reduced.

By setting a guaranteed price that lies above world price levels, the policy-maker will induce greater production of the product. The experience within the EU is that this has moved production of many crops to levels that lie above domestic consumption needs. The excess production then needs to be sold onto the external (world) market, but clearly this can only be done with the use of unit export refunds. There is no impact on the domestic price of this policy, but it does lead to downward pressure on world prices.

Under the Uruguay Round settlement, the EU has agreed to reduce its volume of subsidised exports as well as its total expenditure on subsidised exports. These goals can be achieved in a number of ways. First, if the guaranteed price is reduced then in effect the incentive to produce is reduced and thus the excess supply is also reduced. In turn this means the volume available for export will decline. The effect on world prices is to see them rise, *ceteris paribus*, as the volume of subsidised supply decreases. In turn, this would imply a reduction in the size of the unit export refund as world prices rise and EU prices fall. In the extreme case of no guaranteed price, the world price and domestic price will equate.

Second, if the export refund is fixed and then reduced, then the volume of exports that can be supported is reduced. Again, this implies that world prices will rise and hence exporters from third countries will benefit.

15.4.3 Evaluation of policy reforms

A number of studies have sought to evaluate the impact of sugar policy reform at a number of levels, varying from single country (or trading bloc) level to global liberalisation of the world market. Clearly, such a task is not simple and the results depend on the assumptions employed, with the result that the impact of similar reforms produces quite different outcomes from a range of models.

Borrell and Pearce (1999) provide a summary of works that examine liberalisation in sugar markets in a number of scenarios. Table 15.5 replicates some of this information.

Focusing firstly on liberalisation of EU policies alone, there have been several studies which have attempted to measure the impact of reform of both domestic and international aspects of the EU's regime. A report by NEI (2000) provides a 'quick and dirty static estimate' (p. 37) of the impact of a 10 per cent reduction in EU production quotas on world prices. Simply by using a correlation between EU stock/consumption ratios and New York spot prices, they suggest a 10 per cent cut in quotas would lead to a 1.5 million tonne reduction in supply (assuming no increase in C-sugar). In turn, this supply reduction would lead to an increase in world price of about $15 tonne or 8 per cent of world price.

Frandsen et al. (2001), using a general equilibrium type approach, show how two different scenarios, cutting quotas and cutting intervention prices, can impact on the EU and third countries. The former would lead to a more inefficient distribution of production in the EU and would have an impact on production and trade in third countries. If, however, the latter route is chosen and B-sugar is eliminated via price reductions, border protection falls by 25 per cent and the EU sees production falling by 19 per cent. The shortfall in supplies is met by exports from third countries, generally non-ACP countries such as Brazil, and world trade increases by 10 per cent as subsidised EU exports diminish.

Table 15.5 *Summary of the impact of liberalisation on world market prices*

Authors	Study base period	Price effect % change	Scenario
Anderson and Tyers (1986)	1987	10%	Liberalisation by East Asia and Western Europe
OECD (1988)	1979–81	1.1%	Reduction in assistance to OECD sugar producers
Webb, Roningen and Dixit (1987)	1984	53%	Complete trade liberalisation, twelve commodities
Huff and Moreddu (1990)	1982–8	25%	Multilateral trade liberalisation
Martin et al. (1990)	1980–3	60%	Multilateral trade liberalisation
Lord and Barry (1990)	1990	10–30%	Multilateral trade liberalisation
ABARE (1993)	2000 baseline	5.30%	Implementation of UR agreement
USDA (1994)	2000 baseline	2–5%	Implementation of UR agreement
UNCTAD (1995)	2000 baseline	5%	Implementation of UR agreement
Wong, Sturgiss and Borrell (1989)	1985–2004 simulation	8%	OECD price liberalisation
Wong, Sturgiss and Borrell (1989)	1985–2004 simulation	33%	Liberalisation of Japan, EU and US markets

Source: Adapted from Borrell and Pearce (1999), table 11, p. 18

The longer-term impact of EU policies suggested by Borrell and Duncan (1990) is viewed as reducing world prices by about 17 per cent, which leads to lower annual incomes for Australia and Brazil of $160 million (in 1984 prices).

Borrell and Pearce (1999) use a model of trade behaviour in twenty-four regions for seven types of sweeteners (the Global Sweetener Model (GSM)) to compare the outcomes in 2008 of the results of liberalising all markets in 2000 while retaining existing policies. In the case of liberalisation, EU prices fall by 25 per cent while world prices rise by 38 per cent, and EU imports increase by 7 million tonnes.

Borrell and Hubbard (2000) use a simplified version of a G-TAP model to examine the costs of the EU and the impact liberalisation would have, and do so by using a simulation-based approach. They suggest that liberalising EU policies completely would lead to an increase in consumption in the EU of 7 million tonnes while exports would be 5 million tonnes lower. In addition, if all OECD countries dismantle their policies, the world price would rise between 30 and 38 per cent, while EU sugar prices would fall by 40 per cent. CEFS (1999) show that a 25 per cent increase in world prices would result from the CAP regime for sugar being removed but that a 50 per cent drop in the EU price would be required to make it equate with the world price.

CIE (2002) extend Borrell and Pearce's (1999) work using the GSM and suggest that doubling import quotas by 2012 will lead to world prices rising by only 3 per cent and EU prices falling by 9.2 per cent. However, export subsidies will need to rise to deal with increased surpluses. Alternatively, halving the intervention price by 2012 will cause EU and world prices to equate, EU prices falling by 49 per cent and world prices rising by 16 per cent. Finally, they examine the effect of halving export subsidies by 2012 and the results show that this would raise world prices by 1 per cent while complete removal raises them by 2 per cent.

Other papers have a more global view of liberalisation. Anderson and Tyers (1986) suggest liberalisation by East Asia and Western Europe would cause world prices to rise by 10 per cent whereas the OECD's evaluation of a 10 per cent reduction in assistance to OECD sugar producers would only lead to a 1 per cent rise in world prices.

Multilateral trade models give different results. Huff and Moreddu (1990) suggest a 25 per cent rise in world prices would result from this form of policy reform, while Martin et al. (1990) suggest a 60 per cent rise. Lord and Barry (1990) are more conservative and suggest multilateral liberalisation would result in a rise of between 10 and 30 per cent.

Simply implementing the Uruguay Round agreements would raise world prices by between 2 and 5 per cent (USDA, 1994), 5 per cent (UNCTAD, 1995) and by 5.3 per cent (ABARE, 1993).

In terms of the ACP countries, the EC (2000) believed that a 25 per cent reduction in the EU sugar price would result in an income loss of 250 million ECU per annum. Borrell and Hubbard (2000) imply such a cut in prices would lead to a loss of 400 million ECU per annum. However, some of this loss would be partly offset by selling more exports on the world market where prices would rise by the aforementioned 30–38 per cent.

15.5 Impact of reduction of EU export subsidies on ACP countries

In addition to the possibility of reductions in subsidised exports by the EU resulting from the current case brought at the WTO by Brazil and Australia, there are other potential sources of reform of EU and other OECD countries' sugar policies that may have an impact on world and EU policies. It will be instructive therefore to compare the implications for ACP export earnings of varying intensities of sugar trade policy reforms; from marginal reforms which might follow from the current WTO case through to total reforms which fully liberalise OECD (including EU) policies.

15.5.1 *Current WTO case*

Under the Uruguay Round Agricultural Agreement, the EU made commitments relating to sugar on import duties, on the volume of subsidised exports and on the total value of export subsidies. The case brought by Brazil and Australia relates to the volume of subsidised exports. In the year 2000/01 the subsidised quantity had to be 21 per cent lower than in the base period (1986/7–1988/9). These limits do not include either the export of sugar quantities equivalent to the preferential imports from the Sugar Protocol ACP countries, India, Brazil and Cuba, or sugar exported as food aid. Net of these quantities, the quantity of directly or explicitly subsidised exports for the base period (1986/90) was 1,612 thousand tonnes. As a result, the UR Agreement implied a commitment to limit subsidised exports to 1,273.5 thousand tonnes.

Table 15.6 shows the three-year average (up to 2000/1) level of exports by the EU, with 2,643 thousand tonnes of C-sugar exported with refund and 3,141 thousand tonnes of C-sugar exported. If we take 1,700 thousand tonnes as being equivalent to the preferential and other exports excluded from the UR commitment and view the UR commitment defining 'subsidised' exports to *exclude* C-sugar, then it is clear that *there is no breach of the UR commitment* (2,643 − 1,700) being less than the 1,273.5 UR limit. If, however, we take combined exports of sugar with export refunds and C-sugar exports as capturing the quantity of subsidised exports, then total 'subsidised' exports net of preferential sugar would be (2,643 + 3,141 − 1,700) or 4,084 thousand tonnes. Reducing this to the UR limit would require a reduction of 'subsidised' exports of 2810.5 thousand tonnes or by 68.8 per cent.

15.5.2 *Other wider reforms*

The scale of wider reforms is, of necessity, difficult to specify quantitatively, except in the case of full liberalisation. In order to set an approximate limit on the effects of OECD sugar reform, we investigate the impact on ACP

Table 15.6 *Exports to third countries by EU countries (three-year average for 1998/99, 1999/00 and 2000/01) ('000 tonnes)*

	Sugar exported with export refund	C-sugar exports
Denmark	164	126
Germany	332	881
Greece	7	0
Spain	70	139
France	836	1,107
Ireland	8	19
Italy	266	34
Netherlands	51	156
Austria	25	164
Portugal	47	0
Finland	17	3
Sweden	36	50
Belgium	494	135
UK	290	327
EU '15'	2,643	3,141

Source: European Commission

export earnings and income transfers of a removal of all import and export distortions by all OECD countries. Our representation (based on an assessment of the evidence reviewed in the previous section) of the price adjustment process imposes a full equalisation of prices ($P^c_w = P^e_{EU}$) at 26.28 (cents/kg). For less extreme reforms we consider two other cases: the possible effects of further multilateral trade negotiations (MTN) and major CAP reform. The nature of the reforms assumed and the associated world and EU price estimates are summarised in table 15.7.

These four sets of price (P_w and P_{EU}) combinations are used to re-estimate the change in income transfer to the ACP Sugar Protocol countries, relative to the 2001 estimated level identified in table 15.2.

15.5.3 Alternative simulated reform effects on Sugar Protocol exporters

For each policy reform case we derive two sets of estimates, one assuming constant quantities of exports being supplied by each ACP Sugar Protocol exporter to the EU and non-EU markets and one with quantity

Table 15.7 *Summary of sugar trade policy reform simulations*

Reform option	Nature of reform simulation represented	Simulated prices (cents/kg)	% change relative to 2001
(A) Current WTO Case	– Reduction of EU subsidised exports to UR commitment (assuming C-sugar is implicitly subsidised)	$P_w = 22.28$ $P_{EU} = 47.12$	+17% −7%
(B) (A) + Further MTN Reforms	– Further reduction of EU export market distortions by 21 percentage points – Reduction by EU of import-side distortions by 20 percentage points	$P_w = 24.54$ $P_{EU} = 42.23$	+29% −16%
(C) (B) + Major CAP Reform	– Elimination of EU export subsidies on sugar – Further reduction of domestic market distortions by 20 percentage points	$P_w = 25.01$ $P_{EU} = 37.88$	+31% −25%
(D) Full OECD Liberalisation	– Removal of all OECD export subsidies – Removal of all OECD protection of domestic production	$P_w = 26.28$ $P_{EU} = 26.28$	+38% −52%

adjustments assuming unitary export supply elasticity. The perfectly inelastic values might be thought of as representing either shorter-term outcomes or ones where there are capacity (e.g. land area) constraints on supply expansion or land or other factor specificities which restrict diversification out of sugar into alternative activities. Certainly in the case of the less ambitious reforms then there may be little incentive to reduce production below protocol quotas, if the return to protocol sugar production significantly remains higher than to non-EU export sugar or to alternative forms of agricultural activity. For these circumstances the perfectly inelastic results may be better focused on. For longer-term effects and for large-scale sugar reforms it may be more appropriate to focus on the unitary elastic supply values. A unitary value is chosen for presentational reasons, rather than because there are strong priors or clear indicators from the existing empirical work about the appropriate elasticity to use for each country. Agricultural export supply is often viewed as being relatively inelastic, but it can be expected to be more elastic downwards in the long run if production becomes uncompetitive as received prices fall. Note, therefore, for the present exercise that the unit elastic results will understate the fall in income transfer from the EU if export supply is more elastic, while overstating the fall if export supply is less elastic.

The simulations explicitly identify the *change* in income transfer to each of the protocol exporters and for these countries as a whole (all in 2001 prices), the fall in the gross income transfer from the EU, and the net effect once allowance is made for the increase in export earnings from any sales to non-EU markets at the raised world price (P_w).[4]

The results for simulation A ('current WTO case') are set out in table 15.8. Overall there is a predicted decline in the net income transfer of $ 16.0 million if export volumes remain fixed and a decline of $ 13.4 million if volumes adjust (unit elastic case). This overall net decline is between about 2.7 per cent and 3.3 per cent of the current (2001) transfer. There is, however, marked inter-country variation in the pattern of effects. For all the countries currently receiving an income transfer from the EU, there is a decline in the direct or gross transfer, as a result of the imposed fall in the EU import price; this being consistently greater if there is quantity adjustment

[4] It should be noted of course that what is labelled as changes in income transfers might alternatively be interpreted as the changes in sugar export earnings from the EU ('transfer from EU'), in sugar export earnings from non-EU markets ('non-EU Xs earnings') and in total sugar export earnings ('net transfer').

Table 15.8 *Estimated change in gross and net income transfer to Sugar Protocol exporters with 'current WTO case' (US $ '000, 2001 prices)*

	Change in:					
	fixed supplies			unitary elastic export supply		
	transfer from EU	non-EU Xs earnings	net transfer	transfer from EU	non-EU Xs earnings	net transfer
Barbados	−1,709	0	−1,709	−1,822	0	−1,822
Belize	−1,563	1,551	−12	−1,666	1,815	149
Congo, Rep.	−68	1,507	1,439	−73	1,763	1,690
Côte d'Ivoire	−345	1,296	951	−368	1,517	1,149
Fiji	−5,159	3,044	−2,114	−5,498	3,563	−1,936
Guyana	−6,439	1,892	−4,547	−6,863	2,214	−4,649
Jamaica	−4,904	298	−4,606	−5,227	349	−4,879
Kenya	−126	0	−126	−134	0	−134
Madagascar	−522	203	−320	−557	237	−320
Malawi	−1,296	1,066	−231	−1,382	1,247	−135
Mauritius	−19,104	1,957	−17,147	−20,361	2,290	−18,071
St Kitts	0	567	567	0	663	663
Suriname	0	0	0	0	0	0
Swaziland	−5,960	10,976	5,016	−6,352	12,844	6,492
Tanzania	−468	0	−468	−499	0	−499
Trinidad & Tobago	−1,550	471	−1,079	−1,652	551	−1,101
Uganda	0	0	0	0	0	0
Zambia	−511	3,782	3,271	−545	4,426	3,881
Zimbabwe	−2,106	7,181	5,075	−2,245	8,403	6,158
Protocol Total	−51,832	35,790	−16,042	−55,243	41,880	−13,363

also (i.e. in the unit elastic case). By contrast, there is a rise in income on non-EU sugar exports following the world price rise. Overall, it is not sufficient to offset the direct, gross fall, but for some countries it is. As a result, six countries (Congo, Côte d'Ivoire, St Kitts, Swaziland, Zambia and Zimbabwe) are predicted to gain in net income terms (if supplies are fixed), and seven (above, plus Belize) if there are quantity adjustments. By contrast, a few countries more than offset these gains, with Mauritius predicted to experience a net income loss greater than the overall loss (for both elasticity assumptions). Indeed in the unit elastic case the net losses represent about 10 per cent of the current transfer for both Mauritius and Jamaica and about 7.5 per cent and 5 per cent respectively for Guyana and Fiji.

This mixed pattern of country results is driven by two factors. First, any reforms required to satisfy the EU's Uruguay Round Commitments will concentrate relatively narrowly on subsidised exports. It will as a result have greater impact on world than on EU import prices. In this simulation of the 'current WTO case' we assume that the former rises by 17 per cent and the latter falls only by 6 per cent. This is important when we consider the second critical factor, namely the marked inter-country differences in the relative importance of EU and non-EU sugar trade among the individual ACP protocol exporters. The net gaining countries are those with a relatively high share of non-EU exports – all with over 50 per cent of their total trade with non-EU countries – while the major losers are those with a high share of their sugar trade directed towards the EU.

The qualitative pattern of the results for the first simulation is generally repeated across all the reform cases considered. It is in general the magnitude of the gross and net income transfers that change. Figure 15.3 summarises the changes in transfers for the 'current WTO case' and the three wider reforms simulated for the ACP protocol countries combined.[5]

Figure 15.3 illustrates the progressive increase in the fall in gross and net income transfer through simulations A to D. It also illustrates that the gross loss (or direct loss of income on EU exports) consistently exceeds the net loss (adjusted for increases in non-EU export earnings), and that overall both gross and net income declines are greater where there is allowance for quantity adjustments (with unitary elasticity). Note that the overall, actual (current) income transfer is about $ 490 million, and therefore for neither

[5] The detailed results for the other cases are available from the authors on request.

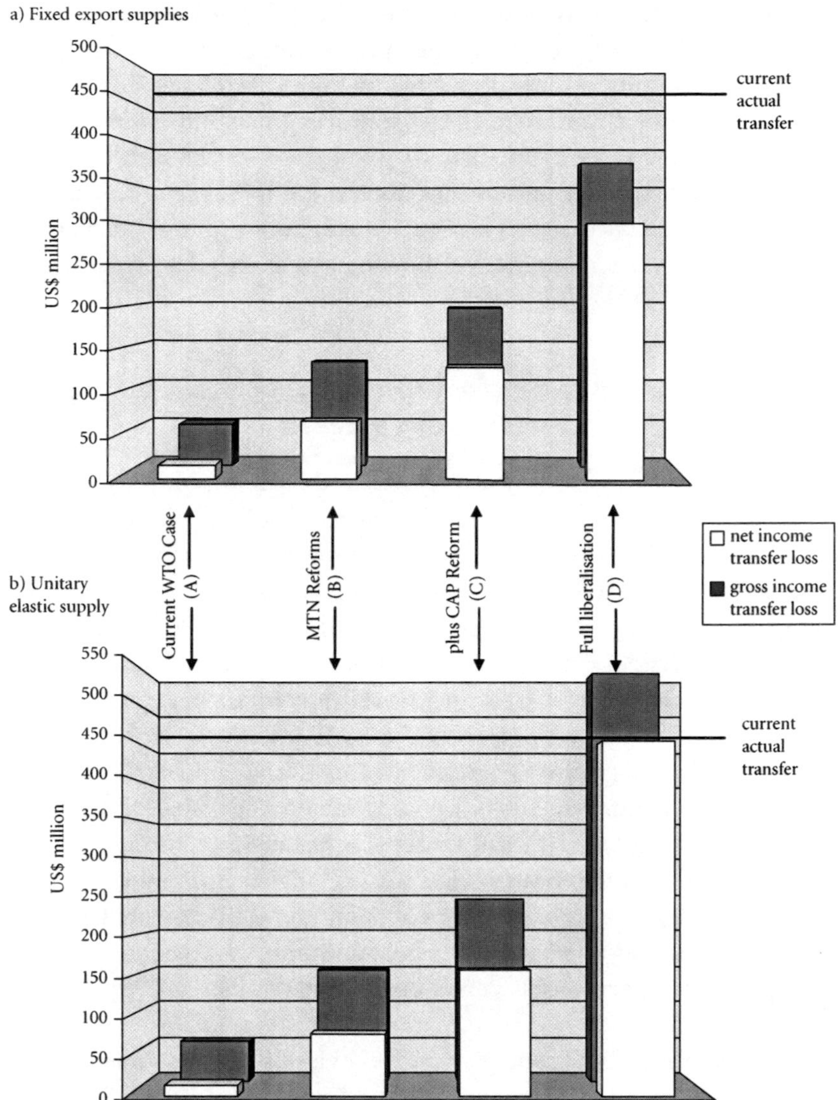

Figure 15.3 Summary gross and net income transfer losses for all protocol countries

assumption about quantity adjustment is the transfer fully eliminated in net terms.

Given the mixture of net gainers and losers in the simulations, it means that the national shares of the actual current transfer understate how the burden of the losses falls on specific countries. Take the case of Mauritius, with 36.9 per cent of the actual (current) total transfer. It is evident that Mauritius accounts for a larger proportion of the overall net fall (about 45 per cent). However, the nature of the quantity adjustment assumed makes a significant difference in this case to whether the actual transfer is fully eliminated or not. Mauritius' current transfer is $ 180.7 million. With fixed supplies it would fall in net terms by $ 134.6 million and by $ 199.6 million if export supply is unitary elastic following a total liberalisation of OECD sugar markets.

15.5.4 Alternative perspectives: effects on non-protocol ACP sugar exporters and importers

Since reforms will affect the world as well as the EU import price of sugar, any reform may affect the imports or exports or both of the non-protocol ACP countries. The clear expectation from the earlier analysis and empirical simulations is that reforms will raise the world price of sugar, and in doing so raise the cost (or opportunity cost) of importing sugar and the earnings from exporting sugar. For illustrative purposes we have taken the current volumes of imports and exports of thirty-nine non-protocol ACP countries, and re-valued this trade at the world prices predicted for the two extreme policy reform cases ('current WTO case' and 'full OECD liberalisation'). We are assuming no quantity adjustments, and so may overstate the increase in the import cost and understate the export earnings increase. Subject to this caution, one can take some guidance from table 15.9 as to the scale of the effect on non-protocol countries as a whole and as to the distribution of the gains and losses across countries. (Section a) reports the change in export values, section b) in import values and section c) on the net effect.)

The table shows this group of countries as a whole to be worse off in net terms (−$121 million) from full liberalisation and (−$54 million) from limited liberalisation. Indeed the vast majority of countries would lose in net accounting terms. Although there are several countries whose export earnings will rise, there are only a few that gain in net terms (Dominican Republic, Ethiopia, South Africa and Papua New Guinea). Indeed if export supply is responsive (even if import demand is not very responsive), the number of countries which would be net gainers from liberalisation is likely to increase.

Table 15.9 *Estimated change in value of sugar exports, imports and net trade of non-protocol ACP countries*

	a) Exports		b) Imports		c)Net trade	
	Current WTO case	Full OECD liberalisation	Current WTO case	Full OECD liberalisation	Current WTO case	Full OECD liberalisation
	('000 US $) (assuming fixed quantities)	('000 US $)	('000 US $) (assuming fixed quantities)	('000 US $)	('000 US $) (assuming fixed quantities)	('000 US $)
Angola	1,134	2,534	5,133	11,470	−3,999	−8,936
Bahamas	0	0	272	609	−272	−609
Benin	4	10	632	1,412	−627	−1,402
Botswana	0	0	1,484	3,317	−1,484	−3,317
Burkina Faso	0	0	679	1,516	−678	−1,516
Burundi	0	0	64	143	−64	−143
Cameroon, Utd Rep.	380	850	1,093	2,443	−713	−1,593
Cape Verde	0	0	1,142	2,552	−1,142	−2,552
Central Afr. Rep.	0	0	38	85	−38	−85
Chad	0	0	839	1,875	−839	−1,875
Comoros	0	0	267	597	−267	−597
Congo, Dem. Rep.	0	0	372	830	−372	−830
Djibouti	0	0	414	925	−414	−925
Dominican Rep.	5,050	11,285	842	1,882	4,208	9,402
Eritrea	0	0	249	555	−249	−555
Ethiopia	1,620	3,620	1,078	2,410	542	1,210
Gabon	0	0	0	0	0	0
Gambia	2,106	4,706	4,025	8,995	−1,919	−4,289
Ghana	3	7	5,750	12,848	−5,747	−12,841
Guinea	0	0	2,280	5,094	−2,280	−5,094

Table 15.9 (*cont.*)

	a) Exports		b) Imports		c)Net trade	
	Current WTO case	Full OECD liberalisation	Current WTO case	Full OECD liberalisation	Current WTO case	Full OECD liberalisation
	('000 US $) (assuming fixed quantities)	('000 US $)	('000 US $) (assuming fixed quantities)	('000 US $)	('000 US $) (assuming fixed quantities)	('000 US $)
Guinea Bissau	0	0	99	221	−99	−221
Haiti	0	0	5,214	11,652	−5,214	−11,652
Liberia	0	0	272	608	−272	−608
Mali	1	1	1,517	3,391	−1,517	−3,390
Mauritania	0	0	4,436	9,912	−4,436	−9,912
Mozambique	1,200	2,682	1,752	3,916	−552	−1,233
Namibia	0	0	1,484	3,317	−1,484	−3,317
Niger	0	0	1,369	3,060	−1,369	−3,060
Nigeria	0	0	39,187	87,566	−39,187	−87,566
Papua N. Guinea	285	637	26	58	259	580
Rwanda	324	724	648	1,449	−324	−725
Senegal	0	0	2,029	4,534	−2,029	−4,534
Sierra Leone	0	0	434	970	−434	−970
Somalia	2,430	5,430	7,266	16,236	−4,836	−10,806
South Africa	39,399	88,039	5,689	12,713	33,709	75,326
Sudan	1,933	4,319	3,083	6,889	−1,150	−2,570
Togo	0	0	986	2,204	−986	−2,204
Uganda	0	0	1,111	2,482	−1,111	−2,482
Western Samoa	0	0	0	0	0	0
Non-protocol total	54,852	122,571	109,169	243,946	−54,317	−121,375

15.6 Conclusions

Initially we take the world price of sugar as given, and estimate the total income transfer to each Sugar Protocol exporter arising from the excess in 2001 of the EU import price over the world price. The estimated total value of the income transfer element for all the ACP protocol exporters of the current EU sugar regime is about $490 million in 2001 (at 2001 prices), which is equivalent to nearly 60 per cent of the total value of these countries' sugar exports to the EU.

Mauritius receives the largest share of the transfer (about 37 per cent), with Mauritius, Fiji, Guyana, Jamaica and Swaziland receiving about 80 per cent of the total transfer. Any reforms of the EU sugar regime which lower the EU import price can be expected therefore to have uneven adjustment implications across the ACP Sugar Protocol countries.

Although the current transfer is equivalent to about 60 per cent of the sugar export earnings from EU sales for all the countries, there are marked variations in the importance of the EU sugar market and of sugar trade for the countries concerned. As a result, the current transfer ranges from being equivalent to about 12 per cent of Mauritius' and Guyana's total exports, down to accounting for considerably less than 1 percent of the value of total exports in several, in particular African, countries.

The current income transfer also makes very different contributions to income and production across the protocol countries. For six countries (Barbados, Belize, Fiji, Guyana, Mauritius and Swaziland) the current transfer is equivalent to over 50 dollars per head of their population. In the case of Mauritius it is equivalent to 150 dollars. The significance of these figures in GDP terms depends on the size and average incomes of the economies. It is only for five countries that the total transfer is equivalent to more than 1 per cent of GDP, but for some the percentage is substantial (e.g. Guyana at 8.7 per cent and Mauritius at 4 per cent). It is for these countries that there are corresponding significant production and employment implications arising from the transfer and its removal.

Any reform of the EU sugar regime will tend to lower the EU price and reduce the world price. Taking sensible indicators from the existing literature, we argue that full liberalisation of all OECD sugar markets and trade would raise the world price by 38 per cent. This would in turn imply a 52 per cent reduction in EU import prices as prices equalised with full liberalisation. We take these values as our basis for representing the effects of alternative degrees of reform on world and EU prices, if reforms are progressively intensified from the current situation. For all of the policy simulations we find that:

- the protocol exporters overall will experience a fall in the net income transfer, the fall increasing as the degree of OECD liberalisation increases (from about \$16 million for the partial reform to nearly \$300 million for full liberalisation (with fixed quantities of \$13 million to about \$450 million (with quantity adjustments);
- there will be protocol countries that consistently gain and lose in net income transfer terms. The losers (e.g. Barbados, Fiji, Guyana, Jamaica and Mauritius) are those that export sugar only or predominantly to the EU and the gainers (e.g. Congo, Côte d'Ivoire and Zambia) are those with significant exports to non-EU markets. The scale of the individual net losers tends, however, to be considerably larger in absolute terms than the net gainers. For example, the largest net gainer from partial reform ('current WTO case') is Swaziland (+\$6.5 million), while the greatest net loss is that experienced by Mauritius (−\$18 million);
- the magnitude of both the net gains and net losses from reform tends to increase if allowance is made for the possibility of export-quantity effects.

Besides identifying the importance of the changes in net income transfer relative to the individual countries' trade, income and production levels, the chapter also illustrates that non-protocol ACP countries will be affected by changes in world prices of sugar. The reforms can be expected to raise both the cost of sugar imports and earnings on sugar exports. Again there are also likely to be net gainers and losers from reform in this set of countries.

Reforming the EU sugar regime, whether it is piecemeal change or complete liberalisation, has significant effects on the ACP Sugar Protocol exporting countries in terms of changes in transfers of income. The extent to which this varies between the countries depends on their reliance on sugar exports for export earnings and also the degree to which they rely on the EU as their main sugar trading partner. Countries relying heavily on sugar exports, and in turn heavily on the EU market, will be highly vulnerable to the negative effects of EU policy reform. These countries will need to diversify their export base away from sugar through policy initiatives of their own and with EU support.

Bibliography

Anderson, K. and Tyers, R. (1986), 'Agricultural Policies of Industrial Countries and their Effects on Traditional Food Exporters', *Economic Record*, 62, pp. 385–99

Borrell, B. and Duncan, R. (1990), 'A Survey of the Costs of World Sugar Policies', *World Bank Research Observer*, 7(2), pp. 171–94

Borrell, B. and Hubbard, L. (2000), 'Global Economic Effects of the EU Common Agricultural Policy', *Economic Affairs*, 20(2), pp. 18–26

Borrell, B. and Pearce, D. (1999), 'Sugar: The Taste Test of Trade Liberalisation', Centre for International Economics Report, September 1999, Canberra and Sydney

Centre for International Economics (CIE) (2002), 'Targets for OECD Sugar Market Liberalisation', Report, October 2002, Canberra and Sydney

Frandsen, S. E., Jensen, H. G., Yu, W. and Walter-Jorgensen, A. (2001), 'Modelling the EU Sugar Policy – A Study of Policy Reform Scenaros', Working Paper No. 13/2001, Danish Research Institute of Food Economics

Hannah, A. C. (1998), 'The World Sugar Market and Reform', *PROSI Magazine*, No. 348, International Relations, January 1998. Also available at: http://www.prosi.net/mag98/348jan/hanna348.htm

Huff, H. B., and Moreddu, C. (1990), 'The Ministerial Mandate Trade Model (MTM)', *OECD Economic Review*, vol. 13. Special issue on modelling the effects of agricultural policies

Lord, R. and Barry, R. (1990), *The World Sugar Market, Government Intervention and Multilateral Policy Reform*, USDA, Washington, D.C.

McDonald, S. (1996), 'Reform of the EU's Sugar Policies and ACP Countries', *Development Policy Review*, 14(2), pp. 131–49

NEI (2000), ' Evaluation of the Common Organisation of the Markets in the Sugar Sector', NEI, Rotterdam

OECD (1988), *Agricultural Policies, Markets and Trade, Monitoring and Outlook 1988*, Paris

United Nations Conference on Trade and Development (1995), 'Analysis of the Evolution of Prices and Trade of Commodities to be Expected in the Light of the Results of the Uruguay Round', TDB – Standing Committee on Commodities, 4th session, 30 October 1995

Webb, A. T., Ronningen, V. O. and Dixit, P. (1987), 'Analysing Agricultural Trade Liberalisation for the Pacific Basin', paper presented at the Livestock and Feedgrains Federation Working Group of the Pacific Economic Co-operation Conference, 20–22 October, Napier, New Zealand

Wong, G., Sturgiss, R. and Borrell, B. (1989), 'The Economic Consequences of International Sugar Trade Reform', ABARE Discussion Paper no. 98.7, AGPS, Canberra

16

Analysis of the impact of opening up the EU import market for canned tuna on ACP countries

ELIZABETH BENNETT, HELENE REY-VALETTE AND ZHEN KUN WANG

16.1 Introduction: background to the WTO decision

On 5 June 2003 the European Commission published Regulation 975/2003 which spelled the beginning of the end of protection for canned tuna producers based in ACP countries. In July that same year a 25,000 tonnes (MT) quota of reduced tariff canned tuna from certain Asian countries was opened and by mid-September had been used up.

Under the Lomé Convention, ACP countries (by and large, the ex-colonies of EU countries) had enjoyed 0 per cent tariff on their canned tuna trade into the EU since 1982. Although this trade was subject to strict rules of origin (see box 16.1), the benefit of preferential trading arrangements with the EU had enabled a number of ACP countries to develop significant capacity in canned tuna production in the face of stiff competition from some of the biggest producers in the world (see figure 16.1).

Box 16.1 Rules of origin

The 'rules of origin' were drawn up by the EU specifically to protect duty-free imports from abuse (the same rules do not apply to imports that are subject to tariffs). As far as the rules of origin apply to fish imports, these ensure that (a) ACP countries (as opposed to third countries) are benefiting from the Lomé Agreement and (b) that the EU is protected from abuse of the fisheries by third parties. Under the rules of origin, fish must be caught within national waters (i.e. up to the 12-mile limit) despite the fact that UNCLOS recognises a 200 nm limit to national waters; fish must also be landed from wholly owned national vessels or vessels operating under a joint venture.[1]

Derogation from the rules of origin is possible, but for the purposes of derogation, all ACP states are considered to be one unit: thus all ACP states currently hold quota for 8,000 MT of canned tuna and 2,000 MT loins that are free from the rules of origin. This quota must be shared by all tuna-pro\ducing ACP states (Gorel, personal communication, 2003; Grynberg, 1997; Gakunu, nd). For most ACP tuna canneries, without the derogation from the rules of origin, production would be very difficult. In the case of Mauritius, under the rules of origin they have to buy (import) nearly all their tuna caught in the Indian Ocean mainly by French and Spanish fishing vessels. The high costs of running EU-owned vessels due to various EU regulations relating to the environment, marine preservation, sanitary standards and fishermen's working conditions cause the fish caught by them to be relatively expensive.

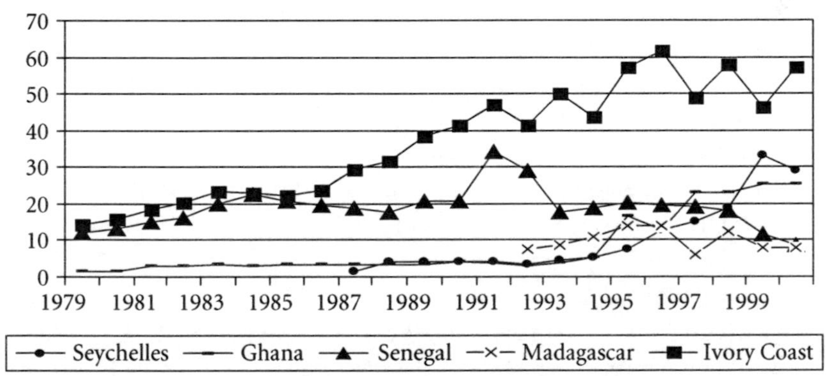

Source: Globefish, Commodity Update Tuna, July 2002

Figure 16.1 Evolution of ACP production of canned tuna (MT)

However, Thailand and the Philippines, two very important global producers (see box 16.2) who were subject to a 24 per cent tariff on their canned tuna trade with the EU, considered this situation to be against their legitimate interests, in contravention of the MFN treatment expected by

[1] See Grynberg, 1997 for a complete explanation of the rules of origin issue.

WTO members, and petitioned the EC to reconsider their Preferential Tariff Treatment.

Lengthy consultations between the parties failed to achieve a mutually acceptable solution and the matter was referred to mediation under the auspices of the WTO. In December 2002, the Mediator suggested one means of addressing the situation would be for the EC to open an MFN-based Tariff Quota of 25,000 tonnes for 2003 at an in-quota tariff rate of

Box 16.2 Growth in Asian production of canned tuna

Since the 1970s, the share of developing countries, especially Asian ones, in world tuna production has increased. Between 1965 and 1997, both Japan and the USA saw a drop in their share of the world market whilst over the same period Asian countries saw their share of world production rise from 9 per cent to 40 per cent. World tuna production remains nonetheless dominated by a few countries. Although there are more than thirty producing countries, the leading ten (Japan, Taiwan, Indonesia, Spain, Korea, the United States, the Philippines, Mexico, France and Ecuador in decreasing order for the period 1978–97) represent 75 per cent of the total world catch (Fishstat, FAO). In the case of canning, international supply is dominated by Thailand, which represented 37 per cent of world exports on average over the period 1993–7 (Globefish).

The increasing number of producing and processing countries has led to greater trade and a more international market. Between 1976 and 1997, the production of tuna raw material grew at an average rate of 2.98 per cent per annum compared with an increase of 4.58 per cent in international trade. In the case of canning, the production growth rate was 4.05 per cent per annum compared with 9.84 per cent in international trade. A succession of three big commercial crises has led to concentration in the processing sector, which in turn has disconnected price formation and fishing company operating costs.

Production analysis shows various trends and country groups. Generally there has been a continuous growth in world production of canned tuna, although in the United States, the leading producer (together with Thailand), production has remained relatively stable over the period. Within the Asian group of countries, Thai production has grown spectacularly, replacing Japanese production, which has fallen dramatically.

12 per cent *ad valorem* on imports of canned tuna from the non-ACP states.

The European Commission agreed that the WTO Mediator's opinion represented a reasonable proposal, although significant canned tuna producers within the EU (notably Spain) vehemently opposed this move (see box 16.3). The Commission indicated that the establishment of a 25,000 tonnes quota at a 12 per cent tariff would not prejudice either ACP imports or EC production of canned tuna. Neither the European tuna interests nor the ACP countries were convinced. Although the quota represented just 4.6 per cent of tuna consumption in the EC in 2000 and 9 per cent of total imports in 2001, interested parties argued that in fact the market for canned tuna in the EU was highly segmented and complex and that there would be serious consequences.

But it was not just the ACP countries that were likely to be affected. Spain is the third largest producer of canned tuna in the world and was worried about the impact of the decision on canneries – many of which are located in fisheries-dependent regions of the country. France, with considerable investments in a number of canneries located in ACP countries, was also worried about how this measure would impact upon its commercial concerns.

Although some observers of EU policy regarded this decision as a sensible step forward to bring the EU's stand on free trade in line with its own policies exercised at home, others were more sceptical. They questioned whether the policy of a 24 per cent tariff on Asian canned tuna was there to protect the EU industry or to protect the ACP industries (Brus, 2001); the true agenda behind the EU's decision to tax Asian tuna at 24 per cent is likely to influence the direction of future negotiations on this issue.

Despite the EC's belief that there would be no economic fall-out for ACP countries from this change in policy towards canned tuna from Asia, there was sufficient concern within certain institutions in Europe to establish just what the impact might be and which parts of the industry were likely to be most affected. During the summer of 2003 a series of in-depth interviews were conducted with tuna canneries and fishing companies in four ACP countries (Senegal, Ghana, Mauritius and the Seychelles) and two key European players (Spain and France). These interviews were then followed up in early 2004 in addition to a review of the actual impact on supermarkets in the UK (the most significant buyers of the product in the largest single EU market to be affected by the change in tariff). The results contradict the initial optimism of the EC.

Box 16.3 The terms of the Agreement

The European Commission agreed it would be appropriate to allocate country-specific shares of the canned tuna quota to those countries having substantial interests in supplying canned tuna on the basis of the quantities supplied by each of them under non-preferential conditions during a representative period of time. Of the 25,000 tonnes, Thailand was allocated 52 per cent, 36 per cent went to the Philippines, Indonesia was given 11 per cent and the remaining 1 per cent was assigned to imports originating in other third countries. In order to ensure that the quota was administered efficiently and to bring the Asian producers into line with some of the restrictions facing the ACP countries, it was agreed that a certificate of origin must be required for imports of canned tuna from Thailand, the Philippines and Indonesia. In a cautionary move, the EC also agreed to open the quota annually for an initial period of five years. After the first year, the quota would rise to 25,750 tonnes.

Because the organisation of the market for canned tuna in the EU is so important to understanding where and how the impacts might make themselves apparent, we start with a brief examination of the EU market for canned tuna. We then present a brief synopsis of the tuna industries in each of the case-study countries. They demonstrate widely different scales of production and dependence on the industry. We then examine what the impacts have been – both in terms of the industry itself and in terms of the wider economy.

16.2 The European market for tuna

Europe is the leading world market for canned tuna: 530,000 tonnes are consumed each year, of which 280,000 tonnes are imported. Consumption within Europe has increased dramatically, rising from around 490,000 tonnes in 1996 to 560,000 tonnes just five years later in 2001 (see figure 16.3).

Five European countries represent 84 per cent of the European market (table 16.1): Italy (22 per cent), UK (20 per cent), Spain (16 per cent), France (16 per cent) and Germany (11 per cent) (FIAC, 2002).

Table 16.1 *National canned tuna markets within Europe (MT, average 1999–2001)*

Country	Market size
Italy	118,435
UK	108,072
Spain	89,587
France	86,161
Germany	59,069
Portugal	15,745
Netherlands	12,228
Belgium	11,306
Finland	6,110
Greece	5,912
Denmark	5,799
Sweden	5,106
Austria	4,936
Ireland	3,558

Source: FIAC, 2002

Canned tuna imports to Europe come from a wide variety of sources. Currently around 70 per cent of products are from tariff-free ACP or SGP-drug[2] states and just under a quarter are from Asia with a tariff of 24 per cent (see figure 16.2).

In terms of the four case-study countries, the destination of their canned tuna exports within Europe differs. Whilst Senegal's primary market within the EU is France (taking 43 per cent of her exports); the UK is the primary destination for Ghanaian (54 per cent), Seychellois (40 per cent) and Mauritian (90 per cent) canned tuna exports.

The UK's importance as a consumer of canned tuna is one of the keys to understanding how and why ACP countries are affected by the recent change in EU policy towards Asian canned tuna (see box 16.4). However, there is a considerable level of intra-EU trade of canned tuna too (see

[2] SGP countries are as follows (tuna producers are shown with an asterisk (*): Colombia (*), Venezuela (*), Peru (*), Ecuador (*), Costa Rica (*weak), Panama, Guatemala, Nicaragua, El Salvador (* weak), Bolivia and Honduras. This particular system set up by the EU is defined as a quota of 20,000 tonnes per country (FAO, 1995) and expires in 2004 (FIAC. Pers. Comm. 2003). The system is questioned by the WTO, which argues against the clause concerning drug producing countries, because this only concerns Latin America and in the absence of official data, the clause is difficult to manage.

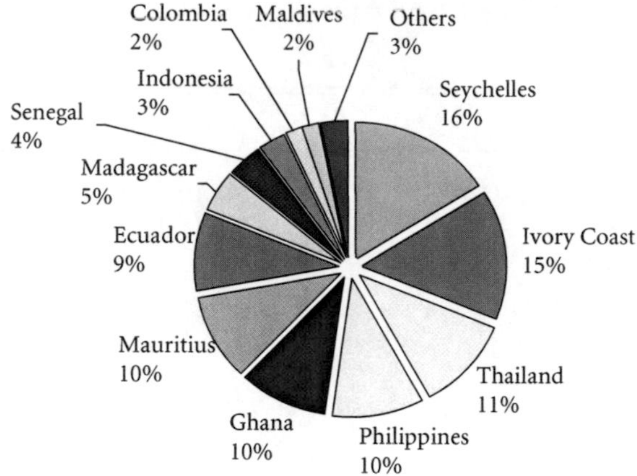

Figure 16.2 Relative importance of canned tuna suppliers to EU market (2001)

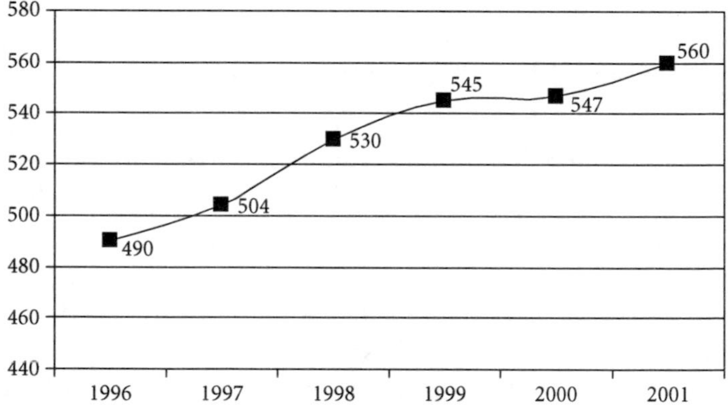

Figure 16.3 Evolution of the European canned tuna market (MT)

table 16.2). Spain is not only the third largest producer in the world, but also the principal source of canned tuna produced in the EU. This complex web of production and supply complicates the unravelling of the cause and effect of the impact of reduced tuna tariffs on the ACP producers, as will become apparent.

The type of canned tuna is a major factor in determining where it is likely to be sold. Broadly speaking, whilst southern European consumers prefer their canned tuna packaged in olive oil (which explains why much of that tuna is packaged in Europe itself – shipping olive oil to West Africa would be prohibitively expensive), northern European consumers prefer theirs

Box 16.4 The UK market for canned tuna

Spain and France may be major players in the production and distribution of canned tuna within Europe, but the UK is the single largest consumer of canned tuna in northern Europe and the most important single destination for tuna exports into the EU from Ghana, Mauritius and the Seychelles.

The tuna-canning market has seen a remarkable growth in the UK, driven by its popularity as a cheap, healthy food product. In 2002, Africa was the main supplying region (accounting for more than half of the total UK imports of canned tuna), led by the Seychelles (21 per cent of total imports, with 29,400 MT), Mauritius (17 per cent, with 23,400 MT) and Ghana (13.9 per cent, with 19,100 MT). All three have increased their presence on the UK canned tuna market in recent years with growing shares of total imports. More recently, in 2002, imports from the Seychelles increased by 26 per cent and from Mauritius by 4 per cent. The UK also relies quite heavily on imports from Asia (24 per cent of total), in particular from Thailand, the Philippines and Indonesia, all of which have recorded a rise in exports to the UK in 2002 (+4 per cent, + 42 per cent and + 45 per cent respectively) compared to 2001. Thailand, which was the main exporter of canned tuna to the UK in 1996, has lost ground recently going from a market share of a quarter in 1996 down to just 12 per cent in 2002.

Two privately owned brands (Princes and John West), controlled by powerful international groups (Mitsubishi Group for the former and Heinz for the latter), supply the majority of the UK market. Princes holds a 22 per cent share of the UK canned fish market, selling 1.2 million cans of tuna per week; their leading brand of canned tuna holds 21 per cent of the UK canned tuna market. Both companies operate an integrated network of canneries and have exclusive partnership agreements with fishing companies operating out of the Seychelles, Mauritius and Ghana.

The fish market in the UK is dominated by the big supermarkets. Tesco is the leading retailer (19.6 per cent of the market share), with canned fish giving them the edge over Asda. Other supermarkets (Sainsbury's: holding 16.6 per cent of the market share, and Marks and Spencers: 8.3 per cent) are also major canned fish retailers though they are more geared to the quality fresh fish market.

Table 16.2 *Main sources and destinations of intra-EU trade in canned tuna (MT)*

Main suppliers	Main importers						
	Italy	France	UK	Portugal	Germany	Austria	Belgium
Spain	31,113	17,653	5,538	3,493			
Netherlands		5,146			16,061	1,026	1,011
Germany	1,083	2,033	7,131			1,123	2,766
France			1,719		9,080		1,476

packaged in brine. As a consequence of these differing preferences, Senegalese production is largely in olive oil while that of the other three study countries tends to be in brine. Asian tuna tends to be packed in brine and as a result is destined for northern European markets. The switch from oil to brine is not easy, but small companies are often flexible enough to do this.

In order to be able to assess the likely impact of the EU change in policy on ACP canned tuna producers, it is vital to understand the basic structure of the sector in each country. The rest of this chapter is organised as follows. First we provide a brief introduction to the history of tuna fishing, the structure of the canning sector, the role that tuna plays in the export economy and an assessment of the key constraints facing the industry in each of the study countries. We then look at the potential and actual impacts that the change in policy has had upon the four study countries – and also on the UK market which is the main market affected so far. Finally, we present some possible options open to the ACP countries and some conclusions.

16.3 Case study 1: Senegal

Fishing occupies an important place in the Senegalese economy. Since 1986, it has represented 12 per cent of primary sector GDP, 2.3 per cent of total GDP and employs 15 per cent of the economically active population. It is the most important export for the country (making up around a third of total exports).

16.3.1 Development of the sector

Exploratory fishing trips funded by French canners in 1953 saw the sector develop under the influence of fishermen from Brittany and the Basque region. These fishermen transferred their live-bait pole and line fishery (a Californian technique) from the Bay of Biscay to the West African coast with spectacular results. The number of vessels operating out of Senegal almost doubled in the first four years: by 1957 there were ninety pole and line vessels in the area and by 1960 it was considered necessary to limit the amount of effort to sixty vessels so that they matched the canning capacity in Dakar. From 1966, fishing zones gradually shifted south-east to the Gulf of Guinea so that by 1970 landings in Abidjan in Côte d'Ivoire exceeded those in Dakar and in 1974 the French moved their fishing companies to Pointe Noire and the port of Abidjan, making Abidjan the new focus for tuna activities in the Eastern Atlantic. In the meantime, the Spanish fishing fleet took over tuna activity in Dakar and the Senegalese government had begun to develop a national fleet through the creation in 1962 of SOSAP (Société Sénégalaise d'Armement à la Pêche). But, in common with other developing country forays into parastatal fishing fleet formation, SOSAP was declared bankrupt in 1976, which effectively left the tuna sector in Dakar dependent on foreign vessels.

The first canning companies appeared in 1955 and by 1960 there were six units operating in Dakar. From 1960 until early 1972 these six canneries went through a series of buyouts and mergers such that by 1973 three canneries existed: Interco which was Senegalese owned (closed in 2002); SE-SNCDS which was a Senegalese–French operation (until the French withdrew in 1997 leaving the state to take up the slack until total collapse in 1999); and PFS which is a mixed Senegalese company. Table 16.3 gives a brief summary of each of the three companies.

16.3.2 *Key features of the canning industry*

With the reduced strategic importance of the port of Dakar and the much reduced level of fishing activity there, just 20 per cent of the tuna processed in the canneries comes from the fleet based in the city. Most of the tuna (68 per cent) comes from boats based elsewhere and a further 12 per cent comes from foreign freighters. All but 0.5 per cent of the cannery production is exported – the local market is very small. The cannery sector is intricately linked to the fishmeal sector: 60 per cent of cannery output (waste) goes to the fishmeal sector which in turn exports some 32 per cent of this output.

The canneries tend to rely upon hyper- and supermarkets and import brokers or wholesalers. In the case of hyper- and supermarkets, canneries

Table 16.3 *Summary of Senegalese canning sector*

	SNCDS Société Nouvelle des Conserveries Sénégalaise (ex CDS)	**Interco** Intercontinental des conserveries (ex SAPAL)	**PFS** Pêcheries Frigorifiques du Sénégal (ex SAIB et Pêche et froid Sénégal)
Annual production capacity[3]	20,000 tonnes	14,000 tonnes	15,000 tonnes
Volume purchased in 2002	8,889 tonnes	221 tonnes	8,724 tonnes
Production 2001	4,241 tonnes[4]	1,305 tonnes	4,530 tonnes
Employment[5]	1,340	Cessation of activity[6]	1,100
	140 permanent		125 permanent
	1,200 casual		800 casual on average

[3] There has been a continuous development in unit size, from a few tonnes in the 1960s to around 20,000 tonnes at the end of the 1990s. The latest factory of Pêche et Froid in Madagascar can handle 40,000 tonnes a year and American units can reach 100,000 tonnes (Mongruel, 2000).

[4] Originally the company SAIB specialised in large cans (Charneau, 1988).

[5] Despite overall employment stability, there has been a decline in permanent jobs since the evaluation undertaken in 1986 by Charneau (1988): 1,133 permanent workers (403 SNCD, 430 SAPAL and 300 SAIB) plus around 1,600 to 1,700 temporary workers, giving around 3,000 jobs in the canneries. Moreover, Charneau (1988) emphasises the low labour productivity and particularly the absenteeism which he estimates at 20 per cent for the SAIB company, where the problem is considered to be less serious than in the other canneries.

[6] The number of jobs in Interco is difficult to estimate because of the irregular nature of its activity during the years before its cessation. Overall evaluations of sector employment indicate 3,500 jobs, which implies that Interco must have provided some 1,000 jobs.

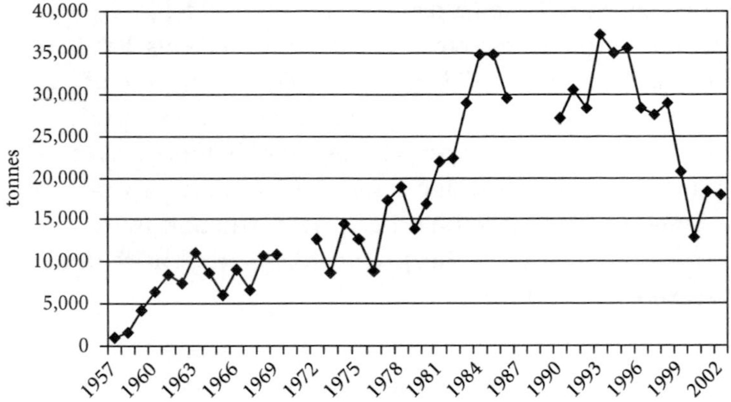

Source: Charneau (1988) until 1988 then DOPM
Figure 16.4 Evolution of tuna purchases by Dakar canneries

must be given a reference, which requires lengthy formalities, with visits on site from hyper- and supermarket representatives to verify the production process. This leads to a certain loyalty. Prices are negotiated through computerised calls for tender by the hyper- and supermarkets who always put their suppliers in competition. However, the hyper- and supermarkets try to diversify their suppliers in order to avoid monopolies or interruptions to supply.

The EU has a tuna fishing agreement with Senegal, and it is this agreement which provides much of the tuna that makes its way to the canneries. The agreement stipulates that a certain percentage of catch must be landed at Dakar. Most of the tuna, however, is not caught within the Senegalese EEZ which provided just a third of landings on average during the 1990s. Landings have fluctuated greatly over the past ten years (see figure 16.4), adding to the already parlous state of the industry. Landings are dependent upon a number of things: fishing strategies pursued by fishing companies, price differentials which can make transshipment more or less attractive, especially towards Spain, and local canning industry demand. Within the European fleet, pole and line vessel landings are becoming increasingly important, which is an advantage (they can offer a quality label of 'line fished tuna'), but because catches are smaller in size and therefore require more labour this also acts as a constraint on the industry.

Over the past ten years, Senegalese canneries have faced various problems which have left them in a crisis situation. Only one of the three companies has operated on a regular basis since 1996. Meeting standards imposed by European directives on trade agreements has necessitated heavy investment (5 billion CFA francs in 1995) and periods of cessation of activity of variable duration depending on the companies. Heavily indebted (partly because of restructuring work but mainly because of the need to fund their cash flow), and destabilised by the large price fall of 1998, Dakar canneries have, since 1998, been faced with downward pressure on the price of the finished product whilst the average price of Senegalese seafood exports has tended to rise since 1998.

16.3.3 Role of tuna in the export market

In a bid to shore up an industry in crisis, Senegal has increasingly diversified its markets – since the late 1990s it has targeted the UK and Belgium and diversification has also occurred through the development of Senegalese exports of canned tuna to some African countries, principally North Africa, Ghana and Gabon. But such tuna exports remain low compared to the European market mainly because the market within Africa is very limited.

Spain and Côte d'Ivoire are the main competitors to Senegalese producers. More recently, Senegalese canneries have also identified products from Ghana and Madagascar which target the French market; and, depending on the dollar exchange rate, Latin American production, since measures have been set up in favour of Scheting Plough (SGP) drugs, can be a serious competitor when the dollar is weak. Thai and Asian competition is less noticeable on the quality markets targeted by Senegalese canneries but since 2003 Asian competition has begun to be felt by Senegalese pole and line vessels on the French, Italian and Belgian markets.

16.3.4 Key constraints facing the industry

In order to make the most of their production capacity the canneries need supplies of some 38,000 tonnes, but since 1990 they have purchased on average just 26,775 tonnes and this figure has decreased markedly since 1998. Whenever there is a lack of supply they have to rely on freight from Côte d'Ivoire, which increases the fish purchase price. Unfortunately, Senegal is ill placed in terms of freight routes: few freighters pass by its coasts, except towards Spain, because the Atlantic Ocean is the least

Table 16.4 *Summary of main strengths and constraints in Senegal*

Strengths	Constraints
• Good quality products (two successive procedures of product separation – originally demanded by the English market) • Good expertise in product control • Important know-how • Partial positioning on ranges of luxury and new products • Potential to generalise and formalise the label 'Line fished tuna' • Client countries' policy to diversify suppliers to avoid shortages and benefit from competition • Wide range with diversified supply (canning and nature of the products)	• No commercial representation in client countries • Recurrent cash flow problems and high banking costs as banking conditions are ill adapted to the sector • Processing capacity development in Mauritania, closer to the local fishing zones of Spanish tuna vessels • Little value extracted from fishmeal and oil • Energy wasted during the sealing process which could be reduced by the use of turbines (as is done by Spanish producers) • Low labour productivity

productive of all the oceans. This 'isolation' of Senegal, indeed of African countries in general, leads to higher costs of access to the spot market than for Thailand. Moreover, repeated crises, the unreliability of some Senegalese canneries, together with landing costs and delays in Dakar, have given the port a bad name and freighters now refuse to put into port there. The only stability comes from the landing requirements under the fishing agreement but it is feared that vessels may soon prefer to pay the fines for non-landing rather than land in Dakar, as is already the case with demersal species.

The organisation of stevedores' work in the port of Dakar has considerably slowed down handling, which leads to very high landing times and costs compared to Abidjan (160 tonnes/day versus 250 tonnes in Abidjan) and higher prices for some inputs. The comparison of product storage costs (highly dependent on energy costs) shows that these costs are very high in Senegal where in 1997 they were evaluated at 620 CFA francs per tonne compared with 403 CFA francs per tonne for the first 100 m^3 and 532 francs/tonne thereafter in Côte d'Ivoire (Discussion days, Côte d'Ivoire, 1997).

In a market dominated by large international companies with a continuous concentration process, the small size of Senegalese companies represents a handicap, the more so because they compete with one another and have no common national marketing policy. Mergers, or understandings between companies, or at least a common positioning strategy on international trade fairs, or even the creation of a national brand 'Products from Senegal' or 'Senegalese pole and line tuna' should be envisaged.

16.4 Case study 2: Ghana

Although agriculture is the mainstay of the Ghanaian economy and, in terms of volume and value, has long been the principal export earner, the fisheries sector along the 500 km coastline is also locally important. The fisheries sector contributes 3 per cent to GDP, accounts for 5 per cent of the agricultural GDP and 10 per cent of the labour force.

16.4.1 Development of the sector

There is a long tradition of artisanal fishing for tuna and other large pelagics in Ghana, but it was not until 1959 that intensive fishing for tuna began in Ghana when a fleet of tuna vessels was introduced by Starkist International (now a division of Heinz). One of the key factors behind the introduction of this fleet was the abundant supplies of anchovy for bait – a close relationship grew between the tuna fleet and the semi-industrial anchovy fishermen, a relationship that continues today. In 1962, the State Fishing Corporation was established. This was based in Tema and it imported a large fleet of trawlers whose fishing activities occurred outside the continental shelf of Ghana and as far away as Angola, Senegal and Mauritania on bilateral agreements. The expansion of the tuna fishing industry took off in the early 1990s, peaking in about 1997 and again in 1999. It has been on the decline since then (see figure 16.5).

Stocks of tuna in Ghanaian waters are not considered to be overexploited and are in fact thought to be the only significant species able to sustain large increases in production. Estimates made in 1998 for the maximum sustainable annual take of tuna in the East Atlantic are of about 200,000 tonnes, of which 40 per cent can be taken in Ghana's economic zone. Ghana's tuna fishing potential has also been increased by the recent provision, financed by Japanese aid, of tuna landing facilities. However, with factories already

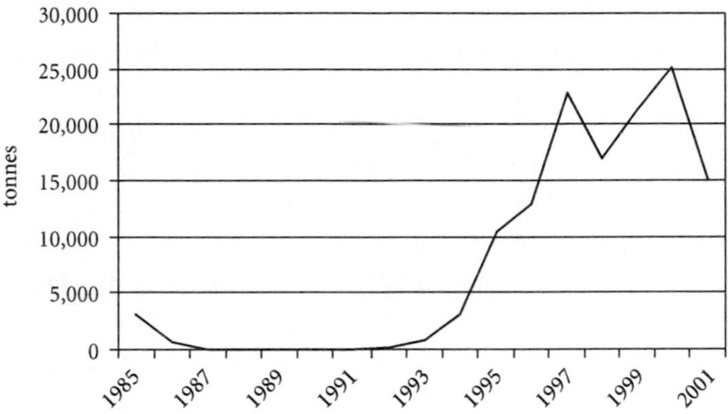

Source: Figis database, FAO

Figure 16.5 Evolution of canned tuna production in Ghana

working to capacity, increased catch is only likely to be of use to Ghana if further investment is forthcoming in the canning sector: which, given the eroding preferences with the EU, is unlikely in the current climate.

Fishing within the Ghanaian EEZ has always been reserved for Ghanaians or for joint ventures where Ghanaians held at least 25 per cent of the company share. Recent changes to the Fisheries Law (2002) now see that minimum stake increased to 50 per cent, an issue which is proving controversial within the tuna sector. Despite repeated requests to open up negotiations, Ghana has never had a fishing agreement with the EU.

16.4.2 Key features of the canning industry

The tuna industry in Ghana is usefully characterised by the fishing sector and the canning sector. One fishing company is part-owned by Heinz (who also own one of the canneries) but this is the only example of a direct tie-in between company and cannery.

There are currently thirty-six tuna vessels operating in Ghanaian waters: twenty-six pole and line (also referred to as bait boats in some literature because of the way they fish) and ten purse seiners. The vessels are owned by the eight registered fishing companies that target tuna (two of these companies are currently undergoing a merger). All the companies are based in Tema.

The fishing companies exhibit a range of different structures. TTV is majority owned by Heinz and is linked directly to the Heinz factory. World Marine is a very small joint Korean–Ghanaian operation. The other companies are wholly owned by Ghanaians. While most of them land at Tema, some also land at Abidjan (a two-day round trip away) when prices there are better than those in Tema. By law, Ghanaian companies must also deposit 10 per cent of their catch on the local market, although the stipulation appears to have no ill effect on the canning industry.

There are currently five tuna canneries in Ghana, all located in Tema: PFC, GAFCO, Quality Food Processing, Myroc Food Processing and Tonelli. The sector is dominated by PFC (majority owned by Heinz) which is by far the largest cannery in terms of production and numbers employed.

All the canneries send the bulk of their production to Europe and most of that to the UK and Germany. There is a market for canned tuna within the ECOWAS region, but it is very small and there is no room for expansion. Likewise, whilst one company sends the product to North Africa, this market is also small and accounts for only a small part of business. Compared to other producer countries, it is interesting to note that the Ghanaian sector is able to support a wide variety of canneries.

Tonelli is a small, wholly Ghanaian-owned cannery operating in the Free Zone in Tema. It has been in operation since the winter of 1995/6 when a bacon factory was converted into a tuna processing facility. It exports to the EU market and has, through an agent, secured a supply contract with Morrisons supermarkets. Before its entry into the EU market it was selling within West and Central Africa. The current division of its output is 95 per cent to the EU, the remaining 5 per cent going to West Africa, though this is a very small market with little room for expansion.

Ghana Agro-Food Company Ltd (GAFCO) was established as a state-owned venture in 1995. It is now a joint venture with 25 per cent held by the Ghanaian government and the remaining 75 per cent owned by a Swiss family concern. The plant processes a number of food items. The largest is the canning division (which is the second largest in Ghana); the flour mill is the second largest division and the third biggest operator in the country, and finally there is the feed mill which is the largest in Ghana. The company also trades in a variety of products. The canned tuna destined for Europe is mostly packed in brine and is a mixture of flakes, chunks and solids; a small segment of the business exports tuna in oil (olive, sunflower and soya), mostly destined for southern Europe. The tuna for the African market is packed in oil and includes a variety of local recipes and spicy sauces.

GAFCO exports around 92 per cent of its canned tuna production to the EU. The remainder is distributed within the West African region – mainly

Table 16.5 *Structure of a selection of the Ghanaian canning sector*

	GAFCO	PFC	Tonelli
Number of employees		1,802	100
Year company established	1995	1976	1995/6
Ownership breakdown	25% Ghanaian 75% Swiss	HJ Heinz Ltd + nominal Ghanaian ownership	Family owned
Throughput		75 MT/day	10–15 MT/day
Contractual obligations	None	John West	Morrisons in UK

Nigeria. Of the share that is exported to the EU, 80 per cent goes to the UK, the remaining 20 per cent going to the Netherlands and Germany, and a very small share to Denmark.

The largest canning concern in Ghana is the Pioneer Food Cannery (PFC) which is owned by HJ Heinz which commands 22 per cent of the world's canned tuna market. The newly refurbished and expanded plant was formally opened by the President of Ghana in 1994. The original formation of PFC began operation in 1976, producing canned tuna for export to Europe and for local consumption in Ghana. Rapidly decreasing tuna prices on the world market, and rising costs due to the ongoing economic crisis in the region, forced the factory to cease canning operations in May 1990, though it continued to process frozen loins for onward shipment to other Heinz-owned canneries (Heinz by this stage owned 50 per cent of PFC). Following Heinz's acquisition of the remaining shares in the company, the expansion programme took place, with distribution to the French market though Paul Paulet being a prime new market for the plant (Guillotreau and Le Roy, 2000: 4). When the new plant was opened in 1994 it was capable of processing 80 MT of tuna/day. In 2004 the plant was processing close to 175 MT/day. A report in November 2002 envisaged this capacity expanding further to 200 MT by June 2003, though with the recent tariff changes this is not necessarily the case any longer.

16.4.3 Role of tuna in the export sector

Agriculture is the mainstay of the Ghanaian export economy and within this, tuna, as a non-traditional agricultural export (NTAX), is an important contributor. Over 80 per cent of Ghanaian NTAX are value-added products, with raw material goods now representing an increasingly small proportion of NTAX. Canned tuna represents a very important segment of the NTAX sector, accounting for just over 14 per cent of total NTAX by value, the single largest contributor. Up to a quarter of Ghana's exports (by value) are sent to other countries in West Africa (many, but not all, within ECOWAS) but the ECOWAS market is comparatively small and chances of expansion into higher value goods are limited due to the relative size of the middle classes in neighbouring countries and the purchasing power of those potential customers.

However, although tuna is an important source of foreign exchange for Ghana (and by weight, the most valuable) it is not the only source. Recent promotion of other goods (timber in particular) has helped broaden the export sector base, potentially making the country less susceptible to external forces. What is more, although the EU is a major trading partner, Ghana has strong and well-established links to other countries in the region which provide an export market. Overall, whilst there is a heavy reliance on tuna, this reliance is not exclusive.

Ghana's main competitors in the tuna canning export market are Mauritius, the Seychelles and the Asian producers who all produce tuna in brine destined for northern European markets.

The Ghanaian tuna sector is reasonably healthy – so much so that Tonelli felt it worth taking the risk to venture into the European canned tuna market comparatively recently. However, the industry in Ghana suffers from a number of structural constraints.

16.4.4 Key constraints facing the industry

The cost of employing labour in the canneries in Ghana is high compared to its competitors. This is not so much governed by the level of wages but by the cost of employment (benefits, cost of uniforms, laundry services – demanded by UK supermarkets). Active and powerful labour unions within Ghana have also contributed to the rise in labour costs through demands for working hours, working conditions and leave entitlements.

Ghanaian energy costs are high. Ghana has no domestic oil reserves so all oil products are imported, driving up costs. Cannery managers are not able to rely 100 per cent on the national grid and have to run their own

Table 16.6 *Strengths and constraints facing the industry in Ghana*

Strengths	Constraints
• Potential to increase catch rates: local stocks are not overexploited • Ghanaian tuna is not shipped in from elsewhere, so there is an opportunity to market tuna as from identifiable sources • Ghana has a long-standing stable political environment and relatively stable economy, both of which may encourage further foreign investment • Comparatively well-established infrastructure • Well placed in development terms in the ECOWAS region	• Comparatively high labour costs • Comparatively high shipping costs to Europe • Little room to increase exports of canned tuna within the region • Power supply has to be supplemented on site, utilities not well organised, labour force not well educated and infrastructure could be better • Energy costs are comparatively higher • Cost of producing cans: sheet metal has to be imported • Distance from richest fishing grounds (WPO) • Productivity of workers (which is low in comparison to Asia)

back-up power units in case of failure. This adds more costs to the overall production.

Despite their proximity to Europe, the coastal nations of West Africa are no longer on major shipping routes. Shipping goods from Tema to Europe is thus far more expensive than comparative costs from Asia.

Ghana's freedom to purchase tuna at the best price is constrained by regulations laid down by the EU regarding product origin (see box 16.1). Ghana is able to produce its own cans for use in the canneries (a distinct advantage over some other ACP producers) but still has to import the sheet metal to make those cans, which contributes to the overall high costs of production.

16.5 Case study 3: Mauritius

The Republic of Mauritius is a maritime state with an Exclusive Economic Zone of 1.7 million square kilometres. The fisheries sector in Mauritius represents approximately 1 per cent of the total GDP, which is of minor significance to the national economy as a whole when compared to tourism which contributes twenty times as much value to the economy.

16.5.1 Development of the sector

Although Mauritius has a very large EEZ due to its large number of islands, it is situated in relatively poor tropical waters; tuna migration routes enter the EEZ of Mauritius, but only just (the tuna migrate from the Maldives across the exclusive zone of the Seychelles down to the south of Mozambique). Despite these disadvantages and the fact that the nation has to rely upon imports from the Seychelles for its cannery, Mauritius has succeeded in developing a thriving tuna cannery sector which processes some 22,000 tonnes of tuna a year.

Tuna fishing has experienced ups and downs. The catch by locally based vessels rose reasonably steadily until the early 1990s, since when it has dropped considerably (see figure 16.6). This rise and fall in catch rates reflects the fortunes of the domestic tuna fleet which is now obsolete. Faced with few tuna resources within its own EEZ and a failing domestic fleet, Mauritius began to import tuna from the Seychelles which lies squarely within rich tuna fishing grounds. Mauritius is heavily dependent upon the ability to import tuna – and, because of the EU Rules of Origin, this places an added constraint on the industry.

Over fifty purse seiners, which operate in the South-West Indian Ocean, land around 260,000 tonnes of tuna in the region yearly. At present, there are no long-line tuna fishing boats registered in Mauritius but there is a large international fleet which uses Port-Louis as a transshipment base. Because Mauritius does not have the capacity fully to tap the migratory tuna stocks available in its waters, it has entered into a fishing agreement with the European Union since 1990, allowing European vessels to fish in the EEZ of Mauritius. The most recent agreement lapsed at the end of December 2003; there is no indication, as yet, of a further agreement. The agreement, which related exclusively to tuna, provided fishing opportunities for forty-three tuna seiners, forty surface longliners and an average annual tonnage of 25 GT per month for line fishing. The total financial compensation is €412,500 and a financial contribution of €206,250 towards science and technology programmes, studies and training programmes.

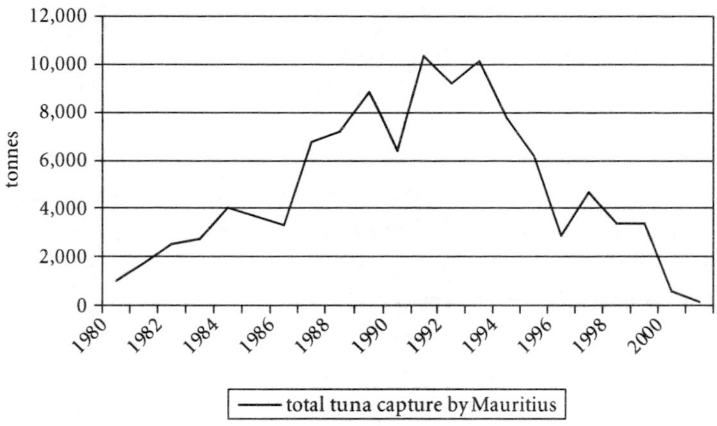

Source: FAOFISHSTAT+

Figure 16.6 Tuna catches landed by Mauritius, 1980–2000

Tuna canning was first set up in Mauritius in 1972 by the Mauritius Tuna Fishing and Canning Enterprise (MTFCE), a joint Mauritian–Japanese venture. Because of space problems, MTFCE was split between two sites: Caudan and Riche Terre. This split-site arrangement, however, meant that MTFCE was unable to comply fully with EU environment and sanitary standards (necessary for importing food into the EU) and so building a new factory became urgent. To raise the necessary finance, a UK private company, Princes Ltd, acquired the assets of MTFCE in April 1999 and established Princes Tuna (Mauritius) Limited. This new company is jointly owned by Princes Ltd (64 per cent) and Ireland Blyth Ltd, a Mauritian public company (36 per cent). In September 2000, the new factory was commissioned at Riche Terre and the modern factory has been operating and expanding its production of canned tuna since then. Princes Tuna (Mauritius) Ltd operates a purse seiner (*Lady Sushil I*) which meets a small percentage of its tuna consumption.

16.5.2 *Structure of the canning sector*

There is only one cannery on Mauritius. In 1999, MTFCE employed 1,200 people, processed about 120 tonnes of raw (frozen) tuna and produced 75 tonnes of canned tuna per day. The total tuna processed was 28,000 tonnes in 1999. By 2002 when MTFCE had become Princes Tuna (Mauritius) Ltd and moved to the new factory, the tuna cannery had increased its employment by

54 per cent compared with 1999, employing 1,845 people. About half of its workforce are foreign employees from Sri Lanka and Madagascar. The cannery processed 182 tonnes of raw tuna and produced 116 tonnes of canned tuna per day. The tuna processed in 2002 was 44,707 tonnes, about a 60 per cent increase relative to 1999.

Port Louis is an important port of transshipment for the Far East Asian tuna longliners, which are landing or transshipping an average of 17,500 tonnes per year. These activities, alongside those of the canneries, mean that associated trades (stevedoring, shipping agents, etc.) are also reliant upon the future of the tuna fishery. What is more, the cannery is also a significant consumer of electricity and water.

16.5.3 Role of tuna in the export sector

More than 95 per cent of Mauritian canned tuna is for export to the EU markets where the UK is the main consumer, accounting for 90 per cent of total Mauritian canned tuna exports in 2000. Other EU markets for Mauritian canned tuna are Germany (3 per cent), Sweden (3 per cent) and the Netherlands (2 per cent). The concentration of Mauritian canned tuna export to the UK market is due to the fact that Princes Tuna (Mauritius) Ltd is owned by Princes Ltd, a private UK company. The latter has traditional marketing networks in the UK. The concentration of Mauritian canned tuna exports in a few northern European markets brings it into head-to-head competition with Thailand, Indonesia and the Philippines.

Although 95 per cent of Mauritian canned tuna goes to the EU market, and the quantity produced has risen steadily throughout the 1990s the same dependence is not exercised in reverse: Mauritius held only 3 per cent of the EU market in 2000. Expansion outside the EU is also fraught with the same difficulties experiences by Ghana and Senegal: the regional African markets for canned tuna exports are too small. Even given the geographic proximity of Mauritius to South Africa, there is little hope of expanding the market sufficiently there in the near future.

With a population of 1.1 million, Mauritius is much larger than other islands in the Indian Ocean and has a diversified economy. However, it is important to see the contribution of tuna within the context of the wider economy. Mauritius has long been an exporter of clothing, but is currently facing difficulties in this sector due to the phase-out of the Multi Fibre Agreement. Mauritius is also an exporter of sugar which, currently, is

Table 16.7 *Main strengths and constraints on the industry in Mauritius*

Strengths	Constraints
• Recent significant investment in the • Princes Tuna (Mauritius) cannery gives confidence to the sector • Princes Tuna has well-established markets in the UK that may be able to withstand any shocks	• There is a lack of adequately trained skippers and master fishermen for purse-seine or long-line fisheries and a shortage of trained seamen and fishermen • Cumbersome and lengthy immigration procedures for foreign crews working onMauritian-flagged vessels deter incoming investment • High costs of production • Existing ageing fleet operating on banks are unable to operate on the high seas which cover the migratory track of tuna • Tuna are highly migratory and only pass through the EEZ for a short period. Catches are concentrated outside the zone

protected on EU markets, but, like tuna, is coming under increasing pressure from other, larger sugar producers to have those preferences reduced. So while the economic value of the tuna cannery may be slight, its value to those employed there (in a climate of impending employment problems, should the textile and sugar sectors also suffer from reduced tariffs in other markets) is certainly great and of symbolic value to the islands.

16.5.4 *Key constraints facing the industry*

With limited tuna now being caught and landed in Mauritius, the key constraint for Mauritius is the cost of raw material which has to be shipped in from the Seychelles – at a cost of $115 per tonne, which automatically affects profits in the cannery. The cannery is also affected (more than most) by the stringent rules of origin. Like their counterparts in West Africa, shipping costs are comparatively more expensive than those experienced by Asian exporters because there are far fewer vessels travelling along that route. This contributes to the high cost of the product.

16.6 Case study 4: The Seychelles

The tuna fishing industry is one of the most important sources of foreign exchange in the Seychelles, a group of small islands in the Western Indian Ocean. Tourism is very important to the economy, yet the fisheries sector (as a whole) has overtaken tourism as the biggest foreign exchange earner. In 2001, exports of canned tuna alone generated 771.2 million rupees (compared with the whole tourist industry at 770 million rupees), accounting for 91 per cent of the total fish export and 87 per cent of the total Seychelles' visible export.

16.6.1 *Development of the sector*

The Seychelles are located in rich tuna fishing grounds and have thus been in a prime position to take advantage of the economic benefits therein. A variety of nations fish for tuna in the waters, although the EU is the single largest group. In 2002 (the latest year for which figures are available), the EU had thirty-six purse seiners (from Spain, France and Italy) operating in the Seychelles EEZ under licence and there are a further seventeen from other countries. There were also 190 long-liners operating in the EEZ: 130 from Taiwan and 57 from Japan. The Seychelles itself had seven purse seiners operating in the EEZ.

The Seychelles has a fishing agreement with the EU which allows forty purse seiners and twenty-seven long-liners to fish in the Seychelles EEZ. The agreement also carries a significant compensation component whereby the EU pays the Seychelles €2.3 million a year for its fishing boats to fish in the Seychelles water, based on a catch of 46,000 tonnes a year, in addition to the licence fee paid by boats' owners. And, for the three-year period covered by the agreement, the EU contributes another €3.48 million to the Seychelles fishing sector.

16.6.2 *Structure of the canning sector*

Expansion of the canning sector, which was rapid in the 1990s, is symptomatic of expansion in the fisheries sector as a whole. Total fish processing capacity has grown from around 20,000 metric tonnes in 1995 to around 70,000 metric tonnes in 1999. Total production has also grown constantly over the same period, from around 12,000 metric tonnes in 1995 to over

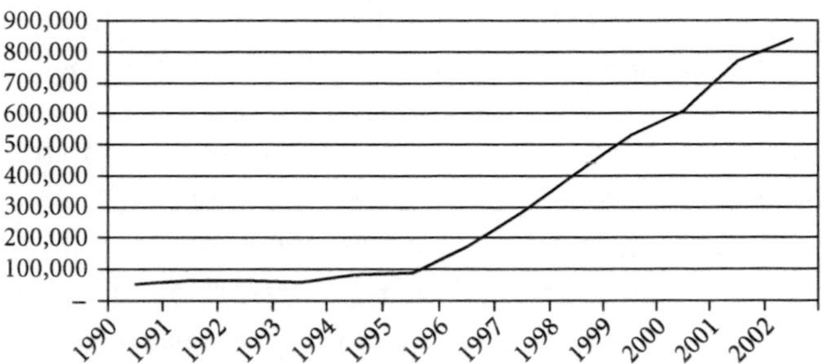

Source: IOT data, February 2004

Figure 16.7 Value of Seychelles canned tuna exports in SR ('000s), 1990–2002

23,000 metric tonnes in 1998. With further investment planned, total capacity and production of fish and fish products are expected to increase further in the future in order to meet the demand. How this expansion will be affected by the change in preferences of canned tuna remains to be seen. The total value of canned tuna exports has also grown steadily over the years, to reach approximately US $159 million in 2002, from only US $16 million in 1995.[7]

The main import for the production of canned tuna is raw or whole tuna. This is bought principally from foreign purse seiners that land at Port Victoria or transship to other vessels that then come into the port. Due to the very small internal economy, most machinery, components and packaging materials are imported. Whilst this would normally increase costs, the facilities of the SITZ (Seychelles International Trade Zone) have helped keep added costs to a minimum.

There is just one tuna cannery in operation on the islands: Indian Ocean Tuna (Seychelles) Ltd (IOT) which is a joint venture between Heinz and the Seychelles government. When IOT was established in 1987, it had a capacity of 50 tonnes per day or around 15,000 tonnes per year. Since its acquisition by Heinz in 1995, the production capacity of the plant has constantly grown to reach an estimated 350 metric tonnes per day by the turn of the century. Exports of canned tuna in terms of volume have also grown steadily. IOT processed 90,000 tonnes and produced 360 million cans in 2002.

IOT was previously called 'Conserverie de L'Ocean Indien'. In 1995, the cannery was acquired by Heinz who bought 60 per cent of the shares (the

[7] These prices converted at 1 Seychelles Rupee = 0.19 dollar in February 2004.

Seychelles government holding the other 40 per cent) and its name then changed to Indian Ocean Tuna Ltd. This facility is the second largest tuna cannery in the world after Starkist Samoa. IOT produces about 14 per cent of the canned tuna bought in the EU and is the largest volume supplier of canned tuna to the UK. However, it only uses one third of the 300,000 tonnes of tuna landed in the Seychelles each year – Princes Tuna in Mauritius buys 40,000 tonnes and the rest is transshipped in large refrigerated ships, mainly to Europe. The cannery is the single largest purchaser of electricity and water on the islands (purchasing 8 per cent of the power produced) and has contributed to making Port Victoria the biggest tuna transshipment and landing port in the world.

Facing such stringent cost disadvantages, IOT is exceptionally efficient; it has invested heavily in capital equipment to reduce manual labour requirements in the areas of non-fish cleaning. This increased investment in automation improves labour productivity. For example, the Seychelles' high labour cost is compensated for by a high level of labour efficiency, measured in tonnes of tuna processed per person per year. A worker at the Seychelles tuna cannery can process 36.8 tonnes of tuna per year, compared to 21 tonnes per person per year in Mauritius and 20 tonnes per person per year in Ghana. Similarly, although it pays a much higher price for water than Ghana, its utilisation rate of water is much lower than Ghana. The Seychelles tuna cannery consumes 5.25 m^3 of water to process one tonne of tuna fish, while in the Ghana tuna cannery the corresponding figure is 11.00 m^3/tonne.

16.6.3 Role of tuna in export sector

IOT contributes a considerable amount to the Seychelles economy; it brings in the most foreign exchange earnings and employs over 10 per cent of the working population as the single largest private employer. The Seychelles tuna cannery sells its output mainly under brand name in Europe; the free-tariff and free-quota market access to the EU was a very important element in determining Heinz's investment in the Seychelles tuna cannery.

The Seychelles is highly dependent on the European market for its canned tuna exports. Within the EU, the UK and France were both lead importers in 2002, followed by Italy and Germany. However, the Seychellois share of the EU market is comparatively small compared to

Table 16.8 *Strengths and constraints for the Seychelles industry*

Strengths	Constraints
• Extensive EEZ within rich tuna grounds • A policy environment that provides incentives to support export-oriented fishing investment • A diverse pool of skilled labour and a long history of political stability • Experienced fisheries-related workforce • Well-established position on EU markets	• Small population requiring additional hiring costs of overseas workers • Comparatively high employment costs per worker • Small internal economy without manufacturing base which requires import of canning inputs • Seasonal water supply problems • Rules of origin regulations

intra- and inter-EU imports, but it is the largest single source of canned tuna compared to rival ACP producers.

The fishery sector accounted for 14 per cent of the total employment (4,600 people) in 2001. There are 1,100 fishermen in the sector, 1,000 employed in industrial fishery services (stevedoring, ship repair, ship chandelling and bunkering, etc.) and a further 2,500 in the tuna cannery. The employment in the tuna cannery accounted for 54 per cent of total employment in the fisheries sector, and 7.6 per cent of total employment in the Seychelles. The small island population means, however, a severe shortage of labour and much of the labour in the cannery is from overseas.

16.6.4 *Key constraints facing the industry*

The Seychelles is a small island country with a total population of 80,000 and so has high labour costs compared with larger countries and has to source many workers from overseas. The cannery is the biggest private employer in the Seychelles. About half of the workers in the cannery are local employees and the other half are foreign employees, mainly from the Philippines, Kenya and Madagascar.

Water, electricity and fuel prices are all relatively expensive due to the poor local production conditions. For example, the cannery pays for water at \$2.64/m^3, while in Ghana the cannery pays US \$0.40/m^3. All the other important ingredients for canning tuna – vegetable oil, cans, and materials for secondary and tertiary packaging – are imported.

As with other ACP countries, rules of origin mean that the ability to access cheaper tuna is a constraint, and, with the added restrictions applied to the tuna vessels operating under the EU fishing agreement, freedom to source raw material is a constraint to competitive production.

16.7 Summary of case studies

The case studies presented offer a wide variety of insights into the canned tuna industry in ACP countries – the results are summarised in table 16.9. Senegal appears to have been in rapid decline for a while and in danger of total industry collapse if reduced production is the consequence of the tariff decision. Ghana, on the other hand, has a much broader base to its industry (with six operational canneries), optimism in the sector (a new cannery opened recently) and much less dependence on the sector as a whole in terms of the wider economy. Unlike their island counterparts, both Senegal and Ghana have a long history of industrial tuna fishing. The Seychelles and Mauritius both suffer from the economic constraints placed on small economies. They have to import many of the inputs for the sector, they are short of labour and water and costs of production are high. Yet, the two examples are quite different. Whilst the Seychelles is very dependent upon the income from the sector, Mauritius has diversified its economy into other export sectors (textiles and sugar) and the luxury tourism market. All the countries face considerable cost difficulties – labour costs are higher than for their Asian counterparts as are the costs of shipping the product to Europe. Work productivity is also lower than in Asia. All the study countries are dependent upon the European market – although Senegal's dependence is on southern European consumers whereas the other three are dependent upon markets in the north.

16.8 Potential and actual impacts of opening the European market to Asian canned tuna

This section looks at each case-study country individually, and then assesses the impact on an EU-wide basis.

Table 16.9 *Case study summary*

	Cost of labour[a]	Number of canneries	Owned by multinational?	% tuna export reliance on EU market	Strengths	Constraints
Senegal	Approx $4.27	3	No	89% (43% to France) in 2001	Potential to exploit local line-caught tuna	High cost of labour High shipping costs Access to product
Ghana	$4.00	5	1 (Heinz)	Over 90% (54% to the UK) in 2000	Locally caught product Diversity of canneries	High cost of labour High shipping costs
Seychelles	$19.15	1	Yes (Heinz)	97.3% (40% to the UK) in 2003	Well-established position in EU markets	High cost of labour High cost of inputs
Mauritius	$4.27	1	Yes (Princes)	95% (90% to the UK)	Well-established markets and outlets in UK	High cost of labour High cost of raw material

[a] Figure for Seychelles due in part to overvalued Rupee

Source: Winters and Wang report based on Heinz calculations for all except Senegal (Rey Vallette report)

16.8.1 Senegal

Establishing the extent of the impact on Senegal is somewhat complicated by the perilous state of the industry to begin with. In other words, it is difficult on face value to determine whether any decline in the Senegalese sector is wholly attributable to the loss of preferential marketing to the EU or partially due to the precarious health of the sector over all.

Irrespective of the source of the decline, with reduced value of its exports on the European market (−15 per cent since 1999, which is added to the large fall in 1998) and with a profitability crisis in the sector, there is considerable fear that in the short term at least international competition will force companies to lower their prices to ensure the competitiveness of their products. With the recent fall in the value of the dollar (in late 2003) and the potential rise in competitiveness of the product from Latin America (also afforded preferential trading tariffs into the EU) there is a possibility that Senegal could be impacted from two sides.

Experts within the sector argue that if, in the medium term, more structural solutions cannot be adopted (such as targeting quality markets or developing new products) so as to achieve substantial productivity gains, the future of the sector cannot be assured. In fact, if substantial competitive gains are not realised, the risk is that Senegalese canners will disappear and the pole and line vessels will depart.

Moreover, even if the reduction in customs duties is for the moment limited, the tendency will be for it to be generalised. It is therefore realistic to envisage thc restructuring of the Senegalese tuna sector in the context of international market liberalisation, a situation which could happen in the future (following the Cancun meeting in September 2003).

It is possible for instance that a marked drop in cannery demand could accelerate the shift in landings (including landing quotas under the agreement) towards Abidjan, worsening the supply difficulties faced by companies. Moreover, the transfer of lost North European markets (Germany, UK and Belgium) to North African markets is optimistic given the (so far) limited nature of exports to North Africa.

An evaluation of the facts for Senegal reveals indirect effects on the fishery sector (tuna companies based in Dakar) and the fishmeal sector (a single company in 2003). It also finds that strategic impacts (risk that the activities might disappear) on other suppliers may be considered negligible, even for closely related sectors such as can manufacturing, because of

Table 16.10 *Possible impacts for Senegal*

Canneries
(Impact 1) Loss of northern European markets (Germany, United Kingdom and Belgium), i.e. 1,612 tonnes on average over 2000/2001. Even on the hypothesis that this production can be switched to North African markets (which is optimistic, and assumes significant growth of these to-date limited markets), the reduction in value added related to the difference in value between the northern country markets and those of Morocco and Tunisia, which was 30 per cent in 2001, must be taken into account.
(Impact 2) Increased competition on southern European markets, which represent on average, over 2000/2001, 60 per cent of the export volume, leading to a marked reduction in selling prices on these markets. On the basis of the 15 per cent reduction already recorded over the three years between 1999 and 2001, the reduction could be between 15 per cent and 30 per cent, the latter figure being the decrease observed between 1998 and 1999.
Fishing companies
(Impact 1) The fall in fish purchase price (30 per cent) is carried over to the fishing companies, leading to a reduction in their value added and also to risks weakening the units leading possibly to the disappearance of some of them (this element has not been evaluated).
(Impact 2) If the canneries cease or substantially decrease their activity, the tuna fleet based in Dakar would not be threatened in the short term because of the possibility to transship, so long as the transport routes of Spanish cargo are not changed by relocation. In the medium term, in the case of global market liberalisation and a crisis in the sector, a substantial reduction in tuna activity is to be feared.
Fishmeal factory
(Impact 1) If we assume that canneries maintain their level of activity, the only impact would be on prices, with no major consequences at the macroeconomic level as this segment is one of the few profitable ones in the sector according to the 1997 evaluation (loss of profits for the company).
(Impact 2) If the canneries cease or substantially decrease their activity, there would be a great impact on the fishmeal company because it depends heavily on the canneries for its supply. It could lead to the closure of the remaining unit.

the increased use by canners of imported products. It is probable that the search for productivity gains will increase the dependence on imports. Similarly, the share of port activity related to tuna is not very important and will only be marginally affected (estimated at 2 per cent of port turnover by Charneau (1988) in 1986).

Evaluating the impact from the point of view of the product, everything suggests that low-priced product markets will be the most exposed to competition, in particular Germany, the United Kingdom and Northern European countries where Thai products are already well implanted. However, despite a downward trend in the relative importance of Asian imports in these countries, Thailand remains the main supplier in both cases.

Senegalese market shares in these countries appear to be marginal. Over the 1996–2000 period on average they represent 1,148 tonnes for the United Kingdom and 272 tonnes for Germany. However, the impact for Senegal could be indirect: southern European producers who had only recently penetrated these markets could be pushed back into their own markets (France, Spain, Italy) and these represent an important proportion of Senegalese exports.

During a follow-up interview in early 2004, the largest Senegalese producer reported that production had fallen by 22 per cent compared to the same period the previous year. However, this statement was qualified by the fact that the strong rise of the euro against the dollar (up 24 per cent) may also have had an impact.

16.8.2 Ghana

The European market for tuna is highly segmented. Ghana stands alone as the West African nation reliant upon markets in Northern Europe (which is also the main destination for Thai and Filipino product). The UK, Ghana's largest single market in the EU, accounts for over half of Ghana's exports – but also for over half the exports from Thailand and Indonesia and a quarter of the exports from the Philippines. In other words, as far as the UK market is concerned, Ghana is in direct competition with the three major non-ACP countries that now have access to reduced tariff quotas for canned tuna.

Latest figures available indicate that total Ghanaian exports of canned tuna (in 2000) were 25,100 MT. Exports to the EU amounted to 22,600 MT in 2002 (down from 26,064 in 2000) or just 4.79 per cent of total EU imports – of those, 54 per cent went to the UK. Under Regulation 975/2003, the quota

Table 16.11 *Summary of possible impacts for Ghana*

Canneries
(Impact 1) Loss of northern European markets (United Kingdom), i.e. 19,100 tonnes based on 2002 figures. Given that it is assumed that non-ACP tuna will target northern European markets, and Ghana's current export is under the 25,000 tonnes quota, this is not entirely infeasible, though it is unlikely that it would lose all of this in one quota-year.
(Impact 2) Reduced production leads to reduced employment, impacting on socio-economic profile of Tema; smaller companies that have just started to invest in EU market are forced out of business or have to contract back to the ECOWAS/North African market.
Fishing companies
(Impact 1) With falling income from canned tuna exports to northern European and no possibility of acquiring market share in southern Europe (which is, hypothetically, oversubscribed by canneries in traditional exporting countries such as Senegal and Côte d'Ivoire), Ghana has to allow EU access to its EEZ through a fishing agreement to maintain employment in the tuna sector in Ghana.
(Impact 2) Falling purchases by Ghanaian canneries force companies to sell to Abidjan more frequently, although Abidjan could now be oversupplied due to a shift in activities of the Senegalese fleet. Fishing companies refocus their activities on other fish stocks – many of them have only recently begun to target tuna stocks. Those fishing companies heavily tied into canneries (TTV, for example) are harder hit than those with more diversified markets.

set for 2003/2004 is 25,000 MT, marginally more than the current Ghanaian export to the EU. What this means is that there is a potential for Ghana to lose its entire share of the UK market to Asian canned tuna. Most commentators doubted that this would be the case, but all acknowledged that Ghana would be sure to lose at least some of that share in the shake up of the UK market for canned tuna which will almost certainly follow the change in EU policy.

In a duty-free situation, as far as costs go, Ghanaian tuna is (marginally) more expensive per unit than Thai tuna and considerably more expensive than Indonesian or Filipino tuna. It is more expensive also than Senegalese or Ivorian tuna which may well impact on intra-ACP country competition as their overall market share in the EU is reduced. But, because they are currently targeting different markets, this price difference is unlikely to be an issue. However, once the 24 per cent tariff has been added to the cost of tuna from non-ACP countries, Ghanaian tuna becomes more competitive: it is cheaper than Thai tuna and only marginally more expensive than tuna from Indonesia or the Philippines. Thus it is conceivable that Ghana might lose ground to tuna from Indonesia or the Philippines, but this would have happened anyway under the old regime of a blanket tariff of 24 per cent.

The fact that the European tuna market is split into two distinct halves means that any increase in Thai exports is likely to target the northern European market (for which the bulk of Ghana's exports are currently destined). Increasing exports to southern European markets is therefore a feasible option. GAFCO, however, maintain that practically this is very difficult. Numerous barriers to exporting to southern Europe were mentioned by producers in Ghana, including delays in verifying paperwork and delayed container shipment. These barriers cause real problems but are hard to prove and thus take action upon.

Reviewing the situation in Ghana in early 2004, some five months after the quota was opened, revealed that in fact turnover was down by about 30 per cent – although without further analysis it is not possible to say if this is due directly and entirely to the arrival of cheaper tuna from Asia or to other factors.

16.8.3 Mauritius

It is perhaps fortunate for Mauritius that tuna specifically and fishing in general represent such a small proportion of the nation's GDP; far more income is earned from the thriving tourism sector. Any decrease in production, therefore, will have an immediate impact upon the tuna sector but its impact on the overall economy will be negligible. However, this comment only holds true if one assumes that other export-driven industries on the island (textiles and sugar, for example) are able to absorb the excess labour and make up the difference. In the light of increasing talk of across-the-board tariff reductions, the continued protection of Mauritian markets to the EU seems unlikely.

Sources in Mauritius in January 2004 confirmed that, whilst the number of cases of canned tuna sold in 2003 was up by 289,000, the profit margin on each case was down by 11 Rupees. This reduced profit margin was a direct result of having to lower prices in order to compete with the amount of

Table 16.12 *Summary of impacts for Mauritius*

Cannery
(Impact 1) Loss of northern European markets (United Kingdom), i.e. 15,440 tonnes based on latest (2000) figures. This is below the 25,000 tonnes quota but it is unlikely that all the Mauritian market share would be used up by the quota.
(Impact 2) Reduced production would lead to staff reductions impacting upon the socio-economic profile of the island, although the other strong economic sectors would minimise this impact.

cheaper tuna coming in from Thailand. More specifically, profit margins from July 2003 (i.e. after the quota came into effect) were down 8 Rupees a case compared to the six months prior to the reduction in tariff on Thai tuna.

16.8.4 *Seychelles*

The tuna sector in the Seychelles is dependent upon just one cannery owned by Heinz. Any indication that production is no longer economically viable could lead to the withdrawal of that foreign investment which would have catastrophic consequences for the Seychelles. With no significant other industry to take up the slack, any erosion of preferences for the import of Seychelles tuna into the EU will have widespread economic consequences. However, there is little likelihood that the Seychelles will lose its tuna sector overnight. Rather it would appear that a gradual reduction in tariffs for non-ACP tuna, will slowly increase the comparative costs of Seychellois tuna, causing the industry to decline slowly.

The cannery confirmed that Heinz had experienced an impact in their canned tuna sector, but was unable to quantify this impact.

16.8.5 *Europe*

The 25,000 tonnes quota of reduced tariff tuna had been all but used up by the end of September 2003, but it was not possible to determine which Member States had imported tuna from that quota. Interviewing a number of supermarkets in the UK and France, it was possible to deduce that in fact the UK had taken the largest share of this quota – and, ironically, the bulk of it had been bought by Princes Tuna, who also own the cannery in Mauritius.

Table 16.13 *Summary of impacts for the Seychelles*

Canneries
(Impact 1) Loss of northern European markets (United Kingdom), i.e. 17,711 tonnes on 2000 data. Given that it is assumed that non-ACP tuna will target northern European markets, and the Seychelles' current export is under the 25,000 tonnes quota, this is not entirely infeasible, though it is unlikely that it would lose all of this in one quota-year.
(Impact 2) Reduced production leads to reduced employment, impacting on the socio-economic profile of the islands. With entire production loss being felt by just one cannery (no room for inter-cannery competition), there is a real chance that the cannery may cease to be economically viable and close.
Fishing companies
(Impact 1) There is no reason to suppose that EU tuna fisheries agreements would cease to be economic, however. The nation could therefore continue to collect rent from the tuna fishery, although this would mean a considerable drop in tuna-related income compared to the current situation.

A major UK supermarket noted that their sourcing of canned tuna had not changed noticeably as a result of the change in EU policy: the Seychelles and Mauritius still provide the bulk of their stock. The supermarket buyer noted that buying decisions for products involved a large range of components, of which price was just one. The conditions provided in the canneries for their workers and the quality of the product are also factors. So, the decision to continue to source tuna from the Seychelles and Mauritius could be due to customer demands for corporate social responsibility (CSR) regarding working conditions in the canneries. This fact was borne out by one of the canneries in Ghana who confirmed, back in July 2003, that many of the working conditions in the cannery (free laundry service, social club and subsidised canteen) were all conditions laid down by the major supermarkets as part of their CSR policy.

A major UK manufacturer and distributor with close financial links to the canning sector in the Indian Ocean reported that they had imported 66 per cent more product from Thailand in 2003 compared to 2002 and that the average price per case was £5 cheaper than the previous year. Because of the overall competitive nature of the marketplace in the UK,

Table 16.14 *Synthesis of main impacts (potential and actual)*

	Potential impacts	Actual impacts
Senegal	Loss of position in southern European markets further harming a fragile sector	Production reported to have reduced 22 per cent
Ghana	Reduced production with potential loss of jobs. No large negative economic impacts predicted but localised socio-economic impacts in Tema a possibility	Reported 30 per cent loss of turnover
Seychelles	Reduced production with catastrophic results for a small island economy	Reported drop in profits as have to compete with imports of cheaper tuna
Mauritius	Reduced production with minimal national impact, but potentially sizeable impact if other sectors suffer equal reduction in tariff protection	Cannery reports a drop in profits; production in the region has gone up, but prices down to compete with Thai product

they had been forced to increase imports from Thailand even though they had tuna interests in the Indian Ocean.

In France, the Société de Vente des Pêcheurs Français remarked that in fact 2003 was an exceptionally good year. Although sales of Asian tuna had increased, so had those from the Seychelles and Mauritius – a fact also supported by one of the canneries in the Indian Ocean that reported increased production (but also reduced profits).

Supermarkets do not appear to have radically changed their buying policies faced with potentially cheaper products from Asia. This could be because contracts are established so far in advance that any real effect will not be discernible until the next quota comes into effect in July 2004 (Brus, personal communication, 2004); or it could be that buying decisions are in fact more complex and price is just one issue (as noted above).

So, it would appear that impacts have indeed been felt, but have not played out quite as simply as had at first been assumed, with the UK absorbing much of the quota and much of that being bought up by a company with vested interests in the sector in the Indian Ocean.

16.9 Next steps

Information collected during interviews with industry experts demonstrated that canned tuna production in ACP countries was not a lost cause. A number of suggestions were offered as to how industries in these countries might change to withstand the potential for excessive losses.

Shifting tuna exports to countries outside the EU is a possibility for all the ACP countries but African food products often suffer from a negative image in the global market and small economies mean markets are very thin. Exploiting the unique position of the West African product is another possibility. Unlike Thai tuna which is often transshipped from a wide geographical area, all but a small proportion of Ghanaian tuna is caught by Ghanaian vessels, much of it within Ghanaian waters. It would thus be relatively easy to exploit the northern European desire for 'locally identifiable' produce rather than homogenous global products. In much the same way that Kenya is now synonymous with coffee, Ghana and Senegal could become synonymous with locally identifiable tuna caught by local fishermen. The large quantity of line-caught tuna originating in all ACP countries is also a quality that sets this tuna apart from the seiner-caught tuna from the large Asian producers. Again, the ACP countries could tap into the growing market for environmentally sensitive foods in the northern European markets. Exploring diversification into quality products within the tuna sector is also a possibility: there is certainly a growing UK market for canned tuna in ready-made sandwich fillings and in 'exotic' sauces. The use of pouches rather than cans for packaging is also an avenue that may be worth exploring to give ACP tuna an edge over their Asian rivals.

Finally, in terms of understanding the interplay between ACP producers, the complexities of the EU market and the potential threat from large-scale Asian producers, more work needs to be done to understand the 'cause and effect' so that more concrete development options might be offered to ACP tuna producers. Specifically:

- Detailed economic analysis of the sector needs to be conducted to establish which factors have impacted upon production in ACP countries and what drives supermarket decisions.

- Without concrete information on which markets absorbed the quota (and are thus likely to absorb the next tranche), it is still not possible to establish which ACP countries are likely to be hardest hit.
- Further monitoring of the situation needs to be conducted. The quota for 2003 has been used up; only when the next quota comes on line will it be possible to track any changes conclusively.

16.10 Conclusions

The ACP African countries have been very successful in taking advantage of preferential market access to the EU canned tuna markets. They have enjoyed tariff-free, quota-free market access to the EU, while other suppliers such as Thailand and the Philippines face a 24 per cent tariff. The ACP canned tuna exporters have replaced many other suppliers, growing into dominant suppliers in the EU markets since the 1990s. The four countries represented in this study, to a greater or lesser extent, have dramatically increased their exports of canned tuna to the EU market in terms of both absolute quantities and market share throughout the 1990s.

Under pressure from the Asian canned tuna suppliers, the EU has adopted the WTO mediator's suggestion to allow a quota of 25,000 tonnes of canned tuna from Thailand, the Philippines and Indonesia at an in-quota tariff rate of 12 per cent rather than the customary 24 per cent. As the tariff opened in July 2003 there were real fears that ACP production would be severely compromised because they are unable to compete against the higher production levels and cheaper product coming from Asia. This fear has not been completely realised, although there is evidence that production in West Africa and profits in the Indian Ocean have reduced by up to 30 per cent in some cases. Whether the effect felt on European markets is entirely due to the quota (as opposed to exchange rates, catch rates or a combination of these) is not possible to determine without further analysis.

EU imports of canned tuna are not evenly distributed across members' markets. The Asian exporters, Thailand, the Philippines and Indonesia, mainly supply the UK, and, to a much lesser extent, Germany. Spain, the largest canned tuna producer in the EU, imports very little from outside sources. France imports nearly all her tuna from Francophone African countries, Senegal and Côte d'Ivoire in particular. Mauritius and the Seychelles send the bulk of their canned tuna to the UK as does Ghana, whilst the Senegalese product is destined for French and southern

European markets. The greatest competition due to this policy change is likely, therefore, to be felt on the UK market. Current analysis of the situation, however, does not provide a clear picture of how the tariff has impacted upon supplies.

Although the tuna canning industry in all four countries is a very important contributor to the local economy in terms of employment and, for Ghana and the Seychelles, contribution to GDP, the industry is also very uncompetitive compared to its Asian market rivals. Protected and supported by the Lomé Convention, Ghanaian, Mauritian and Seychellois tuna had been able to establish a small niche in the northern European market but, with the gradual reduction in trade preferences, this position is under threat. Similarly, the exemption from customs duties has enabled a historically important tuna activity to continue in Senegal even if the Senegalese market share has steadily declined over the years. As noted by a number of authors, none of the countries in this study are alone in this position. Many African countries have failed to achieve the levels of success of their Asian counterparts, even allowing for the generous trade preferences afforded them. Despite this, cannery owners in Ghana in particular considered tuna to be one of the few successes of the Lomé Convention.

Tuna represents a significant part of Ghana's NTAX and a significant part of its exports to the EU, but it is not wholly dependent upon tuna. Similarly, in the case of Senegal, the macroeconomic importance of the tuna sector is limited compared to other fisheries and even more so when compared to other activities. Any reduction in the monies earned from tuna will have a direct impact on the economy of Tema and will impact on the national economy, but Ghana does have other sectors it can fall back on. What is more, the impact on Senegal is likely to be small, not least because it holds but a very small share of the EU canned tuna market. However, since 1998 the tuna sector in general and the canneries in particular have been facing an economic crisis, and this measure, without major restructuring, could have serious consequences and even call into question the very future of tuna fishing in Senegal.

Tuna canning in Mauritius is a comparatively new sector, with a large investment being made there by Princes in 2000. However, unlike in the other three countries, tuna canning is a very small part of the overall economy: textiles, tourism and sugar providing much greater and longer-standing sources of income. So, whilst Mauritius will undoubtedly feel the effect of the quotas, the effect will be far less drastic than in Ghana, Senegal or the Seychelles. The Seychelles, on the other hand, is highly dependent on tuna which makes up 95 per cent of its exports and 40 per cent of its imports. With few other resources to fall back on, any significant reduction in the industry in the Seychelles will be keenly felt.

The impact of the adoption of the 25,000 tonnes quota could be worsened by the current risk of a generalised reduction in customs duties, which, after the Doha meeting, follows from the results of the WTO negotiating groups on the levelling of market access custom duties.[8] ACP and SPG drug countries must organise themselves to respond to the proposal and particularly try to obtain a more progressive reduction in the case of tuna. The French position is to request special treatment for tuna (the other product similarly affected is sugar) with customs duties reduced in the end to 15 per cent but in two successive steps of 21 per cent and 18 per cent so as to make the reduction process progressive (FIAC note of 22 July 2003). The reduced customs duty quota does not include a clause on product origin and it is still not known whether the levelling measures will eliminate the origin clause for ACP countries in order to allow them to get their supplies from more advantageous spot markets. However, Senegal, Ghana, the Seychelles and Mauritius will always be at a disadvantage on these markets because of transport costs as they are so far from the major fishing zones.

Whilst the free-trade advocates might argue that ACP countries need to be acclimatised to the world market and forced to adapt to enable them to compete without preferential treatment, the reality is that without substantial assistance, many of these countries, and the countries represented in this study are no exception, will find it increasingly difficult to compete in the canned tuna market and will have to reduce their participation.

[8] A first framework paper was produced by the EU Trade Commission in October 2002. Faced with contradictory and inflexible positions, the president of the group, M. Girard (of Swiss nationality), submitted on 16 May 2003, a document of his own to be used as a basis for negotiations (as quoted in CRS Report for Congress, 'World Trade Organisation Negotiations: The Doha Development Agenda', August 2004). According to this document, the reduction in duties will take place sectorally using a general formula based on average volumes from 1999 to 2001 (reference period), with a coefficient per product which is the determining factor. For example, with a coefficient of 0.5, which for the moment appears to be the value adopted by the negotiating group, the final customs duty rate will go from 24 per cent to a rate between 2 per cent and 4 per cent, depending on the base rates which are adopted. To obtain a final rate of 15 per cent, which is the French position (FIAC note of 22 July 2003), the product coefficient would have to be between 4 and 5. The negotiation and the adoption of this measure should have taken place at the WTO meeting in Cancun from 10 to 14 September 2003. The absence of agreement at this meeting merely postpones the negotiation.

One of the most important consequences of the recent change in policy is not so much the impact of the 25,000 tonnes quota (although that is a concern) but the 'slippery slope' nature of trade policy change which possibly presages further erosion of preferences which would have far more negative impacts on ACP tuna canneries and could threaten their competitiveness and their survival. Evidence suggests that lobbying by ACP countries, compared to their Asian market rivals, was poor in the run up to the decision by the EU. More effective lobbying (as is being orchestrated by the Seychelles government) needs to be put in place to ensure that ACP countries are proactive in the face of future trade policy changes rather than having to react to the global quest for tariff-free international markets.

References

Brus, H. (2001). 'The Bangkok Bottleneck', www.atuna.com/opinions/my%20opinion/archive/the_bangkok_bottleneck.htm, last accessed 2 July 2003

Charneau, D. (1988). 'L'économie du thon au Sénégal: intégration nationale et internationalisation de la filière'. *CRODT Document Scientifique* no. 109, April 1988, 192 pp.

DOPM. *Rapport Annuel*, 1993, 1994, 1995, 1996, 1997, 1998, 1999, 2000, 2001

FIAC (2002). 'Rapport Economique 2002. Produits de la Mer', 16 pp.

FIAC (2003). 'Compte rendu de la réunions des pays ACP producteurs et exportateurs de Thon du 04 Juin 2003', 6 pp.

FIAC 'Note sur la position des conserveurs français par rapport aux mesures d'écrêtement', 2 pp.

Gakunu, P. (nd). 'What Future for Trade?' Courier publication. http://europa.eu.int/comm/development/body/publications/courier/courier181/en/en_017_ni.pdf, last accessed 3 July 2003

Grynberg, R. (1997). *Handicapped Infants and Delinquent Parents: Lomé Convention Rules of Origin and the Solomon Islands Tuna Industry*. ECDPM Working Paper no. 37, Maastricht, ECDPM

Guillotreau, P. and Le Roy, F. (2000). *Raising Rival Costs in Tuna Industry*, Conférence IFET, New Orleans

UNCTAD/WTO (1999). 'Sub Regional Trade Expansion in Southern Africa: Supply Survey on Seychelles' Fish and Fish Products, July–August 1999', http://www.intracen.org/sstp/Survey/fish/fishsey.html, last accessed 12 January 2004

Wang, Z. K. and Winters, A. (2003). 'Impact of Opening of EU Import Market for Canned Tuna on Seychelles and Mauritius'. Report presented to the Commonwealth Secretariat, London, unpublished

PART IV

Negotiating issues and institutional arrangements

17

WTO fisheries subsidies negotiations: implications for ACP fisheries access arrangements and sustainable management

ROMAN GRYNBERG

17.1 Introduction

After almost five years of discussion at the Committee on Trade and Environment, WTO members embarked upon negotiations on fisheries subsidies as a result of the decision reached by ministers at the 4th Ministerial Conference of the WTO at Doha. The ministerial decision was couched in language that explicitly recognised the importance of the sector to developing countries and clearly implied the development of appropriate special and differential treatment rules.[1] Yet despite the language, the principal submission[2] by the 'Friends of Fish', the majority of which are developing countries,[3] there has been no substantive call for special and differential treatment from developing countries.[4]

This chapter begins by briefly considering both the economic case for fisheries subsidies disciplines and the evidence of the magnitude of those subsidies. The analysis proceeds to consider the existing subsidies rules in the WTO and perceived weaknesses that may exist in those rules, and then reviews the negotiating positions of various WTO members in the

The views expressed in this chapter are those of the author and not necessarily those of the Commonwealth Secretariat or any of its members.

[1] WTO Ministerial Declaration, WT/MIN(01)/DEC/1, 20 November 2001, para. 28:

> In the context of these negotiations, participants shall also aim to clarify and improve WTO disciplines on fisheries subsidies, taking into account the importance of this sector to developing countries.

[2] Negotiating Group on Rules, TN/RL/W/3, 24 April 2002.

[3] The principal proponents of enhanced fisheries subsidies rules at the WTO include Australia, Chile, Ecuador, Iceland, New Zealand, Peru, the Philippines and the USA.

[4] China has called for special and differential treatment provisions in very broad terms without specifying the content of such provisions. Negotiating Group on Rules, TN/RL/W/9, 20 June 2002.

Negotiating Group on Rules which is considering the fisheries subsidies issue. The chapter attempts to explain the need for special and differential treatment of developing coastal states in the current round of WTO negotiations in terms of the particular development needs of coastal states.

Particular reference is made to the situation in the Pacific island states, which are the source of 45 per cent of the world's tuna landings and for which, as some of the world's smallest and most vulnerable island states, the fisheries subsidies issue is of vital economic importance. It will be argued that two of the world's smallest and most vulnerable LDCs, Kiribati and Tuvalu, neither of which is conducting an unsustainable fisheries policy, are exposed to the greatest risk from the current negotiations if they should result in new fisheries access disciplines. The last section of the chapter deals with the implications of the proposed disciplines for ACP states in a number of areas and proposes several policy options that ACP governments may wish to pursue to minimise the possibility of new fisheries disciplines adversely affecting their development and fisheries policies.

17.2 Existing economic theory and empirical evidence on subsidies

The question of fisheries depletion in open access fisheries has been studied for many decades by natural resource economists. What is in large measure agreed is that, in the absence of property rights, fish stock depletion will occur in open access fisheries.[5] It is also widely accepted that this will occur whether or not there are subsidies.[6] The only role that subsidies play, if one accepts the direction of causality, is that they accelerate the rate of depletion. Only where there is some form of property rights arrangements can the natural tendency of depletion in the commons be arrested.[7] It is on this basis that economists have attempted to develop systems of tradable quotas as a mechanism of checking the tendency towards depletion in the open access fisheries. However, where a sustainable management regime exists[8]

[5] H. S. Gordon, 'The Economic Theory of a Common Property Resource: The Fishery', *Journal of Political Economy*, vol. 62, 124–42 (1954).

[6] See R. Aaronson, 'Ocean Fisheries Management: Recent International Developments', *Marine Policy* (September 1993); G. Porter, *Fisheries Subsidies and Overfishing: Towards a Structured Discussion*, UNEP, Geneva (2002), p. 11.

[7] A. D. Scott, 'The Fishery: The Objectives of Sole Ownership', *Journal of Political Economy*, vol. 63, 116–24 (1955).

[8] O. Flaaten and P. Wallis, 'Government Financial Transfers to Fishing Industries in OECD Countries', OECD (2000), http://oecd.org/agr/fish/publication.htm.

or where a system of tradable quotas is created[9] then subsidies simply become rents that are transferred to either producers or consumers depending upon the particular market situation. This raises the key policy question of whether the current negotiations at the WTO on enhanced fisheries subsidies disciplines constitute a 'second best' approach to fisheries management when devising appropriate sustainable management policies in more appropriate fora such as the FAO has been more politically difficult than devising enforceable WTO rules.[10]

While there has been considerable discussion of subsidies in the marine products sector there has been no systematic attempt to quantify these subsidies until the late 1980s and 1990s when there was a flurry of research activity to attempt to determine the magnitude of the subsidies involved. The research results have indicated that these subsidies have been of a significant order of magnitude. While the order of magnitude is in dispute, the fact that they are substantial is not in dispute. The estimates originally made by the FAO suggested that in 1989 subsidies were US $22 billion when measured in terms of operating costs only and US $54 billion when all investment costs were included.[11] This study was followed by research by APEC,[12] OECD[13] and World Bank,[14] all providing different estimates of the magnitude of subsidies. Regrettably, neither the WTO estimates stemming from notifications nor the research undertaken by international organisations has as yet provided sufficient and accurate time series on fisheries subsidies to allow economists to disentangle the direction of causality, i.e. whether fish stock depletion is the result of subsidies or whether subsidies are caused by depletion leading to governments increasing transfers to sustain the fisheries.

[9] R. Aaronson, 'Fisheries Subsidies, Overcapitalization and Economic Losses' in A. Hatcher and C. Robinson (eds.), *Overcapacity, Overcapitalisation, and Subsidies in European Fisheries, Proceedings of the First Workshop of the EU Concerted Action and the Common Fisheries Policy*, University of Portsmouth (October 1998).

[10] Japan has asserted that any possible adverse effect of fisheries subsidies on stock depletion could be addressed with an appropriate management regime, WT/CTE/W/173.

[11] FAO, *Marine Fisheries and the Law of the Sea: A Decade of Change*, Rome (1992).

[12] Asia–Pacific Economic Cooperation (APEC), Fisheries Working Group, 'Study into the Nature and Extent of Subsidies in the Fisheries Sector in APEC Member Countries' (2000).

[13] See *Transition to Responsible Fisheries: Economic and Policy Implications*, Paris (2000); also *Transition to Responsible Fisheries, Government Financial Transfers and Resource Sustainability: Case Studies* (AGRI/FI), Paris (2000). It is worthy of note that the OECD does not refer to subsidies, which may be construed as having WTO implications, but 'government transfers'.

[14] M. Milazzo, *Subsidies in World Fisheries: A Re-Examination*, World Bank, Washington (2000).

17.3 Existing WTO rules on subsidies

During the Uruguay Round, largely as a result of the EU position, fisheries were left out of the Agreement on Agriculture. This left fisheries subject to the more rigorous disciplines of the Agreement on Subsidies and Countervailing Measures (ASCM). Fisheries were covered by the ASCM agreed during the Uruguay Round in the course of the Negotiations on Resource Based Products but they were not included as part of the Final Act of the Uruguay Round. The ASCM provides for two types of subsidies relevant to the fisheries sector – prohibited and actionable subsidies.[15] In the definition of a prohibited subsidy,[16] which is a subsidy 'contingent in fact or in law' upon exports, the article is prefixed with the proviso that certain subsidies were prohibited 'except as provided in the Agreement on Agriculture'.[17] As the fisheries sector is bound by the disciplines of the ASCM, there exist adequate provisions to deal with many, but by no means all, of the subsidies that are currently found in the sector. When defining the adverse effects of actionable subsidies, the ASCM states: 'This Article does not apply to subsidies maintained on agricultural products as provided in article 13 of the Agreement on Agriculture.'[18]

During the implementation period of the Uruguay Round reduction commitments in agriculture the ASCM was not intended to cover all products not covered by the Agreement on Agriculture.[19] The two principal forms of subsidies discussed above, prohibited and actionable subsidies, cover various subventions that are offered by coastal states to their fisheries sector. Subsidies are defined, *inter alia*, as existing if:[20]

- there is a financial contribution by a government or any member public body within the territory of a member
- a government practice involves a direct transfer of funds (e.g. grants, loans and equity infusions), potential direct transfers of funds or liabilities (e.g. loan guarantees)

[15] For a full and complete analysis of the application of existing WTO fisheries subsidies rules see C. D. Stone, 'Too Many Fishing Boats, Too Few Fish: Can Trade Laws Trim Subsidies and Restore the Balance in Global Fisheries?' *Ecology Law Quarterly*, vol. 24, 505–43 (1997).

[16] Article 3 ASCM.

[17] There are clear exemptions from these provisions under the covered agreements which would allow least developed countries and those with a GNP per capita of less than USD 1,000 to be exempted from these disciplines, Annex VII ASCM.

[18] Article 5 ASCM.

[19] *Agreement on Agriculture*, Article 13, Due Restraint or Peace Clause.

[20] Article 1 ASCM.

or

- there is any form of income and price support in the sense of Article XVI of GATT 1994

and

- a benefit is thereby conferred.

This definition may not include certain types of payments or subsidies for access by fishing fleets that may be 'flag-of-convenience' registered and hence defined as 'outside the territory' of the member offering the subsidy. Also, subsidies that may be offered in the form of foreign aid in lieu of access may not be covered under the current definition of subsidy, and hence one of the main forms of fisheries subsidies that are under attack by environmental NGOs (WWF and Greenpeace) would not be covered by the ASCM. It is precisely this potentially extraterritorial application of fisheries subsidies disciplines to distant-water fishing nations' development assistance that should necessarily be of principal concern to developing countries.

However, the definition is adequate to cover many of the domestic subsidies that are currently available from distant-water fishing nations. These subsidies include low interest loans, tax exemptions, vessel buy-back schemes, direct payments as income and price support schemes.

The two types of subsidies that are of principal concern in the ASCM, prohibited and actionable subsidies, are prevalent to varying degrees in the fisheries.[21] Prohibited subsidies are defined as those that are 'contingent in law or in fact . . . upon export performance'.[22] Given the broad listing of prohibited export subsidies in the ASCM[23] and the broad interpretation normally given these subventions, there is no doubt that many of the provisions currently applied to coastal fishing fleets of developed countries would be considered in the category of prohibited export subsidies. The problem, as has been noted in the submissions during the current WTO

[21] Part IV provisions of the ASCM allow for what are normally referred to as Green Box measures, i.e. non-actionable subsidies such as research, assistance to disadvantaged regions and environmental measures. The exceptions for disadvantaged areas, when applied to fisheries, constitute a very significant weakening of any disciplines on fisheries subsidies given the coincidence of fisheries with disadvantaged areas both in Europe and in North America.

[22] Article 3 ASCM defines this standard as being met 'when the facts demonstrate that the granting of a subsidy, without having been made legally contingent upon export performance, is in fact tied to *actual or anticipated* export earnings'.

[23] See Annex 1 ASCM.

negotiations by the 'Friends of Fish', is that the subsidies notifications are at a level of aggregation that makes it not possible to determine precisely which species of fish are being targeted. However, even where the existing range of subsidies is not covered under the broad definition of prohibited subsidies there remain actionable subsidies that have 'adverse effects' upon the domestic industry of a WTO member. Adverse effects are defined to exist when there is:[24]

(a) injury to the domestic industry of another Member
(b) nullification and impairment of benefits accruing directly or indirectly to other members under GATT 1994, in particular the benefits of concessions bound under Article II of GATT 1994
(c) serious prejudice.

It is the third provision that is of particular interest in the fisheries because the ASCM offers a quantitative measure of serious prejudice which is deemed to exist, *inter alia*, when 'the total ad valorem subsidization of a product exceed[s] 5 per cent'.[25] This definition of serious prejudice would imply that, unless the FAO, World Bank and other estimates reviewed above are totally in error, there is *prima facie* evidence of the adverse effects of actionable subsidies. Redress for subsidies can be through the immediate application of countervailing duty measures.[26] New Zealand has argued in a recent communication that the heterogeneity of fish stocks makes remedies, including countervailing measures, difficult to apply.[27] However, for fish-exporting countries such as Iceland, New Zealand or Australia which do not import fish from fish-subsidising countries countervailing duties are an ineffective form of redress. This has been raised by several countries. But where countervailing duties are inappropriate the ASCM also permits resort to the WTO Dispute Settlement Mechanism. Should the DSM find in favour of a complainant experiencing injury to the domestic industry or nullification and

[24] Article 5 ASCM.

[25] Article 6(a) ASCM. Other situations that can be deemed to be serious prejudice and are of relevance to fisheries include subsidies to cover the operating losses of an enterprise or an industry and the forgiveness of debt.

[26] Articles 17 and 19 ASCM.

[27] TN/RL/W/3 and TN/RL/W12. While there is no doubt that fish stocks are heterogeneous in nature and this creates difficulties in the definition of 'like products' for the purpose of the application of countervailing measures, this is not unique to fish. More significantly, heterogeneity does not preclude the determination of injury or serious prejudice as there is no obligation in footnote 46 ASCM for the like products to be identical.

impairment or serious prejudice it would allow redress through the imposition of duties in other sectors.

This raises the obvious question of why the subsidies issue is in need of new rules when the WTO's Dispute Settlement Mechanism could readily be employed as a means of dealing with WTO members that are employing prohibited or actionable subsidies. As argued by New Zealand, given the heterogeneity of fish species proof of serious prejudice is difficult, as any dispute may founder on an appropriate definition of like products. Once again the possibility of the use of nullification and impairment provisions in the ASCM would address the concerns of those WTO members unable to employ countervailing duties because of the structure of their fisheries sector. Second, as subsidies for fishing fleets are so pervasive among developed WTO members, negotiations are being chosen essentially for political and diplomatic reasons. In the increasingly litigious 'tit-for-tat' environment at the WTO it is difficult to find a developed WTO member with substantive trade interests in the sector that could not be accused of applying actionable subsidies. Moreover, given the informational requirements involved in successful litigation, a fisheries subsidies discipline based upon a methodology that forces countries to notify their subsidies in a precise manner similar to the traffic light approach found in the Agreement on Agriculture seems an architecture that will find support amongst many 'Friends of Fish'.

17.4 The post-Doha fisheries negotiations and the concerns of developing coastal states

17.4.1 The negotiations

What then should be the concerns of the developing world with regard to the development of possible new disciplines on the fisheries sector. For over 200 years developed countries have provided subsidies to their fisheries sector as part of a mercantilist policy of development of fisheries, maritime transport, food security and national defence.[28] Now these subsidies, correctly or otherwise, are seen as undermining fisheries

[28] Indeed Adam Smith, in *The Wealth of Nations*, criticised bounties provided by Britain to its own whaling fleet but in the end recognised the key role the subsidies played in the national defence. Japan and France used subsidies in the nineteenth century to develop their own distant water fleets.

sustainability and hence are about to be subjected to possibly entirely new disciplines. There remains considerable disagreement in the Negotiating Group on Rules on the need for new disciplines and whether the provisions of the ASCM are adequate.[29] New Zealand has argued that, given the heterogeneous nature of fish stocks, it is not possible to use existing ASCM disciplines to challenge the actions of WTO members offering what are viewed as illegal subsidies.[30]

The question now arises as to precisely what type of architecture, if any, will evolve in order to accommodate the perceived shortcoming of the ASCM in the area of fisheries. This depends in large measure on political as well as technical considerations. With most WTO issues it is the commercial interests that count when issues are being traded off at the end of the round. In the case of fisheries, the proponents are a mixed collection of countries with commercial interests and those which believe that fisheries subsidies disciplines will constitute an important step towards environmental sustainability. The only two developed countries where a substantial and clearly demonstrable commercial interest is at stake are Iceland and New Zealand, both nations with highly efficient and competitive fishing fleets, but neither are politically significant. In the case of Iceland, fisheries constitute 75 per cent of export earnings and hence the government simply cannot compete with other WTO members on subsidies, i.e. in the Icelandic economy fisheries cannot subsidise fisheries. In the case of New Zealand, which has pursued a policy of aggressive unilateral liberalisation, there is also an ideological opposition to such subsidies which, according to OECD estimates, are virtually non-existent.[31] Both countries and their fishing industries would benefit substantially from the exit of less efficient suppliers that currently rely on subsidies.

[29] Japan has argued that the current rules are adequate (Negotiating Group on Rules, TN/RL/W/11, 2 July 2002) and that the matter should be addressed at the FAO (Negotiating Group on Rules, TN/RL/W/9, 8–10 July 2002) which possesses the fisheries expertise to address such a complex issue. [30] Negotiating Group on Rules, TN/RL/W/11, 2 July 2002.

[31] OECD, *Transition to Responsible Fisheries – Economic and Policy Implications*, Paris (2000). New Zealand government transfers to the national fisheries are approximately 1.5 per cent of the estimated value of the New Zealand catch in 1996 (p. 145). In the case of Iceland the comparable figure is 4.6 per cent of the value of the catch. While no comparable figures were provided by Japan, the EU, reputedly amongst the largest providers of subsidies, granted 639 million Euros, equal to approximately 7 per cent of the value of 1997 landings. If one includes the cost of general services under the Common Fisheries Policy, this figure rises to 14 per cent of the value of the catch (p. 140).

The USA is a key player backing the current fisheries subsidies initiative.[32] It has now tabled a supportive paper on fisheries subsidies[33] but, given the very wide diversity of its own fisheries interests (the New England, Gulf, Pacific west coast and distant-water fleets all have quite different interests), its long-term support may depend not so much on direct commercial interests but on how much the current US administration wishes to demonstrate that it has an environmental agenda in multilateral trade negotiations. Similarly, Australia appears to have strong political, as opposed to strictly commercial, interests in the subject. Those developing countries which are part of the 'Friends of Fish' all have substantial international fisheries trade interests but are also unlikely to be willing or able to 'pay' for fisheries disciplines when the crunch comes. The real powerhouses behind the fisheries subsidies negotiations are the environmental NGOs, Greenpeace and WWF backed by UNEP.

During the Uruguay Round, political opposition to the inclusion of fisheries under the reduction commitment disciplines of the Agreement on Agriculture came from the EU and those countries called 'the Friends of Fisheries'.[34] However, if recent proposed changes to the EU Common Fisheries Policy actually succeed, then the EU will be removed as an active obstacle to fisheries subsidies reform at the WTO.[35] Thus far in the Doha Round the EU has remained uncharacteristically silent and if the CFP reform is blocked by the 'Friends of Fisheries' then the EU will certainly become a more active protagonist.[36] The most vocal political opposition now comes from Japan, Korea and other Asian countries. For most OECD countries, fish is just one alternative to beef or lamb, but in Japan – with its long mercantilist tradition in the fisheries and where an older generation still vividly remembers the hunger at the end of the Second World War – food security issues for the nation's main source of animal protein remain

[32] On the basis of OECD data, p. 148, the USA is by far the most prolific provider of transfers to the fisheries sector. In 1997, the last year for which comparable OECD data were available, the US provided transfers of $724 million in constant 1990 dollars from a catch of $3 billion, i.e. 24 per cent of the value of the catch. This makes the US the largest user of transfers of any OECD country for which comparable data were available. (Data from Japan were not available.)

[33] Negotiating Group on Rules, TN/RL/W/21, 10 October 2002.

[34] This is a group of EC members who have substantial fisheries interests and includes, amongst others, France and Spain.

[35] At the Johannesburg Earth Summit, the European Union took an active role as protagonist for the agreement to limit fish catches to sustainable levels.

[36] The EU has uncharacteristically remained silent on the Fisheries Subsidies issue in the Negotiating Group.

a high priority. It is Japan's vital fisheries interests that will create the single largest barrier to a new architecture with enhanced disciplines.

WTO members in the Negotiating Group on Rules have not yet resolved or even openly discussed the technical issues pertaining to the possible architecture of enhanced disciplines. However, the environmental NGOs and UNEP have a much clearer picture and are well ahead of most WTO members in terms of enunciating architecture for future disciplines. If there is to be a new architecture it will employ a methodology that would be related to the one employed in the Uruguay Round negotiations on agriculture where countries disclose their support measures to fisheries and then make appropriate reduction commitments based upon some sort of traffic light system, i.e. red, green and amber.

It is instructive to consider briefly the options that have been presented by various non-state parties on the WTO and Fisheries Subsidies issue as to possible architectural arrangements for a WTO agreement.[37] In 2000 three separate subsidies nomenclatures were developed for categorising subsidies by the USA,[38] the OECD[39] and APEC,[40] all of which either directly or indirectly categorise subsidies such as access fees and tax and access fee exemptions that are of trade and commercial interest to coastal developing countries.[41] The architecture that emerges would almost certainly limit the capacity of developed countries to contribute to access fees and of developing countries to domesticate their fisheries. Such an architecture would require detailed notification of a variety of measures and also likely require commitments to reductions in support measures as well as commitments to the abolition of certain types of subsidies. If the normal type of special and differential approach provisions seen in the reduction commitments in the Agreement on Agriculture are extended to fisheries, then most developing coastal states would not be absolved from some level of bound reductions. It is precisely these measures that should be of concern to developing countries as many of the measures that will be discussed below are vital to the downstream processing of marine resources.

[37] The architectural options come from G. Porter, *Fisheries Subsidies and Overfishing: Towards a Structured Approach*, UNEP, Geneva (2001).

[38] WT/CTE/W/154.

[39] OECD, *Transition to Responsible Fisheries: Economics and Policy Implications*, Paris (2000).

[40] APEC, Fisheries Working Group, 'Study into the Nature and Extent of Subsidies in the Fisheries Sector in APEC Member Countries'.

[41] Access fee exemption provisions for local fishers may well constitute a prima facie violation of GATT 1947 National Treatment obligations.

While a traffic light architecture seems the most likely to emerge, if economic reason is to have any influence on the disciplines then, unless disciplines are imposed within the context of the fisheries management regime and the particular national context, it would make little sense. To make reduction commitments where an appropriate fisheries management regime is in place would be futile and have no effect on sustainability, but to accept such an approach would imply something that WTO negotiators have long resisted, that criteria from other areas, e.g. environment or agriculture would become a pre-condition for the application of disciplines. If negotiators agree on an architecture it will be based solely on commercial criteria, i.e. whether a subsidy exists in a particular category, irrespective of whether the fisheries regime is sustainable or otherwise.[42]

If WTO members are unable to agree on a new architecture then what is likely to emerge is an annex to the ASCM which will have little commercial import and do little or nothing to protect fish stocks. Given the opposition to such an architecture from Japan and the relative weakness of its principal proponents, a new architecture is by no means a 'done deal' unless the environmental NGOs are able to exert their considerable pressure on both the US and the EU. What is becoming an increasingly popular option in Geneva to increase bargaining leverage is to file a dispute, such as has occurred in the case of the Australia/Brazil challenge to EU sugar subsidies and the Brazilian challenge to the US cotton regime. In the case of fisheries, such a challenge to the fisheries regimes of several larger WTO members is possible, despite New Zealand's protestations to the contrary.

17.4.2 The concerns of small vulnerable coastal states

The experience that developing countries have had with the WTO disciplines over the last few years requires a highly precautionary approach to any new disciplines. Few developing country missions in Geneva have had time to consider fisheries subsidies as they are widely seen by them as a peripheral issue to their principal trade interests. In the past, and often quite unintentionally, small developing countries have found themselves as third parties

42 Porter, *Fisheries Subsidies*, pp. 34–5. The architecture proposed by Porter, which foresees a matrix that would include evaluation of whether a particular fisheries management regime imposes weak or strong output controls, would require an evaluation from experts in fisheries as a pre-condition to imposing trade rules. Irrespective of the economic or environmental virtues of such a methodology, it would certainly prove extremely unpalatable to trade negotiators.

'by-catch' in trade disputes between larger WTO members. The experience with the banana panels, the ensuing pressure on tuna margins of preference[43] and the current dispute over the EU sugar regime[44] have all resulted in developing countries experiencing the consequences of 'judicial activism' in the multilateral trading system between much larger players. It is precisely the interaction of past disciplines cast small which catch 'big fish' and 'small by-catch' along with ad hoc judicial activism that has created much of the developing world's discomfort with further disciplines. The WTO's net has been cast far too small and too wide and without adequate consideration of the development, as opposed to adjustment, needs of its members.

Fisheries activities in small, vulnerable coastal states come under three separate categories:

a) Revenue generation from access fees for distant-water fleets
b) Domestic and foreign fishers operating for export in the EEZ and territorial sea to supply canneries, loining facilities and domestic processing facilities
c) Artisanal fisheries within the territorial sea for the domestic and export market.

In the fisheries sector of many small, vulnerable coastal states governments have been attempting to localise the distant-water fisheries as well as develop linkages between in-shore fishery in the territorial sea and other sectors of their economies which include tourism, a substantial consumer of both domestic and imported marine products in coastal states. The section below considers the interests and concerns of small coastal states in each of these areas of fisheries activities as it pertains to the WTO negotiations.

17.4.2.1 Revenue generation from access fees

It is widely, though incorrectly, assumed that fish stocks are in decline in all marine environments. This is not the case, and in those coastal states which have a substantial surplus fish stock in their exclusive economic zones and

[43] Thailand and the Philippines placed considerable pressure on the EU at the Doha Ministerial Conference to lower their MFN tariff on canned tuna in response to demands from the ACP group for a waiver for the trade provisions of the Cotonou Agreement. Thailand and the Philippines have sought mediation at the WTO over EU MFN canned tuna tariffs.

[44] Australia, Request for Consultation, European Communities – Export Subsidies on Sugar, WT/DS265/1, 1 October 2002; Brazil, Request for Consultation, European Communities – Export Subsidies on Sugar, WT/DS266/1, 1 October 2002.

which have practised prudent fisheries management policies there are stocks in excess of the existing sustainable catch capacity of the domestic fleets. In these countries, many of which are least developed countries, significant government revenue has been generated from access fees from developed and developing country distant-water fishing fleets.

The access fees that Pacific island states negotiate are through state-to-state agreements and through commercial agreements between states and private companies. In the state-to-state agreements the distant-water fishing nations (DWFN) also provide invaluable development assistance. A recent submission to the Negotiating Group on Rules (TN/RL/W/3, para. 14) has served to heighten concerns amongst small, vulnerable states that the intention of negotiations in this area may, by design or by default, result in disciplines on fisheries access fees. This submission argues that

> the fisheries sector is distinctive in that, in addition to the standard market addressed in the SCM rules, fisheries sector subsidies can also distort access to productive resources, and can have negative effects from an environmental or developmental perspective.

As has been argued above, these disciplines on access agreements are designed directly as a result of the experience with the EU in West Africa. However, as we shall see below, the experience in other regions with access agreements is quite different.

17.4.2.2 Domestic and foreign fishers operating for export in the EEZ and territorial sea to supply canneries, loining facilities and domestic processing facilities

Access fees, while significant to some marine-resource-rich small, vulnerable states, have generally only been significant to the least developed and most vulnerable. A far more common concern pertaining to the current negotiations on fisheries subsidies is the potential impact that new disciplines may have upon fisheries activities geared towards domestic processing and subsequent export. This is a far more widespread concern as many of the small, vulnerable coastal states that do not offer access to distant-water fishing nations have nevertheless sought to develop domestic capacity to use their own marine resources for development purposes. Many of these domestic facilities have formed strategic partnerships with fleets from distant-water fishing nations to develop and land catches from the EEZ of small, vulnerable coastal states.

In order to attract local and foreign investment in the fisheries, many developing and least developed small, vulnerable states have offered incentives to both local and foreign fishers to supply domestic processing facilities. These incentives are vital if small, vulnerable coastal states are to develop their fisheries sectors. The right of coastal states to domesticate their fisheries sector is assured under UNCLOS and any possible WTO disciplines should not undermine the fundamental principles of the Law of the Sea.

There has been some early discussion of the methodology to be employed in any possible fisheries subsidies negotiations. While the ASCM has considerable weaknesses as it pertains to special and differential treatment for developing countries, the need for departure from its methodology is as yet to be demonstrated.

17.4.2.3 Artisanal fisheries for export and domestic markets

Any new fisheries subsidy disciplines on distant-water and local fleets as suggested by the proponents of such disciplines would impact on a large number of small, vulnerable coastal states. However, heightened subsidies disciplines, if crafted without sufficient understanding or consideration of the particular circumstances of artisanal fishers, could affect the development efforts of all small, vulnerable coastal states in the fisheries sector. The artisanal fisheries sector remains central to the subsistence and monetised livelihood of coastal populations throughout the developing world in general and in small, vulnerable coastal states in particular. Those involved in artisanal fisheries in the territorial sea are normally from low-income groups. Moreover, in many coastal developing states women disproportionately dominate the subsistence component of the artisanal sector.

In many small, vulnerable states governments have specific programmes to assist these groups, often including direct assistance for the purchase of monetised inputs. This type of government assistance to low-income, low-technology fishers to raise income levels by expanding into monetised activities for the domestic and speciality export market is vital to the development efforts of small, vulnerable coastal states and to raising the standard of living of what are often very-low-income groups. As a result, any disciplines that may be developed on fisheries subsidies must be crafted so that they exempt government programmes to raise income levels of artisanal fishers.

All these matters can conceivably be addressed if the size of the WTO's net is cast large enough to provide for appropriate escape for the by-catch. The judicious use of appropriate *de minimis* and special and differential provisions could provide a genuine development space. The question is whether, in the rush to write yet more disciplines, the genuine and legitimate concerns of the WTO's most vulnerable members will be missed.

17.5 Fisheries subsidies disciplines: the case of Pacific ACP fisheries access arrangements

This section considers some of the implied disciplines that the current negotiations at the WTO appear to suggest. It will be argued that the disciplines implied from the negotiating position and the new fisheries subsidies architecture suggest possible future WTO disciplines that could endanger the position of the Pacific island states and other coastal developing states that remain highly dependent upon revenues and development assistance stemming from access fees.[45] The analysis of possible WTO provisions will be reviewed in light of the various access provisions of the predominant regional fisheries access arrangements. These include treaty arrangements with the USA, emerging arrangements with the European Union and private bilateral access arrangements.

17.5.1 Fisheries access arrangements with the USA

The most significant access arrangement in the South Pacific is the multilateral arrangement between the Pacific islands and the USA, the Treaty on Fisheries Between the Governments of Certain Pacific Island States and the Government of the United States of America (the US Treaty),[46] originally negotiated in 1987 and revised in 1993. The US Treaty creates a multilateral framework to regulate access of US purse seine vessels in the EEZs of the

[45] T. Kingston, 'The Current Status and Benefits of the Pacific Island Fisheries Industry' in D. Zachary et al. (eds.), *Towards a Prosperous Pacific: Building a Sustainable Tuna Industry in the Pacific Islands*, Maui Pacific Centre, Hawaii (1997), pp. 73–81. The Marshall Islands obtained 25 per cent of government revenue from fisheries access fees in 1992/3. The equivalent figures for other island states were Kiribati 45 per cent in 1991; Federated States of Micronesia 25 per cent in 1993, Tuvalu 11 per cent in 1990 and Solomon Islands 5 per cent in 1993.

[46] Forum Fisheries Agency, Treaty on Fisheries Between the Governments of Certain Pacific Island States and the Government of the United States of America (the Multilateral Treaty on Fisheries), Honiara, 1994.

South Pacific island states which are members of the Forum Fisheries Agency.[47]

The financial terms of the revised US Treaty (currently US $21 million per annum) fall into three categories: (a) annual industry payments representing licence fees for a maximum of fifty-five purse seine vessels and technical assistance; (b) observer programme costs paid by industry; and (c) economic development assistance provided by the US Government pursuant to a related agreement between the US Government and the Forum Fisheries Agency.[48] Under current arrangements in the Multilateral Treaty, USAID pays approximately US $18 million of the US $21 million of annual returns to the beneficiaries.[49] This accounts for almost a third of total access fees derived by Pacific Island states but is less than 20 per cent of total DWFN catch in their EEZ.[50]

Studies by the World Bank[51] suggest that the current 4 per cent average access fee is only as high as it is because of the 10–11 per cent return received from the US, which is subsidising the agreement through USAID. In the past two decades two factors, both now related to events at the WTO, have pushed the US fleet into the Central and Western Pacific and away from the Eastern Pacific which was the traditional fishing ground of the US fleet. The first is that in the Western Pacific tuna and dolphin do not school together and hence canneries using fish caught by US purse seniers could continue to use the 'dolphin friendly' label and continue to use the profitable purse seine fishing technique. However, with recent amendments to the US Mammal Protection Act made necessary as a result of the Second Tuna–Dolphin case there has been a redefinition of 'dolphin friendly' which will increase the permissible dolphin by-catch and may well help to pull the US fleet back to the Eastern Pacific closer to the previous bases of Pago Pago and San Diego.

The second factor bringing the US fleet into the Central and Western Pacific has been the US Treaty itself which not only provides substantial subsidies but also allows purse seine operators to fish throughout the EEZ of the

[47] The parties to the Multilateral Treaty include Australia, Cook Islands, Federated Stares of Micronesia, Fiji, Kiribati, Marshall Islands, Nauru, New Zealand, Niue, Papua New Guinea, Samoa, Solomon Islands, Tonga, Tuvalu and Vanuatu.

[48] See Schedule 3, Multilateral Treaty.

[49] S. Tarte, *The European Union and the Western Pacific Tuna Fishery*, Strasbourg, France (October 2002).

[50] Forum Fisheries Agency.

[51] World Bank, *Pacific Island Economies: Building a Resilient Economic Base for the Twenty-First Century*, Report No. 13803-EAP, Washington (February 1995), p. viii.

members of the FFA under one access agreement.[52] Should new subsidies disciplines now proposed be negotiated, then the US Treaty in its present form would have to be revised. This would put further pressure on the US purse seiners to shift operations to the Eastern Pacific. Without the US Treaty, the average access fee for Pacific Island countries would drop to 3 per cent.[53]

17.5.2 EU fisheries partnership agreements

The EU has been a relatively new entrant into the resource-rich waters of the South Pacific. The first fisheries access agreement was signed between Kiribati and the EU in July 2002.[54] The three-year agreement is a bilateral access agreement which foresees six EU purse seine fishing vessels in the Kiribati EEZ in the first year along with twelve long-liners.[55] Receipts will be set at €546,000, but in the second year of the agreement the benefits to Kiribati decrease to €416,000 when vessel levels will fall to four purse seine vessels, though this can increase to eleven purse seine vessels with an additional payment of €65,000 per vessel. The component paid by the industry is the highest of any previous EU access agreement and is set at €35/tonne landed.[56] The method of calculating the licence fee in the EU agreement, it will be argued, compounds the fisheries management difficulties faced by policy-makers in the sector by providing a substantial and direct incentive to under-reporting. It should be noted that approximately 17 per cent of the total cost of fisheries access was met by ship owners, with the balance coming from EU public funds.[57]

[52] If the US purse seiners paid the US government the equivalent of the USAID contribution in licence fees then this would not be a subsidy.

[53] This estimate is based on tuna prices existing in 1997.

[54] The agreement grants access to French, Spanish and Portuguese vessels.

[55] Even this initially modest agreement between the EU and Kiribati has proven to be quite controversial as there was considerable debate as to whether Kiribati provision of access for EU purse seiners violated their obligation to limit access under the Palau arrangement (Arrangement for the Management of the Western Pacific Purse Seine Fishery – 1995). See www.spc.org.nc/OceanFish/Hmtl/SCTB/SCTB14/FT5_Opnai_Clark.pdf. For a complete analysis of the Palau arrangement see T. Aquorau and A. Bergin, 'Ocean Governance in the Western Pacific Purse Seine Fishery – the Palau Arrangement', *Marine Policy*, vol. 21, no. 2, 173–86 (1997).

[56] In earlier tuna access agreements, such as the Seychelles–EU arrangement, the amount paid by the industry was set at €25/tonne.

[57] IFREMER, CEMARE, CEP, 199. Evaluation of Fishing Agreements Concluded by the European Community, European Contract No. 97/S 240-152919.10.12.1197 IFREMER/CEMARE/CEP Ref. APC02 quoted in B. Gorez and B. O'Roidan, 'A Report on the Future of European Union–ACP Fisheries Relations', Commonwealth Secretariat (February 2002), p. 17.

The relationship in fisheries between the EU and the ACP states in general has, by and large, been dominated by this type of 'cash for access' type arrangement with only some notable exceptions.[58] However, at the very end of 2002 the European Commission launched a new policy initiative on fisheries that foresaw the development of 'fisheries partnership agreements'.[59] It is envisaged that the partnership agreements will result in the creation of a framework agreement with ACP countries in the area of fisheries. These fisheries agreements will have the overall objectives of sustainability, good governance and poverty eradication[60] but have the specific objectives of protecting EU fisheries interests (including access) and fostering developing countries' capabilities to exploit their marine resource. The potential for policy conflict is apparent.

The current EU access arrangements are highly subsidised and result in incentive mechanisms that exacerbate unsustainable practices. The estimate of the extent of subsidy in the current EU access arrangement is 83 per cent of total cost. This is very similar to that of the USA where the public contribution is 84 per cent of total payment.

17.5.3 Japan, Korea and Taiwan

While US and, to a lesser degree, EU fisheries access agreements are state-to-state and transparent in nature, agreements with East Asian DWFN are highly opaque because they are of a commercial nature. In the case of Japan, there is a Head agreement with South Pacific nations but access is negotiated by individual companies with individual governments. The access fee is negotiated in the subsidiary agreement which is based on a per-trip basis but is paid wholly by the Japanese companies.[61] Significantly, like the US arrangement, the fisheries access is not dependent upon declared catch and hence is not as corrosive as other arrangements. Japan has also successfully decoupled, in law if not entirely in fact, its access arrangements

[58] This type of 'first generation agreement' was followed by 'second generation agreements', e.g. EU–Argentina, which saw the creation of joint ventures. In Mozambique the EU has also pursued fisheries joint ventures.

[59] Communication from the Commission on an Integrated Framework for Fisheries Partnership Agreements with Third Countries, Brussels, 23 December 2002, COM (2002)637 final.

[60] Ibid., p. 5.

[61] Japan has fisheries agreements with the Federated States of Micronesia, Kiribati, Marshall Islands, Nauru, Palau, Solomon Islands and Tuvalu. There is also a fisheries agreement with Fiji but Japanese fishing vessels do not fish in Fiji waters.

from its development assistance. Access is not subsidised but becomes, in the view of Pacific Island countries, a *conditio sine qua non* of Japanese development assistance to the fisheries sector.[62]

Other DWFN such as Korea and Taiwan negotiate bilateral commercial agreements between individual ministries and fishing companies which are not agreements between sovereign states. Little or nothing is publicly known about these agreements except that the access fee is normally based on a percentage of the previous year's catch. In a recent publication, Forum Fisheries Agency officials described the access formula used by Pacific Island states:[63]

> In the FFA region, the access fees are largely determined using the previous year's catch and effort data as supplied by the DWFN, the market price and set percentage rate of return. The standard access fee formula is as follows:
>
> Access = Average Price of Tuna × Average Catch per Vessel × Minimum Rate of Return

This access fee formula or variants thereof have been used by Pacific Island countries as a method for calculating access fees for over a decade.[64] On the basis of current estimates, US purse seine owners are paying USD 120,000 for access as compared with USD 250,000 for access from Japan, Korea and Taiwan.[65] EU purse seiners will pay an extra €65,000 (USD 70,000) for access. However, what the Pacific island receives is approximately five times more than what the US vessel owner pays because of the contributions of USAID.

This formula contrasts sharply with the access arrangement in the US Treaty which is highly subsidised but, more importantly, is not in any way related to catch levels or declared catch and hence creates no incentive for under-reporting or misreporting. In the formula above the more the fisherman reports the more he will pay next year in access fees. Scientists and

[62] The Government of Japan normally denies that there exists any link between its fisheries technical assistance and access agreements. The US government also denies that the Multilateral Treaty has any subsidy component.

[63] J. Tamate and G. Joseph, 'The Experience in the Pacific on Negotiating Fishing Agreements' in K. Lankester, P. Diouf and S. Khandy (eds.), *Proceedings of Two Workshops held in Senegal and Mauritania on Fisheries Access in West Africa*, WWF (2002), p. 94.

[64] See R. Grynberg and M. Powell, *Taxation in the Island Nations of the South Pacific*, Australian National University, NCDS, Canberra (1994), vol. I.

[65] See Tarte, *EU and Western Pacific Tuna Fishery*, p. 6.

policy-makers are keenly aware that there are economic incentives to under-report or to report fish caught in the EEZ as being caught on the high seas. These policy-makers and scientists are confident that they are able to build into their own catch estimates margins of error which will take into account the magnitude of the misreporting and hence assure the sustainability of the region's fisheries. Whether this confidence is justifiable will only be tested in time as more pressure is put on the resource with the entry of new DWFNs into the Pacific and the EU's desire for enhanced access into ACP waters brings effort levels close to estimated sustainable yields. However, suffice it to say that a system of access fees that provides financial incentives to misreport only further compounds fisheries management problems in the region because biological accuracy of recruitment is notoriously poor in the tuna fisheries.

It will be argued that the differences between the nature of the agreements bear heavily on the issue of sustainability of the fisheries but in the exact opposite way to that predicted by the opponents of fisheries subsidies disciplines. The US agreement with extensive subsidies is far more conducive to sustainability because it is multilateral in nature, transparent to all parties and in large measure respectful of environmental and marine standards established in the Pacific Islands. The US Treaty is widely regarded in fisheries circles as a model and US Distant Water Fishing Fleet behaviour in terms of sustainability and monitoring is exemplary. The USA is widely seen as the DWFN that is least involved in under-reporting and misreporting. The reason for this is because the treaty is based on access fees that are decoupled from fish catches. Thus whether the US fleet reports catches on the high seas or on the EEZ of the Pacific island countries will not affect the amount it will pay in the coming years. Thus the US Treaty imposes an access fee regime that is equivalent to a lump sum tax and does not distort behaviour.

17.5.4 Revenue estimates from Pacific ACP access arrangements

For many years data on the economic importance and magnitude of access fees has not been publicly available in the Pacific island states or indeed in many coastal states. National governments and regional fisheries organisations, operating under instruction from their members, have jealously guarded what they have seen as 'commercially sensitive' data on fisheries access fees and the revenues generated from the fisheries. Table 17.1 is the

Table 17.1 *1999 access fees and gross domestic product*

	Access fees (USD)	GDP (USD)	Access fees (% of GDP)
Kiribati	$20,600,000	$48,123,871	42.81%
Tuvalu	$5,900,000	$13,848,788	42.60%
FSM	$15,400,000	$229,869,864	6.70%
Nauru	$3,400,000	$51,612,903	6.59%
Marshall Islands	$4,982,600	$97,311,800	5.12%
Niue	$151,793	$7,514,077	2.02%
Palau	$800,000	$113,484,869	0.70%
Cook Islands	$169,072	$82,371,930	0.21%
PNG	$5,840,000	$3,415,590,478	0.17%
Tonga	$152,041	$157,018,257	0.10%
Solomon Islands	$273,458	$279,593,229	0.10%
Vanuatu	$218,448	$226,280,313	0.09%
Samoa	$188,616	$233,506,665	0.08%
Fiji	$212,000	$1,821,334,281	0.01%

Source: FFA: R. Gillet and C. Lightfoot, *The Contribution of Fisheries to the Economies of the Pacific Island Countries*, Honiara (2001)

first country-specific estimate of the significance of access fees to Pacific island countries.

The most significant observation regarding this data is the importance of access fees to the economies of the region. One quarter of total Pacific access fees come from payments made by USAID under the terms of the US Treaty. What is also significant is that access fees as a percentage of GDP tend to be greatest in those countries with the least developed fisheries sectors and they are very often smallest as a portion of GDP in those countries with relatively developed fisheries export sectors. This is in large measure a result of the fact that many coastal states, including Pacific island countries, have used access fees as a proxy development levy or export tax. The WTO compatibility of these arrangements should be of concern to Pacific island countries that are members of the WTO.

Table 17.2 covers estimates of access fees for two groups of countries, Pacific WTO members, i.e. Papua New Guinea, Fiji and the Solomon Islands, and resource-rich non-WTO members who may nonetheless be affected by WTO disciplines. In those countries where there are abundant marine resources, e.g. Kiribati, Marshall Islands, Nauru, FSM and Tuvalu, one finds that almost no fish exports pass through the territory of these

Table 17.2 *Exports and access fees of selected Pacific countries (1999)*

Country	Estimated exports (USD)	Estimated catch[a] (MT)	Estimated value of catch (USD)	Access fees (USD)	Access fees as % of catch
Fiji	$23,000,000[b]	15,600	$40,000,000	$212,000	0.053%
Federated States of Micronesia	$4,623,000[c]	134,499	$180,000,000	$15,400,00	8.6%
Kiribati	$2,302,000[d]	138,000	$139,000,000	$20,600,000	14.8%
Marshall Islands	473,000	33,217	$50,000,000	$4,984,000	9.96%
Nauru	0	41,000	$37,000,000	$3,400,00	9.2%
Papua New Guinea	$48,000,000	141,000 (85,000)	$140,000,000 ($75,000,000)	$5,840,000	4.1% (7.3%)[e]
Solomon Islands	$5,000,000	74,000	$70,600,000	$273,000	0.3%
Tuvalu	$4,500	40,532	$37,400,000	$5,900,000	15.8%

[a)] Based on total commercial (non-subsistence) catch

[b)] These estimates are based on official figures of the Fiji Fisheries Division. The Reserve Bank of Fiji estimates that these figures are $28,000,000. The EU estimates that these figures are closer to $40,000,000.

[c)] These are 1997 estimates for FSM.

[d)] Kiribati exports are dominated by live aquarium fish.

[e)] The bracketed estimates for PNG are based on the assumption that all access fees are paid only by offshore foreign-based vessels.

Source: FFA: R. Gillet and C. Lightfoot, *The Contribution of Fisheries to the Economies of the Pacific Island Countries*, Honiara (2001)

states. However, one finds that where exports are substantial access fees are minimal because governments have used them as a means of providing incentives to localisation.

Cross-country comparisons of percentage access fees are always fraught with difficulty for many reasons. As mentioned above, relatively advanced marine product exporting countries such as Fiji, the Solomon Islands and Papua New Guinea have, as a matter of development policy, developed a diversified and 'domestic' fisheries sector where no or almost no access fees are paid by local and locally based fishers. This has been achieved with massive subsidies to these sectors. In Fiji this virtual absence of government earnings from access fees is compounded by the loss of tax revenues stemming from tax incentives to the export sector. Thus a very high rent sector such as the export of sashimi-grade tuna operates in an almost tax-free environment.[66] Moreover, there is evidence that operators in this sector are involved in the massive and systematic under-reporting of exports, as has been highlighted by the EU as well as the Reserve Bank. This absence of access fees for local fishers accounts for the relatively low percentage access fees found for Fiji and PNG.[67] In the Fiji and PNG canned tuna sectors no access fee is paid for tuna used in the cannery which is processed domestically. In the demersal export fisheries in PNG, where there are only domestic fishers, there is an exemption from access fees. Thus it may not be possible to compare access fee arrangements between countries with significantly different fisheries sectors.

The data in table 17.2 cannot easily be reconciled with the World Bank estimates of fisheries catch returns in the region. Indeed, the estimates of access fee returns from FSM and Kiribati, two of the most resource-rich countries in the South Pacific and countries with almost no export sectors, are two to three times the estimates of the World Bank. How are such inconsistencies possible? These inconsistencies are not statistical aberrations but are significant in explaining observed behaviour in the Pacific tuna fisheries. The estimates above are determined by dividing the known access fees by the estimated value of the catch. The numerator i.e. access fees are part of government revenue and are relatively accurate as they are presented to parliament in government budget estimates. It is the denominator, the volume and unit value of fish, which is the most difficult to verify as it comes from reported catch levels multiplied by estimated price. The catch estimates of the distant-water fishing fleets are reputed to be notoriously inaccurate.

It is worth considering three groups of countries in the above sample. The first is Kiribati and Tuvalu, two of the poorest LDCs in the Pacific but which are resource rich and overwhelmingly dependent upon access fees paid under the US Treaty. The US fleet has over the last few years become increasingly dependent upon the EEZ of Kiribati and Tuvalu as these countries are most proximate to their traditional fishing grounds in the Eastern Pacific. In 1999 approximately 40 per cent of the tuna caught in the Kiribati

[66] Fiji has a long tradition of offering tax-free status to marginal garment factories as well as high-rent-earning sectors such as gold mining and sashimi grade tuna.

[67] This exemption from access fees in Fiji has in the past extended to foreign fishers operating under licence to domestic fishers.

EEZ was caught by US purse seiners (56,000 tonnes) and 90 per cent of the tuna caught in Tuvalu (36,000 tonnes). The very high estimates of return to both Kiribati and Tuvalu are real and reflect the way access fees are paid under the terms of the US Treaty. These access fees paid by the USA are not in any way linked to the market price of tuna but reflect the volumes caught in the EEZ of the various signatories. Thus in a low-price year such as 1999 it is entirely possible, given that the bulk of the US fleet was fishing in the Kiribati and Tuvalu EEZ, that this is an accurate reflection of the *ad valorem* rate of access fees.

The second group of countries include Nauru, the Federated States of Micronesia and the Marshall Islands which appear to generate access fees approximately twice those estimated by the World Bank, in the vicinity 8.6–9.9 per cent of estimated catch. In this case it is not possible to reconcile the estimates easily. From the data available in 1999 these apparently high rates of return cannot be explained by the presence of the US tuna fleet as it was not operating in the EEZ of the FSM or the Marshall Islands and was only a minor player in the EEZ of Nauru (15 per cent of total Nauru catch in 1999).

The third group of countries, PNG, the Solomon Islands and Fiji, have as a matter of policy developed a domestic tuna resource sector by using access fees, along with a host of other measures, to subsidise domestication of their industry. This has been a significant investment in the development of a commercial advantage in marine resource exports. As a result, access fess have been minimal, though PNG has earned access fees from agreements with Taipei and, to a lesser degree, the USA.[68]

17.6 Implications of WTO disciplines on fisheries subsidies

The clamour for fisheries subsidies disciplines at the WTO has been strenuously supported by the NGOs and the IGOs (UNEP, FAO, APEC, World Bank, WTO). The nexus between fisheries subsidies and stock depletion is now the accepted wisdom such that policy-makers no longer even consider the internal dynamics of the global capture fisheries. However, even if, by some *deus ex machina*, effective subsidies disciplines

[68] It is reported that PNG tuna caught by Filipino and PNG vessels bound for the Madang tuna cannery and export to the EU have been free of access fees. This accounts for approximately 50 per cent of PNG exports in 1999.

are negotiated at the WTO, the dynamics of rising global population, rapid economic growth which has increased income and demand for fish and the application of sophisticated technology to the last primitive hunter-gatherer activity will mean that the global fisheries will not survive unless global disciplines to limit access to sustainable levels are negotiated in the appropriate forum, i.e. the FAO or the UN. To discuss this dynamic of fisheries depletion is today profoundly unfashionable because it is to lay the blame for fish stock depletion on what are in effect the very pillars of our modern society – the application of advanced technology and rapid population and economic growth. Instead the NGOs and the IGOs prefer to pretend to address the issue of fish stock depletion by attempting to negotiate what will ultimately be weak disciplines at the WTO.

Disputing the logical veracity and factual foundations of an argument made by those who are large, rich and powerful by those who are small, poor and vulnerable may prove satisfying but it normally overlooks the inevitable outcome. It is best to consider policy responses to the threats posed by those changes in policy. The challenges posed by these disciplines include:

- the potential loss of a substantial portion of the GDP of Kiribati and Tuvalu, two of the smallest and most environmentally and economically vulnerable LDCs in the ACP group;
- losses of revenue to a large number of other ACP countries dependent upon revenues from subsidised access agreements;
- dismantling of economic incentives to domestication through elimination of subsidies to local fishers.

The responses by ACP countries to the challenges posed should be based upon:

- seeking special and differential treatment in fisheries negotiations that recognise the needs of developing coastal states to maintain revenues from sustainable access arrangements, subventions to domestic and artisanal fishers;
- developing access agreements that decouple development assistance from fisheries access arrangements such as is found in the Japanese agreements with the Pacific ACP. In the case of the fisheries partnership agreements, development assistance to the fisheries sector should not be linked to EU access;

- where possible, replacing access fees with income-withholding taxes for DWFNs. This will permit differential rates for local and foreign fishers.

There is much irony in a situation where two of the world's most environmentally vulnerable states, threatened by unsustainability caused by the immediate consequences of global warming, are threatened with economic collapse as a result of WTO negotiations in an international trade body attempting to protect the environment. This outcome is all the more unpalatable given that there is no evidence of unsustainable fisheries in Kiribati and Tuvalu and that the first victim of the negotiations would likely be the very access agreement most closely associated with good fisheries management practice in the region, i.e. the US Treaty. The outcome becomes demonstrably inequitable and unjust when one considers that the disciplines are being negotiated in the WTO, a forum in which both Kiribati and Tuvalu are not members and from which they were excluded at the end of the Uruguay Round.[69]

[69] Kiribati and Tuvalu were GATT de facto members until the end of the Uruguay Round. As they did not seek accession prior to the creation of the WTO, they would now have to accede like all other countries. Countries such as the Solomon Islands which were also GATT de facto members obtained WTO membership easily at the end of the Uruguay Round because they submitted their offers within the stipulated period.

18

Plurilateral financial standards and their regulation: the experience of small developing states

ROMAN GRYNBERG, SACHA SILVA AND JAN YVES REMY

18.1 Introduction

A recent WTO proposal[1] presented by the small Caribbean island of Antigua and Barbuda on behalf of some small states, aimed at ensuring greater fairness and participation by all in the process of setting genuinely international standards for the regulation of financial services, has brought to the fore an issue that has been silently brewing in the midst of services negotiations at the WTO. The question of how to ensure that the international regulation of financial services becomes an inclusive process for small developing states[2] has in recent years assumed paramount importance in securing their economic growth and viability within the multilateral trading system.

One of the great ironies of the post-Cold War period of globalisation has been that while it has been associated with trade and economic liberalisation, it has also been coupled with the creation of a number of standard-setting bodies which have in turn spawned a multiplication of what are essentially plurilateral standards and regulations. These international standards, to the extent they existed in the past, did not involve small developing states which were outside the global process of integration.

[1] See proposal presented to the WTO Committee on Financial Services (S/FIN/W/29/Rev.1) by the representative of Antigua and Barbuda on 6 October 2003. The proponents listed in the communication are Antigua and Barbuda, Belize, Fiji, Guyana, Papua New Guinea, Maldives, Solomon Islands and St Kitts and Nevis.

[2] Employing the Commonwealth Secretariat criteria, small states in this context refer to states of relatively small populations (i.e. less than 1.5 million) which are characterised by their vulnerability in the areas of defence and security, environmental disasters, limited human resources, and lack of economic resources. They range in size from micro-states such as St Kitts and Nevis, Nauru, Niue and Tuvalu with less than 50,000 people each, to countries like Botswana, the Gambia and Mauritius. (Source: Commonwealth Small States' website: http://www.commonwealthsmallstates.org.)

However, many of these small developing states which have now developed not inconsiderable export-oriented offshore financial services sectors are faced with implementing increasingly complex external regulations as part of their integration into the multilateral system and the WTO.[3]

While small developing states have almost invariably been excluded from the process of formulation of international financial standards and regulations, they have, by and large, been unwilling objects of international regulatory authorities. This is not because of any lack of solidarity on their part with the stated goal of these bodies in ensuring stability and security within the international financial system. However, small developing states' consistent absence from the formulation process means that they have little or no say in the development of standards or regulations, many of which have negative effects on their development prospects. This absence from the formulation process has already had important consequences for the development and ultimate legitimacy of the financial standards emerging from these standard-setting bodies and the process of globalisation of financial regulations. Further, there is growing evidence that the application of these standards, at times coercive, risks being extended to other international fora, such as multilateral financial and trade institutions like the WTO.

In part I of this chapter the experiences which small developing states have encountered with some of the multinational bodies formulating standards for the regulation of the international financial services sector are illustrated. Three of these standards, and the bodies from which they derive, will be considered in detail – the OECD's Harmful Tax Initiative (HTI); those standards developed by the Financial Action Task Force (FATF) to combat money laundering; and, most recently, the financial regulations under the revised Basel Capital Accord. All three organisations have established international standards that affect – either through coercion or threat of coercion, as in the case of the HTI, or 'voluntarily' through the norms of developed countries, as in the case of the Basel

[3] The small developing states that have developed offshore financial service sectors are normally but not exclusively small island states. In the Caribbean Antigua and Barbuda, Barbados, Bahamas, Bermuda, Belize, British Virgin Islands, Cayman Islands, Jamaica and St Kitts and Nevis have substantial offshore financial service sectors. In the Pacific Cook Islands, Marshall Islands, Nauru, Niue, Tuvalu, Samoa and Vanuatu have all developed offshore financial service sectors. In the Indian Ocean only Mauritius has thus far been successful in developing an offshore centre.

Capital Accord – the competitive provision of financial services in and by small developing countries. The experience of these countries highlights the limited participation and impact in formulating these standards, and the continuing constraints and obstacles they face in the formation, implementation of and compliance with standards set by industrialised, developed and, to a much lesser degree, a selected group of large developing countries.

Then, in part II of this chapter we briefly explore how the issue of international regulation of financial services is relevant to the more general, but very crucial, WTO negotiations about domestic regulation of services under the General Agreement on Trade in Services (GATS) and the Annex on Financial Services (FSA). It is argued that these discussions offer developing countries, and in particular small states, the greatest potential for ensuring their participation in the setting of internationally harmonised standards which affect their trade in services, and the means for seeking redress through improvements and/or further elaboration of the text of GATS and/or FSA. Precedents for promoting participation by all WTO members and harmonisation in the standard-setting process do exist under the current WTO/GATT framework, through collaboration and co-operation with relevant international organisations which have the appropriate expertise. Given a more positive political climate and will, much can be done in Services negotiations to strengthen the role of the WTO in limiting the impact of the arbitrary introduction of plurilateral standards by developed and/or large developing countries.

Part I

18.2 Overview of characteristics of the standard-setting bodies

The increasing number of financial standard-setting bodies[4] reflects to a large degree the effects of an increasing number of international financial crises, and developed-country perceptions that inadequate supervision in

[4] There are presently thirteen major standards issued by ten standard-setting bodies, ranging from the major multilateral institutions (IMF, World Bank, OECD) to private-sector bodies such as the International Accounting Standards Board. There are currently efforts underway to develop several other initiatives in areas such as tax policy and international reserves management.

developing economies is a chronic source of instability in financial markets. Some of the standard-setting bodies in question grew out of a series of G-7 initiatives immediately following the Asian Crisis, and their origins have resulted in overlapping membership between the various fora.[5] It is immediately apparent that the standard-setting bodies are 'universal' only at the G-10 level, and that universality begins to break down at the level of the G-22, where only the largest developing countries are represented. Several multilateral and international financial institutions, drawing from much more universal memberships, are limited to observer status. For many small developing states the 'similarity of composition and the complementary interlocking programmes of these organisations are perceived as suggesting a single agenda – that of the major developed countries'.[6]

These standard-setting bodies, which comprise mostly developed countries, form the backbone of the codes and standards regime by not only formulating and revising the content of the standards, but also monitoring compliance by both members and non-members. Increasingly, these standards have been adopted by multilateral agencies, international financial institutions and the private sector to guide trade, lending, aid and investment decisions. The result has been a dramatic expansion of *de facto* jurisdiction of the standard-setting bodies beyond their G-7 origins.[7]

The extension of the codes and standards regime to small developing states has occurred in the near-absence of involvement by the affected jurisdictions at the formulation stage – nor any substantial consideration of their interests – in spite of the adverse impact of many of the proposed regulatory changes.[8] The institutional processes producing the initiatives of major concern for these purposes – the OECD HTI, the FATF '40+8' Anti-Money Laundering and Counter-Terrorist Financing (AML/CTF) Guidelines and the Basel Capital Accord – all, to varying degrees, exhibit common characteristics which effectively preclude the emergence of truly multilateral standards. These include:

[5] See Appendix 18.1, 'Overlapping Memberships in Key Standard-Setting Bodies'.

[6] Society of Trust and Estate Practitioners (2002).

[7] Many standard-setting bodies seem to hold a contradictory position on this issue. The Basel Committee, for example, has repeatedly stressed that it is not a policy-making body, yet that its basic principles are that 'no foreign banking establishment should escape supervision; and that supervision should be adequate', i.e. conforming to standards issued by the Committee (BCBS, 2002).

[8] This topic will be addressed in section 18.4.

1. The membership and the decision-making processes of the standard-setting bodies are dominated by industrialised economies and only the largest developing countries. In most cases, membership has been extended to large developing economies only after the standards in question were drafted and approved.
2. The standard-setting bodies have realised, after a considerable delay, that developing country participation is a major concern. However, the result of outreach efforts has been that small developing states are included as observers by invitation only, conditioned on prior commitment to the standards in full, and with little or no substantial decision-making power. In addition, many fora established on behalf of small developing states have not been treated as equal partners in the standard-setting process.
3. The lack of representation leads to justifiable concerns regarding the legitimacy of the standards initiatives and the threat to the sovereignty of targeted jurisdictions.

The standards emerging from these fora have been plagued by a fundamental breach of the principle of due process – a universal set of rules created by non-multilateral, non-representative bodies where the concerns of small developing states have been consistently and often purposely ignored. The failure of the standard-setting bodies to abide by basic principles of corporate governance[9] – transparency, accountability and the protection of minority stakeholders – has raised serious questions regarding the legitimacy of the standards process.

Several initiatives have greatly impacted the legislative structures and economic well-being of small developing states, in spite of justifiable concerns about the legal and economic bases of the standards themselves. In fact, the practices characterising the standard-setting process by these organisations have raised several questions about sovereignty, legitimacy, equality and fairness. As an illustration, we take the case of the OECD's HTI (see details below), which in particular has come under great scrutiny by developing country supervisors, multilateral institutions, tax policy administrators and think-tanks who feel that its very foundation is questionable.[10] They feel that the HTI violates

[9] Ironically, the standards on corporate governance are an OECD initiative.

[10] For an overview of the main arguments, see Dwyer (2000) and Hay (2001). For further reading, visit the Center for Freedom and Prosperity website at www.freedomandprosperity.org.

several basic tenets of contemporary international law, namely that states or international organisations cannot intervene in the territory, nor in areas under the jurisdiction, of other states. Although the OECD has gone to great lengths to stress that it does not intend to dictate tax policy to jurisdictions, nor is it attempting to harmonise taxes on a global level, many jurisdictions under scrutiny feel that the HTI will undermine their sovereignty in determining their domestic tax policies.[11]

Another contentious issue surrounds the unilateral means employed for determining whose domestic tax regime was 'harmful' and whose was not. Developing countries widely feel that the OECD has unilaterally determined that tax practices are harmful in so far as they hinder the application of residence-based income taxation in OECD countries. The abstention of Switzerland, Luxembourg, Portugal and Belgium, coupled with reservations expressed by the US government in face of non-compliance by some US states,[12] has forced the OECD to retract several 'non-core' principles since the 1998 Report.[13] The OECD is unlikely to be an impartial referee in regulating a market where its members have a significant commercial interest, as the OECD membership is dominated by high-tax, developed nations who are the principal participants in the market for cross-border financial services. However, the OECD is by no means a monolith and some of its members, like Switzerland, Luxembourg, Austria and Belgium, have commercial interests similar to those of the jurisdictions targeted by the OECD's HTI. Indeed, as subsequent events have demonstrated, it is the presence of a large number of OECD countries that are themselves involved in what the OECD considers harmful activities that has served to undermine the legitimacy of the initiative.

[11] See, for instance, 'Offshore Tax Havens Reject Calls for Transparency', at http://www.twnside.org/title/havens.htm.

[12] Society of Estate and Trust Practitioners (2002).

[13] The OECD has dropped the 'no substantial activities' criterion from its list of criteria. The other criteria for deciding whether a country is a tax haven are the absence of taxes or very low taxes, the lack of effective exchange of information with other tax authorities, and a lack of transparency on its tax regime. The OECD has stressed that it does not consider the presence of zero or nominal taxes alone to indicate a harmful tax regime, simply that it is 'a gateway criterion to determine those situations in which an analysis of the other criteria is necessary'. This came as a result of pressure from jurisdictions who felt the OECD was conflating tax avoidance with tax evasion.

18.3 Small developing states' experiences with standard-setting bodies

18.3.1 Membership and participation

18.3.1.1 The OECD[14]

The OECD is a thirty-member organisation of what are developed economies with a select few EU accession states and large developing countries. The OECD's Harmful Tax Initiative has come under great scrutiny for its perceived lack of inclusion of non-OECD members and focus on non-OECD jurisdictions, principally from representatives of small developing states who were the initial targets of Harmful Tax efforts. The OECD's response was to create its own Global Forum on Taxation (GFT), which ostensibly is open to non-OECD members as well. Attendance at the GFT, however, is by OECD invitation only, and jurisdictions targeted by the OECD were allowed to participate only *after* they had committed to the principles of the HTI. In addition, the role of the GFT in actually formulating the standards is very much in doubt, and many developing countries feel that the GFT is a consultative body in which developing countries have no substantive input in standard formation. The Committee on Fiscal Affairs has a number of working groups[15] to explore the implementation of specific elements of the HTI; these groups include a small number of developing countries but are nonetheless predominantly OECD-member bodies.

Despite the large number of expert fora considering tax co-operation from the perspective of both OECD and non-OECD countries, such as the

[14] Present OECD member states (with dates of accession) are Austria (1961), Belgium (1961), Canada (1961), Denmark (1961), France (1961), Germany (1961), Greece (1961), Iceland (1961), Ireland (1961), Italy (1961), Luxembourg (1961), Netherlands (1961), Norway (1961), Portugal (1961), Spain (1961), Sweden (1961), Switzerland (1961), Turkey (1961), United Kingdom (1961), United States (1961), Japan (1964), Finland (1969), Australia (1971), New Zealand (1973), Mexico (1994), Czech Republic (1995), Korea (1996), Hungary (1996) and Poland (1996). It is explicitly designed and mandated by its own legislation to promote the interests of its member states. The mandate for the HTI arose from a 1996 meeting of the OECD Council of Ministers (comprising member state representatives). Much of the initial HTI work was undertaken by the OECD's Committee on Fiscal Affairs, whose 1998 'Harmful Tax Practices: An Emerging Global Issue' report was produced with little consultation outside of a core group of experts drawn from OECD member states. (McIntyre, 2002).

[15] These working groups include the Forum on Harmful Tax Practices, the Global Forum Working Group on Effective Exchange of Information, the Working Party on Tax Evasion and Avoidance, and the Joint Ad Hoc Group on Accounts.

International Tax and Investment Organisation (ITIO), the Commonwealth Association of Tax Administrators, and the UN Ad Hoc Group of Experts on International Co-operation on Tax Matters, the OECD has refused to create any formal channels for these organisations to participate in the formulation and adoption of the HTI guidelines. The OECD also refused, with the exception of selected conferences or peripheral fora, to allow full participation by multilateral institutions such as the IMF and World Bank, though these organisations are seen by many small developing states as honest brokers in the process.

Concerns that small developing states' interests were being ignored were fuelled by a list of seventeen questions submitted in March 2001 to the OECD by the ITIO, seeking to clarify several fundamental points regarding the HTI.[16] The questions sought to identify whether the OECD was ensuring a 'level playing field' for both members and non-members, and whether it supported the creation of a 'truly inclusive' forum where non-OECD members would be treated as equal partners in the formulation, adoption and assessment of the standards. These seventeen questions remained without a response for five months until a high-level intervention (by the co-chair of the OECD's Joint Working Group).[17] The written responses, none of which were seen as plain and explicit, were received only two weeks before an OECD deadline for jurisdictions to sign onto the HTI or face the threat of sanctions.

18.3.1.2 FATF

The original framework for international coordination of anti-money laundering efforts was established by the Basel Committee in 1988.[18] FATF, which meets under the auspices of the OECD, was established by the G-7 Heads of State and President of the European Commission in 1989 to

[16] The ITIO (www.itio.org) was established in March 2001 as a forum for small developing economies to discuss international tax and investment measures such as the OECD's Harmful Tax Initiative. Members currently comprise Anguilla, Antigua and Barbuda, Bahamas, Barbados, Belize, British Virgin Islands, Cayman Islands, Cook Islands, Malaysia, St Kitts and Nevis, St Lucia, Turks and Caicos Islands and Vanuatu. For a list of questions submitted to the OECD by the ITIO, see 'Offshore Jurisdictions Push OECD to Respond to Questions', TaxNews.com, June 2001. [17] Sanders (2001).

[18] The 'first significant step towards the international preventive regulation of financial institutions with respect to money laundering' was the Basel Committee's 1988 *Statement of Principles on the Prevention of Criminal Use of the Banking System for the Purpose of Money-Laundering*, which was drafted by the United States representatives from the Federal Reserve, the Federal Deposit Insurance Corporation and the Comptroller of the Currency (Castle and Broomhall, 1998).

continue these efforts. The original FATF membership (the 'FATF-16') was restricted to developed economies, comprising the G-7 member states, the European Commission and eight other developed economies. Less than a year after FATF's creation, a series of consultations between three internal working groups (chaired by OECD states and drawing upon experts from FATF-16 member countries) produced the FATF Forty Recommendations, which became the basis for its subsequent work.

Only after 1991, after the approval of the Forty Recommendations, did FATF expand its membership[19] to include a few large developing states, and three of the largest developing economies (Argentina, Brazil and Mexico) did not become members until 2000. Invitations issued to potential members were explicitly conditioned on full prior acceptance of the Forty Recommendations.[20] Further FATF expansion has been thrown into doubt by a controversial 1994 agreement to restrict the FATF membership in order to facilitate decision-making and manageability.[21] Additionally, any future FATF expansion will be explicitly limited to strategically important countries, indefinitely postponing the possibility of small developing country participation in FATF decision-making. In 1996, FATF revised its Forty Recommendations to reflect its new membership, although there is a widespread feeling that these changes were 'not dramatic'.[22] In 2001, FATF members, in an extraordinary Plenary Session a month after the 11 September terrorist attacks, expanded their mandate by issuing the eight Special Recommendations on Terrorist Financing. FATF then invited all non-FATF countries 'to participate on the same terms as FATF members', although this participation is mostly limited to completing

[19] Present FATF members are Argentina, Australia, Austria, Belgium, Brazil, Canada, Denmark, European Commission, Finland, France, Germany, Greece, Gulf Co-operation Council, Hong Kong SAR, Iceland, Ireland, Italy, Japan, Luxembourg, Mexico, the Netherlands, New Zealand, Norway, Portugal, Singapore, Spain, Sweden, Switzerland, Turkey, United Kingdom and the United States.

[20] FATF Press Communiqué, 4 June 1991, available at http://www1.oecd.org/fatf/pdf/PR-19910604_en.pdf.

[21] The 1994 FATF Annual Report states that 'there was agreement that a significant increase in the size of the FATF would prejudice its flexibility and efficiency. Hence it was decided that there should be no more than a very limited expansion. However, the FATF will be examining further the possibility of setting up additional regional task forces [i.e. regional bodies].'

[22] The British Bankers' Association criticised the Public Consultation Paper issued by FATF for the 1996 Review, raising concerns that the 'open consultation period [given] has been relatively short, with much of it occurring over traditional holiday months, [to review a] lengthy, and at times difficult document'.

self-assessments and occasional consultations (by FATF invitation) on selected elements of the Special Recommendations.

FATF has established several 'FATF-style' regional bodies[23] which include many small developing states. Preconditions for membership in these bodies include full acceptance of the Forty Recommendations, the completion of annual self-assessments and periodic on-site assessments by FATF delegations. The role of these regional groups, many of which represent the only means of participation for small developing states, is deliberately restricted.[24] They are granted only observer status within FATF and its thrice-yearly Plenary Meetings, where decisions are made by consensus of FATF members. The regional bodies' role is largely limited to conducting mutual evaluations of economies outside the core FATF membership and, on occasion, adding regionally specific principles to the Forty Recommendations.[25]

18.3.1.3 The Basel Committee

The Basel Committee on Banking Supervision, established in 1974 by the central bank Governors of the G-10, comprises nearly thirty technical working groups and task forces. Its membership, however, is exclusively drawn from the regulatory bodies, finance ministries and central banks of thirteen developed economies.[26] The Basel Committee has published two interrelated standards – the Basel Capital Accord and the Basel Core Principles for Effective Banking Supervision.

The Basel Committee is but one of three committees[27] of the Bank for International Settlements (BIS). Before 1996, the membership of the BIS was limited to the G-10, Switzerland, and a small number of EU accession and

[23] These are the Asia/Pacific Group on Money Laundering (APG), Caribbean Financial Action Task Force (CFATF), Council of Europe PC-R-EV, Eastern and Southern Africa Anti-Money Laundering Group (ESAAMLG), and the Financial Action Task Force on Money Laundering in South America (GAFISUD).

[24] This is based in FATF policy, which states that 'FATF's strategy for contacts with non-member countries has continued to be based on [the] principle that activities are oriented towards encouraging countries to adopt the FATF Recommendations and on monitoring and reinforcing this process rather than on the provision of routine training and technical assistance' (FATF 1996).

[25] In 1990, the Caribbean nations under CFATF developed nineteen additional recommendations (the 'Aruba Recommendations') to complement the FATF Forty Recommendations.

[26] The Committee's members are Belgium, Canada, France, Germany, Italy, Japan, Luxembourg, the Netherlands, Spain, Sweden, Switzerland, United Kingdom and United States.

[27] The three committees are the Basel Committee on Banking Supervision (BCBS), the Committee on the Global Financial System, and the Committee on Payment and Settlement Systems.

large developing countries (including South Africa and Turkey). In 1996, several large developing countries were invited to join the BIS[28] – however, the invitation list was restricted to those countries with the largest GDP, populations and financial centres. The BIS Board of Directors has an even more limited membership: it comprises the Governors of the central banks of Belgium, France, Germany, Italy and the UK and the Chairman of the Board of Governors of the US Federal Reserve, each of whom appoints another member of the same nationality. The Statutes of the BIS also provide for the election to the Board of not more than nine Governors of other member central banks. The elected members of the Board are currently all from developed countries (Canada, Japan, the Netherlands, Sweden and Switzerland).[29]

The Basel Committee meets four times a year, and its technical working groups and task forces also meet at regular intervals. The Basel Committee meetings, attended by the G-10 central bank Governors, are fora in which key decisions are made, including substantive changes to the financial standards and the functions and operations of the Committees themselves. While the Committee meetings are increasingly focused on emerging-market developments, still too often the perspective is that of the impact on G-10 economies. Many of the meetings in which developing countries are discussed are attended exclusively by G-10 representatives.[30]

Outreach efforts by the Basel Committee to developing states began with the Basel Core Principles for Effective Banking Supervision. To provide a forum to discuss implementation issues, the Committee's narrow working group of G-10 countries was supplemented by representatives from Chile, China, the Czech Republic, Hong Kong, Mexico, Russia and Thailand. In addition, the so-called Core Principles Liaison Group also included representatives from Argentina, Brazil, Hungary, India, Indonesia, Korea, Malaysia, Poland and Singapore.

Despite BIS claims to the contrary,[31] the influence of non-G-10 countries on the process of formulating and revising Basel guidelines has been

[28] Those countries invited to join were Brazil, India, China, Korea, Saudi Arabia, Hong Kong, Mexico, Singapore and Russia.

[29] This lack of developing country representation extends to the BIS staff as well – though the staff draws from twenty-nine countries, developing countries remain underrepresented (Griffith-Jones and Kimmis, 1998). [30] Ibid.

[31] Daniele Nouy, Secretary-General of the Basel Committee, told a World Bank Workshop in December 2000 that the Basel Core Principles were 'the first truly G-10/non-G-10 joint product'. This view is disputed in Andrew Walter's forthcoming volume, *The Political Economy of Global Financial Regulatory Standards: Implementation in East Asia.*

greatly exaggerated, and largely limited to providing feedback on implementation issues rather than participating in the formulation of the standards, which remains the jurisdiction of the Committee members. The perception that developing countries were being relegated to 'junior partner' status led to a near-boycott of the recent Basel II consultations by the Executives Meeting of East Asia–Pacific Central Banks (EMEAP), an alternative grouping of East Asian central bankers. Other Basel initiatives have seen little progress on this issue: the Committee recently established the Joint Forum on Financial Conglomerates to co-ordinate standard-setting efforts with the International Organisation of Securities Commissions (IOSCO) and the International Association of Insurance Supervisors (IAIS). The membership of the Forum, however, is restricted to the thirteen Committee members, with the EU Commission granted observer status.

Arguments traditionally put forward for such limited membership include the facilitation of consensus and quick decision-making, and the fact that the legitimacy of the Committee's work depends on the quality of its membership, reflecting the sophistication of a country's financial markets and the calibre of its supervisors.[32] This ignores the general acknowledgement that supervisors, banks and markets in a number of countries have now attained high levels of sophistication, and that an expansion of BIS membership may not be incompatible with its consensus-driven *modus operandi*. Despite these considerations, small developing country participation on the key BIS Committees continues to be on an ad hoc, informal basis.[33]

18.4 Effective implementation: obstacles and impacts

The dominance of standard-setting bodies by developed countries has resulted in a highly restricted view of the effects of implementing the standards. All but absent from the debate has been the consideration of adverse effects of adopting the standards on small developing countries.[34] The

[32] Cornford (2000).

[33] For a proposal aimed at increasing developing country representation in the BIS and the Basel Committee, see Griffith-Jones, 'Proposal for Increasing Developing Country Participation in Global Financial Governance', available at http://www.ids.ac.uk/ids/global/finance/pdfs/prop. pdf.

[34] A separate issue is the consequences of *not* adopting the standards (e.g. being placed on a list of non-cooperative states), which will be addressed in the following section of this chapter.

implementation of a number of guidelines will negatively impact the competitiveness of many developing economies. These jurisdictions acknowledge the need for increased prudential regulation because:

> [a]ppropriate regulation is generally accepted to be proportionate to the risks and benefits associated with the activity being regulated . . . [d]isproportionate and excessive regulation applied selectively to particular market participants burdens those participants with a competitive disadvantage. In an efficient market, unevenly applied regulatory burdens shift demand from one service provider (or jurisdiction) to another, as users search for a cost-efficient, low friction service. Regulatory limitations on services offered also shift demand.[35]

In addition, adoption of several standards threatens to restrict further the access of such states to international finance and make major lenders increasingly risk-averse to developing country lending.

Another fundamental concern which, until recently, was a peripheral issue for many standard-setting bodies, is that of resources for implementing the standards. Many developing countries with small administrations find that the adoption of the standards requires complex and onerous regulatory and administrative structures well beyond their current institutional capacity. Many small developing states require considerable resources to determine practical requirements and develop appropriate capacities to understand and address the technical issues involved in joining each initiative or in meeting its requirements. The provision of technical assistance remains largely on an ad hoc basis or is simply left to other multilateral institutions who face resource constraints of their own. Many standard-setting bodies have promised to provide technical assistance, yet have not created formal assistance programmes for implementing their own guidelines, or, even if they have, these have failed to deliver. As a result, there is an acute shortage of resources for implementation that has yet to be adequately addressed. The standard-setting bodies have created a 'no-win' regime for small developing states, who are being told to adopt measures which impose substantial fiscal costs, while at the same time eroding their financial standing and competitiveness in financial markets.

35 Stikeman and Elliot (2002).

18.4.1 The OECD

The OECD's HTI has attracted widespread criticism over its possible implications for the development strategies of many small states for whom the export of financial services is a major source of foreign exchange and a viable supply of development finance in jurisdictions with few or no natural resources and limited access to international finance.[36]

The HTI originally called for preferential tax rates which are available to offshore entities to be available to domestic businesses of the same type. This effectively eliminates crucial economic development measures such as export processing zones, tax holidays for export industries and special tax exemptions for exporters and foreign investors,[37] many of which have been used as successful development strategies by several small developing states such as Mauritius and Dubai. This provision was only removed after considerable opposition from targeted jurisdictions.

Additional concerns have been raised over the dramatic increase in the scope and remit of the HTI to include all geographically mobile service industries.[38] By covering all 'geographically mobile service industries', the HTI extends the OECD's possible remit to include banking, leasing, free zones, distribution centres, service centres, shipping, headquarters regimes, insurance, factoring, funds management, airport zones, international business centres, offices of foreign companies, co-ordination centres and logistics centres. The OECD can also expand its list at any time to any country to include anything else it defines as geographically mobile.[39] For many resource-poor small developing states with minuscule domestic markets, these service industries underpin their economic development strategies. The prospect of regulation in these industries by the OECD, whose membership is dominated by the major market contenders in financial services, raised justifiable questions regarding the legitimacy of their mandate and commercial conflicts of interest.

[36] See CARICOM (2000) for further details on the importance of the offshore banking sector for small Caribbean states.

[37] This is despite the recognition by the WTO, in its 1995 Agreement on Subsidies and Countervailing Measures, of the importance of subsidies for economic development for poorer developing states (Biswas, 2001).

[38] See, for instance, 'OECD Moves Forward in Counteracting Harmful Tax Practices' issued in Paris on 24 November 1999 (http://www1.oecd.org/media/release/nw99-114a.htm).

[39] Ministry of Industry and International Business (2001b).

These concerns have led to a widespread feeling that the HTI, rather than focusing efforts to hinder illegal tax evasion, will effectively create non-tariff barriers to the trade in financial services and place small developing states at a competitive disadvantage by placing onerous regulations inappropriate to the size and development status of these jurisdictions. The implications for the competitive position of many small states were suggested by the Financial Stability Forum's *Report of the Working Group on Offshore Centres*, which linked the rise of London as the largest offshore banking sector to regulations imposed on the US banking sector.[40] The continued abstention of non-compliant OECD jurisdictions such as Switzerland and Luxembourg, both major offshore financial centres, has raised fears of possible client migration to OECD jurisdictions which continue to provide 'harmful' tax incentives. Adopting the HTI guidelines, for many small developing states, threatens to remove a major source of development finance and economic growth, while increasing their reliance on a dwindling flow of developing country aid.

Jurisdictions targeted by the OECD HTI have called for OECD technical assistance and expertise to determine not only the implications of compliance, but also options available to affected jurisdictions for loss of business, before the deadline for compliance. The OECD has recently acknowledged the shortfall in resources among small developing states but has failed thus far to elaborate any specific offers of technical assistance. A small number of multilateral and regional bodies[41] have attempted to address the resource gap; however, donor efforts remain on a country-by-country basis and country demand far exceeds donor supply.

18.4.2 FATF

The FATF anti-money laundering and counter-terrorist financing measures pose significant implementation problems for the financial sector supervisors of many small developing states. Many supervisors are already overburdened with increasingly complex prudential regulations in the banking sector. The extension of their responsibilities to monitor both the

[40] These included capital controls through the Interest Equalisation Tax of 1964, the Foreign Credit and Exchange Act of 1965, cash reserve requirements on deposits imposed in 1977 and a ceiling on time deposits in 1979 (Hay, 2001).

[41] Such as the Commonwealth Secretariat, the Caribbean Development Bank and the Pacific Financial Technical Assistance Centre.

transactions and the internal controls of non-bank financial intermediaries threatens to weaken their primary activities in the absence of considerable technical assistance.[42] Compliance with FATF guidelines requires considerable (and expensive) revisions of current legislation, adding supervisory responsibility towards mutual assistance in criminal matters, forfeiture of the proceeds of crime, criminalising money laundering and extradition financial supervision, customer identification and suspicious activity reporting. Many of these legislative reforms must be further tailored to the specific circumstance of each economy. For example, many small developing economies are sustained by informal banking practices and cash-based transactions (the FATF guidelines, in line with G-7 practice, implicitly assume that most legal economic activity is credit-based).

> This phenomenon is not easily countered . . . [and] raises the larger issue of the feasibility of establishing reporting regimes in economies commonly exhibiting financial practices at variance with the dominant practices of the most developed state economies. Accordingly, it would be appropriate to develop the concept of 'suspicious transaction' on a case-by-case basis, developing reporting mechanisms and compliance schemes in tandem with this knowledge.[43]

For many small developing states, the costs of developing this sort of 'tailor-made' AML/CTF legislation is highly prohibitive. Compliance with several FATF guidelines requires sophisticated statistical infrastructure which is beyond the current resource capabilities of most developing economies.[44] Although increasing amounts of technical assistance are being made available by multilateral bodies, current levels of assistance are still far below requirements in many developing economies.[45]

A proposed solution for establishing FATF-compliant institutions (such as a Financial Intelligence Unit) has been the creation of regulatory bodies on a regional level, such as a Regional Supervisory Authority. However, this has proven difficult in many regions ideally suited for such a development. Many Caribbean jurisdictions, for example, enjoy close cooperation on a number of issues through several joint fora. However, CFATF members found that limited resources are already strained by conducting mutual

[42] Riechel (2000). [43] Castle (1999).

[44] See PFTAC (2002), which explores this issue in depth for Pacific island economies.

[45] Ibid. See tables 5 and 6 in Castle (1999) for current and planned technical assistance activities for anti-money laundering and counter-terrorist financing in the Asia–Pacific region.

evaluations, and the Secretariat was not able to complete a comprehensive regional technical assistance and training needs analysis until April 2002, well past the FATF compliance deadline. CFATF members found that:

> limited human and financial resources are severely strained, which mitigates against timely and full compliance with international standards. The various international initiatives have required the CFATF secretariat to attend several meetings that were not anticipated and for which no budgetary provisions were made, straining our core work – the mutual evaluation program . . . [there is a] growing fatigue and frustration of many countries, particularly the small ones, with the demands of various international initiatives, which generate unceasing requests to provide information – to many different organizations that do not appear to have coordinated their efforts.[46]

Such regional solutions, given the complexities of co-ordinating legal and criminal cooperation between sovereign states, are highly unlikely within the timeframe proposed by FATF.[47] Thus small developing states face a double blow: they are given impractical FATF deadlines (given current levels of resources), and then face the possibility of being placed on the list of non-cooperative countries and territories (NCCT) for 'obstructing international co-operation against money laundering'; that is, failing to provide adequate resources towards anti-money laundering infrastructure.[48]

18.4.3 The Basel Committee

The landmark 1988 Basel Capital Accord, setting the minimum capital level requirement for internationally active banks in over 100 subscriber jurisdictions, was criticised from many quarters for its adverse impact on developing country financial systems and distortions in the international banking industry leading up to the Asian financial crisis in late 1997. In response to many of these concerns, the Basel Committee began work on a New Capital Accord (Basel II),[49] which sought to alleviate concerns of both

[46] World Bank and IMF (2002). [47] Ibid.

[48] The FATF lists both 'the failure to provide the administrative and judicial authorities with the necessary financial, human or technical resources to ensure adequate oversight and to conduct investigations' and the 'absence of a financial intelligence unit or of an equivalent mechanism' as grounds for inclusion on its 'blacklist' (FATF, 2000).

[49] The text of the new Basel II proposal is available from the BIS website at http://www.bis.org/publ/bcbsca01.pdf. For an excellent analysis of the content of the new Accord, and its implications for developing countries, see Cornford (2000).

developing country regulators and representatives from major internationally active banks. Unfortunately, it does not appear clear that the concerns of these two groups of stakeholders were adequately balanced, with Basel II having a potentially negative impact on small developing states.

Under the 1998 Accord, uniform risk weights were assigned according to the type and perceived riskiness of the borrower. Borrowers were categorised according to OECD/non-OECD status and whether the borrowing institution was a sovereign, corporation or bank. Also included within the risk profile was the loan's maturity (i.e. short- or long-term). The new Accord proposes a Standardised Approach (a slight modification of the 1998 Accord) and a new Internal Ratings Based Approach (IRB).[50] The IRB approach was intentionally designed to make greater use of banks' own internal risk management systems, and reduce perverse incentives created by crude distinctions contained in the 1998 Accord.[51] Nonetheless, the implications for small developing states of the switch to an IRB system by large internationally active banks are profound.

The primary effect of the adoption of the IRB approach will be increased lending costs and a reduction in bank lending for small developing states. The IRB approach links capital requirements and risk weights to a country's credit rating. The highly convex shape of the IRB curve[52] reveals that while at high ratings the IRB approach gives lower capital requirements, at lower ratings the IRB approach can give very significantly increased capital requirements. The highly exponential rise of risk weightings along the spectrum of probability of default (PD) will have several effects. First, many lower-rated sovereigns, which include many small developing states, may experience prohibitive increases in lending costs. A study by Powell (2001) estimates the increase in the costs of funds for countries rated below BBB to be around 235 basis points (which increases to 260 basis points once Mexico and Korea are excluded), and that for countries rated BB the increase is calculated at 384 basis points.[53] The clear implications are that many parts of the developing world will no longer be able to

[50] The IRB approach is itself split into a Foundation Internal Ratings Based Approach and an Advanced Internal Ratings Based Approach.

[51] Griffith-Jones and Spratt (2001).

[52] See table 4, 'Potential Impact in Risk Weightings Implied by Basel II' in Reisen (2001) for a detailed breakdown of the IRB curve.

[53] To place these numbers in dollar terms, Powell calculates that the increased capital requirements for countries rated below BBB amounts to about $93 billion on total liabilities of those countries to BIS reporting banks of some $530 billion. Excluding Mexico, the relevant figures are about $80 billion on a stock of just over $400 billion (Powell, 2001).

access international finance on sustainable terms, and that the effects will be most pronounced in those lowest-rated countries in greatest need of finance.

Another implication is the coexistence of two 'types' of banking: sophisticated banks using the IRB approach (which decreases the incentive to hold lower-rated loans), decreasing potentially risky lending, alongside less sophisticated banks (using the standardised approach) who retain an incentive to hold risky loans, with the perverse result of concentrating high-risk loans in the hands of banks with relatively low credit risk expertise.[54]

The IRB approach will also increase the pro-cyclical tendencies of major bank lending which will serve to exacerbate financial crises. During an upswing, average PD will fall, raising ratings, and under the IRB approach the exponentially lower capital requirements will increase incentives to lend. During a downturn, the chain of events reverses. If banks' lending is constrained by regulatory capital requirements, and as capital is difficult to raise in recessions, there is a serious risk of credit crunches in recession.[55] As lending by multilateral agencies has become more uncertain after the recent crises in Asia, Russia and Argentina, the implications of IRB-driven pro-cyclical lending are a cause for concern among small developing states. The pro-cyclical elements of the IRB approach are compounded by other elements in the Basel Capital Accord, namely provisions setting lower risk weights for claims of a shorter duration. The Accord sets the risk weight for emerging-market lending at 20 per cent for claims of less than one year, but 100 per cent for claims of more than one year. These provisions effectively discourage interbank lending to small developing states, and tilt the structure of developing country capital imports towards short-term debt, which has been identified as the single most important precursor of financial crises.[56]

A seminal paper by Persaud (2000) examined the role of market expectations and risk management systems, and found that in the short run, market participants were increasingly prone to herding behaviour and contagion. The key realisation was that market participants behave strategically (i.e. vis-à-vis one another) yet risk management systems, such as the

[54] The Basel Committee has modified the IRB curve since the January 2001 consultative paper. The BCBS has flattened the IRB curve, implying lower capital requirements for lower-rated borrowers. While this is an improvement on the January 2001 proposal for small developing states, it still implies higher capital requirements than the existing 1998 Accord.

[55] Griffith-Jones et al. (2002).

[56] Reisen (2001).

Daily Earnings at Risk (DEAR) limit, measure risk statically (i.e. at a point in time, without strategic considerations). Persaud portrays a vicious cycle of a rise in market volatility leading to the DEAR limits of some banks being hit. Several banks then sell the same asset simultaneously, raising market volatility, which hit more banks' DEAR limits. Paradoxically, it is precisely the adoption of uniform risk management systems (such as the IRB) that leads to widespread herding and contagion.[57] On this issue, Griffith-Jones and Spratt (2001) note that:

> the view that greater risk sensitivity may have pro-cyclical results is not disputed by the Basel Committee. Rather, it is argued that the benefits will outweigh the costs. However, as is the case with much of the New Accord, the trade-offs in terms of costs and benefits are viewed in terms of their impact on the major banks. For the developing world, it is likely that they will feel the costs disproportionately (reduced lending coupled with increased scale of crises) while simultaneously attracting none of the benefits.

Introducing the IRB approach alongside the standardised risk weights will also have the effect of increasing consolidation in the banking industry, with serious implications for financial access for many small developing states. Most major internationally active banks are expected to adopt the IRB approach, thereby enhancing their competitive advantages through the use of more sophisticated (and therefore lower) capital requirements. In many small developing economies, this implies increasing control of the domestic banking sector, and an increase in the proportion of banks using the harmful IRB approach, and a concomitant decrease in lending for all but the most highly rated sovereigns.[58]

The new Accord's reliance on credit ratings agencies also poses additional, and highly significant, risks for small developing economies. There is a widespread view that the performance of such agencies, most notably in the Asian crisis, has been plagued by highly pro-cyclical behaviour, such as

[57] 'The paradox is that if one or two banks followed a DEAR limit and others did not, those banks would have an effective risk management system that at the margin would support the financial system. But if every bank were to follow the same approach, given that these banks follow each other into and out of markets, the DEAR limit would contribute to systemic risk. It is ironic, therefore, that the Basel Committee on Banking Supervision is supporting the rapid adoption of these systems across all banks and encouraging investors to follow suit' (Persaud, 2000).

[58] Griffith-Jones and Spratt (2001).

the large and swift downgrading of sovereigns.[59] The new Accord sets out eligibility criteria for agencies regarding their objectivity, independence, transparency and size. However, there are concerns that despite these minimum eligibility criteria, there may be a 'race to the bottom' to provide 'convenient' (i.e. market-following) ratings which even the larger, more reputable agencies may find difficult to resist.[60] This consideration is further reinforced by evidence that major credit rating agencies often disagree in ratings for the same sovereigns, and that the differential widens substantially for lower-rated sovereigns. Cornford (2000) notes that a 1995 survey of two large credit rating agencies showed agreement of AA/Aa or above in 67 per cent of the cases, for other ratings of investment grade in 56 per cent of the cases, and for ratings below investment grade in 29 per cent of the cases. The low level of agreement for lower-rated sovereigns, which includes the vast majority of small developing states, is especially troubling as it makes changes in ratings consensus particularly difficult to forecast.[61]

Many observers find it unsurprising that the IRB approach contains numerous inconsistencies with the goals of small developing economies, as the system is essentially based on the current (and highly complex) practices of the large G-10 based private banks. Powell (2001) notes that the focus of the Basel Committee has been to produce general principles instead of a detailed methodology. While this may be appropriate for large banks that have been developing these methodologies for some time, many small developing country authorities find the new Basel guidelines extremely difficult to implement or adapt to domestic conditions. The proposed move towards the 'two-tiered' (IRB and standardised) approach places the financial authorities in a difficult position:

> They may attempt to implement an IRB approach as described in the proposals. In this case they will face several difficulties and the calibration may not be appropriate. A sub-alternative may be to attempt to adapt the approach to the particular emerging country circumstances . . . It is likely that, given the proposals as they stand, most authorities will choose to implement the standardised approach. In that case . . . very little will change and the new proposals will not

[59] Thailand, for example, was downgraded four notches by both Moody's and Standard and Poor's between July 1997 and early 1998; Indonesia five notches by Moody's and six by Standard and Poor's between June 1997 and early 1998; and Republic of Korea six notches by Moody's and no less than ten by Standard and Poor's during the same period (Cornford, 2000).

[60] Powell (2001). [61] Cornford (2000).

> imply a significant advance over the 1988 Accord. From the standpoint of emerging economies, this would be a lost opportunity. Put crudely, the new standard was not designed for them.[62]

It is precisely the inability of banks in emerging markets and small states to implement the IRB that lies at the heart of the trade issue. Banks unable to implement this approach to risk evaluation will be forced to maintain the standard approach to risk assessment. This in turn will raise capital cost requirements for many of these banks and will make them either targets for takeover or uncompetitive on local capital markets. It is precisely this effect that will have trade and commercial implications for the supply of financial services.

The implementation of the proposed Basel II Accord also places additional strains on the supervisory institutions of small developing states, which has led to a widespread feeling that implementation will be very complicated and demanding, if not impossible in the medium term.[63] The new Accord's market disclosure requirements (the so-called 'third pillar') allow market participants accurately to assess indicators of capital adequacy such as risk assessments, risk exposures and management processes. While these changes in reporting requirements may impose minor costs on large banks,[64] for many less sophisticated banks (which comprise the overwhelming majority in small developing states) implementation will pose significant challenges. Many developing country banks do not have robust ratings systems or historical data to estimate many IRB parameters, and the transition period of three years envisaged by the new Accord may not be long enough to build such databases.[65]

Effective implementation of Basel II will also require significant upgrading of prudential supervision by domestic authorities. The new Accord requires supervisors not only to monitor capital adequacy levels, but also to review in detail the risk profile, risk management process and internal

62 Powell (2001). 63 Griffith-Jones and Spratt (2001).

64 Indeed, this is the explicit assumption of the Committee, which 'does not expect the incremental costs of making such information public to be high, since banks will be collecting this data for internal purposes and they will be benefiting from the more risk sensitive capital requirements that result from the use of bank specific inputs' (BCBS, 2001b).

65 This problem is not restricted to developing country banks. The Basel Committee conducted an initial survey of large internationally active banks in order to estimate the quantitative effects of the proposal on their capital requirements. The Committee was disappointed in the modest number of banks worldwide that could provide meaningful distributions of credit quality, even for their corporate portfolios (Reserve Bank of India, 2001).

controls of all banks operating in their jurisdiction. Many financial institutions in small developing economies have operated in environments with at best lax rules regarding transparency, and the new Accord will require additional implementation of accounting and auditing standards to make risk-weighted capital-to-asset ratios work. The limited development of capital markets in many small developing economies further constrains the ability of both regulatory authorities and market agents to assess the quality of capital reported by banks, especially in situations where asset ownership is very concentrated.[66]

In light of the 'assessment fatigue' facing many financial regulators in small developing economies, the Basel Committee no longer proposes adherence to the IMF's SDDS, the Committee's Core Principles for Effective Banking Supervision, or the IOSCO's thirty Objectives and Principles of Securities Regulation as preconditions for preferential risk weights. Nonetheless, the new Accord 'will represent a quantum increase in the complexity of supervisors' responsibilities in most countries, and probably a corresponding increase in the tasks involved in assessment exercises'.[67]

18.5 Assessment, compliance and small developing states

The methodologies for both assessing levels of compliance and disciplining non-compliant jurisdictions are key elements in the coverage and legitimacy of the standard-setting bodies. The assessment and compliance regimes are the means by which the guidelines are propagated and reinforced in a variety of jurisdictions, and each standard-setting body has developed its own methodologies tailored to its own unique circumstances and vision.

For many small developing states, the means by which the standards in question have been assessed and enforced have raised justifiable questions of whether or not a 'level playing field' exists vis-à-vis the members of the standard-setting bodies. There are concerns that jurisdictions which are

[66] 'In situations where asset ownership, both financial and real, is very concentrated, supervisors face difficulties in determining whether shareholders' wealth is really at risk when they supply equity capital to a bank, since shareholders can finance their capital contribution from a related party, including non-financial corporations. Accounting capital, therefore, does not necessarily reflect the "true" riskiness of banks' (Latin American Shadow Regulatory Committee, 2001).

[67] Cornford (2000).

members of the standard-setting bodies are being treated more leniently than non-members, and that disproportionate attention is being focused on small developing states. Many standard-setting bodies have opted for a 'name and shame' approach, producing lists of dissenting states and suggested guidelines for sanctions under the name of 'co-ordinated defensive measures'. The process by which these so-called 'blacklists' are produced remains, in many standard-setting bodies, one in which the basic principles of corporate governance (namely transparency, accountability and the protection of minority shareholders) are all but absent.

Various standard-setting bodies have opted to 'outsource' the assessment of jurisdictions to multilateral financial institutions (MFIs). While the MFIs draw from a more universal membership, they face considerable capacity constraints in their global surveillance activities, compromising the periodicity of assessment data and coverage of small developing economies. Additionally, the manner in which MFI assessments are interpreted by the market threatens to exacerbate contagion and herding in developing country financial crises.

Many standard-setting bodies have faced criticism regarding the feasibility of assessing a wide number of unique domestic financial systems against a single set of criteria, then enforcing compliance to a fixed deadline with guidelines that are often vague and inconsistently revised. The methodologies of assessment and enforcement suffer from a 'one-size-fits-all' approach, ignoring the need for flexible, feasible deadlines which account for different stages of development, institutional capacity and economic structure.[68] Although the standard-setting bodies recognise the need for a wide, participatory dialogue, far too often the reality is one in which targeted jurisdictions are involved only 'at the receiving end', where dialogue is restricted to how the jurisdictions will comply and in what timeframe.

More fundamentally, inclusion on such a 'blacklist' has potentially devastating effects on the economic prospects of targeted jurisdictions, well beyond the sector targeted by the OECD. There are justifiable concerns that forcing legislative reform through highly coercive, unilateral, sanctions-based regimes will undermine country ownership, decrease the effectiveness of global financial standards, and further marginalise small developing states in structuring the international financial system.

[68] IMF (2001).

18.5.1 *The OECD*

The HTI methodology for determining jurisdictional compliance is centred on the Forum on Harmful Tax Practices, an OECD-member body established by the 1998 OECD HT Report. The Forum, which reports to the OECD's Committee on Fiscal Affairs,[69] oversees a number of study groups comprised largely of experts drawn from OECD member countries. These study groups determine which jurisdictions should be considered tax havens based on the HTI guidelines, with individual members given a jurisdiction to assess. The 1998 Report's 'List of Uncooperative Tax Havens', listing forty-seven target jurisdictions, was drawn up using a combination of published sources and discussions within the OECD study groups. The targeted jurisdictions were given a deadline of 31 July 2001 to make an explicit commitment to implement the OECD guidelines. The jurisdictions were given six months to formulate an 'acceptable' schedule of changes, describing a series of target dates to ensure that the 'harmful' aspects of their tax policies were removed by 31 December 2005. If the OECD's Committee on Fiscal Affairs at any time felt that a jurisdiction had not met its target dates, or not made 'concrete and significant action' during the first year of the commitment, the Committee placed the jurisdiction on their List of Uncooperative Tax Havens.

The 1998 Report came under immediate and intense criticism by both independent experts and targeted jurisdictions on a number of issues. First, many small developing states felt that the so-called blacklist had been drawn up with a 'subjective, largely anecdotal, non-introspective and non-benchmarked approach . . . [lacking] any form of scholarly research methodology'.[70] Indeed, the OECD's claim that it engaged targeted jurisdictions in a bilateral dialogue was undermined by the widespread perception that

> the classification of jurisdictions as tax havens was effected by the OECD without reference to those targeted. Subsequently, the acceptability or otherwise of a commitment demanded by the OECD and given by any of those jurisdictions was determined exclusively by the OECD. Only after such a commitment is deemed acceptable is that jurisdiction invited to join the Global Forum which will determine the implementation plans and the form of exchange of information agreements to be utilised by all those jurisdictions going forward.[71]

[69] The Committee on Fiscal Affairs, in turn, is overseen by the OECD Council of Ministers.

[70] Society of Trust and Estate Practitioners (2002). [71] Ibid.

With no clear, formal channels for the substantive participation of small developing states, the OECD has given the impression to many supervisors in targeted jurisdictions that it is solely interested in 'dialogue' which results in jurisdictions adopting the HTI guidelines, viewing any decision not to comply as 'political' rather than grounded in legitimate concerns over the appropriateness of the guidelines or the feasibility of timelines imposed for compliance.[72]

Perhaps the most contentious part of the OECD HTI assessment process has been the perceived bias against non-OECD members, and small developing economies in particular. The 1998 Report focused almost exclusively on financial vehicles established in non-OECD countries, despite the fact that OECD member states account for 80 per cent of trade in non-resident financial services (i.e. offshore banking).[73] Grynberg and Chilala (2001) note the 'subtle difference in language in the OECD report between its dealings with OECD members' preferential regimes as "potentially" harmful . . . and those of non-OECD measures which are deemed unambiguously harmful', although in reality many OECD offshore centres lag substantially behind their non-OECD counterparts in adopting prudential regulations.[74]

The 1998 Report excluded several prominent OECD financial centres,[75] most notably Switzerland and Luxembourg, from the List of Uncooperative Tax Havens despite the substantial legislative limitations on their abilities to exchange financial information and compromise client privacy. Both countries have dissented from the entire HTI initiative and, despite the fact that these non-cooperating OECD jurisdictions are the principal competitors

[72] The fundamental approach of the OECD has been to encourage non-compliant jurisdictions to 'associate themselves with the 1998 Report and to agree to its principles; and hold regional seminars that will encourage and assist nonmember economies to remove features of their preferential regimes that are potentially harmful' (OECD, 2001).

[73] 'The restricted focus is curious, particularly as the initial report of the FSF acknowledged difficulty in distinguishing so-called "offshore activity" within the major developed states from that in smaller and developing states' (Society of Trust and Estate Practitioners, 2002).

[74] See Society of Trust and Estate Practitioners (2001) for a detailed comparison.

[75] The OECD Report failed to address potentially 'harmful' offshore regimes such as the United States, the United Kingdom, Ireland, the Netherlands and Hungary (with its regime of Hungarian Offshore Companies, which has attracted considerable attention in the tax world). Excluded as well were holding company regimes for Ireland, the Netherlands, Germany and Switzerland. The report indicates that the OECD Forum 'reached no conclusions' as to whether these are harmful preferential regimes in the light of 'complexities raised by such regimes, including their possible interaction with tax treaties and with general principles of domestic law'. There are few indications as to whether the same 'complexities' were explored for non-OECD jurisdictions (Louis, 2000).

for non-resident financial services, the OECD has been reluctant to impose the same measures threatened to non-OECD jurisdictions.[76] The OECD claims that there is 'only one distinction: cooperative versus uncooperative'; however the Swiss Economics Minister was able to announce that Swiss banking secrecy laws were 'not negotiable' with no apparent threat of OECD sanctions. The Republic of Nauru, in contrast, whose financial sector is marginal compared to that of Switzerland, came under considerable OECD pressure when it dissented from its inclusion on the OECD List. The continued abstentions of Switzerland and Luxembourg were recently joined by Portugal and Belgium, who both dissented from the 2001 OECD HTI Report. Many states in the US, such as Delaware, Montana and Colorado, have also indicated that they will not implement the commitment given by the US federal government. Controversially, the 1998 Report additionally proposed that sanctions against non-OECD jurisdictions would apply two years earlier than their OECD counterparts.[77]

The perceived inequities in the treatment of non-OECD jurisdictions was highlighted in a May 2001 statement by the US Treasury Secretary Paul O'Neill, who stated that 'in order for the OECD initiative to have the legitimacy it needs to succeed, jurisdictions inside the OECD must be treated no more severely than similarly situated OECD Member Countries'. Secretary O'Neill additionally warned that 'OECD Member Countries should hold themselves to standards and timelines at least as rigorous as those to which they hold jurisdictions that are not part of the OECD.'[78]

The public criticism by the Treasury Secretary lent credibility to the concerns of small developing states, although several issues remain. The list of criteria by which the OECD determines a tax regime to be 'harmful' has been criticised as excessively vague, and upon publication of the List of Uncooperative Tax Havens in the 1998 Report, many targeted jurisdictions were unclear as to the steps required to comply with the HTI. The OECD,

[76] This is unsurprising, as the OECD 1960 Convention 'provides that, if an OECD Member abstains from voting on a decision or recommendation, such abstention will not invalidate the decision or recommendation. It will apply to the other Members, but not to the abstaining Member. Another provision of the reconstitution helps to balance accomplishing the goals of the OECD with the sovereignty of its Members: an OECD decision does not bind any Member until it has complied with the requirements of its own constitutional procedures' (Zagaris, 2001).

[77] This distinction has since been removed.

[78] Secretary O'Neill further objected to the perception that the OECD was attempting to harmonise tax rates and stifle global tax competition. For a full text of his statement, see http://www.ustreas.gov/press/releases/po366.htm.

in turn, failed to complete the six 'application notes' (defining commitments for listed jurisdictions) in time for the initial July 2001 deadline. Jurisdictions were effectively being asked to sign, under threat of collective sanction, up to commitments which the OECD itself had not accurately defined.[79] In response to US and small developing state criticism, the OECD has also been forced to drop several 'non-core' elements of the initiative such as the 'no substantial activities' and 'ring fencing' criteria, and focus exclusively on commitments to transparency and effective information exchange. Nevertheless, non-transparent OECD jurisdictions such as Switzerland continue to operate freely without threat of sanction.

The OECD's 'co-ordinated defensive measures' raise justifiable concerns that the measures are little more than 'punitive sanctions . . . applied on a collective or bilateral basis'.[80] The list of proposed sanctions includes:

i. To disallow deductions, exemptions, credits or other allowances related to transactions with Uncooperative Tax Havens or transactions taking advantage of their harmful tax practices;
ii. To require comprehensive information reporting rules for transactions involving Uncooperative Tax Havens or taking advantage of their harmful tax practices, supported by substantial penalties for inaccurate reporting or non-reporting of such transactions;
iii. To impose withholding taxes on certain payments to residents of Uncooperative Tax Havens;
iv. To enhance audit and enforcement activities with respect to Uncooperative Tax Havens and transactions taking advantage of their harmful tax practices;
v. To ensure that any existing and new domestic defensive measures against harmful tax practices are also applicable to transactions with Uncooperative Tax Havens and to transactions taking advantage of their harmful tax practices;
vi. Not to enter into any comprehensive income tax conventions with Uncooperative Tax Havens, and to consider terminating any such existing conventions unless certain conditions are met;
vii. To impose transactional charges or levies on certain transactions involving Uncooperative Tax Havens.[81]

[79] Grynberg and Chilala (2001). The six application notes covered transparency/exchange of information, transfer pricing, ring fencing, holding companies, fund management and shipping.
[80] Ibid. [81] OECD (2000).

In addition to this list, the OECD had also recommended to its members that they review all non-essential aid to listed jurisdictions. This process, characterised by Secretary O'Neill as 'highly coercive', had been criticised by many multilateral institutions such as the IMF[82] which have called upon the OECD to adopt a more voluntary and cooperative approach to non-compliant jurisdictions. There were concerns that the OECD's 'blacklist' approach would tarnish the entire financial sectors of many small developing states, many of which depend on legitimate financial activity to achieve key development goals. Although several of the 1998 criteria have been dropped from the OECD's list, inclusion on the Uncooperative Tax Haven list has further maligned the financial sectors of small developing states in the eyes of many investors and development NGOs.[83]

18.5.2 FATF

The FATF model of compliance assessment rests on the twin pillars of self-assessment and mutual evaluation.[84] In the self-assessment exercise, each country must complete a common questionnaire on a yearly basis, providing detailed information on compliance with the Forty Recommendations. Each member country is then examined in turn by the FATF on the basis of an on-site visit conducted by a team of three or four selected experts from the legal, financial and law enforcement fields from FATF member governments. The FATF delegation then produces a Mutual Evaluation Report, which is sent to the examined jurisdiction for comment within twenty-one days. On the basis of the Mutual Evaluation Report and the completed self-assessment, the FATF Secretariat produces a draft report which is then submitted to FATF members at its Plenary Session, which debates the report[85] before its approval and inclusion in the Annual Report. These procedures have been adopted, with minor revisions, by each of the FATF-style regional bodies. For the recently developed eight Special Recommendations on

[82] The IMF has recently launched its own series of offshore financial centre assessments which are available at http://www.imf.org/external/np/ofca/ofca.asp.

[83] See UNCTAD (2001) and Persaud (2001).

[84] The FATF evaluation procedure is described in detail in FATF (2001).

[85] The debate includes representatives from the examined jurisdiction, the FATF delegation and FATF member states. However, FATF itself admits that 'the discussion time was generally reduced to about two hours or less per report, and this may have contributed to the reduced level of debate. The mutual evaluation discussions also became somewhat formal and less productive' (FATF, 2001).

Terrorist Financing, the first phase of implementation consisted of a self-assessment by all FATF members and regional bodies (completed in January 2002), with an invitation to all non-FATF jurisdictions to 'participate on the same terms as FATF members', although participation has thus far been limited to completing a standard self-assessment against the Special Recommendations and commenting on the Recommendations by FATF invitation.

The most controversial element of FATF's compliance methodology is the Non-Cooperative Countries and Territories (NCCTs) Initiative, which published the first NCCT list in the February 2000 Report on Non-Cooperative Countries and Territories.[86] The FATF secretariat, prior to publication of the 2000 Report, developed a set of criteria for evaluating NCCTs based on the Forty Recommendations. Jurisdictions determined to be 'non-cooperative' are first publicly identified by FATF, both on its website and in periodic press releases. The 2000 Report includes a list of suggested 'collective and co-ordinated countermeasures to better protect their financial systems and economies'.[87] FATF members have also agreed to issue advisories to countries on the NCCT list, requiring them to take extra care in business undertaken with counterparties in listed jurisdictions. The bulk of the NCCT work is undertaken by the FATF Ad Hoc Group on Non-Cooperative Countries and Territories, whose scope extends to jurisdiction both within and outside the FATF membership. The NCCT approach has also been adopted for the eight Special Recommendations, with a target date of June 2002 to identify publicly and begin countermeasures against non-compliant jurisdictions. The FATF NCCT approach served as a model for the OECD's List of Uncooperative Tax Havens, and regrettably shares many elements threatening the viability and interests of small developing economies.

The process by which countries have been selected for the NCCT list, much like the OECD HTI work, shows considerable bias against non-FATF economies. Jurisdictions targeted by the 2000 Report were alarmed by a review of twenty-nine jurisdictions which preceded the Report. Rather than an objective assessment of possible money-laundering regimes in a wide range of countries, FATF members instead were invited to nominate those jurisdictions where they had experienced 'difficulties' in the past, who were then examined by the Ad Hoc Group. Many of the same

[86] FATF (2000). [87] Ibid.

nominating FATF members were involved in evaluating the targeted jurisdictions for the 2000 Report and its NCCT list. In light of this subjective selection process, it came as no surprise to many observers that the 2000 Report, much like the first 1998 OECD HTI Report, focused exclusively on non-FATF jurisdictions, and included an NCCT list dominated by small developing states.[88] The Report notably failed to include a single evaluation of a FATF member economy, despite clear evidence that substantial money-laundering activities exist in many FATF members' jurisdictions, including Switzerland and Luxembourg (who both abstained from the OECD's HTI), the United States, Brazil, Mexico and Argentina.[89]

There have been concerns raised that the adoption of the eight Special Recommendations has been marked by relative leniency for non-compliant FATF members. For example, the June 2002 deadline for the NCCT list publication and the beginning of countermeasures has come and gone without any FATF action. Many observers feel that this is unsurprising considering the FATF acknowledgement that

> there is still some work to be done by the FATF to ensure that its members have fully implemented the Special Recommendations. With regard to Special Recommendation 8 (Non-profit organisations), for example, FATF members decided to give additional consideration of this issue before proceeding to a full analysis of the self-assessment results. With regard to SR 1 (Ratification and implementation of UN instruments), the self-assessment results show only four FATF members at full implementation.[90]

It is apparent that FATF views its guidelines as negotiable (i.e. in need of 'additional consideration') in the case of non-compliance by FATF members, while imposing them as 'best practice' on dissenting non-FATF jurisdictions. In addition, given the broad sweep of the FATF guidelines and the general complexity of financial sector reform, many small developing states felt that they were given too little time to determine the exact

[88] The 2000 Report singled out Bahamas, Cayman Islands, Cook Islands, Dominica, Israel, Lebanon, Liechtenstein, Marshall Islands, Nauru, Niue, Panama, Philippines, Russia, St Kitts and Nevis and St Vincent and the Grenadines as having 'serious systemic problems'.

[89] See Economist (2001) and Society of Trust and Estate Practitioners (2002) for evidence on money laundering in FATF economies. The absence of FATF member jurisdictions is significant as FATF has pledged to 'focus our attention on financial centres whose activities are of such character or significant size that, if there are shortcomings in their systems, they could undermine existing anti-money laundering regimes'.

[90] FATF (2002).

requirements for FATF compliance. In the case of the eight Special Recommendations, adopted only a month after the 9/11 attacks, the interpretative Guidance Notes were not disseminated until two months before the proposed deadline for compliance.

The FATF countermeasures have been criticised, much like the OECD's 'defensive measures', as being an overly harsh form of collective punishment, with an asymmetric and significantly negative impact on small developing economies. Possible countermeasures include:

i. Stringent requirements for identifying clients and enhancement of advisories, including jurisdiction-specific financial advisories, to financial institutions for identification of the beneficial owners before business relationships are established with individuals or companies from these countries;
ii. Enhanced relevant reporting mechanisms or systematic reporting of financial transactions on the basis that financial transactions with such countries are more likely to be suspicious;
iii. In considering requests for approving the establishment in FATF member countries of subsidiaries or branches or representative offices of banks, taking into account the fact that the relevant bank is from an NCCT;
iv. Warning non-financial sector businesses that transactions with entities within the NCCTs might run the risk of money laundering;
v. Consideration of whether it is desirable and feasible to condition, restrict, target or even prohibit financial transactions with such jurisdictions; and
vi. Prevent financial institutions located in identified non-cooperating countries or territories from using facilities (for example, information technology facilities) located in the FATF members' territory.

These countermeasures, in many small developing economies, stigmatise the investment climate of entire economies, far beyond the sector targeted by the NCCT criteria. In many small developing states, where the export of legitimate financial services is a primary source of foreign exchange, the effect has been devastating. Ferrance (2000) examined the effects of US and UK advisories on Antigua and Barbuda's financial services sector.[91] The relative costs of transacting business in the jurisdiction increased

[91] Ferrance (2000).

dramatically for several businesses operating in the jurisdiction, on average by 25 per cent! This resulted in several major banks closing their branches, not due to perceptions of money laundering, but simply due to increased cost. New investment in the financial services sector effectively stopped, with the resulting multiplier effect in the larger economy. The advisories conferred disproportionate bargaining power upon businesses wishing to establish a presence in the jurisdiction, forcing the government to increase incentives such as tax breaks and duty concessions further, leading to large falls in government revenues. Finally, the action by the US and UK governments by agreement with FATF caused a number of other non-FATF jurisdictions to follow suit, creating yet another multiplier effect.

The overwhelmingly negative implications of the FATF sanctions regime for many small developing states led to considerable criticism from many multilateral bodies. The IMF, in response to pressure from developing country directors on its Executive Board, has insisted that FATF members adopt a more 'universal, cooperative approach'.[92] The IMF has since placed a condition for a joint AML/CFT ROSC pilot project, stating that 'the FATF not undertake a further round of the non-cooperative countries and territories (NCCT) initiative, at least during the period of the [one-year] pilot project'.

18.5.3 The Basel Committee

The Basel Committee does not conduct formal assessments of jurisdictional adherence to its standards, nor has it issued any OECD- or FATF-style guidelines for coordinated action in case of non-compliant jurisdictions. These tasks have been left to multilateral financial institutions (MFIs) such as the IMF and World Bank, regional development banks and private sector bodies.

Indeed, it was stressed in several of the meetings held at the BIS that there was a fairly sharp and important distinction, broadly seen as desirable, whereby institutions like the BIS and the Committees linked to it formulated standards and norms for financial sectors and institutions like the IMF and the World Bank, which help disseminate them and survey their implementation in developing countries.[93]

[92] Eduardo Aninat, deputy managing director of the IMF, quoted in 'FATF to Soften Approach on "Naming and Shaming" ', TaxNews.com, 3 October 2002.

[93] Griffith-Jones and Kimmis (1999).

The primary focus of MFIs has been on the so-called 'second pillar' of the new Basel Capital Accord, which addresses the role of domestic authorities in monitoring capital adequacy and internal controls within their jurisdiction. The Basel Committee has deflected a considerable amount of criticism by 'outsourcing' its assessment and enforcement processes to multilateral bodies, many of which are seen as more cognisant of small developing country concerns. Nonetheless, the involvement of these bodies does not address several fundamental problems.

First, many MFIs face considerable capacity constraints in their ever-expanding surveillance role in the global financial system, leading to a bias against small developing countries. The IMF is currently charged with monitoring eleven codes and standards for a membership of 184 countries, regularly publishing Reports on the Observance of Standards and Codes, or ROSCs. However, the IMF as of September 2002 had only published 227 ROSCs for sixty-eight economies, with the vast majority of ROSCs focused on a small number of EU accession states and large developing countries.[94] The IMF has now moved towards publishing ROSCs as part of their Financial Sector Assessment Program (FSAP) evaluations of members' domestic financial systems. This approach, however, has only yielded two dozen FSAPs in the space of two years, and once again the focus is primarily on EU accession and large developing economies. The lack of periodicity in the publication of compliance and the MFI focus on economies deemed systematically vital means that small developing states, despite substantial legislative progress, must endure disproportionately lengthy delays before they are evaluated by MFIs, resulting in an unreasonable persistence in market opinions.[95]

In an effort to disseminate compliance information rapidly, several initiatives have converted MFI assessments into a quantified 'score'.[96] The move towards quantitative compliance assessment has overwhelmingly negative implications for small developing states. In all economies, compliance in one set of standards (such as those produced by the Basel

[94] IMF (2002a). A joint IMF–World Bank ROSC project has not fared much better, producing only thirty-three ROSCs since the beginning of the project.

[95] The issue of surveillance by the Bretton Woods institutions is explored further in ODI (2002).

[96] See www.estandardsforum.com for an example of a private-sector initiative to provide quantitative compliance information to the market. Countries are given ratings of 'full compliance', 'compliance in progress', 'enacted' (i.e. the necessary legislation has been approved), 'intent declared' (i.e. by a credible authority that implementation will take place), 'no compliance' or 'no assessment available'.

Committee) is linked to compliance in others (most notably accounting and auditing, payments and settlements systems and securities regulations).[97] In many small developing states, many of whom face a number of infeasible deadlines to implement various standards, a binary 'compliant/non-compliant' approach threatens to create a one-way expectation and increased herding among market participants, where a simple numerical score ignores the complex and interrelated nature of financial reform.[98] As noted earlier, the standards regime, rather than mitigating the effects of contagion and herding in emerging-market lending, threatens instead to exacerbate financial crises.

Regrettably, OECD- and FATF-style coercive elements have become increasingly part of the MFI-led assessment of Basel Committee guidelines. MFIs are increasingly incorporating Basel and other standards as part of lending conditionality, which many small and developing countries see as a thinly veiled attempt to introduce compulsory standards adoption. The IMF, for example, has recently included 'a positive assessment of policies and progress towards adherence to internationally accepted standards', including compliance with several elements of the 'second pillar' of Basel II, as eligibility criteria for access to its Contingent Credit Lines. Although MFI conditionality represents a less blatant form of coercion than the OECD and FATF regimes, it nonetheless threatens to undermine small and developing country ownership of financial standards further.

Part II

18.6 Financial services in the WTO

The question that naturally arises is to what extent can, or should, the standards created within these plurilateral bodies but outside the formal framework of the WTO – without the formal participation of many small developing countries – affect the tenor and content of negotiations and obligations at the WTO. As far as impact on the WTO negotiations is concerned, all of the developed country members of the standard-setting bodies are members of the WTO, but less than half of small developing states with substantial financial services sectors are full-fledged WTO

[97] ODI (2002). [98] For a discussion of this issue in the Indian context, see Anant (2001).

members or observers.[99] Nevertheless, the discussion is important for the current WTO members, and may become more real in the future for those who will eventually become members. As mentioned above, the proliferation of these standards has threatened, and stands increasingly to threaten, the competitive trade advantage small states have thus far managed to obtain in the financial services sector. Being the international body whose exclusive preserve is the creation, maintenance and enforcement of a legal framework for the multilateral trade in, *inter alia*, services, debate about the impact of such regulatory standards has inevitably spilled over into negotiating rooms in the WTO.

This issue takes centre stage in the context of framing disciplines under Article VI for the domestic regulation of services under the General Agreement for Trade in Services (GATS), and more specifically for prudential regulation under the Financial Services Annex (FSA). Whilst the WTO is chiefly concerned with the liberalisation of trade in goods and services, and by extension financial services, the importance of regulation, and a growing awareness of its effects on trade, means that the WTO has become germane to discussions about regulation. Bodies like the Basel Committee, FATF and the OECD, which operate at an international level, are increasingly becoming concerned about the regulation of activities that affect the stability and security of the international financial system, and, as discussed above, their concern has been marked by a proliferation of standards that are affecting the financial services product of many small states, many of whom specialise mainly, or at times exclusively, in the trade of financial services. It is not beyond the realm of possibility that standards produced in these bodies could enter discussions in the WTO about regulation of measures and, by extension, inform the nature of obligations and commitments that small states will assume and be adjudged by, by a WTO panel or the Appellate Body.

The chink in the GATS armour which arguably provides the most direct means for the introduction of these financial standards is a sub-paragraph in Article VI allowing for international standards formulated in international organisations to be 'take[n] account of' in determining conformity

[99] Of the small states with important financial services sectors (based on note 3 above), only Antigua and Barbuda, Barbados, Belize, Jamaica, Mauritius and St Kitts and Nevis are WTO Members; the Bahamas, Samoa and Vanuatu are currently observers. However, the following small states are not (as yet) WTO members or observers: Bermuda, British Virgin Islands, Cayman Islands, Cook Islands, Marshall Islands, Nauru, Niue and Tuvalu.

with regulatory obligations and disciplines under the GATS.[100] This explicit reference to international bodies presents a potential basis for increasing harmonisation of international regulatory standards by consideration of the standards developed in bodies with specific expertise in relevant areas. As it is currently articulated, the provision is temporary in nature, and concerned only with the use of international organisations in so far as they can provide guidance for informing and determining WTO members' compliance with disciplines upon which regulatory measures should be based. The provision therefore is not as far reaching or strongly formulated as other WTO Agreements that seek to harmonise international regulatory standards that affect trade. For instance, harmonisation of international standards is already encouraged in GATT Agreements – the Technical Barriers for Trade (TBT) and Sanitary and Phyto-Sanitary (SPS) Agreements – and provides a means for promoting uniformity and greater inclusiveness of all in the setting of standards that affect international trade in goods.

The GATS however, with its cursory reference to international standards bodies, does not give clear guidance on how to strike the optimal balance between harmonising international regulatory standards and ensuring that individual governments retain the ability to respond to their own domestic needs. Arguably, however, the reference in the text to due consideration being taken of standards emerging from international organisations manifests a WTO preference for countries voluntarily collaborating with each other, through the aegis of specific relevant bodies, in standardising the regulatory measures that affect trade in services. To the extent that such co-operation and harmonisation complements a voluntary, participatory and consensual process by all WTO members in formulating and implementing standards, this approach towards domestic regulatory standardisation would be useful and could provide the means for the development of a database of standards that could inform adjudication by the WTO. However, if standards formulated and applied in a non-transparent, unfair and at times coercive manner become the starting point from which to judge a member's compliance with regulatory disciplines, then the WTO risks replicating and promoting unilateralism, discrimination and lack of openness in international trade relations.

[100] See Article VI(5)(b) of GATS. Other possible entry points could be provisions for the mutual recognition by countries of each other's standards, on the basis of mutually agreed criteria, under GATS Article VII and FSA Article 3.

We turn first to the domestic regulation debate generally at the WTO, and then to the issue of international regulation and harmonisation.

18.6.1 Background to domestic regulation at the WTO

As alluded to above, the wider issue concerns the relationship between trade liberalisation and domestic regulation of the services sector.[101] Whilst the ultimate aim of the services negotiations, as in all WTO negotiations, is the gradual liberalisation of international trade, this is pursued through the elimination of restrictions, and not through deregulation. More explicitly, the preamble of the GATS recognises the right of governments to 'regulate and introduce new regulations in order to meet national policy objectives', bearing in mind the asymmetries in development of services regulatory frameworks within different member countries.[102] More specifically, the importance of domestic regulation warrants its specific treatment in the GATS under Article VI.

The Financial Services sector provides a good illustration of the importance of regulation as it is undoubtedly one of the more heavily regulated service sectors under the GATS. The FSA is annexed to the GATS and establishes a legal framework for trade in financial services.[103] Trade in these financial sectors has become increasingly competitive, global and diversified, and because this sector constitutes one of the basic infrastructures of an economy and a country's development, governments are under constant pressure to protect their financial sectors from both domestic and foreign disruptions.[104] This 'protection' often takes the form of regulation, conducted with a view to the particular social, economic and other policy objectives of a country. As in the GATS, there is allowance under Article 2(a) of the FSA for governments to exercise some degree of regulatory autonomy, but in this case, only if the measures taken are for 'prudential reasons'.[105] This exemption has been often referred to as the 'prudential

[101] Note, for instance, WTO Symposium on Assessment of Trade in Services, 14–15 March 2002; OECD–World Bank Services Expert Meeting, 4–5 March 2002.

[102] See GATS Preamble at fourth paragraph.

[103] Its coverage extends to all insurance and insurance-related services, and all banking and other financial services (excluding insurance). See Article 5 of FSA.

[104] See the Note by the WTO Secretariat at WTO Document S/C/W/72.

[105] Article 2(a) of the FSA is located under the general heading 'Domestic Regulation' and states that: 'Notwithstanding any other provisions of the Agreement, a Member shall not be prevented from taking measures for prudential reasons, including for the protection of investors,

carve-out', and although its exact scope and nature is left undefined, it is an implicit recognition that governments must be allowed some latitude in conducting their regulatory functions.

However, both GATS and the FSA are first and foremost trade agreements, and a member's right to regulate must not be a guise for protectionism that unduly restricts trade. As the permissible extent of a member's right to regulate could not be concluded at the time that the WTO Agreement was agreed to, WTO members decided that the process of determining the acceptable limits for the exercise of this right by governments, in a multilateral context, would continue until January 2005. The task facing negotiators therefore is to develop disciplines for the domestic regulation of the services sector generally. The effects, if any, that these disciplines will have on the regulation of the Financial Services are far from clear, and neither the texts of the GATS and the FSA, nor discussions emerging from the various negotiating groups of the WTO, clarify the matter.

18.6.2 Domestic regulation: GATS Article VI(4) and (5) and Article (2)(a) of the FSA

Although there has been some debate about the applicability of Article VI(4) to all sectors, regardless of whether specific sectoral commitments have been undertaken, the article on domestic regulation as a whole is intended to promote reasonableness, objectivity and impartiality in administration, formulation and application of regulatory measures. Specifically, Article VI(4) mandates the Council for Trade in Services to 'develop any necessary disciplines' that will guide member states, and presumably dispute settlement panels, in assessing the WTO compatibility of their regulatory measures[106] – i.e. those measures relating to qualification requirements and procedures, technical standards and licensing requirements.[107] The Council for Trade in Services has since delegated this role to

depositors, policy holders or persons to whom a fiduciary duty is owed by a financial service supplier, or to ensure the integrity and stability of the financial system. Where such measures do not conform with the provisions of the Agreement, they shall not be used as a means of avoiding the Member's commitments or obligations under the Agreement.'

[106] 'Measures' is ascribed a wide meaning in the GATS Article XXVII(a) and includes 'any measure by a member, whether in the form of a law, regulation, rule, procedure, decision, administrative action, or any other form . . .'.

[107] See GATS Article VI(4).

the Working Party on Domestic Regulation (WPDR),[108] whose task is to frame the disciplines on the following basis, i.e. they must be:

(a) based on *objective and transparent* criteria, such as competence and the ability to supply the service;
(b) *not more burdensome than necessary* to ensure the quality of the service (commonly referred to as the requirement of 'necessity');
(c) in the case of licensing procedures, not in themselves a restriction on the supply of the service.

In the interim negotiating period, Article VI(5)(a) ensures that any such new measures undertaken by member states do not have the effect of nullifying and impairing commitments in a manner that is not compliant with the criteria listed in Article VI(4) (above); or that is unreasonable in light of the specific commitments made by that member. Further, Article VI(5)(b) allows 'account to be taken' of international standards in determining compliance with Article VI(5)(a). It is noteworthy, however, that this provision, being contingent and complementary to the temporary Article 5(a), only applies for as long as disciplines remain to be finally negotiated.

There is no guidance as to whether, or how, the disciplines negotiated under Article VI(4) of the GATS are intended to affect, or in any way relate to, domestic regulation of financial measures. Of course to the extent that the FSA 'prudential carve-out' is the most obvious starting point for assessing the WTO compatibility of financial regulatory measures, a panel would have to decide first and foremost whether a member country's financial measure was taken for 'prudential reasons'. In its entirety, Article 2(a) provides that:

> Notwithstanding any other provisions of the Agreement, a Member shall not be prevented from taking measures for prudential reasons, including for the protection of investors, depositors, policy holders or persons to whom a fiduciary duty is owed by financial supplier, or to ensure the integrity and stability of the financial system. Where such measures do not conform with the provisions of the Agreement, they

[108] The mandate for the Working Party on Domestic Regulation (WPDR) was given by the Council for Trade in Services on 26 April 1999 (S/L/70). The WPDR took over the function of the Working Party on Professional Services, and has been assigned the task of carrying out the mandate under Article VI(4). According to this mandate, the WPDR must develop generally applicable disciplines and *may* develop disciplines as appropriate for individual sectors or groups thereof.

> shall not be used as a means of avoiding the Member's commitments or obligations under the Agreement.

A number of academics have suggested possible ways in which this prudential carve-out could be interpreted.[109] Given that the text itself provides little guidance as to the basis upon which 'prudential reasons' should be interpreted, save in so far as the inclusive list of reasons enumerated may give some general direction, and that there may be a suggestion from the last sentence that it authorises departure from other GATS provisions once the intention is not to evade other commitments, a panel might nevertheless be led to the conclusion that the more overarching disciplines on domestic regulation in Article VI(4) should in some way inform its analysis. Indeed, the WTO Secretariat itself has suggested that Article VI(4) and (5) could have some bearing on the interpretation of prudential measures:

> Although technically, Article VI:4 and 5 may not be applicable to prudential measures, questions may remain as to whether [prudential measures] are based on *objective and transparent* criteria, or are *not more burdensome than necessary.*[110] (emphasis added)

This reference to the exact wording of Article VI(4) suggests that there should be a cross-fertilisation in analysis of the two agreements. Would, for instance, disciplines formulated under Article VI(4) apply to and inform an analysis of what constitutes 'prudential' for the purposes of Article 2 of the FSA? To the extent therefore, even in the interim period of negotiations, that international standards could inform what is 'objective and transparent' and 'not more burdensome than necessary', there is a possibility for the entry of standards developed outside the WTO to guide a panel or the Appellate Body.[111] Alternatively, and more directly, the term 'prudential' could acquire a generic meaning that is informed by standards developed in bodies that have specific expertise in the development of financial standards. This is not as fanciful as might first appear. Consider, for example,

[109] See, for instance, Trachtman, 'Addressing Regulatory Divergence through International Standards: Financial Services' in Mattoo and Suave (2003) at p. 30, where she suggests that a panel could approach such an analysis along the lines adopted by the Appellate Body in United States–Shrimp for the interpretation of Article XX(g) of the GATT.

[110] See the Note by the WTO Secretariat at WTO Document S/C/W/72, at footnote 50.

[111] The FSA is subject to the far-reaching grasp of the dispute settlement mechanism of the WTO: Article 4 of the FSA states that: 'Panels for disputes on prudential issues and other financial matters shall have the necessary expertise relevant to the specific financial service under dispute.'

a recent WTO proposal by a developed country which in effect would encourage the wholesale, indiscriminate adoption of plurilateral standards into the WTO, by designating certain organisations as 'relevant international forums' for the purposes of promoting 'solid prudential regulation'.[112] According to the proposal, these organisations could include the Basel Committee, the IAIS, IOSOC and the Joint Forum on Financial Conglomerates, but would not seem to preclude the OECD and FATF. This is a troubling proposition for small states in so far as it does not suggest the use of these standards as mere guidelines for a mutually supportive relationship between the WTO and these other standard-setting bodies, whereby the WTO would adapt standards and application of standards in light of its own organisational objectives. The proposal therefore would not go very far in addressing the concerns of small states not party to the standard-formulating exercises occurring in these plurilateral bodies.

Although some countries have initiated and proposed discussions on how to define and interpret Article 2(a) in the context of the GATS,[113] such attempts have met with staunch resistance by WTO members generally. Members appear weary of other countries using the 'prudential carve-out' as a pretext for unilateral introduction and imposition of their own domestic and international financial standards. For the moment however, any discussion about the link between domestic regulation generally and Financial Services specifically is at best academic, as no substantial discussion has yet taken place in the WTO. Members seem to be content for the moment with discussing the issue horizontally, i.e. generally relevant across all sectors, rather than according to the specificities of any particular sector.[114]

112 See Switzerland's proposal to the Special Session in WTO Document S/CSS/W/71.

113 See, for example, the attempt by Australia at WTO Document S/FIN/5, at paragraph 5.

114 Current negotiations on domestic regulation, and specifically on domestic regulation of financial services, have not taken place in a mutually supportive or complementary way, although the mandate does not preclude it. (WTO Document S/L/70 at paragraph 3: 'In fulfilling its task, the Working Party shall develop generally applicable disciplines and may develop disciplines as appropriate for individual sectors or groups thereof.') Most countries in the WPDR have supported an initial approach that develops horizontal cross-sectoral disciplines, and if necessary particularises them according to the needs of specific sectors. Not much movement has been made beyond this first phase, although possible aspects of a financial regulatory framework have been discussed in parallel sessions of the Committee on Trade in Financial Services and have been the subject of proposals in Special Sessions of the Council on Trade in Services, but there has not been a coherent co-ordinated approach towards domestic regulation under the GATS and FSA.

18.6.3 International standardisation and harmonisation

The preceding discussion suggests that external plurilateral financial standards could potentially enter the sphere of WTO negotiations most directly through Article VI(5)(b) of the GATS. It might prove useful to consider it in more detail.

GATS Article VI(5)(b) provides that account shall be taken of international standards of *relevant* international organisations[115] in determining whether regulatory measures taken are compatible with the principles of necessity, transparency and objectivity enumerated in Article VI(4). 'Relevant organisations' is defined further to refer to international bodies whose membership is open to the relevant bodies of at least all WTO members.[116] Presumably, this reference to international bodies with inclusive membership points towards a preference by the WTO for resort to bodies which have specific expertise and from which as wide a range of input from WTO members can be ensured. However, the reference to 'open' membership might not go far enough in checking the influence of the plurilateral bodies like the OECD, FATF and Basel Committees, and promoting a truly genuine harmonisation process. Surely enough, these bodies may not qualify under Article VI(5)(b), as their membership is exclusive of many small states, but this does not address the underlying concern that small states have that their interests are not being fully integrated or accommodated in the process of formulating these standards in the first place. Further, even if formal membership into these organisations were opened up to all, this does not necessarily translate into participation in the process of formulating standards, if for instance small states lack the technical, human and financial resources to make meaningful contributions.

The most recent proposal presented to the WTO by Antigua and Barbuda goes some way in trying to ensure this sort of effective inclusion of small states. First, the proposal would have members further define 'open' to ensure actual participation by all countries, through a requirement *inter*

[115] See footnote 3 of GATS Article VI(5)(b).

[116] This provision in effect creates a presumption in favour of requirements based on international standards. Presumably, such a provision could constitute a strong incentive for the use of international standards. Note that similarly a strong presumption in favour of international standards is contained in Article 2.5 of the TBT Agreement and Article 3.2 of the SPS Agreement (which also incorporates a necessity test). Similarly, in the Accountancy Sector the mandate of the working party encouraged Members to work towards harmonising common international standards.

alia that qualifying organisations include provision of technical assistance for countries that could not otherwise participate in standard-setting activities, presumably through lack of human resources/financial capacity.[117]

Secondly, the proposal recommends that the WTO assume a more prominent role in the standard-setting process, as a facilitator of participation between different member states and/or bodies for the creation of truly international standards.[118] Although the proposal goes further in the role it ascribes to the WTO,[119] it borrows much from the collaborative approach to regulation employed in the SPS and TBT Agreements and is intended to involve all parties in the process at a multilateral level. Both the TBT and SPS Agreements, in their preambles and in certain provisions of the main text, recognise the difficulties presented to developing countries in the formulation, application and compliance with regulatory and technical requirements and standards provided for under the Agreements. Special and differential treatment is provided for respectively in Articles 12 and 10, and in each there is explicit mention of the need to encourage and facilitate the active participation of developing countries in the relevant international organisations. Provisions in the TBT Agreement go further in *inter alia* exhorting Members to take reasonable measures as may be available to them to ensure that international standardising bodies and international systems facilitate *active and representative participation* in the relevant bodies,[120] that technical standards and regulations be appropriate to their development, financial and trade needs[121] and that technical assistance be provided in the preparation and application of technical regulations.[122]

Both Agreements go even further and contain specific provisions which seek to promote international harmonisation through co-operation with relevant international bodies. The SPS Agreement does so under the aegis of Article 3, dedicated entirely to, and entitled, 'Harmonisation'. Under the TBT Agreement it is integrated into Article 2 which is concerned more generally with the preparation, adoption and application of technical

[117] See Antigua and Barbuda proposal (above) for insertion at proposed new Article VI(5), footnote 3.

[118] See Antigua and Barbuda proposal (above) at proposed new paragraph 5(c). The proposal would place the WTO Secretariat at the centre of notification and consultation activities concerning standards being set by member states.

[119] Note, for instance, that the proposal seeks to ensure that input given by countries via the notification and consultative process is to be taken account of and reflected in the development of standards (above, at proposed new Article VI(5)(c)(D)).

[120] See TBT Agreement at Article 12.5. [121] Ibid., at Article 12.4. [122] Ibid., at Article 12.7.

regulatory measures. Within these articles, members are encouraged to play as full a part 'within the limits of their resources' in the preparation of standards in the international standard-setting bodies.[123] The SPS Agreement goes as far as naming the relevant bodies, i.e. the Codex Alimentarius Commission, the International Office of Epizootics and organisations working with the International Plant Protection Convention.[124] WTO members are charged with the responsibility of working within these bodies to raise the level of standards and keep them under constant review, and in the process, ensure that they are harmonised. As a further illustration of how genuine multilateralisation can be enabled via the WTO, the TBT Agreement similarly encourages members to work with international bodies, but where international standards are absent or where technical standards deviate from those created in international bodies, the Agreement allows for a process of notification and consultation among WTO members, through the WTO Secretariat, where new technical regulations are being developed for use by countries.[125]

There is precedent within the text of the WTO Agreement for the WTO to act as a facilitator and liaise with other organisations in harmonisation of international standards. Although the present GATS and FSA are relatively weak in comparison with other Agreements, there is certainly a case for the WTO to operate as a medium which promotes and enables the participation of all countries in the process of standard setting for services.

18.7 Conclusion

The international financial standards considered in this chapter are of two varieties. The Basel Accord falls into the generic and common category of voluntary standards which are not forcefully imposed on WTO members. Indeed, developing countries which were not party to the formation of these standards are not legally obliged to implement them. However, small developing countries and local financial institutions in those countries that fail to implement the risk assessment techniques, for technical or financial reasons, will find themselves at a considerable competitive disadvantage in domestic and overseas markets. Equally, the standards imposed of the second type – those imposed by sanction or threat of sanction like those

[123] See TBT Agreement at Article 2.6 and SPS Agreement at Article 3.4.
[124] See SPS Agreement at Article 3.
[125] See TBT Agreement at Article 2.9.

developed under OECD and FATF – place the small states obliged to comply with them at a substantial disadvantage in competing for the supply of financial services from larger jurisdictions.

In addition to these concerns about loss of competitive advantage, the chapter highlighted a growing concern for small states, that in deciding what standards to apply in assessing the WTO-compliance of a regulatory measure, panels and the Appellate Body will feel unconstrained in incorporating substantive standards that are developed in these plurilateral fora via loopholes in the GATS and FSA, that could be closed off or filled if the requisite political intent of the WTO membership is secured.

The chapter recounts clearly the unfortunate experiences of the small states with some standard-setting bodies. Although it is encouraging that they have responded in some cases by collectively demanding, under the umbrella of organisations like the ITIO,[126] that a 'level playing field' be obtained in the financial services sector, there undoubtedly remains much to do inside the WTO in order to ensure the effective participation and inclusion of small states in these processes. Within the WTO, their immediate aim must be to arrest any sort of replication of coercive and non-transparent behaviour. There is much merit in the WTO capitalising on the work taking place in regulatory bodies, and establishing a collaborative framework for the coherent development and application of regulatory standards that benefits from truly multilateral and transparent participation.[127] This has occurred in the context of the GATT, and the existence of precedents in the TBT and SPS Agreements which clearly aspire to espouse and enact WTO principles of fairness, transparency and multilateralism in the formation and application of international regulatory standards means that the same can be replicated in the GATS.

The Antigua and Barbuda proposal is the only one on the table that seeks to address squarely the situation of small states, mainly through the mechanism of GATS Domestic Regulation provisions. Apart from encouraging WTO developed members to provide more technical assistance to small, developing countries for their increased participation in the standard-setting process being undertaken by the more developed countries, it also

[126] See, for instance, work being done by the ITIO on their website: www.itio.org.

[127] There is permissibility for such interaction with outside bodies under the GATS: 'Article XXVI: Relationship with Other International Organizations: The General Council shall make appropriate arrangements for consultation and cooperation with the United Nations and its specialized agencies as well as with other intergovernmental organizations concerned with services.'

goes further and suggests that the WTO should act as facilitator of a more inclusive and participatory standard-setting process. Of course, the WTO *cannot* prevent sovereign states from forming associations with each other, as they deem fit, and formulating codes and practices for the conduct of their financial business and activity; indeed, many of the standards developed in the various standard-setting bodies such as the OECD, Basel Committee and FATF are ostensibly created with laudatory and worthwhile intentions in mind, i.e. to ensure that governments carry out and conduct their financial policies in conformity with guidelines that are safe and secure, and promote international financial stability. Surely these ends are desirable and will inure to the benefit of all, including small states. Rather the issue is that, as the situation exists currently, these standards create a trade advantage for those involved in their formation at the expense of those who are not.

The answer for small states is not to recoil from the challenges of negotiations with other WTO members, but to engage fully in redressing the problems through the refining and redefining of existing obligations, and where necessary creating new ones. Indeed, the window has been granted in the context of finalising disciplines for domestic regulation, but equally small states have a work programme within the Working Group on Small Economies whose specific mandate exhorts all members to facilitate the fuller integration of small, vulnerable economies into the multilateral trading system.

Small states must lead this discussion as it is clearly in their interest to do this sooner rather than later. It is clear that the process of formulating standards in the various plurilateral bodies is continuing unabated and is unlikely to wane in intensity. Whilst ensuring that they obtain a louder voice in these plurilateral fora, small states would do well to launch a co-ordinated and simultaneous attack on the WTO in order to secure their rightful place as equals in the international financial services sector.

Appendix 18.1

Table 1 *Overlapping memberships in key standard-setting bodies*

Country	G-7	G-10	Basel	OECD	FATF	G-22
Argentina					✓	✓
Australia				✓	✓	✓
Brazil					✓	✓
Canada	✓	✓	✓	✓	✓	✓
China						✓
France	✓	✓	✓	✓	✓	✓
Germany	✓	✓	✓	✓	✓	✓
Hong Kong					✓	✓
India						✓
Indonesia						✓
Italy	✓	✓	✓	✓	✓	✓
Japan	✓	✓	✓	✓	✓	✓
Malaysia						✓
Mexico				✓	✓	✓
Netherlands		✓	✓	✓	✓	✓
Poland				✓		✓
Russia						✓
Singapore					✓	✓
South Africa						✓
South Korea				✓		✓
Thailand						✓
Turkey				✓	✓	✓
UK	✓	✓	✓	✓	✓	✓
US	✓	✓	✓	✓	✓	✓

Bibliography

Anant, T. C. (2001). 'Implementation of Financial Standards and Codes: Lessons from the Indian Experience'. Background paper for the Overseas Development Institute/Commonwealth Secretariat Conference 'International Standards and Codes: The Developing Country Perspective', 21 June 2002, London

BCBS (2001a). 'The New Basle Capital Accord: An Explanatory Note'. Bank for International Settlements, Basel

BCBS (2001b). 'Consultative Document: Pillar 3 (Market Discipline)'. Bank for International Settlements, Basel

BCBS (2002). 'About the Basel Committee'. BIS website at www.bis.org

Biswas, R. (2001). *Global Competition in Offshore Business Services: Prospects for Developing Countries.* Commonwealth Heads of Government Reference Book 2001, Commonwealth Secretariat, London

Brownbridge, M. and Kirkpatrick, C. (2000). 'Financial Regulation in Developing Countries'. *Journal of Development Studies*, 37/1

Caprio, G., Honohan, P. and Stiglitz, J. E. (2001). *Financial Liberalization: How Far, How Fast?* Cambridge University Press

CARICOM (2000). 'The OECD Harmful Tax Initiative: Impact of the Proposals on Small Developing CARICOM States'. Available at www.foreign.gov.bb

Castle, A. (1999). *Money Laundering in the Asia Pacific: Regional Challenges and Opportunities for International Co-operation.* International Centre for Criminal Law Reform and Criminal Justice Policy, Vancouver

Castle, A. and Broomhall, B. (1998). *The International Money Laundering Regime and the Asia Pacific: Pairing Multilateral Co-operation with Domestic Institutional Reform.* International Centre for Criminal Law Reform and Criminal Justice Policy, Vancouver

Cornford, A. (2000). 'The Basel Committee's Proposals for Revised Capital Standards: Rationale, Design and Possible Incidence'. Background paper for UN/ECE Regional Conference, 'Financing for International Development', 6–7 December 2000

(2001). 'The Basel Committee's Proposals for Revised Capital Standards: Mark 2 and the State of Play'. UNCTAD Discussion Paper No. 68. Geneva, UNCTAD

DFID (2001). *Technical Assistance for Standards and Codes (TASC) Facility. Project Submission.* Department for International Development (DFID), London

Dwyer, T. (2000). '"Harmful" Tax Competition and the Future of Offshore Financial Centres'. *Pacific Economic Bulletin*, vol. 15, no. 1

EMEPG (2001). *Rebuilding the International Financial Architecture.* Emerging Markets Eminent Persons Group, Seoul

Evans, J. L. (1997). *International Efforts to Contain Money Laundering.* International Centre for Criminal Law Reform and Criminal Justice Policy, Vancouver

FATF (1996). *Annual Report.* Financial Action Task Force on Money Laundering, Paris

FATF (2000). *Review to Identify Non-Cooperative Countries or Territories: Increasing the Worldwide Effectiveness of Anti-Money Laundering Measures.* Financial Action Task Force on Money Laundering, Paris

FATF (2001). *Review of FATF Anti-Money Laundering Systems and Mutual Evaluation Procedures 1992–1999.* Financial Action Task Force on Money Laundering, Paris

FATF (2002). *Annual Report 2001–2.* Financial Action Task Force on Money Laundering, Paris

Ferrance, W. (2000). 'Case Study: Antigua and Barbuda'. CFATF Conference

Griffith-Jones, S. (2000). 'Developing Countries and the Global Financial System'. Commonwealth Secretariat, World Bank and IMF Conference, London, June

Griffith-Jones, S. and Gottschalk, R. (2002). 'Enhancing Private Flows to Developing Countries in the New International Context'. Commonwealth Secretariat, World Bank and Commonwealth Business Council Conference, August

Griffith-Jones, S. and Kimmis, J. (1999). 'The BIS and its Role in International Financial Governance'. *International Monetary and Financial Issues for the 1990s – Research Papers for the Group of Twenty-Four* – vol. XI. United Nations publication, sales no. E.99.II.D.25. New York and Geneva

Griffith-Jones, S. and Spratt, S. (2001). *Will the Proposed New Basel Capital Accord Have a Net Negative Effect on Developing Countries?* Institute of Development Studies, 2001

Griffith-Jones, S. and Spratt, S. (2002). 'The New Basle Accord and Developing Countries'. UNU-WIDER Discussion Paper No. 2002/36, March

Griffith-Jones, S., Spratt, S. and Segoviano, M. (2002). *The Onward March of Basel II – Can the Interests of Developing Countries be Protected?* Institute of Development Studies, University of Sussex

Grynberg, R. and Chilala, B. (2001). 'WTO Compatibility of the OECD "Defensive Measures" Against "Harmful Tax Competition"'. *Journal of World Investment*, September

Hay, R. J. (2001). 'Offshore Financial Centres and the Supranationals: Collision or Cohabitation?' *The Chase Journal*, New York

IMF (2001). *Assessing the Implementation of Standards: A Review of Experience and Next Steps.* Prepared by Staffs of the International Monetary Fund and the World Bank, January

IMF (2002a). *Quarterly Report on the Assessment of Standards and Codes – November 2002.* International Monetary Fund, Washington

IMF (2002b). *Intensified Work on Anti-Money Laundering and Combating Financing of Terrorism.* Joint Progress Report on the Work of the IMF and World Bank. International Monetary Fund, Washington

Latin American Shadow Regulatory Committee (2001). 'Statement No. 2', April, Caracas, Venezuela

Louis (2000). 'Blacklist'. *Tax Notes*, CCH Canadian Ltd

Mattoo, A. and Suave, P. (2003). Editors. *Domestic Regulation and Services Trade Liberalisation*, co-published by the World Bank and Oxford University Press

Mcintyre, J. (2002). 'Options for Greater International Coordination and Cooperation in the Tax Treaty Area'. *Bulletin for International Fiscal Documentation*, 250–3. Wayne State University Law School, June

Ministry of Industry and International Business (2001a). *Barbados Global E-Letter*, March

Ministry of Industry and International Business (2001b). *Barbados Global E-Letter*, April

ODI (2002). *Conference Report on International Standards and Codes: The Developing Country Perspective*. Overseas Development Institute/ Commonwealth Secretariat

OECD (2000). *Towards Global Tax Co-operation: Report to the 2000 Ministerial Council Meeting and Recommendations by the Committee on Fiscal Affairs*. Organisation for Economic Co-operation and Development, Paris

Parody, S. (2000). 'Statement'. CFATF Conference

Persaud, A. (2000). *Sending the Herd Off the Cliff Edge: The Disturbing Interaction Between Herding and Market-Sensitive Risk Management Practices*. Institute of International Finance, Washington

Persaud, B. (2001). 'A Major Issue for Small States'. *The Round Table*, no. 359, April

PFTAC (2002). *Overview of Statistical Operations and Coordination of Technical Assistance in the Region*. Pacific Financial Technical Assistance Center, Suva

Powell, A. (2001). *A Capital Accord for Emerging Economies*? World Bank

Reisen, H. (2001). 'Will Basel II Contribute to Convergence in International Capital Flows'. Mimeo, OECD Development Centre, OECD, Paris

Reserve Bank of India (2001). *Comments of the Reserve Bank of India on the New Basel Capital Accord*. Reserve Bank of India, New Delhi

Riechel, K. W. (2000). 'Cooperation in Financial Sector Regulation and Supervision: The Case of Pacific Island Countries'. Background document, Forum Economic Ministers Meeting, Pacific Island Forum Secretariat, Fiji

Sanders, R. (2001). 'The Future of Financial Services in the Caribbean'. PriceWaterhouseCoopers Conference on Financial Services Investment Practice, Nassau, September

Society of Trust and Estate Practitioners (2002). *Towards a Level Playing Field: Regulating Corporate Vehicles in Cross-Border Transactions*. Review commissioned by the International Tax and Investment Organisation (ITIO) and STEP, conducted by Stikeman and Elliot

UNCTAD (2001). *Trade and Development Report 2001*. United Nations, New York and Geneva

World Bank and IMF (2002). 'Anti-Money Laundering and Combating the Financing of Terrorism. Regional Videoconference: Latin America and Caribbean Region (Brazil, Colombia, Guatemala, Jamaica, and Mexico)'. World Bank, Washington

Zagaris, B. (2001). *Exchange of Tax Information Policies at the Millennium: Balancing Enforcement with Due Process and International Human Rights*. International Platform Association, Washington

19

Export processing zones and the WTO Agreement on Subsidies and Countervailing Measures

DAVID ROBERTSON

19.1 Introduction

Many of the Commonwealth's developing countries have established export processing zones (EPZs) as trade policy instruments designed to promote non-traditional exports. Typically, these programmes provide that if a company locates a manufacturing facility within a geographically delimited zone, and exports all or most of its products, it will be provided with a number of incentives. These incentives range from exemption from various direct and indirect taxes and customs duties to provision of a number of free or low-cost services. EPZs located in developing countries typically provide the greatest number of incentives.

The WTO's Agreement on Subsidies and Countervailing Measures (SCM) contains specific definitions, restrictions and implementation deadlines in relation to the use of export subsidies. These rules may affect incentives granted to EPZ companies in Commonwealth developing countries that are currently WTO Members or are contemplating accession.

This chapter aims to highlight some of the potential conflicts between the SCM Agreement and EPZ incentives. It should be borne in mind, however, that each EPZ will have particular regulatory characteristics and that each Commonwealth WTO Member may have differing bilateral or regional obligations. The comments made in this chapter can, therefore, only be general in nature and should not substitute a case-by-case review of EPZ incentives.

19.2 Agreement on Subsidies and Countervailing Measures

The SCM Agreement came into effect on 1 January 1995 and builds on Article XVI of the General Agreement on Tariffs and Trade 1947 (GATT) and the earlier Agreement on Interpretation of and Application of

Articles VI, XVI and XXIII. The SCM Agreement provides a more or less complete code in relation to the use of subsidies that reference back to GATT 1947 and the earlier Agreement on Interpretation is not necessary in most instances.

19.2.1 Definition of subsidy

The rules contained in the SCM Agreement apply only to subsidies as defined within the Agreement. A subsidy is defined in Article 1 as a financial contribution by a government or any public body, including a direct transfer of funds (e.g. grants, loans and equity infusion), government revenue that is forgone (e.g. tax credits), provision of goods or services by a government, other than infrastructure, and income or price support.

This very broad definition is qualified by two provisos. First, to become subject to the rules in the SCM Agreement, a subsidy must confer a benefit on the recipient, and secondly, it must be specific, namely, available only to an enterprise or industry or group of enterprises or industries within the jurisdiction of the authority granting the subsidy. Article 2.2 specifically provides that 'a subsidy which is limited to certain enterprises located within a designated geographical region . . . shall be specific'. Subsidies extended on the basis of administrative delineation would also be specific.

The general definition of subsidy is further refined by specifying two categories of subsidies: *prohibited export subsidies* and *actionable subsidies.* These two categories are also referred to as 'red light' and 'yellow light' subsidies. Until 2000 there was a third category of *non-actionable subsidy*, which has been discontinued.

19.2.2 Prohibited export subsidies

Prohibited export subsidies are those '. . . contingent, in law or fact . . . upon export performance . . . and those contingent . . . upon the use of domestic over imported goods'. Prohibited export subsidies are described further by reference to Annex I of the SCM Agreement, which provides an illustrative list. Annex 1 includes as prohibited export subsidies a number of the incentives that might be offered to EPZ companies, including:

- transport or freight charge subsidies on export shipment provided or mandated by the government;

- the provision by governments of export credit guarantees or insurance programmes at premiums that are adequate to cover the long-term operating costs and losses of the programmes; and,
- the full or partial exemption, remission, or deferral in relation to exports, of direct taxes or social welfare charges paid or payable by industrial or commercial enterprises. (Direct taxes are defined as taxes on wages, profits, interests, rents, royalties, and all other forms of income, and taxes on ownership of real property.)

Developed WTO Members are prohibited from granting or maintaining prohibited export subsidies. However, the SCM Agreement recognises that subsidies may play an important role in the economic development of developing countries. Accordingly, least-developed countries (as designated by the United Nations), and developing countries with a GNP per capita of less than $1,000, are exempted from the prohibition on prohibited export subsidies indefinitely, or at least for so long as their GNP remains below the specified level.

Developing countries, other than least developed and those with a GNP below $1,000 per capita, were exempted from this prohibition until the end of 2002. However, they were required to phase out prohibited export subsidies within the eight-year implementation period, preferably in a progressive manner, and they were not allowed to increase their level of export subsidies.

If a developing country requires an extension of the period of exemption in relation to prohibited export subsidies, Article 27.4 of the SCM Agreement provides that it may enter into consultation with the Committee on Subsidies and Countervailing Measures (the Committee) to determine whether an extension of the period is justified. These consultations were to be initiated at least one year before the end of the exemption period, i.e. by the end of 2001. If, having taken into account all relevant economic, financial and development needs, the Committee is of the view that the extension is justified then the subsidy will be subject to annual reviews from then on.

It is worth noting that developing countries may be reluctant to apply for extensions on the grounds that to do so could create unease amongst existing or prospective EPZ companies. The alternative is to develop a strategy for bringing the incentive packages within the SCM Agreement rules.

A further exemption is provided in relation to the prohibition against subsidies in the form of domestic content requirements or preferential treatment for domestic over imported inputs. Developing countries were exempted from this prohibition until 2000. Least developed countries were exempt until the end of 2002.

19.2.3 Some further examples of measures likely to constitute prohibited export subsidies

Each of the following measures may, subject to the particular circumstances of the EPZ concerned, constitute a prohibited export subsidy:

- exemption from taxes on real estate;
- exemption from taxes on profits as well as of any other tax determined on the basis of gross or net income, dividends paid to shareholders or income or sales;
- income tax exemptions based on locating plant in areas of 'lesser development';
- income tax exemptions based on reinvestment in the host country;
- exemption from taxes on remittances abroad;
- provision of non-chargeable customs processing services; and
- the provision of public administrative services to EPZ manufacturers on a non-chargeable basis, such as assistance in selection of personnel, advice regarding government regulatory requirements and assistance with housing and educational needs of personnel.

19.2.4 Actionable subsidies

The second category of subsidies is actionable subsidies. These subsidies are defined by reference to the effect they have on another WTO Member. Therefore, if a subsidy falls within the Article 1 definition of subsidy, confers a benefit on the recipient and is specific, but is not a prohibited export subsidy, then the following test will be applied to determine whether it is an actionable subsidy:

> *Article 5*
>
> No Member should cause, through the use of any subsidy referred to in paragraphs 1 and 2 of Article 1, adverse effects to the interests of other Members, i.e.
>
> (a) injury to the domestic industry of another Member;
> (b) nullification or impairment of benefits accruing directly or indirectly to other Members;
> (c) serious prejudice to the interests of another Member.

Serious prejudice is deemed to exist in certain circumstances, namely where the total *ad valorem* subsidisation of a product exceeds 5 per cent of its value or where subsidies are paid to cover operating losses sustained by an industry. Where serious prejudice is deemed to exist, the burden of proof is on the subsidising Member to show that the subsidies in question do not cause serious prejudice to the complaining Member. This presumption of serious prejudice, however, only applies in relation to developed countries. For developing countries serious prejudice must be demonstrated by positive evidence.

Further, where a developing country maintains an actionable subsidy, i.e. one which causes adverse effects to the interests of other Members as per Article 5, a remedy will only be granted where the subsidy in question also displaces or impedes imports of like products into that country, or injures a domestic market in another country. In other words, the threshold to be reached before a remedy will be granted in response to an actionable subsidy is raised for developing countries.

19.2.5 Some examples of measures likely to constitute actionable subsidies

The measures listed below may, depending on the particular circumstances of the EPZ concerned, constitute actionable subsidies:

- exemption from import charges on the importation of raw materials, machinery and any other components necessary for EPZ company manufacturing (where the same exemptions are granted to imports for the manufacture of like products for domestic consumption);
- exemption from municipal taxes;
- exemption from stamp duty or transaction taxes; and
- exemption of sales and consumption taxes on purchases of goods and services.

19.2.6 Non-actionable subsidies

The final category of subsidy recognised by the SCM Agreement was non-actionable. Article 8 provides that subsidies which are not specific and certain other specific subsidies, e.g. industrial research subsidies, assistance to disadvantaged regions and subsidies to implement environmental requirements, are non-actionable. Members relying on the exemptions in Article 8 had to notify the Committee. However, Article 31 of the SCM Agreement provides that Article 8, amongst others, would apply only for a provisional period of five years. The Committee was then faced with the task of deciding whether to extend Article 8's application. The Committee failed to reach a consensus on an extension before 31 December 1999. Accordingly, this exemption no longer applies and previously non-actionable subsidies will now be treated in the same way as other subsidies.

This raises the question of whether subsidies previously notified under Article 8 continue to enjoy their exempt status, and if so for how long.

19.2.7 Notifications

The SCM Agreement builds on the obligation contained in Article XVI of GATT 1947 that Members must notify any subsidy that they maintain. Article 25 of the SCM Agreement requires Members to notify any specific subsidy within the broad definition of Article 1, i.e. *prohibited export subsidies*, and actionable subsidies as well as any non-actionable subsidies. Notifications are to be submitted by 30 June each year and Members may bring to the attention of the Committee any Member's failure to notify.

19.2.8 Remedies

Where a WTO Member maintains a prohibited subsidy the aggrieved WTO Member may initiate the SCM Agreement dispute settlement process, which includes an expedited timetable for action by the Dispute Settlement Body. If it is found that the subsidy is indeed prohibited, it must be immediately withdrawn. If this is not done within the specified time period, the complaining Member may be authorised to take countermeasures.

It is worth noting that in the *Australia – Subsidies Provided to Producers and Exporters of Automotive Leather* case, a dispute between the United States and Australian Governments resulted in a WTO Panel ordering that the exporter concerned repay A$30 million of export assistance to the Australian Government. A sanction of this type passed through to a corporation clearly demonstrates the risks that EPZ companies will be evaluating in relation to the incentives they receive.

An alternative course of action open to the aggrieved WTO Member, once a prohibited export subsidy is established, is to initiate a countervailing duty investigation with a view to imposing an additional import duty on the product or products concerned from the subsidising country. Before an aggrieved Member may impose a countervailing duty, it must comply with the detailed obligations contained in the SCM Agreement regarding the conduct of a countervailing duty investigation and the findings of a subsidy, injury, and a causal link between the two.

Affected Members can take action against a Member maintaining an actionable subsidy in the same way as for prohibited subsidies. In the event that it is determined that *adverse effects*, as defined in the SCM Agreement, exist, the subsidising Member must withdraw the subsidy or remove the adverse effects. Alternatively, a countervailing duty investigation may be commenced once the existence of an actionable subsidy has been established.

The SCM Agreement provides that a countervailing duty investigation of a product originating from a developing country is to be terminated if it is determined that the level of the subsidies does not exceed 2 per cent (3 per cent for some developing Members) of the value of the product, or if the subsidised imports from the developing country concerned amount to less than 4 per cent of the total imports of the *like product* into the aggrieved country.

Finally, a countervailing duty investigation will also be terminated in circumstances where the amount of the subsidy is de minimis or where the volume of exports or the injury is negligible.

19.2.9 What are the main issues for Commonwealth Governments with EPZ?

19.2.9.1 Illegal prohibited export subsidies

Several of the preferential incentives typically provided to companies in EPZs fall squarely within the definition of prohibited export subsidy as described in Article 3 and the illustrative list in Annex I. For example:

- the exemption or partial remission of direct taxes such as wage taxes, profit taxes, rents, royalties and property taxes;
- transport or freight charge subsidies on export shipment provided or mandated by the government; and,

- the provision of export credit guarantees or discounted insurance programmes.

It is important to note that the SCM Agreement is not targeting duty-free imports and exports. Rather, the Agreement targets the set of fiscal incentives, such as tax breaks and utility subsidies, which are offered on a preferential basis to exporters. If these measures were applied nationwide and to companies other than exporters, they would not be considered discriminatory and therefore would probably not be subject to WTO regulation. However, where these fiscal incentives are provided to EPZ firms on a preferential basis they become prohibited export subsidies (as described above) and are viewed as being an export subsidy for the EPZ companies' exported goods.

Therefore, developing Commonwealth countries with active EPZs and a per capita GNP of US $1,000 technically had until 2003 to remove the prohibited subsidies or realign EPZ incentive schemes with national norms. Where this was not done these countries faced disciplinary actions and countervailing measures from trade partners.

As discussed above, the least developed Commonwealth countries and those with a GNP per capita of less than US $1,000 are exempt from this restriction on prohibited subsidies.

19.2.9.2 Illegal local content requirements

Prohibited export subsidies include both subsidies contingent on export performance and those contingent on the use of domestic over imported goods (Article 3.1(b)). The phase-out period for these local content subsidies was slightly different to that for export performance subsidies. Developing countries were required to remove all such subsidies by the end of 2000. Least developed countries had until the end of 2002 to remove local content subsidies. Local content requirements may also conflict with a country's obligations under the WTO Agreement on Trade Related Investment Measures.

19.2.9.3 Introduced prohibited export subsidies

It should be remembered that the eight-year period before developing countries were prohibited from maintaining prohibited export subsidies, i.e. until 2003, was intended to be a phase-out period. Article 27.4 of the SCM Agreement provides that a developing country 'shall not increase the: level of its export subsidies'. Accordingly, where Commonwealth developing countries have increased, or are proposing to increase, the level of subsidies or introduce new subsidies, a careful assessment should be made as to whether the subsidy falls within the definition of *prohibited export subsidy*. Where such subsidies have already been introduced, there is of course the possibility of retaliation from a trade partner.

19.2.9.4 Extended time-limits for specific prohibited export subsidies

For all developing Commonwealth countries there was room in the SCM Agreement for a one-year extension of the exemption in relation to particular prohibited export subsidies, with annual consultation regarding further yearly extensions. These consultations were to be initiated by the end of 2001.

19.2.9.5 Illegal actionable subsidies

Where a Commonwealth country maintains an actionable subsidy, i.e. one which causes adverse effects to the interests of another Member and exceeds the de minimis thresholds, that country may become the focus of a direct challenge to the subsidy or a countervailing duty investigation, potentially resulting in the country being forced to withdraw the subsidy or remove the adverse effects, or the country's exporters facing a higher duty on exports to certain foreign markets. It should be noted that, while least developed countries or those with a GNP per capita below $1,000 are exempt from the restrictions on prohibited export subsidies, there is no exemption in relation to actionable subsidies. Therefore, if such a country were to export sufficient levels of subsidised product to pass the de minimis thresholds, an aggrieved country could take action against it.

19.2.9.6 Failure to notify subsidies

Article 25 of the SCM Agreement requires Members to notify any subsidies being maintained by 30 June each year. This includes an obligation to notify that no subsidies at all are maintained.

19.2.9.7 New round of negotiations

The issues raised above all presume that the SCM Agreement remains unamended. However, developing countries, including Commonwealth developing countries, may decide that the export subsidy exemptions for developing and least developed countries should be extended as part of any future negotiating round.

20

The accession of Vanuatu to the WTO: lessons for the multilateral trading system

ROMAN GRYNBERG AND ROY MICKEY JOY

20.1 Introduction

At present six least developed countries have formally sought accession to the World Trade Organisation (WTO).[1] This chapter examines the accession process of Vanuatu, a small least developed country (LDC) in the Western Pacific,[2] an experience that brings to the fore two fundamental – or perhaps over-arching – weaknesses of WTO Accession under the terms of Article XII of the Marrakesh Agreement.[3] The process normally proceeds through two logical stages. In the first, referred to as the 'protocol or multilateral stage', members examine the trade regime of individual applicants, seeking clarification of, and often reforms to, the conduct of trade where they deem aspects to be in violation of existing WTO rules. Clearly, this stage of the accession process – wherein self-interested WTO members examine the WTO conformity of an applicant's trade regime, with neither the operation of any rules for the process of examination nor the applicant's having right of recourse to any review – is akin to having a complainant at a panel act as the sole panelist. It is this first and most significant of the inherent flaws in the accession process, and the ensuing abuse of power, that has resulted in the proliferation of 'WTO-plus' demands on new WTO applicants.

This chapter was written in early 2000. An epilogue was added in May 2004 to bring readers up to date with Vanuatu's situation.

[1] These include Nepal, Cambodia, Laos, Samoa, Sudan and Vanuatu.

[2] Vanuatu, at the time of writing, was still classified by ECOSOC as a least developed country but was under threat of graduation to developing country status from 1997.

[3] Article XII states:

> Any state or separate customs territory possessing full autonomy in the conduct of its external commercial relations and of the other matters provided for in this Agreement and the Multilateral Trade Agreements may accede to this agreement, on terms to be agreed between it and the WTO.

In the second stage, commonly referred to as the 'bilateral stage', applicants negotiate with individual WTO members on the terms of their goods offer, agricultural schedules and service sector commitments. While it remains one of the enduring convenient cliches of the multilateral trading system that the WTO is a 'rule-based system', the actuality is that accession is inherently power-based and hence the very antithesis of the WTO's credo. The reality of all law and rules is that they mask power relations in a society, and certainly the WTO is no exception. Consequently it should come as no surprise that this bilateral stage of the accession process is flawed by virtue of the fact that the negotiation of accession, unlike normal GATT and WTO negotiations, offers the applicant no possibility of imposing a marginal cost on the *demandeur.*

The central thesis of this chapter is that in their submissions to the Seattle Ministerial Conference, the EU[4] and the Melanesian Spearhead Group[5] have taken a misguided approach to the reform of the accession process. The weakness of their approach lies in the fact that it fails to focus on the nature of the inherent flaws of the process itself, focusing instead on the development status of the applicant, i.e. whether it is an LDC or a developing country. The length and costliness of the WTO accession process are explained by the two inherent flaws in it, rather than by the development status of a particular applicant. Accession is biased against the applicant and the process gives enormous powers to the WTO members to extract concessions that would not be possible in a genuinely rule-based system. Indeed, the reason the process is unlikely ever to be reformed lies in these inherent flaws and the power they give as a consequence to the large WTO members (i.e. the Quad – the USA, the EU, Japan and Canada) vis-à-vis developing countries and countries in transition (the categories to which recent WTO applicants normally belong). But it is also one of the reasons why the process must be reformed if the WTO is to establish its legitimacy as a real rule-based system that serves all members and not just the most powerful.

20.2 The Vanuatu economy

Vanuatu is both small and highly dispersed, with eighty islands covering a land area of 12,189 sq km spread over an EEZ of 710,000 sq km of ocean.[6]

[4] WT/GC/W/153. [5] WT/GC/W/378.

[6] Vanuatu became an independent country only in 1980, following an intervention by Papua New Guinean military forces to put down an insurrection by French separatists on the island

The country's economy is minuscule – the total 1997 GDP was USD 200 million – and equally characterised by smallness and dispersion – a population of 170,000 shared a GDP/capita of USD 1,200. The economy is highly dualistic in nature, the vast majority of the population living in rural subsistence. Real GDP has grown at 3 per cent since independence and the population has grown at 2.9 per cent, resulting in a virtually stagnant real per capita income over the period. Vanuatu's main exports are beef, copra and cocoa. Agriculture accounts for approximately 25 per cent of GDP. The main markets for Vanuatu exports are the EU and Japan. Indeed, for a country that has been independent from the UK and France since 1980, Vanuatu remains almost unnaturally dependent upon trade with the EU, largely as a result on the one hand of access to EU imports via neighbouring New Caledonia, and on the other, the viability of copra exports to the EU because of Stabex and the Lomé Convention. This dependence, though, dropped sharply in the late 1990s.

Increasingly, the service sector has come to dominate the economy. Tourism and earnings from the Finance Centre constitute the largest sources of foreign exchange earnings. Also growing in importance has been housing construction in Port Vila, where there is a significant and high-income expatriate population.[7] This accounts for the high GDP per capita in comparison to the country's other Melanesian neighbours, the Solomon Islands and Papua New Guinea.[8]

One of the most significant structural features of the economy has been the absence of any direct taxes. Vanuatu is one of the few tax havens to maintain no domestic internal direct taxes alongside the system of no taxes in the tax haven. This absence of income taxes – and until the economic reforms that began in 1997, the absence of any other significant source of government tax revenue – was to shape the nature of the reform programme and the bilateral accession negotiations to the WTO. Furthermore,

of Espiritu Santo. Until then the country had been ruled as an Anglo-French condominium since 1906, after some twenty years of a joint Anglo-French naval commission that attempted to safeguard a degree of order after turbulent years of mission, trading and 'blackbirding' activity.

[7] The presence of this high-income expatriate community in Port Vila greatly skews the economic indicators for Vanuatu. The resultant GDP/capita may well lead ECOSOC to graduate Vanuatu to developing country status, thus further compounding the nation's difficulties with accession to the WTO.

[8] In 1997 the Solomon Islands GDP/capita was USD 640 and Papua New Guinea's GDP/capita was USD 1,200. However, the Asian economic crisis has resulted in a collapse of the local unit in Papua New Guinea, leading to a fall in GDP/capita to approximately USD 700–800 in 1999.

given the tax structure, it was evident that with high and common triple-digit applied rates, a fundamental reform of the Vanuatu taxation system would be a precondition for WTO accession.[9]

In 1998 Vanuatu signed an agreement with the Asian Development Bank for the implementation of the Comprehensive Reform Programme (CRP). This structural adjustment programme stemmed from a crisis of economic and political governance in which:

- the Vanuatu public service had become increasingly politicised and less professional;
- decisions regarding investment and work permits were seen as increasingly politicised and highly arbitrary in nature;
- governments changed through parliamentary votes of no-confidence an average of two times in any one year in the period 1996–8;
- a series of very damaging reports regarding the public misconduct of several leaders was published by the Ombudsman in 1996–7; and
- rioting occurred in the capital Port Vila in January 1998, as a result of revelations that funds from the Vanuatu National Provident Fund (VNPF) had been improperly used by political leaders. The consequent run on the VNPF funds necessitated government injections that would raise the deficit to an unparalleled 14 per cent of GDP.[10]

This combination of events, in conjunction with an abortive attempt to devalue the local currency in late March 1998, led to a collapse of economic and political confidence in Vanuatu.[11] In order to restore public confidence in the beleaguered processes of political and economic governance, the Vanuatu government agreed to the implementation of the CRP. This was regarded as a *sine qua non* for accession to the WTO, because many of the reforms, while not directly trade related, were certainly investment related.

[9] For the most recent and comprehensive economic analysis of the Vanuatu economy, see Asian Development Bank (ADB), *Vanuatu: Economic Performance, Policy and Reform Issues* (Manila: Asian Development Bank, 1997).

[10] B. Knapman and C. Saldanha, *Reforms in the Pacific: An Assessment of the Asian Development Bank's Assistance for the Reform Programs in the Pacific* (Manila: Asian Development Bank, 1999), p. 144.

[11] On the morning of Friday, 27 March 1998, the Governor of the Reserve Bank of Vanuatu devalued the currency by 20 per cent without the permission of the Minister of Finance or the Prime Minister (on what was the last day of his appointment and that of the government). That afternoon the Minister of Finance reversed the devaluation. A new government sworn in on 30 March upheld the reversal of the devaluation.

20.3 The process of accession

20.3.1 Systemic and protocol issues: from WTO to 'WTO plus'

The accession of Vanuatu has gone ahead very much alongside the country's more significant reform process undertaken in conjunction with the Asian Development Bank, which has acted as the multilateral agency responsible for the small island states of the Western and Central Pacific.[12] This reform process, still underway in Vanuatu, formed the basis of the trade, investment and general commercial reforms that have been at the heart of Vanuatu's WTO accession. The fact that Vanuatu is undergoing a structural reform process under the supervision of a multilateral agency while simultaneously negotiating accession to the WTO is a situation shared with most applicants to the WTO.[13] In fact accession, which involves a series of at best politically incomprehensible and often unpopular commercial and economic reforms, is best disguised under a structural adjustment or a round of multilateral trade negotiations. Trying to explain to any public and its political leadership the range of necessary reforms to bring a trade regime into conformity with its WTO obligations is extremely difficult, no less so in developing countries, especially following the negative publicity in the wake of the Seattle Ministerial Conference.

As all applicants must, Vanuatu submitted to the WTO Working Party a memorandum of foreign trade in 1996. The data gathering involved in the preparation of this memorandum of foreign trade was extremely useful because it forced Vanuatu to examine trade policies as well as serving to complement many of the reforms that were contemplated under the CRP. This section of the chapter reviews the trade and investment regime in place at the commencement of the accession process, and the reforms agreed to and requested by WTO members.

[12] Only when the structural adjustment programmes are for the largest economies of the Central and Western Pacific (Papua New Guinea, Fiji and Solomon Islands) is the intervention of the World Bank deemed necessary. In the recent structural adjustment programmes of the smallest states (Vanuatu, Cook Islands, Marshall Islands and Federated States of Micronesia) the ADB has acted as the lead agency.

[13] UNCTAD, 'Accession to the World Trade Organisation: The Process and Issues', Discussion Paper, May 1998.

20.3.1.1 The trade regime

In 1996 almost two-thirds of total tax revenue was generated through international trade taxes. This trade-based tax represented approximately one-half of total government revenue, making Vanuatu one of the most trade-tax-dependent economies in the region. Moreover, the official figure masked the fact that many of the other taxes, such as business licences and service taxes, were in fact surcharges on import duty.

The trade taxes were both import and export taxes. Import duties prior to the reform process were in fifty-four different bands and ranged from zero to 207 per cent. The range of nominal taxes by broad economic classification is depicted in table 20.1.

The high dependence upon import duties had three separate effects. First, it raised the cost structure and made exports less competitive. Second, it provided what were often inadvertent incentives to highly inefficient import substituting industries. Third, in order to provide incentives to investment, a system of exemptions from import duties (as there were no direct taxes) further complicated and rendered opaque the system of taxes. The latter two effects came to constitute serious impediments to Vanuatu's accession, even after its reform programme had been put in place.

The other source of trade tax revenue lay in the existence of export taxes. In 1990, Vanuatu levied export taxes of 8 per cent on copra and 7 per cent on cocoa exports. Taxes on exports were lowered to 3 per cent in 1995 and Vanuatu continued to maintain export taxes of 3 per cent on a range of exports. Higher rates of export taxes existed on unprocessed timber exports and trochus shell. Like so many of Vanuatu's tax measures, this was clearly not intended to be a disincentive to exports. Without direct taxes it was not possible to tax in any other way the quasi-rents being derived from resource sectors, and the government's measures were meant to capture part of the economic rents being derived by exporters. In the process this also acted as a further disincentive to exports.

The reform programme begun at the behest of the ADB made significant advances towards resolving many of the WTO accession issues. Import duties were simplified and dramatically lowered although, as will become evident, in the subsequent bilateral negotiations several significant tariff peaks remained. However, while the ADB eliminated the business licence regime and export taxes, phased out service taxes and simplified the import

Table 20.1 *Duty rates by broad economic classification*

	1990	1995
Consumer	47.0	36.5
Intermediate	17.7	23.1
Capital	8.0	10.6
Fuel (motor spirits)	128.7	151.7
Cars	19.3	21.0
Total	25.1	26.1

Source: Statistics Office, Trade Statistics, 1996

duty system, the actual effect was to make Vanuatu dependent upon a very narrow range of taxes. Subsequent to the reforms, Value Added Tax (VAT) and import duties have become the principal sources of revenue. Without this reform no credible goods offer was possible; but following the reform, the narrowing of the range of taxes rendered it more difficult for Vanuatu to make bilateral concessions that would further limit import duties.

The trade regime in Vanuatu also contained several elements that were of doubtful WTO compatibility. The first requiring reform was the 3 per cent surcharge paid for imports of five staple products: flour, rice, fish, tobacco and sugar.[14] This particular provision meant, as a revenue-raising measure, that those with import licences for these products were paying a commission to the Vanuatu Cooperative Federation. In 1999, the Government of Vanuatu abolished the import licences for these products, as well as the surcharge. There are presently no import licences in Vanuatu.[15]

The powers granted Vanuatu provincial governments to raise taxes on imports constituted a second measure requiring reform.[16] Given the very

[14] *Laws of Vanuatu*, Import of Goods Control Act [Cap.176].

[15] Perhaps one of the most interesting experiences of Vanuatu with WTO-liberalisation measures was the elimination of import licences for rice. Following the reform of the trade regime, the government began to issue licenses freely and in 1999 twenty-six licenses were offered, as opposed to the monopoly arrangement that existed prior to WTO reforms. Despite the liberalization, the elimination of monopoly and the lowering of duties, rice imports continue to be handled by only one trader – the same monopolist as prior to the reforms. The reason is that the Australian exporter is unwilling to sell to small local buyers who have a limited track record. Prices have not changed and, given the ni-Vanuatu preference for Australian 'Calrose' rice, there is unlikely to be a diversion to other sources of supply such as Thailand. Thus far the liberalization of trade in staple products seems to have had no visible effect.

[16] *Laws of Vanuatu*, Provincial Government Act 1994.

narrow tax base and the very weak administrative capacity in the field of taxation, the then existing practice of provincial governments raising import duties would not be WTO compatible. The Government of Vanuatu made a commitment in its protocol not to allow sub-national governments to raise import duties.[17]

The power of the Minister of Trade to use import restrictions in a manner inconsistent with WTO rules was also limited by protocol agreement. In the past the minister was empowered to limit imports where this was deemed to be in the national interest.[18] The use of these powers has been limited to WTO-compatible quantitative restrictions as permitted under Article XX and the various safety contingency provisions. Vanuatu maintained no other quantitative restrictions on trade.[19]

The existence of the so-called 'service tax' at 7 per cent of imports was also called into question by WTO members. Clearly, as the tax was well in excess of any conceivable ports and services charge based on a user-pays system, this was quite correctly seen as a surcharge on import duties. The tax was eliminated and replaced by the 12.5 per cent Value Added Tax.

Several institutional issues that are protocol matters arose from the very outset. The absence of WTO-compatible Customs Valuation legislation, as well as legislation recognising the Agreement on Rules of Origin, was seen by WTO members as an area requiring reform.[20] It was here that the most profound differences of view began to emerge between Vanuatu and WTO Working Party members.[21] Developing countries should implement the

[17] This matter was resolved by a protocol commitment not to allow sub-national governments to impose taxes that are in violation of WTO obligations. This procedure can be policed because all revenue-raising measures of sub-national governments must be approved by the Vanuatu national government.

[18] Over a period of two years, WTO members raised a considerable number of questions over the import ban on potatoes, which had been imposed to help develop the Irish potato production capacity of the island of Tanna. The Trade division agreed in 1998 to tarifficate the measure, only to be informed subsequently by the Customs Department that the restriction had been officially rescinded in 1993. In small countries with high staff and government turnover, this lack of knowledge about the conduct of policy is common. The WTO is most useful in providing the clarity and transparency that is often missing because, in a particular country, knowledge of the institutions of trade is widely dispersed.

[19] The only trade restriction maintained was on the import of T-shirts with a Vanuatu motif, a measure that existed to protect the local and tourist-oriented screen print industry. This ban has now been replaced with a high tariff.

[20] Until its revision of legislation, Vanuatu continued to use the Brussels valuation system.

[21] The Working Party on the Accession of Vanuatu is normally composed of the Quad (USA, EU, Japan and Canada) with Australia, New Zealand and Switzerland in attendance. In general only

Agreement on the Interpretation of Article VII of GATT 1994 by 2000. Some WTO members, despite public protestations to the contrary, remain unsympathetic to the Special and Differential Treatment (SDT) provisions and in some cases are hostile to them. Vanuatu, recognising this fact and in order to minimise the hostility from Working Party members, decided to pursue only those SDT provisions that were necessary to assure efficient implementation. It was also clear that WTO members were, during accession negotiations, totally uninterested in the question of the development status of Vanuatu. This was particularly so for some of the largest WTO members. Thus Vanuatu requested a two-year transition to allow for training. The USA, though appearing willing to accept a shorter transition, did not accept this request.

20.3.1.2 The investment regime

The investment regime in Vanuatu prior to the implementation of the Comprehensive Reform Programme was described by the ADB as 'uninviting'.[22] Prior to the reforms, decisions regarding business licences for foreign investment and work permits were often highly political. Decisions were made either at the ministerial level or even at the level of the council of ministers. Business licences and work permits were subject to regular renewal and decisions on their renewal and continuation were widely seen by the business community in Vanuatu as political in nature, arbitrary and often opaque.[23]

By making specific access commitments under the terms of GATS, WTO applicants and members by definition make express commitment regarding the movement of capital.[24] WTO applicants frequently do not

the larger and better-financed WTO members with global trade interests are able to devote resources to the accession of small states. In late 1999 the three WTO members of the Melanesian Spearhead Group (Papua New Guinea, Solomon Islands and Fiji) also joined the Working Party. Nevertheless, the Working Party is in large measure driven by the Quad and Australia and New Zealand. [22] ADB, *Vanuatu*, p. 89.

[23] Vanuatu, prior to the CRP, had become infamous for the 'Green letter', which gave the Minister of Immigration the right to remove residence permits, without reason or the right of appeal. This arbitrary right has now been removed: all work permits now carry terms of termination specified in law and all work permit holders have a clear right of appeal.

[24] GATS, Article XVI, para. 1, footnote 8 states:

> If a member undertakes a market access commitment in relation to the mode of supply referred to in subparagraph 2(a) of Article I and if the cross-border movement of capital is an essential part of that service itself, that member is thereby committed to allow such movement of capital . . .

understand this: it was certainly not clear at the beginning of accession that Vanuatu had to create transparent and open investment rules in order to become a member of the WTO. What were seen as highly intrusive demands were justified on the grounds that without an appropriate investment climate all GATS obligations in terms of mode 1 and 3 access were meaningless. In a bargaining situation for WTO accession where the applicant has no power, this, of course, raises the question of what are the proper limits to the demands of WTO members. On the basis of experience, the response unfortunately seems to be: whatever can be extracted from the applicant.

Perhaps the most sensitive issue raised during the protocol stage of Vanuatu's accession was the issue of land. Members of the Working Party during the protocol or multilateral stage argued that Vanuatu should consider a revision of its land laws as they did not provide for adequate access and protection of property. Vanuatu, perhaps even more so than other countries of Melanesia, has a particular sensitivity with regard to the nature and significance of land ownership. Freehold land was abolished at independence and all land previously privately owned, which was mainly in the hands of European colonialists, reverted to its traditional owners.[25] Despite an initial shock to investor confidence, the absence of freehold has not acted as a constraint on very substantial foreign investment in real estate in Vanuatu. Conflicts over delineation of property rights under traditional title do act as a constraint to investment but no government in Melanesia has successfully managed to deal with the matter, which would involve the state in the delineation of often overlapping traditional titles. WTO members also wanted to see some improvement in land law administration. Whether or not such sensitive issues are now properly within the purview of the WTO raises very serious issues for the countries of Melanesia, the Pacific Islands and the developing world in general. However, it seems fair to say that any government in Melanesia in general or Vanuatu in particular that attempts to reform land laws and delineate custom title can count its longevity in days, if not shorter units.

Because the implications of this footnote have not been the subject of interpretation by a panel, there is no jurisprudence to act as a guide. However, a very broad interpretation of the obligation to 'allow such movement of capital' could well be expected once the matter is tested.

[25] The name Vanuatu, literally 'our land', was chosen as an expression of the indissoluble spiritual relationship between the ni-Vanuatu population and their land.

20.3.1.3 Other protocol issues

A host of multilateral issues arose relating to the implementation of agreements. Vanuatu was asked by the USA to join both the Agreement on Government Procurement and the Agreement on Civil Aircraft. These demands, like so many other US demands to small acceding countries at the WTO, were systemic in nature. They did not in any way reflect a perception that US trade interests were otherwise likely to be impaired: Vanuatu, as an LDC, neither has any government procurement contracts of a sufficient value to induce any US interest in tendering[26] nor does it buy or produce aircraft.[27] Vanuatu has thus far refused to accede to these discriminatory and largely irrelevant plurilateral agreements.

The USA has also refused the request by Vanuatu for a two-year transition for the implementation of TRIPs. Vanuatu offered to WTO members to have the TRIPs legislation in place on the date of accession but is unwilling to commit to full implementation in less than two years because it lacks an agency and the proper level of training to make such a goal achievable.[28]

In the area of agriculture, several issues of some importance arose. Vanuatu was prohibited from joining the WTO if it insisted on using Special Safeguard Provisions (Article 5). WTO members argued that these, as 'Uruguay Round methodologies', were not available to acceding countries.[29] Vanuatu, having 'tarifficated' its quantitative restrictions in potatoes, felt that it should have rights to use SSG provisions. WTO members, despite the LDC status of Vanuatu, denied this request.

26 Virtually all large (i.e. greater than USD 1 million) construction and procurement contracts are normally made using the procurement rules of the donor agency involved.

27 Air Vanuatu, the national carrier, either leases or wet leases aircraft.

28 Vanuatu is the biological home of one of the world's most fashionable 'green' indigenous sedatives, the root crop 'kava'. Kava as a traditional beverage has been consumed by ni-Vanuatu and many other Pacific islanders since long before the arrival of Europeans. Its sedative qualities were known throughout the Pacific region. However, large pharmaceutical companies in the USA and the EU now produce, and have patented, kava pills. Apart from the export of the unprocessed root, Vanuatu gains nothing from this high-value and increasingly popular natural sedative. Its implementation of TRIPs compliant legislation will also do nothing to protect the one IPR issue it has, the indigenous intellectual property rights.

Article 27.3 of the TRIPs provides for *sui generis* legislation that can protect, through national legislation, against the piracy of indigenous intellectual property. However, in the absence of an international standard for the protection of such IPRs, Vanuatu has no claim in the national courts of those large developed countries that do not recognise such collectively owned rights.

29 This prohibitive stance is not factually defensible as both Bulgaria and Panama acceded with SSG provisions in their schedule.

The most difficult agricultural area was that of export subsidies. Vanuatu occasionally offers agricultural price supports to some of its poorest copra farmers when prices fall to catastrophically low levels. Given that large WTO members such as the EU and the USA offer massive subsidies to temperate edible oils, the USD 1 million in price supports that had been offered for copra producers in 1996 should not have been problematic. However, because these were funded by Stabex funds under the Lomé IV Convention, [30] it was argued that since the money was aid, it could not be used as a subsidy. Thus Vanuatu was in the paradoxical position of having to argue that it was subsidising exports, yet given that the EU funds could be used in any of a number of ways, their use as subsidy was a matter of choice for the government. The EU does not oblige ACP countries to use Stabex funds for export subsidies, though this is accepted as part of the Stabex 'Framework of Mutual Obligations' agreed between the EU and the ACP recipient.[31]

Some WTO members have publicly stated that they would not permit any country with agricultural export subsidies to join the WTO. This position has no grounding in WTO rules because LDCs are not obliged to make export subsidy commitments.[32] In the end, Vanuatu decided that it would not be able to join the WTO if its ES1 schedule contained any export subsidies and, for this reason, accepted the interpretation that Stabex was aid. In the future, some of the poorest farmers in Vanuatu will have to bear the full brunt of price fluctuations in a distorted and volatile edible oil market, solely because it was in the interests of WTO members.

[30] Throughout the four Lomé Conventions, Stabex funding was amongst the most innovative instruments devised by the EU, for it provided funding to compensate exporters for shortfalls of earnings for their exports to the EU. This helped stabilise export earnings in ACP countries while simultaneously assuring EU access to agricultural exports, which was a high policy priority in the 1970s. Because Stabex was paid only to those who exported to the EU, it was responsible for the continuation of the copra trade between Vanuatu and the EU. With the advent of all-destinations derogation in the Stabex provisions of Lomé IV (Article 189, paras. 2 and 3) this incentive to export to the EU declined after 1980. Stabex was abolished at the end of Lomé IV and is not found in the successor Convention to be signed in 2000.

[31] Lomé IV, Article 186, para. 2.

[32] Article 9, Agreement on Agriculture, does not prohibit export subsidies. Article 15 excludes LDCs from all reduction commitments under the agreement.

20.3.2 Bilateral issues: goods offer and service commitments

At an informal Working Party meeting in October 1999, Vanuatu presented a complete package for its accession to the WTO.[33] This package included a draft goods offer, service sector commitments and agricultural schedules as well as a draft protocol of accession. By the standards of other WTO members of a similar development status, Vanuatu's offer was extremely generous. Yet despite successful bilateral trade negotiations with all of its trading partners, the negotiations with the USA – which does not trade with the tiny nation[34] – failed in key areas that remain vital to Vanuatu's trade and economic interests.

The disagreements with the USA were over a range of issues, including the broad parameters of the goods offer, the extent of service commitment, and several crucial protocol issues pertaining to the transition periods of LDCs. However, USA objections, which stem from its vital trade interests, have nothing to do with bilateral trade with Vanuatu. The problem lies rather in the fact that any concession the USA might offer to Vanuatu might be urged as a precedent for extension to other more significant WTO applicants.

While Vanuatu has resolved many of the outstanding issues with its bilateral partners, its failure to do so with the USA is also in many ways 'systemic'. Given that the USA places the greatest demands upon acceding countries – and this is well known among accession negotiators – assumptions have developed regarding US behaviour that allow WTO members to play what accession negotiators now term 'good cop–bad cop'. Other Quad members and the Cairns group, aware that the USA will take a hard line with applicants, are able to make less strident demands. This strategy will minimise the political costs of attempting to extract concessions from acceding countries, some of whom are close political allies.

20.3.2.1 The goods offer

Vanuatu's goods offer in the October 1999 package to the WTO involved binding the entire tariff at an average rate of duty of 39 per cent plus a 10 per cent bound rate for Other Duties and Charges (ODC). Following bilateral negotiations with the EU, it was agreed to roll the ODC into the bound rate. Over 60 per cent of bound tariffs in the Vanuatu offer (see table 20.2)

[33] The WTO frequently argues that it attempts to keep Working Party meetings to a minimum for LDCs, usually two. This is factually correct, but there is a need for numerous 'informal' meetings, for some of which the applicant has no resources to attend.

[34] Total bilateral trade between Vanuatu and the USA was less than USD 1 million in 1998.

Table 20.2 *Simple average rates of* ad valorem *duty by HS Chapter, offer of October 1999*

HS 96 Chapter	Average rate	HS 96 Chapter	Average rate	HS 96 Chapter	Average rate	HS 96 Chapter	Average rate
1	30	25	30	49	33	73	30
2	28	26	30	50	30	74	30
3	55	27	63	51	30	75	30
4	30	28	30	52	30	76	36
5	30	29	30	53	30	77	
6	55	30	25	54	30	78	30
7	54	31	30	55	30	79	30
8	30	32	36	56	30	80	30
9	30	33	30	57	30	81	30
10	30	34	40	58	30	82	30
11	30	35	30	59	30	83	50
12	30	36	30	60	30	84	27
13	30	37	30	61	32	85	26
14	30	38	30	62	30	86	30
15	30	39	32	63	30	87	32
16	30	40	30	64	30	88	0
17	30	41	30	65	30	89	37
18	30	42	30	66	30	90	33
19	30	43	30	67	30	91	45

20	39	44	30	68	30	92	35
21	34	45	30	69	30	93	200
22	205	46	30	70	30	94	55
23	30	47	30	71	30	95	35
24	450	48	30	72	30	96	30
Average for agriculture	58	Average for intermediate goods	31	Average for final goods	30	97	30

Table 20.3 *Average rate of WTO bound* ad valorem *tariffs for various Pacific Island WTO members*

	Development status (recent GDP/capita – USD)	Average bound rate of tariff	Year of WTO membership
Fiji	Developing country (USD 2,200)	40%	1995
Papua New Guinea	Developing country (USD 1,020)	40%* 45% for agriculture	1995
Solomon Islands	Least developed country (USD 700)	80%	1995
Vanuatu	Least developed country (USD 1,020)	49%	1999 offer

*PNG average bound rates for non-agricultural goods are scheduled to decrease to 30 per cent by 2007.

are below the applied rates that existed at the time of the commencement of the accession negotiations in 1995. Vanuatu's structure of bound tariffs is also common for an enclave economy in that it has a clear 'reverse escalation' in its offer. This stems from high rates of duty for competing agricultural products and very high rates of duty for sin goods (chapters 22 and 24). The average rate of duty on agricultural products was 58 per cent, decreasing to 31 per cent for intermediate goods (chapters 25–60) and 30 per cent for final goods.

However, Vanuatu not only agreed to a very moderate bound rate of tariff given its continuing reliance on import duty revenue, it also offered a rate very similar to that of countries in the region that applied to join the GATT/WTO only several months prior to Vanuatu. Table 20.3 presents the average rate of bound *ad valorem* duty in the tariff offers of various Pacific Island WTO members. It demonstrates that Vanuatu has made offers not dissimilar to those made by much larger and more developed countries in the region, and much lower than offers made by least developed countries such as the Solomon Islands.[35]

[35] Both Vanuatu and Solomon Islands were GATT *de facto* members prior to the completion of the Uruguay Round. However, Vanuatu moved at a slower pace to submit its application to the GATT before the expiry of the *de facto* provisions. As a result, it was subject to WTO rather than GATT standards of accession, which have progressively increased since 1995 under pressure from the Quad.

Table 20.4 *Service sector commitments by Pacific Island countries*

	Number of areas covered by commitments
Fiji	2
Papua New Guinea	18
Solomon Islands	9
Vanuatu	18

Vanuatu has also agreed to zero-for-zero commitments in more than 160 tariff lines and is in full conformity with zero-for-zero initiatives in information technology. It has offered to provide duty-free access for aircraft and parts and pharmaceuticals by 2005. No other least developed country made offers even remotely close to those of Vanuatu during the Uruguay Round.

20.3.2.2 Service sector commitments

In the service sector the commitments made by Vanuatu are far more extensive than those made by other WTO members from the region. Table 20.4 summarises the number of areas covered in GATS commitments by Pacific Island countries during the Uruguay Round.

Thus Vanuatu, an LDC, has made service sector commitments with clear and unambiguous market opening commitments in eighteen areas. This is more than four times the average for LDCs and twice that of the Solomon Islands, which is the most obvious case for comparison.

20.3.2.3 Bilateral negotiations

Following the presentation of its package to the WTO Working Party, Vanuatu began bilateral negotiations with WTO members. In the space of two days negotiations were virtually completed with the EU, Australia, New Zealand, Japan, Canada and Switzerland. In the case of some countries, the issues under negotiation were systemic and had nothing to do with bilateral issues.[36] In other cases – such as Australia and New Zealand, which are major sources of imports for Vanuatu – the negotiations were more substantive. In none of these cases were the negotiations particularly difficult

[36] Many of the bilateral negotiations were regarding a standard set of Initial Negotiating Rights (INRs) that had little to do with actual bilateral trade. In some cases, such as the Canadian demand that canola oil be treated the same as other edible oils, they were pro forma demands made of all acceding countries to assure that Canada's market position in the edible oil market is not eroded vis-à-vis competing products from the USA.

as they resulted in no substantive demands from bilateral trading partners for Vanuatu to move away from its essential position, as outlined in its October 1999 accession package.

Only in negotiations with the USA were the demands such that no agreement was possible. The USA demanded that Vanuatu lower its bound tariff to around 15–25 per cent, from its current average of 49 per cent. The US demand for a reduction of the bound rate of import duty to 25 per cent would result in a complete loss of flexibility in the taxation system. Should there be a particularly severe natural disaster – a relatively common cause of decreased revenue and increased expenditure in this part of the world – the Vanuatu government would not be in a position to raise import duties. This is particularly significant because, as noted, Vanuatu, in its Comprehensive Reform Programme, introduced a VAT and eliminated a host of other taxes such as business licences and service tax. This has meant that the government is now heavily dependent upon import duties and a VAT that still has administrative teething problems. Understandably, the complete elimination of flexibility in the taxation regime that acceptance of the US demands would mean is unacceptable to the Government of Vanuatu.

The USA has objected to the tariff peaks in chapters 22, 24 and 93. It has become one of the clichés of accession negotiations that in the end the negotiations always come down to 'booze and cigarettes'; but now the USA, clearly under pressure from its own gun lobby, is putting pressure on acceding countries to liberalise the trade in weapons. The US has argued that if Vanuatu wishes to restrict the trade in any of the categories of commodities – alcohol, tobacco and weapons – then tariffs are an inappropriate measure. The USTR, arguing that restrictions should be undertaken using other trade-neutral taxes, has insisted on removal of the tariff peaks in these areas of vital US trade interest. The unacceptability of allowing such tariff peaks clearly rests on the implications that would flow on for other accession negotiations. While there are revenue concerns on tobacco and alcohol and a desire to prohibit weapons completely, there is a protective interest in alcohol. In a counter offer to the USA, Vanuatu has agreed to impose a trade-neutral excise tax in these three areas and leave the tariff peak at 50 per cent in the case of chapters 24 and 93, in addition to agreeing to bind all alcohol tariffs at their applied rate. Given the structure of its economy and its high vulnerability, Vanuatu cannot accept the US demands on general tariffs.

In the service sector the USA has added a further demand for the opening of the telecommunications sector. In Vanuatu this is not legally possible as France Telecom and Cable and Wireless, the two strategic partners in Vanuatu's telecom condominium arrangement, have an ironclad 'gateway monopoly' until 2012. A USA counter proposal has demanded that Vanuatu make commitments to open the telecommunications sector in 2012. Vanuatu has replied that to do so would discourage the strategic partners from investing further in the improvement of the telecommunications infrastructure. In 2012 Vanuatu would be likely to find itself far behind the rest of the world in telecommunications, an area vital to a small vulnerable country highly dependent upon tourism and the service sector.

Vanuatu has requested transitional arrangements, only for two years, in the application of the Agreement on Customs Valuation and the TRIPs, though a much longer time is permitted to LDC WTO members. The USA has not agreed even to these moderate requests for transition. Vanuatu has indicated that unless there is a moderation of US demands, it will withdraw its application for WTO membership.

20.4 Conclusion

The USA has no bilateral trading interest in Vanuatu. Its demands are systemic in nature rather than country specific. The placing of these demands on an LDC is occurring only because of the precedent that not doing so would create vis-à-vis other applicants to the WTO. This is not a conclusion drawn by Vanuatu negotiators. It comes as a verbal *mea culpa* from developed country negotiators trying to explain why such patently unreasonable demands are being placed upon an LDC that is of no economic significance. Vanuatu is simply 'collateral damage' in the so-called 'rule-based system', a system that when it comes to the accession process is in reality based purely upon power.

WTO officials are fond of saying that the multilateral trading system is a rule-based system. Yet the accession process has no rules, except precedent and power, and is the very antithesis of what the members publicly state to be the intention and design of the WTO. Accession, because the applicant is not a WTO member and has no rights, is power based. More importantly, the applicant cannot inflict any marginal cost on the WTO members when they demand progressively more trade concessions. The accession process is inherently flawed by this latter factor rather than simply by the size disparity between LDCs and small vulnerable states like Vanuatu on the one hand and large WTO members such as the USA, the EU and Japan on the other.

One of the most used of the many clichés repeated at WTO ministerial conferences is the desire of members 'to integrate the least developed countries into the multilateral trading system'. Yet the experience of Vanuatu has been the exact opposite. Once ministers have finished their diplomatic speeches, the job of trade officials is 'business as usual', to wit the extraction of the maximum concessions possible irrespective of the development needs or status of the applicant.

Not until the WTO lives by its promises and creates a genuinely rule-based system will least developed and highly vulnerable countries be able to take their proper place at the WTO. At present, accession is a power-based process within which the applicant – even the largest and seemingly most powerful, such as China – has no real power to inflict any marginal cost on a *demandeur.* The negotiation of WTO accession, fundamentally flawed and lawless, is in desperate need of reform for it only serves to undermine further the credibility – in tatters since Seattle – of the 'rule-based' multilateral trading system.

Two simple and completely WTO-compatible reforms to the accession process would bring to an end much of the current power-based system. WTO members in the protocol or multilateral stage have a perfectly legitimate right to assure themselves that the trade regime of an applicant is in conformity with its WTO obligations. However, as mentioned in the introduction, the enormous power that this bestows upon WTO members must eventually be abused whenever a complainant acts as judge. The result has been obvious and predictable – the proliferation of 'WTO-plus' demands on new applicants. The reform that would resolve this would be to have a panel of experts decide whether an applicant's trade regime is in conformity with existing WTO rules. This is exactly the right bestowed upon all WTO members during a dispute, and no WTO member would countenance a system where panelists reviewing the WTO compatibility of their trade regime were complainants. Thus a report of a panel of experts would fulfil the perfectly legitimate demands of WTO members that there be a review of the trade regime of applicants. This report could then act as the basis for negotiation of necessary reforms of the trade regime of WTO applicants.

While extension of the system of panel reports to WTO applicants would greatly relieve the multilateral track, an equally simple reform would end the excessive bilateral demands in the goods sector. Under the GATT system, in order to facilitate negotiations and simultaneously keep small members out of tariff negotiations, members applied the provisions of Article XVIII limiting negotiations to principal suppliers only.[37] This would mean that countries supplying only negligible quantities of imports to an applicant would not have negotiating rights in the bilateral stage of negotiations.

Only those who are extraordinarily naive would believe that the system of accession will be reformed. The reasons are simple. First, the beneficiaries of the reform, which is to say those who are applying for WTO access, have no voice in the WTO as they are by definition outside the multilateral trading system. Once they become members they rarely wish to discuss what is an embarrassing and highly intrusive process. Secondly, those who would have to pay for the reforms would be the WTO proponents, who gain nothing and have to expend scarce political capital in its reform. The losers would also be the WTO members, who would no longer be able to extract the trade concessions from applicants. Indeed, given the very large countries currently attempting to gain access, there can be no doubt that few WTO members would wish to see such reform. The accession process will remain power based, because WTO members benefit from that state of affairs. This will only serve further to undermine the credibility of the rule-based system.

20.5 Epilogue

Vanuatu's accession stalled at Doha, due to disagreements on the liberalisation of wholesale and retail sectors. They have since remained an observer at the WTO. Recently however Vanuatu has tried to reactivate their accession process.

In the intervening period the WTO General Council adopted a decision[38] recommending that restraint be shown by members in seeking

[37] The principal supplier is the country with the largest portion of the GATT market for a particular product. This proposal has already been made in the context of submissions for accelerating the accession negotiations for LDCs. It was made in preparation for the Seattle Ministerial Conference by Fiji, Papua New Guinea and Solomon Islands (WT/GC/W/378).

[38] WT/L/508.

concessions from acceding LDCs. The decision also streamlines the accession process, allows acceding LDCs to take advantage of special and differential treatment, and enhances trade-related technical assistance and capacity-building.

Also in this period, Cambodia and Nepal, both LDCs, acceded to the WTO. As the first LDCs to accede, their accessions provide potential precedents for future accessions of LDCs.

Vanuatu wishes to accede on terms that are acceptable to the majority of local businesses, to the public service and to civil society. It remains to be seen whether the changes that occurred within the WTO during Vanuatu's stalled accession will allow them to accede on more favourable terms.

INDEX